PATHWAYS
❖
NUMBER TWO

The Geometry of the Triangle

Gerry Leversha

The United Kingdom Mathematics Trust

The Geometry of the Triangle

© 2013 United Kingdom Mathematics Trust

All rights reserved. No part of this publication may be reproduced or transmitted in any form or by any means, electronic or mechanical, including photocopy, recording, or any information storage and retrieval system, without permission in writing from the publisher.

Published by The United Kingdom Mathematics Trust.
School of Mathematics, University of Leeds,
Leeds, LS2 9JT, United Kingdom
http://www.ukmt.org.uk

First published 2013.

ISBN 978-1-906001-17-9

Printed in the UK for the UKMT by Charlesworth Press, Wakefield.
http://www.charlesworth.com

Typographic design by Andrew Jobbings of Arbelos.
http://www.arbelos.co.uk

Typeset with LaTeX.

The books published by the United Kingdom Mathematics Trust are grouped into series.

❖

The EXCURSIONS IN MATHEMATICS series consists of monographs which focus on a particular topic of interest and investigate it in some detail, using a wide range of ideas and techniques. They are aimed at high school students, undergraduates and others who are prepared to pursue a subject in some depth, but do not require specialised knowledge.
1. *The Backbone of Pascal's Triangle*, Martin Griffiths
2. *A Prime Puzzle*, Martin Griffiths

❖

The HANDBOOKS series is aimed particularly at students at secondary school who are interested in acquiring the knowledge and skills which are useful for tackling challenging problems, such as those posed in the competitions administered by the UKMT and similar organisations.
1. *Plane Euclidean Geometry: Theory and Problems*, A D Gardiner and C J Bradley
2. *Introduction to Inequalities*, C J Bradley
3. *A Mathematical Olympiad Primer*, Geoff C Smith
4. *Introduction to Number Theory*, C J Bradley
5. *A Problem Solver's Handbook*, Andrew Jobbings

❖

The PATHWAYS series aims to provide classroom teaching material for use in secondary schools. Each title develops a subject in more depth and in more detail than is normally required by public examinations or national curricula.
1. *Crossing the Bridge*, Gerry Leversha
2. *The Geometry of the Triangle*, Gerry Leversha

❖

The PROBLEMS series consists of collections of high-quality and original problems of Olympiad standard.
1. *New Problems in Euclidean Geometry*, David Monk

❖

The YEARBOOKS series documents all the UKMT activities, including details of all the challenge papers and solutions, lists of high scorers, accounts of the IMO and Olympiad training camps, and other information about the Trust's work during each year.

Contents

Series Editor's Foreword	xi
Preface	xiii
Notation and definitions	xxi

1 Introduction   1
- 1.1 The four main centres 1
- 1.2 Locus arguments 2
- 1.3 Homothetic figures 3
- 1.4 Centres of mass 5
- 1.5 Shifting the focus 6
- 1.6 Cyclic quadrilaterals 7

2 The principal triangle centres   9
- 2.1 The circumcentre and circumcircle 9
- 2.2 The centroid 14
- 2.3 The incentre and excentres 15
- 2.4 The orthocentre 20
- 2.5 Fagnano's problem 23

3 The Euler line   27
- 3.1 An important collinearity 27
- 3.2 The nine-point circle 28
- 3.3 Distances between triangle centres 31
- 3.4 Orthocentric quadrilaterals 34
- 3.5 Three more points on the Euler line 36
- 3.6 The power of a point 37

4 Simson lines — 41
  4.1 The Simson line — 41
  4.2 Another look at the nine-point circle — 46
  4.3 Miquel circles — 48

5 Cross-ratio — 51
  5.1 The cross-ratio of a range — 51
  5.2 The cross-ratio of a pencil — 56
  5.3 Harmonic ranges — 59
  5.4 Centres of similitude — 63
  5.5 Apollonius circles — 64
  5.6 The complete quadrangle — 66

6 Cevians and pedal triangles — 69
  6.1 Ceva and Menelaus — 69
  6.2 Centres of similitude — 75
  6.3 Pedal triangles — 77

7 Conjugates — 81
  7.1 Three types of conjugacy — 81
  7.2 Characterising isogonal conjugates — 84
  7.3 Isogonal conjugates and pedal triangles — 88
  7.4 Isotomic and cyclocevian conjugates — 90
  7.5 Pedal-cevian points — 92
  7.6 Droz-Farny circles — 93

8 The symmedian point — 99
  8.1 Symmedians — 99
  8.2 Parallels and antiparallels — 103
  8.3 Quadrangles — 108
  8.4 Pedal properties — 110

9 Centres related to the incentre — 113
  9.1 The Gergonne point — 113
  9.2 The Nagel point — 114
  9.3 The Spieker centre and circle — 116
  9.4 A notation for triangle centres — 119
  9.5 The Fuhrmann circle — 120
  9.6 The Bevan point — 122
  9.7 The Adams circle — 123

9.8	Barycentric coordinates	124

10 Triangles in perspective — 127
10.1	Desargues' theorem	127
10.2	Duality	132
10.3	Pascal's theorem	136
10.4	Three triangles in perspective	139

11 The isogonic centres — 143
11.1	Isogonic centres	144
11.2	Kiepert's theorem	147
11.3	The Napoleon points	149
11.4	The Lester circle	151

12 The Vecten and Kosnita points — 157
12.1	The Vecten points	157
12.2	Flanks	160
12.3	The Kosnita triangle	162
12.4	Three homothetic triangles	166

13 Circumcevian triangles — 171
13.1	Forming circumcevian triangles	171
13.2	The circumorthic triangle	173
13.3	The circummedial triangle	177
13.4	The circummidarc triangle	180

14 The Morley configuration — 185
14.1	Morley's theorem	185
14.2	External trisectors	190
14.3	The lighthouse theorem	194
14.4	More equilateral triangles	195

15 Spiral similarities — 199
15.1	Spiral similarity	199
15.2	Finding the centre	201
15.3	Triangles of correspondence	204
15.4	The circle of similitude	208
15.5	The invariable points	212

16 Brocard geometry — 217
- 16.1 The Brocard points — 217
- 16.2 The Brocard triangles and circle — 221
- 16.3 Brocard triangles and perspective — 227
- 16.4 The Brocard configuration and spiral similarities — 230
- 16.5 The Steiner and Tarry points — 234

17 Lemoine, Tucker and Taylor circles — 237
- 17.1 Lemoine circles — 237
- 17.2 Miquel points — 241
- 17.3 Tucker circles — 244
- 17.4 Tucker centres — 247
- 17.5 The Taylor circle — 248

18 Poles, polars and radical axes — 251
- 18.1 Pole and polar — 251
- 18.2 The radical axis — 255
- 18.3 Coaxal circles — 260

19 The isodynamic points — 265
- 19.1 The Apollonius circles — 265
- 19.2 A coaxal system — 268
- 19.3 The pedal triangles — 273
- 19.4 The isogonic centres and the isodynamic points — 274

20 Inversion — 277
- 20.1 Transformation properties — 277
- 20.2 Angles and tangency — 281
- 20.3 Proof by inversion — 284
- 20.4 The Kosnita and reflection triangles revisited — 286
- 20.5 Inarc circles — 288
- 20.6 Poncelet's porism — 291

21 The Feuerbach points — 295
- 21.1 Feuerbach's theorem — 295
- 21.2 A proof using inversion — 297
- 21.3 Consequences — 298
- 21.4 A proof using spiral similarities — 300
- 21.5 A proof using the Simson line — 303
- 21.6 The Feuerbach triangle — 305

22 Soddy circles — 309
- 22.1 Touching circles 309
- 22.2 The Soddy circles 311
- 22.3 The Soddy radii 314
- 22.4 The isoperimetric and equal detour points 317
- 22.5 The Soddy line 318
- 22.6 Gergonne's construction 320
- 22.7 Ratios on the Soddy line 324
- 22.8 The limiting case 329

23 The Mittenpunkt and the Clawson point — 331
- 23.1 The excentral triangle 331
- 23.2 The Mittenpunkt 333
- 23.3 The extangents triangle 336
- 23.4 More on the intouch triangle 338
- 23.5 The Clawson point 342

24 Partition triangles — 347
- 24.1 Some easy facts about partitions 348
- 24.2 Some triangles in perspective 350
- 24.3 Some concurrent Euler lines 352
- 24.4 Some connections between triangle centres 355
- 24.5 Van Lamoen's circle 358

25 What lies beyond — 363
- 25.1 The equiparallelian point 363
- 25.2 The Malfatti circles 365
- 25.3 The Parry circle 367
- 25.4 The Apollonius point 369
- 25.5 The Kenmotu point 370

Appendix A   Barycentric and areal coordinates — 373

Appendix B   Solutions to the exercises — 389

Appendix C   An index of geometers — 523

Bibliography — 531

Index — 535

Series Editor's Foreword

This book is part of a series whose aim is to provide classroom teaching material for use in secondary schools. Each title will try to develop a subject in more depth and in more detail than is normally required by public examinations or national curricula. Particular attention is paid to sound pedagogical principles, such as the need for logical clarity in arguments, the importance of learning to tackle multi-stage problems and the recognition of connections between different parts of the subject. The bulk of the text is devoted to carefully constructed exercises, either for classroom discussion or for individual study.

I hope that every secondary school will have these books in its library. The prices have been set so low that many good students will wish to purchase their own copies. Schools wishing to give out large numbers of copies of these books as prizes should note that discounts may be negotiated with the UKMT office.

London, UK   GERRY LEVERSHA

About the author

Gerry Leversha taught mathematics in secondary schools for over thirty years and has also been involved in the work of the UKMT, both in the setting and marking of various Olympiads and as Chair of the Publications Committee. He is also the editor of *The Mathematical Gazette*, the journal of the Mathematical Association, and is a regular speaker at conferences and summer schools. His interests include music, film and literature, wine and cooking, as well as playing tennis and mountain walking, and his current ambition is to complete the ascent of all 284 Munros in the Scottish Highlands.

Preface

The triangle is the simplest of all geometrical figures. With two lines in a plane, there is not much to say; either they meet in a unique point or they are parallel. So, for anything interesting to happen, we need three lines, which will usually meet in a triangle. This is because the first two lines normally meet in a point, and the third does not, in general, pass through that point.

Starting from a basic triangle, we can now begin to construct new points and lines. We can identify the midpoint of and draw the perpendicular bisector of any line segment joining two points. For any angle formed from two intersecting lines, there are two angle bisectors. Through any three points not on the same line, there is a unique circle. New triangles can be formed from any three non-collinear points. By combining these operations, our simple triangle turns into a complex configuration containing many lines, points, circles and triangles.

Of course, complicated configurations are not usually interesting. A spider's web attracts our attention, not because the threads are arranged in a random arrangement, but because it exhibits a structure which appeals to our aesthetic sense. This might be a question of symmetry or formal balance or the presence of sub-patterns within the web. What sort of features must a geometrical configuration need to display before it is deemed to be worthy of notice?

We might, for example, discover three lines within it which do not create a new triangle because they are concurrent; they pass through a common point. When this occurs, there is usually a good reason for it and the point is often given a special name. In the context of triangles, such points are sometimes called triangle centres. These centres have been extensively studied and they are seen to have many interesting properties and interconnections, and the purpose of this book is to exhibit some of the most important of these.

Again, if we choose three points in the configuration, it is significant when they are collinear. It turns out that there are many important such lines associated with a triangle. Furthermore, we can examine the arrangement of points on a line by calculating various ratios. A noteworthy example of this is when four points form a harmonic range, since such a relationship can lead to the creation of new collinearities. It is also interesting when we discover a circle which passes through more than three significant points, particularly when they arise in quite dissimilar ways.

I hope that in this short sketch I have clarified my motives in writing this book. In *Crossing the Bridge* [19], I attempted to get a foothold on the continent of triangle geometry, introducing the principal centres and even exploring a little further, including as a climax the proof by inversion of Feuerbach's theorem. Here, my aim is to survey part of the vast hinterland which lies beyond the well-trodden coastal fringe.

What purpose is served by revisiting material which has already been treated very competently elsewhere? First, I believe that this is a more comprehensive account than is available in any other modern text and that readers will find it useful to have a whole galaxy of results in one place. Secondly, I think I have been able to organise the journey in an illuminating way, highlighting various techniques as the exploration progresses and showing connections between new territory and that which has been previously visited. Examples of this include the identification of several configurations as variations on the underlying theme of the complete quadrangle, the use of different forms of conjugacy as a way of creating new centres from old, the focus on centres of similitude of familiar circles and the search for centres of perspective. Finally, I have attempted, so far as is possible, to use classical Euclidean methods throughout. As I explain later, I believe this will be more familiar to more readers than other approaches and I also think it sheds more light than algebraic approaches.

The structure of the book

Familiarity is assumed with the elementary Euclidean methods that used to be taught in school; these are exemplified by the content of *Crossing the Bridge*. Beyond that, all the techniques used are carefully explained.

Thus there are chapters on cross-ratio, Simson lines, Cevians and centres of similitude, triangles in perspective, spiral similarities, radical axes and inversion. It is hoped that these do not interrupt the flow of the narrative too much.

The itinerary through triangle geometry begins with the most familiar triangle centres, the nine-point circle and the Euler line. The Gergonne, Nagel, Spieker and symmedian points are introduced as examples of different types of conjugacy. The consequences of placing triangles around the reference triangle are explored, leading to the isogonic centres, Napoleon points and a remarkable theorem due to June Lester. Circumcevian triangles provide an example of a perspective argument, and the existence of the Exeter point is justified using synthetic methods. The extraordinary theorem due to Morley is then explored along with various extensions.

There is then a survey of Brocard geometry, which forms a sort of independent archipelago in the triangle continent, approaching both by classical and transformational methods, leading on to the Lemoine circles and the Steiner and Tarry points. The theory of radical axes and coaxal circles is used to investigate Taylor circles and the isodynamic points. Feuerbach's theorem on the incircles, excircles and nine-point circle is then proved using a variety of methods, including inversion and spiral similarity as well as more constructive methods. Then we meet the Soddy line and the Mittenpunkt, associated with a network of collinearities. Finally, we look at the process of subdividing a triangle into parts. I hope that this approach emphasises that the subject of triangle geometry is still developing and perhaps readers of this book will be able to contribute to its progress.

Sets of exercises are incorporated in the text and the reader is recommended to attempt to solve the problems, although full solutions are given in appendix B. Appendix A is a brief account of barycentric coordinates. There is a glossary showing all the notation and definitions used and there is also a brief biographical survey of some of the mathematicians whose names crop up in the text.

Synthetic or algebraic?

The current expositions of triangle geometry, and particularly those on the Web, nearly all employ the technique of areal coordinates. This is particularly true whenever the geometry becomes difficult, and so it applies to virtually all of the more obscure results described in the book. There are good reasons for this, and, ironically, the least of these is the mathematical facility of the algebraic approach.

A major drawback in traditional Euclidean methods is the bugbear of diagram dependency. In any reasonably complex configuration the question of uniqueness is going to rear its head. Does the foot of a perpendicular from a point to a line segment meet it between the two endpoints or on the segment produced? When four points are chosen on a line or on a circle, does it matter which order they are placed? What happens if two lines which are supposed to meet are in fact parallel? What happens if two of the points coalesce? The beauty of an algebraic approach is that many of these problems simply disappear, and a single simple proof works for all possible configurations. By the additional expedient of introducing points on the line at infinity, the issue of parallel lines is also resolved.

When it comes to the identification of newly-discovered points of concurrency, the areal approach also comes into its own. One simply 'looks up' the areal coordinates in a glossary, and at once it becomes clear whether a 'new' point really is new or whether it is some 'familiar' point masquerading in a different guise. Moreover, the relationships between points and lines – concurrency, collinearity, concyclicity, harmonic proportion, the different forms of conjugacy – become crystal clear as algebraic relationships, so that geometry takes on an algebraic structure. This is exemplified beautifully by Bradley's elegant book *The Algebra of Geometry* [5].

Why, then, even bother to adopt a traditional Euclidean approach? What is the point of eschewing a viewpoint which not only simplifies the analysis but avoids ambiguity? Why make mathematics difficult?

I can only plead on the basis of a sort of intuitive aesthetic feeling. For me, a synthetic proof, despite doubts about its universal applicability and the possible need to consider limiting special cases, still conveys an element of spatial understanding which is absent from an algebraic demonstration. The existence of the centroid of a triangle can be rigorously determined from vector algebra, but is that really as convincing as an argument based on the homothecy of the reference triangle and its medial triangle? Whilst some areal proofs are short and elegant, many are actually rather lengthy and involve significant manipulations which are best handled using computer algebra applications. Having gone through this process, are we really any the wiser as to the reasons for the result? I would much prefer a synthetic argument which reduces a concurrency to some property of loci, or an appeal to Desargues' theorem on triangles in perspective, or the recognition that two elements in the configuration can be transformed to one another by a spiral similarity. So, whether or not the reader agrees with my prejudice, this is the philosophy underlying the book.

There are, however, a number of results which I have been unable to demonstrate using classical arguments. The most important of these is the existence of the Kiepert hyperbola, but there are also some concurrencies and collinearities which appear to elude Euclidean methods. Appendix A defines barycentric coordinates and lists the principal results concerning them. The Kiepert hyperbola, along with other material which depends on the use of these methods, is discussed there.

A note on directed angles

There are several places in this text where the existence of distinct diagrams for the same result really does make the exposition tiresomely fussy. This is particularly the case where different variants of a diagram lead to separate proofs which are identical apart from the fact that some angles are replaced by their supplements. One way of resolving this problem is to use the concept of directed or oriented angles. The essential idea is to define the angle between two lines so that it can sometimes refer to the acute and sometimes to the obtuse angle which they create. By consistently making this choice, several configurations can be treated in exactly the same way.

Given two lines $\mathcal{L}$ and $\mathcal{L}'$, the *directed angle* $\mathcal{L} \measuredangle \mathcal{L}'$ is defined as that angle through which $\mathcal{L}$ must be rotated in a positive (anti-clockwise) direction in order to coincide with $\mathcal{L}'$. Given three distinct points A, B and C, the directed angle $\measuredangle ABC$ is then defined as $AB \measuredangle BC$.

In this definition, a line is understood simply in terms of its direction, not in its sense. Thus the line AB is identical to the line BA. As a consequence, two directed angles are to be considered as equal if they differ by multiples of $180°$. As an example, consider $\triangle ABC$, where the triangle is drawn in an anticlockwise direction (see figure 1).

The interior angles of the triangle are described by the directed angles $\measuredangle CBA$, $\measuredangle ACB$ and $\measuredangle BAC$.

Figure 1

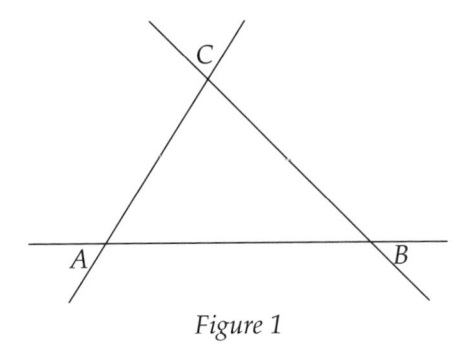

The exterior angles of the triangle are described by the directed angles $\measuredangle ABC$, $\measuredangle BCA$ and $\measuredangle CAB$.

The advantage of using directed angles becomes clear when we consider two circle theorems which are part of the GCSE syllabus. Here is a result stated in the language of directed angles.

Let A, B, C and D be four distinct points on a circle. Then $\measuredangle ABC = \measuredangle ADC$.

Now let us translate this into the ordinary language of Euclidean geometry.

If A, B, C and D appear in that order as we move anticlockwise around the circle, then this statement says that the exterior angle at B is equal to the interior angle at D (see figure 2).

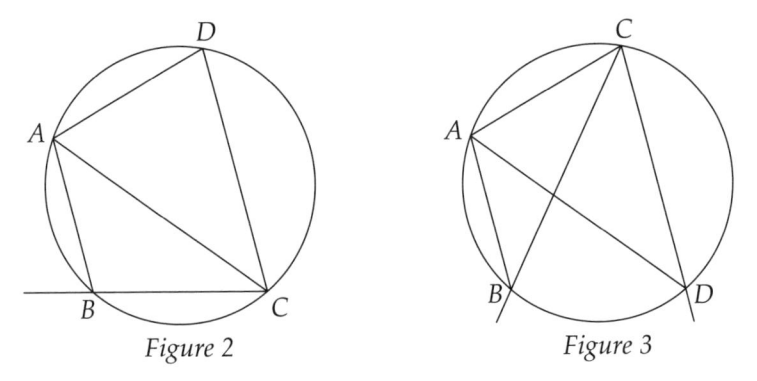

Figure 2

Figure 3

In other words, opposite angles of a cyclic quadrilateral are supplementary.

Now suppose the order is A, B, D, C. The statement now asserts that the exterior angles of the two triangles at B and D are equal (see figure 3).

In other words, angles in the same segment are equal.

However, after some thought, I have decided not to adopt this approach. Such proofs, despite their technical advantages, lack the intuitive nature of arguments using standard angle notation, and there is something to be said for not obscuring the familiar in new language. Besides, if I were to use directed angles in some places, I would really have to use them everywhere, and the expense of making some proofs concise would be a global recourse to the unfamiliar. I have, however, indicated places where directed angles would have been especially useful, such as the treatment of Miquel circles and some of the results in Brocard geometry. The reader who wishes to translate the relevant arguments into the language of directed angles is welcome to do so, or to search for them in the literature.

Acknowledgements

This book would have been impossible without the support of a large number of people. I would like to thank James Gazet for reading the text and making many useful suggestions for improving it, particularly the earlier chapters. John Silvester has been a great help in commenting on the existing literature and helping fill gaps in my narrative. I have been inspired by a number of books, both classic texts such as Johnson [16], Altshiller-Court [1] and Maxwell [20] and modern treatments like Honsberger [14]. The internet has also been a great source of stimulation, pointing me to key papers in journals and relevant insights on geometrical websites such as *Forum Geometricorum* and *Hyacinthos*. Then there is the remarkable website developed by Clark Kimberling, which is unsurpassed as an encyclopaedia of triangle centres together with their interrelationships. All of this is acknowledged in the bibliography. Last but by no means least I am indebted to Andrew Jobbings, not only for his elegant typesetting and exquisite diagrams but for his meticulous criticism of my errors and textual infelicities, as well as suggestions of where to find additional material. Without his contribution this book would not have been possible.

Notation and definitions

As far as practicable, I have tried to establish a consistent use of notation for important points associated with the triangle. This has required the employment of both the Greek and the Roman alphabet as well as an extensive use of subscripts. The aim is to reserve many labels so that they have an exclusive meaning; for instance, A_1 will always stand for the midpoint of the side BC of $\triangle ABC$.

In two instances, the Morley and Brocard triangles, there is some duplication of notation. The context is very clear in these cases, however, and there should not be any confusion.

Of course, it is also necessary to label other points which are significant only in the context of particular proofs or arguments. Again, it should be clear that these labels are not being used in the conventional way.

Notation

Standard points

A, B, C vertices of the reference triangle

A_1, B_1, C_1 midpoints of BC, CA, AB

A^*, B^*, C^* images of A, B, C under reflection in BC, CA, AB

D, E, F feet of the perpendiculars from A, B, C to BC, CA, AB

K_A, K_B, K_C intersections of the symmedians with BC, CA, AB

N_A, N_B, N_C circumcentres of the equilateral triangles drawn outwardly on BC, CA, AB

N_a, N_b, N_c circumcentres of the equilateral triangles drawn inwardly on BC, CA, AB

O_A, O_B, O_C circumcentres of $\triangle COB$, $\triangle AOC$ and $\triangle BOA$
P, Q, R points of tangency of incircle with BC, CA, AB
P_A, Q_A, R_A points of tangency of excircle opposite A with BC, CA, AB
U, V, W Euler points, the midpoints of AH, BH and CH
V_A, V_B, V_C centres of three squares drawn outwardly on BC, CA, AB
V_a, V_b, V_c centres of three squares drawn inwardly on BC, CA, AB
X, Y, Z intersections of internal angle bisectors at A, B, C with BC, CA, AB
X', Y', Z' intersections of external angle bisectors at A, B, C with BC, CA, AB
$X_B, \ldots, Z_A$ intersections of Adams circle with BC, CA, AB

Lengths, distances, areas, cross-ratios

a, b, c side lengths of BC, CA, AB
h_A, h_B, h_C lengths of altitudes from A, B, C
R circumradius
r inradius
r_A, r_B, r_C exradii
s semiperimeter
$\pi(X, I)$ perpendicular distance from X to I
Δ area of $\triangle ABC$
$[AB \ldots X]$ area of the polygon $AB \ldots X$
$(A, C; B, D)$ cross-ratio of the range A, B, C, D
$(a, c; b, d)$ cross-ratio of the pencil a, b, c, d

Homothecies

α enlargement, centre O, scale factor 2 *page 167*
θ enlargement, centre G, scale factor $-\frac{1}{2}$ *page 5*
λ enlargement, centre Λ_1 *page 167*
ϕ enlargement, centre Φ_1 *page 167*
μ enlargement, centre M_* *page 332*

Other

C_i, C_e	internal and external centres of similitude of two circles
$V(A, B, C, D)$	pencil consisting of VA, VB, VC, VD
ω	Brocard angle
$⌾_{ABC}P$	circumcevian triangle of $\triangle ABC$ with respect to P
$⌾P$	same as $⌾_{ABC}P$
$\triangle\!\!\!\triangle X$	partition triangles of X
$Y_{\triangle\!\!\!\triangle} X$	triangle composed of the centres Y of $\triangle\!\!\!\triangle X$
$X_{\triangle\!\!\!\triangle}$	triangle composed of the centres X of $\triangle\!\!\!\triangle X$

Triangle centres and other significant points

$P \triangle\!\!\!\triangle XYZ$ is the centre notation for a triangle.

In the following list, the Kimberling reference X_n is given when the point is classified as a triangle centre, together with the first appearance of the point in the book.

A^*	Apollonius point	X_{181}	page 369
A_1^*	first Ajima-Malfatti point	X_{179}	page 365
A_2^*	second Ajima-Malfatti point	X_{180}	page 365
C^*	Clawson point	X_{19}	page 343
E_1	first Eppstein point	X_{481}	page 319
E_2	second Eppstein point	X_{482}	page 319
E^*	Exeter point	X_{22}	page 179
F^*	Fuhrmann centre	X_{355}	page 120
F_1	first isogonic centre	X_{13}	page 145
F_2	second isogonic centre	X_{14}	page 146
G	centroid	X_2	page 5
G_1	inner Griffiths point	X_{1373}	page 323
G_2	outer Griffiths point	X_{1374}	page 323
G_E	centroid of excentral triangle	X_{165}	page 333
G_I	Weill point	X_{354}	page 333

G_l	far-out point	X_{23}	page 368
H	orthocentre	X_4	page 6
H_I	orthocentre of intouch triangle	X_{65}	page 333
I	incentre	X_1	page 3
I_A, I_B, I_C	excentres opposite A, B, C		page 15
J	Feuerbach point	X_{11}	page 296
J_A, J_B, J_C	Feuerbach points of excircles		page 296
J_1, J_2	isodynamic points	X_{15}, X_{16}	page 267
K	symmedian point	X_6	page 99
K_1	symmedian point of the medial triangle $\triangle A_1 B_1 C_1$	X_{141}	page 351
K^*	Kosnita point	X_{54}	page 163
K_*	inverse Kosnita point	X_{1157}	page 287
K_1^*	first Kenmotu point	X_{371}	page 370
K_2^*	second Kenmotu point	X_{372}	page 371
L	Brocard centre	X_{182}	page 223
M	Nagel point	X_8	page 114
M^*	Mittenpunkt	X_9	page 333
M_*	isogonal Mittenpunkt	X_{57}	page 335
M_1	first Morley centre	X_{356}	page 185
M_2	second Morley centre	X_{357}	page 188
M_3	Morley-Yff centre	X_{358}	page 189
N	nine-point centre	X_5	page 28
N_1	medial centre	X_{140}	page 36
O	circumcentre	X_3	page 2
O_I	internal centre of similitude of Kosnita and tangential circles		page 168
O_K	circumcentre of Kosnita triangle	X_{1658}	page 168
O_T	circumcentre of tangential triangle	X_{26}	page 168
O_{vL}	centre of van Lamoen triangle	X_{1153}	page 360
P^*	centre of Parry circle	X_{351}	page 367
$P_=$	equiparallelian point	X_{192}	page 364

Q	centre of orthocentroidal disc	X_{381}	*page 36*
R_1	inner Rigby point	X_{1371}	*page 323*
R_2	outer Rigby point	X_{1372}	*page 323*
S	Spieker centre	X_{10}	*page 116*
S_i	inner Soddy centre	X_{176}	*page 312*
S_o	outer Soddy centre	X_{175}	*page 313*
T	Tarry point	X_{98}	*page 234*
V_i	inner Vecten point	X_{486}	*page 159*
V_o	outer Vecten point	X_{485}	*page 158*
Γ	Gergonne point	X_7	*page 113*
Θ	Bevan point	X_{40}	*page 122*
Λ	de Longchamps point	X_{20}	*page 36*
Λ_1	Lambda point; external centre of similitude of circumcircle and incircle of circumorthic triangle	X_{24}	*page 167*
Λ_2	internal centre of similitude of circumcircle and incircle of circumorthic triangle	X_{378}	*page 168*
Ξ	homothetic centre of OoI triangle and reference triangle		*page 184*
Π_1	Pi point ; external centre of similitude of circumcircles of Kosnita and reference triangles		*page 175*
Π_2	internal centre of similitude of circumcircles of Kosnita and reference triangles		*page 175*
σ_e	external centre of similitude of incircle and circumcircle	X_{56}	*page 181*
σ_i	internal centre of similitude of incircle and circumcircle	X_{55}	*page 181*
Σ	Steiner point	X_{99}	*page 234*
Y	Schiffler point	X_{21}	*page 352*

Φ_1	Phi point; external centre of similitude of circumcircle and incircle of orthic triangle	X_{25}	*page 167*
Φ_2	internal centre of similitude of circumcircle and incircle of orthic triangle	X_{1593}	*page 167*
Ψ_1	outer Napoleon point	X_{17}	*page 149*
Ψ_2	inner Napoleon point	X_{18}	*page 149*
Ω_1	first Brocard point		*page 218*
Ω_2	second Brocard point		*page 218*
Ω_3	third Brocard point	X_{76}	*page 227*

Definitions

altitude	a line from a vertex perpendicular to the opposite side
angle bisector	a line which bisects the angle at a vertex; it can be internal or external
antiparallel	see page 104
cevian	see page 72
circumcevian triangle	see page 172
cyclocevian conjugate	see page 83
exmedian	a side of the anti-complementary $\triangle A^*B^*C^*$
exsymmedian	a side of the tangential triangle $\triangle T_A T_B T_C$
harmonic pencil	a pencil with cross-ratio equal to -1
harmonic range	a range with cross-ratio equal to -1
isogonal conjugate point	see page 81
isogonal conjugate line	see page 82
isotomic conjugate	see page 82
median	a line segment from a vertex to the midpoint of the opposite side
pedal-cevian point	see page 92
perpendicular bisector	a line through the midpoint of a side and perpendicular to that side
symmedian	a line through a vertex isogonally conjugate to a median

Special lines and axes

antiorthic axis	axis of perspective of reference triangle and excentral triangle
Brocard axis	the line including the diameter of the Brocard circle
Euler line	the line through O, G, H and many other centres
Fermat axis	the line through the two isogonic centres
Gergonne line	axis of perspective of reference triangle and intouch triangle
Morley axis	axis of perspective of reference, Morley and adjunct Morley triangles
orthic axis	axis of perspective of reference triangle and orthic triangle
Lemoine line	axis of perspective of reference triangle and tangential triangle
Simson line	line joining feet of perpendiculars from point on circumcircle to triangle

Triangles

adjunct Morley triangle, first	$\triangle PQR$	see page 189
adjunct Morley triangle, second	$\triangle P^*Q^*R^*$	see page 192
adjunct Morley triangle, third	$\triangle P^{**}Q^{**}R^{**}$	see page 193
anti-complementary triangle	$\triangle A^*B^*C^*$	lines through the vertices parallel to the opposite sides
Brocard triangle, first	$\triangle PQR$	see page 221
Brocard triangle, second	$\triangle P^*Q^*R^*$	see page 224
circummedial triangle	$\triangle A'_1 A'_2 A'_3$	the circumcevian triangle of $\triangle ABC$ with respect to the centroid

circummidarc triangle	$\triangle X'Y'Z'$	the circumcevian triangle of $\triangle ABC$ with respect to the incentre
circumorthic triangle	$\triangle D'E'F'$	the circumcevian triangle of $\triangle ABC$ with respect to the orthocentre
Euler triangle	$\triangle UVW$	formed by the midpoints of AH, BH and CH
excentral triangle	$\triangle I_A I_B I_C$	formed by the excentres
extangents triangle	$\triangle U_A U_B U_C$	formed by the external tangents to the three excircles
extouch triangle	$\triangle P_A Q_B R_C$	formed by the points of contact of the three excircles internal to the sides
A-extouch triangle	$\triangle P_A Q_A R_A$	formed by the points of contact of the excircle opposite A with the sides — one internal and two external
Fuhrmann triangle	$\triangle F_A F_B F_C$	see page 120
incentral triangle	$\triangle XYZ$	formed by the points where the internal angle bisectors meet the opposite sides
inner Napoleon triangle	$\triangle N_a N_b N_c$	formed by the circumcentres of equilateral triangles drawn inwardly on the sides
inner Soddy triangle	$\triangle E_A E_B E_C$	formed by the points of tangency between the inner Soddy circle and the base circles
inner Vecten triangle	$\triangle V_a V_b V_c$	formed by the centres of squares drawn inwardly on the sides
intouch triangle	$\triangle PQR$	formed by the points of contact of the incircle with the sides
IoCO triangle		intouch of circumorthic triangle
IoO triangle		intouch triangle of $\triangle DEF$

Kosnita triangle	$\triangle O_A O_B O_C$	formed by circumcentres of $\triangle COB$, $\triangle AOC$ and $\triangle BOA$
medial triangle	$\triangle A_1 B_1 C_1$	formed by the midpoints of the sides
Morley triangle, first	$\triangle DEF$	see page 185
Morley triangle, second	$\triangle D^* E^* F^*$	see page 190
Morley triangle, third	$\triangle D^{**} E^{**} F^{**}$	see page 192
OoI triangle		orthic triangle of $\triangle PQR$
OoO triangle		orthic triangle of $\triangle DEF$
orthic triangle	$\triangle DEF$	formed by the feet of the perpendiculars from A, B, C to BC, CA, AB
outer Napoleon triangle	$\triangle N_A N_B N_C$	formed by the circumcentres of equilateral triangles drawn outwardly on the sides
outer Soddy triangle	$\triangle E_A^* E_B^* E_C^*$	formed by the points of tangency between the outer Soddy circle and the base circles
outer Vecten triangle	$\triangle V_a V_b V_c$	formed by centres of squares drawn inwardly on the sides
pedal triangle		formed by the perpendiculars from a point to the sides
reference triangle	$\triangle ABC$	the original triangle
reflection triangle	$\triangle A^* B^* C^*$	formed by reflecting the vertices in the opposite sides
tangential triangle	$\triangle T_A T_B T_C$	formed by the tangents to the circumcircle at the vertices

Circles

Adams circle	see page 123
A-, B- and C-Apollonius circles	see page 265
Apollonius circle	see page 369
Brocard circle	circumcircle of first Brocard triangle
circumcircle	the circle through A, B, C
circle of similitude	(for two given circles) the circle on diameter $C_i C_e$
Droz-Farny circle	see page 94
exarc circle	see page 289
excircles	three circles tangential internally to one side and externally to the other two
Fuhrmann circle	the circumcircle of $\triangle F_A F_B F_C$
inarc circle	see page 289
incircle	the circle tangential internally to all three sides
incentral circle	the circumcircle of $\triangle XYZ$
inner Napoleon circle	the circumcircle of $\triangle N_a N_b N_c$
inner Soddy circle	see page 309
IoO circle	the intouch circle of $\triangle DEF$
Lemoine circle, first	see page 238
Lemoine circle, second	see page 240
Lester circle	see page 154
Miquel circles	see page 49
Morley circle	the circumcircle of the Morley triangle

nine-point circle	the circle through $A_1, B_1, C_1, D, E, F, U, V, W$
orthocentroidal disc	the circle on diameter GH
outer Napoleon circle	the circumcircle of $\triangle N_A N_B N_C$
outer Soddy circle	see page 309
Parry circle	see page 367
pedal circle	the circumcircle of a pedal triangle
Spieker circle	incircle of $\triangle A_1 B_1 C_1$
Taylor circle	see page 249
Tucker circle	see page 245
van Lamoen circle	see page 360

Chapter 1

Introduction

It is customary to label the vertices of a triangle A, B and C, and so the sides are BC, CA and AB. It is helpful to distinguish these sections of lines, which are of finite length, from the lines themselves, which stretch infinitely far in both directions. For that reason, we use the term *line segment* to refer to the part of a line between two definite points. Sometimes we wish to describe half-lines, which start at a particular point and then stretch infinitely far in one direction; these are called *rays*.

The triangle $\triangle ABC$, which functions as the germ from which all the subsequent material follows, will be known as the *reference triangle*. Throughout the book, I have attempted to use a standard notation for the labelling of points within this triangle, and this is given for the reader's convenience on page xxi, together with a glossary of terminology.

1.1 The four main centres

We begin with the four most significant triangle centres. Table 1.1 shows their names, the standard notation for these centres and the lines (or line segments) whose concurrency gives rise to them.

The next task is to show that the lines in question are always concurrent. This is a good opportunity to introduce some elementary proof strategies, which will become very familiar in this book.

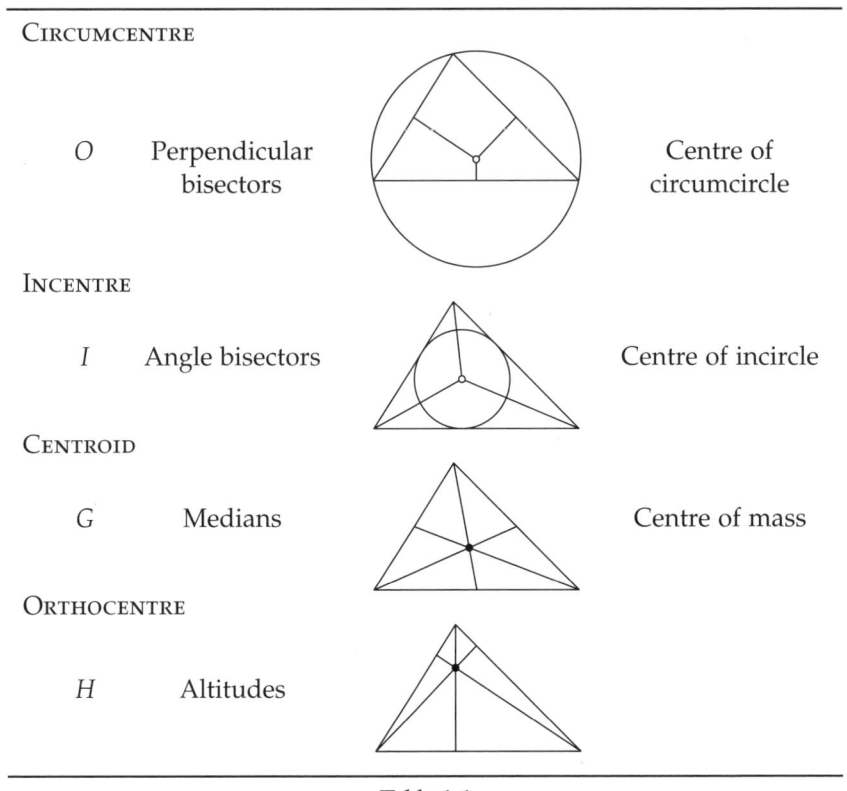

Table 1.1

CIRCUMCENTRE				
	O	Perpendicular bisectors		Centre of circumcircle
INCENTRE				
	I	Angle bisectors		Centre of incircle
CENTROID				
	G	Medians		Centre of mass
ORTHOCENTRE				
	H	Altitudes		

Table 1.1

1.2 Locus arguments

The idea here is to define three lines or line segments in terms of a condition which, if it satisfied by any two of them, is automatically satisfied by the third. This is best illustrated by examples.

The circumcentre

We think of the *perpendicular bisector* of a line segment PQ as being the locus of points which are equidistant from the points P and Q. Consider now the three perpendicular bisectors of the sides of the reference triangle $\triangle ABC$.

Chapter 1: Introduction

The perpendicular bisector of AB consists of points equidistant from A and B, and that of BC consists of points equidistant from B and C. If these two lines meet at O, this point is equidistant from A, B and C. Two observations follow from this:

- The point O, being equidistant from C and A, lies on the perpendicular bisector of CA, and so the three perpendicular bisectors are concurrent at O.
- There is a circle, centre O, which passes through all three vertices of $\triangle ABC$. This is the *circumcircle* of $\triangle ABC$ and its radius is the *circumradius*, which is denoted by R.

The incentre

We think of the *angle bisector* of $\angle PQR$ as being the locus of points which are equidistant from the lines QP and QR. In fact, there are always two angle bisectors and they are at right angles to one other.

Here we are focusing on the *internal* angle bisectors of triangle $\triangle ABC$ at the three vertices, which pass inside the triangle $\triangle ABC$. The angle bisector of $\angle A$ consists of points equidistant from AB and AC, and that of $\angle B$ consists of points equidistant from BC and BA. If these two lines meet at I, this point is equidistant from AB, BC and CA. Again, two observations follow:

- The point I, being equidistant from CA and CB, lies on the angle bisector of $\angle C$, and so the three angle bisectors are concurrent at I.
- There is a circle, with centre I, which touches the three sides of the triangle internally. It is the *incircle* of the triangle and its radius is the *inradius*, which is denoted by r.

1.3 Homothetic figures

If two polygons are similar and their corresponding sides are parallel, they are said to be *homothetic*. This relationship will turn out to be a fundamental key to many of the results in this book.

This is because of the theorem which follows, which states that any two such polygons have a *homothetic centre*, or *centre of similitude*, and that one is the image of the other under an enlargement with this centre and an appropriate scale factor. This transformation will be referred to as a *homothecy*.

Note that the scale factor may be positive (in which case the two triangles are *directly similar*) or negative (when they are *inversely similar*).

Theorem 1.1 *The lines joining corresponding vertices of two homothetic polygons are concurrent.*

PROOF Suppose that AA' and BB' meet at O, and that BB' and CC' meet at O' (see figure 1.1). We shall show that O and O' are the same point.

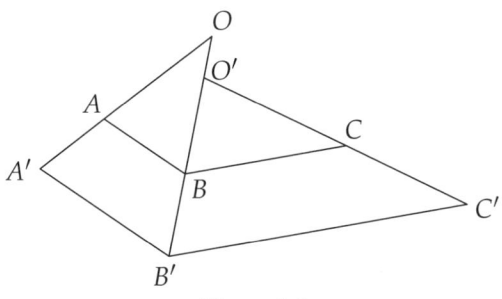

Figure 1.1

From similar triangles we have

$$\frac{OB}{OB'} = \frac{AB}{A'B'} \quad \text{and} \quad \frac{O'B}{O'B'} = \frac{BC}{B'C'}.$$

But we are given that

$$\frac{AB}{BC} = \frac{A'B'}{B'C'},$$

so we can deduce that

$$\frac{OB}{OB'} = \frac{O'B}{O'B'}.$$

However, if O and O' were different points, these two ratios would not be equal. It follows that O coincides with O'. ❑

The argument can clearly be extended to any number of extra vertices of the polygons. This proof indicates that, for triangles, it is sufficient for the sides to be parallel for them to be homothetic. In other words, the fact that the ratios are equal follows from the fact that the sides are parallel. This is not true of polygons in general. For example, a rectangle and a square with corresponding sides parallel are not homothetic, and do not have a homothetic centre (unless the rectangle is actually a square).

The centroid

Let A_1, B_1 and C_1 be the midpoints of the sides BC, CA and AB (see figure 1.2).

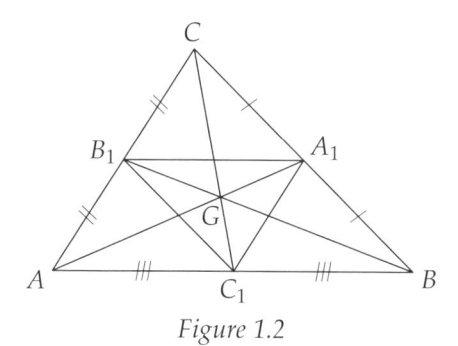

Figure 1.2

By the midpoint theorem, the segments C_1B_1, A_1C_1 and B_1A_1 are parallel to the sides BC, CA and AB and half their length. Hence the triangles $\triangle A_1B_1C_1$ and $\triangle ABC$ are homothetic, so by theorem 1.1 they have a homothetic centre, which is denoted by G.

The triangle $\triangle A_1B_1C_1$ is known as the *medial triangle* of $\triangle ABC$. The triangle $\triangle ABC$ can be transformed into $\triangle A_1B_1C_1$ by an enlargement with centre G and scale factor $-\frac{1}{2}$. Hence G is a point of trisection of each of the three medians of $\triangle ABC$.

We will be making use of this homothecy many times in the course of this book, and it will be useful to refer to it as $\theta : \triangle ABC \to \triangle A_1B_1C_1$.

1.4 Centres of mass

A slightly unexpected technique of proof involves placing masses at the vertices of a triangle and finding the position of their centre of mass. This is essentially equivalent to an argument using vector algebra.

In the case of the centroid, an alternative to the homothetic argument is to imagine three unit masses at the vertices of $\triangle ABC$. The masses at B

and C can be replaced by a single mass of 2 units at A_1. Now this mass and the unit mass at A can be replaced by a single mass of 3 units at G, which divides the median AA_1 in the ratio of $2:1$. As this is the centre of mass of the original three masses, it is a unique point. Now we carry out the same procedure but in a different order. If we begin by replacing the masses at, say, A and C by a single mass at B_1, we would arrive at the same eventual point, but now it is seen to divide the median BB_1 in the ratio of $2:1$, and the argument for CC_1 is the same.

A variation on this argument is to consider the centre of mass of $\triangle ABC$ considered as a *lamina*. We divide this into infinitesimally thin strips parallel to BC. Each of these has centre of mass at its midpoint, and hence the centre of mass of the whole lamina lies somewhere on the line consisting of all these midpoints, which is the median AA_1. But, by the same argument, it must also lie on the other two medians, and hence they are concurrent.

1.5 Shifting the focus

Sometimes a theorem can be proved by viewing the configuration in a different way—adopting a shift of focus. Often this is done simply by embedding the configuration in a more familiar setting so that the result becomes a case of one which is already known. This will turn out to be a very valuable strategy for discovering new results about triangle centres.

The orthocentre

We now establish that the altitudes of a triangle are concurrent. Consider the effect of drawing lines through A, B and C which are parallel to the opposite sides BC, CA and AB. What results is a triangle which is clearly similar to $\triangle ABC$; it is called the *anti-complementary triangle* $\triangle A^*B^*C^*$ (see figure 1.3).

From the parallelograms in figure 1.3, it is clear that $AB^* = BC = C^*A$, so $\triangle ABC$ is the medial triangle of $\triangle A^*B^*C^*$. The altitudes of the reference triangle are now the perpendicular bisectors of the anti-complementary triangle, so they are concurrent at its circumcentre.

This establishes that the orthocentre of a triangle is the circumcentre of its anti-complementary triangle.

Chapter 1: Introduction

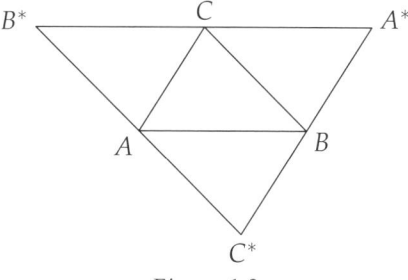

Figure 1.3

1.6 Cyclic quadrilaterals

Finally, of course, there are standard Euclidean arguments. The usual proof of the concurrency of the altitudes is a classic example of one which uses the circle theorems and their converses.

We begin by drawing two altitudes BE and CF, meeting at a point H, and then defining X as the point where AH meets BC (see figure 1.4). We do not assume, initially, that AX is perpendicular to BC.

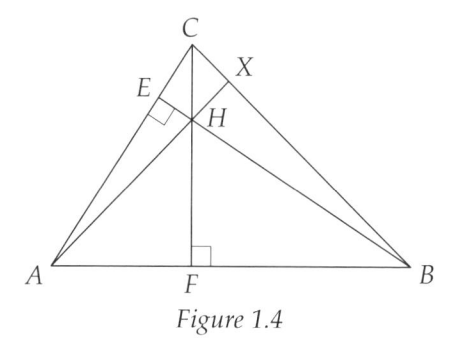

Figure 1.4

First note that the quadrilateral $AFHE$ is cyclic since its opposite angles add to $180°$. (In fact, AH is a diameter of its circumcircle, but we do not need that fact.) It follows, from angles in the same segment, that $\angle EAH = \angle EFH$. Now the quadrilateral $BCEF$ is also cyclic since the angles $\angle BFC$ and $\angle BEC$ are equal (and BC is a diameter). Hence, again from angles in the same segment, $\angle EFC = \angle EBC$.

Now we have $\angle EAH = \angle EBC$ (noting that $\angle EFH$ and $\angle EFC$ are just different names for the same angle). But, since $\angle BEC = 90°$, these are both $90° - \angle C$. It follows that $\angle AXC = 90°$ and so AX is also an altitude. The point X would normally be labelled as D.

Chapter 2

The principal triangle centres

In this chapter, we look in more detail at the four triangle centres which have already been introduced, proving their most important properties and showing why they are important in triangle geometry.

2.1 The circumcentre and circumcircle

There is one useful hint for tackling any geometrical problem involving triangles: *always draw the circumcircle*. Although this is often not necessary, it is generally a good idea and never does any harm.

We can, for instance, use the circumcircle for a neat proof of the sine rule.

The lengths of the sides BC, CA and AB of the reference triangle are written as a, b and c. This has the consequence that the side length opposite a vertex is denoted by the corresponding lower case letter. The area of $\triangle ABC$ is denoted by Δ, and the circumradius of $\triangle ABC$ is R.

Theorem 2.1 (Sine rule)

$$\frac{a}{\sin A} = \frac{b}{\sin B} = \frac{c}{\sin C} = 2R.$$

PROOF Draw a diameter AA' (see figure 2.1).

Figure 2.1   *Figure 2.2*

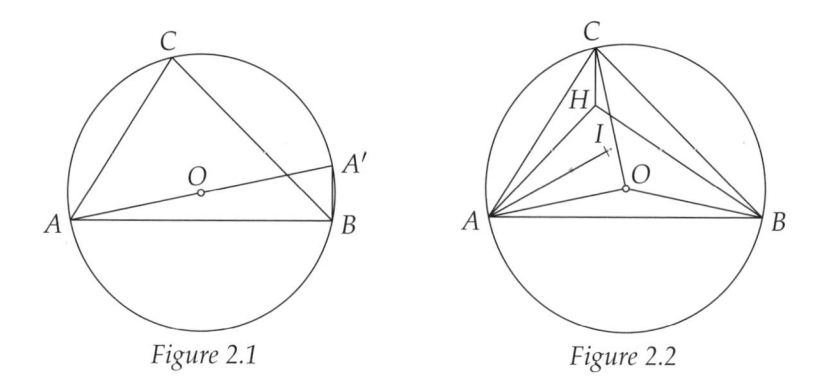

Then $\angle AA'B = \angle ACB = \angle C$ (angles in the same segment), $\angle ABA' = 90°$ (angle in a semicircle) and $AA' = 2R$. So $c = AB = 2R \sin C$ and hence
$$\frac{c}{\sin C} = 2R.$$
The other equalities follow similarly. ☐

Corollary 2.2 $\Delta = \dfrac{abc}{4R}$.

PROOF $\Delta = \frac{1}{2} ab \sin C = \frac{1}{2} ab \left(\dfrac{c}{2R} \right)$ by the sine rule. ☐

We can use the sine rule to derive relationships between significant lengths in a triangle, such as the altitudes and the sides. The feet of the perpendiculars from A, B and C to BC, CA and AB are denoted by D, E and F, and the lengths of the altitudes AD, BE and CF are h_A, h_B and h_C.

Corollary 2.3 $bc = 2R h_A$.

PROOF If we express the area of the triangle in two ways, we have $\frac{1}{2} a h_A = \frac{1}{2} bc \sin A$. By the sine rule, this becomes
$$\tfrac{1}{2} h_A = \tfrac{1}{2} \frac{bca}{2R},$$
and this can be rearranged to give the required result. ☐

Chapter 2: *The principal triangle centres*

Note that we have analogous relationships $ca = 2Rh_B$ and $ab = 2Rh_c$ by cyclic permutation of variables. This will happen frequently throughout this book, so much so that it will usually be taken for granted.

Geometrical facts can also be deduced using the circle theorems.

Theorem 2.4 *AI bisects $\angle HAO$.*

PROOF (See figure 2.2.)
Note first that $\angle AOC = 2\angle B$ (angles at centre and circumference). Since $\triangle AOC$ is isosceles, we have $\angle OAC = 90° - \angle B$. But $\angle BAH = 90° - \angle B$, and so $\angle OAC = \angle BAH$.

Since AI is the angle bisector of $\angle BAC$, it is also the angle bisector of $\angle HAO$. ❏

Theorem 2.5 *The internal angle bisector at A and the perpendicular bisector of BC meet on the circumcircle.*

PROOF Let X' be the point where the internal angle bisector meets the circumcircle again (see figure 2.3).

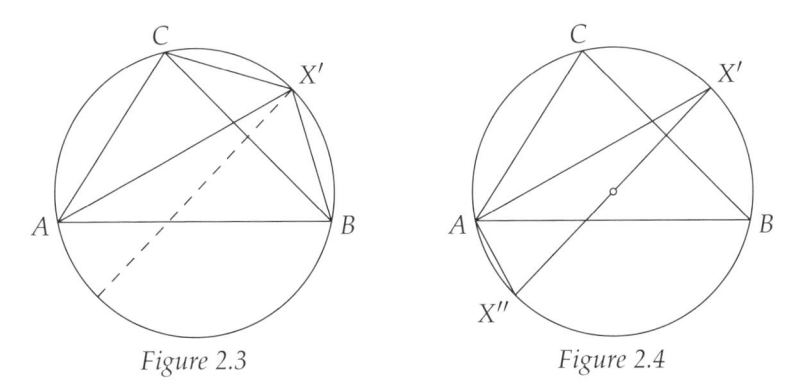

Figure 2.3 Figure 2.4

Since $\angle BAX' = \angle X'AC$, the chords BX' and $X'C$ are equal. Therefore $\triangle BX'C$ is isosceles and the perpendicular bisector of BC passes through X'. Note that this line also passes through the circumcentre, so it is a diameter of the circumcircle. ❏

Corollary 2.6 *The internal and external bisectors at A pass through the ends of the diameter of the circumcircle perpendicular to BC.*

PROOF Let the diameter perpendicular to BC meet the circumcircle at X' and X'' (see figure 2.4). It follows that $\angle X'AX'' = 90°$. However, by theorem 2.5, AX' is the internal angle bisector at A; it follows that AX'' is the external angle bisector. ❑

Similarly Y' and Z' are the points where the internal angle bisectors at B and C meet the circumcircle.

Theorem 2.7 *The incentre I is the orthocentre of the triangle $\triangle X'Y'Z'$.*

PROOF Set as question 2 of exercise 2a. ❑

Exercise 2a

1. Show that the circumcentre is the orthocentre of the medial triangle.

2. Prove theorem 2.7.

3. (a) Prove that $OH = OA + OB + OC$.
   (b) Prove that $OI = OX' + OY' + OZ'$.

4. Prove that the circumcircle of $\triangle BOC$ goes through H if, and only if, it goes through I.

5. Prove that, if the tangent to the circumcircle at A meets BC at T, then $b^2 \times BT = c^2 \times CT$.

6. Prove that, if the internal and external angle bisectors at A meet BC at X and X_1, then the tangent to the circumcircle at A meets BC at the midpoint of XX_1

7. Prove that, if the internal angle bisector at A meets BC at X, then $AX^2 + BX \times CX = bc$.

8. Let P, Q and R be internal points on the sides BC, CA and AB of triangle $\triangle ABC$. Prove that the perpendiculars to the sides at P, Q and R are concurrent at a point $\tilde{O}$ if, and only if,

$$BP^2 + CQ^2 + AR^2 = PC^2 + QA^2 + RB^2.$$

Prove that, if the perpendiculars are concurrent and, in addition,

$$\frac{BP}{PC} = \frac{CQ}{QA} = \frac{AR}{RB},$$

then $\tilde{O}$ is the circumcentre of $\triangle ABC$.

9. Two fixed lines $\mathcal{M}$ and $\mathcal{N}$ intersect at A. Points B and C move on $\mathcal{M}$ and $\mathcal{N}$ so that BC is of constant length. Find, with proof, the locus of the circumcentre of $\triangle ABC$.

10. The triangle $\triangle ABC$ is isosceles with $AB = AC$. Prove that, if X is any point on BC, and P and Q are the circumcentres of $\triangle ABX$ and $\triangle ACX$, then $APXQ$ is a rhombus.

11. Let A, B and C be points on a fixed line, in that order, and let D be a point not on the line. Let the circumcentres of $\triangle ABD$, $\triangle ACD$ and $\triangle BCD$ be X, Y and Z. Prove that the quadrilateral $XYZD$ is cyclic.

12. The diagonals of quadrilateral $ABCD$ meet at X, and the circumcentres of triangles $\triangle ABX$, $\triangle BCX$, $\triangle CDX$ and $\triangle DAX$ are P, Q, R and S. Prove that $PQRS$ is a parallelogram.

13. The quadrilateral $ABCD$ is cyclic, the sides AB and DC produced meet at P and the sides CB and DA produced meet at Q. The circumcircles of $\triangle PBC$ and $\triangle QAB$ meet at a second point R. Prove that P, R and Q are collinear.

14. Two circles, centred at O_1 and O_2, intersect at X and Y. The point A lies on the first circle and B on the second, such that A, X and B are collinear. If C is the intersection of AO_1 and BO_2, prove that Y lies on the circumcircle of $\triangle CO_1O_2$.

2.2 The centroid

Whereas the circle theorems are useful in proofs about the circumcentre, it is often considerations of area and ratio which help to determine properties of the centroid.

Theorem 2.8 *The medians of a triangle divide it into six parts of equal area.*

PROOF The base of the shaded triangle in figure 2.5 is one-half of the base of $\triangle ABC$, and its height is one-third of that of $\triangle ABC$ since G trisects CC_1.

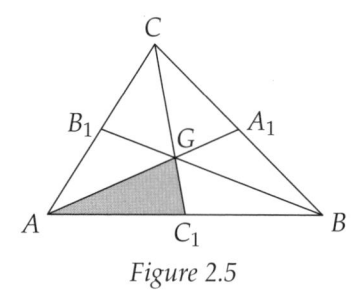

Figure 2.5

This is true of all six triangles around the centroid. ◻

Using the notation $[\ldots]$ to denote the area of a polygon, we have $[AC_1G] = \frac{1}{6}[ABC]$.

Exercise 2b

1. Find the locus of the centroid of a triangle with a fixed base and fixed circumcircle.

2. Prove that the line parallel to BC through G divides the area of the triangle into two parts in the ratio $4:5$.

3. Let X be any point on the median AA_1 and the distances of X from AB and AC be β and γ. Show that $\beta c = \gamma b$.

4. Let M be the midpoint of the median AA_1. Prove that BM trisects AC.

5. Let P be any point. Prove that the centroids of the three triangles $\triangle PBC$, $\triangle PCA$ and $\triangle PAB$ form a triangle which is similar to $\triangle ABC$.

6. Let P, Q and R be points on BC, CA and AB such that
$$\frac{BP}{PC} = \frac{CQ}{QA} = \frac{AR}{RB}.$$
Prove that the centroid of $\triangle PQR$ is G.

7. If $AG = BC$, prove that the medians from B and C are perpendicular.

8. Prove that the medians of $\triangle ABC$ can be rearranged to form another triangle, and find the area of this triangle in terms of the area of $\triangle ABC$.

2.3 The incentre and excentres

It is worth re-emphasising that the locus of points equidistant from two intersecting lines is not a single angle bisector, but a *pair* of angle bisectors which are at right angles to one another. In $\triangle ABC$, this means that we must include not only the internal bisectors of the angles of the vertices, but also their external bisectors as well. These intersect in four points, one of which is the incentre I and the other three are the excentres I_A, I_B and I_C.

The excentre I_A is the centre of a circle which touches the side BC internally and the sides AB and AC produced. The proof of this is almost identical to the ordinary incentre proof. So altogether we have a configuration involving four circles (see figure 2.6). Sometimes these are called the *tritangent* circles since each of them is tangential to three lines.

It is worth clarifying the standard notation used in the configuration.

- The centre of the excircle opposite to A is I_A.
- The points where the incircle touches BC, CA and AB are P, Q and R.

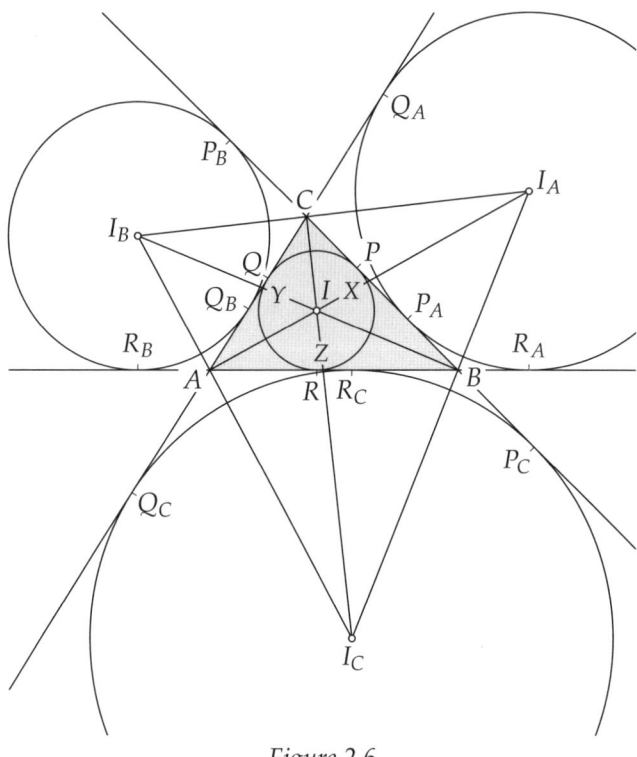

Figure 2.6

- The points where the excircle opposite A touches BC, CA and AB are P_A, Q_A and R_A.
- The radius of the incircle is r and the radius of the excircle opposite A is r_A.
- The semi-perimeter of $\triangle ABC$ is s.
- The internal angle bisectors at A, B and C meet the opposite sides at X, Y and Z.

Theorem 2.9 *The incentre I is the orthocentre of $\triangle I_A I_B I_C$.*

PROOF This follows immediately from the fact that the internal and external bisectors of an angle are perpendicular. ❑

The triangle $\triangle I_A I_B I_C$ is known as the *excentral triangle*.

Theorem 2.10 $AQ = AR = s - a$, $BR = BP = s - b$ and $CP = CQ = s - c$.

Chapter 2: The principal triangle centres

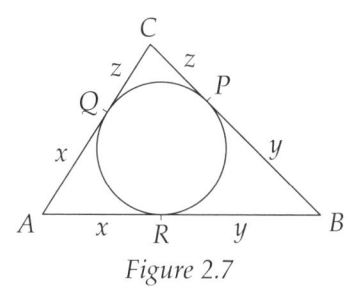

Figure 2.7

PROOF First note that tangents from a point to a circle are equal, so we can label the lengths in figure 2.7 as x, y and z. We now have

$$y + z = a,$$
$$z + x = b$$
and $$x + y = c.$$

A little algebra now yields the desired results. ☐

Theorem 2.11 $AQ_B = AR_B = s - c$, $BP_B = BR_B = s$ and $CP_B = CQ_B = s - a$. Consequently B_1 is the midpoint of QQ_B. There are similar results for the other two sides of $\triangle ABC$.

PROOF The two tangents from B to the excircle opposite B are equal, so $BP_B = BR_B$ (see figure 2.8).

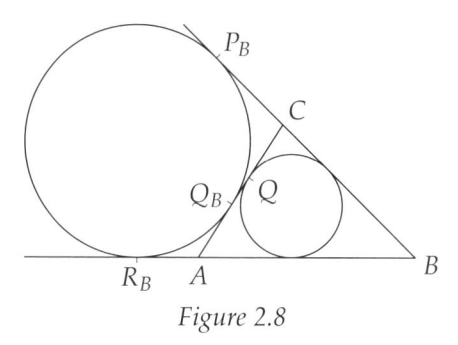

Figure 2.8

But also $AQ_B = AR_B$ and $CP_B = CQ_B$. This means that $2BR_B$ is the perimeter of $\triangle ABC$, so $BR_B = s$. The other formulae follow quickly from this and similar arguments. ☐

Theorem 2.12 $rs = \Delta$ and $r_A(s-a) = \Delta$.

PROOF The areas of the three triangles like the one shown shaded in figure 2.9 are $\frac{1}{2}ra$, $\frac{1}{2}rb$ and $\frac{1}{2}rb$, and their sum is Δ. It follows that $rs = \Delta$.

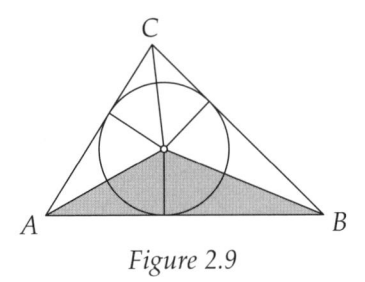

Figure 2.9

The other formula comes from a similar argument applied to triangles grouped around I_A, but it is necessary both to add and subtract areas to make the area of $\triangle ABC$. ❑

Theorem 2.13 *The circle with diameter* II_A *passes through B and C, and its centre is the point* X' *where AI meets the circumcircle of* $\triangle ABC$.

PROOF Since $\angle I_A BI$ is a right angle, B lies on the circle with diameter II_A, and the same is true of C (see figure 2.10).

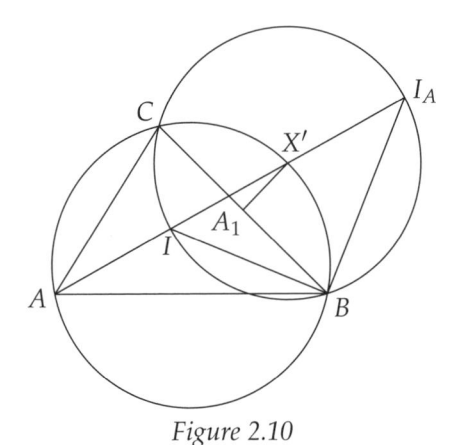

Figure 2.10

By theorem 2.5, $\angle X'A_1C = 90°$. It follows that X' is the centre of the circumcircle of $I_A BIC$. ❑

Chapter 2: The principal triangle centres

Theorem 2.14 *With the standard notation, $r_A + r_B + r_C - r = 4R$.*

PROOF Set as question 3 of exercise 2c. ❑

Exercise 2c

1. Prove that $\triangle I_A R_A B$ is similar to $\triangle BRI$ and that $rr_A = (s-b)(s-c)$. Hence deduce Heron's formula $\Delta = \sqrt{s(s-a)(s-b)(s-c)}$ for the area of $\triangle ABC$. Show also that $rr_A r_B r_C = \Delta^2$.

2. Prove that
$$\frac{1}{r} = \frac{1}{r_A} + \frac{1}{r_B} + \frac{1}{r_C} \quad \text{and} \quad \frac{1}{r} = \frac{1}{h_A} + \frac{1}{h_B} + \frac{1}{h_C}.$$

3. Prove theorem 2.14.

4. Prove that the circle with diameter $I_B I_C$ passes through B and C.

5. Prove that an external bisector of an angle of a triangle is parallel to the line joining the points where the circumcircle is met by the internal bisectors of the other two angles.

6. Prove that an external bisector of an angle of a triangle is parallel to the line joining the points where the circumcircle is met by the external bisectors of the other two angles.

7. Prove that, if $\angle BAC = 90°$, then $\angle BIC = 135°$.

8. Show how to construct three circles, centred at A, B and C, which touch in pairs on the sides of the triangle.

9. Suppose that the quadrilateral $ABCD$ is *inscribable*—it has an incircle which touches all four sides. Prove that the incircles of $\triangle ABD$ and $\triangle ACD$ touch AD at the same point.

10. Prove that the incircles of $\triangle ABP$ and $\triangle ACP$ touch AP at the same point.

11. Prove that, if $\angle BAC = 120°$, then the circle on diameter YZ passes through X.

12. Prove that a triangle is isosceles if, and only if, it has two equal angle bisectors.

13. Let A, B, C and D be four points on a circle. Prove that the incentres of the four triangles $\triangle ABC$, $\triangle ABD$, $\triangle ACD$ and $\triangle BCD$ form a rectangle.

2.4 The orthocentre

In figure 2.11, $\triangle DEF$ is known as the *orthic triangle*.

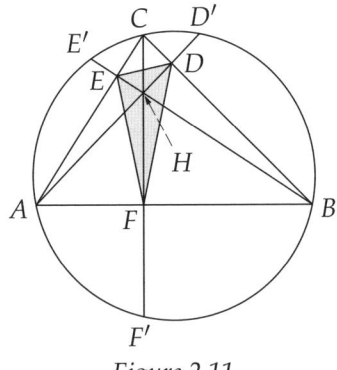

Figure 2.11

Let D', E' and F' be the points where AD, BE and CF meet the circumcircle again.

Theorem 2.15 *The orthocentres of $\triangle BCH$, $\triangle CAH$, $\triangle ABH$ are A, B, C respectively.*

PROOF This follows from consideration of altitudes in the diagram. ☐

Theorem 2.16 $AH \times HD = BH \times HE = CH \times HF$.

PROOF These results follow from cyclic quadrilaterals and the intersecting chords theorem. ❑

Theorem 2.17 *D, E and F are the midpoints of HD′, HE′ and HF′.*

PROOF We show that $\triangle HDC \cong \triangle D'DC$ (see figure 2.12).

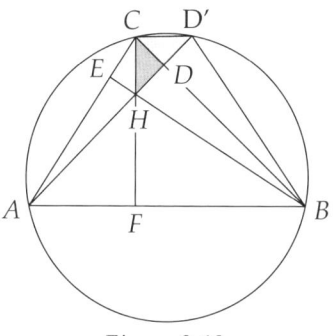

Figure 2.12

We immediately have equal right angles and a common side. The additional fact is that

$$\angle BCD' = \angle BAD'$$
$$= \angle BAD$$
$$= 90° - \angle B$$
$$= \angle FCD$$
$$= \angle HCD$$

and hence we have congruence by ASA. ❑

It follows from this result and the intersecting chords theorem that $BD \times DC = AD \times HD$, and so on.

Theorem 2.18 $\triangle BCH$, $\triangle CAH$ *and* $\triangle ABH$ *all have circumradius R.*

PROOF By a similar argument to the last, $\triangle BCH \cong \triangle BCD'$ and so they have the same circumradius. But the circumcircle of $\triangle BCD'$ is the same as that of $\triangle ABC$. ❑

Figure 2.13

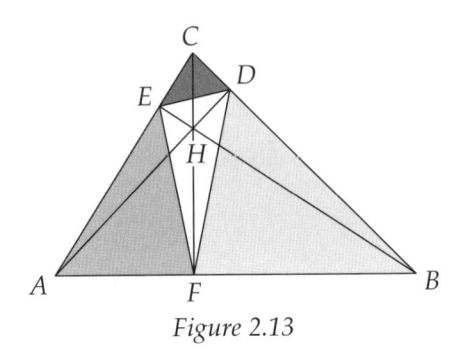

Theorem 2.19 Each of $\triangle AEF$, $\triangle DFB$ and $\triangle DEC$ is similar to $\triangle ABC$ (see figure 2.13).

PROOF We shall prove that $\triangle AEF$ is similar to $\triangle ABC$. This is because they clearly share an angle at A, and also, since $FECB$ is cyclic, $\angle AEF = \angle FBC$. ❑

Corollary 2.20 The two angles either side of E are both $\angle B$, those either side of F are both $\angle C$ and those either side of D are both $\angle A$.

Theorem 2.21 The incentre of the orthic triangle is H and its excentres are A, B and C.

PROOF It follows from corollary 2.20 that DH, EH and FH are the internal angle bisectors of $\triangle DEF$, and hence the sides of $\triangle ABC$ are the external angle bisectors. ❑

Theorem 2.22 The lines AO, BO and CO are perpendicular to EF, FD and DE.

PROOF Set as question 3 of exercise 2d. ❑

Exercise 2d

1. Show that A, B and C are the midpoints of the arcs $E'F'$, $F'D'$ and $D'E'$.

2. Prove that the perpendicular bisector of EF passes through A_1.

3. Prove theorem 2.22.

4. Prove that the lines through D, E and F parallel to AO, BO and CO are concurrent.

5. Prove that the lines through D', E' and F' parallel to AO, BO and CO are concurrent.

6. Let P and Q be the feet of the perpendiculars from B and C to DF and DE. Show that EQ is equal to FP.

7. Prove that the circumcircles of $AFHE$ and $BCEF$ are *orthogonal*—they intersect at right angles.

8. Two circles intersect at P and Q. A variable line through P meets the circles at A and B. Find, with proof, the locus of the orthocentre of $\triangle ABQ$.

2.5 Fagnano's problem

The problem of finding an inscribed triangle of minimum perimeter in an acute-angled triangle was first stated by Giovanni Fagnano in 1775, and his solution used the techniques of the calculus. However, there is an illuminating argument using reflections.

Begin with any point P on the side AB, which is regarded as fixed, and let Q and R be arbitrary points on BC and AC. Reflect the triangle $\triangle ABC$ in the sides BC and AC so that the images of P are P' and P'' (see figure 2.14).

Then
$$PQ + QR + RP = P'Q + QR + RP''$$
since $PQ = P'Q$ and $PR = P''R$. Now the points P' and P'' are fixed, so the distance is minimised when Q and R are positioned so that P', Q, R and P'' are collinear (see figure 2.15).

But now $\triangle CP'P''$ is isosceles since $CP' = CP'' = CP$, and $\angle P'CP'' = 2\angle BCA$. (Note that we require $\triangle ABC$ to be acute in order that this triangle

Figure 2.14   *Figure 2.15*

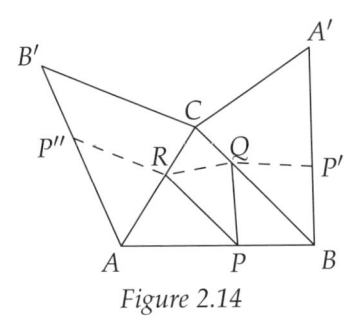

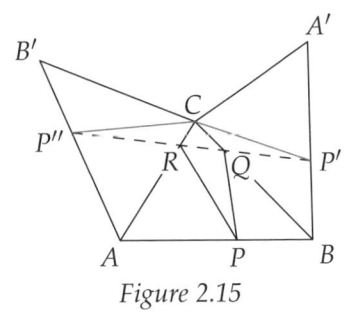

exists.) So the length $P'P''$ is minimised when CP is minimised. Hence the optimal situation is achieved when P is F, the foot of the altitude from C (see figure 2.16).

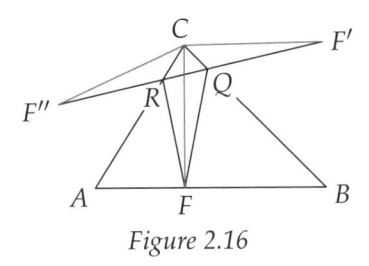

Figure 2.16

Then $\angle CFQ = \angle CF'Q = 90° - \angle C$ and so $\angle BFQ = \angle C$. Similarly $\angle AFR = \angle C$. Hence $\triangle FQR$ is the orthic triangle and Q and R are D and E.

The final step is, in fact, unnecessary. We have shown that the point F on side AB is the only point which produces a unique triangle with minimal perimeter. However, one could equally apply this argument to points on CA to show that E does exactly the same thing. Since the triangle is unique, it must be the same triangle as is generated by F. Similarly, the point D on BC will produce exactly the same minimal triangle, which is therefore $\triangle DEF$.

We have proved the following result.

Theorem 2.23 (Fagnano) *The orthic triangle is the inscribed triangle of minimum perimeter in an acute-angled triangle.*

Notice that this is intuitively suggested by corollary 2.20, if we imagine a billiard ball bouncing off the sides of the triangle with perfectly elastic collisions, and hence following the straight line path in the reflected diagram above.

Of course, this also gives an 'interesting' characterisation of the orthocentre.

We define the *pedal triangle* of a point inside $\triangle ABC$ as that formed by the feet of the perpendiculars to the sides BC, CA and AB.

Fagnano's theorem shows that the orthocentre of a triangle is the point whose pedal triangle has minimal perimeter. However, it is actually more general than this since it applies to all inscribed triangles, and not all such triangles are pedal triangles of a point.

Exercise 2e

1. Prove that the perimeter of the minimal triangle for Fagnano's problem (and hence the orthic triangle) is $\dfrac{2\Delta}{R}$.

2. If $\triangle ABC$ is acute-angled, with orthic triangle $\triangle DEF$, prove that $DE + DF \leq BC$, and determine the conditions for equality.

3. Deduce from the result of either question 1 or question 2 that $R \geq 2r$.

Chapter 3

The Euler line

3.1 An important collinearity

As already mentioned, the reference triangle $\triangle ABC$ and the medial triangle $\triangle A_1B_1C_1$ are homothetic under the enlargement θ with centre G and scale factor $-\frac{1}{2}$. This maps every triangle centre of $\triangle ABC$ to the corresponding triangle centre of $\triangle A_1B_1C_1$, and, in so doing, establishes that these two centres are collinear with G. For example, the centroid of $\triangle ABC$ is mapped to the centroid of $\triangle A_1B_1C_1$, but, as both of these are the point G, this is not saying a great deal.

More significantly, the orthocentre of $\triangle ABC$ is mapped to the orthocentre of $\triangle A_1B_1C_1$. However, the orthocentre of $\triangle A_1B_1C_1$ is the circumcentre of $\triangle ABC$ since the altitudes of the first triangle are the perpendicular bisectors of the second. This means that the three points H, G and O are collinear, and, moreover, $HG = 2GO$. The line containing all three centres is called the *Euler line* of $\triangle ABC$.

Now consider the circumcentre O of $\triangle ABC$, which is mapped to the circumcentre of $\triangle A_1B_1C_1$. Call this new point N (see figure 3.1).

It follows, as before, that N lies on the Euler line and that $OG = 2GN$. All of this can be summarised in the important theorem.

Theorem 3.1 *The points O, G, N and H are collinear and $OG : GN : NH = 2 : 1 : 3$.*

PROOF This follows from the ratios already mentioned; note in particular that N is the midpoint of OH. ❑

Figure 3.1

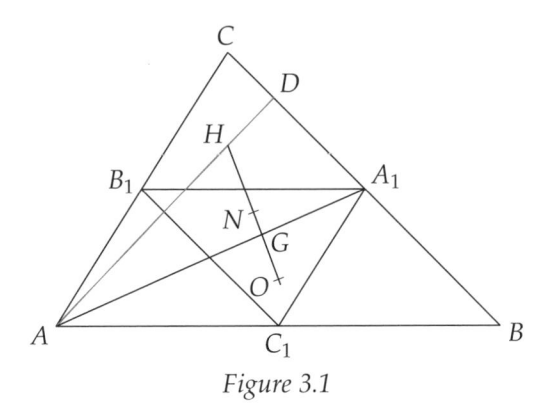

A consequence of theorem 3.1 is that $HN : NG = 3 : 1$ and that $HO : OG$ is the same. However, if we follow the usual convention of denoting 'backward' lengths as negative, then $HO : OG = 3 : -1$. We say that N divides HG *internally* in the same ratio as O divides HG *externally*. This relationship is explored in depth in chapter 5.

Theorem 3.2 $\triangle AHG$ *is similar to* $\triangle A_1 OG$ *and* $AH = 2A_1 O$.

PROOF The similarity follows from the ratios in theorem 3.1 by the SAS condition and the second fact is an immediate consequence. ❑

3.2 The nine-point circle

Theorem 3.3 N *is the centre of a circle containing nine points. They are the midpoints of the sides* A_1, B_1 *and* C_1, *the feet of the altitudes* D, E *and* F, *and the Euler points* U, V *and* W, *the midpoints of* AH, BH *and* CH *(see figure 3.2).*

The circle of theorem 3.3 is the *nine-point circle* and N is the *nine-point centre* of $\triangle ABC$.

PROOF (See figure 3.3.)
Theorem 3.1 shows that $\triangle UHN$ and $\triangle A_1 ON$ are congruent by SAS, and it is then immediate that $NU = NA_1$. Hence N is the centre of the circle on diameter UA_1, and, by the converse of the angle in a semicircle theorem, this passes through D. As N is by definition the circumcentre of $\triangle A_1 B_1 C_1$, we now have five concyclic points A_1, B_1, C_1, D and U, and, by exactly the same argument, E, F, V and W lie on the circle as well.

Chapter 3: The Euler line

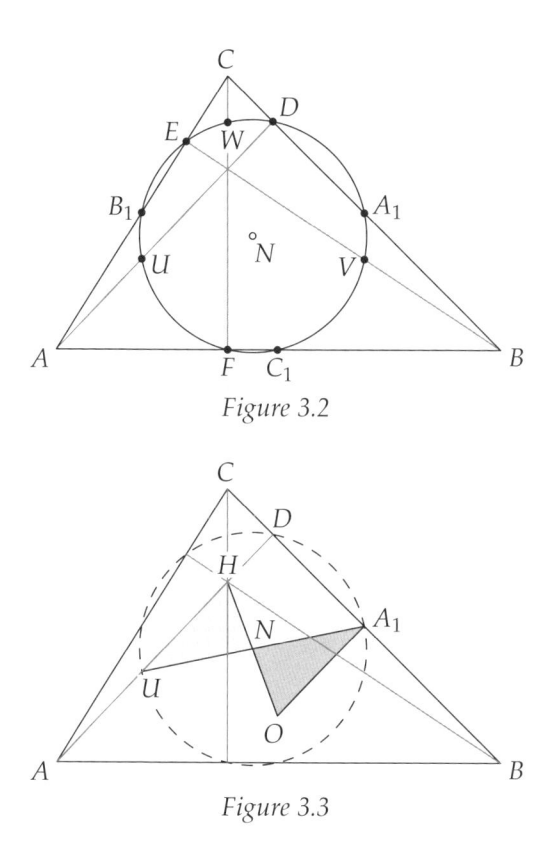

Figure 3.2

Figure 3.3

However, there is nothing special about A_1, D and U, so the other six points also lie on the circle. ❑

Corollary 3.4 *The nine-point circle is the circumcircle of the orthic triangle and of the medial triangle, and it has circumradius $\frac{1}{2}R$.*

PROOF The first statement is simply a restatement of theorem 3.3. The second is a consequence of regarding the nine-point circle as the image of the circumcircle under θ, which takes O to N. ❑

Theorem 3.5 *The tangent to the nine-point circle at A_1 makes an angle of $|\angle C - \angle B|$ with BC.*

PROOF Set as question 10 of exercise 3a. ❑

The next two results will turn out to be useful in chapters 12 and 21.

Lemma 3.6 *Let p_A be the perpendicular distance from N to BC. Then $p_A = \frac{1}{2} R \cos(B - C)$.*

PROOF Set as question 12 of exercise 3a. ❑

As on 15, P, Q and R are the points of contact of the incircle with BC, CA and AB.

Theorem 3.7 *The circumcircle of $\triangle QAR$ passes through the incentre I.*

PROOF Set as question 13 of exercise 3a. ❑

Exercise 3a

1. What is the Euler line of
   (a) an equilateral triangle?
   (b) an isosceles triangle?
   (c) a right-angled triangle?

2. Prove that the Euler line of $\triangle ABC$ is parallel to BC if, and only if, $\tan B \tan C = 3$.

3. Show that the medial triangle $\triangle A_1 B_1 C_1$ is congruent to the *Euler triangle* $\triangle UVW$.

4. Prove that OU is bisected by AA_1.

5. Let PP' be a diameter of the circumcircle of $\triangle ABC$. Show that PG (produced) bisects the line segment HP'.

6. Let P be a fixed point inside a circle, and let APB and CPD be perpendicular chords of the circle, intersecting at P. As these chords rotate about P, what is the locus of the orthocentres of $\triangle ABC$ and $\triangle ABD$?

7. In the same configuration as question 6, what is the locus of the centroids of these two triangles?

Chapter 3: The Euler line 31

8. What happens to the nine-point circle if the triangle is
   (a) right-angled?
   (b) isosceles?

9. Prove that the nine-point circle of $\triangle AB_1C_1$ touches the nine-point circle of $\triangle A_1B_1C_1$.

10. Prove theorem 3.5.

11. Let $\triangle ABC$ be acute-angled with $AB > AC$ and $\angle BAC = 60°$ and suppose that its Euler line meets AB at X and AC at Y. Prove that $\triangle AXY$ is equilateral.

12. Prove lemma 3.6.

13. Prove theorem 3.7.

3.3 Distances between triangle centres

Theorem 3.8 (Euler's formula) *If r and R are the inradius and circumradius of a triangle, then $IO^2 = R(R - 2r)$.*

PROOF Let CI meet the circumcircle at Z' and $Z'Z''$ be a diameter (see figure 3.4).

Now $\angle ICQ = \angle Z'CA = \angle Z'Z''A$ and $\angle CQI = \angle Z''AZ' = 90°$, so $\triangle CQI$ is similar to $\triangle Z''AZ'$ and hence

$$\frac{QI}{AZ'} = \frac{CI}{Z''Z'}.$$

It follows that $QI \times Z''Z' = AZ' \times CI$. But $QI = r$ and $Z''Z' = 2R$, so this common value is $2rR$.

By theorem 2.9 on page 16, I is the orthocentre and $\triangle ABC$ the orthic triangle of $\triangle I_AI_BI_C$, so the circumcircle of $\triangle ABC$ is the nine-point circle of $\triangle I_AI_BI_C$ and Z' is an Euler point. This means that $IZ' = Z'I_C$. Hence Z' is the centre of the circumcircle of $\triangle IAI_A$ and so $AZ' = IZ'$. Hence we have $CI \times IZ' = 2rR$. Now introduce another diameter $XIOY$. By intersecting chords, $CI \times IZ' = XI \times IY = (R - IO)(R + IO)$. The result follows. ☐

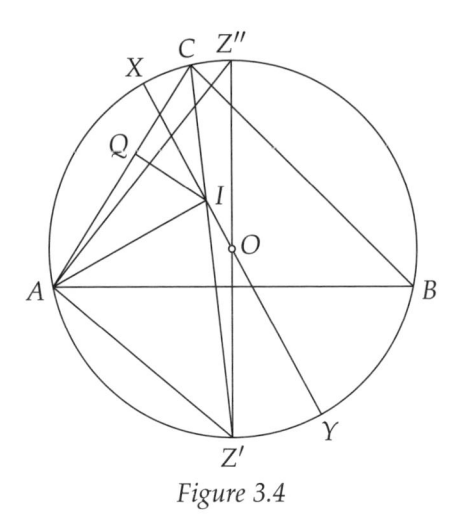

Corollary 3.9 $R \geq 2r$.

PROOF Simply note that $IO \geq 0$. ☐

Theorem 3.10 *In a triangle $\triangle ABC$, with the standard notation,*

$$OH^2 = 9R^2 - (a^2 + b^2 + c^2).$$

PROOF Let X be the foot of the perpendicular from O to AD (see figure 3.5).

We will use the right-angled triangle $\triangle OXH$. Note that

$$OX = A_1 D$$
$$= \tfrac{1}{2}a - b\cos C$$

and that

$$XH = AH + OA_1 - AD$$
$$= 3OA_1 - AD$$
$$= 3R\cos A - b\sin C,$$

Figure 3.5

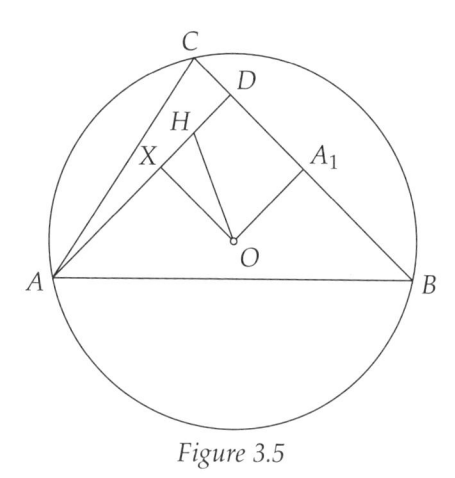

using theorem 3.2. Hence, using the sine and cosine rules,

$$OH^2 = \left(\tfrac{1}{2}a - b\cos C\right)^2 + (3R\cos A - b\sin C)^2$$
$$= \tfrac{1}{4}a^2 + b^2 - ab\cos C - 6bR\sin C \cos A + 9R^2 \cos^2 A$$
$$= \tfrac{1}{4}a^2 + b^2 - ab\cos C - 3bc\cos A + 9R^2 - 9R^2 \sin^2 A$$
$$= \tfrac{1}{4}a^2 + c^2 - \tfrac{1}{2}(a^2 + b^2 - c^2) - \tfrac{3}{2}(b^2 + c^2 - a^2) + 9R^2 - \tfrac{9}{4}a^2$$
$$= 9R^2 - (a^2 + b^2 + c^2). \qquad \square$$

Exercise 3b

1. Under what conditions do we have $R = 2r$?

2. Find an expression for ON^2.

3. (a) Prove that $OH^2 = R^2(1 - 8\cos A \cos B \cos C)$.
   (b) Deduce that $\cos A \cos B \cos C \leq \tfrac{1}{8}$.
   (c) What are the conditions for equality?

4. Prove that the Euler line of $\triangle ABC$ is perpendicular to the median from A if, and only if, $b^2 + c^2 = 2a^2$.

3.4 Orthocentric quadrilaterals

Consider figure 3.6 which features $\triangle ABC$, its orthocentre H and the orthic triangle $\triangle DEF$.

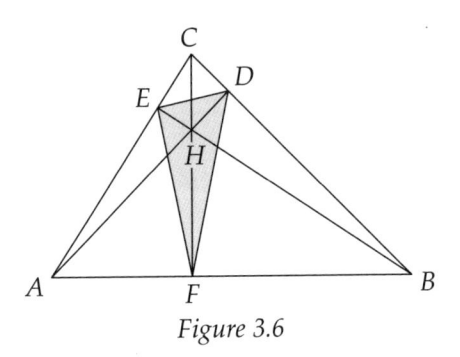

Figure 3.6

By theorem 2.15 on page 20, each of A, B, C and H is the orthocentre of the other three. These four points are said to form an *orthocentric quadrilateral*. The four triangles $\triangle ABC$, $\triangle BCH$, $\triangle CAH$ and $\triangle ABH$ form an *orthocentric group*.

The orthocentric group has the following properties:

- The four triangles of the group have the same orthic triangle.
- The four triangles of the group have the same circumradius.
- The four triangles of the group have the same nine-point centre and circle. The Euler lines of the four triangles of an orthocentric group are concurrent.

The first of these is immediate, the second is theorem 2.18, the third follows from corollary 3.4 and the fourth is true since each Euler line contains the common nine-point centre.

Now consider the effect on this configuration of an enlargement with centre N and scale factor -1. On an Euler line, N is the midpoint of OH, so this mapping takes O to H and H to O. Since all four Euler lines meet at N, it will map one orthocentric quadrilateral, consisting of A, B, C and H, to a second, congruent, orthocentric quadrilateral consisting of the circumcentres of the four triangles of the orthocentric group. At the same time, the common nine-point circle is mapped to itself. Furthermore, this enlargement is invertible, so the process can be reversed. As a consequence, we have the following theorem.

Theorem 3.11 *(i) The circumcentres of the four triangles of the group form an orthocentric quadrilateral.*
(ii) The nine-point circle of the group of circumcentres is the same as that of the original group.
(iii) The points H, C, A and B can be considered as the circumcentres of a second orthocentric group of triangles.

Similarly, an enlargement with centre N and scale factor $-\frac{1}{3}$ takes the points H, C, A and B to the centroids of the four triangles of the group, and as a consequence we have another theorem.

Theorem 3.12 *(i) The centroids of the four triangles of the group form an orthocentric quadrilateral.*
(ii) The nine-point circle of an orthocentric group of triangles and the nine-point circle of the group formed by the centroids are concentric.
(iii) H, C, A and B can be considered as the centroids of another orthocentric group of points having the same nine-point centre.

Exercise 3c

1. Prove that the circumcentres of $\triangle BCH$, $\triangle CAH$ and $\triangle ABH$ form a triangle congruent to $\triangle ABC$ with sides parallel to those of $\triangle ABC$, circumcentre H and orthocentre O.

2. Prove that the centroids of $\triangle BCH$, $\triangle CAH$ and $\triangle ABH$ form a triangle similar to $\triangle ABC$ with sides parallel to those of $\triangle ABC$ and orthocentre G.

3. Prove that the incentre and three excentres form an orthocentric quadrilateral and identify its orthic triangle and nine-point circle. Show that the circumradius of any triangle in this group is equal to the circumdiameter of $\triangle ABC$.

4. Prove that the incentre of the medial triangle $\triangle A_1 B_1 C_1$ is the midpoint of the line segment joining H to the circumcentre of the excentral triangle. (This point is known as the *Spieker centre*, and will be met again in section 9.3.)

3.5 Three more points on the Euler line

If we now carry out an enlargement with centre G and scale factor -2, the reference triangle $\triangle ABC$ maps to the anticomplementary triangle $\triangle A^*B^*C^*$. The orthocentre of $\triangle ABC$ maps to the orthocentre of $\triangle A^*B^*C^*$. This is known as the *de Longchamps point* and is labelled Λ in figure 3.7.

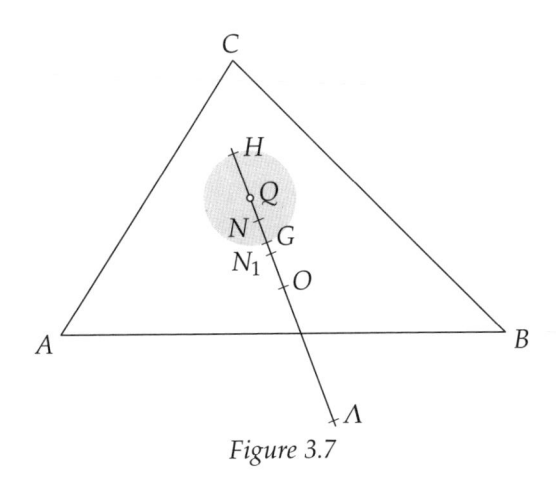

Figure 3.7

Going in the other direction, we can map the reference triangle to the medial triangle $\triangle A_1B_1C_1$ and create the nine-point centre of the medial triangle. This does not have a name, but we will call it the *medial centre* and denote it by N_1. Also marked in figure 3.7 is Q, which is the midpoint of GH. It is the centre of the *orthocentroidal disc*, which has GH as diameter.

The points H, Q, N, G, N_1, O and Λ lie on the Euler line in that order and the distances between them are in fixed ratios, which the reader can calculate.

We could clearly continue doing this sort of thing forever and so create an infinite sequence of centres on the Euler line, but there must be some sort of subjective judgement as to which are *interesting* centres. This presumably means that the centres bear some relationship—such as collinearity, conjugacy, concyclicity—to other centres, triangles or circles. The de Longchamps point, medial centre and orthocentroidal disc have this property and will all make appearances later in this book.

3.6 The power of a point

Suppose we have a fixed circle and a point P. It turns out to be useful to define a quantity which is positive, zero or negative according as the point is outside, on or inside the circle.

The *power of a point* P with respect to a circle with centre O and radius R is defined as $OP^2 - R^2$.

The smallest possible value of the power is $-R^2$, which happens when P coincides with O. It is clear that when P is on the circumference of the circle, the power is zero. For points inside or outside the circle, there is an obvious connection with the theorems about intersecting chords, tangents and secants.

If P lies outside the circle (see figure 3.8), then the power of P is equal to the square of the tangent PT^2, and also to $PA \times PB$. It is a positive quantity.

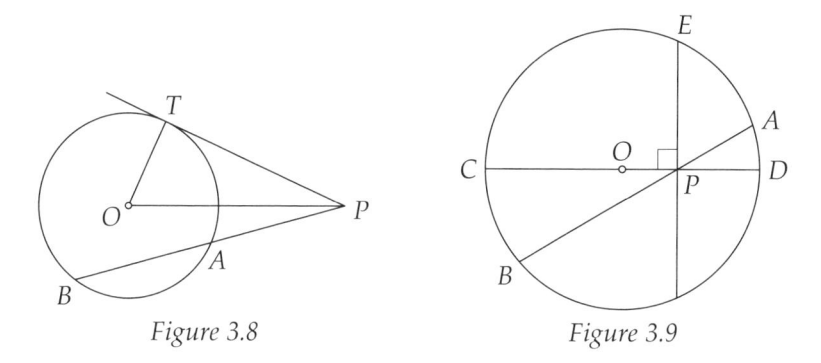

Figure 3.8   Figure 3.9

If P lies inside the circle (see figure 3.9), then the power of P is equal to

$$(OP + R)(OP - R) = -CP \times PD$$
$$= -AP \times PB$$
$$= -PE^2$$

and it is a negative quantity.

Of all the chords through P, that of minimal length is perpendicular to the diameter through P. Therefore we could also think of the power of P as $-\frac{1}{4}m^2$, where m is the length of the minimal chord.

Theorem 3.13 *If a point P is outside a circle C, then the power of P is equal to the square of the radius of a circle with centre P orthogonal to C.*

PROOF Set as question 2 of exercise 3d. ❑

This idea turns out to be useful in various calculations, and avoids the use of a great deal of trigonometrical manipulation which is often involved. Here is an example which uses the concept of power and some facts about the nine-point circle.

Theorem 3.14 *In the standard orthocentre configuration,*

$$AH \times HD = 4R^2 - \tfrac{1}{2}\left(a^2 + b^2 + c^2\right).$$

PROOF (See figure 3.10.)

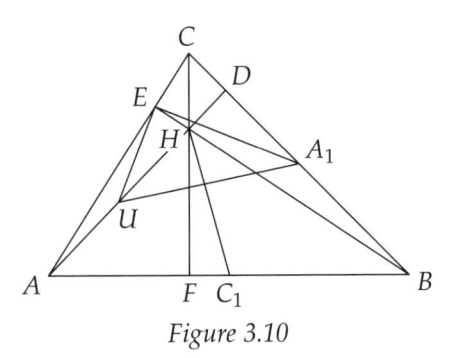

Figure 3.10

Note that $AH \times HD$ is the power of H with respect to the circle on diameter AB. Hence

$$AH \times HD = HC_1^2 - \tfrac{1}{4}c^2.$$

But, by Apollonius' median theorem,

$$2HC_1^2 + \tfrac{1}{2}c^2 = HA^2 + HB^2.$$

So

$$AH \times HD = \tfrac{1}{2}\left(HA^2 + HB^2 - c^2\right).$$

Now UA_1 is the diameter of the nine-point circle, which is R. Also $UE = \tfrac{1}{2}AH$ and $EA_1 = \tfrac{1}{2}a$, so $AH^2 = 4R^2 - a^2$. Similarly $BH^2 = 4R^2 - b^2$. The result follows. ❑

Exercise 3d

1. If $p > -R^2$, what is the locus of a point which has power p with respect to a fixed circle of radius R?

2. Prove theorem 3.13.

3. Let two circles C_1 and C_2, with centres O_1 and O_2, have common chord AB, and suppose that AB is a diameter of C_1. Prove that the power of O_1 with respect to C_2 is $-\frac{1}{4}AB^2$.

Chapter 4

Simson lines

In this chapter, we meet the Simson line. This is an important collinearity arising from points on the circumcircle of a triangle, which turns out to be linked both to the orthocentre and the nine-point circle. We then explore the consequences of a very simple but surprising theorem associated with Miquel.

4.1 The Simson line

Theorem 4.1 *Let P be any point in the plane of $\triangle ABC$, and let L, M and N be the feet of the perpendiculars from P to BC, CA and AB. Then the points L, M and N are collinear if, and only if, P lies on the circumcircle of $\triangle ABC$.*

PROOF (See figure 4.1.)
Note that, for any position of P, we have cyclic quadrilaterals $PNAM$ and $PMCL$. It follows that $\angle AMN = \angle APN = 90° - \angle PAN$ and $\angle LMC = \angle LPC = 90° - \angle PCL$.
Hence L, M and N are collinear if, and only if, $\angle AMN = \angle LMC$, which is true if, and only if, $\angle PAN = \angle PCL$, that is, if and only if, P is on the circumcircle of $\triangle ABC$. ❑

If a different position for P is chosen, then the points L, M and N might well appear in a different order on the line. However, the proof needed will remain essentially the same as that given above. The only change will be that the reason for the final step will change from being

Figure 4.1

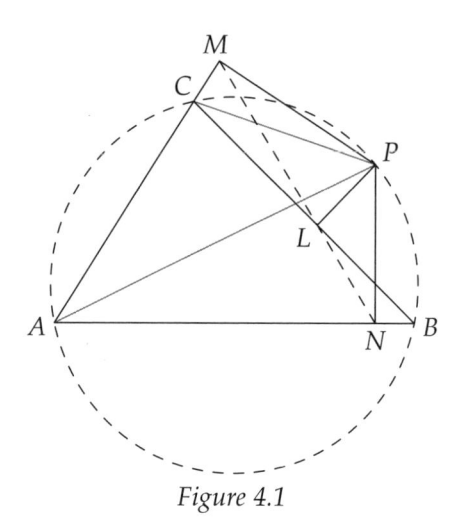

'angles in the same segment' to 'external angle of a cyclic quadrilateral'. As mentioned in the introduction, this 'ambiguity' can be avoided by using the concept of directed angles. Readers will notice that similar examples of diagram dependency occur throughout this chapter, but there will never be a problem about adapting the proofs to fit any possible diagram.

The line so formed is called the *Simson line* of P with respect to $\triangle ABC$. Note that theorem 4.1 allows us to define the circumcircle as the locus of points whose pedal triangle degenerates to a line.

The next couple of results allow us to locate the Simson line of a given point on the circumcircle.

Theorem 4.2 *The Simson line of P is parallel to AL', where L' is the point where PL meets the circumcircle again.*

PROOF (See figure 4.2.)
By exterior angle of a cyclic quadrilateral, $\angle PL'A = \angle PCM$. But $PMCL$ is cyclic, so $\angle PCM = \angle PLM$. Hence AL' is parallel to the Simson line MLN. ❑

Note that similarly defined lines BM' and CN' are also parallel to the Simson line.

Theorem 4.2 allows us to show that there is exactly one Simson line in a given direction. Suppose we want to find the Simson line parallel

Chapter 4: Simson lines   43

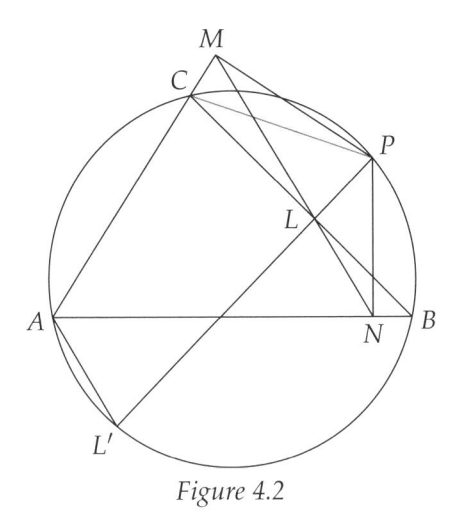

Figure 4.2

to the line $\mathcal{M}$. Draw a line parallel to $\mathcal{M}$ through A, say, meeting the circumcircle at L', and then the chord through L' perpendicular to BC until it meets the circumcircle again at P. Then by theorem 4.2, the Simson line of P has the desired direction. The point P is uniquely determined by $\mathcal{M}$, and as a consequence we can call P the *Simson pole* of $\mathcal{M}$, without any ambiguity.

Theorem 4.3 *The Simson line of P bisects PH.*

PROOF Let AD meet the circumcircle again at D', let PD' intersect BC at K, and let HK and PL intersect at K' (see figure 4.3).
    Since, by theorem 2.17 on page 21, $\triangle HDK$ is congruent to $\triangle D'DK$, we have $\angle AL'P = \angle AD'P = \angle DD'K = \angle DHK' = \angle HK'P$. So HK' is parallel to AL' and also to the Simson line.
    Since PL' is parallel to AD', the arcs AP and $D'L'$ are equal, and so the angles subtended are also equal. Hence $\angle AL'P = \angle D'PL'$. It follows that $\angle KK'L = \angle KPL$ and so L is the midpoint of PK'.
    Now consider $\triangle PHK'$. Since the Simson line passes through the midpoint L of PK' and is parallel to HK', it also bisects PH. This proves the desired result. ❏

Theorem 4.3 allows us to state theorem 4.1 in a different way.

Figure 4.3

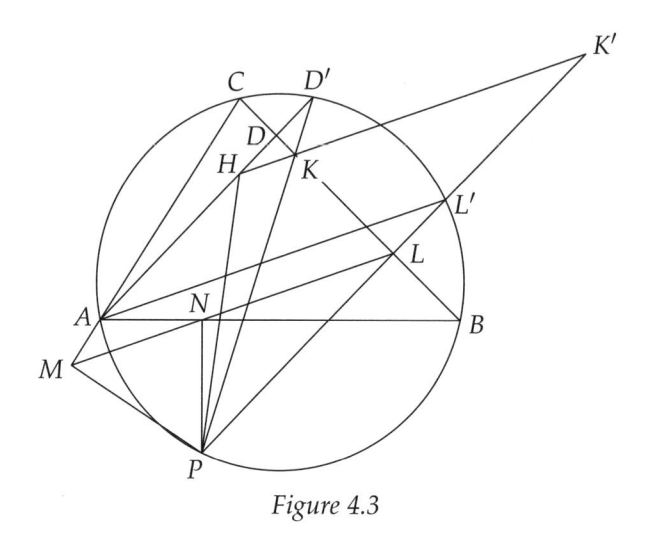

Let P be any point in the plane of $\triangle ABC$, and let P_A, P_B and P_C be the images of P in the sides BC, CA and AB. Then P is on the circumcircle of $\triangle ABC$ if, and only if, P_A, P_B, P_C and H are collinear (see figure 4.4).

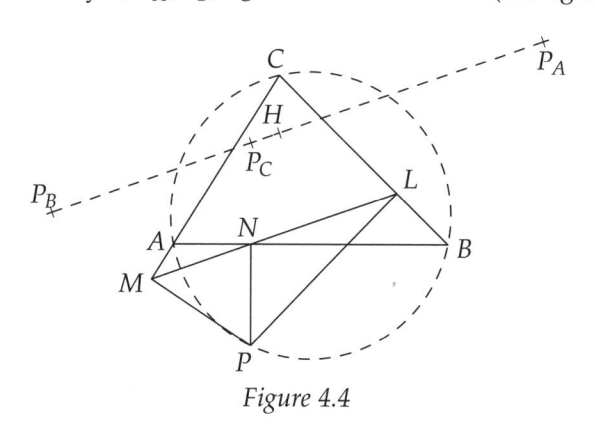

Figure 4.4

To see that this is equivalent, simply find the images of L, M and N under an enlargement with centre P and scale factor 2.

Theorem 4.4 *The Simson line of a point P on the circumcircle intersects PH on the nine-point circle.*

PROOF Set as question 3 of exercise 4a. ☐

Exercise 4a

1. What is the Simson line of a vertex of $\triangle ABC$?

2. What is the Simson line of a point diametrically opposite to a vertex of $\triangle ABC$?

3. Prove theorem 4.4.

4. If the Simson line of P is parallel to CO, prove that PC is parallel to AB.

5. Let D' be the point where the altitude AD cuts the circumcircle again. Prove that the Simson line of D' is through D and perpendicular to the tangent at A.

6. Let PQ be a chord of the circumcircle parallel to BC. Show that Simson line of P is perpendicular to AQ.

7. Prove that, if the perpendicular from A to the Simson line of P intersects the circumcircle again at Q, then PQ is parallel to BC.

8. Suppose that $ABCD$ is a cyclic quadrilateral. Use the Simson line result to prove Ptolemy's theorem, that $AD \times BC + AB \times DC = AC \times DB$.

9. Prove that the feet of the perpendiculars from D to AB, BE, CF and AC are collinear.

10. Let PA, PB and PC be three chords of a circle, and let $\mathcal{C}_1$, $\mathcal{C}_2$ and $\mathcal{C}_3$ be circles with PA, PB and PC as diameters. Prove that these circles intersect in pairs in three collinear points.

11. Let $APBC$ be a cyclic quadrilateral. Prove that the circles through P with centres A, B and C intersect in pairs at three points which are collinear with the orthocentre of $\triangle ABC$.

4.2 Another look at the nine-point circle

We first establish a result about the directions of different Simson lines.

Theorem 4.5 *Suppose P and Q are points on the circumcircle so that $\angle POQ = 2\alpha$; then the angle between the Simson lines of P and Q is α.*

PROOF Draw the usual perpendiculars PJ' and QK' (see figure 4.5).

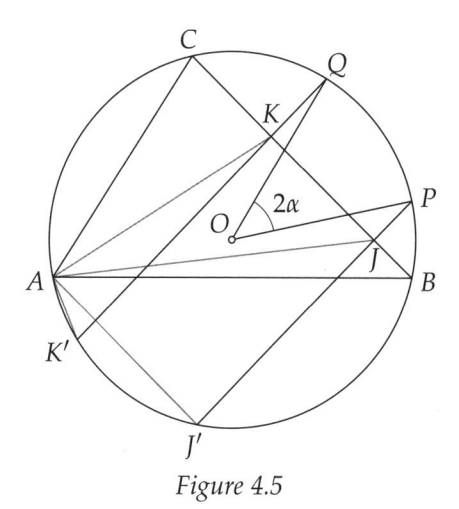

Figure 4.5

Then, by theorem 4.2, the angle between the Simson lines is $\angle J'AK'$. Since PJ' and QK' are parallel, the arcs QP and $K'J'$ are equal, and so $\angle J'AK' = \angle J'PK' = \angle PJ'Q = \frac{1}{2}\angle POQ = \alpha$. □

Corollary 4.6 *If P and Q are diametrically opposite on the circumcircle, then their Simson lines are perpendicular.*

By the result of theorem 4.4, there is clearly a link between the Simson lines of points on the circumcircle and the nine-point circle. In fact, we could define the nine-point circle as the locus of the intersection of the Simson line of P with PH, as P moves around the circumcircle. In addition, we have the following theorem.

Theorem 4.7 *The Simson lines of the points at the ends of a diameter of the circumcircle intersect at right angles on the nine-point circle.*

Chapter 4: Simson lines

PROOF Let P and Q be diametrically opposite points on the circumcircle of $\triangle ABC$. The Simson line of P passes through the midpoint M_P of PH and that of Q through the midpoint M_Q of QH (see figure 4.6).

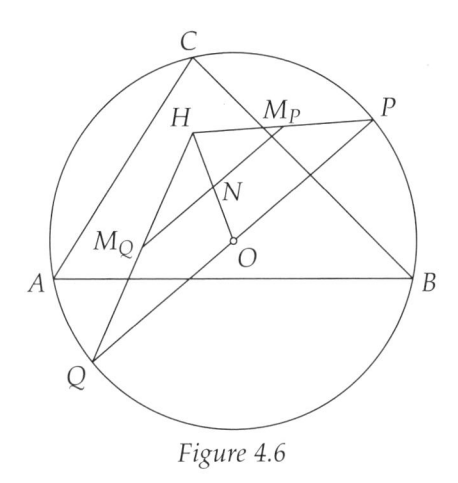

Figure 4.6

An enlargement with centre H and scale factor $\frac{1}{2}$ maps the circumcircle onto the nine-point circle, so $M_P M_Q$ is a diameter of the nine-point circle. Since, by theorem 4.5, the two Simson lines are perpendicular, they meet on this circle. ❑

It follows from theorem 4.7 that it would also be possible to define the nine-point circle as the locus of the intersections of Simson lines of points which are diametrically opposite on the circumcircle.

Exercise 4b

1. Let the Simson lines of points P, Q and R on the circumcircle form a triangle; prove that this is similar to $\triangle PQR$.

2. Prove that, in terms of the result described in theorem 4.7,
   (a) the diameter perpendicular to BC gives rise to A_1;
   (b) the diameter through A gives rise to D;
   (c) the diameter parallel to BC gives rise to U.

3. Prove that, if $ABCD$ is a cyclic quadrilateral, the Simson lines and the nine-point circles of triangles $\triangle BCD$, $\triangle CDA$, $\triangle DAB$ and $\triangle ABC$ are concurrent at a single point.

4.3 Miquel circles

We begin with a simple but surprising theorem on circumcircles associated with a triangle.

Theorem 4.8 (Miquel theorem) *If points P_1, P_2 and P_3 are chosen on the sides BC, CA and AB of $\triangle ABC$, then the circumcircles of $\triangle AP_2P_3$, $\triangle BP_3P_1$ and $\triangle CP_1P_2$ have a point in common.*

There is no need for P_1, P_2 and P_3 to be internal points of the sides of $\triangle ABC$, nor is it necessary for P to lie within the triangle. We will give the argument in the case where all three points are internal to the sides, and the reader can verify that essentially the same proof applies in other cases.

PROOF Suppose that the circumcircles of $\triangle BP_3P_1$ and $\triangle CP_1P_2$ intersect at P (see figure 4.7).

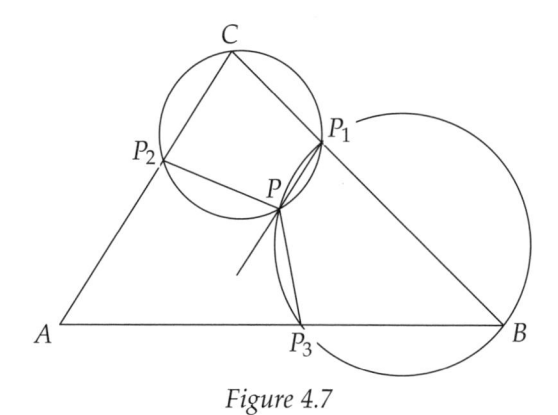

Figure 4.7

Then, by external angles of a cyclic quadrilateral, $\angle P_3PP_2 = \angle B + \angle C = 180° - \angle A$. It follows that quadrilateral AP_3PP_2 is also cyclic, and so the circumcircle of $\triangle AP_2P_3$ passes through P. ∎

Chapter 4: Simson lines

We call P the *Miquel point* of the triangle $\triangle P_1P_2P_3$. This triangle is known as a *Miquel triangle* of P, and the three circles are called *Miquel circles*. Given a point P, there are infinitely many Miquel triangles associated with it. It is enough to pick an arbitrary point P_1 on the line BC and then find P_2 and P_3 on CA and AB which lie on the circumcircles of $\triangle PP_1C$ and $\triangle BP_1P$. Theorem 4.8 now guarantees that the quadrilateral PP_2AP_3 is cyclic.

Corollary 4.9 *In the configuration for theorem 4.8, $\angle BPC = \angle A + \angle P_2P_1P_3$.*

PROOF Set as question 4 of exercise 4c. ❑

A particularly significant instance of the Miquel theorem is when P lies on the circumcircle of $\triangle ABC$. In this case (and only in this case) the points P_1, P_2 and P_3 are collinear, on the Simson line. The three Miquel circles now intersect on the circumcircle, and the Miquel triangle is degenerate. This turns out to be an interesting configuration.

Theorem 4.10 *If a transversal meets the sides BC, CA and AB of $\triangle ABC$ at L, M and N, then the circumcircles of $\triangle ABC$, $\triangle AMN$, $\triangle BNL$ and $\triangle CLM$ have a common point P.*

This is clearly a special case of theorem 4.1, but it can be proved independently.

PROOF Draw the circumcircles of $\triangle ABC$ and $\triangle AMN$ and let their second point of intersection be P. Let U, V, W and X be the feet of the perpendiculars from P to BC, CA, AB and LMN (see figure 4.8).

The Simson line of P with respect to $\triangle ABC$ is UVW, and that of P with respect to $\triangle AMN$ is WVX. These are the same line, so the points U, V, W and X are collinear. Now, by the converse of the Simson line property, P also lies on the circumcircles of $\triangle BNL$ and $\triangle CLM$. ❑

We call P the *Miquel point* of the four lines BCL, CMA, ANB and LMN.

Exercise 4c

1. Prove that the segments PP_1, PP_2 and PP_3 are equally inclined to the sides BC, CA and AB.

Figure 4.8

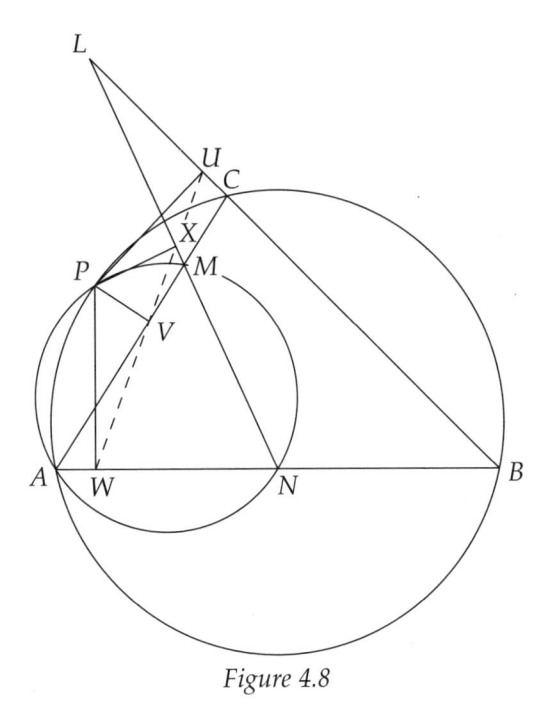

2. Prove that all the Miquel triangles associated with a point P are similar.

3. Prove that the centres of the three Miquel circles form a triangle similar to $\triangle ABC$.

4. Prove corollary 4.9.

5. In the configuration of theorem 4.10, prove that the orthocentres of $\triangle ABC$, $\triangle AMN$, $\triangle BNL$ and $\triangle CLM$ are collinear.

6. In the configuration of theorem 4.10, prove that the circumcentres of $\triangle ABC$, $\triangle AMN$, $\triangle BNL$ and $\triangle CLM$ are concyclic, and that the common circle passes through P.

Chapter 5

Cross-ratio

In the treatment of the Euler line, it was noted that $HN : NG = 3 : 1$ and $HO : OG = 3 : -1$. Ratio properties such as this are abundant in triangle geometry. In fact, what turns out to be particularly significant is a ratio of ratios called the cross-ratio, which is an example of a geometrical invariant.

In this chapter, we turn aside for a while from the investigation of the triangle to study such ratio properties in general. We look at a way in which the cross-ratio can be transferred from one part of a configuration to another, and we relate a particular case, when its value is -1, to angle bisectors and to centres of similitude of circles. Finally we look at a configuration which is a general case of several results about triangle centres.

5.1 The cross-ratio of a range

In previous chapters, we have often used enlargements to produce triangles with parallel sides and we have then been able to deduce ratios of lengths.

The essential result (see figure 5.1) is the intercept theorem which says that, if $A_1B_1C_1$ is parallel to ABC, then

$$\frac{A_1B_1}{AB} = \frac{B_1C_1}{BC}.$$

Figure 5.1

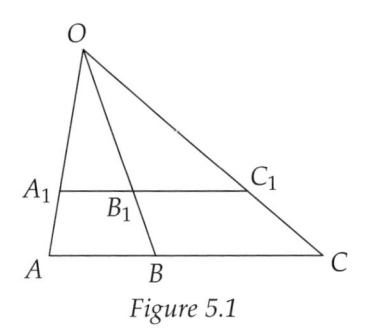

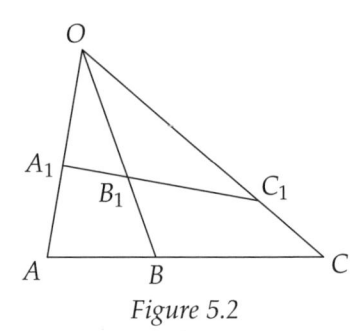

Figure 5.2

This fails, of course, when $A_1B_1C_1$ is not parallel to ABC (see figure 5.2).

However, in figure 5.2, we can apply the sine rule to $\triangle OAB$ and $\triangle OBC$ and get

$$\frac{\sin \angle AOB}{AB} = \frac{\sin \angle OBA}{OA} \quad \text{and} \quad \frac{\sin \angle BOC}{BC} = \frac{\sin \angle OBC}{OC}.$$

But since $\sin \angle OBA = \sin \angle OBC$, this gives

$$\frac{\sin \angle AOB}{\sin \angle BOC} = \frac{AB}{BC} \times \frac{OA}{OC}.$$

Hence, since the left-hand side of this equation depends on the angles between the lines and not on where the points are on the line, we have

$$\frac{AB}{BC} \times \frac{OA}{OC} = \frac{A_1B_1}{B_1C_1} \times \frac{OA_1}{OC_1}.$$

This is still not useful because, unlike the result about parallel lines, each side is dependent on the position of the lines ABC and $A_1B_1C_1$ relative to O. One way to get rid of this dependence is to take a fourth point on each line, D and D_1, with O, D and D_1 collinear (see figure 5.3).

Replacing B by D and B_1 by D_1 in the above, we have

$$\frac{AD}{DC} \times \frac{OA}{OC} = \frac{A_1D_1}{D_1C_1} \times \frac{OA_1}{OC_1}.$$

In this equation, we are using 'directed lengths', so that distances 'to the right' (such as AD) are positive and those 'to the left' (such as DC) are negative. We then divide one equation by the other to produce a result

Chapter 5: Cross-ratio

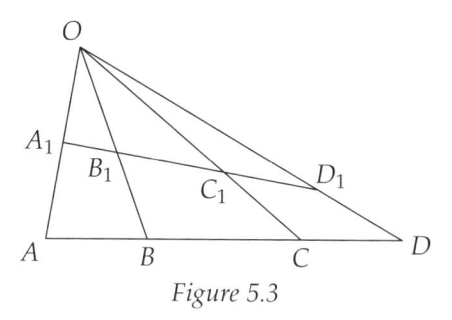

Figure 5.3

about 'ratios of ratios', namely

$$\frac{AB}{BC} \div \frac{AD}{DC} = \frac{A_1B_1}{B_1C_1} \div \frac{A_1D_1}{D_1C_1}.$$

Now we have a quantity which is independent of the directions of the lines $ABCD$ and $A_1B_1C_1D_1$.

This motivates the following definition. Any set of collinear points is said to form a *range*. When there are four distinct collinear points A, B, C and D, their *cross-ratio* $(A, C; B, D)$ is defined by

$$(A, C; B, D) = \frac{AB \times DC}{BC \times AD}.$$

We do not require that the points appear in the line in any particular order since we use the sign convention which has already been mentioned. If, for example, A, B, C and D are arranged from left to right in the printed order, then $(A, C; B, D)$ turns out to be negative. If, however, the order in the line is A, C, B and D, then $(A, C; B, D)$ is positive. In fact the use of the semi-colon in this notation can be thought of as indicating that we are viewing A and C as being a 'fixed' pair of points and we are considering the positions of B and D in relation to them. In the discussion which follows, we treat the four points as if they are in the order A, B, C and D, but it does not matter at all if the actual order is different.

As we have already said, cross-ratio can be considered as a ratio of ratios if we write it as

$$(A, C; B, D) = \frac{AB}{BC} \div \frac{AD}{DC}.$$

Theorem 5.1 (Uniqueness property) *If* $(A, C; B, D) = (A, C; B, E)$, *then the points D and E are identical.*

PROOF This is an immediate consequence of the definition of cross-ratio. ❑

Exercise 5a

In this exercise, positive distances are from left to right.

1. Calculate the value of $(A, C; B, D)$ if
   (a) $AB = BC = CD = 1$;
   (b) $AB = 2, BC = 1, CD = 3$;
   (c) $AB = -5, BC = 1, CD = 6$.

2. If $AB = 2, BC = 2$ and $(A, C; B, D) = -\frac{1}{2}$, what is CD?

3. If $AC = 3, BD = 4$ and $(A, C; B, D) = -1$, what is AD?

4. If $(A, C; B, D) = \frac{5}{2}$, calculate
   (a) $(A, C; D, B)$;
   (b) $(C, A; D, B)$;
   (c) $(D, B; C, A)$.

5. Is it possible to have $AB = BC$ and $(A, C; B, D) = -1$?

6. What is the value of $(H, G; N, O)$ and of $(O, N; G, H)$?

The next few results are technical in the sense that they simply follow from applying the definition of cross-ratio, but we shall see that they are very useful when applying this concept to specific configurations.

Theorem 5.2 (Interchange theorem) *The value of $(A, C; B, D)$ is unchanged if two pairs of points are interchanged, so that*

$$(A, C; B, D) = (C, A; D, B) = (B, D; A, C) = (D, B; C, A).$$

PROOF There are three cases as we can interchange A with B or C or D. The proofs are similar, so we will only deal here with the case where A interchanges with B and C with D. Then

$$(B, D; A, C) = \frac{BA \times CD}{AD \times BC} = \frac{AB \times DC}{BC \times AD} = (A, C; B, D) \qquad ❑$$

Chapter 5: Cross-ratio

Theorem 5.3 (Reciprocal theorem) *If only one pair of A and B or C and D is interchanged, the value of $(A,C;B,D)$ changes to its reciprocal, in other words*

$$(C,A;B,D) = (A,C;D,B) = \frac{1}{(A,C;B,D)}.$$

PROOF Again the proof is a simple check. We have

$$(C,A;B,D) = \frac{CB \times DA}{BA \times CD} = \frac{BC \times AD}{AB \times DC} = \frac{1}{(A,C;B,D)}$$

and the other equality follows from the interchange theorem. ☐

Theorem 5.4 (Complement theorem) *The value of $(A,C;B,D)$ changes to its 'complement' if B and C or A and D are interchanged, in other words*

$$(A,C;B,D) = 1 - (A,B;C,D) = 1 - (D,C;B,A).$$

PROOF This needs a little more algebra. We have

$$(A,B;C,D) + (A,C;B,D) = \frac{AC \times DB}{CB \times AD} + \frac{AB \times DC}{BC \times AD}$$

$$= \frac{AC \times BD - AB \times CD}{BC \times AD}$$

$$= \frac{(AB + BC) \times (BC + CD) - AB \times CD}{BC \times AD}$$

$$= \frac{(AB + BC + CD) \times BC}{BC \times AD}$$

$$= 1. \qquad ☐$$

It is possible to interpret cross-ratio as a sort of generalised directed length. Consider points A, C and B in that order on a line, and define the directed length CB to be one unit. Now allow D to be at the 'point at infinity' such that $AD = -DC$. Then the cross-ratio $(A,C;B,D)$ represents the directed length of AB. This is obvious from the calculation:

$$(A,C;B,D) = \frac{AB \times DC}{BC \times AD} = -\frac{AB}{BC} = \frac{AB}{CB} = AB.$$

Finally, we have three technical lemmas. The proofs are set as questions in exercise 5b.

Lemma 5.5 *For A, B, C and D in order on a line,*

$$AB \times CD + AD \times BC = AC \times BD.$$

Lemma 5.6 *For a range A, B, C, D,*

$$(A, B; D, C) \times (B, C; D, A) \times (C, A; D, B) = -1.$$

Lemma 5.7 *For a range A, B, C, D, E,*

$$(A, B; C, D) \times (A, B; D, E) = (A, B; C, E).$$

Exercise 5b

1. Show that, if the four points of a range are permuted in all 24 possible different orders, then the cross-ratios form the set

$$\left\{ x, 1-x, \frac{1}{x}, \frac{1}{1-x}, \frac{x-1}{1}, \frac{x}{x-1} \right\}.$$

2. Prove lemma 5.5.

3. Prove lemma 5.6.

4. Prove lemma 5.7.

5.2 The cross-ratio of a pencil

If A, B, C, D is a range and V any point not collinear with the range, we can draw rays (or lines) VA, VB, VC and VD. The result is known as a *pencil of rays* with *vertex* V and it is written as $V(A, B, C, D)$.

Given such a pencil, we consider a line in the plane which meets VA, VB, VC and VD at A', B', C' and D' respectively. Such a line is called a *transversal* of the pencil. As we have seen, if a transversal is moved, both the lengths of the line segments inside it such as $A'B'$ and the ratios, such as $A'B' : C'D'$ change. However, the cross-ratio of the range is *invariant*, and this is why this concept is so important. This has already been demonstrated, and is made explicit in the following theorem.

Theorem 5.8 (Invariance of cross-ratio) *Any two transversals of the pencil $V(A, B, C, D)$ create ranges with the same cross-ratio, namely $(A, C; B, D)$.*

The cross-ratio $(A, C; B, D)$ can then be defined as the *cross-ratio of the pencil*; it is written as $V(A, C; B, D)$. An alternative notation is to denote the rays by lower case letters a, b, c and d, and then the cross-ratio is written as $(a, c; b, d)$.

The line at infinity

In question 5 of exercise 5a, we introduced the idea of a point at infinity on a line, and it is worth making this more explicit. It allows us to state that any two lines in a plane meet at a unique point. If the two lines are parallel, this point is a point at infinity. In order for it to be unique, we can now stipulate that any set of parallel lines all pass through a common point at infinity. In fact, they form a pencil of lines whose vertex is this common point. The set of all points of infinity has the property that it meets each line in the plane in precisely one point, so it is itself a line. We are therefore led to the creation of a *line at infinity*. The advantage of doing this is that it permits all of the theorems and results in this book to be true in general, without the creation of special cases or exceptions to deal with the possibility of parallel lines which do not meet.

Theorem 5.9 *If A, B, C, D is a range and U and V are two points not collinear with the points, then $U(A, C; B, D) = V(A, C; B, D)$.*

PROOF The result is immediate from the invariance of cross-ratio. ❑

Theorem 5.10 *Two pencils which have corresponding rays parallel have the same cross-ratio.*

PROOF This follows from the discussion in section 5.1 since the angles are the same. ❑

A consequence of the last three theorems is that cross-ratios can be transferred within and between pencils.

For example, the five ranges shown in figure 5.4 all have the same cross-ratio. (The two pencils $\mathcal{P}_1$ and $\mathcal{P}_2$ have corresponding rays parallel.)

There are also converse results which show that equal cross-ratios imply concurrence of rays.

Figure 5.4

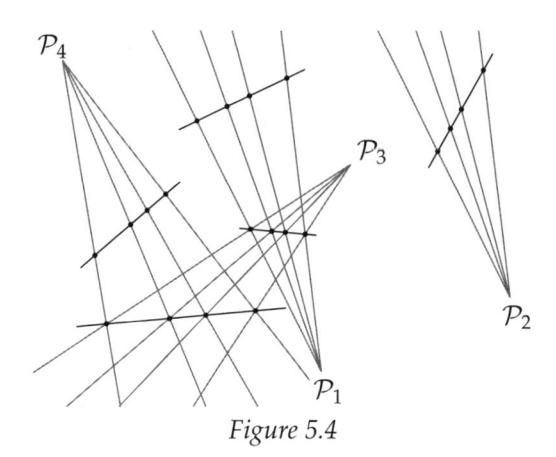

Theorem 5.11 *If the two ranges A, B, C, D and A', B', C', D' are such that $(A,C;B,D) = (A,C';B',D')$, then BB', CC' and DD' are concurrent.*

PROOF Let V be the intersection of BB' and CC' (see figure 5.5). Consider the pencil $V(A,B,C,D)$. By theorem 5.8, the transversal $AB'C'$ cuts VD at a point X with $(A,C;B,D) = (A,C';B',X)$. Hence $(A,C';B',X) = (A,C';B',D')$ and so, by theorem 5.1, X is the same point as D'. ∎

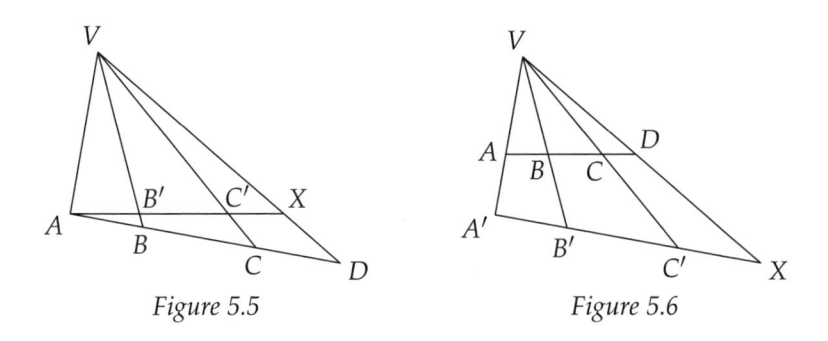

Figure 5.5

Figure 5.6

Theorem 5.12 *If the two ranges A, B, C, D and A', B', C', D' are such that $(A,C;B,D) = (A',C';B',D')$ and AA', BB' and CC' are concurrent at V, then DD' also passes through V.*

PROOF This is simply a generalisation of the last result. Again, consider the pencil $V(A,B,C,D)$ (see figure 5.6). By theorem 5.1, the transversal $A'B'C'$ cuts VD at a point X with $(A,C;B,D) = (A',C';B',X)$.

Hence $(A', C'; B', X) = (A', C'; B', D')$ and so, by theorem 5.1, X is the same point as D'. ❑

Exercise 5c

1. Show that theorem 5.8 is true when the transversal is parallel to one of the rays of the pencil.

2. Let $U(A, B, C, D)$ and $V(A, B, C, D)$ be two pencils containing the range A, B, C, D. Now let A, B', C', D' be a transversal of the pencil $U(A, B, C, D)$ and let A, B'', C'', D'' be a transversal of $V(A, B, C, D)$. Prove that $B'B''$, $C'C''$ and $D'D''$ are concurrent.

3. Let A be a point on the line segment UV, and consider the range A, B, C, D and the two pencils $U(A, B, C, D)$ and $V(A, B, C, D)$. Let a transversal cut $U(A, B, C, D)$ at A', B', C', D' and another cut $V(A, B, C, D)$ at A'', B'', C'', D''. Let the lines UB'' and VB' intersect at B^*, UC'' and VC' at C^* and UD'' and VD' at D^*. Prove that B^*, C^* and D^* are collinear.

5.3 Harmonic ranges

A cross-ratio is *harmonic* if it is equal to -1. A range or a pencil with cross-ratio -1 is a *harmonic range* or a *harmonic pencil*.

Four collinear points A, B, C, D form a harmonic range if, and only if, $(A, C; B, D) = -1$. In other words

$$\frac{AB}{BC} = -\frac{AD}{DC}.$$

Hence we are expressing the fact that B divides AC internally in the same ratio as D divides AC externally.

Alternatively, we can say that:

- ♦ B and D separate A and C harmonically; or
- ♦ B and D are harmonic conjugates with respect to A and C.

Note that if B is the midpoint of AC, then its harmonic conjugate is the point at infinity.

Theorem 5.13 *The range O, G, H, N is harmonic.*

PROOF This is immediate from theorem 3.1 on page 27. ❑

Theorem 5.14 *In $\triangle ABC$, let the internal and external angle bisectors of $\angle A$ cut BC at X and X_1 (see figure 5.7); then B and C separate X and X_1 harmonically.*

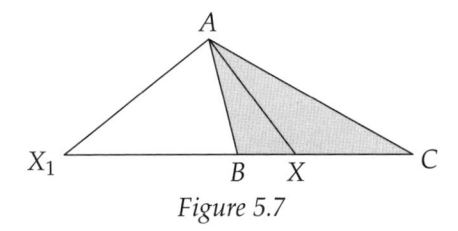

Figure 5.7

PROOF This follows immediately from the angle bisector theorem since

$$\frac{BX}{XC} = \frac{BA}{AC} \quad \text{and} \quad \frac{BX_1}{X_1C} = -\frac{BA}{BC}.$$
❑

Corollary 5.15 *The range A, I, X, I_A is harmonic.*

Theorem 5.14 has an important converse.

Theorem 5.16 *If the lines a, b, c and d, in that order, form a harmonic pencil, and if b and d are perpendicular, then they are the internal and external bisectors of the angle formed by a and c*

PROOF Draw a line parallel to d cutting a, b, c at P, Q, R and cutting d at the point at infinity D (see figure 5.8).
Since $(a, c; b, d) = -1$, we have $(P, R; Q, D) = -1$ and so $PQ = QR$. As PQR is parallel to d, it is perpendicular to b. It follows that b is the internal angle bisector, and so d is the external angle bisector. ❑

Now we prove a number of useful technical results.

Chapter 5: Cross-ratio

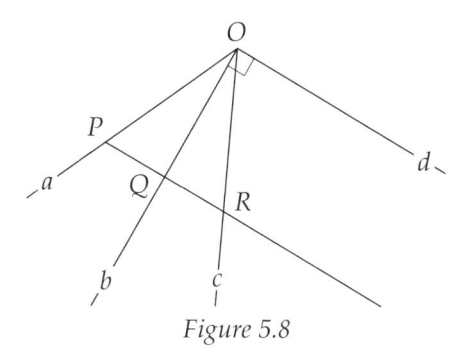

Figure 5.8

Theorem 5.17 *If the cross-ratio $(A, C; B, D)$ is harmonic, so are $(C, A; B, D)$ and $(B, D; A, C)$.*

PROOF The first result follows from the reciprocal theorem (5.3), and it expresses the fact that if B and D separate A and C harmonically, then they also separate C and A harmonically. So A and C occur symmetrically *inside* the pair, and this justifies the language we use in talking about them. The second follows from the interchange theorem (5.2), and it says that if B and D separate A and C harmonically, then A and C separate B and D harmonically. The relationship *between* the pairs is also symmetrical. ❏

Theorem 5.18 *If $(A, B; C, D) = (B, A; C, D)$, where C and D are different points, then A, B, C, D is a harmonic range.*

PROOF By the reciprocal theorem, $(A, B; C, D) = (B, A; C, D)$ implies that $(A, B; C, D) = x = \frac{1}{x}$, and $x \neq 1$ since C and D are different points. Hence $x = -1$ and so A, B, C, D is harmonic. ❏

Theorem 5.19 *If $(A, C; B, D)$ is harmonic and O is the midpoint of AC, then $OA^2 = OC^2 = OB \times OD$.*

PROOF Putting $AB = x$, $AC = y$ and $AD = z$ in the defining property of a harmonic range, we obtain $2xz = xy + yz$. This can be rearranged to

$$\left(\frac{y}{2}\right)^2 = \left(x - \frac{y}{2}\right)\left(z - \frac{y}{2}\right),$$

which is the desired result. ❏

Theorem 5.20 *If O is the midpoint of AC and $OA^2 = OC^2 = OB \times OD$, then $(A, C; B, D)$ is harmonic.*

PROOF This is simply a matter of reversing the argument in the proof of theorem 5.19. ❑

Lemma 5.21 *Let A, B, C, D be a harmonic range and let $\mathcal{L}$ be a fixed line. Let A', B', C', D' be the feet of the perpendiculars from A, B, C, D to $\mathcal{L}$, the projections onto $\mathcal{L}$. Prove that A', B', C', D' is also a harmonic range.*

PROOF Set as question 2 of exercise 5d. ❑

Exercise 5d

1. Prove that if $(A, C; B, D)$ is harmonic, then
$$\frac{2}{AC} = \frac{1}{AB} + \frac{1}{AD}.$$

2. Prove lemma 5.21

3. Show that the points A, I, X, I_A in section 2.3 on page 15 form a harmonic range.

4. Let AP and AQ be tangents from a point A, outside a circle, to the circle, and let ABD be a line intersecting the circle in B and D. Let C be the intersection of AD and PQ. Prove that A, B, C, D is a harmonic range.

5. Let A, B and C be three points in order on a line, and draw an arbitrary circle $\mathcal{C}$ through A and B. Draw the circle with centre C which is orthogonal to $\mathcal{C}$, cutting AB at P and Q. Prove that A, P, C, Q is a harmonic range.

5.4 Centres of similitude

If two circles, of different radii, lie entirely outside one another, then they have both direct and transverse common tangents. Calling their centres O_1 and O_2, we have the configuration shown in figure 5.9.

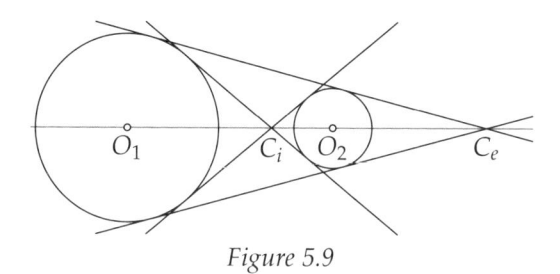

Figure 5.9

The points C_i and C_e, where the common tangents meet O_1O_2, are the *internal* and *external centres of similitude* of the two circles.

Theorem 5.22 *If the radii of the two circles are r_1 and r_2, where, without loss of generality, $r_1 > r_2$, then*

$$\frac{O_1C_i}{C_iO_2} = \frac{r_1}{r_2} = -\frac{O_1C_e}{C_eO_2}.$$

Consequently O_1, C_i, O_2, C_e form a harmonic range.

PROOF The result follows immediately from the similar triangles formed by drawing the radii from the centres to the points of tangency. ☐

If the two circles do not lie entirely outside one another, it is still possible to talk of two centres of similitude. They are defined as two points on the line of centres which satisfy the relationship

$$\frac{O_1C_i}{C_iO_2} = \frac{r_1}{r_2} = -\frac{O_1C_e}{C_eO_2};$$

consequently O_1, C_i, O_2, C_e still form a harmonic range. The circle on diameter C_iC_e is called the *circle of similitude* of the two circles. In the next section, we tie these ideas up with that of Apollonius circles.

5.5 Apollonius circles

The result which follows should be familiar to readers, but for the sake of completeness we provide a statement and proof of it.

Theorem 5.23 *If a point P moves so that its distances from two fixed points B and C are in a constant ratio, then the locus of P is a circle.*

PROOF If the ratio is $\lambda > 1$, we have $BP : PC = \lambda : 1$. Let X and X_1 be the points which divide BC internally and externally in the ratios $\lambda : 1$ and $\lambda : -1$, noting that B, X, C, X_1 is a harmonic range (see figure 5.10).

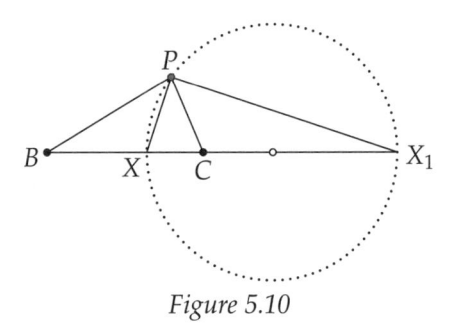

Figure 5.10

Then, by the angle bisector theorem, PX and PX_1 are the internal and external bisectors of $\triangle BPC$, so $\angle XPX_1 = 90°$, and the locus of P is a circle on diameter XX_1. □

Theorem 5.24 *Two circles have centres O_1 and O_2 and radii r_1 and r_2, and P is any point on their circle of similitude. Then $O_1P : O_2P = r_1 : r_2$, and PC_i and PC_e are the internal and external bisectors of $\angle O_1PO_2$ (see figure 5.11).*

PROOF Since $O_1C_i : C_iO_2 = r_1 : r_2$ and $O_1C_e : C_eO_2 = -r_1 : r_2$, it follows that the pencil $P(O_1, C_i, O_2, C_e)$ is harmonic. Also $\angle C_iPC_e = 90°$, so, by theorem 5.16, PC_i and PC_e are internal and external angle bisectors and the circle is an Apollonius circle. □

Theorem 5.25 *Suppose two circles have centres O_1 and O_2 and a circle with centre O_3 touches them, both externally or both internally, at points T_1 and T_2. Then T_1T_2 passes through their external centre of similitude.*

PROOF Set as question 5 of exercise 5e. □

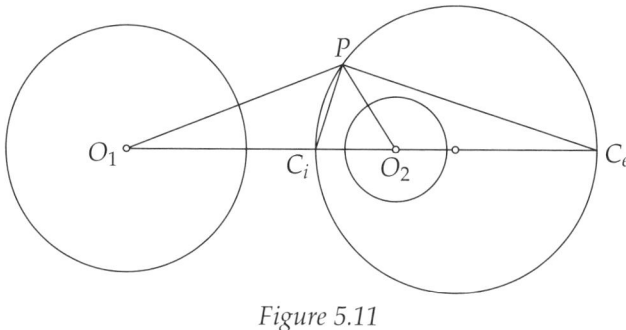

Chapter 5: Cross-ratio

Figure 5.11

Theorem 5.26 *Suppose two circles have centres O_1 and O_2 and a circle with centre O_3 touches them, one internally at T_1 and the other externally at T_2. Then T_1T_2 passes through their internal centre of similitude.*

PROOF Set as question 6 of exercise 5e. ❑

Exercise 5e

1. Identify the internal and external centres of similitude of the circumcircle and the nine-point circle.

2. Two circles meet at X and Y and a direct common tangent touches them at A and B. An arbitrary circle through X and Y meets the tangent at P and Q. Prove that A, P, B, Q is a harmonic range.

3. Let A, C and D be three points in order on a line, and a circle on diameter AC is drawn. The tangent from D to the circle touches it at T, and B is the foot of the perpendicular from T to AC. Prove that A, B, C, D is a harmonic range.

4. The line of centres of two circles cuts off diameters A_1B_1 and A_2B_2. Let a line through a centre of similitude cut the first circle at P_1 and Q_1 and the second at P_2 and Q_2. Prove that $P_1P_2 \times Q_1Q_2$ is constant.

5. Prove theorem 5.25.

6. Prove theorem 5.26.

7. Prove that the circle of similitude of two intersecting circles passes through their points of intersection.

8. Two circles have centres O_1 and O_2; prove that any circle through O_1 and O_2 is orthogonal to the circle of similitude.

5.6 The complete quadrangle

Four distinct points P, Q, R and S are said to form a *quadrangle*. This simply means a figure composed of four angles, those formed at the vertices P, Q, R and S. The quadrangle has three pairs of opposite sides, and these meet in three points which are the vertices of the *diagonal triangle*. In figure 5.12, $\triangle ABC$ is the diagonal triangle since

- QR and SP meet in A;
- RP and QS meet in B;
- PQ and RS meet in C.

(If two sides are parallel, this will meet at a point at infinity. However, we focus on the situation where the diagonal triangle is made up of 'real' points.)

We now focus on BC, one side of the diagonal triangle, which is formed from the pairs RP, QS and PQ, RS and look at the points where this meets the other pair QR, SP. These are labelled U and V in figure 5.12.

Theorem 5.27 *In the diagonal triangle of a complete quadrangle:*

(i) U and V separate C and B harmonically;

(ii) A and V separate Q and R harmonically;

(iii) U and A separate P and S harmonically.

PROOF First consider the pencil $S(C, U, B, V)$. Applying theorem 5.8, we have $(B, C; U, V) = (Q, R; A, V)$. Applying the same theorem to the pencil $P(Q, A, R, V)$, we obtain $(Q, R; A, V) = (C, B; U, V)$. Hence $(B, C; U, V) = (C, B; U, V)$ and so, by theorem 5.19, U and V separate C

Figure 5.12

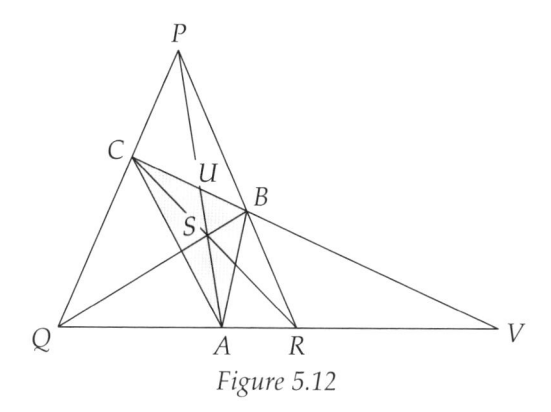

and B harmonically. It follows immediately that $(Q, R; A, V) = -1$ and so A and V separate Q and R harmonically. Finally, by considering the pencil $C(Q, A, R, V)$, we also have $(P, S; A, U) = -1$ and so A and U separate P and S harmonically. ❑

This proof is an excellent example of the sort of arguments which rely on the ease with which cross-ratios can be transferred using different pencils and it justifies the (perhaps) rather tiresome development of results in the first three sections of this chapter.

In the light of this result, reconsider the configuration formed by the excentral triangle and the incentre, interpreting it as a quadrangle formed by the points I, I_A, I_B and I_C (see figure 5.13).

It can be seen that $\triangle ABC$ is the diagonal triangle of this quadrangle. Theorem 5.27(i) gives us the result in question 4 of exercise 5d, and the other two parts give us two other harmonic ranges which arise from this configuration.

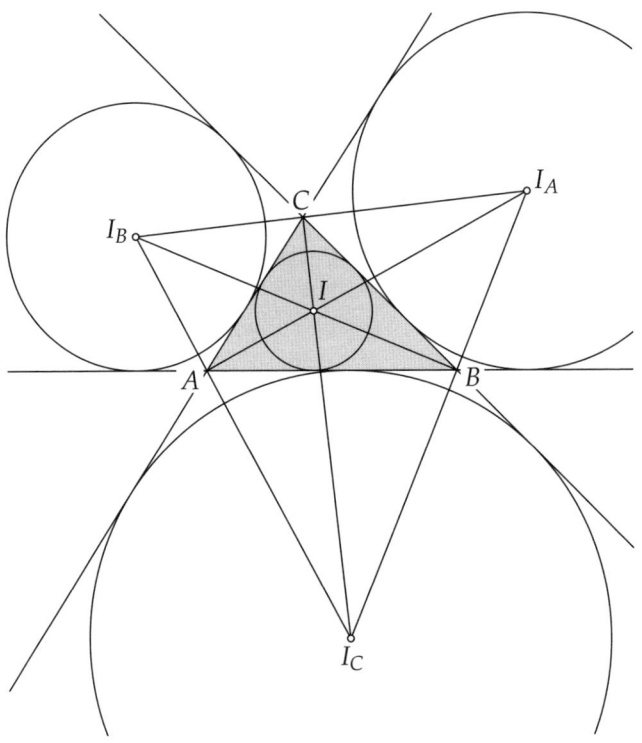

Figure 5.13

Chapter 6

Cevians and pedal triangles

We revisit two theorems which are essential in proving many concurrencies and prove some useful results about pedal triangles.

6.1 Ceva and Menelaus

Theorem 6.1 (Ceva) *Let L, M and N be points on the sides BC, CA and AB of $\triangle ABC$. If the lines AL, BM and CN are concurrent, then*

$$\frac{AN}{NB} \times \frac{BL}{LC} \times \frac{CM}{MA} = 1.$$

Note that the lengths are, as usual, directed, so it possible for one of the points L, M and N to be internal to a side and the other two on the sides produced.

PROOF Let P be the point of intersection of the three lines (see figure 6.1). We shall assume that this is internal to the triangle; if not, then the proof is easily adapted.

It is enough to note that

$$\frac{BL}{LC} = \frac{[BPA]}{[CPA]}$$

and two similar statements, which can be multiplied together. ☐

Figure 6.1

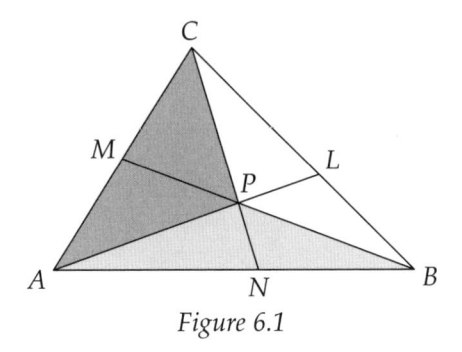

Theorem 6.2 (Converse of Ceva) *Let L, M and N be points on the sides BC, CA and AB of $\triangle ABC$. If*

$$\frac{AN}{NB} \times \frac{BL}{LC} \times \frac{CM}{MA} = 1,$$

then the lines AL, BM and CN are concurrent

PROOF Let BM and CN intersect at P, and let AP meet BC at L' (see figure 6.2).

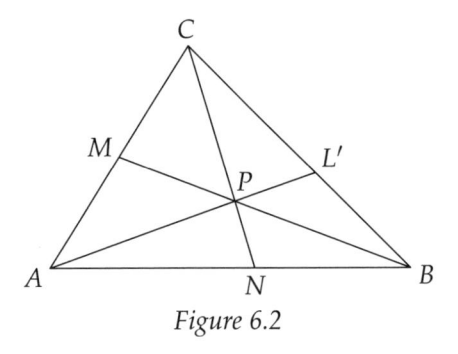

Figure 6.2

Then by Ceva we have

$$\frac{AN}{NB} \times \frac{BL'}{L'C} \times \frac{CM}{MA} = 1.$$

It follows that

$$\frac{BL}{LC} = \frac{BL'}{L'C}$$

and so L and L' are the same point. ❑

Chapter 6: Cevians and pedal triangles

Sometimes it is necessary to use the trigonometrical version of Ceva. By the sine rule on $\triangle NAC$ and $\triangle BCN$ and the fact that the angles either side of N have the same sine, we have

$$\frac{AN}{NB} = \frac{b \sin \angle NCA}{c \sin \angle BCN}.$$

Multiplying three such expressions together and cancelling, we obtain

$$\frac{\sin \angle NCA}{\sin \angle BCN} \times \frac{\sin \angle LAB}{\sin \angle CAL} \times \frac{\sin \angle MBC}{\sin \angle ABM} = 1$$

Again, these should be signed angles, so angles measured anticlockwise are taken as positive and those measured clockwise negative.

Theorem 6.3 (Menelaus) *If a transversal meets the sides BC, CA and AB at L, M and N (see figure 6.3), then*

$$\frac{AN}{NB} \times \frac{BL}{LC} \times \frac{CM}{MA} = -1.$$

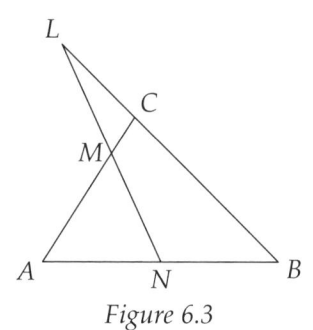

Figure 6.3

Again the lengths are directed, so it possible for the transversal to cut all three sides of the triangle externally. The proof is quite ingenious.

PROOF Draw CN' parallel to LMN (see figure 6.4).
Then it is trivially true that

$$\frac{AN}{NB} \times \frac{BN}{NN'} \times \frac{N'N}{NA} = -1.$$

But, by similar triangles, we have

$$\frac{BL}{LC} = \frac{BN}{NN'} \quad \text{and} \quad \frac{CM}{MA} = \frac{N'N}{NA}$$

and these yield the desired result. ☐

Figure 6.4

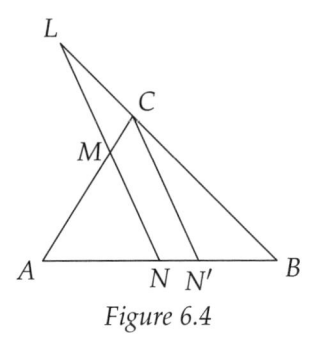

Theorem 6.4 (Converse of Menelaus) *If L, M and N are points on the sides BC, CA and AB, such that*

$$\frac{AN}{NB} \times \frac{BL}{LC} \times \frac{CM}{MA} = -1.$$

then the points are collinear.

PROOF The proof of uses contradiction in exactly the same way as for the converse of Ceva. ❏

Given an arbitrary point P in the plane of $\triangle ABC$, denote by A', B' and C' the points where AP, BP and CP meet BC, CA and AB, possibly produced (see figure 6.5).

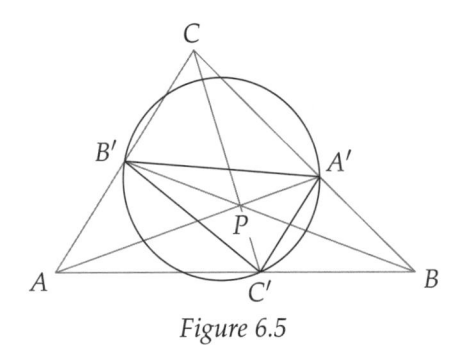

Figure 6.5

The line segments AA', BB' and CC' are known as *cevians*. The triangle $\triangle A'B'C'$ is called the *cevian triangle* of $\triangle ABC$ with respect to P, and its circumcircle is the *cevian circle*.

Some authors use the word 'cevian' to denote any line which joins a vertex of a triangle to a point on the opposite side. In that case, three cevians need not necessarily be concurrent, although it is easy to check whether this is so using Ceva's theorem. However, it seems more convenient to include concurrence in the definition.

An important example of the use of Ceva's theorem is given in the following theorem.

Theorem 6.5 *If P, Q and R are the points of tangency of the incircle of $\triangle ABC$ to the sides BC, CA and AB, then the cevians AP, BQ and CR are concurrent.*

PROOF This follows immediately from theorem 2.10 on page 16 and Ceva's theorem. ❏

The point of concurrency in theorem 6.5 is known as the *Gergonne point* and will be denoted by Γ.

Exercise 6a

1. Use Ceva's theorem to justify the concurrency of
   (a) the medians;
   (b) the internal angle bisectors;
   (c) the altitudes.

2. Prove that the internal angle bisectors of two angles of a triangle and the external angle bisector of the third meet the opposite sides in three collinear points.

3. Prove that the external angle bisectors of the angles of a triangle meet the opposite sides in three collinear points.

4. If $\triangle DEF$ is the orthic triangle of $\triangle ABC$, let EF, FD and DE meet BC, CA and AB at L, M and N respectively. Prove that L, M and N are collinear. (This line is known as the *orthic axis* of $\triangle ABC$.)

5. In the usual Menelaus configuration, let L', M' and N' be the harmonic conjugates of L, M and N with respect to BC, CA and AB. Prove that AL', BM' and CN' are concurrent.

6. Let P be an internal point of an acute angled triangle $\triangle ABC$ and let the internal angle bisectors of $\angle BPC$, $\angle CPA$ and $\angle APB$ meet BC, CA and AB at L, M and N. Prove that AL, BM and CN are concurrent at a point P'. Under what circumstances do P and P' coincide?

7. In the configuration of question 6, let the external angle bisectors of $\angle BPC$, $\angle CPA$ and $\angle APB$ meet the sides BC, CA and AB at L', M' and N'. Prove that these three points are collinear.

8. Let the tangents to the circumcircle of $\triangle ABC$ at A, B and C meet the sides BC, CA and AB at L, M and N. Prove that L, M and N are collinear.

9. Identify the cevians, the cevian triangle and the cevian circle associated with
   (a) the centroid;
   (b) the orthocentre;
   (c) the incentre.

10. The circumcentre is the 'odd-man-out' of the principal triangle centres in the sense that it is not initially defined by means of cevians. If the cevian AO meets BC at P, show that
$$\frac{BP}{PC} = \frac{\sin 2C}{\sin 2B}.$$

11. It is possible to use the concept of cross-ratio to prove Menelaus' theorem. Consider the usual Menelaus configuration together with the line at infinity. Let AB, BC, CA, LMN and AL meet the line at infinity at points U, V, W, X and Y. (See figure 6.6: you are privileged to be able to see this line!)
   (a) Use lemma 5.7 on page 56 to show that
$$(U, W; X, Y) \times (U, W; Y, V) = (U, W; X, V).$$
   (b) Show that it follows that
$$(N, M; X, L) \times (B, C; L, V) = (U, W; X, V).$$

Chapter 6: Cevians and pedal triangles

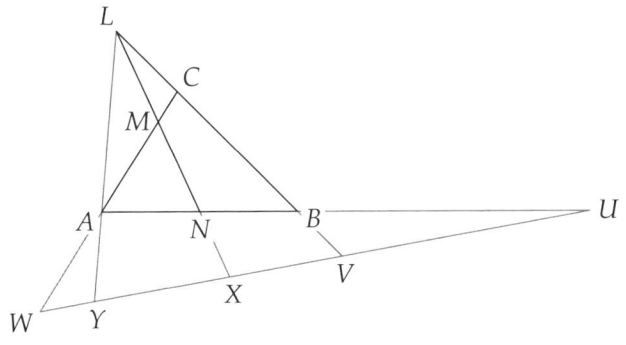

Figure 6.6

(c) Now cycle the three triples (L, M, N), (A, B, C) and (U, V, W) to produce another two similar equations, multiply together their left-hand and right-hand sides, and use lemma 5.6 on page 56 to produce the equation

$$(B, C; L, V) \times (C, A; M, W) \times (A, B; N, U) = -1.$$

(d) Use the interpretation of cross-ratios when one point is on the line at infinity to derive Menelaus' theorem.

12. It is now possible to derive Ceva from Menelaus by appealing to the properties of a complete quadrangle. If NM meets BC at X, deduce that L and X separate B and C harmonically, and hence deduce the Ceva relationship.

6.2 Centres of similitude

The following theorem about three circles in a plane will turn out to be useful.

Theorem 6.6 *The three circles C_A, C_B and C_C have centres A, B and C. The external and internal centres of similitude of C_A and C_B are E_C and I_C, and E_A, I_A, E_B and I_B are defined similarly. Then (see figure 6.7):*

(i) the points E_A, E_B and E_C are collinear;
(ii) the points E_A, I_B and I_C are collinear;
(iii) the lines AE_A, BE_B and CI_C are concurrent;
(iv) the lines AI_A, BI_B and CI_C are concurrent.

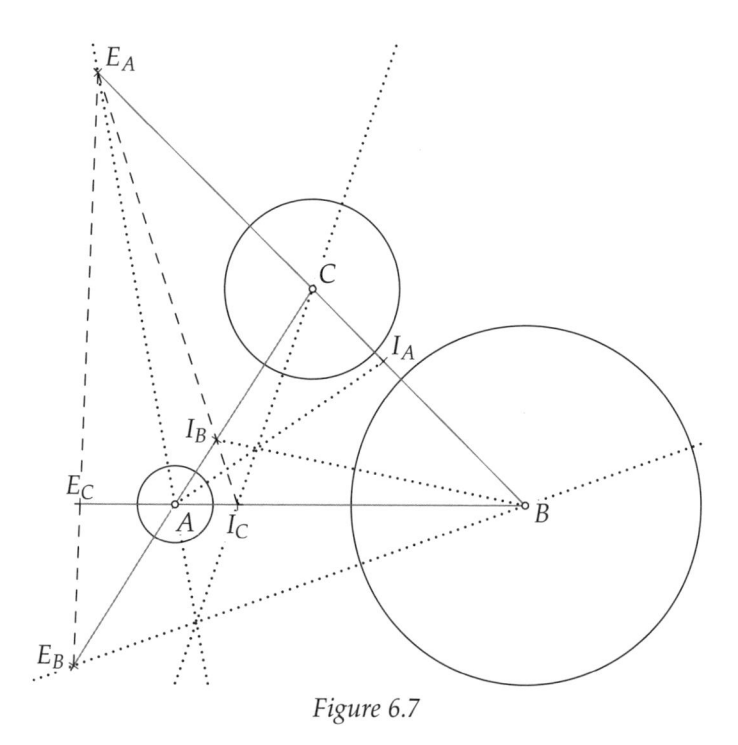

Figure 6.7

Theorem 6.6(i) is known as *Monge's circle theorem*.

PROOF If the radii of the three circles are a, b and c, we have

$$\frac{AE_C}{E_CB} = -\frac{a}{b}, \quad \frac{BE_A}{E_AC} = -\frac{b}{c}, \quad \frac{CE_B}{E_BA} = -\frac{c}{a}$$

and

$$\frac{AI_C}{I_CB} = -\frac{a}{b}, \quad \frac{BI_A}{I_AC} = -\frac{b}{c}, \quad \frac{CI_B}{I_BA} = -\frac{c}{a}.$$

Results (i) and (ii) (in three versions) now follow from theorem 6.4, and (iii) and (iv) follow from theorem 6.2. ❑

Chapter 6: Cevians and pedal triangles

6.3 Pedal triangles

Recall that, given an arbitrary point P in the plane of $\triangle ABC$, the *pedal triangle* $\triangle A''B''C''$ is that formed by the feet of the perpendiculars from P to the three sides (see figure 6.8). Its circumcircle is the *pedal circle* of P.

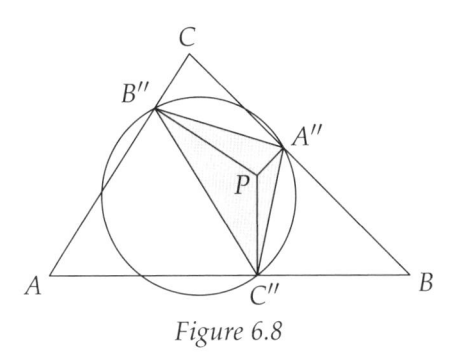

Figure 6.8

Note that a pedal triangle is a special case of a Miquel triangle, and that the pedal triangle of a point on the circumcircle of $\triangle ABC$ is degenerate (since A'', B'' and C'' are collinear on the Simson line).

Theorem 6.7 *If $\triangle A''B''C''$ is the pedal triangle of P, then $\angle APB = \angle C + \angle B''C''A''$ (with similar results for the other angles around P).*

PROOF We use the cyclic quadrilaterals $AC''PB''$ and $BA''PC''$ (see figure 6.9).

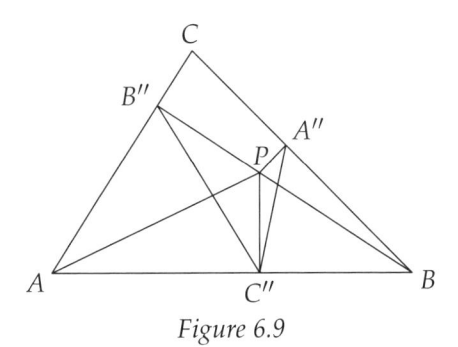

Figure 6.9

Then

$$\angle APB = \angle APC'' + \angle C''PB$$
$$= \angle AB''C'' + \angle C''A''B$$
$$= \angle B''C''C + \angle B''CC'' + \angle A''C''C + \angle C''CA''$$
$$= \angle A''C''B'' + \angle C$$ ❑

Theorem 6.8 *The side lengths of the pedal triangle of P are given by*

$$B''C'' = AP \sin A = \frac{a\, AP}{2R},$$

with similar expressions for $C''A''$ and $A''B''$.

PROOF This follows immediately from the sine rule on the cyclic quadrilateral $AC''PB''$, whose diameter is AP. ❑

Theorem 6.9 *The area of the pedal triangle of P is equal to*

$$\frac{(R^2 - OP^2)\Delta}{4R^2}.$$

PROOF Let AP meet the circumcircle again at A^* (see figure 6.10).

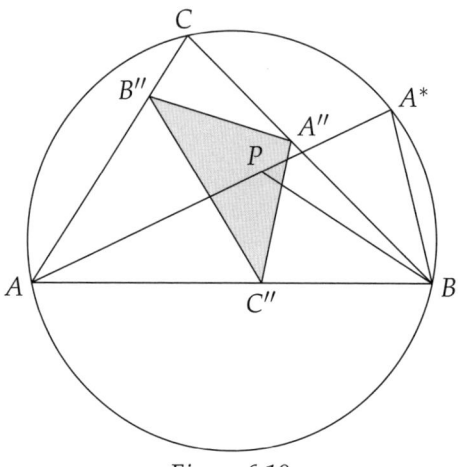

Figure 6.10

The area of the pedal triangle is equal to

$$\tfrac{1}{2}B''C'' \times C''A'' \sin \angle B''C''A''$$

and by theorem 6.7, $\angle B''C''A'' = \angle APB - \angle C$.

But $\angle APB = \angle AA^*B + \angle A^*BP = \angle C + \angle A^*BP$, so now we see that $\angle A''C''B'' = \angle A^*BP$. Now, by the sine rule in $\triangle A^*BP$,

$$\sin \angle A^*BP = \frac{A^*P \sin C}{BP}.$$

So the area we require is

$$\frac{B''C'' \times C''A \times A^*P \sin C}{2BP}.$$

Now we use theorem 6.8 and the sine rule on $\triangle ABC$ to write this as

$$\frac{abc \times AP \times A^*P}{16R^3}.$$

But, by intersecting chords,

$$AP \times A^*P = (R - OP)(R + OP) = R^2 - OP^2,$$

and also

$$\Delta = \frac{abc}{4R}. \qquad \square$$

Exercise 6b

1. Identify the pedal triangle and pedal circle associated with
   (a) the circumcentre;
   (b) the orthocentre;
   (c) the incentre.

2. What is the locus of a point whose pedal triangle has a given area?

3. For which internal point is the pedal triangle of maximum area?

4. For which point in the plane is the pedal triangle of minimum area?

Chapter 7

Conjugates

In this chapter, we look at ways of deriving one concurrency from another. In each case, we begin with a point P and its cevians AL, BM and CN, and define a related point Q by replacing the cevians with new ones. The points P and Q are known as conjugates, and this is a reciprocal relationship: if P is the conjugate of Q, then Q is the conjugate of P.

7.1 Three types of conjugacy

Theorem 7.1 (Isogonal conjugacy) *If the point P is defined by cevians AL, BM and CN, and AL'', BM'' and CN'' are the reflections of the rays AL, BM and CN in the internal angle bisectors at A, B and C, then these are concurrent in P'', the* isogonal conjugate *of P (see figure 7.1).*

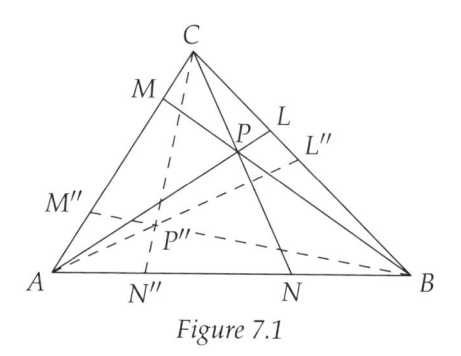

Figure 7.1

PROOF The result follows from the version of Ceva's theorem in terms of sines of angles. ❏

An alternative way of describing the relationship is to say $\angle CAL'' = \angle LAB$, $\angle ABM'' = \angle MBC$ and $\angle BCN'' = \angle NCA$. These are signed angles, so they are allowed to be negative. We also refer to pairs of lines through a vertex as isogonally conjugate if they make equal angles with the angle bisector at that vertex. The theorem then states that if three cevians are concurrent, so are their isogonal conjugates.

What is the isogonal conjugate of a point on the circumcircle of the triangle? Let P be on the circumcircle and let the isogonal conjugates of the lines AP, BP and CP be AQ, BR and CS (see figure 7.2).

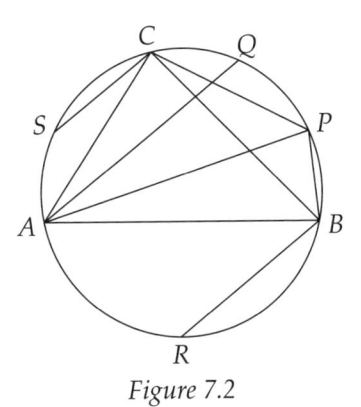

Figure 7.2

Note that $\angle RBA = \angle CBP = \angle CAP = \angle BAQ$ and $\angle ACS = \angle PCB = \angle PAB = \angle CAQ$, so the lines AQ, BR and CS are parallel, and the isogonal conjugate of P lies at infinity.

Theorem 7.2 (Isotomic conjugacy) *If the point P is defined by cevians AL, BM and CN, and if L', M' and N' are the reflections of L, M and N in the midpoints A_1, B_1 and C_1 of the sides, then the cevians AL', BM' and CN' are concurrent in P', the* isotomic conjugate *of P (see figure 7.3).*

PROOF The result is immediate from Ceva's theorem. ❏

Another way of defining L', M' and N' is to say that $BL = L'C$, $CM = M'A$ and $AN = N'B$. These are signed distances, so if L is on CB produced, then L' is on BC produced.

Chapter 7: Conjugates

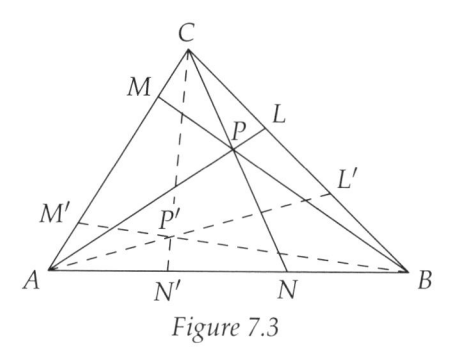

Figure 7.3

Theorem 7.3 (Cyclocevian conjugacy) *If the point P, not on a side, is defined by cevians AL, BM and CN, and if L*, M* and N* are the points where the circumcircle of $\triangle LMN$ meets the respective sides again, then the cevians AL*, BM* and CN* are concurrent in P*, the* cyclocevian conjugate *of P (see figure 7.4).*

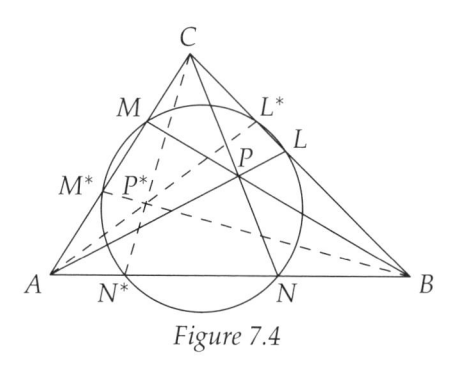

Figure 7.4

PROOF The result follows from Ceva and the intersecting chords theorem. ❑

Note that, if P is on a side, the points L, M and N are collinear and this construction breaks down.

Exercise 7a

1. What is the isogonal conjugate of the orthocentre?

2. Which point is its own isogonal conjugate?

3. What is the isotomic conjugate of a point on a side of the triangle?

4. Which internal point of $\triangle ABC$ is its own isotomic conjugate?

5. Prove that the vertices of the anti-complementary triangle $\triangle A^*B^*C^*$ are also isotomically self-conjugate.

6. What is the cyclocevian conjugate of the orthocentre?

7. What is the only point which is its own cyclocevian conjugate?

7.2 Characterising isogonal conjugates

Of these three relationships, isogonal conjugacy turn out to be the most significant. It would be useful to be able to recognise isogonally conjugate lines in other ways than that given by the definition. For example, suppose that we can show that two lines are isogonally conjugate by one of the alternative characterisations which follow. We could then deduce that the angles between the lines and the sides are equal. Thus we have increased the range of techniques available for proving facts about triangles.

The first new characterisation concerns the circumcircle of $\triangle ABC$.

Theorem 7.4 *Let P and Q be points on the circumcircle of $\triangle ABC$. Then AP and AQ are isogonally conjugate lines if, and only if, PQ is parallel to BC.*

PROOF Let AX' be the angle bisector at A; by corollary 2.6 on page 11, OX' is the perpendicular bisector of BC (see figure 7.5).

If AP and AQ are isogonal conjugates, then AX' is also the angle bisector of $\angle PAQ$ and so OX' is the perpendicular bisector of PQ. Hence PQ is parallel to BC.

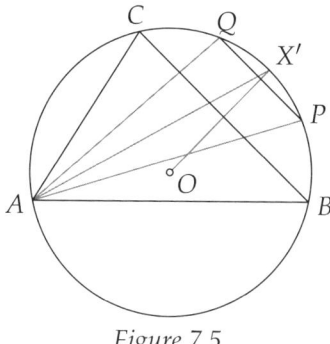

Figure 7.5

Conversely, suppose that PQ is parallel to BC. Then OX' is the common perpendicular bisector of these two line segments, and the arcs PX' and $X'Q$ are equal. Hence, by corollary 2.6 on page 11, AX' is the bisector of $\angle PAQ$ and the lines are indeed isogonal conjugates. ❏

A second characterisation concerns ratios of perpendicular distances.

Lemma 7.5 *Let $\mathcal{R}$ be a ray through the vertex A of a triangle and let P be an arbitrary point on it. Let p_B and p_C be the lengths of the perpendiculars from P to the sides CA and AB. The ratio $p_B : p_C$ is independent of the position of P (see figure 7.6).*

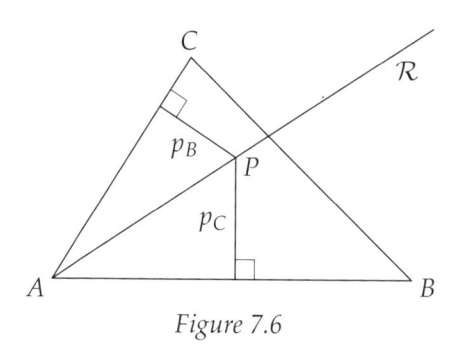

Figure 7.6

PROOF This is immediate from similar triangles. ❏

It follows from lemma 7.5 that the ratio $p_B : p_C$ is an *invariant* of the ray $\mathcal{R}$. If we know the value of this ratio, the ray is uniquely defined.

Theorem 7.6 *As in lemma 7.5, let p_B and p_C be the perpendicular distances from P to CA and AB, and let q_B and q_C be the corresponding distances from Q. Then AP and AQ are isogonally conjugate lines if, and only if,*

$$\frac{p_C}{p_B} = \frac{q_B}{q_C}.$$

What this is saying is the two lines, considered as rays through a vertex, have reciprocal ratio invariants.

PROOF Let R, S, U and V be the feet of the perpendiculars from P to AB, P to CA, Q to CA and Q to AB respectively.

The quadrilaterals $ARPS$ and $AUQV$ are cyclic, so $\angle RPS = \angle UQV = 180° - \angle A$ (see figure 7.7).

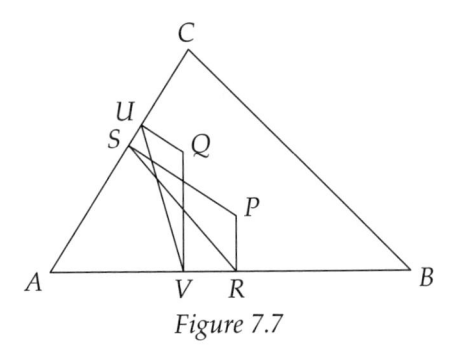

Figure 7.7

Now

$$\frac{p_C}{p_B} = \frac{q_B}{q_C}$$

if, and only if,

$$\frac{PR}{PS} = \frac{QU}{QV}$$

if, and only if, $\triangle RPS$ and $\triangle UQV$ are similar, which is the case if, and only if,

$$\angle RSP = \angle UQV,$$

that is,

$$\angle RAP = \angle UAQ$$

and this is equivalent to the fact that AP and AQ are isogonally conjugate lines. ❑

Chapter 7: Conjugates 87

A third result characterises isogonally conjugate points in terms of the angles around P and Q.

Theorem 7.7 *P and Q are isogonal conjugates if, and only if,*

$$\angle BPC + \angle BQC = 180° + \angle A,$$
$$\angle CPA + \angle CQA = 180° + \angle B$$
$$\text{and} \quad \angle APB + \angle AQB = 180° + \angle C.$$

PROOF First note that, if we add together the first and second equation, we have

$$\angle BPC + \angle BQC + \angle CPA + \angle CQA = 180° + \angle A + 180° + \angle B,$$

that is,

$$360° - \angle APB + 360° - \angle AQB = 360° + 180° - \angle C,$$

which is the third equation. Therefore there are only two independent relationships here.

Suppose now that P and Q are isogonal conjugates (see figure 7.8).

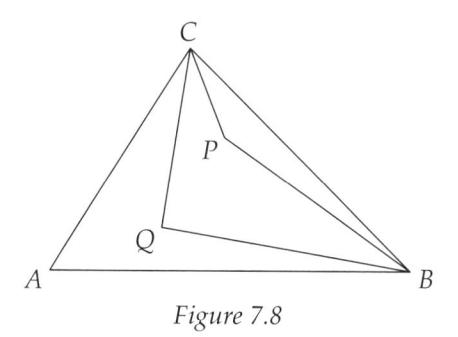

Figure 7.8

Then $\angle ABP = \angle CBQ$ and $\angle ACQ = \angle BCP$, and so

$$\angle BPC + \angle BQC = (180° - \angle CBP - \angle BCP) + (180° - \angle CBQ - \angle BCQ)$$
$$= (180° - \angle CBP - \angle ACQ) + (180° - \angle ABP - \angle BCQ)$$
$$= 180° + 180° - \angle B - \angle C$$
$$= 180° + \angle A.$$

The other relationships follow similarly.

We must now prove the converse result. Suppose that the three equations are true and that the point P is fixed. Then the angles around the point Q are uniquely determined. But this means that the point Q is also determined since it is the intersection of three fixed circles. However, it is known that the isogonal conjugate of P satisfies these relationships. Hence Q must be that point. ☐

7.3 Isogonal conjugates and pedal triangles

The next theorem generalises theorem 2.22 on page 22, about the orthocentre and circumcentre.

Theorem 7.8 *Let $\triangle A''B''C''$ be the pedal triangle of P and let Q be the isogonal conjugate of P. Then $B''C''$, $C''A''$ and $A''B''$ are perpendicular to AQ, BQ and CQ.*

PROOF We focus on AQ and $B''C''$. Let T be the intersection of AQ and $B''C''$ (see figure 7.9).

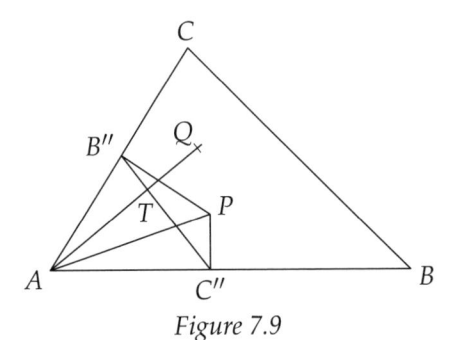

Figure 7.9

Because $PC''AB''$ is cyclic, $\angle TB''A = \angle C''B''A = \angle C''PA$. Because P and Q are isogonal conjugates, $\angle TAB'' = \angle C''AP$. Hence the triangles $\triangle TAB''$ and $\triangle C''AP$ are similar and $\angle ATB''$ is a right angle. The same is clearly true for the other vertices. ☐

Equivalently, we have shown that the perpendiculars from the vertices of $\triangle ABC$ to the corresponding sides of the pedal triangle of a point P are concurrent in the isogonal conjugate of P. This result has an important consequence.

Chapter 7: Conjugates

Theorem 7.9 *Isogonal conjugates share the same pedal circle and its centre is at their midpoint.*

PROOF Let P and Q be isogonal conjugates, with pedal triangles $\triangle DEF$ and $\triangle D^*E^*F^*$. By theorem 7.8, AP is perpendicular to E^*F^*; denote the intersection by R (see figure 7.10).

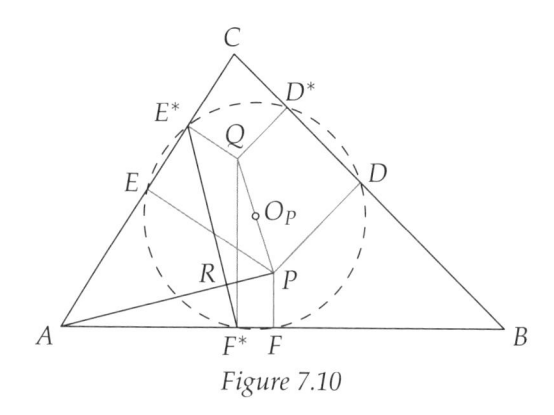

Figure 7.10

Then quadrilaterals FF^*RP and PRE^*E are cyclic, and so, by intersecting chords, $AF \times AF^* = AP \times AR = AE \times AE^*$.

It follows that F, F^*, E, E^* are concyclic and their circumcentre is on the perpendicular bisectors of FF^* and EE^*. Hence it is the midpoint O_P of PQ. We can now apply exactly the same argument to show that D, D^*, E and E^* are concyclic, and their circumcentre is also O_P. Hence the two circumcircles are identical, and the result follows. ❑

Again, if we take P and Q to be the orthocentre and circumcentre, we have a well-known result about the nine-point circle; it is the circumcircle of the orthic and medial triangles. The converse of this theorem is also true.

Corollary 7.10 *Let the pedal circle of a point P cut the sides in three more points. These points are the vertices of the pedal triangle of the isogonal conjugate of P.*

PROOF By theorem 7.9, the pedal circle of Q, the isogonal conjugate of P, is identical to the pedal circle of P, so the three new points form the pedal triangle of Q. ❑

Exercise 7b

1. Let the images of a point P by reflection in the sides BC, CA and AB be P_a, P_b and P_c. Prove that the circumcentre of $\triangle P_a P_b P_c$ is the isogonal conjugate of P.

2. Let P be a point on the circumcircle of $\triangle ABC$. Prove that the Simson line of P is perpendicular to the lines which are isogonally conjugate to AP, BP and CP.

3. Let P and Q be isogonal conjugates, and let AP and AQ meet the side BC at P_A and Q_A and the circumcircle of $\triangle ABC$ at P^* and Q^* respectively. Prove that $AP^* \times AQ_A = AQ^* \times AP_A = bc$.

4. With the notation of question 3, prove that

$$\frac{BP_A \times BQ_A}{CP_A \times CQ_A} = \frac{c^2}{b^2}.$$

5. A transversal meets the sides BC, CA and AB in L, M and N. Let L', M' and N' be the points where the isogonal conjugates of AL, BM and CN meet BC, CA and AB. Prove that L', M' and N' are collinear.

7.4 Isotomic and cyclocevian conjugates

Theorem 7.11 *In the isotomic configuration, the areas of triangles $\triangle LMN$ and $\triangle L'M'N'$ are equal.*

PROOF (See figure 7.11.)
Since $CM = M'A$ and $AN = N'B$, we have

$$[CMN] = [M'AN] = [M'N'B]$$

because triangles on the same base with the same height have equal area.

Chapter 7: Conjugates

Figure 7.11

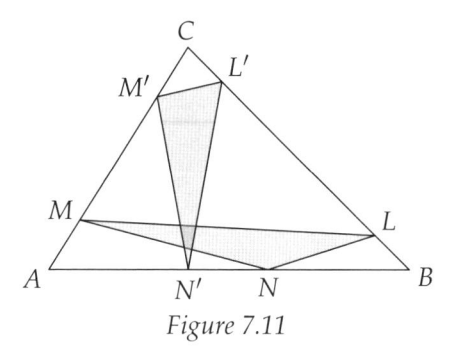

Now let MN meet CB at X. Then

$$\frac{[CMN]}{[LMN]} = \frac{p_C}{p_L} = \frac{XC}{XL}$$

(where p_C and p_L are the perpendicular distances of C and L from MN (see figure 7.12) and similarly, if $N'M'$ meets BC at X',

$$\frac{[M'N'B]}{[M'N'L']} = \frac{X'B}{X'L'}.$$

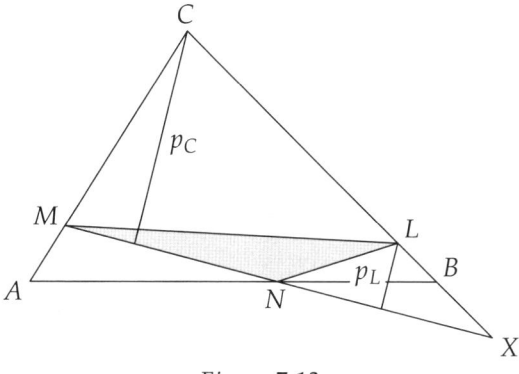

Figure 7.12

We now apply Menelaus' theorem to the transversal MNX to obtain

$$\frac{AN}{NB} \times \frac{BX}{XC} \times \frac{CM}{MA} = -1.$$

Similarly we have
$$\frac{AN'}{N'B} \times \frac{BX'}{X'C} \times \frac{CM'}{M'A} = -1.$$
But $AN = N'B$, $AN' = NB$, $CM' = MA$ and $CM = M'A$, and so $XC \times CX' = XB \times BX'$. By considering the line $XBCX'$, it follows that $XC = BX'$ and, since $BL = L'C$, we have $XL = L'X'$. From this we deduce that
$$[LMN] = [CMN] \times \frac{XL}{XC} = [M'N'B] \times \frac{X'L'}{X'B} = [L'M'N']. \qquad \square$$

Theorem 7.12 *In the cyclocevian configuration,*
$$\angle LMN + \angle L^*M^*N^* + \angle ABC = 180°.$$

PROOF (See figure 7.13.)

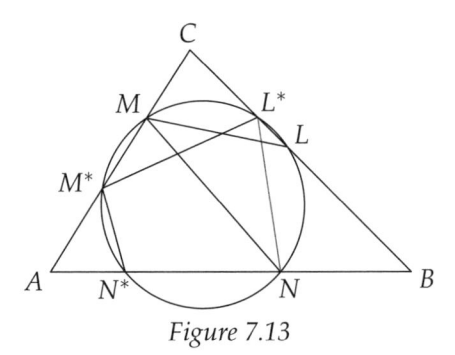

Figure 7.13

Since $\angle LMN = \angle LL^*N = \angle BL^*N$ and $\angle L^*M^*N^* = \angle L^*NB$, the result follows immediately from the angle sum of $\triangle BNL^*$. $\qquad \square$

7.5 Pedal-cevian points

A point P is a *pedal-cevian point* if its pedal triangle is the cevian triangle of a point $\widehat{P}$. We say that P is the pedal-cevian point of $\widehat{P}$.

The circumcentre is pedal-cevian since its pedal triangle is the medial triangle, and this is the cevian triangle of the centroid. Hence $\widehat{O} = G$. The orthocentre is pedal-cevian since its pedal triangle is the orthic triangle, and this is the cevian triangle of the orthocentre. Hence $\widehat{H} = H$. It is clear after a little thought that this is the only self pedal-cevian point.

Exercise 7c

1. A transversal meets the sides BC, CA and AB in L, M and N. Prove that L', M' and N', the isotomic conjugates of L, M and N, are collinear.

2. If AL, BM and CN are concurrent cevians, and L^*, M^* and N^* are the points where the circumcircle of $\triangle LMN$ meets the respective sides again, prove that the Miquel points of $\triangle LMN$ and $\triangle L^*M^*N^*$ are isogonal conjugates.

3. Show that the incentre is a pedal-cevian point.

4. If P is a pedal-cevian point, prove that its image under reflection in O is also pedal-cevian.

5. If P is a pedal-cevian point, prove that its isogonal conjugate is also pedal-cevian.

6. Prove that the de Longchamps point is pedal-cevian and $\widehat{\Lambda}$ is the isotomic conjugate of H.

7.6 Droz-Farny circles

Theorem 7.13 *Let P and Q be isogonal conjugates with respect to $\triangle ABC$, and let $\triangle XYZ$ be the pedal triangle of P. Let circles with centres X, Y and Z through Q cut the sides of $\triangle ABC$ at six points. Then these six points lie on a circle with centre P. Similarly, there is a circle with centre Q. These two circles have the same radius.*

PROOF In figure 7.14, X_1 and X_2 are the intersections of the circle with centre X and radius XQ with the line BC, and Y_1, Y_2, Z_1 and Z_2 are defined similarly. The midpoint of PQ is M.

Using Apollonius' median theorem on $\triangle XPQ$, we have $XQ^2 + XP^2 = 2XM^2 + 2MP^2$.

Figure 7.14

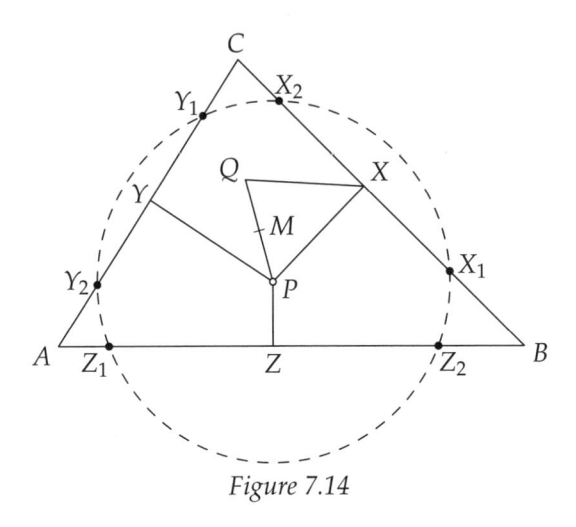

Hence

$$PX_1^2 = PX^2 + XX_1^2 = PX^2 + XQ^2 = 2XM^2 + 2MP^2.$$

But this depends only upon MP, which is $\frac{1}{2}PQ$, and MX, which, by theorem 7.9, is the radius of the pedal circle of P, and so is the same for PY_1 and PZ_1. Again using theorem 7.9, the same expression holds for the circle centred at Q. ◻

The circles with centres P and Q are known as the *Droz-Farny circles* of the pair (P, Q). However, there are another six significant points on these circles.

Theorem 7.14 *Let $\triangle UVW$ be the pedal triangle of Q. The circles with centres A, B and C through Q meet $\triangle UVW$ at six points on the Droz-Farny circle of P.*

PROOF Figure 7.15 shows the side UV meeting the Droz-Farny circle with centre P at U_1 and V_2. It is enough to show that the circle with centre C through Q also passes through U_1 and V_2.

By theorem 7.8, CP is perpendicular to UV and so it bisects the chord U_1V_2 at N. Hence $CU_1 = CV_2$.

Chapter 7: Conjugates

Figure 7.15

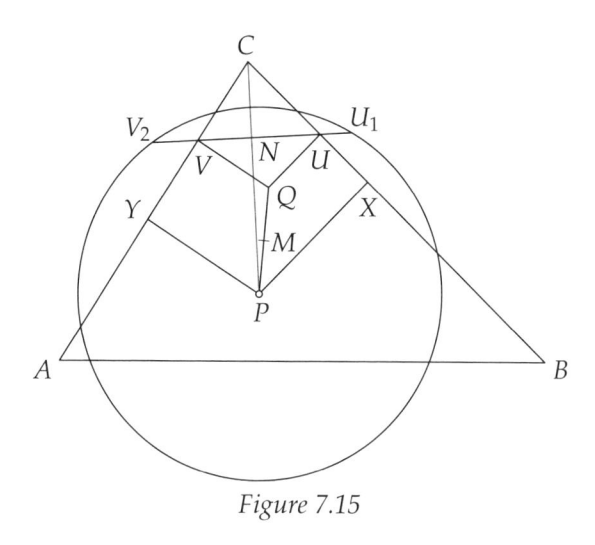

Now

$$CU_1^2 = CN^2 + NU_1^2$$
$$= CN^2 + PU_1^2 - PN^2$$
$$= PU_1^2 + CP(2CN - CP).$$

The quadrilateral $NPYV$ is cyclic, so $CN \times CP = CV \times CY$. By the proof of theorem 7.13, $PU_1^2 = 2XM^2 + 2MP^2$, so

$$CU_1^2 = 2XM^2 + 2MP^2 + 2CV \times CY - CP^2.$$

By Apollonius' median theorem on $\triangle CPQ$, we have $CP^2 + CQ^2 = 2CM^2 + 2MP^2$ and so we can simplify further to obtain

$$CU_1^2 = 2XM^2 + 2CV \times CY - 2CM^2 + CQ^2.$$

But, by theorem 7.9, the common pedal triangle of P and Q has centre M and radius XM. Hence the term $CV \times CY$ is the power of C with respect to this circle and is equal to $CM^2 - XM^2$. It follows that $CU_1 = CQ$ as required. The argument for the other two vertices is the same. ❏

It is worth showing the entire configuration on one diagram (see figure 7.16). Recall that the points X_1, X_2, Y_1, Y_2, Z_1 and Z_2 are on circles with centres X, Y and Z through Q, and that the points U_1, U_2, V_1, V_2, W_1 and W_2 are on circles with centres A, B and C through Q, and bear in mind that there are another twelve points on the Droz-Farny circle of Q.

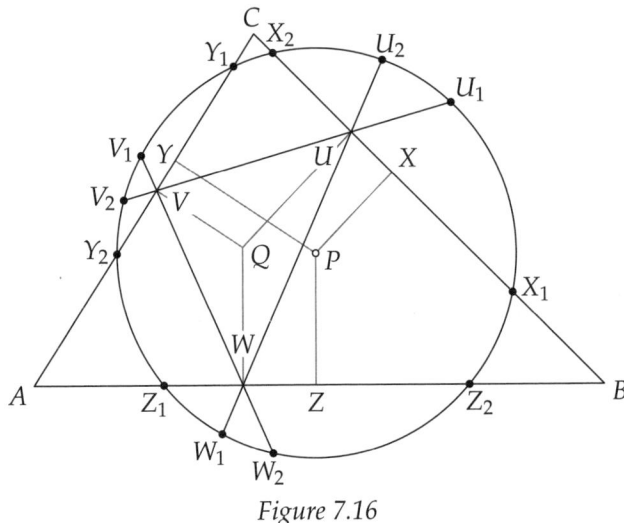

Figure 7.16

The name of Droz-Farny circles is often applied to the special case where the two isogonal conjugates are the orthocentre and circumcentre. The following exercise focuses on some special features of this configuration.

Exercise 7d

1. Prove that a circle with centre H which cuts all three sides of the medial triangle $\triangle A_1 B_1 C_1$ does so in six points which lie (in pairs) on three equal circles centred at A, B and C.

2. Conversely, prove that if three equal circles centred at A, B and C cut the medial triangle in six points, they lie on a circle with centre H.

3. In this configuration, let ρ be the radius of the circles centred at A, B and C and let ρ_0 be the radius of the circle with centre H. Prove that

$$\rho_0^2 + \tfrac{1}{2}(a^2 + b^2 + c^2) = 4R^2 + \rho^2.$$

4. Derive a formula for the radius of the Droz-Farny circle(s) of (O, H) in terms of a, b, c and R.

Chapter 8

The symmedian point

In this chapter, we meet the symmedian point, which has many significant properties, providing a link between the 'elementary' centres familiar in school geometry and more sophisticated configurations such as that associated with Brocard.

8.1 Symmedians

The isogonal conjugate of the centroid is called the *symmedian point*. It is sometimes referred to as the Lemoine point or Grebe point, and will be denoted by K. The cevians through K are known as *symmedians*. We denote by K_A, K_B and K_C the points at which they meet the opposite sides of $\triangle ABC$ (see figure 8.1).

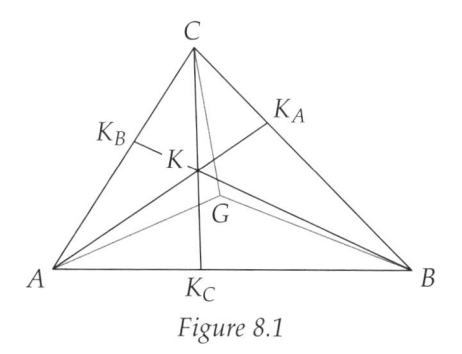

Figure 8.1

In the next two results, we use the invariance mentioned in lemma 7.5 on page 85.

Theorem 8.1 *If p_A, p_B and p_C are the distances of P to the sides BC, CA and AB, then P is the symmedian point of $\triangle ABC$ if, and only if,*

$$\frac{p_A}{a} = \frac{p_B}{b} = \frac{p_C}{c}.$$

PROOF Let K be the symmedian point, AA_1 the median through A and X, Y, U and V be the feet of the perpendiculars from K and A_1 to AB and CA (see figure 8.2).

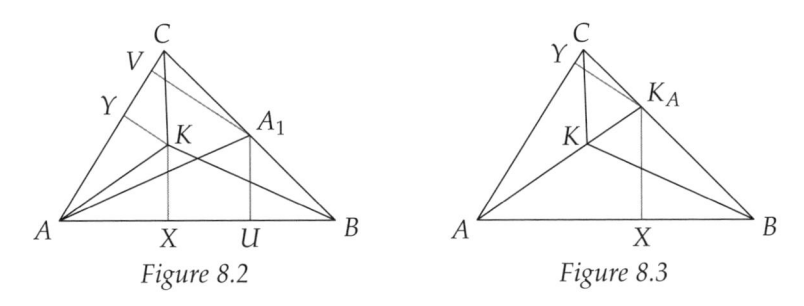

Figure 8.2   Figure 8.3

As $\triangle AA_1C$ and $\triangle AA_1B$ have equal areas, we have

$$\frac{A_1U}{A_1V} = \frac{b}{c},$$

and hence, by theorem 7.6 on page 86,

$$\frac{KX}{KY} = \frac{c}{b}.$$

The result follows.

This argument is easily reversible to give the converse implication. ❑

Corollary 8.2 $BK_A : K_AC = c^2 : b^2.$

PROOF (See figure 8.3.) We use areas, together with the result of theorem 8.1, to obtain

$$\frac{BK_A}{K_AC} = \frac{[ABK_A]}{[ACK_a]} = \frac{p_Cc}{p_Bb} = \frac{c^2}{b^2}.$$

❑

Corollary 8.2 gives another justification, using Ceva's theorem, of the concurrency of the symmedians.

Corollary 8.3 *The perpendicular distance of K from BC is*

$$\frac{2a\Delta}{a^2 + b^2 + c^2}.$$

PROOF Set as question 5 of exercise 8a. ❏

Theorem 8.4 *Let T_A be the point of intersection of the tangents at B and C to the circumcircle. Then AT_A is a symmedian of $\triangle ABC$.*

PROOF Let U be the point on AB such that $\angle AUT_A = \angle ACB$, and let UT_A meet AC at V (see figure 8.4).

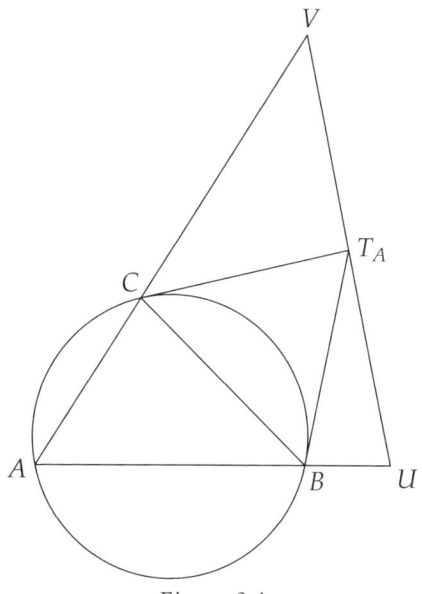

Figure 8.4

Then $\angle VUA = \angle BCA$ and, by the alternate segment theorem, we have $\angle UBT_A = \angle BCA$ and $\angle VCT_A = \angle CBA$. Hence the triangles $\triangle T_A UB$ and $\triangle T_A VC$ are isosceles, and so $T_A V = T_A C = T_A B = T_A U$ and T_A is the midpoint of UV. But $\triangle AVU$ and $\triangle ABC$ are similar (and oppositely oriented) and hence the median AT_A of $\triangle AVU$ is the symmedian of $\triangle ABC$, as claimed. ❏

The triangle $\triangle T_A T_B T_C$ is known as the *tangential triangle*. Theorem 8.4 leads to a diagram showing the relationship between the reference triangle $\triangle ABC$ and its tangential triangle (see figure 8.5).

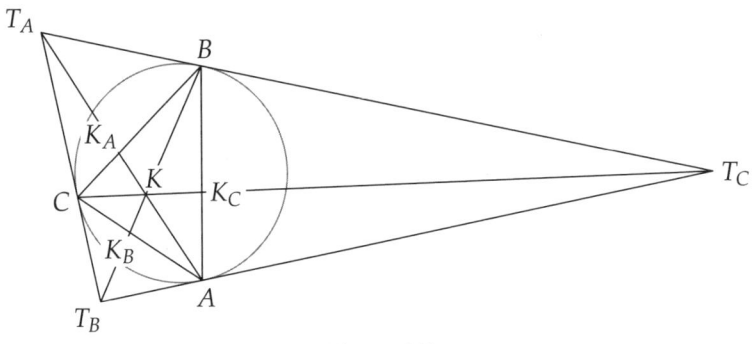

Figure 8.5

The three symmedians are AT_A, BT_B and CT_C, and they are concurrent at the symmedian point K.

Exercise 8a

1. Prove that the symmedians of $\triangle ABC$ bisect the sides of the orthic triangle $\triangle DEF$.

2. Prove that the symmedian through A of $\triangle AEF$ bisects BC.

3. If $\triangle ABC$ is right-angled at A, prove that its symmedian point is the midpoint of AD.

4. Prove that K divides AK_A in the ratio $b^2 + c^2 : a^2$.

5. Prove corollary 8.3.

6. Prove that the perpendicular distance of T_A from BC is
$$\frac{2a\Delta}{b^2 + c^2 - a^2}.$$

7. Prove that the line OK is perpendicular to the symmedian from A if, and only if, $b^2 + c^2 = 2a^2$.

8. Denoting by $\mathcal{C}$ the circumcircle of $\triangle ABC$, let X be the intersection of $A_1 H$ with $\mathcal{C}$ and Y be the intersection of XD with $\mathcal{C}$. Prove that AY is the symmedian through A.

8.2 Parallels and antiparallels

The definition of what it means for lines to be parallel has had an enormous impact on the history of geometry. In Euclid's axiom system, the fifth axiom was for some two thousand years the centre of controversy. Could this axiom be deduced from the other axioms of geometry? Is there some simpler (and obvious) axiom which implies it? As readers will doubtless know, this debate was only resolved with the demonstration of the independence of the parallel axiom by the invention of non-Euclidean geometries. Today the position is simple—lines are parallel if, and only if, alternate angles (for example) are equal. It then turns out that if two lines are parallel to a third, then they are parallel to one another.

It turns out to be useful to introduce the concept of antiparallel line segments. The situation, however, is not as straightforward as with parallel lines. Antiparallels are only defined in relation to a given angle, and it is not true that two segments which are antiparallel to the same segment are antiparallel to each other. The definition we will use can be motivated by considering the problem of cutting off, from a given triangle, a triangle which is similar to it. This can be done in two ways.

The obvious way to do this is to draw a line segment UV which is parallel to the base BC (see figure 8.6). This means that U is on AB and V is on AC, and it produces a triangle $\triangle AUV$ which is similar to $\triangle ABC$.

But equally well we could choose U on AC and V on AB and still have $\triangle AUV$ similar to $\triangle ABC$ (see figure 8.7). In this case the quadrilateral $BCUV$ is cyclic.

In figure 8.6, we can go ahead to say that the line UV is parallel to the line BC, and indeed any transversal will exhibit the same equal angle properties. But in the case of antiparallels the definition will be stated in terms of the configuration as a whole:

Figure 8.6 *Figure 8.7*

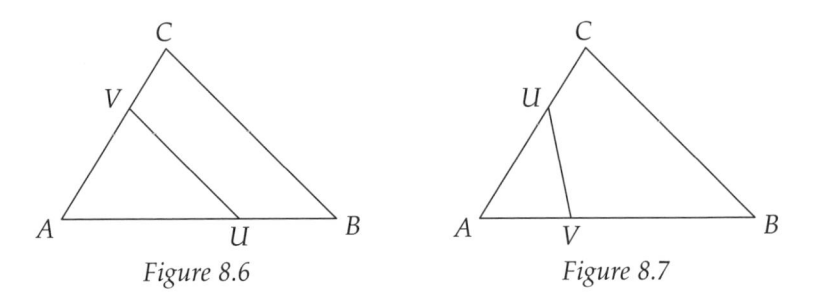

The line segment VU is *antiparallel* to BC with respect to AVB and AUC if, and only if, $\angle AVU = \angle ACB$.

We can make this definition without mentioning A since it can be introduced as the intersection of BV and CU.

It is clearly necessary that BV and CU are not parallel. This prompts an equivalent definition:

The line segment VU is *antiparallel* to BC with respect to AVB and AUC if, and only if, quadrilateral $BCUV$ is cyclic.

Immediately we have the fact that VU is antiparallel to BC if, and only if, VB is antiparallel to UC.

Note, however, that if D is any point on the line BC apart from C, then it is not true that VU is antiparallel to BD (see figure 8.8).

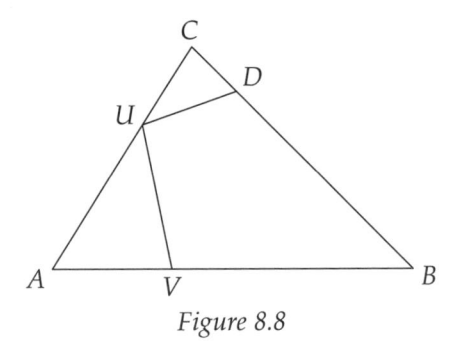

Figure 8.8

It therefore makes no sense to say that the lines VU and BC are antiparallel, without reference to any other lines, points or angles. However, we can say that one pair of lines is antiparallel with respect to another pair. For instance, it makes perfect sense to say that the lines VU and BC

are antiparallel with respect to the lines VB and UC since that is drawing attention to the cyclic quadrilateral which is formed.

We also have to be a little careful about the relationship between the concepts of parallel and antiparallel. For example, suppose that (as segments)

(i) VU is antiparallel to BC and

(ii) V_1U_1 is antiparallel to BC

relating to two *different* points A and A_1. Then it is certainly not true that VU is parallel to V_1U_1 (see figure 8.9).

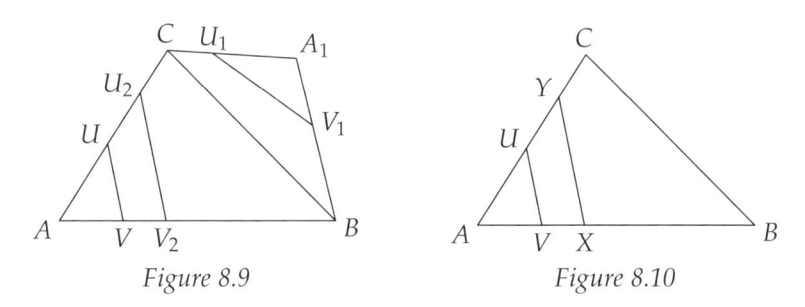

Figure 8.9   Figure 8.10

If, however, V_2U_2 is antiparallel to BC with respect to the *same* point A, then it does follow that VU is parallel to V_2U_2.

It is also true that if VU is antiparallel to BC, a line parallel to VU yields a segment XY which is also antiparallel to VU. Of course X and Y have to be the points where the line meets AB and AC (see figure 8.10).

In the extreme case where X and Y coincide at A, it becomes the tangent to the circumcircle of $\triangle ABC$, and we do allow ourselves to say that this tangent is antiparallel to BC.

Theorem 8.5 *The diameter of the circumcircle of $\triangle ABC$ at A is perpendicular to any line segment antiparallel to BC.*

PROOF Set as question 3 of exercise 8b.   ❑

We now look at two equivalent characterisations of antiparallel line segments.

Theorem 8.6 *Let the angle bisector at A meet VU at X_1 and BC at X. Then VU and BC are antiparallel with respect to $\triangle ABC$ if, and only if, $\angle AX_1U = \angle AXB$.*

This property is, of course, analogous to that of corresponding angles for parallel lines.

PROOF (See figure 8.11.)

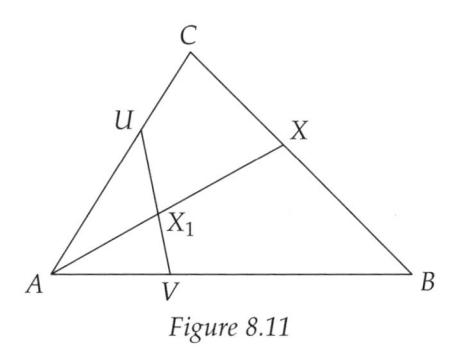

Figure 8.11

It is a simple angle chase to show that $\angle AX_1U = \angle AXB$ if, and only if, $\angle AUV = \angle ABC$, which is the case if, and only if, $BCUV$ is cyclic. ❑

It is also possible to characterise parallel segments in terms of a median: UV is parallel to BC if, and only if, it is bisected by the median AA_1 (see figure 8.12). So the median is the locus of the midpoints of chords parallel to the base of the triangle.

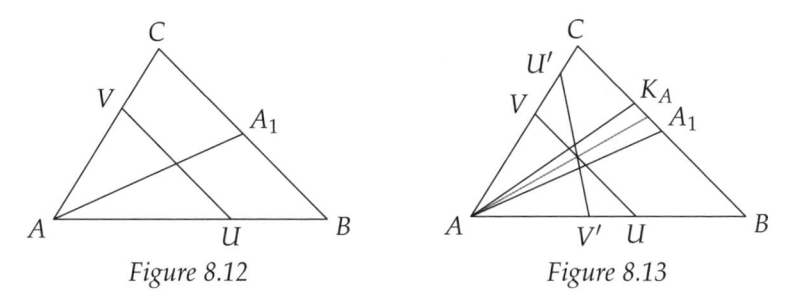

Figure 8.12   *Figure 8.13*

Now we can reflect the chord and the median in the angle bisector at A to produce the corresponding criterion for antiparallels.

Theorem 8.7 *For U' and V' on AC and AB, $V'U'$ is antiparallel to BC if, and only if, it is bisected by the symmedian AK_A.*

Note that U' and V' map to U and V under reflection in the angle bisector because they lie on the sides, which are equally inclined to the axis of reflection (see figure 8.13). So the symmedian is the locus of the midpoints of chords antiparallel to the base of the triangle. Note that, in the proof of theorem 8.4, we used this idea since the segments BC and $U'V'$ are antiparallel, and the median of the triangle containing BC becomes the symmedian of the triangle containing $U'V'$.

Theorem 8.8 *In $\triangle ABC$, let UV be antiparallel to AC and ST be antiparallel to AB, and let X be the intersection of UV and ST. If $UV = ST$, then AX is a symmedian.*

PROOF Set as question 5 of exercise 8b. ☐

Exercise 8b

1. Prove that, if $\triangle ABC$ is isosceles, then a line is parallel to BC if, and only if, it is antiparallel to BC.

2. Prove that a side FE of the orthic triangle of $\triangle ABC$ is antiparallel to BC. (Hence the result of question 1 of exercise 8a is seen to be a special case of theorem 8.7.)

3. Prove theorem 8.5.

4. If VU and BC are antiparallel with respect to $\triangle ABC$, and a transversal AX_1X, which cuts VU at X_1 and BC at X, is such that $\angle AX_1U = \angle AXB$, then the transversal is the internal angle bisector of $\angle BAC$.

5. Prove theorem 8.8.

6. Let D' be the point where the altitude AD of $\triangle ABC$ meets the circumcircle. Prove that the Simson line of D' is antiparallel to BC with respect to $\triangle ABC$.

8.3 Quadrangles

An alternative proof of theorem 8.4 uses the properties of harmonic ranges.

PROOF OF THEOREM 8.4 Let $X'X''$ be the diameter of the circumcircle perpendicular to BC. Then $X'X''$ passes through A_1 (see figure 8.14) and by corollary 2.6 on page 11, AX' and AX'' are the internal and external angle bisectors of $\angle BAC$.

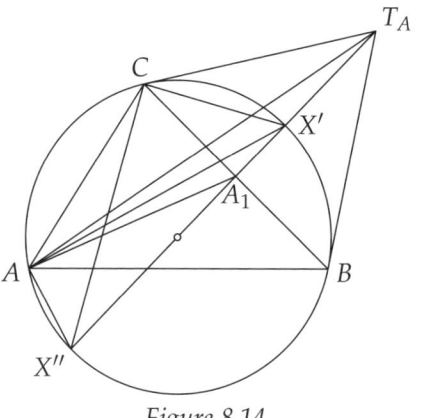

Figure 8.14

First, note that $\angle T_A C X' = \angle C X'' X' = \angle X' C A_1$ so CX' is the internal angle bisector of $\angle A_1 C T_A$, and, since it is perpendicular, CX'' is the external angle bisector. It follows from corollary 5.15 on page 60 that X'', A_1, X', T_A is a harmonic range, and so $A(X'', A_1, X', T_A)$ is a harmonic pencil. But $\angle X'' A X' = 90°$ and so, by theorem 5.16 on page 60, AX' is the bisector of $\angle A_1 A T_A$. Since AA_1 is a median and AX' is an angle bisector of $\triangle ABC$, it follows by definition that AT_A is a symmedian. ☐

In view of this connection, we briefly revisit the subject matter of section 5.6 on page 66. Here the configuration consisting of the excentral triangle and the incentre was interpreted as a complete quadrangle with diagonal triangle $\triangle ABC$.

Another example of this concerns the anticomplementary triangle and the centroid (see figure 8.15). This can be viewed as a quadrangle $A^* B^* C^* G$ and its diagonal triangle $\triangle ABC$.

In theorem 5.27 on page 66, the point U becomes A_1 and V the point at infinity on BC and $B^* C^*$. Of the three harmonic ranges in theorem 5.27,

Chapter 8: The symmedian point 109

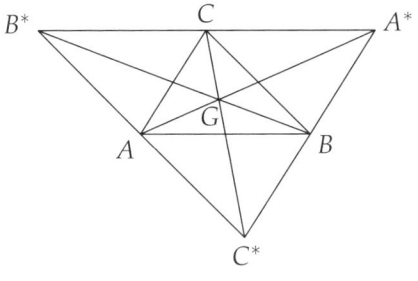

Figure 8.15

that in (iii) is A, G, A_1, A^* and the other two express the fact that the harmonic conjugate of a midpoint is at infinity.

Note also that the centroid G of $\triangle ABC$ is also the centroid of $\triangle A^*B^*C^*$. This is another similarity between this diagram and that showing the incentre and the excentres. By analogy with the external angle bisectors in $\triangle I_A I_B I_C$, the sides of $\triangle A^*B^*C^*$ are sometimes called *exmedians*.

Now consider the tangential triangle and the symmedian point (see figure 8.16). Again we think of $T_A T_B T_C K$ as a quadrangle with diagonal triangle $\triangle ABC$. This time, in terms of theorem 5.27, the point U becomes K_A and V becomes K_A^*. Now we have three harmonic ranges, namely (a) A, K, K_A, T_A, (b) T_B, A, T_C, K_A^* and (c) C, K_A, B, K_A^*.

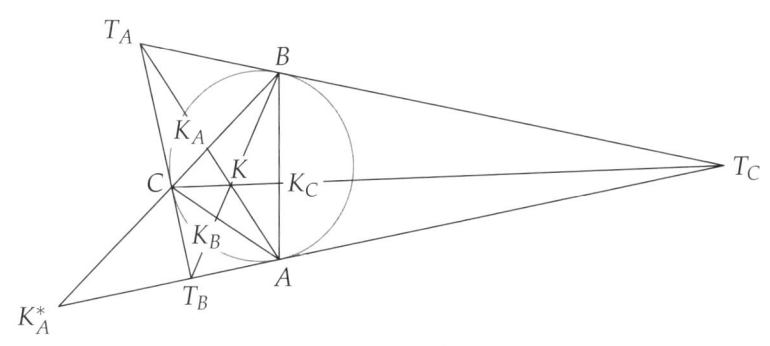

Figure 8.16

By analogy with the two previous diagrams, the sides of the tangential triangle are sometimes called *exsymmedians*, and the points T_A, T_B and T_C are the *exsymmedian points*.

8.4 Pedal properties

Theorem 8.9 *The symmedian point is the unique point which is the centroid of its pedal triangle.*

PROOF Set as question 4 of exercise 8c. ❑

One of the most celebrated properties of the symmedian point arises from a minimisation problem. For a point P in the plane of $\triangle ABC$, let the *pedal sum* be the sum of the squares of the distances of P from the vertices of its pedal triangle, that is, $PD^2 + PE^2 + PF^2$.

Theorem 8.10 *The symmedian point is the point inside a triangle with minimal pedal sum.*

PROOF Let the distances of an internal point P from AB, BC and CA be p_C, p_B and p_A. Then $ap_A + bp_B + cp_C = 2\Delta$, which is constant. Hence, by the Cauchy-Schwartz inequality,

$$4\Delta^2 \leq \left(a^2 + b^2 + c^2\right)\left(p_A^2 + p_B^2 + p_C^2\right),$$

with equality if, and only if,

$$\frac{p_A}{a} = \frac{p_B}{b} = \frac{p_C}{c}.$$

Hence the pedal sum is minimised when this happens, but by theorem 8.1, this means that P is the symmedian point. ❑

Exercise 8c

1. Let X be the intersection of the altitude AD of $\triangle ABC$ with the line A_1K; prove that X is the midpoint of AD. In other words, the three lines from the midpoints of the sides of $\triangle ABC$ to the midpoints of the corresponding altitudes are concurrent at the symmedian point.

2. Prove that the orthocentre of a triangle is the isotomic conjugate of the symmedian point of its anti-complementary triangle.

3. Let the symmedians of $\triangle ABC$ meet the circumcircle again at A^*, B^* and C^*. Prove that K is the symmedian point of $\triangle A^*B^*C^*$.

4. Prove theorem 8.9.

Chapter 9

Centres related to the incentre

Three triangle centres—the Gergonne, Nagel and Spieker points—are related to the incentre in a manner which is reminiscent of the Euler line. The Adams and Fuhrmann circles turn out to have connections to these new centres.

9.1 The Gergonne point

By theorem 6.5 on page 73, the intouch triangle $\triangle PQR$ is cevian, and the point of concurrency is the Gergonne point Γ (see figure 9.1).

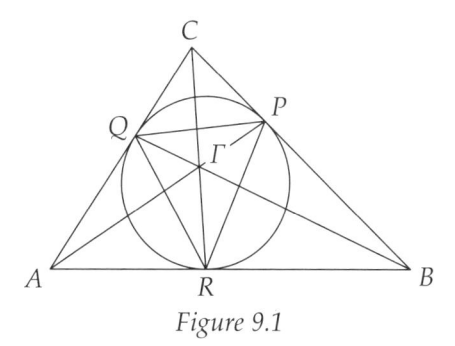

Figure 9.1

Theorem 9.1 *The Gergonne point of $\triangle ABC$ is the symmedian point of its intouch triangle.*

PROOF From the point of view of the intouch triangle $\triangle PQR$, the incircle of $\triangle ABC$ is its circumcircle, and so $\triangle ABC$ is its tangential triangle. Hence, by theorem 8.4 on page 101, Γ is the symmedian point of $\triangle PQR$. ❑

Lemma 9.2 *Let p_A and p_B be the perpendicular distances from Γ to BC and CA. Then*
$$\frac{p_A}{p_B} = \frac{b(s-b)}{a(s-a)}.$$

PROOF Set as question 1 of exercise 9a. ❑

Lemma 9.3 *With p_A defined as in lemma 9.2, prove that*
$$p_A = \frac{2r_A \Delta}{a(r_A + r_B + r_C)} = \frac{2r_A \Delta}{a(4R + r)}.$$

PROOF Set as question 2 of exercise 9a. ❑

9.2 The Nagel point

The isotomic conjugate of the Gergonne point of $\triangle ABC$ is known as the *Nagel point*. We will denote it by M (as N is already in use for the nine-point centre).

Theorem 9.4 *The cevians of the Nagel point are the lines AP_A, BQ_B and CR_C, connecting each vertex to the point of contact of the corresponding excircle with the opposite side (see figure 9.2).*

PROOF This is immediate from the definition of isotomic conjugates and theorem 2.11 on page 17. ❑

Lemma 9.5 *Let r_A and r_B be the perpendicular distances from M to BC and CA. Then*
$$\frac{r_B}{r_A} = \frac{a(s-b)}{b(s-a)}.$$

PROOF Set as question 3 of exercise 9a. ❑

Chapter 9: Centres related to the incentre 115

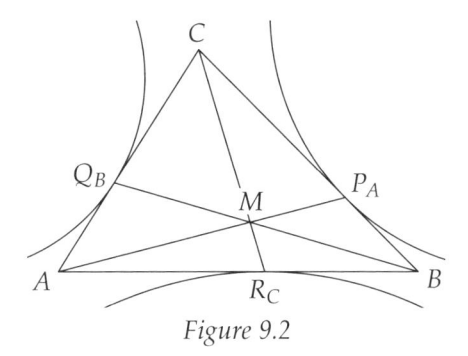

Figure 9.2

Theorem 9.6 *The incentre of $\triangle ABC$ is the Nagel point of its medial triangle.*

PROOF First note that A is the external centre of similitude of the incircle and the excircle opposite to it. Let X be the point where AP_A intersects the incircle for the first time (see figure 9.3); under the enlargement it follows that the tangent at X is parallel to BC. Hence XP is a diameter of the incircle.

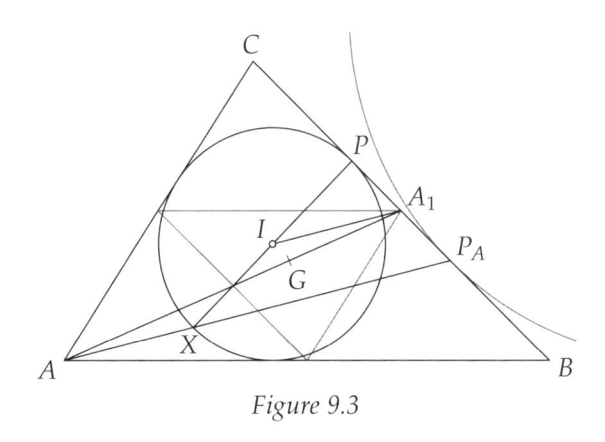

Figure 9.3

By theorem 2.11 on page 17, A_1 is the midpoint of PP_A, so $\triangle PIA_1$ is similar to $\triangle PXP_A$ and IA_1 is parallel to XP_A.

Let θ be the familiar enlargement with centre G and scale factor $-\frac{1}{2}$, which maps $\triangle ABC$ to the medial triangle $\triangle A_1B_1C_1$. It follows that θ maps A to A_1 and the ray AP_A to the ray A_1I. Since it does this for all three cevians P_AA, Q_BB and R_CC, it takes the Nagel point of $\triangle ABC$ to that of $\triangle A_1B_1C_1$. But the three lines IA_1, IB_1 and IC_1 meet at I, so this is the Nagel point of $\triangle A_1B_1C_1$. ❑

Corollary 9.7 *The points I, G and M are collinear and G trisects IM.*

PROOF This is immediate since the centre of θ is G. ❑

Corollary 9.8 *The Nagel point is the incentre of the anti-complementary triangle $\triangle A^*B^*C^*$.*

9.3 The Spieker centre and circle

Again we make use of the enlargement θ. This maps the incentre I of $\triangle ABC$ to the incentre of $\triangle A_1B_1C_1$, which is known as the *Spieker centre S*. The incircle of $\triangle A_1B_1C_1$, with centre S, is known as the *Spieker circle* (see figure 9.4).

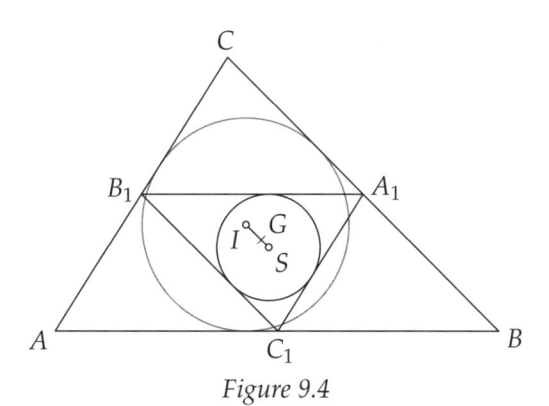

Figure 9.4

Two immediate consequences of this definition are that:
(i) I, G and S are collinear, and $IG = 2GS$;
(ii) the radius of the Spieker circle is $\frac{1}{2}r$.

Theorem 9.9 *Let A_1S meet another side of $\triangle ABC$ internally at X. Then the transversal A_1X bisects the perimeter of $\triangle ABC$.*

X could, of course, lie on either BA or CA.

Figure 9.5

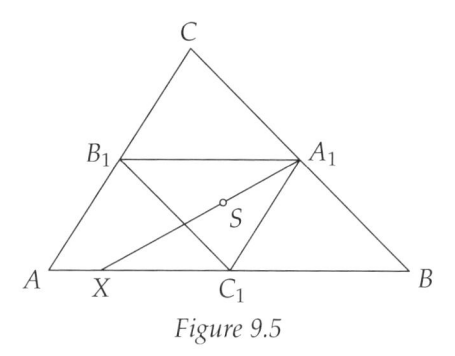

PROOF Since $\angle C_1 A_1 X = \angle B_1 A_1 X$ and $B_1 A_1$ is parallel to AB, it follows that $A_1 C_1 = X C_1$ (see figure 9.5).

Hence $A_1 B + B C_1 + C_1 X = A_1 B + B C_1 + C_1 A_1$, which is the perimeter of $\triangle A_1 B C_1$ and therefore half that of $\triangle ABC$. ❑

Note that the Nagel point has a similar property, in that the three lines AP_A each bisect the perimeter of $\triangle ABC$. This is immediate from theorem 2.11 on page 17.

The inverse enlargement θ^{-1}, with centre G and scale factor -2, takes I to the Nagel point M. This immediately produces four collinear points.

Theorem 9.10 *I, G, S and M form a harmonic range.*

The ratios, just as on the Euler line, are $IG : GS : SM = 2 : 1 : 3$. Note also that S is the midpoint of IM.

It is worth considering these two harmonic ranges drawn on the same diagram (see figure 9.6).

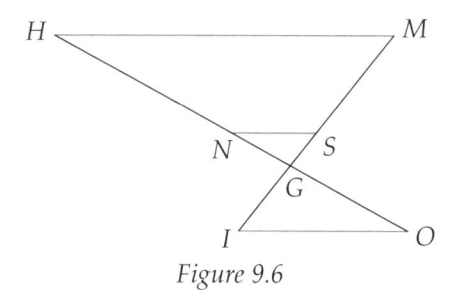

Figure 9.6

Note that $HM \parallel IO \parallel NS$ and that the lengths are in the ratio $4:2:1$. Also, if we think of correspondences of the form

$$\text{incentre} \longleftrightarrow \text{circumcentre,}$$
$$\text{Spieker centre} \longleftrightarrow \text{nine-point centre,}$$
$$\text{Nagel point} \longleftrightarrow \text{orthocentre,}$$

we can start looking for other analogies, such as

$$\text{Spieker circle} \longleftrightarrow \text{nine-point circle.}$$

Whilst being no substitute for rigorous proof, these may be an intuitive guide to discovering new results.

Theorem 9.11 *G is the internal and M the external centre of similitude of the Spieker circle and the incircle.*

PROOF The first result follows immediately from the enlargement θ (which has a negative scale factor), and the second is a consequence of the fact that we have a harmonic range. This result is analogous to the fact that G is the internal and H the external centre of similitude of the nine-point circle and the circumcircle. ❑

Theorem 9.12 *Let U, V and W be the midpoints of MA, MB and MC. Then the Spieker circle is the incircle of $\triangle UVW$.*

PROOF By theorem 9.11, M is the centre of an enlargement of scale factor 2, mapping the Spieker circle to the incircle. Let P' be the intersection of MP with the Spieker circle (see figure 9.7).

The tangent to the Spieker circle at P' is parallel to BC, the tangent to the incircle at P, and this intersects MB and MC at V and W. ❑

Note that U, V and W are analogous to the Euler points on the nine-point circle.

Exercise 9a

1. Prove lemma 9.2.

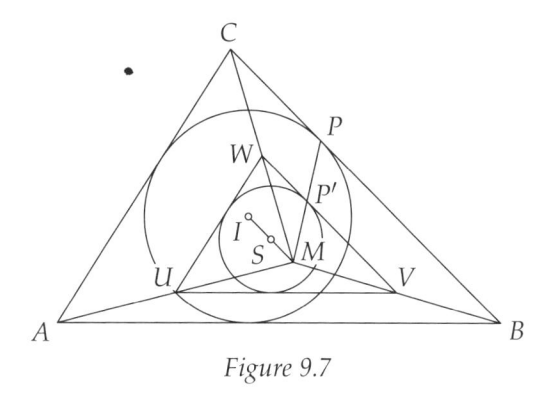

Figure 9.7

2. Prove lemma 9.3.

3. Prove lemma 9.5.

4. Prove that the lines through A_1, B_1 and C_1 perpendicular to PQ, QR and RP are concurrent in the Spieker centre.

5. Prove that the points of contact of the Spieker circle with $\triangle A_1 B_1 C_1$ and $\triangle UVW$ are diametrically opposite.

6. Prove that IU is bisected by the median AA_1.

7. Prove that $\dfrac{AM}{AP_A} = \dfrac{a}{s}$.

9.4 A notation for triangle centres

The process which I call 'shifting the focus' has now been illustrated several times, and it turns out that it is useful to have a notation to express what we are doing when we focus on a particular triangle and investigate its triangle centres.

We shall use the notation $P \triangle XYZ$ to mean that P is a 'centre' in $\triangle XYZ$. For instance, $O \triangle ABC$ is just O, the circumcentre of the reference triangle, and in this case we will omit the triangle.

Exercise 9b

In terms of the reference triangle $\triangle ABC$, identify:

1. $O \triangle A^*B^*C^*$.

2. $N \triangle A^*B^*C^*$.

3. $I \triangle A^*B^*C^*$.

4. $S \triangle A^*B^*C^*$.

5. $K \triangle PQR$.

6. $H \triangle I_A I_B I_C$.

7. $I \triangle DEF$.

8. $I_D \triangle DEF$.

9.5 The Fuhrmann circle

Let X', Y' and Z' be the points of intersection of the angle bisectors at A, B and C with the circumcircle, and F_A, F_B and F_C be the images of X', Y' and Z' after reflection in the sides BC, CA and AB (see figure 9.8).

The triangle $\triangle F_A F_B F_C$ is the *Fuhrmann triangle* and its circumcircle is the *Fuhrmann circle*. The centre of the Fuhrmann circle, known as the *Fuhrmann centre*, will be denoted by F^*.

Theorem 9.13 *HM is a diameter of the Fuhrmann circle.*

PROOF Consider the diameter $X'OX''$ of the circumcircle, which also passes through A_1 and F_A. It is parallel to AH, so $X''F_A = 2R - 2A_1X' = 2OA_1 = AH$. Hence AHF_AX'' is a parallelogram (see figure 9.9).

But $\angle X'AX'' = 90°$ and so HF_A is perpendicular to AX' since it is parallel to AX''.

Chapter 9: Centres related to the incentre

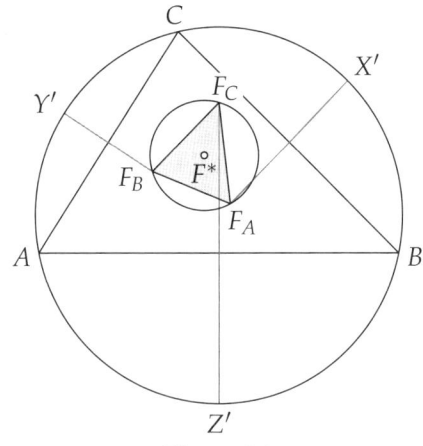

Figure 9.8

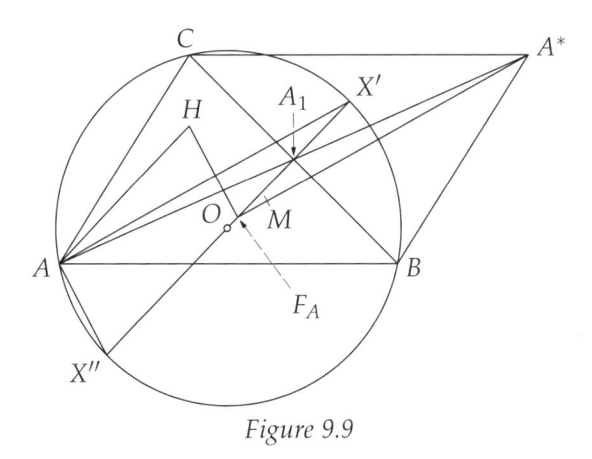

Figure 9.9

Now let A^* be the vertex of the anticomplementary triangle opposite A, so $AA_1 = A_1A^*$. Since $X'A_1 = A_1F_A$, it follows that $AX'A^*F_A$ is a parallelogram and F_AA^* is parallel to AX'. But AX' is the angle bisector of $\angle CAB$ and so A^*F_A is the angle bisector of $\angle B^*A^*C^*$.

Hence, by corollary 9.8, the Nagel point M lies on A^*F_A. It follows that $\angle HF_AM = 90°$. So the circle on diameter HM contains the point F_A. As, by symmetry, it also contains F_B and F_C, it is the Fuhrmann circle. ☐

9.6 The Bevan point

The *Bevan point*, which will be denoted Θ, is the circumcentre of the excentral triangle. In the notation introduced in section 9.4, $\Theta = O\triangle I_A I_B I_C$.

It turns out that there is an intriguing web of relationships between this point and other triangle centres including the Nagel point, Spieker centre, de Longchamps point and incentre.

Theorem 9.14 *Each of the following triples of points is collinear:*

(i) *the incentre, the circumcentre and the Bevan point;*
(ii) *the Nagel point, the Bevan point and the de Longchamps point;*
(iii) *the orthocentre, the Spieker centre and the Bevan point;*
(iv) *the circumcentre, the Spieker centre and the Fuhrmann centre.*

PROOF We begin with the Euler line, which includes H, N, G, O and Λ. The ratios along this line are $3 : 1 : 2 : 6$ (see figure 9.10).

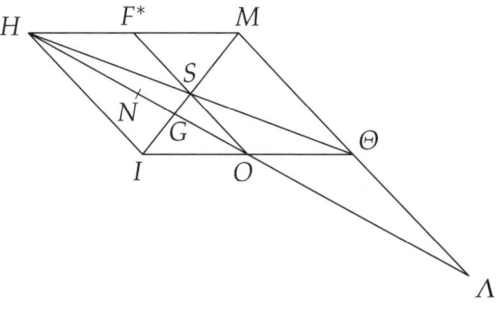

Figure 9.10

Now, by theorem 2.9 on page 16, $I = H\triangle I_A I_B I_C$ and, since the circumcircle of $\triangle ABC$ is the nine-point circle of $\triangle I_A I_B I_C$, $O = N\triangle I_A I_B I_C$. Hence I, O and Θ are collinear on the Euler line of $\triangle I_A I_B I_C$, with O at the midpoint of $I\Theta$.

Also, by theorem 9.10, I, G, S and M are collinear, with ratios $2 : 1 : 3$. Hence, by the midpoint theorem, SO is parallel to $M\Theta$ and half its length. Hence $M\Theta$ meets GO at a point such that $GO : OX = 1 : 3$, and so X is Λ, the de Longchamps point.

But also we have $IG : GS = 2 : 1 = HG : GO$, so HI is parallel to SO. Hence it is also parallel to and equal to $M\Theta$. It follows that H, S and Θ

are collinear, with S at the midpoint of $H\Theta$, and also that OS meets HM at its midpoint, which is the Fuhrmann centre F^*. ☐

9.7 The Adams circle

Recall that P, Q and R are the points where the incircle of $\triangle ABC$ is tangential to the sides.

Theorem 9.15 *Let Y_A and Z_A on AC and AB be such that $Y_A Z_A$ passes through Γ and is parallel to QR. Analogously, define points Z_B, X_B, Y_A and Z_A (see figure 9.11). Then the six points so defined lie on a circle with centre I.*

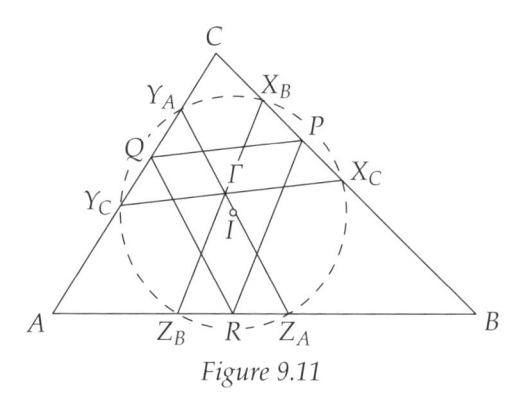

Figure 9.11

The circle given by theorem 9.15 is known as the *Adams circle* of $\triangle ABC$.

PROOF Since $Y_A Z_A$ is parallel to QR, we see that $\triangle AY_A Z_A$ is similar to $\triangle AQR$, which is isosceles, so $Y_A Q = Z_A R$, and similarly $Z_B R = X_B P$ and $X_C P = Y_C Q$.

Now consider the effect of drawing lines through A and Γ parallel to BC cutting the rays PQ and PR at X, U, Y and V (see figure 9.12).

Then $PX_B = V\Gamma$, $X_C P = \Gamma U$ from the parallelograms, and

$$\frac{V\Gamma}{\Gamma U} = \frac{YA}{AX}$$

by similar triangles. But $\triangle AYR$ is similar to $\triangle BPR$ and is therefore isosceles, as is $\triangle AXQ$. Hence $AY = AR = AQ = AX$ by tangents, and so $PX_B = X_C P$. It follows that all six segments of this type are equal in

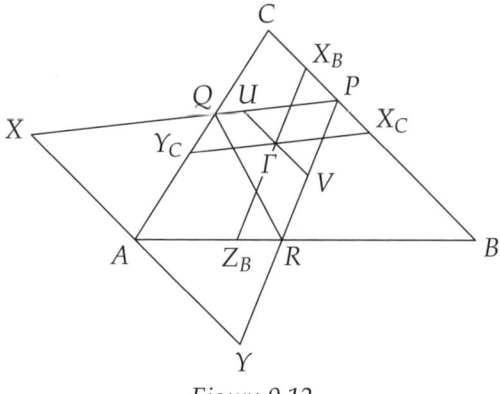

Figure 9.12

length. But the incentre I is equidistant from P, Q and R, and these are the feet of perpendiculars from I to the sides, so the result follows from the six congruent triangles about the incentre. ❑

9.8 Barycentric coordinates

In section 1.4 on page 5, the existence of the centroid was shown by placing equal masses at the vertices of $\triangle ABC$ and calculating the position of their centre of mass. A similar, but different, argument showed that G was also the centre of mass of the lamina $\triangle ABC$.

We now examine other distributions of masses at the vertices which can demonstrate the existence of triangle centres. In general, the principle we are using is the following one:

- If masses m and n are placed at points A and B, they are equivalent to a single mass $m + n$ placed at a point C on AB, where $AC : CB = n : m$.

Theorem 9.16 *If P is the centre of mass of masses λ, μ and ν placed at A, B and C, then the areas of the triangles $\triangle BCP$, $\triangle CAP$ and $\triangle ABP$ are in the ratio $\lambda : \mu : \nu$.*

PROOF Let L be the centre of mass of μ and ν on BC. It is immediate that

$$\frac{LP}{LA} = \frac{\lambda}{\lambda + \mu + \nu} = \frac{[BCP]}{[BCA]}.$$

The result now follows. ☐

The point P is said to have *barycentric coordinates* (λ, μ, ν). Note that these are not unique and that the same point is given by the barycentric coordinates $(k\lambda, k\mu, k\nu)$ for any positive k. When k is chosen so that $k(\lambda + \mu + \nu) = 1$, the coordinates are said to be *normalised*, and then they are also known as *areal coordinates*. Thus the centroid has barycentric coordinates $(1,1,1)$ and areal coordinates $(\frac{1}{3}, \frac{1}{3}, \frac{1}{3})$.

In fact, it is perfectly reasonable to allow λ, μ and ν to take zero or negative values (so long as they are their sum is not zero). This allows every point in the plane to be described using barycentric or areal coordinates.

A related technique is to consider $\triangle ABC$ to be a framework of uniform rods of appropriate mass. One must be careful since this is not 'equivalent' to using masses at the vertices.

Exercise 9c

1. Prove that the Fuhrmann circle cuts each altitude of $\triangle ABC$ at a distance of $2r$ from the vertex.

2. Prove that the nine-point centre is the midpoint of IF^*.

3. What are the barycentric coordinates of the vertices A, B and C and the midpoints of the sides A_1, B_1 and C_1?

4. Find the barycentric coordinates of:
   (a) the incentre I;
   (b) the excentre I_A.

5. Find the centre of mass of the following distributions of masses at the vertices A, B and C:
   (a) a^2, b^2 and c^2;
   (b) $s-a$, $s-b$ and $s-c$;
   (c) $(s-b)(s-c)$, $(s-c)(s-a)$ and $(s-a)(s-b)$;
   (d) $b+c$, $c+a$ and $a+b$.

6. Determine the centre of mass of a triangular framework of uniform rods of equal mass.

7. Determine the centre of mass of a triangular framework of uniform rods of equal density.

8. Find the barycentric coordinates of the following points in terms of trigonometrical ratios of the angles of $\triangle ABC$:
   (a) the circumcentre O;
   (b) the orthocentre H.

Chapter 10

Triangles in perspective

In order to discover more interesting triangle centres, we first develop some theoretical results about triangles which are in perspective. The principal theorem, associated with Desargues, is one of the fundamental results of projective geometry. We also explore the principle of duality, meet a remarkable theorem due to Blaise Pascal and prove some theorems involving three triangles in perspective.

10.1 Desargues' theorem

Suppose that we have a pencil of three lines with vertex O, and that there are points A, A' on one line, B, B' on the second and C, C' on the third (see figure 10.1).

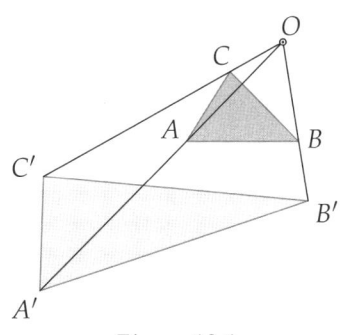

Figure 10.1

The two triangles $\triangle ABC$ and $\triangle A'B'C'$ which are produced are said to be in *perspective*, and O is called the *centre of perspective* or *perspector*.

Note that we are talking about lines here, not just rays, so it is possible for corresponding vertices to be on opposite sides or on the same side of the vertex. It is quite likely that the two triangles will overlap, as they do in figure 10.2.

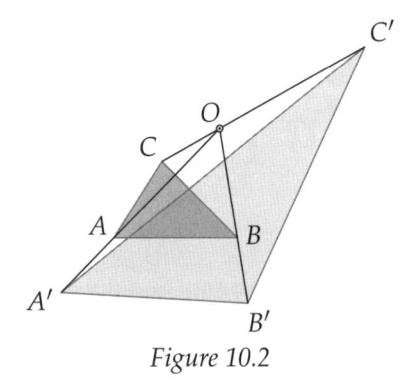

Figure 10.2

Also note that this is a much weaker relationship than homothecy. Homothetic triangles are similar and their corresponding sides are parallel, and there is a homothetic centre from which one can be mapped onto the other by an enlargement. Clearly all homothetic triangles are in perspective, but most triangles in perspective are not homothetic. To put this another way, the homothetic centre is the perspector in the case of homothecy, but most perspectors are not homothetic centres.

There is a very important necessary and sufficient condition for triangles to be in perspective. The proof consists of writing down a sequence of equations about ratios which exhibit a degree of symmetry, which are then combined algebraically to produce something new. This type of argument is common in projective geometry; another example occurs in the proof of Pappus's theorem later in this chapter.

Theorem 10.1 (Desargues) *If the triangles $\triangle ABC$ and $\triangle A'B'C'$ are in perspective, then the intersections of corresponding pairs of sides are collinear.*

In figure 10.3, L is the intersection of BC and $B'C'$, M of CA and $C'A'$, and N of AB and $A'B'$.

The line LMN is known as the *axis of perspective*.

Chapter 10: Triangles in perspective

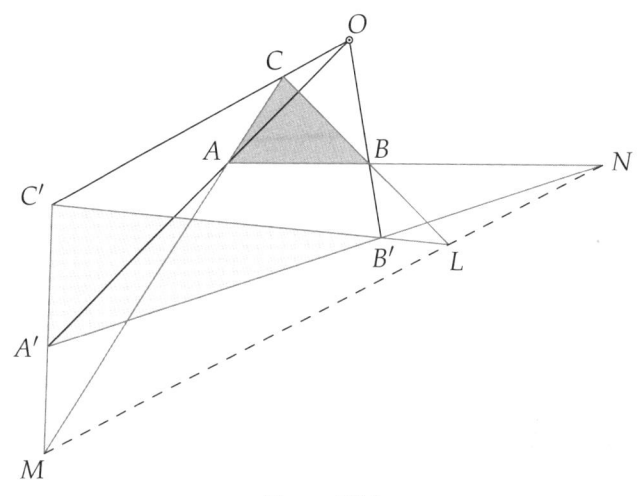

Figure 10.3

PROOF This is proved using Menelaus' theorem. From $\triangle OBC$ with transversal $LB'C'$, we have

$$\frac{OB'}{B'B} \times \frac{BL}{LC} \times \frac{CC'}{C'O} = -1.$$

Similarly from $\triangle OCA$ with transversal $MC'A'$,

$$\frac{OC'}{C'C} \times \frac{CM}{MA} \times \frac{AA'}{A'O} = -1,$$

and from $\triangle OAB$ with transversal $NA'B'$

$$\frac{OA'}{A'A} \times \frac{AN}{NB} \times \frac{BB'}{B'O} = -1.$$

Multiplying these together, we obtain

$$\frac{AN}{NB} \times \frac{BL}{LC} \times \frac{CM}{MA} = -1,$$

and the converse of Menelaus shows that L, M and N are collinear. ❏

Desargues' theorem is also true in three dimensions, and it is interesting that the proof is actually easier in this case. Suppose that $\triangle ABC$ and

△A'B'C' are in different planes. Then L, M and N are in both planes, and so they lie on their line of intersection. If the planes are parallel, this is the line at infinity.

Remarkably, the converse of Desargues' theorem is proved using the theorem itself.

Theorem 10.2 (Converse of Desargues) *If △ABC and △A'B'C' are two coplanar triangles with the property that L, M and N, the points of intersection of BC and B'C', CA and C'A', and AB and A'B', are collinear, then the lines AA', BB' and CC' are concurrent (see figure 10.4).*

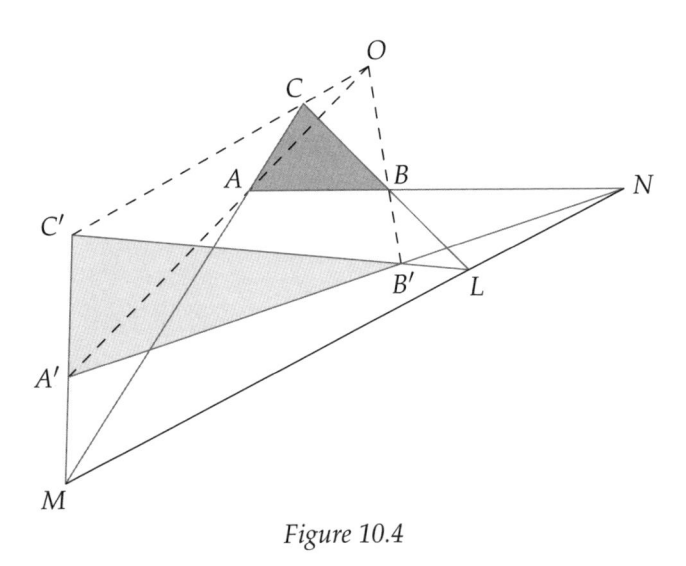

Figure 10.4

PROOF Let O be the intersection of BB' and CC'. Now △BB'N and △CC'M are in perspective from L. The corresponding line pairs meet at O, A and A', so it follows from Desargues' theorem that these three points are collinear. ❑

In the exercise which follows, you will be asked to recognise some examples of triangles in perspective and identify the perspector in each case. In some cases, the axis of perspective has been given a name. When the triangles are actually homothetic, this is the line at infinity, and this happens when we consider:

- triangle $\triangle ABC$ and its medial triangle $\triangle A_1B_1C_1$, with perspector G;
- triangle $\triangle ABC$ and its anticomplementary triangle $\triangle A^*B^*C^*$, with perspector G.

The more interesting situation occurs when the two triangles are not homothetic. In the case of $\triangle ABC$ and its orthic triangle $\triangle DEF$, where the perspector is H, the axis of perspective is the orthic axis, already encountered in question 4 of exercise 6a.

Exercise 10a

1. Show that the reference triangle $\triangle ABC$ and its excentral triangle $\triangle I_A I_B I_C$ are in perspective and identify the perspector. (The axis of perspective is called the *antiorthic axis*.)

2. Show that the reference triangle $\triangle ABC$ and its intouch triangle $\triangle PQR$ are in perspective and identify the perspector. (The axis of perspective is called the *Gergonne line*.)

3. The *extouch triangle* $\triangle P_A Q_B R_C$ is formed by the points of contact of the three excircles which are internal to the sides BC, CA and AB. Show that the reference triangle $\triangle ABC$ and its extouch triangle are in perspective and identify the perspector.

4. Prove that the reference triangle $\triangle ABC$ and its tangential triangle $\triangle T_A T_B T_C$ are in perspective and identify the perspector. (The axis of perspective is called the *Lemoine line*.)

5. Let A, B, C and D form a complete quadrangle. Show that each of the triangles $\triangle ABC$, $\triangle BCD$, $\triangle CDA$ and $\triangle DAB$ is in perspective with its diagonal triangle $\triangle PQR$, and identify the perspector in each case.

10.2 Duality

There are two fundamental facts which are important in plane geometry:
- A unique line can be drawn joining two given points.
- A unique point can be found lying on two given lines.

We will need to invoke the line and points at infinity to make these facts true in general, but for the moment we suppose this does not happen. However, the reader should check that the results proved are still true when lines are parallel. It now turns out that the concepts of collinearity—three points which lie on the same line—and concurrency—three lines which pass through the same point—are analogous. Often a theorem about collinearity can be paired with one about concurrency, and occasionally the two concepts play an equal role in the same result. Indeed, Desargues' theorem is an example of such a phenomenon.

It is therefore useful to develop a way of looking at geometrical configurations which allows us to switch our attention easily between points and lines. In essence, there are two different ways of viewing geometry. One of these viewpoints begins with the point as the fundamental concept, and then lines arise as the joins of points. The other starts with the line as the underlying idea, and defines points as intersections of lines. If a result involving collinearity or concurrency is shown to be true for one viewpoint, then there is an analogous result which is true for the other. This is known as the *principle of duality*.

This means that even the simplest of figures, the triangle, can be viewed in two ways.

The triangle

We denote the line opposite to the vertex A by $\mathcal{A}$, and similarly with $\mathcal{B}$ and $\mathcal{C}$ (see figure 10.5). We shall denote the intersection of $\mathcal{B}$ and $\mathcal{C}$ by $\mathcal{B} \cap \mathcal{C}$, or, where there is no ambiguity, simply by $\mathcal{BC}$; thus $A = \mathcal{BC}$, $B = \mathcal{CA}$, $C = \mathcal{AB}$. Also, in more familiar notation, we denote the join of B and C by BC, so that $\mathcal{A} = BC$.

We can now consider the two propositions $A = \mathcal{BC}$ and $\mathcal{A} = BC$ as *dual statements*. The triangle in figure 10.5 can be considered

- as three points A, B, C and their joins $\mathcal{C} = AB$, $\mathcal{A} = BC$, $\mathcal{B} = CA$;
- as three lines $\mathcal{A}$, $\mathcal{B}$, $\mathcal{C}$ and their intersections $C = \mathcal{AB}$, $A = \mathcal{BC}$, $B = \mathcal{CA}$.

Chapter 10: Triangles in perspective

Figure 10.5

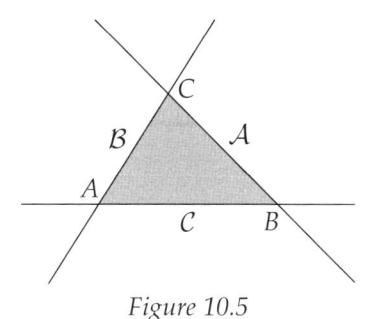

Hence the triangle is a self-dual figure because if we shift our viewpoint from one version to the other, the figure does not change.

If we were very precise, we should actually distinguish between the *triangle* $\triangle ABC$, where the points are fundamental and the sides are derived, and the *trilateral* $\triangle \mathcal{ABC}$, where the lines are fundamental and the vertices are a consequence. However, this is so counter-intuitive that we will not, unless absolutely necessary, do so.

Range and pencil

The concepts of a range and a pencil are dual to one another because:

- a range is a set of points $A, B, C, \ldots$, which lie on a common line $\mathcal{V}$;
- a pencil is a set of lines $\mathcal{A}, \mathcal{B}, \mathcal{C}, \ldots$, which pass through a common point V.

If we have a point V and a set of points $A, B, C, \ldots$, we can define a pencil by considering the lines $VA, VB, VC, \ldots$. The dual statement says that if we have a line $\mathcal{V}$ and a set of lines $\mathcal{A}, \mathcal{B}, \mathcal{C}, \ldots$, we can define a range by considering the points $\mathcal{VA}, \mathcal{VB}, \mathcal{VC}, \ldots$.

Quadrangle and quadrilateral

We can also revisit the concept of the quadrangle introduced in section 5.6. This consists of four points A, B, C, D, which define six lines (see figure 10.6).

These lines form three pairs of *opposite sides* BC and AD, CA and BD, AB and CD, and we can define three more points, $P = BC \cap AD$, $Q = CA \cap BD$, $R = AB \cap CD$.

Figure 10.6

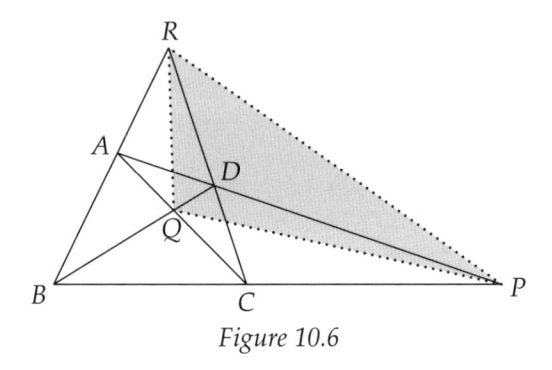

$\triangle PQR$ is then the *diagonal triangle* of the quadrangle.

Now let us examine the dual concept, which is known as a *quadrilateral*. This consists of four lines $\mathcal{A}$, $\mathcal{B}$, $\mathcal{C}$, $\mathcal{D}$, which define six points (see figure 10.7).

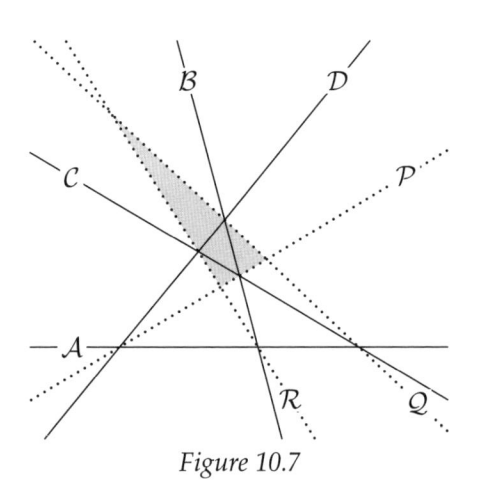

Figure 10.7

These points form three pairs of vertices $\mathcal{BC}$ and $\mathcal{AD}$, $\mathcal{CA}$ and $\mathcal{BD}$, $\mathcal{AB}$ and $\mathcal{CD}$, which are thought of as *opposite vertices* and define three more sides $\mathcal{P}$, $\mathcal{Q}$, $\mathcal{R}$.

$\triangle \mathcal{PQR}$ is then the *diagonal triangle* (or *trilateral*) of the quadrilateral.

Dual theorems

Now we look at the process of changing a theorem into its dual, and we shall use Desargues' theorem as our example. The technique is to examine the statement of theorem 10.1 carefully, reformulating each step, if necessary, so that the relationship between lines and points is made explicit, and then to translate it into the dual statement.

STATEMENT

We have a pencil of lines $\mathcal{A}, \mathcal{B}, \mathcal{C}$.

The points A, A' lie on $\mathcal{A}$;
B, B' lie on $\mathcal{B}$;
and C, C' lie on $\mathcal{C}$.

The intersections of BC and $B'C'$, CA and $C'A'$, AB and $A'B'$ are L, M and N.

Then L, M, N are collinear.

DUAL STATEMENT

We have a range of points A, B, C.

The lines $\mathcal{A}, \mathcal{A}'$ pass through A;
$\mathcal{B}, \mathcal{B}'$ pass through B;
and $\mathcal{C}, \mathcal{C}'$ pass through C.

The joins of $\mathcal{BC}$ and $\mathcal{B}'\mathcal{C}'$, $\mathcal{CA}$ and $\mathcal{C}'\mathcal{A}'$, $\mathcal{AB}$ and $\mathcal{A}'\mathcal{B}'$ are $\mathcal{L}, \mathcal{M}$ and $\mathcal{N}$.

Then $\mathcal{L}, \mathcal{M}, \mathcal{N}$ are concurrent.

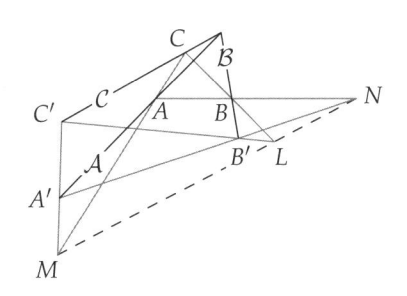

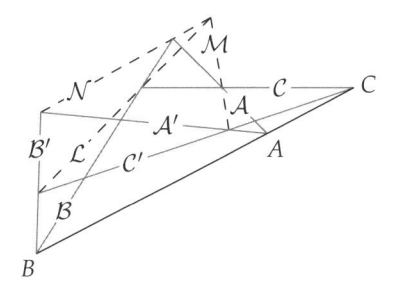

It turns out that we have exactly the same diagram except for the renaming of certain points and lines. The original theorem says that if two triangles are in perspective, then corresponding sides join in an axis of perspective. The dual theorem starts with the axis of perspective and concludes that the two trilaterals have a perspector. The converse of Desargues' theorem is its dual.

Exercise 10b

For each of the results below, draw the diagram and form the dual theorem.

1. If a hexagon is inscribed in a circle, then the intersections of opposite sides are collinear.

2. In triangle $\triangle ABC$, the lines AP, BQ and CR are concurrent (at the Gergonne point).

3. Two fixed lines $\mathcal{X}$ and $\mathcal{Y}$ meet at A. From a fixed point B, two variable lines are drawn. One cuts $\mathcal{X}$ at P and $\mathcal{Y}$ at Q, and the other cuts $\mathcal{X}$ at R and $\mathcal{Y}$ at S. The intersection of PS and QR is on a fixed line through A.

10.3 Pascal's theorem

We begin with a result which gives a necessary and sufficient condition for two triangles to be in perspective.

Theorem 10.3 *(See figure 10.8.)* Let $\triangle A_1 B_1 C_1$ and $\triangle A_2 B_2 C_2$ be any two triangles (such that no two sides are parallel), and intersections are defined as follows:

$$P_1 = B_1 C_1 \cap B_2 C_2, \quad P_2 = C_1 A_1 \cap C_2 A_2, \quad P_3 = A_1 B_1 \cap A_2 B_2,$$
$$Q_1 = B_1 C_1 \cap C_2 A_2, \quad Q_2 = C_1 A_1 \cap A_2 B_2, \quad Q_3 = A_1 B_1 \cap B_2 C_2,$$
$$R_1 = B_1 C_1 \cap A_2 B_2, \quad R_2 = C_1 A_1 \cap B_2 C_2, \quad R_3 = A_1 B_1 \cap C_2 A_2.$$

Then $\triangle A_1 B_1 C_1$ and $\triangle A_2 B_2 C_2$ are in perspective (in the sense indicated by the order of the vertices) if, and only if,

$$\frac{A_1 Q_3}{Q_3 B_1} \times \frac{B_1 Q_1}{Q_1 C_1} \times \frac{C_1 Q_2}{Q_2 A_1} = \frac{R_3 B_1}{A_1 R_3} \times \frac{R_1 C_1}{B_1 R_1} \times \frac{R_2 A_1}{C_1 R_2}.$$

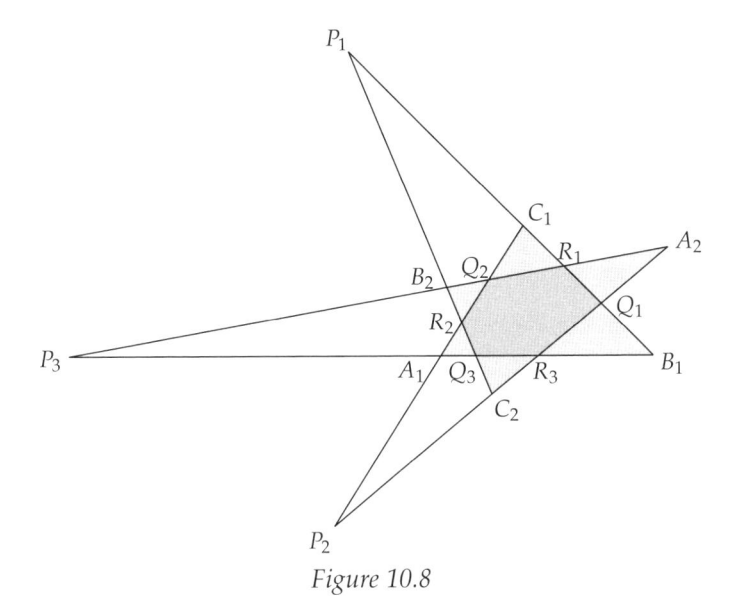

Chapter 10: Triangles in perspective 137

Figure 10.8

PROOF We may use Menelaus' theorem for the triangle $\triangle A_1B_1C_1$ and the transversals $P_1Q_3R_2$, $P_2Q_1R_3$ and $P_3Q_2R_1$ to obtain the statements

$$\frac{A_1Q_3}{Q_3B_1} \times \frac{B_1P_1}{P_1C_1} \times \frac{C_1R_2}{R_2A_1} = -1,$$

$$\frac{A_1R_3}{R_3B_1} \times \frac{B_1Q_1}{Q_1C_1} \times \frac{C_1P_2}{P_2A_1} = -1$$

and $\quad\dfrac{A_1P_3}{P_3B_1} \times \dfrac{B_1R_1}{R_1C_1} \times \dfrac{C_1Q_2}{Q_2A_1} = -1.$

Now, by Desargues' theorem, the triangles are in perspective if, and only if, P_1, P_2 and P_3 are collinear and, again by Menelaus' theorem, this is equivalent to

$$\frac{B_1P_1}{P_1C_1} \times \frac{C_1P_2}{P_2A_1} \times \frac{A_1P_3}{P_3B_1} = -1.$$

Multiplying the first three equations together and dividing by the last produces the required relationship. ❑

Corollary 10.4 *If, taking the order of vertices into account, $\triangle A_1B_1C_1$ and $\triangle A_2B_2C_2$ are in perspective and $\triangle A_1B_1C_1$ and $\triangle B_2C_2A_2$ are in perspective, then $\triangle A_1B_1C_1$ and $\triangle C_2A_2B_2$ are also in perspective.*

PROOF This follows at once from theorem 10.3 since the two statements equivalent to the first two perspectivities can be multiplied to produce one equivalent to the third. The statement can be stated in the more straightforward form: if two triangles are in perspective in two ways, then they are also in perspective in the third. ❑

Theorem 10.5 (Pascal's theorem) *If the six points P, R', Q, P', R, Q' lie on a circle in any order, then the intersections $PQ' \cap P'Q$, $QR' \cap Q'R$ and $RP' \cap R'P$ are collinear.*

PROOF Form the triangle $\triangle ABC$ by extending the lines $P'Q$, $R'P$ and $Q'R$ and finding their intersections, and, similarly, form $\triangle DEF$ from the lines PQ', RP' and QR' (see figure 10.9).

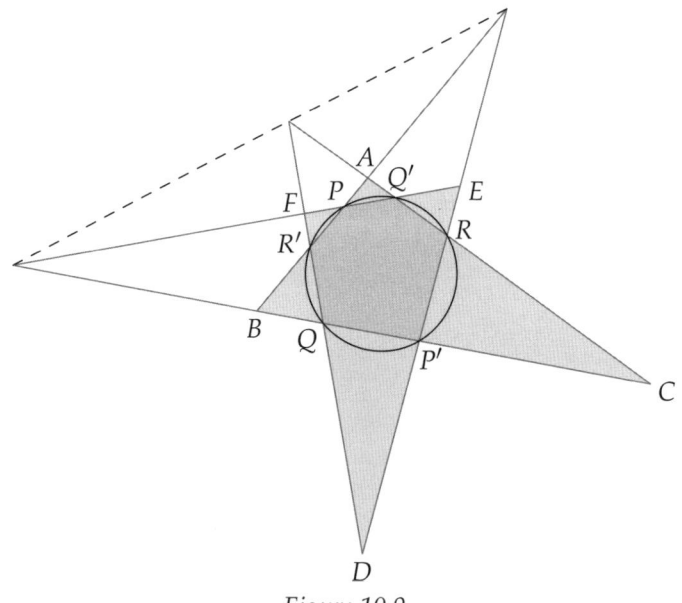

Figure 10.9

By the tangent-secant theorem, we have

$$AP \times AR' = AQ' \times AR,$$
$$BQ \times BP' = BR' \times BP$$
and $$CR \times CQ' = CP' \times CQ.$$

Multiplying and rearranging, we obtain

$$\frac{AP}{PB} \times \frac{BQ}{QC} \times \frac{CR}{RA} = \frac{R'B}{AR'} \times \frac{P'C}{BP'} \times \frac{Q'A}{CQ'}.$$

Hence, by theorem 10.3, the triangles $\triangle ABC$ and $\triangle DEF$ are in perspective, and now Desargues' theorem guarantees the existence of an axis of perspective. This turns out to be the required collinearity. ☐

Pascal's theorem (and its dual, Brianchon's theorem) are true not just for a circle but for any conic.

10.4 Three triangles in perspective

Finally we prove some results which involve perspective relations between three triangles. These may appear to be rather dry and technical, but they will turn out to be very useful in demonstrating some collinearities. In chapter 12, for example, a synthetic proof (not involving areal coordinates) is given of the existence of the Exeter point, which lies on the Euler line of the reference triangle.

Theorem 10.6 *If three triangles are in perspective with a common perspector, then the three axes of perspective are concurrent (see figure 10.10).*

PROOF In figure 10.10, the perspector is O and the triangles are $\triangle A_1 B_1 C_1$, $\triangle A_2 B_2 C_2$ and $\triangle A_3 B_3 C_3$, where corresponding letters lie on the same line of the pencil. Denote the side $A_1 B_1$ by C_1 and the join of C_1, C_2 by C_{12}, with similar notation for the other permutations of suffices. Consider $\triangle A_{12} A_{23} A_{13}$ and $\triangle B_{12} B_{23} B_{13}$.

Now $A_{12} A_{13}$ and $B_{12} B_{13}$ meet at C_1, $A_{12} A_{23}$ and $B_{12} B_{23}$ meet at C_2 and $A_{13} A_{23}$ and $B_{13} B_{23}$ meet at C_3. These three points are collinear, so by the converse of Desargues' theorem (see page 130) $\triangle A_{12} A_{23} A_{13}$ and $\triangle B_{12} B_{23} B_{13}$ have a perspector. But $A_{12} B_{12}$, $A_{23} B_{23}$ and $A_{13} B_{13}$ are the axes of perspective of the original three triangles, and hence these three axes are concurrent at the point labelled P. ☐

Theorem 10.6 concerns three triangles with a common perspector, and it turns out to be useful in deducing collinearities in triangle geometry. However, we also consider triangles which are *pairwise* in perspective.

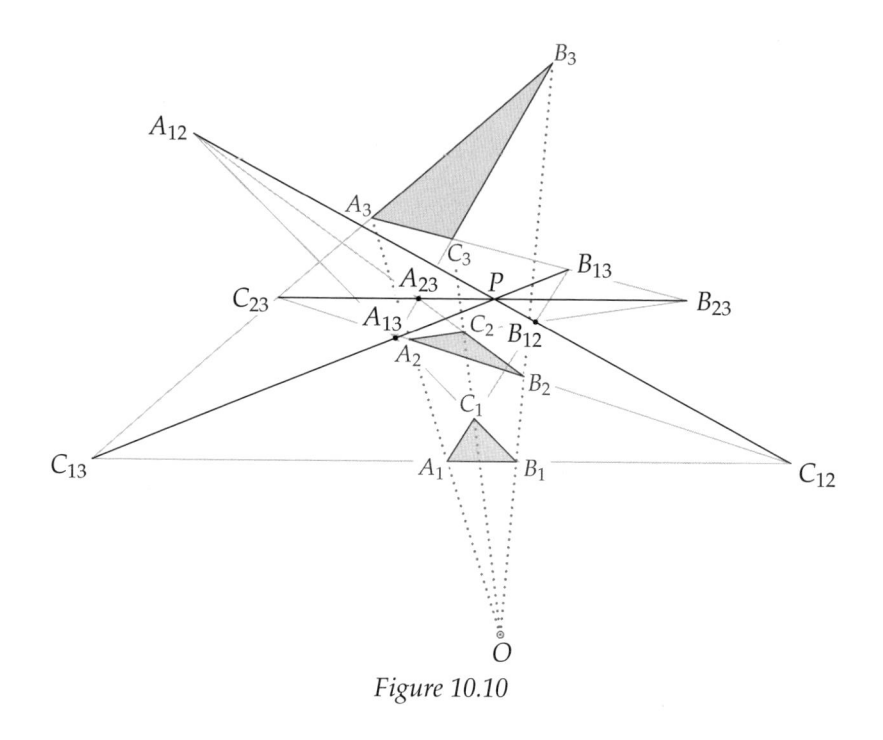

Figure 10.10

In other words, triangles T_1 and T_2 are in perspective with one centre, triangles T_2 and T_3 in perspective with another centre and T_1 and T_3 in perspective with a third.

Theorem 10.7 *If three triangles are in perspective in pairs, and the three axes of perspective are concurrent, then the triangles have a common perspector.*

PROOF We consider the concurrent axes as forming a pencil, and apply theorem 10.6 to the triangles $\triangle A_{12}A_{23}A_{13}$, $\triangle B_{12}B_{23}B_{13}$ and $\triangle C_{12}C_{23}C_{13}$. It follows that their axes of perspective are concurrent, but these are the lines $A_1A_2A_3$, $B_1B_2B_3$ and $C_1C_2C_3$ which therefore meet in a common perspector. ❏

Theorem 10.8 *If three triangles are in perspective in pairs with their perspectors collinear, then they share the same axis of perspective (see figure 10.11).*

PROOF This is the dual of theorem 10.6. The pencil is replaced by a range of three points, with a pencil of three lines through each. The sides

Chapter 10: Triangles in perspective 141

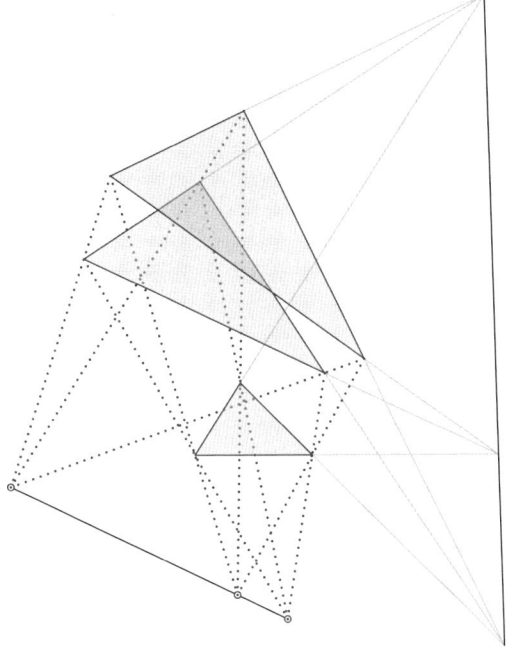

Figure 10.11

of the triangles become intersections of corresponding lines from each pencil, and the intersections of corresponding sides become the sides of the three triangles in perspective. The three axes of perspective become the intersections of pairs of sides, and the concurrency of the axes becomes the collinearity of these points. ❏

Theorem 10.9 *If three triangles which are in perspective in pairs have a common axis of perspective, then their perspectors are collinear.*

PROOF This can be thought of either as the dual of theorem 10.8 or simply as a consequence of theorem 10.7. ❏

A special case of theorem 10.9 is when three triangles are homothetic. Then the common axis of perspective is the line at infinity, and it follows that the homothetic centres are collinear.

Exercise 10c

1. In triangle $\triangle ABC$ let AL, BM and CN be (concurrent) Cevians. Prove that $\triangle ABC$ is in perspective with $\triangle L_1 M_1 N_1$, the medial triangle of $\triangle LMN$.

2. In triangle $\triangle ABC$ let AL, BM and CN be (concurrent) Cevians. Let the midpoints of AL, BM and CN be L', M' and N'. Prove that $\triangle L'M'N'$ is in perspective with $\triangle A_1 B_1 C_1$, the medial triangle of $\triangle ABC$.

3. Let triangles $\triangle ABC$ and $\triangle A'B'C'$ be in perspective, and suppose that $P = BC' \cap B'C$, $Q = CA' \cap C'A$ and $R = AB' \cap A'B$. Prove that $\triangle PQR$ is in perspective with both $\triangle ABC$ and $\triangle A'B'C'$, and that the three perspectors are collinear.

4. Let P and P^* be isogonal conjugates in the triangle $\triangle ABC$, and let their pedal triangles be $\triangle DEF$ and $\triangle D^*E^*F^*$. Prove that the points $EF^* \cap FE^*$, $FD^* \cap F^*D$ and $DE^* \cap D^*E$ are collinear with P and P^*.

Chapter 11

The isogonic centres

Perhaps the most celebrated result in all of Euclidean geometry is the theorem attributed to Pythagoras. One way of interpreting the result is to build squares on the three sides of the triangle and to state the theorem in terms of their areas (see figure 11.1).

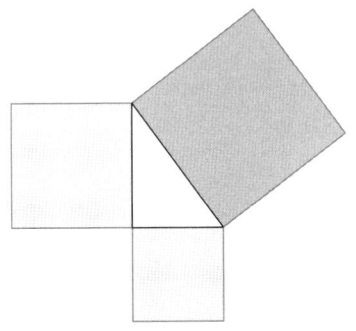

Figure 11.1

But in fact these figures do not have to be squares. Any similar shapes, whose area is proportional to the square of the side on which they are constructed, would do—semicircles, pentagons, or triangles, for instance. And there is no particular reason why the shapes have to be built externally; they might all be facing inwards, for example.

We begin by constructing equilateral triangles on the sides of the triangle; this idea gives rise to the isogonic centres. This result is then generalised to similar isosceles triangles and familiar triangle centres become part of a larger picture involving a rectangular hyperbola. The final result in the chapter is a surprising theorem due to June Lester.

11.1 Isogonic centres

Theorem 11.1 *If equilateral triangles $\triangle CBX$, $\triangle ACY$ and $\triangle BAZ$ are placed externally on the sides of $\triangle ABC$, the three line segments AX, BY and CZ are equal, concurrent and inclined at $120°$ to one another.*

PROOF Let the circumcircles of $\triangle BAZ$ and $\triangle ACY$ meet at F_1 (see figure 11.2).

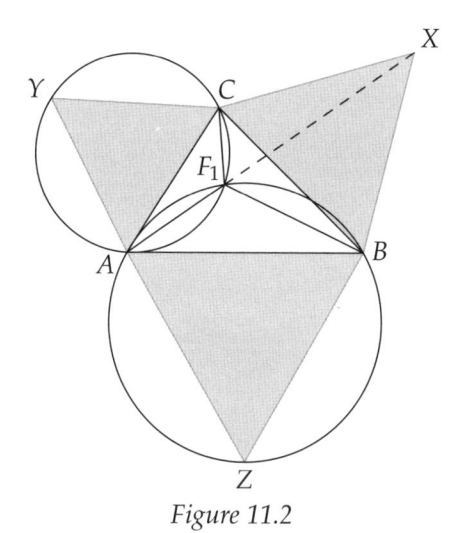

Figure 11.2

Then $\angle AF_1B = \angle AF_1C = 120°$ and so $\angle CF_1B = 120°$. Hence quadrilateral CF_1BX is cyclic and the circumcircle of $\triangle CBX$ also passes through F_1. It follows that $\angle XF_1B = \angle XCB = 60°$ and so the points A, F_1 and X are collinear. The same is true for C, F_1 and Z and for B, F_1 and Y.

Finally, $\triangle AZC \equiv \triangle ABY$ by SAS and so $BY = CZ$, and, similarly, AX is the same length.

Figure 11.2 shows the case in which all of the angles of $\triangle ABC$ are smaller than $120°$. If one of the angles is greater than (or equal to) $120°$, then the point F_1 is outside the triangle (see figure 11.3), but apart from the fact that $\angle AF_1B = \angle CF_1A = 60°$, the proof works in precisely the same way. ❑

Chapter 11: The isogonic centres 145

Figure 11.3

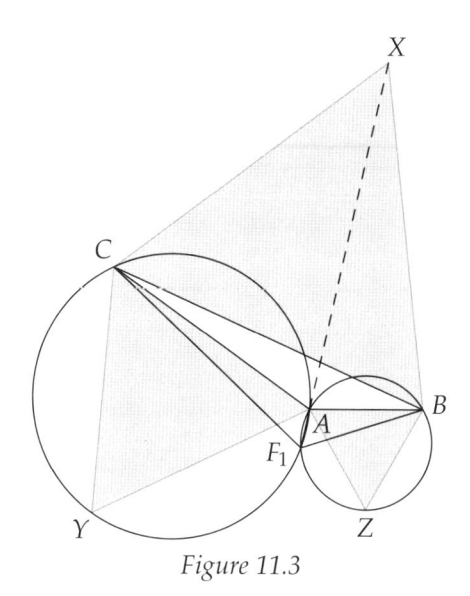

The point F_1 is known as the *first isogonic centre* of $\triangle ABC$. In the language of chapter 10, F_1 is the perspector of $\triangle ABC$ and $\triangle XYZ$.

It is also called the *Fermat point*, but strictly speaking this is inaccurate. The name comes from a problem posed by Fermat and solved by Torricelli: determine a point P inside $\triangle ABC$ for which the sum $PA + PB + PC$ is a minimum. If all three angles of the triangle are less than 120°, then F_1 is indeed the required point. If, however, there is a vertex with an angle of 120° or greater, then this vertex is the Fermat point.

Theorem 11.2 *If $\triangle ABC$ has no angle of 120° or greater, then the Fermat point is the first isogonic centre.*

PROOF Let P be an arbitrary point within $\triangle ABC$. Construct equilateral triangles $\triangle CPQ$ and $\triangle CBR$ (see figure 11.4). Note that the position of R is independent of P.

It follows that $\triangle CQR$ is congruent to $\triangle CPB$. Then $AP + BP + CP = AP + QR + PQ$ and this is minimised when A, P, Q and R are collinear.

Hence $\angle APC = \angle CQR = 120°$, so $\angle CPB = 120°$ and P is the first isogonic centre. ❑

Theorem 11.3 *If equilateral triangles $\triangle BCX$, $\triangle CAY$ and $\triangle ABZ$ are placed internally on the sides of $\triangle ABC$, the three lines AX, BY and CZ are concurrent.*

Figure 11.4

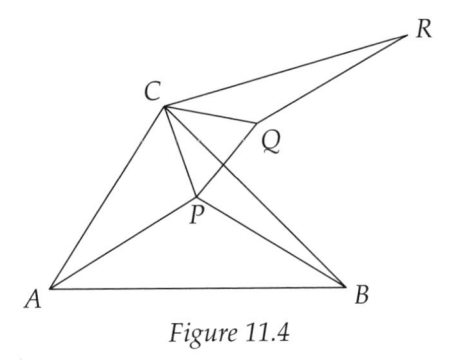

PROOF A similar argument to that in the proof of theorem 11.1 shows that the three circumcircles pass through a common point F_2 and that this is the point of concurrency of AX, BY and CZ, forming two angles of 60° at F_2 (see figure 11.5).

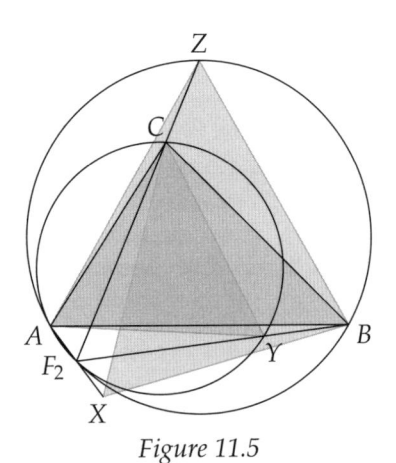

Figure 11.5

Once more we have two possible diagrams according to whether or not $\triangle ABC$ has one or two angles greater than 60°. (If $\triangle ABC$ is equilateral, the diagram becomes degenerate.) ❑

Predictably, F_2 is known as the *second isogonic centre* of $\triangle ABC$. The line $F_1 F_2$ is called the *Fermat axis* of $\triangle ABC$.

Chapter 11: The isogonic centres

Exercise 11a

1. Denoting the new vertices of the outwardly-facing triangles as X_1, Y_1 and Z_1 and those of the inwardly-facing triangles as X_2, Y_2 and Z_2, prove that the triangles $\triangle AZ_2Y_1$, $\triangle AZ_1Y_2$, $\triangle Z_2BX_1$, $\triangle Z_1BX_2$, $\triangle Y_2X_1C$, $\triangle Y_1X_2C$ and $\triangle ABC$ are all congruent.

2. If F_1 lies inside $\triangle ABC$, prove that

   $$F_1A + F_1B + F_1C = AX + BY + CZ.$$

   How is this amended if F_1 lies outside $\triangle ABC$?

3. Suppose that F_2 lies on the opposite side of BC to A. Prove that $AX = F_2B + F_2C - F_2A$.

4. Suppose that $\angle BAC = 60°$. In the usual configuration, prove that

   $$[ABC] + [BXC] = [CYA] + [AZB].$$

5. Let three triangles $\triangle CBX$, $\triangle ACY$ and $\triangle BAZ$ be constructed on the sides of $\triangle ABC$ with the condition that $\angle X + \angle Y + \angle Z = 180°$. Prove that the circumcircles of the triangles have a common point.

6. Let three similar triangles $\triangle CBX$, $\triangle CYA$ and $\triangle ZBA$ be constructed on the sides of $\triangle ABC$. Prove that the circumcircles of the triangles have a common point.

11.2 Kiepert's theorem

The following theorem is due to Ludwig Kiepert, so it seems sensible to name it after him.

Theorem 11.4 (Kiepert) *On the sides of $\triangle ABC$, similar isosceles triangles $\triangle CBX$, $\triangle ACY$ and $\triangle BAZ$ are constructed, facing all outwards or all inwards. Then the lines AX, BY and CZ are concurrent.*

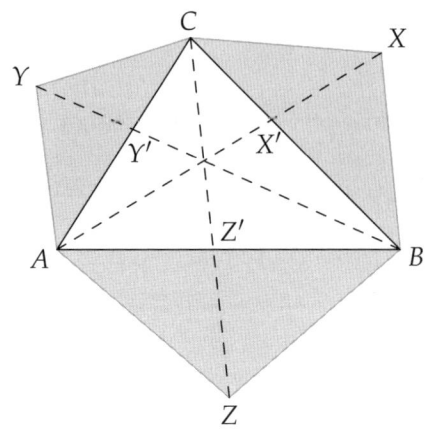

Figure 11.6

PROOF Let the common base angles be α and let AX, BY and CZ meet BC, CA and AB at X', Y' and Z' (see figure 11.6).

By the sine rule on $\triangle BXX'$ and $\triangle CXX'$, we have

$$\frac{BX'}{CX'} = \frac{\sin \angle BXX'}{\sin \angle CXX'}.$$

Similarly, by the sine rule on $\triangle ABX$ and $\triangle AXC$ we have

$$\frac{\sin \angle BXX'}{\sin \angle CX'X} = \frac{c \sin(B + \alpha)}{b \sin(C + \alpha)}.$$

After obtaining similar values for the other intersections, we now apply the converse of Ceva's theorem to prove the concurrency. ❑

We have shown that the triangles $\triangle ABC$ and $\triangle XYZ$ are in perspective, and hence have a centre and axis of perspective.

This important result can be used to justify a range of concurrencies. When α is $60°$, the perspector is the first isogonic centre. When α is zero, it is the centroid. As α approaches $90°$, and the vertices move off to infinity, it becomes the orthocentre. By taking α as negative, we can view the isosceles triangles as facing inward rather than outward, an example of this being the second isogonic centre.

An obvious question concerns the locus of the perspector as α changes. This turns out to be a rectangular hyperbola. For details, see page 376 in appendix A.

Chapter 11: The isogonic centres   149

11.3 The Napoleon points

In figure 11.2 on page 144, let N_A, N_B and N_C be the circumcentres of $\triangle CBX$, $\triangle ACY$ and $\triangle BAZ$.

Theorem 11.5 *The triangles $\triangle ABC$ and $\triangle N_A N_B N_C$ are in perspective.*

PROOF (See figure 11.7.)

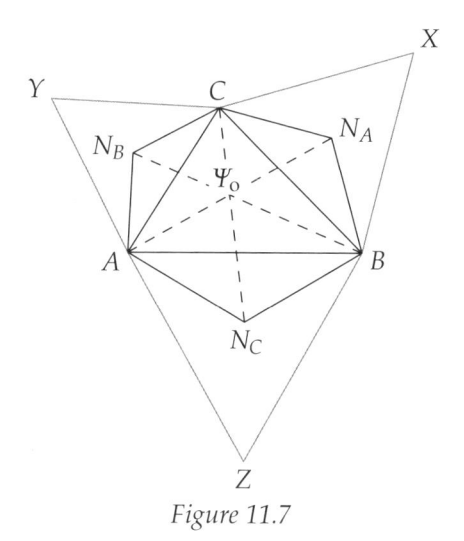

Figure 11.7

The triangles $\triangle CBN_A$, $\triangle ACN_B$ and $\triangle BAN_C$ are isosceles, so, by theorem 11.4, with $\alpha = 30°$, the lines AN_A, BN_B and CN_C are concurrent. ❑

The perspector is known as the *outer Napoleon point*, and will be referred to as Ψ_o.

Theorem 11.6 (Napoleon) *The triangle $\triangle N_A N_B N_C$ is equilateral.*

PROOF Set as question 3 of exercise 11b.   ❑

Triangle $\triangle N_A N_B N_C$ is the *outer Napoleon triangle*.
The proof of theorem 11.6 works equally well if the triangles are drawn inwardly, so we also have an *inner Napoleon point* Ψ_i, which is the point of concurrency of the lines joining the vertices of $\triangle ABC$ to the triangle which is formed by the circumcentres of the inwardly-facing equilateral

triangles; this corresponds to taking α as $-30°$ in Kiepert's theorem. The triangle so formed is the *inner Napoleon triangle* and is also equilateral. We will denote this triangle by $\triangle N_a N_b N_c$.

The circumcircles of the Napoleon triangles are called the *outer* and *inner Napoleon circles* (see figure 11.8).

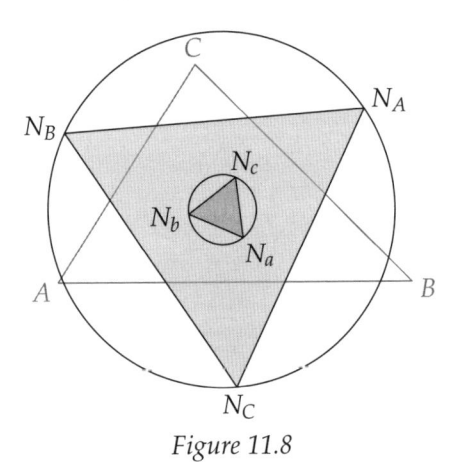

Figure 11.8

Theorem 11.7 *The two Napoleon circles are concentric and their centre is the centroid of* $\triangle ABC$.

PROOF (See figure 11.9.)

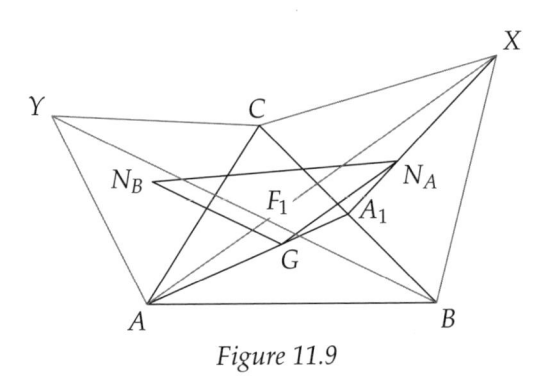

Figure 11.9

Since $A_1 X = 3 A_1 N_A$ and $A_1 A = 3 A_1 G$, we see that $N_A G$ and XA are parallel. Similarly $N_B G \parallel YB$, and so $\angle N_A G N_B = \angle X F_1 Y$.

However, by theorem 11.1, this angle is 120°, as are the other two angles surrounding G. It follows that G is the circumcentre of $\triangle N_A N_B N_C$.
This proof works equally well when the triangles are drawn inwardly. It follows that G is the centre of both Napoleon circles. ❑

Theorem 11.8 *The first isogonic centre lies on the inner Napoleon circle and the second isogonic centre lies on the outer Napoleon circle.*

PROOF Set as question 4 of exercise 11b. ❑

Exercise 11b

1. Prove that $\triangle XYZ$ is in perspective with both Napoleon triangles.

2. Prove that the areas of the two Napoleon triangles differ by Δ, the area of $\triangle ABC$.

3. Prove theorem 11.6.

4. Prove theorem 11.8

11.4 The Lester circle

It is not often that new theorems in geometry are discovered, but this happened in 1996 when June Lester announced that, in any scalene triangle, the circumcentre, nine-point centre and two isogonic centres were concyclic. Her proof used areal coordinates and some formidable calculations involving complex numbers.

Since then, a number of attempts have been made to find a simpler proof using either projective or Euclidean methods. The most successful of these was achieved by Nikolai Beluhov in 2012 in [2], based on an insight of Paul Yiu in [26]. He proves a lemma about triangles in general and then uses this in the case of the configuration of isogonic centres and Napoleon points.

In this account, we present an adapted version of Beluhov's proof.

Lemma 11.9 $N_B G$ and $N_b G$ are the perpendicular bisectors of $N_b F_1$ and $N_B F_2$ respectively.

PROOF Since $\angle CN_b A = 120°$, it follows that N_b lies on the circumcircle of $\triangle ACY$ (see figure 11.10).

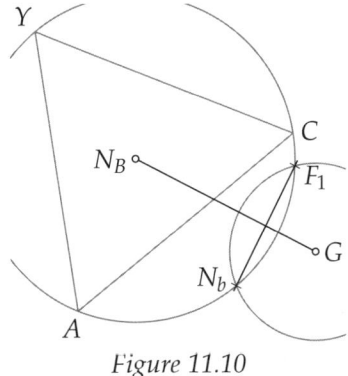

Figure 11.10

Hence, by theorem 11.8, the segment $N_b F_1$ is the common chord of the circumcircles of $\triangle ACY$ and the inner Napoleon circle, and as such it is bisected by their line of centres, which is $N_B G$. The other claim is proved in exactly the same way. ❏

Theorem 11.10 Let T and U be the intersections of $F_1 F_2$ and $N_b N_B$ with the tangent to the circumcircle of $\triangle F_1 G F_2$ at G. Then $TG = GU$.

PROOF First note that, by lemma 11.9, the triangles $\triangle N_b G N_B$ and $\triangle F_1 G N_B$ are congruent since one is the reflection of the other in the line $N_B G$. By the same lemma, there is the same relationship between the triangles $\triangle N_b G N_B$ and $\triangle N_b G F_2$. In fact, $\triangle N_b G F_2$ can be rotated about G by an angle of $2\angle N_b G F_2$ to produce $\triangle F_1 G N_B$ (see figure 11.11).

A convenient way of proving that $TG = GU$ is to consider the effect of rotating $\triangle N_b G N_B$ through $180°$ about G to produce $\triangle N'_b G N'_B$ and then prove that N'_b, T and N'_B are collinear. This is represented by a dashed line in figure 11.11, and we must be very careful not to assume that it is a line in the proof which follows.

Note that $N'_b F_1$ is parallel to $N_B N'_B$ as a result of the congruence of $\triangle N'_b G N'_B$ and $\triangle F_1 G N_B$. Now construct M on $N_B N'_B$ so that $GN'_b F_1 M$ is a parallelogram. In the same way, construct N on $N_b N'_b$ so that $GNF_2 N'_B$ is

Chapter 11: The isogonic centres

Figure 11.11

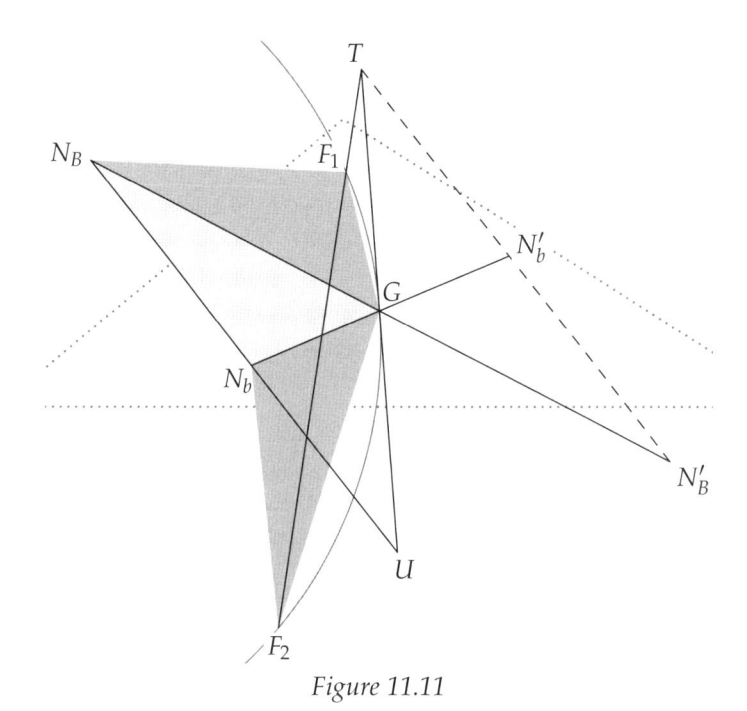

a parallelogram. Also, construct R such that $RTGN'_b$ is a parallelogram. The effect of these constructions is shown in figure 11.12.

Now, by the alternate segment theorem, $\triangle TF_1G$ and $\triangle TGF_2$ are similar. Therefore it is possible to map the first to the second using a reflection in the angle bisector of $\angle GTF_1$ followed by an enlargement with centre T in the ratio $F_2G : GF_1$. The same transformation, α say, maps GN'_bF_1M to $F_2NGN'_B$.

Now $\angle TRN'_b = \angle TGN'_b$ and, by means of α, $\angle TGN'_b = \angle TF_2N$. It follows that $\angle TRN'_b = \angle F_2F_1N'_b$ and hence N'_bRTF_1 is cyclic.

Finally we have

$$\begin{aligned}\angle F_2TN'_B &= \angle GTM &&\text{(by } \alpha^{-1}\text{)} \\ &= \angle N'_bRF_1 &&\text{(parallel lines)} \\ &= \angle N'_bTF_1 &&\text{(cyclic quadrilateral).}\end{aligned}$$

This shows that N'_b, T and N'_B are collinear, as required. ∎

Figure 11.12

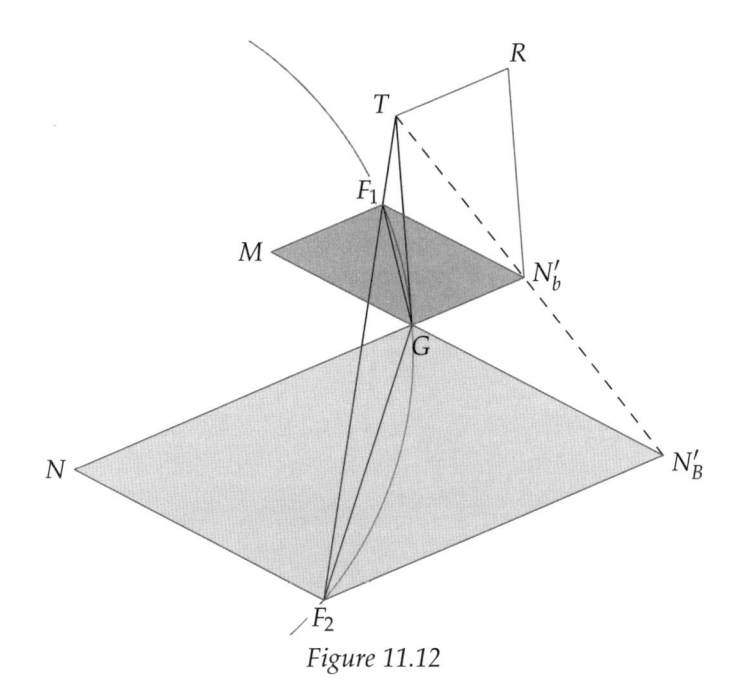

Note that this result is actually a general one about three congruent triangles arranged in a pattern. It could have been presented by relabelling $\triangle N_B G N_b$ as $\triangle RPQ$, say, reflecting it twice and producing a tangent line with points on it such that $TP = PU$. This was Beluhov's own formulation.

Corollary 11.11 *The intersection of the Fermat axis and the Euler line is the centre of the orthocentroidal disc (see figure 11.13).*

PROOF In theorem 11.10, there is no particular reason to use the points N_b and N_B rather than N_a and N_A or N_c and N_C. In each case, the circumcircle of $\triangle F_1 G F_2$ is the same circle, and the point T is unchanged. It follows, then, that U is the same point in all three versions, and that it lies on $N_a N_A$, $N_b N_B$ and $N_c N_C$. These are the perpendicular bisectors of the sides of $\triangle ABC$ and U is therefore the circumcentre O. It follows that T is Q, the centre of the orthocentroidal disc, and that the tangent is the Euler line. □

Theorem 11.12 (Lester) *The points F_1, F_2, O and N are concyclic.*

The circumcircle is known as the *Lester circle* (see figure 11.14).

Chapter 11: The isogonic centres   155

Figure 11.13   *Figure 11.14*

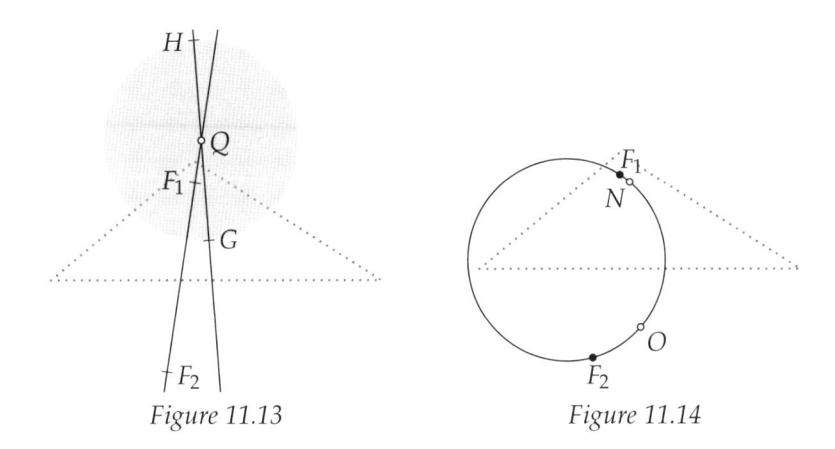

PROOF From theorems 3.1 and 5.19 on page 27 and on page 61, $QG^2 = QN \times QO$. But, by corollary 11.11 and the tangent-secant theorem, $QG^2 = QF_1 \times QF_2$. Hence $QN \times QO = QF_1 \times QF_2$ and the result follows. ☐

Exercise 11c

1. Prove that the circumcircle of $\triangle F_2 H F_1$ is tangential to the Euler line.

2. Prove that the orthocentroidal disc is orthogonal to the Lester circle.

3. Prove that the orthocentroidal disc is orthogonal to the circumcircles of $\triangle F_2 G F_1$ and $\triangle F_2 H F_1$.

Chapter 12

The Vecten and Kosnita points

In this chapter, we investigate other configurations, constructed in a similar way to the isogonic centres, which give rise to triangles in perspective. As a result, we identify a number of other significant points on the Euler line.

12.1 The Vecten points

Here we return to figure 11.1, but now with a general triangle. Let V_A, V_B and V_C be the centres of the three squares (which we will call *Vecten squares*) erected externally on the sides of $\triangle ABC$ (see figure 12.1).

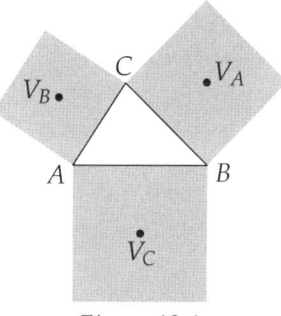

Figure 12.1

Theorem 12.1 *The triangles $\triangle V_A V_B V_C$ and $\triangle ABC$ are in perspective (see figure 12.2).*

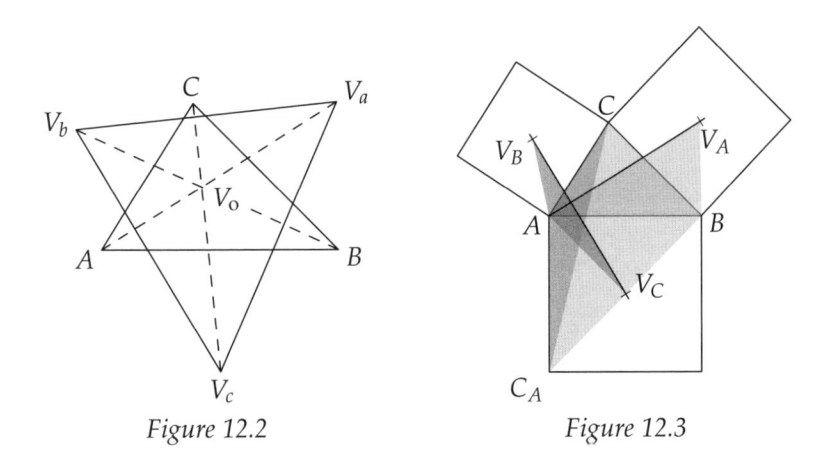

Figure 12.2

Figure 12.3

PROOF This follows from Kiepert's theorem with $\alpha = 45°$. ❏

The perspector is known as the *outer Vecten point*, and will be denoted by V_o. The triangle $\triangle V_A V_B V_C$ is the *outer Vecten triangle*.

This configuration yields another interesting result.

Theorem 12.2 *The line segments $V_A A$ and $V_B V_C$ are equal and perpendicular.*

PROOF Label the outer vertex of the square opposite C next to A as C_A (see figure 12.3). Note that the triangle $\triangle BV_A A$ is mapped to $\triangle BCC_A$ under a rotation of 45° about B and an enlargement with centre B and scale factor $\sqrt{2}$, and that the triangle $\triangle AC_A C$ is mapped to $\triangle AV_C V_B$ by a rotation of 45° about A and an enlargement with centre A and scale factor $\frac{1}{2}\sqrt{2}$.

It follows that, under the combined effect of all of these transformations, $V_A A$ is mapped to $V_C V_B$, preserving its length and rotating it through 90°. ❏

The transformations described in the last proof, being a combination of rotations and enlargements, are known as spiral similarities, and will be investigated in more depth in chapter 15.

Chapter 12: The Vecten and Kosnita points 159

Corollary 12.3 *The outer Vecten point is the orthocentre of the outer Vecten triangle.*

Predictably, we obtain a similar result by constructing squares facing internally on the sides. Their centres form the *inner Vecten triangle* $\triangle V_a V_b V_c$, which is also in perspective with $\triangle ABC$, the perspector being the *inner Vecten point* V_i. Both Vecten points lie on the Kiepert hyperbola.

Lemma 12.4 *The line segments $A_1 V_B$ and $A_1 V_C$ are equal and perpendicular.*

PROOF Note that $B_1 A_1 = AC_1 = C_1 V_C$, and similarly $B_1 V_B = C_1 A_1$ (see figure 12.4).

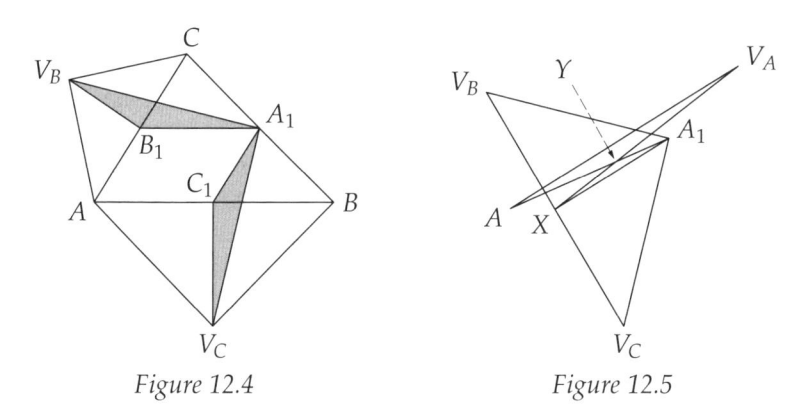

Figure 12.4   Figure 12.5

Also $\angle A_1 C_1 V_C = \angle V_B B_1 A_1 = \angle A + 90°$ so, by SAS, $\triangle B_1 A_1 V_B$ is congruent to $\triangle C_1 V_C A_1$. Finally $V_C C_1$ is perpendicular to AB which is parallel to $B_1 A_1$, so $A_1 V_C$ is perpendicular to $V_B A_1$ as required. ❏

Theorem 12.5 *The triangles $\triangle ABC$, $\triangle V_A V_B V_C$ and $\triangle V_a V_b V_c$ have the same centroid.*

PROOF Let X be the midpoint of $V_B V_C$ (see figure 12.5). By lemma 12.4, $\triangle A_1 V_B V_C$ is an isosceles right-angled triangle, and so $A_1 X$ is perpendicular to $V_B V_C$ and half its length. Hence, by theorem 12.2, $A_1 X$ is parallel to AV_A and half its length. Thus, if Y is the intersection of AA_1 and $V_A X$, it divides each segment in the ratio 2 : 1. Therefore Y is the centroid G of $\triangle ABC$ and also the centroid of the outer Vecten triangle.

The argument for the inner Vecten triangle is similar. ❏

Exercise 12a

1. Let $\triangle A'B'C'$ be the triangle produced by extending the sides of the Vecten squares which are parallel to the sides of $\triangle ABC$. It is clear that $\triangle A'B'C'$ is homothetic to $\triangle ABC$. Prove that the homothetic centre is the symmedian point of $\triangle ABC$.

2. Prove that the area of the outer Vecten triangle is $\Delta + \frac{1}{8}(a^2 + b^2 + c^2)$. What is the corresponding expression for the inner Vecten triangle?

3. Denote the vertices of the Vecten squares using the notation in the proof of theorem 12.2. Prove that CC_A, BB_A and B_CC_B are concurrent.

4. Denoting the point of concurrency in question 3 by X, and defining Y and Z similarly, prove that $\triangle ABC$ and $\triangle XYZ$ are in perspective.

5. Prove that the intersection of AA_B and BB_A lies on the altitude CF.

6. Prove that V_c is the midpoint of A_BB_A.

12.2 Flanks

The three triangles $\triangle C_AAB_A$, $\triangle A_BBC_B$ and $\triangle B_CCA_C$, which are shown shaded in figure 12.6, are known as the flanks of $\triangle ABC$.

Note that $\triangle ABC$ is one of the flanks of $\triangle C_AAB_A$, and so on.

Theorem 12.6 *The flanks have area equal to that of $\triangle ABC$.*

PROOF This follows immediately from the area formula since $\angle BAC$ and $\angle B_AAC_A$ (and so on) are supplementary. ☐

Theorem 12.7 *The medians of the flanks from A, B and C are collinear with the altitudes of $\triangle ABC$, and are equal in length to $\frac{1}{2}a$, $\frac{1}{2}b$ and $\frac{1}{2}c$.*

Chapter 12: The Vecten and Kosnita points

Figure 12.6

Figure 12.7

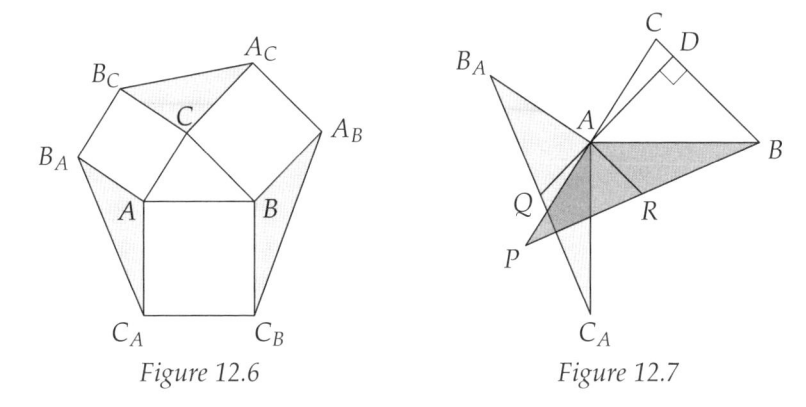

PROOF Rotate the flank $\triangle C_A AB_A$ through 90° about A (see figure 12.7). Then C_A goes to B, B_A goes to P and the midpoint Q goes to R, with A and R the midpoints of PC and PB. Hence RA is parallel to BC and half its length.
By rotating back, we see that the results follow. ❑

Much of the material about flanks can be found in papers by Warburton [24] and van Lamoen [23].

Exercise 12b

1. Let G_A, G_B and G_C be the centroids of the flanks. Prove that $\triangle G_A G_B G_C$ and $\triangle ABC$ are in perspective and identify the perspector.

2. Let H_A, H_B and H_C be the orthocentres of the flanks. Prove that $\triangle H_A H_B H_C$ and $\triangle ABC$ are in perspective and identify the perspector.

3. Let O_A, O_B and O_C be the circumcentres of the flanks. Prove that $\triangle O_A O_B O_C$ and $\triangle ABC$ are in perspective and identify the perspector.

4. Let K_A, K_B and K_C be the symmedian points of the flanks. Prove that $\triangle K_A K_B K_C$ and $\triangle ABC$ are in perspective and identify the perspector.

5. Let I_A, I_B and I_C be the incentres of the flanks. Prove that $\triangle I_A I_B I_C$ and $\triangle ABC$ are in perspective and identify the perspector.

12.3 The Kosnita triangle

We begin with a result which is a variation on Kiepert's theorem.

Lemma 12.8 *On the sides of $\triangle ABC$, three isosceles triangles $\triangle CBX$, $\triangle ACY$ and $\triangle BAZ$ are constructed externally, with base angles $2\angle A - 90°$, $2\angle B - 90°$ and $2\angle C - 90°$. Then the lines AX, BY and CZ are concurrent. (If a base angle is negative, the triangle will be facing inwards.)*

PROOF (See figure 12.8.)

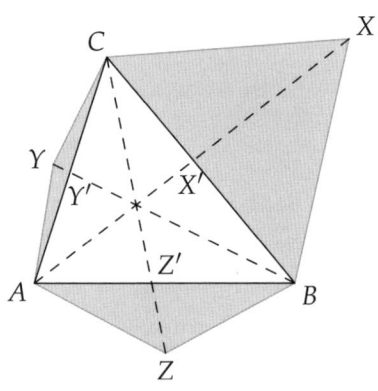

Figure 12.8

The proof proceeds in precisely the same way as that of theorem 11.4 on page 147. Thus we obtain, for example,

$$\frac{BX'}{X'C} = \frac{c\sin(B + 2A - 90°)}{b\sin(C + 2A - 90°)}$$
$$= \frac{c\sin(90° + A - C)}{b\sin(90° + A - B)}$$
$$= \frac{c\cos(A - C)}{b\cos(A - B)}$$

and the resulting Ceva expression is

$$\frac{\cos(A - C)\cos(B - A)\cos(C - B)}{\cos(A - B)\cos(B - C)\cos(C - A)} = 1.$$

The result follows. ❏

Theorem 12.9 *Let O_A, O_B and O_C be the circumcentres of triangles $\triangle COB$, $\triangle AOC$ and $\triangle BOA$. The triangles $\triangle O_A O_B O_C$ and $\triangle ABC$ are in perspective (see figure 12.9).*

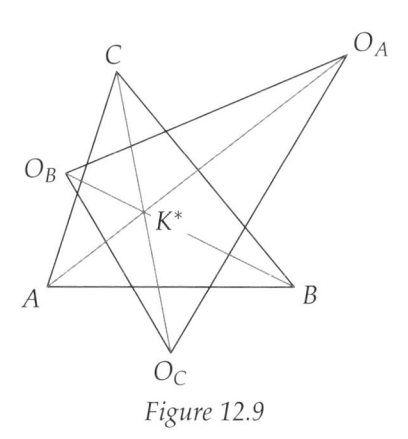

Figure 12.9

PROOF Set as question 1 of exercise 12c. ❏

The triangle $\triangle O_A O_B O_C$ is known as the *Kosnita triangle*, and the perspector of the two triangles is the *Kosnita point*. We will denote it by K^*.

Theorem 12.10 *The Kosnita point is the isogonal conjugate of the nine-point centre of* $\triangle ABC$.

PROOF We calculate the ratio of the perpendicular distances of O_A from AB and CA, which we denote by p_C and p_B (see figure 12.10).

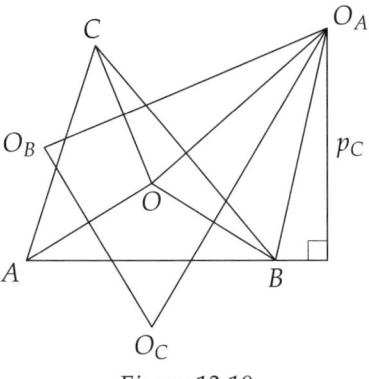

Figure 12.10

Note that $\angle O_A BA = 2\angle A + \angle B - 90°$ so $p_C = BO_A \cos(A - C)$ and $p_B = CO_A \cos(A - B)$ and hence

$$\frac{p_B}{p_C} = \frac{\cos(A - B)}{\cos(A - C)}$$

since BO_A and CO_A are radii of the Kosnita triangle and thus equal.

Similarly, for the nine-point centre, we have, by lemma 3.6 on page 30,

$$\frac{p_C^*}{p_B^*} = \frac{\cos(A - B)}{\cos(A - C)}$$

By theorem 7.6 on page 86, we see that AO_A and AN are isogonal conjugates, and the result follows by considering the other two vertices B and C. ❏

We now prove a surprising result about the Kosnita point, which involves the triangle formed by reflecting the vertices of $\triangle ABC$ in the opposite sides. This is known as the *reflection triangle* of $\triangle ABC$ and is denoted by $\triangle A^*B^*C^*$ (see figure 12.11). For more detail, see the article by Grinberg [10].

Let A_* be the intersection of GA^* with BC, and define B_*, C_* similarly. We begin with a preliminary lemma.

Chapter 12: The Vecten and Kosnita points

Figure 12.11

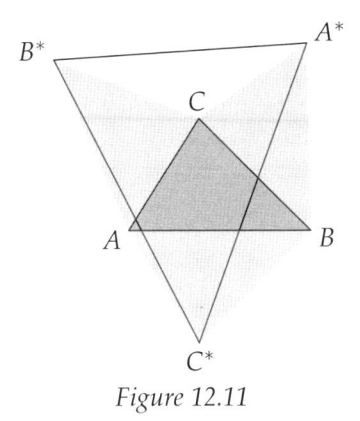

Lemma 12.11 $GA_* : GA^* = 1 : 4$.

PROOF Set as question 2 of exercise 12c. ☐

Theorem 12.12 *The pedal triangle of the nine-point centre N is $\triangle A_*B_*C_*$.*

PROOF Let $\triangle A_1 B_1 C_1$ be the medial triangle and let the median AA_1 meet $C_1 B_1$ at A_2 (see figure 12.12).

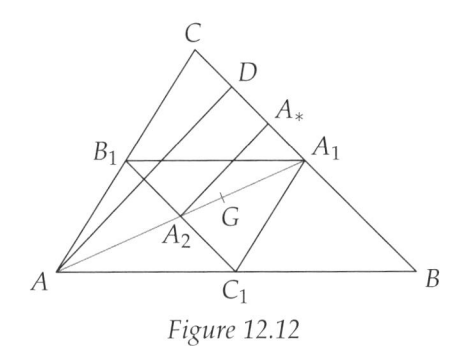

Figure 12.12

By lemma 12.11 and the intercept theorem, $A_2 A_*$ is parallel to AD and hence perpendicular to both $B_1 C_1$ and BC. Hence $A_2 A_*$ contains the circumcentre of $\triangle A_1 B_1 C_1$, which is the nine-point centre of $\triangle ABC$. Since the same is true for B_* and C_*, the result follows. ☐

Theorem 12.13 *Let O^* be the circumcentre of the reflection triangle. Then the Kosnita point is the midpoint of the segment OO^*.*

PROOF By theorem 12.10, the Kosnita point K^* is the isogonal conjugate of N, and hence, by theorem 7.9 on page 89, K^* and N share the same pedal circle, and its centre is X, the midpoint of K^*N (see figure 12.13).

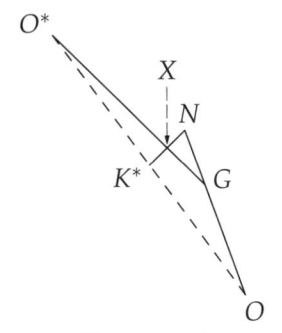

Figure 12.13

Hence, by lemma 12.11, O^* lies on GX and $GX : GO^* = 1 : 4$. Now we have

$$\frac{GO^*}{O^*X} \times \frac{XK^*}{K^*N} \times \frac{NO}{OG} = \frac{4}{-3} \times \frac{1}{-2} \times \frac{3}{-2} = -1,$$

so by the converse of Menelaus' theorem on $\triangle GXN$, the points O^*, K^* and O are collinear. Finally, we apply Menelaus to $\triangle GO^*O$ and the transversal NXK^* to obtain

$$\frac{1}{3} \times \frac{OK^*}{K^*O} \times \frac{3}{-1} = -1,$$

so $OK^* = K^*O^*$ as claimed. □

12.4 Three homothetic triangles

We now identify some more triangle centres on the Euler line, exploiting the fact that the orthic, Kosnita and tangential triangles are all homothetic to each other.

Theorem 12.14 *The Kosnita triangle and the tangential triangle are homothetic.*

PROOF The side O_BO_A of the Kosnita triangle is parallel to the side T_BT_A of the tangential triangle since both are perpendicular to OA, and the

Chapter 12: The Vecten and Kosnita points

same is true of the other two sides. Therefore there is a homothecy, which we will call α, with centre O and scale factor 2, which takes $\triangle O_A O_B O_C$ to $\triangle T_A T_B T_C$. ❏

Equivalently, note that O is the incentre of both triangles and that the intouch triangle of the Kosnita triangle is homothetic to $\triangle ABC$.

Theorem 12.15 *The orthic triangle is homothetic to both the Kosnita and tangential triangles.*

PROOF By theorem 2.22 on page 22, the sides of the orthic triangle are perpendicular to OA, OB and OC, so they are parallel to the sides of the other two triangles. ❏

We shall denote the homothetic centre of the orthic and tangential triangles by Φ_1. It has no agreed name, so we will call it the *Phi point*. It is also convenient to denote the homothecy which takes $\triangle DEF$ to $\triangle T_A T_B T_C$ by ϕ.

Theorem 12.16 *The Phi point lies on the Euler line of $\triangle ABC$.*

PROOF The homothecy ϕ maps $I \triangle DEF$, which by theorem 2.21 on page 22 is H, to $I \triangle T_A T_B T_C$, which is O. It follows that Φ_1, O and H are collinear on the Euler line. ❏

We can also think of Φ_1 as the external centre of similitude of the incircle of $\triangle DEF$ and the circumcircle of $\triangle ABC$. There is also an internal centre of similitude, which we will call Φ_2, and this also lies on the line of centres, which is the Euler line.

Corollary 12.17 Φ_1, H, Φ_2, O *is a harmonic range.*

PROOF This follows from theorem 5.22 on page 63. ❏

Now we can follow the same logic in dealing with the homothecy between the orthic and Kosnita triangles. The homothetic centre is denoted by Λ_1, and will turn out to be quite a significant triangle centre, despite having no standard name. We will call it the *Lambda point*, and denote the homothecy which takes $\triangle DEF$ to $\triangle O_A O_B O_C$ by λ.

Theorem 12.18 *The Lambda point lies on the Euler line of $\triangle ABC$.*

PROOF The homothecy λ maps $I \triangle DEF$, which by theorem 2.21 on page 22 is H, to $I \triangle O_A O_B O_C$, which by theorem 12.14 is O. The result follows. ☐

Again we can think of Λ_1 as the external centre of similitude of the incircle of $\triangle DEF$ and the incircle of $\triangle O_A O_B O_C$, and then define Λ_2 as the internal centre of similitude. There is an obvious consequence.

Corollary 12.19 $\Lambda_1, H, \Lambda_2, O$ is a harmonic range.

Now we turn our attention to the circumcentres. Denote $O \triangle O_A O_B O_C$ by O_K and $O \triangle T_A T_B T_C$ by O_T.

Theorem 12.20 *The circumcentres of the Kosnita and tangential triangles lie on the Euler line of $\triangle ABC$.*

PROOF The homothecy ϕ takes $O \triangle DEF$, which is N, to $O \triangle T_A T_B T_C$, which is O_T, and, since Φ_1 and N are on the Euler line, so is O_T. The same argument applies to the homothecy λ which takes $O \triangle DEF$ to $O \triangle O_A O_B O_C$, which is O_K. ☐

We have two further consequences.

Theorem 12.21 *The circumcentre of the Kosnita triangle is the midpoint of OO_T.*

PROOF This is immediate from the homothecy α. ☐

Another way of stating this is that O is the external centre of similitude of the circumcircles of the Kosnita and tangential triangles. Hence there is also an internal centre of similitude, which divides $O_K O_T$ in the ratio $1:2$. We shall call this point O_I.

Corollary 12.22 O, O_K, O_I, O_T is a harmonic range.

Finally in this chapter, we state a result without proof.

Theorem 12.23 Λ_1, K and K^* are collinear.

Exercise 12c

1. Prove theorem 12.9.

2. Prove lemma 12.11.

3. Prove that Φ_1, N, O, O_T is a harmonic range.

4. Prove that Λ_1, Φ_1, H, O is a harmonic range.

Chapter 13

Circumcevian triangles

Now we focus on an operation which creates new triangles concyclic with the reference triangle $\triangle ABC$. In the process, we discover several new triangle centres. Some of these, including the Exeter point, lie on the Euler line.

13.1 Forming circumcevian triangles

Suppose that P is a point in the plane of $\triangle ABC$ (which is not one of the vertices and not on the circumcircle), and let A', B' and C' be the other intersections of AP, BP and CP with the circumcircle of $\triangle ABC$ (see figure 13.1).

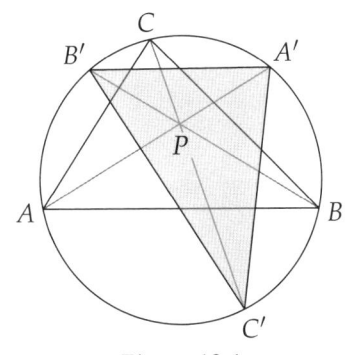

Figure 13.1

Then $\triangle A'B'C'$ called the *circumcevian triangle* of $\triangle ABC$ with respect to P, and will be denoted $⌀_{ABC}P$ or simply $⌀P$.

The circumcevian triangle of the circumcentre $⌀O$ is of little interest, being congruent to $\triangle ABC$. Other such triangles are more significant, and have special names.

* $⌀H$ is the *circumorthic triangle*;
* $⌀G$ is the *circummedial triangle*;
* $⌀I$ is the *circummidarc triangle*.

Theorem 13.1 *The circumcevian triangle with respect to a point P and the pedal triangle of P are similar.*

PROOF Let the pedal triangle of P be $\triangle A''B''C''$ (see figure 13.2).

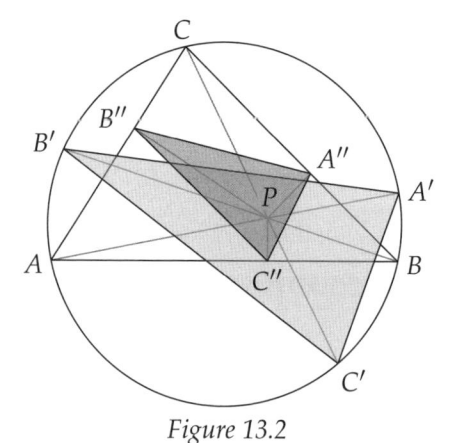

Figure 13.2

From the cyclic quadrilateral $PB''AC''$, we have $\angle PB''C'' = \angle PAC''$. However $\angle PAC'' = \angle A'AB = \angle A'B'B$ and so $\angle PB''C'' = \angle A'B'B$.

But similarly $\angle A''B''P = \angle BB'C'$ and hence $\angle A''B''C'' = \angle A'B'C$.

The similarity follows, but note that, in general, these two triangles are not homothetic since the corresponding sides are not parallel. ☐

Exercise 13a

In this exercise, the order of the vertices in the triangle descriptions is significant.

1. Under what circumstances is $⌀P$ congruent to $\triangle ABC$?

2. Under what circumstances is △P congruent to △ACB?

3. Under what circumstances is △P congruent to △BCA?

4. Under what circumstances is △P congruent to △BAC?

5. Under what circumstances is △P congruent to △CAB?

6. Under what circumstances is △P congruent to △CBA?

13.2 The circumorthic triangle

It will often be convenient to use a more suggestive notation for a circumcevian triangle. For instance, the circumorthic triangle will be called $\triangle D'E'F'$ to emphasise the link with the orthic triangle $\triangle DEF$ (see figure 13.3).

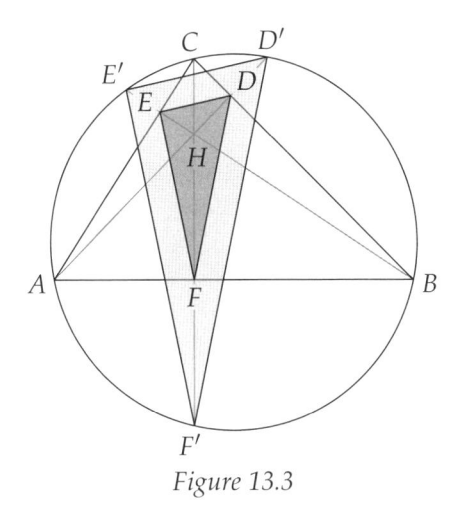

Figure 13.3

The pedal triangle of H is $\triangle DEF$, and so, by theorem 13.1, $\triangle D'E'F'$ is similar to $\triangle DEF$.

However, we already knew that and more since, by theorem 2.17 on page 21, $\triangle DEF$ and $\triangle D'E'F'$ are homothetic under an enlargement with centre H and scale factor 2.

It follows that the circumorthic triangle is also homothetic to the tangential and Kosnita triangles, as discussed in section 12.4.

Theorem 13.2 *The homothetic centre of the triangles $\triangle D'E'F'$ and $\triangle T_A T_B T_C$ is the Lambda point Λ_1.*

PROOF By definition, the homothecy λ, with centre Λ_1, takes H to O and $\triangle DEF$ to $\triangle O_A O_B O_C$ (see figure 13.4).

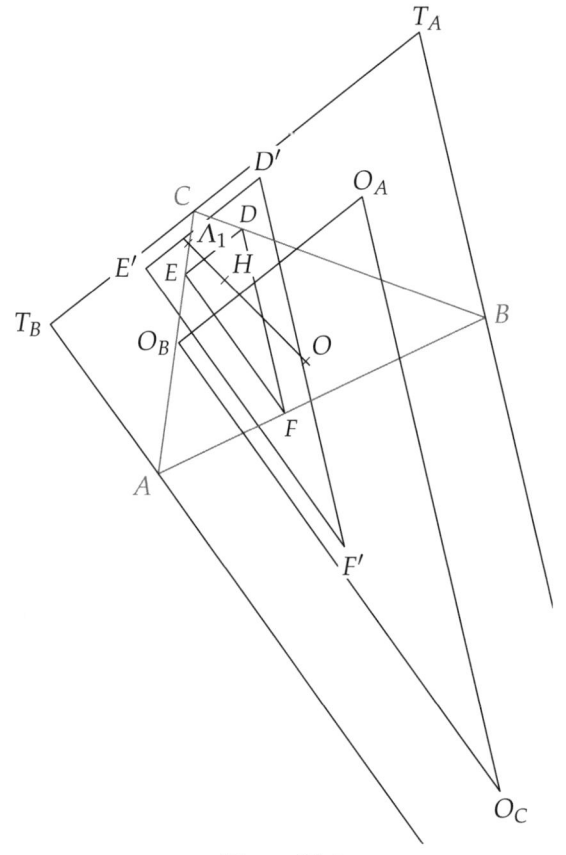

Figure 13.4

Now enlarge $\triangle DEF$ from its incentre H by a scale factor of 2 to produce $\triangle D'E'F'$, and enlarge $\triangle O_A O_B O_C$ from its incentre O by a scale factor of 2 to produce $\triangle T_A T_B T_C$.
It follows that λ maps $\triangle D'E'F'$ to $\triangle T_A T_B T_C$. ❏

Note that Λ_1 and Λ_2 can also be thought of as the external and internal centres of similitude of the incircles of these two triangles, and that the incircle of $\triangle T_A T_B T_C$ is the circumcircle of $\triangle ABC$.
The intouch triangle of $\triangle D'E'F'$ is known as the *intouch-of-circumorthic triangle* or *IoCO triangle*.

Corollary 13.3 *The IoCO triangle is homothetic to $\triangle ABC$ with centre Λ_1.*

PROOF This follows from the fact that $\triangle ABC$ is the intouch triangle of $\triangle T_A T_B T_C$. ❏

There is one more homothecy to consider, that between the Kosnita and circumorthic triangles. We shall denote the centre of this enlargement by Π_1 and note that the enlargement takes H to O and O to O_K, so Π_1 too lies on the Euler line. The point Π_1 is also the external centre of similitude of the circumcircle of $\triangle O_A O_B O_C$ and the circumcircle of $\triangle ABC$ and will be called the *Pi point*. The internal centre of similitude Π_2 is also on the Euler line.

Theorem 13.4 Π_1, O, Π_2, O_K *is a harmonic range.*

PROOF This follows by theorem 5.18 on page 61. ❏

It is worthwhile summarising the relationships between the various triangles, circles and points on the Euler line, introduced in sections 12.4 and 13.2. This is done in figure 13.5 and tables 13.1 and 13.2.

Triangle	Incentre	Circumcentre
Kosnita	O	O_K
orthic	H	N
circumorthic	H	O
tangential	O	O_T

Table 13.1: Triangle centres

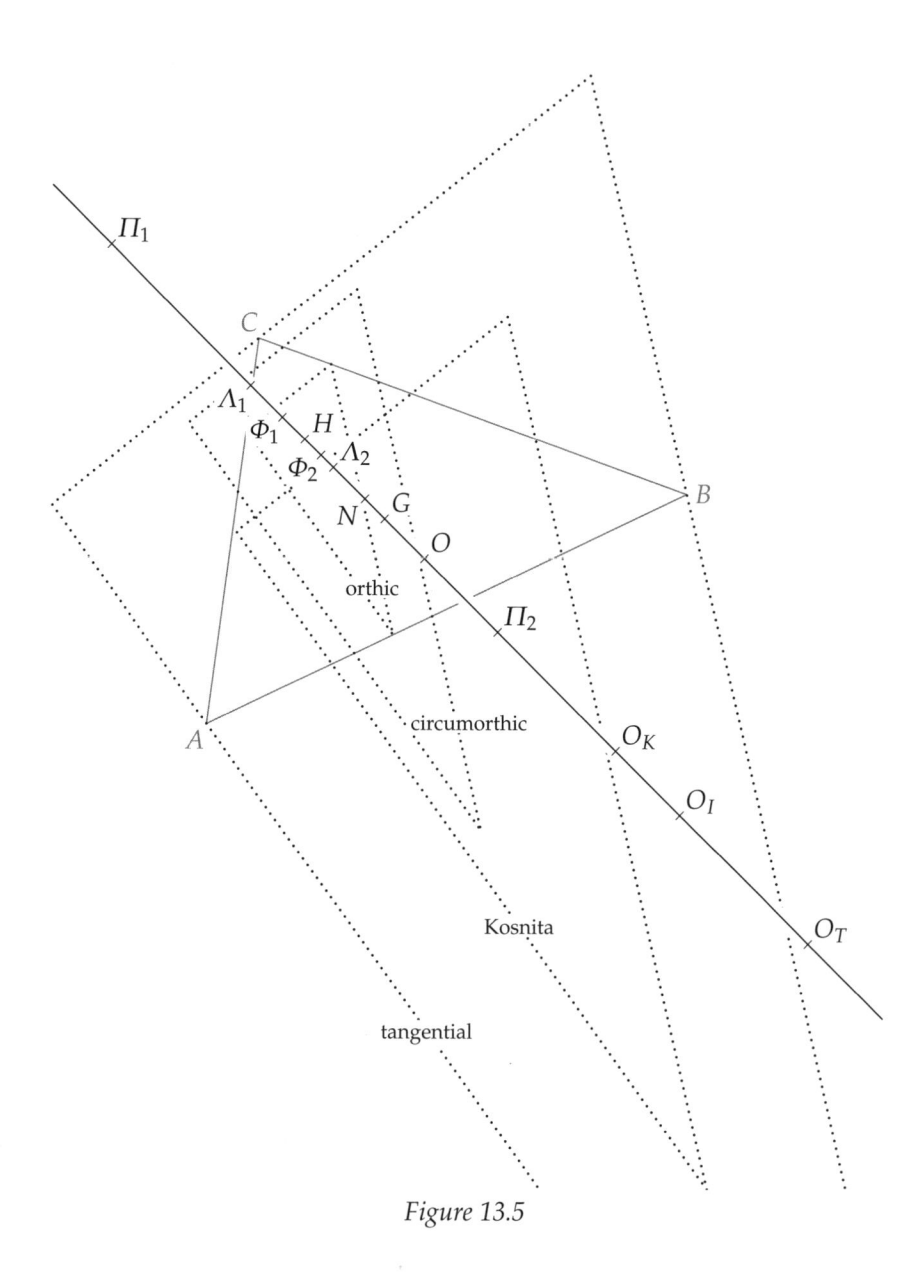

Figure 13.5

Chapter 13: Circumcevian triangles

Triangles	Homothetic centre	Harmonic ranges Incircles	Circumcircles
orthic, circumorthic	H	*concentric*	H, N, G, O
orthic, Kosnita	Λ_1	$\Lambda_1, H, \Lambda_2, O$	$\Lambda_1, N, \Lambda_2, O_K$
orthic, tangential	Φ_1	Φ_1, H, Φ_2, O	Φ_1, N, Φ_2, O_T
circumorthic, Kosnita	Π_1	Π_1, H, Π_2, O	Π_1, O, Π_2, O_K
circumorthic, tangential	Λ_1	$\Lambda_1, H, \Lambda_2, O$	$\Lambda_1, O, \Lambda_2, O_T$
Kosnita, tangential	O	*concentric*	O, O_K, O_I, O_T

Table 13.2: Homothetic triangles associated with $\triangle ABC$

One could, of course, extend the idea of table 13.2 by looking at nine-point circles, say, but then the range will not in general lie on the Euler line.

13.3 The circummedial triangle

We now turn our attention to the circummedial triangle, denoted by $\triangle A_1'B_1'C_1'$. Our aim is to prove the existence of a point on the Euler line, which was shown, at a computers-in-mathematics workshop in Phillips Exeter Academy in 1986, to be the perspector of the circummedial and tangential triangles of $\triangle ABC$. As a result, this point was christened the *Exeter point*, and we shall supply a Euclidean proof that it exists. We begin with two lemmas.

Lemma 13.5 *Suppose that two circles C_1 and C_2 are tangential at A, with C_2 inside C_1. Then the locus of points which have equal tangents to C_1 and C_2 is the common tangent.*

PROOF Let the centres be O_1 and O_2 and the radii r_1 and r_2 with $r_1 > r_2$. Let P be a point on the locus and let Q be the foot of the perpendicular from P to the line of centres, which passes through A (see figure 13.6).

Then, by section 3.6, P has equal power with respect to both circles. Hence $O_1P^2 - r_1^2 = O_2P^2 - r_2^2$, and so, by Pythagoras' theorem, $O_1Q^2 - r_1^2 = O_2Q^2 - r_2^2$. Now let $AQ = x$. Then $(r_1 - x)^2 - r_1^2 = (r_2 - x)^2 - r_2^2$ and so $x = 0$. It follows that Q coincides with A. ∎

Figure 13.6

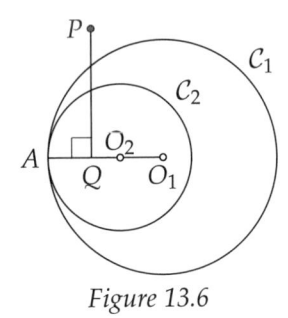

This is a special case of a much more general result, which will be the focus of chapter 18.

Lemma 13.6 *Let X be the intersection of the lines B_1C_1 and $B_1'C_1'$. Then XA is a tangent to the circumcircles of both $\triangle ABC$ and $\triangle AB_1C_1$.*

PROOF By angle-chasing (see figure 13.7) $\angle B_1C_1C = \angle C_1'CB = \angle C_1'B_1'B = \angle C_1'B_1'B_1$ and so $C_1B_1B_1'C_1'$ is cyclic.

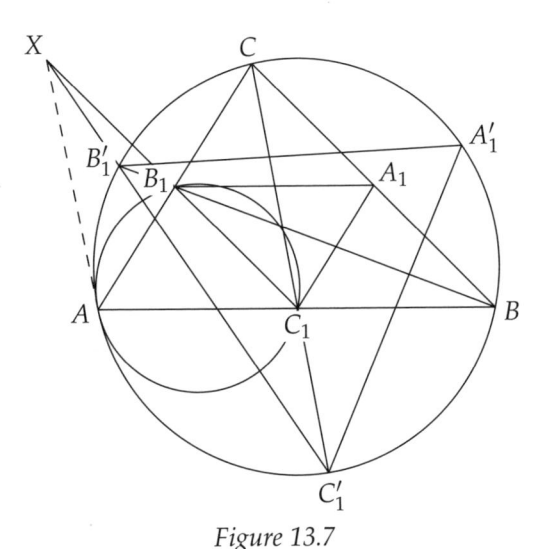

Figure 13.7

Hence $XC_1' \times XB_1' = XC_1 \times XB_1$ and X has equal tangents to both circumcircles. But they are tangent at A, and so, by lemma 13.5, X lies on the common tangent. ❏

Chapter 13: Circumcevian triangles

Theorem 13.7 *The circummedial and tangential triangles are in perspective, and their perspector lies on the Euler line.*

PROOF By lemma 13.6, the points X, T_C, A and T_B are collinear.

Triangles $\triangle A_1 B_1 C_1$ and $\triangle A_1' B_1' C_1'$ are in perspective (with centre G) and so their axis of perspective passes through X. Also $\triangle A_1 B_1 C_1$ and $\triangle T_A T_B T_C$ are in perspective (with centre O) and so their axis of perspective passes through X. But there is nothing special about X; if we define analogous points Y and Z, we see all three triangles share a common axis of perspective through X, Y and Z.

Hence, by the converse of Desargues' theorem, triangles $\triangle A_1' B_1' C_1'$ and $\triangle T_A T_B T_C$ are also in perspective. Since the three axes of perspective are identical, theorem 10.9 on page 141 shows that the three perspectors are collinear. Hence the point lies on the Euler line. ❑

The perspector given by theorem 13.7 is the *Exeter point*, which will be denoted by E^*.

The perspectors used in the proof of theorem 13.7 are illustrated in figure 13.8 and listed in table 13.3. This proof first appeared in [22], along with other material in this and the previous chapter.

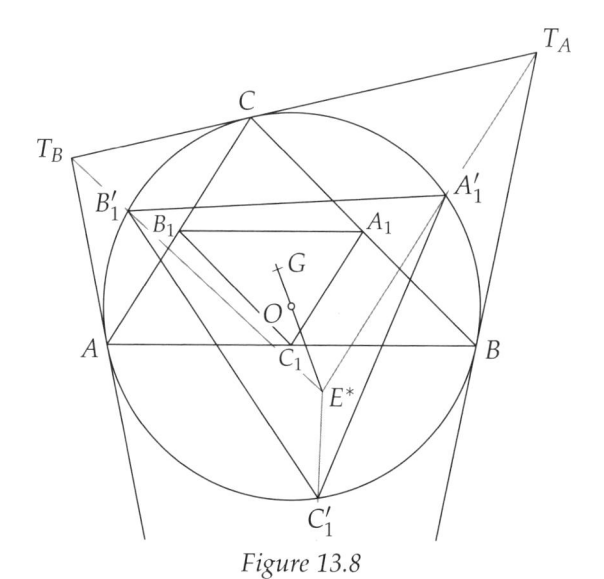

Figure 13.8

Triangles		Perspector	
reference, tangential	$\triangle ABC, \triangle T_A T_B T_C$	centroid	G
reference, medial	$\triangle ABC, \triangle A_1 B_1 C_1$	circumcentre	O
circummedial, tangential	$\triangle A'_1 B'_1 C'_1, \triangle T_A T_B T_C$	Exeter point	E^*

Table 13.3: Perspectors in the proof of theorem 13.7

13.4 The circummidarc triangle

We now examine the circumcevian triangle of the incentre I (see figure 13.9).

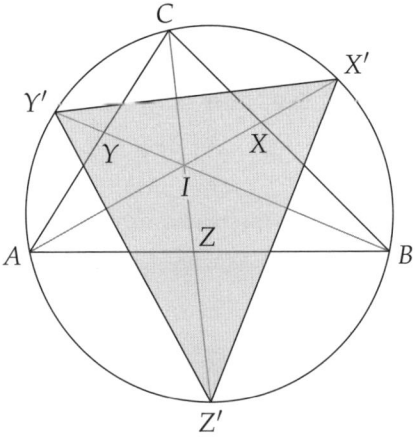

Figure 13.9

The cevians through I meet the sides of $\triangle ABC$ at the points X, Y and Z, and therefore a natural notation for the circummidarc triangle which results is $\triangle X'Y'Z'$. Note that X', Y' and Z' bisect the arcs BC, CA and AB of the circumcircle.

However, I is the orthocentre of the circummidarc triangle, and so we can consider $\triangle ABC$ as the circumorthic triangle of $\triangle X'Y'Z'$. This immediately presents us with a 'free' result.

Theorem 13.8 *The intouch triangle of $\triangle ABC$ is homothetic to the circummidarc triangle, and the homothetic centre is collinear with the incentre I and the circumcentre O of $\triangle ABC$.*

PROOF This is nothing more than a restatement of corollary 13.3, taking $\triangle X'Y'Z'$ as the reference triangle and $\triangle ABC$ as its circumorthic triangle. The corollary states that $\triangle PQR$ and $\triangle X'Y'Z'$ are homothetic with centre on the Euler line of $\triangle X'Y'Z'$. We only need to identify this line (see figure 13.10).

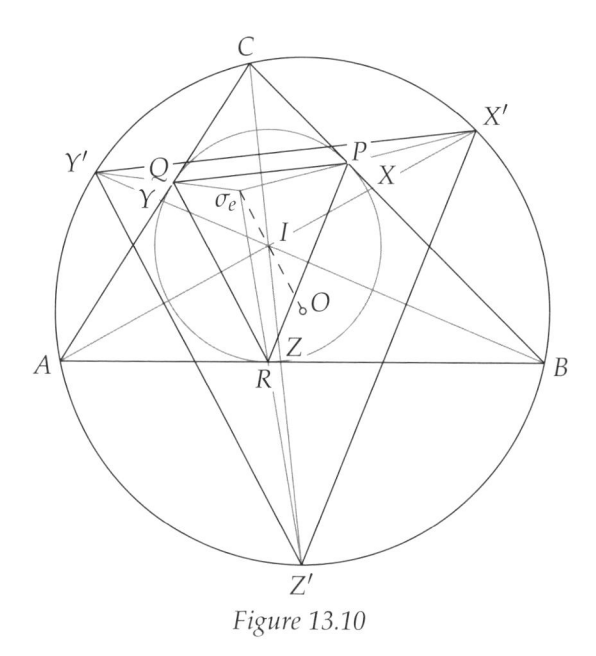

Figure 13.10

The circumcentre of $\triangle X'Y'Z'$ is, of course, the same as the circumcentre of $\triangle ABC$, and the orthocentre of $\triangle X'Y'Z'$ is the incentre of $\triangle ABC$. It follows that O and I are collinear with the homothetic centre. ❑

We will call the new point σ_e. It is the external centre of similitude of the incircle and circumcircle of $\triangle ABC$. It follows that σ_i, the internal centre of similitude of the incircle and circumcentre, also lies on IO. These points can be constructed in another way.

Let UV be a diameter of the circumcircle perpendicular to BC (see figure 13.11).

Then UP and VP meet IO at σ_e and σ_i. Note that

$$\frac{I\sigma_i}{\sigma_i O} = \frac{r}{R} \text{ and } \frac{I\sigma_e}{\sigma_e O} = -\frac{r}{R}.$$

Figure 13.11

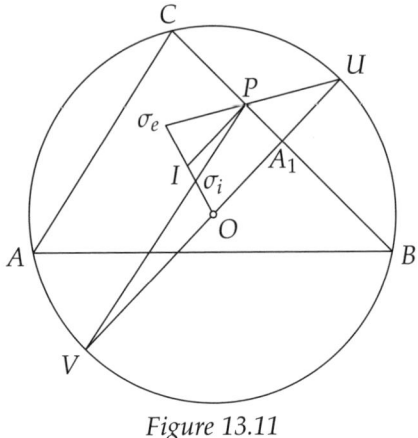

As always, the internal and external centres of similitude separate the centres of the circles harmonically.

Theorem 13.9 σ_i is the isogonal conjugate of the Gergonne point.

PROOF Let the perpendicular distances from σ_i to BC and CA be q_A and q_B, and those from Γ to BC and CA be p_A and p_B. Note that $OA_1 = R\cos A$ (see figure 13.12).

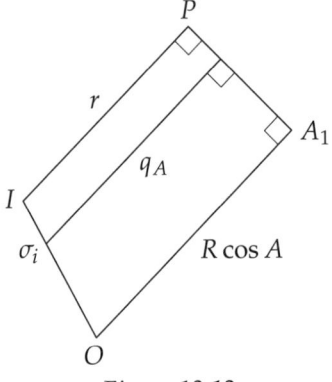

Figure 13.12

Then, by proportion,

$$q_A = \frac{Rr + rR\cos A}{r + R}$$

$$= \frac{rR}{r+R}\left(1 + \frac{b^2 + c^2 - a^2}{2bc}\right)$$

$$= \frac{rR}{r+R}\left(\frac{(b+c)^2 - a^2}{2bc}\right)$$

$$= \frac{2rR}{r+R}\left(\frac{s(s-a)}{bc}\right).$$

Hence

$$\frac{q_A}{q_B} = \frac{a(s-a)}{b(s-b)}.$$

But, by lemma 9.2 on page 114,

$$\frac{p_B}{p_A} = \frac{a(s-a)}{b(s-b)},$$

and so, by theorem 7.6 on page 86, the lines $A\sigma_i$ and $A\Gamma$ are isogonal conjugates. By symmetry for the other vertices, the result follows. ❑

Theorem 13.10 σ_e *is the isogonal conjugate of the Nagel point.*

PROOF This is analogous to the proof of theorem 13.9, so some of the detail is omitted. Let the perpendicular distance of σ_e from BC be s_A. Then, by proportion,

$$s_A = \frac{Rr - rR\cos A}{R - r}$$

$$= \frac{2rR}{R - r}\left(\frac{(s-b)(s-c)}{bc}\right).$$

Hence

$$\frac{s_A}{s_B} = \frac{a(s-b)}{b(s-a)}.$$

But, by lemma 9.5 on page 114,

$$\frac{r_B}{r_A} = \frac{a(s-b)}{b(s-a)}$$

and so, by theorem 7.6 on page 86, the result follows. ❑

Exercise 13b

1. Define the *OoO* or *orthic-of-orthic triangle* of $\triangle ABC$ as the orthic triangle of $\triangle DEF$. Prove that Λ_1 is the perspector of $\triangle ABC$ and the OoO triangle.

2. Define the *OoI* or *orthic-of-intouch triangle* of $\triangle ABC$ as the orthic triangle of the intouch triangle $\triangle PQR$. Prove that the OoI triangle is homothetic to triangle $\triangle ABC$ and that the homothetic centre, denoted by Ξ, lies on the Euler line of $\triangle PQR$.

3. Define the *IoO* or *intouch-of-orthic triangle* of $\triangle ABC$ as the intouch triangle of the orthic triangle $\triangle DEF$. Prove that the OoI and IoO triangles are homothetic and that the homothetic centre is collinear with Π_1 and Ξ.

4. The intouch triangle is $\triangle PQR$ and the *A*-, *B*-, and *C*-extouch triangles are $\triangle P_A Q_A R_A$, $\triangle P_B Q_B R_B$ and $\triangle P_C Q_C R_C$. Prove that the Euler lines of these four triangles are concurrent.

5. Prove that the Fuhrmann and circummidarc triangles are similar.

Chapter 14

The Morley configuration

The result which is the subject of this chapter is surprising and elegant. However, being about angle trisectors, it is rather an isolated outpost in triangle geometry. It was discovered by Frank Morley in about 1899.

14.1 Morley's theorem

Theorem 14.1 *The adjacent trisectors (those closest to the sides) of a triangle intersect in the vertices of an equilateral triangle.*

The triangle so formed is called the *Morley triangle* of $\triangle ABC$ (see figure 14.1). Being equilateral, all of its triangle centres are coincident at a single point, which is the first *Morley centre* M_1. Its circumcircle is the *Morley circle*.

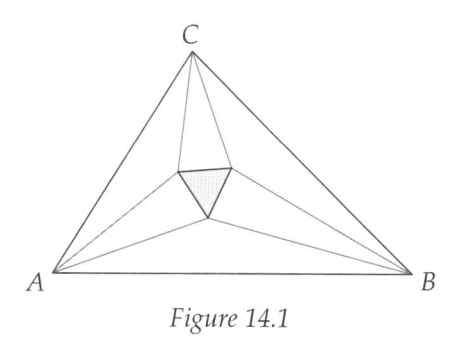

Figure 14.1

There are several proofs, all of which rely on 'knowing the result in advance', in that they begin by constructing the equilateral triangle and then showing that it is formed using trisectors.

PROOF Let the adjacent trisectors of $\angle B$ and $\angle C$ meet at D, and the other trisectors of these angles meet at P (see figure 14.2). Then it is immediate that D is the incentre of $\triangle PBC$ and $\angle DPC = \angle DPB$. Construct E and F on CP and BP such that $\angle PDF = \angle PDE = 30°$. Then $\triangle PDF$ and $\triangle PDE$ are congruent (AAS) and hence $DF = DE$. It follows that $\triangle DEF$ is equilateral.

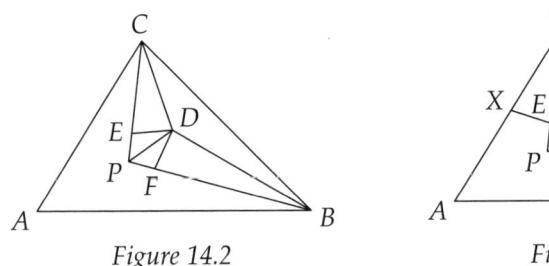

Figure 14.2 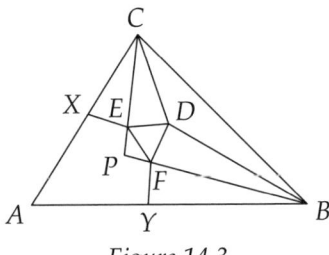   Figure 14.3

It remains to show that AE and AF are the trisectors of $\angle A$.

Now let X and Y be the images of D under reflection in CP and BP (see figure 14.3). It is clear that X and Y lie on CA and BA and that the triangles $\triangle BDF$ and $\triangle BYF$ are congruent, as are $\triangle CDE$ and $\triangle CXE$. Also $YF = DF = FE = ED = EX$.

Now

$$\angle PFE = \angle PEF = 90° - \tfrac{1}{2}\angle BPC$$

but

$$\angle BPC = 180° - \tfrac{2}{3}(\angle B + \angle C),$$

so

$$\angle PFE = \tfrac{1}{3}(\angle B + \angle C) = 60° - \tfrac{1}{3}\angle A$$

and hence

$$\angle PFD = 120° - \tfrac{1}{3}\angle A = \angle PFY.$$

It follows that $\angle YFE = 180° - \tfrac{2}{3}\angle A$, and a similar calculation shows that $\angle FEX$ has the same value.

Chapter 14: The Morley configuration

Now let the internal bisectors of $\angle YFE$ and $\angle FEX$ meet at Z (see figure 14.4). Then Z is the centre of the circle $YFEX$, $\angle YFZ = \angle FYZ = 90° - \frac{1}{3}\angle A$ and $\angle YZX = 3\angle YZF = 2\angle A$. It follows that A also lies on this circle.

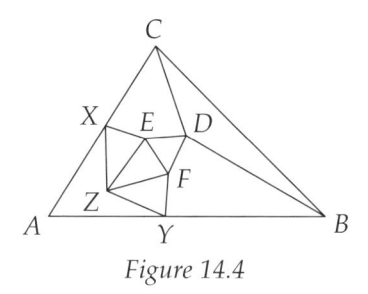

Figure 14.4

Finally, since equal chords subtend equal angles, we have $\angle YAF = \angle FAE = \angle EAX$ as required. ◻

An alternative way of describing this argument is to construct a sort of jigsaw, starting with the equilateral Morley triangle and adding triangles of the appropriate shape around it, checking that everything fits together properly and that we end up with the trisected $\triangle ABC$ (see [7]).

Corollary 14.2 *The angle between the sides BC of the reference triangle and EF of the Morley triangle is* $\frac{1}{3}|\angle B - \angle C|$.

PROOF From the proof of theorem 14.1, $\angle PFE = 60° - \frac{1}{3}\angle A$ and $\angle PBC = \frac{2}{3}\angle B$. It follows that the angle between FE and BC is $60° - \frac{1}{3}\angle A - \frac{2}{3}\angle B$. But this is $\frac{1}{3}(\angle C - \angle B)$ since $\angle A = 180° - \angle B - \angle C$. In the diagram used, $\angle B < \angle C$; had it been the other way around, we would have obtained $\frac{1}{3}(\angle B - \angle C)$. ◻

Theorem 14.3 *The Morley triangle is in perspective with* $\triangle ABC$.

PROOF We will use Ceva's theorem on $\triangle DEF$. Let BE and DF intersect at Y (see figure 14.5).
Then, since $\triangle DEF$ is equilateral,

$$\frac{DY}{YF} = \frac{\sin \angle DEB}{\sin \angle FEB}$$

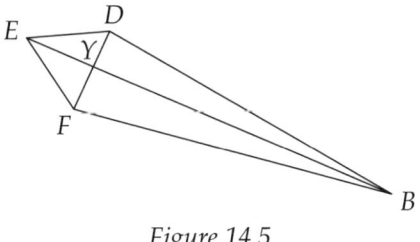

Figure 14.5

by the sine rule, and also

$$\frac{BD}{\sin \angle DEB} = \frac{BE}{\sin \angle BDE} \quad \text{and} \quad \frac{BF}{\sin \angle FEB} = \frac{BE}{\sin \angle BFE}.$$

Combining these, we have

$$\frac{DY}{YF} = \frac{BD \sin(120° + \tfrac{1}{3}C)}{BF \sin(120° + \tfrac{1}{3}A)},$$

with similar results for the other two sides. Hence

$$\frac{DY \times FX \times EZ}{YF \times XE \times ZD} = \frac{BD \times AF \times CE}{BF \times AE \times CD}.$$

But

$$\frac{BD}{CD} = \frac{\sin \tfrac{1}{3}C}{\sin \tfrac{1}{3}B}$$

(and two similar results) so the result follows by Ceva. □

The perspector is known as the *second Morley centre* of $\triangle ABC$ and will be denoted by M_2 (see figure 14.6).

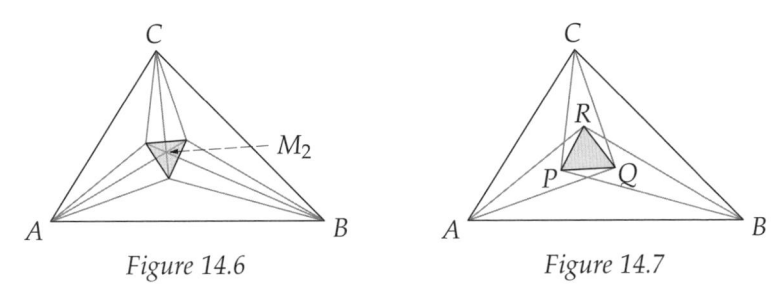

Figure 14.6

Figure 14.7

Let the points Q and R be defined analogously to P as the intersections of the non-adjacent angle trisectors. The triangle so formed, which is not in general equilateral, is called the *adjunct Morley triangle* (see figure 14.7).

Theorem 14.4 *The adjunct Morley triangle and the Morley triangle are in perspective, with perspector M_1, the* first Morley centre.

PROOF Set as question 2 of exercise 14a. ❏

Theorem 14.5 *The adjunct Morley triangle is in perspective with $\triangle ABC$, and the perspector is the isogonal conjugate of M_2.*

The perspector is called the *Morley-Yff centre*, and will be denoted by M_3.

PROOF Set as question 4 of exercise 14a. ❏

Theorem 14.6 *The three points M_1, M_2 and M_3 are collinear.*

PROOF This is best proved using barycentric coordinates. See page 382 of appendix A. ❏

We shall refer to the line $M_1 M_2 M_3$ as the *first Morley line*.

Exercise 14a

1. Prove that the side length of the Morley triangle is

    $8R \sin \tfrac{1}{3} A \sin \tfrac{1}{3} B \sin \tfrac{1}{3} C.$

2. Prove theorem 14.4.

3. Prove that the first Morley centre is the first isogonic centre of the adjunct Morley triangle.

4. Prove theorem 14.5.

14.2 External trisectors

Any angle has two angle bisectors, and when the angle is a vertex of a triangle, it is normal to think of these as internal and external bisectors. In the case of trisectors the situation is a little more complicated since an angle at the vertex of a triangle has three trisectors. Figure 14.8 shows an acute angle $\angle ABC$ which is part of a circle with centre B. The point A' is diametrically opposite to A on the circle.

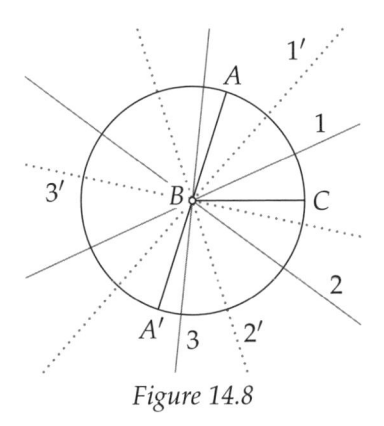

Figure 14.8

Line 1 is the internal trisector, which trisects the minor arc CA. Line 2 is the first 'external trisector', which trisects the minor arc CA'. Line 3 is the second 'external trisector', which trisects the major arc $CA'A$.

The 'other' trisectors $1'$, $2'$, $3'$ trisect the minor arc AC, the minor arc $A'C$ and the major arc $A'AC$. We can think of the three types as trisecting the acute, obtuse and reflex angles at the vertex.

Note that the lines 1, 2 and 3 are inclined at 60° to one another. Another way of saying this is that they are at *equal angular distances*. The same is true of $1'$, $2'$ and $3'$.

In section 14.1 we considered the internal trisectors 1 at $\angle CBA$ and $1'$ at $\angle ACB$ which met at the vertex D of the first Morley triangle. We now consider what happens when we use the trisectors 2 at $\angle CBA'$ and $2'$ at $\angle ACB'$, which we can think of as 'adjacent obtuse trisectors'.

Theorem 14.7 *The adjacent obtuse trisectors of a triangle meet in the vertices of an equilateral triangle.*

We shall call this equilateral triangle the *second Morley triangle* (see figure 14.9); so the original one becomes the *first Morley triangle*.

Chapter 14: The Morley configuration 191

Figure 14.9

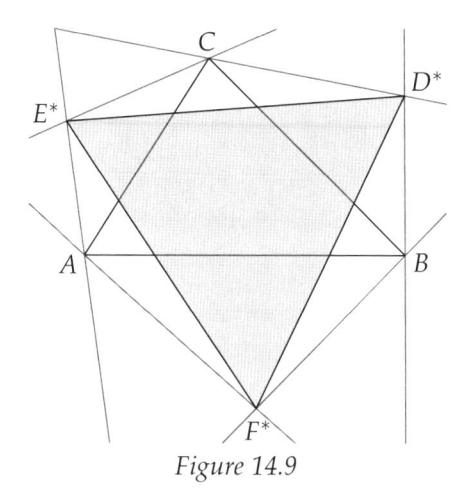

PROOF The proof mirrors that of theorem 14.1.
Let the adjacent obtuse trisectors at B and C meet at D^*, and the other obtuse trisectors of these angles meet at P^* (see figure 14.10). (If we select $\angle A$ to be acute, then these lines will meet on the same side of BC as D^*.) Then D^* is the incentre of $\triangle BCP^*$ and P^*D^* is the bisector of $\angle BP^*C$. Now construct points E^* on P^*C and F^* on P^*B such that $\angle P^*D^*E^* = \angle P^*D^*F^* = 150°$. Again we have congruent triangles $\triangle P^*D^*F^*$ and $\triangle P^*D^*E^*$, and also $\angle F^*D^*E^* = 60°$, so $\triangle D^*E^*F^*$ is equilateral. It remains only to show that AE^* and AF^* are external angle trisectors.

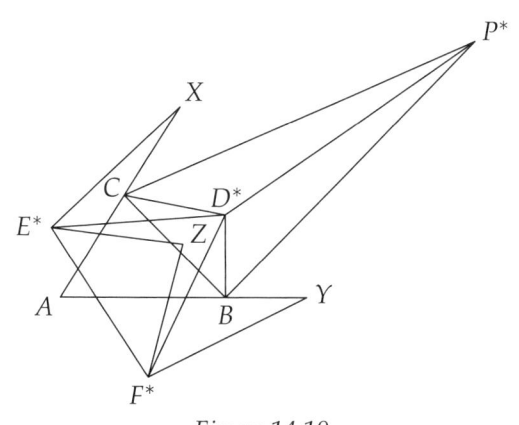

Figure 14.10

Now let X and Y be the images of D^* under reflection in CP^* and BP^*. As before, there follows a bit of angle-chasing. It turns out that $\angle BP^*C = 60° - \frac{2}{3}\angle A$, $\angle P^*F^*E^* = 60° + \frac{1}{3}\angle A$, $\angle P^*F^*D^* = \angle P^*F^*Y = \frac{1}{3}\angle A$ and $\angle YF^*E^* = 60° + \frac{2}{3}\angle A$. A similar exercise gives the same value for $\angle XE^*F^*$. As before, let Z be the intersection of the bisectors of $\angle XE^*F^*$ and $\angle YF^*E^*$ and the centre of the circumcircle of YF^*E^*X. A short calculation shows that $\angle YZX = 2\angle YAX$, so A is also on the circle. The final step is a little different. By equal chords, we have $\angle F^*AY = \angle E^*AX = 180° - \angle F^*AE^*$ (since they clearly cannot be equal to F^*AE^*), and now a little work gives $\angle F^*AY = \angle E^*AX = 60° - \frac{1}{3}\angle A$ as required. ❏

Theorem 14.8 *The first and second Morley triangles are homothetic.*

PROOF By corollary 14.2, the angle between BE and CF is $\frac{1}{3}(\angle B - \angle C)$, and by a similar argument for the second triangle, that between BC and E^*F^* is

$$(60° + \tfrac{1}{3}\angle A) - \tfrac{2}{3}(180° - \angle B) = \tfrac{1}{3}(\angle B - \angle C).$$

So FE and F^*E^* are parallel, with analogous results for the other two pairs of sides. ❏

Given the similarity between the proofs for the first and second Morley triangles, it is no surprise that the other results in section 14.1 also have counterparts. Thus we have a second adjunct Morley triangle $\triangle P^*Q^*R^*$, and the three triangles $\triangle ABC$, $\triangle D^*E^*F^*$ and $\triangle P^*Q^*R^*$ are pairwise in perspective with the three perspectors collinear in the *second Morley line*.

We now carry out exactly the same construction but for the 'reflex angle trisectors'. In terms of the notation used above, these would be the trisectors 3 at B and $3'$ at C.

Theorem 14.9 *The adjacent reflex trisectors of a triangle meet in the vertices of an equilateral triangle.*

We shall call this equilateral triangle the *third Morley triangle* (see figure 14.11), denoted by $\triangle D^{**}E^{**}F^{**}$.

PROOF Set as question 1 of exercise 14b. ❏

Theorem 14.10 *The first and third Morley triangles are homothetic, although the homothecy is inverse.*

Chapter 14: The Morley configuration 193

Figure 14.11

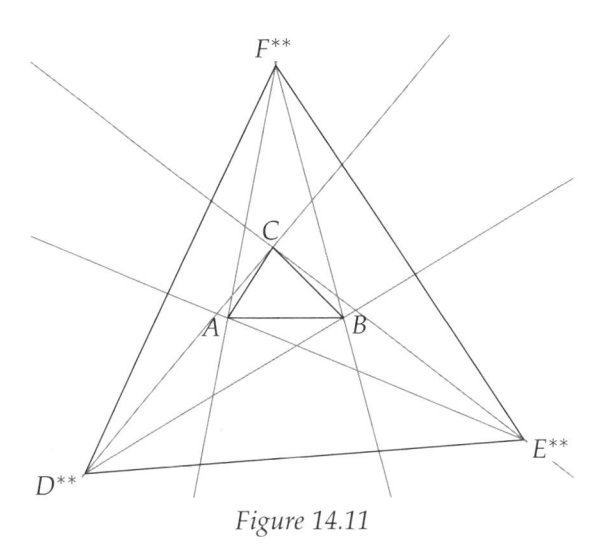

PROOF Set as question 2 of exercise 14b. ☐

Again we have a third adjunct Morley triangle $\triangle P^{**}Q^{**}R^{**}$, and the three triangles $\triangle ABC$, $\triangle D^{**}E^{**}F^{**}$ and $\triangle P^{**}Q^{**}R^{**}$ are pairwise in perspective with the three perspectors collinear in the *third Morley line*.

We name the three Morley lines $\mathcal{L}_1$, $\mathcal{L}_2$ and $\mathcal{L}_3$ and we denote by M_i^j the ith Morley centre of the jth Morley triangle (for $1 \leq i,j \leq 3$). Clearly M_1^1, M_2^1 and M_3^1 lie on $\mathcal{L}_1$, by definition, but there are also some unexpected relationships.

Theorem 14.11 *With the above notation for the Morley lines and centres:*
 (i) *the point M_1^3 lies on $\mathcal{L}_1$;*
 (ii) *the point M_1^1 lies on $\mathcal{L}_2$;*
 (iii) *the point M_1^2 lies on $\mathcal{L}_3$.*

PROOF The proof uses barycentric coordinates. ☐

Exercise 14b

1. Prove theorem 14.9.

2. Prove theorem 14.10.

14.3 The lighthouse theorem

A theorem due to Richard Guy [11] turns out to be particularly useful in investigating this configuration further. He imagines lighthouses with rotating beams at the n vertices of a polygon. Each lighthouse sends out a pencil of n lines at equal angular distances. He goes on to show that this gives rise to a configuration involving n^2 points which are the vertices of n regular n-gons. We use the special case when $n = 3$ to derive a pleasing 'gasket' of equilateral triangles related to the Morley triangles.

A set S of three lines through a point P which make three angles of $60°$ is known as a *set of spokes* at P. We can label the lines anticlockwise, beginning anywhere, as s_1, s_2 and s_3.

Theorem 14.12 *Let S be a set of spokes at B and let T be a set at C. Suppose that s_i and t_i intersect at X_i, for $i = 1, 2, 3$. Then $\triangle X_1 X_2 X_3$ is an equilateral triangle (see figure 14.12).*

PROOF Since $\angle X_2 B X_3 = 60° = \angle X_2 C X_3$, it follows that $X_2 X_3 CB$ is cyclic. Similarly $X_1 B X_2 C$ is cyclic, so there is a circle through X_1, X_2, X_3, B and C. Hence all the angles in $\triangle X_1 X_2 X_3$ are $60°$ and the result follows. □

In the diagram, the spoke s_1 at B can be chosen as the one which makes an angle $\beta < 60°$ with BC, measuring anticlockwise. Similarly the spoke t_1 at C is chosen as that which makes an angle $\gamma < 60°$ with CB, but this time measuring clockwise. In the given diagram $\beta \leq \gamma$, but if $\beta > \gamma$ we have a similar situation by reflecting the diagram in the perpendicular bisector of BC.

Corollary 14.13 *The line $X_3 X_2$ makes an angle of $\beta - \gamma$ with BC.*

Figure 14.12

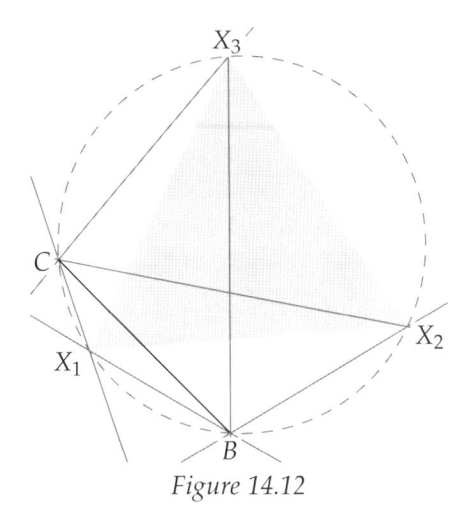

This corollary can be stated in the general case by using directed angles.

PROOF We have $\angle BX_3X_2 = \gamma + 60°$, by external angle of a cyclic quadrilateral, and $\angle X_3BC = 120° - \beta$. Hence the angle between X_3X_2 and BC is $180° - (\gamma + 60°) - (120° - \beta) = \beta - \gamma$. □

Now we can relabel T by cyclically permuting the spokes to t_2, t_3, t_1 and apply the theorem again to produce a second equilateral triangle, and then do this again to produce a third one. Since the effect of this on γ is increase it by 60° each time, the resulting triangles have parallel sides. This produces three homothetic equilateral triangles (see figure 14.13).

14.4 More equilateral triangles

The relevance of the lighthouse theorem is that the six trisectors at each vertex can be considered as two sets of spokes. These have already been identified in section 14.2 as the set 1, 2, 3 and the set 1', 2', 3'. As we have seen, sets of spokes at two adjacent vertices yield three equilateral triangles. There are four ways of choosing which sets of spokes to use, so there are twelve such possible triangles. This can be repeated for each of the three sides, leading to a total of 36 triangles.

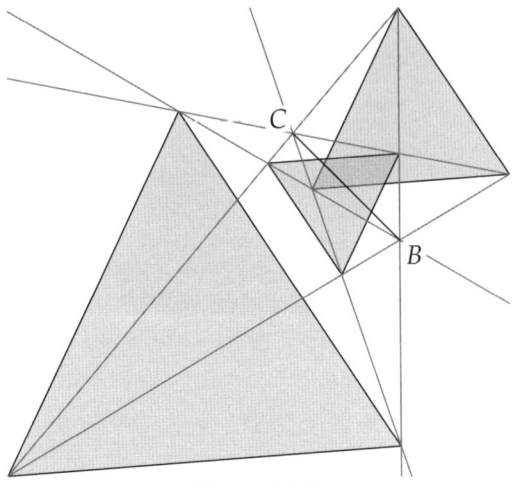

Figure 14.13

However, to obtain an *interesting* set of triangles, we need to be careful. If we restrict ourselves to spokes which lead to adjacent internal trisectors, we obtain triangles which are related to the Morley triangles. Hence we choose the trisectors 1, 2, 3 around B and $1'$, $2'$, $3'$ around C, distinguished by the appropriate suffix, and denote by X_{ij} the point of intersection of i_B and j'_C, where $1 \leq i, j \leq 3$. There are nine such points which form three equilateral triangles (see figure 14.14). Each of the six trisectors contains three of the points, and each of the points lies on two trisectors. We can also make three important identifications, namely $X_{11} \equiv D$, $X_{22} \equiv D^*$, $X_{33} \equiv D^{**}$.

Now, by corollary 14.13, one of the sides of $\triangle X_{11} X_{32} X_{23}$ is inclined at an angle of $\frac{1}{3}(\angle B - \angle C)$ to BC. Hence it is parallel to the side of a Morley triangle, and it must be the side $X_{32} X_{23}$. It follows, since the triangles are equilateral, that each of the three new triangles is homothetic to all three Morley triangles.

The same is true of all the triangles generated by this procedure. It is now instructive to produce a diagram showing all nine triangles, but we can no longer use the X_{ij} notation for the points since we will not know which pair of vertices they come from.

The result is a remarkable 'gasket' (see figure 14.15). In the process of building up this configuration, the vertices of the Morley triangles function as 'fixed points', and, since the directions of the various triangle sides are

Chapter 14: The Morley configuration 197

Figure 14.14

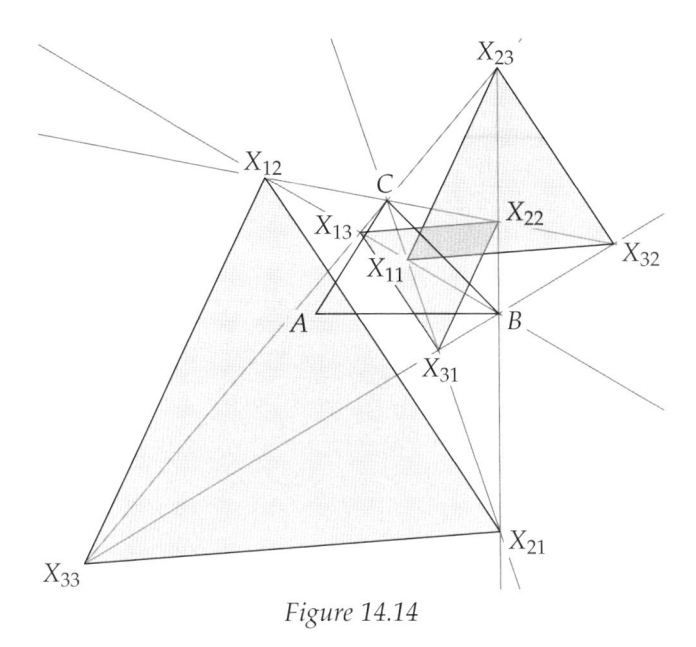

in fixed directions relative to these points, they 'overlay' each other in the way shown in the diagram. It would be very tedious to explain in detail how this happens and the best way to understand what is going on is to construct the gasket for yourself. Apart from A, B and C, there are 27 points in the gasket, which lie on nine lines, with six points on each line and two lines through each point.

We now add the six trisectors around B to the diagram (see figure 14.16). Since each trisector is responsible for three points which are vertices of equilateral triangles, there are six collinearities including the vertex B and three points in the gasket. When we include all three vertices of $\triangle ABC$, we have eighteen such collinearities.

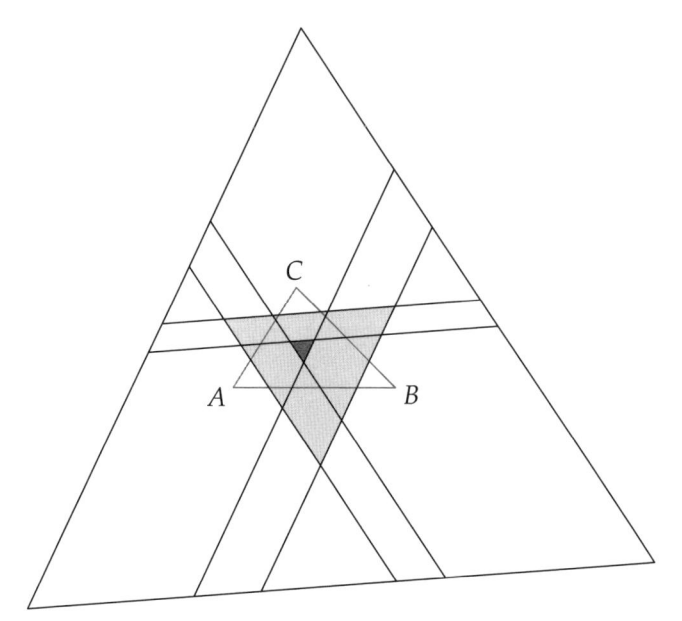

Figure 14.15

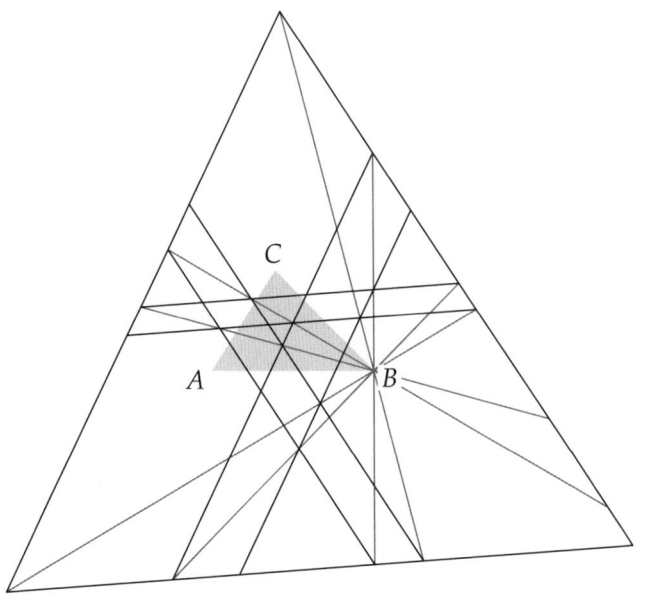

Figure 14.16

Chapter 15

Spiral similarities

We have already made extensive use of the idea of homothecy, which concerns two similar figures (often, but not necessarily, triangles) whose corresponding sides are parallel. A consequence of this is the joins of corresponding vertices are concurrent at the homothetic centre. Then one figure can be transformed into the other by an enlargement with either a positive or negative scale factor, according as the similarity is direct or inverse.

This method has turned out to be fruitful because we are able to deduce new facts about the centres of one triangle by using known facts about the centres of the other. In the case of circles we have emphasized the internal and external centres of similitude.

In this chapter, we generalise our ideas to include figures which are directly similar but differently orientated.

15.1 Spiral similarity

Suppose we have a fixed point O, a fixed angle θ and a fixed positive real number k, known as the scale factor. A *spiral similarity* is the result of combining a rotation of θ about O with an enlargement of k with centre O. Clearly these transformations are commutative; the order in which they are done does not matter. Some authors call this transformation a *homology*, but there is no general agreement on the meaning of this word, and the term spiral similarity is unambiguous.

Figure 15.1 shows an example of a spiral similarity which maps $\triangle ABC$ to $\triangle A'B'C'$. The angle of the similarity (measured anti-clockwise) is $\angle COC'$ and the scale factor is $\dfrac{OC'}{OC}$.

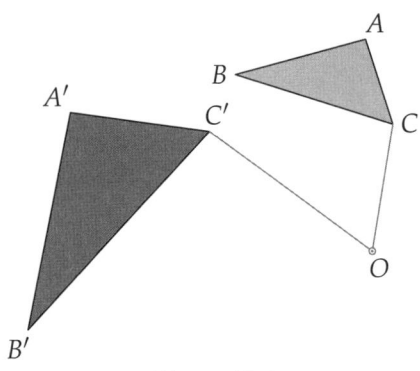

Figure 15.1

It is worthwhile making a few definitions concerning a spiral similarity.

- A_1 and A_2 are *corresponding points* if the transformation maps A_1 to A_2.
- $A_1 B_1$ and $A_2 B_2$ are *corresponding segments* if the transformation takes A_1 to B_1 and A_2 to B_2. It is then clear that it maps each point of the first segment to a unique point of the second.
- ℓ_1 and ℓ_2 are *corresponding lines* if the transformation maps the whole of the first line to the whole of the second.

It is immediate that the scale factor in figure 15.1 can also be expressed as $\dfrac{A'B'}{AB}$. A third way, which turns out to be particularly useful, is to use the ratio of the perpendicular distances of $A'B'$ and AB from O. In fact, once we know the centre, we do not even need to know the specific points A, B, A' and B'. It is sufficient just to know two corresponding lines in order to determine θ and k. In figure 15.2, ℓ_1 and ℓ_2 are two corresponding lines, and X_1 and X_2 are the feet of the perpendiculars from O. Then the angle of rotation is $\angle X_1 O X_2$ and the scale factor is $\dfrac{OX_2}{OX_1}$.

Note also that a spiral similarity with centre O, angle θ and scale factor k can be inverted by means of one with centre O, angle $-\theta$ and scale factor $\frac{1}{k}$.

Figure 15.2

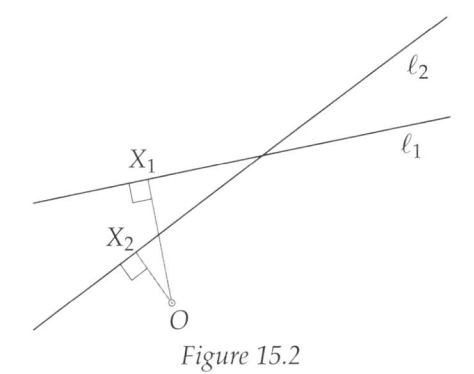

15.2 Finding the centre

Suppose now that we are given two triangles which are directly similar and it is our task to determine the centre of similitude. The fact that the corresponding angles are equal, and that they are in the same order around the triangles, is enough to convince us that there must exist such a centre. If we find one point which satisfies the conditions to be the centre, then it is unique. It is the only point in the plane which does not move under the transformation; if there were two different centres O_1 and O_2, then the transformation with centre O_1 would cause O_2 to move, and so O_2 could not possibly be the centre.

In fact, all we need to determine the centre of similitude is one pair of sides, for example AB and $A'B'$. The two sides BC and CA would automatically be mapped to the correct $B'C'$ and $C'A'$ once we have established the correct centre, scale factor and angle.

Theorem 15.1 *Any two non-parallel segments define a centre of similitude.*

PROOF Let AB and $A'B'$ intersect in X, and draw the circumcircles of $\triangle AXA'$ and $\triangle BXB'$, meeting in a second point O (see figure 15.3).

Now $\angle OAB = \angle OA'B'$ and $\angle OBA = \angle OB'A'$ by the circle theorems, and so $\triangle OAB$ and $\triangle PA'B'$ are similar. Hence a rotation with centre O followed by an enlargement of the appropriate scale factor will take AB to $A'B'$, as required. ❏

We now consider ways in which this construction goes wrong. The first is when the segments are parallel. If, in addition, they are equal in

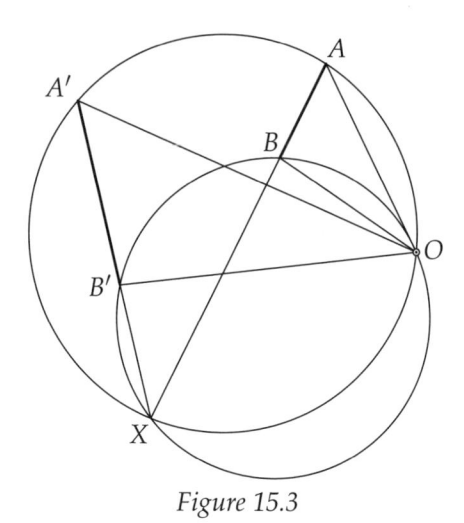

Figure 15.3

length, then all that is needed to map one to the other is a translation (and the two triangles will then be congruent and in the same orientation). If they are unequal in length, then we have a homothecy and the centre of similitude is just the homothetic centre.

It is possible that the two circles turn out to be tangential at X (see figure 15.4). However, this is no problem: what has happened is that we have placed AB and $A'B'$ in such a way that the two lines already intersect in the centre of similitude.

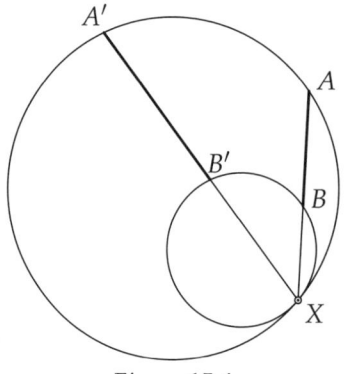

Figure 15.4 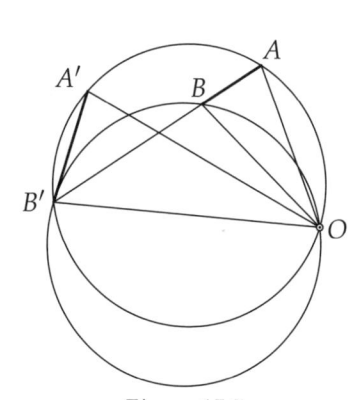 *Figure 15.5*

But it is also possible that the point X coincides with one of the points A, B, A' and B'. In that case, we need to modify the diagram slightly (see figure 15.5).

Suppose that X and B' coincide, so B' lies on AB. Now we draw the circumcircle of $\triangle B'AA'$ as before, but the degenerate triangle $\triangle BB'B'$ suggests that we construct a circle through B tangential to $A'B'$ at B'. If these two circles intersect at O, then $\angle OAB = \angle OA'B'$ as before, and $\angle OBA = \angle BB'O + \angle BOB' = \angle BB'O + \angle BB'A' = \angle OB'A'$. Again we have the desired similarity.

Note that throughout we have assumed that the similarity between triangles is direct. If it is inverse, there is a theorem that one can be transformed to the other either by means of a *glide reflection*, which is a combination of a translation and a reflection, or a *dilative reflection*, which is a combination of a reflection and an enlargement. We shall not pursue this idea further, but refer the reader to an excellent account in [25].

Exercise 15a

1. Prove that, if AA' and BB' intersect at Y, then the centre of similitude O is the intersection of the circumcircles of $\triangle ABY$ and $\triangle A'B'Y$.

2. Triangle $\triangle AB'C'$ is similar to the fixed triangle $\triangle ABC$, and B' moves on a straight line through B. Prove that the locus of C' is a straight line through C.

3. For the triangle $\triangle ABC$, let $\mathcal{C}_1$ be the circle through B and tangent to AC at A and $\mathcal{C}_2$ the circle through C and tangent to AB at A. Let D be the second point of intersection of $\mathcal{C}_1$ and $\mathcal{C}_2$ and E be the point where the line AD meets the circumcircle of $\triangle ABC$. Prove that D is the midpoint of AE.

4. Prove that, in the configuration of question 3, AD is a symmedian of $\triangle ABC$.

15.3 Triangles of correspondence

We now investigate what happens when three directly similar figures occur in the same diagram. In order to motivate the rather technical nature of the results, we will develop the general theory at the same time as focusing on a special case which involves the orthic configuration.

If $\triangle DEF$ is the orthic triangle of $\triangle ABC$, then the three triangles $\triangle AFE$, $\triangle DFB$ and $\triangle DCE$ are all similar to $\triangle ABC$ (see figure 15.6). Hence they can be mapped to one another using spiral similarities. The three spiral similarities are given in table 15.1.

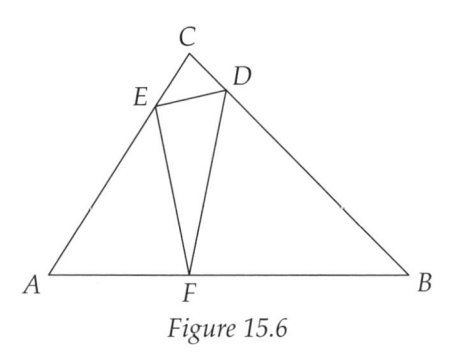

Figure 15.6

Centre	Angle	Scale factor	From	To
D	$180° - \angle A$	$\cos B \sec C$	$\triangle DCE$	$\triangle DFB$
E	$180° - \angle B$	$\cos C \sec A$	$\triangle AFE$	$\triangle DCE$
F	$180° - \angle C$	$\cos A \sec B$	$\triangle DFB$	$\triangle AFE$

Table 15.1

In general, suppose we have three similar triangles which we will call $\mathcal{F}_1$, $\mathcal{F}_2$ and $\mathcal{F}_3$. By theorem 15.1, we need only know three corresponding segments, one in each of the figures, and we can then deduce the centres of similitude, which will be denoted by O_1, O_2 and O_3. In order to maintain symmetry, O_1 is used to indicate the centre of similitude of $\mathcal{F}_2$ and $\mathcal{F}_3$, O_2 of $\mathcal{F}_3$ and $\mathcal{F}_1$ and O_3 of $\mathcal{F}_1$ and $\mathcal{F}_2$. Note that the centre O_3 is completely determined by the first two similarities. In the example, $\mathcal{F}_1$, $\mathcal{F}_2$ and $\mathcal{F}_3$ are $\triangle AFE$, $\triangle DFB$ and $\triangle DCE$ and O_1, O_2 and O_3 are D, E and F.

If two of O_1, O_2 and O_3 are identical, so is the third. Then $\mathcal{F}_1$, $\mathcal{F}_2$ and $\mathcal{F}_3$ share the same centre of similitude and the geometry is simple; we

Chapter 15: Spiral similarities 205

shall assume that this is not the case. If the spiral similarities involve no rotation, then they are homothecies and O_1, O_2 and O_3 will be collinear; we also exclude this case. With these assumptions, O_1, O_2 and O_3 are either collinear or they form a triangle. This is called the *triangle of similitude*, and its circumcircle is known as the *circle of similitude*. In the example, the circle of similitude is the nine-point circle of $\triangle ABC$ since it is the circumcircle of the orthic triangle. We will use the results in this and the following section to deduce further properties of this circle. We shall assume that the triangle of similitude is not degenerate, but the reader can easily adapt the treatment which follows in the case when the centres of similitude are collinear.

Once these centres are known, the three spiral similarities can be deduced from one corresponding line ℓ_1, ℓ_2 and ℓ_3 in each figure. Suppose that these meet in three points P_1, P_2 and P_3, where again P_1 is the intersection of ℓ_2 and ℓ_3, and so on. We shall call $\triangle P_1 P_2 P_3$ a *triangle of correspondence*. It is possible that this triangle degenerates into a point, when the three corresponding lines are concurrent. There are infinitely many possible triangles of correspondence for three similar figures. It is important to understand that we are *not* claiming that $P_2 P_3$, $P_3 P_1$ and $P_1 P_2$ are corresponding *segments* under the three transformations.

Figure 15.7 shows an example of this situation. A useful shorthand is to refer to a spiral similarity by its centre. If the angles of rotation for O_1 and O_2 are θ_1 and θ_2, that for O_3 is $-(\theta_1 + \theta_2)$. If the scale factors for O_1 and O_2 are k_1 and k_2, then the scale factor for O_3 is $\frac{1}{k_1 k_2}$.

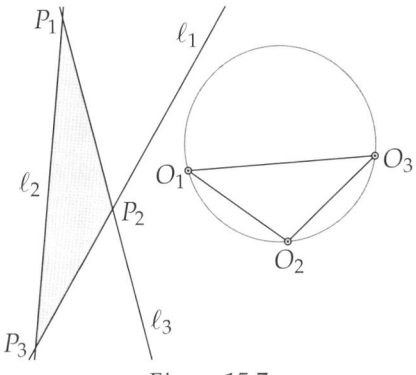

Figure 15.7

Theorem 15.2 *For given similar figures $\mathcal{F}_1$, $\mathcal{F}_2$ and $\mathcal{F}_3$, all triangles of correspondence are directly similar.*

PROOF The angle between the lines ℓ_2 and ℓ_3 is θ_1, that between ℓ_3 and ℓ_1 is θ_2 and that between ℓ_1 and ℓ_1 is $-(\theta_1 + \theta_2)$. These angles determine the relative directions of the lines uniquely. ❑

Theorem 15.3 *For all triangles of correspondence $\triangle P_1 P_2 P_3$, angles $\angle O_1 P_1 P_2$ and $\angle O_1 P_1 P_3$ are constant.*

PROOF Note that $\frac{O_1 X_2}{O_1 X_3} = k_1$ and $\angle P_3 P_1 P_2 = \theta_1$, both of which are constant (see figure 15.8).

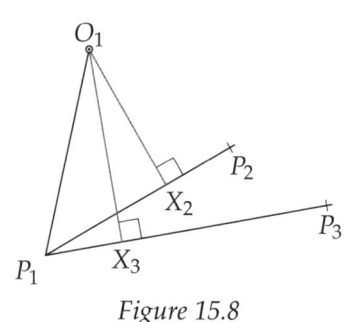

Figure 15.8

It is clear by trigonometry that the angles $\angle O_1 P_1 P_2$ and $\angle O_1 P_1 P_3$ are now determined. ❑

Examples

Now we identify some triangles of correspondence arising from the orthic configuration. Note that the order of vertices is important in describing these triangles. The starting point is to decide on a corresponding line from each of the triangles $\triangle AFE$, $\triangle DFB$ and $\triangle DCE$.

(a) An obvious example is a corresponding side from each of the triangles. For instance, the segments FE, FB and CE form $\triangle AEF$ which is therefore a triangle of correspondence. Similarly $\triangle DBF$ and $\triangle DEC$ are triangles of correspondence.

(b) We can use any corresponding cevians from the three triangles. These must relate to a particular vertex—for example, A in $\triangle AFE$

and D in the other two triangles. We might, for example, choose altitudes, angle bisectors, medians or symmedians.

If we use altitudes, the triangle of correspondence is $\triangle DYX$ (see figure 15.9). Since the triangle is formed by rotating two sides through 90°, $\angle XDY$ is equal to $\angle A$. Similarly $\angle DYX = \angle FEA = \angle B$ and $\angle DXY = \angle EFA = \angle C$. Hence $\triangle DYX$ is similar to the original triangles $\triangle AEF$, $\triangle DBF$ and $\triangle DEC$.

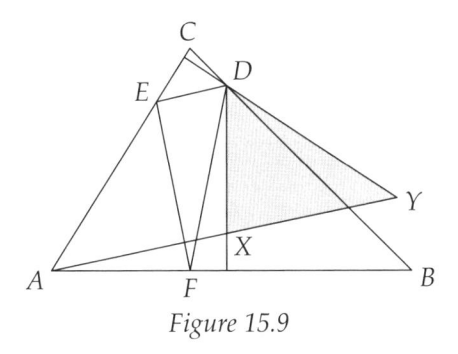

Figure 15.9

Essentially the same argument applies to any triangle of correspondence constructed from cevians.

(c) We could use the perpendicular bisectors of AE, DE and DB (see figure 15.10).

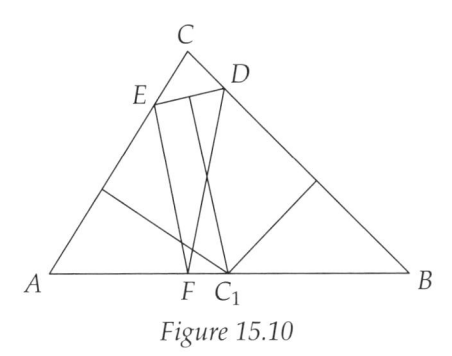

Figure 15.10

By the midpoint theorem applied to $\triangle ADB$, the perpendicular bisector of DB passes through C_1, and the same is true of the perpendicular bisector of AE. The circumcentre of the cyclic quadrilateral

$ABDE$ is C_1, so it lies on the perpendicular bisector of DE. So this triangle degenerates to the point C_1.

(d) We could use corresponding sides of the medial triangles of $\triangle AFE$, $\triangle DFB$ and $\triangle DCE$. In figure 15.11, QR passes through the midpoints of AF and AE; RP and PQ are defined in the same way. It is immediate that $\triangle PQR$ is homothetic to $\triangle AEF$.

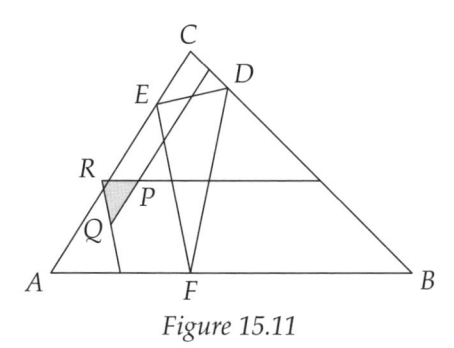

Figure 15.11

An enlargement with centre D and scale factor $\frac{1}{2}$ takes the lines AB and AC to the lines RP and QP, so P is the midpoint of the altitude AD.

15.4 The circle of similitude

We now have a group of theorems which relate triangles of correspondence to the circle of similitude.

It will be convenient to denote the perpendicular distance from a point X to a line ℓ by $\pi(X, \ell)$.

Theorem 15.4 *The lines P_1O_1, P_2O_2 and P_3O_3 are concurrent at a point K, which is on the circle of similitude.*

PROOF As O_1 is the centre of similitude of ℓ_2 and ℓ_3, it satisfies

$$\frac{\pi(O_1, \ell_3)}{\pi(O_1, \ell_2)} = k_1.$$

The locus of all points X such that

$$\frac{\pi(X, \ell_3)}{\pi(X, \ell_2)} = k_1$$

Chapter 15: Spiral similarities

Figure 15.12

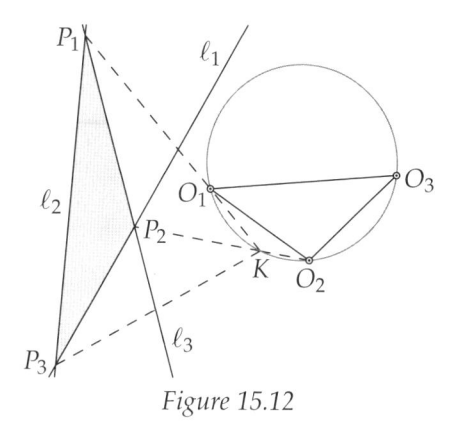

is the line P_1O_1. Similarly, P_2O_2 is the locus of points such that

$$\frac{\pi(X,\ell_1)}{\pi(X,\ell_3)} = k_2.$$

These lines meet at a point K which satisfies both properties, so

$$\frac{\pi(K,\ell_2)}{\pi(K,\ell_1)} = \frac{1}{k_1k_2} = k_3.$$

Hence K lies on the line P_3O_3.

By theorem 15.2, all triangles of correspondence are similar. Also the directions of P_1K, P_2K and P_3K are determined by the scale factors, so the angles $\angle P_1KP_2$, $\angle P_2KP_3$ and $\angle P_3KP_1$ are also fixed, and this fixes the angles $\angle O_1KO_2$, $\angle O_2KO_3$ and $\angle O_3KO_1$. Therefore K lies on a circle with three fixed chords O_1O_2, O_2O_3 and O_3O_1, which is the circumcircle of $\triangle O_1O_2O_3$. □

A consequence of this result is that the circle of similitude can be thought of as the locus of the point K, for all such triangles of correspondence.

Corollary 15.5 *The three centres of similitude are collinear if, and only if, the lines P_1O_1, P_2O_2 and P_3O_3 are parallel for any triangle of correspondence $\triangle P_1P_2P_3$.*

PROOF The point K guaranteed by theorem 15.4 is now at infinity on the line $O_1O_2O_3$. □

Theorem 15.6 *The centre of similitude of any two triangles of correspondence lies on the circle of similitude.*

PROOF Let the triangles of correspondence be $\triangle P_1P_2P_3$ and $\triangle Q_1Q_2Q_3$. We first deal with the case when the sides of $\triangle Q_1Q_2Q_3$ are parallel to those of $\triangle P_1P_2P_3$ (see figure 15.13).

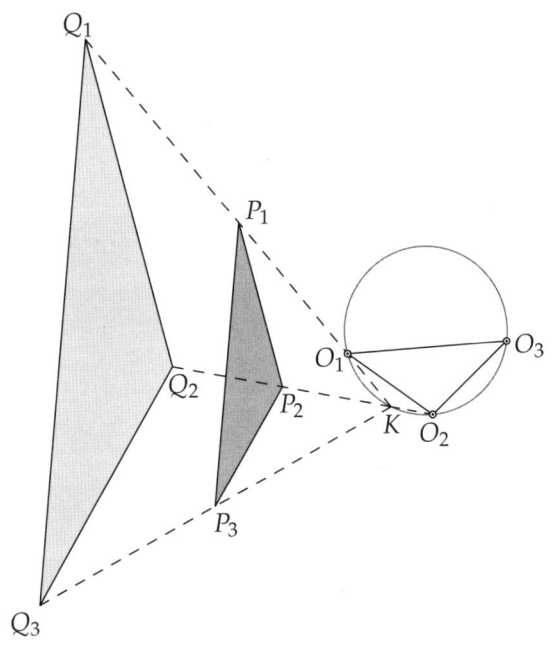

Figure 15.13

Since O_1 is a centre of similitude,

$$\frac{\pi(O_1, Q_1Q_2)}{\pi(O_1, Q_1Q_3)} = \frac{\pi(O_1, P_1P_2)}{\pi(O_1, P_1P_3)}.$$

Hence O_1, P_1 and Q_1 are collinear, and hence, by theorem 15.4, K is on Q_1P_1. A similar argument shows that Q_2P_2 and Q_3P_3 also pass through K, which lies on the circle of similitude.

Note that K is the homothetic centre of $\triangle P_1P_2P_3$ and $\triangle Q_1Q_2Q_3$.

Now we deal with the more general case (see figure 15.14).

Triangles $\triangle P_1P_2P_3$ and $\triangle Q_1Q_2Q_3$ are similar by theorem 15.2. Let A_1 denote the intersection of P_2P_3 and Q_2Q_3 and define A_2 and A_3 in the same way. The required centre of similitude is the second intersection of the circumcircles of $\triangle P_1Q_1A_3$ and $\triangle P_2Q_2A_3$ and is labelled Y in figure 15.14.

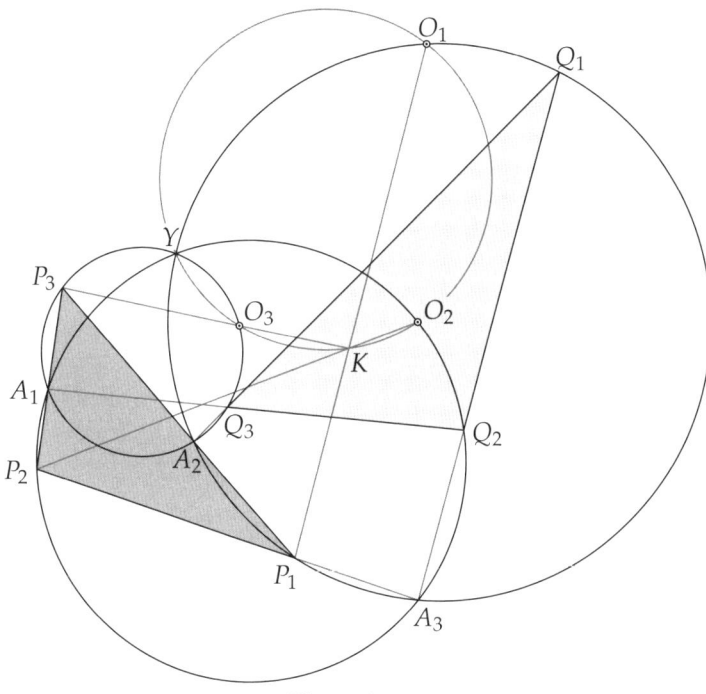

Figure 15.14

Since $\angle P_3P_1P_2 = \angle Q_3Q_1Q_2$, it follows that $A_2P_1A_3Q_1$ is cyclic, and $A_3Q_2A_1P_2$ is cyclic since $\angle P_3P_2P_1 = \angle Q_3Q_2Q_1$.

Now $\angle A_2YA_3 = \angle P_1$ and $\angle A_1YA_3 = 180° - \angle P_2$, so $\angle A_1YA_2 = \angle A_1YA_3 - \angle A_2YA_3 = \angle P_3$. Hence Y also lies on the circumcircle of $\triangle A_1A_2P_3$ (as does Q_3).

It remains to show that Y lies on the circle of similitude.

By theorem 15.1, O_1 lies on the circumcircle of $\triangle A_2A_3P_1$, and similarly O_2 and O_3 lie on the circumcircles of $\triangle A_3A_1P_2$ and $\triangle A_1A_2P_3$. By theorem 15.4, P_1O_1, P_2O_2 and P_3O_3 are concurrent at a point K on the circle of similitude. Hence $\angle KO_2Y = \angle P_2O_2Y = 180° - \angle P_2A_1Y$ and $\angle KO_3Y = 180° - \angle P_3O_3Y = \angle P_3A_1Y$.

But $\angle P_2A_1Y + \angle P_3A_1Y = 180°$, so $\angle KO_2Y + \angle KO_3Y = 180°$, and so K, O_2, O_3 and Y are concyclic, as required. ❑

Examples

We illustrate these results for our examples of triangles of correspondence (see page 206).

(c) If we use perpendicular bisectors, then theorem 15.4 shows that C_1 lies on the circle of similitude. This is an independent justification that the nine-point circle passes through the midpoints of the sides.

(d) Using $\triangle PQR$ and theorem 15.4, we see that DP, EQ and FR are concurrent on the nine-point circle. By theorem 15.6, the point of concurrency is their homothetic centre. Since it is on the altitude AD, it is the Euler point U.

15.5 The invariable points

We now examine what happens when a triangle of correspondence is degenerate.

Theorem 15.7 *If three lines forming a triangle of correspondence are concurrent, then they meet on the circle of similitude and they pass through three fixed points on the circle of similitude.*

PROOF Let the three lines ℓ_1, ℓ_2 and ℓ_3 meet at a point W. Choose any non-degenerate triangle of correspondence $\triangle P_1P_2P_3$ whose sides are parallel to these three lines (so P_2P_3 is parallel to ℓ_1, and so on). As a consequence, $\pi(O_3, P_2P_3)$ and $\pi(O_3, P_3P_1)$ are proportional to $\pi(O_3, \ell_1)$ and $\pi(O_3, \ell_2)$. Hence O_3P_3 passes through W, as do O_1P_1 and O_2P_2. Now we apply theorem 15.4 to $\triangle P_1P_2P_3$ and the degenerate triangle consisting of point W alone; this shows that W is on the circle of similitude.

Let J_1, J_2 and J_3 be the second intersections of ℓ_1, ℓ_2 and ℓ_3 with the circle of similitude (see figure 15.15). By theorem 15.3, the angles $\angle O_1P_1P_2$, $\angle O_1P_2P_3$ and $O_1P_3P_1$ are fixed, but these are equal to $\angle O_1WJ_3$, O_1WJ_1 and O_1WJ_2. Hence the points J_1, J_2 and J_3 are also fixed. ◻

The fixed points J_1, J_2 and J_3 given by theorem 15.7 are known as the *invariable points* of the system of similar figures, and $\triangle J_1J_2J_3$ is the *invariable triangle*.

Corollary 15.8 *The invariable points are corresponding under the three spiral similarities.*

Chapter 15: Spiral similarities 213

Figure 15.15

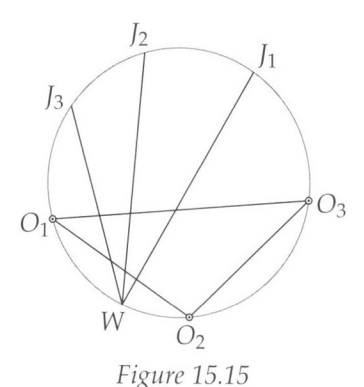

PROOF From the proof of theorem 15.7, $\angle J_2 O_1 J_3 = \angle J_2 W J_3 = \theta_1$ and

$$\frac{\pi(O_1, J_2 W)}{\pi(O_1, J_3 W)} = \frac{\pi(O_1 \ell_2)}{\pi(O_1, \ell_3)} = k_1.$$

Hence the spiral similarity with centre O_1 maps J_2 to J_3. The same is true for the other two centres. ❑

Corollary 15.9 *The invariable triangle is inversely similar to any triangle of correspondence.*

PROOF From the proof of theorem 15.7, $\angle J_1 J_2 J_3 = \angle J_1 W J_3 = \angle P_3 P_2 P_1$ since $W J_1$ is parallel to $P_2 P_3$ and $W J_3$ is parallel to $P_1 P_2$. The same argument works for the other angles. ❑

Theorem 15.10 *The invariable triangle and the triangle of similitude are in perspective.*

PROOF Let p_{12} and p_{13} be the perpendicular distances from O_1 to $J_1 J_2$ and $J_1 J_3$ (see figure 15.16).
Then
$$\frac{p_{12}}{p_{13}} = \frac{O_1 J_2}{O_1 J_3} = k_1,$$

with similar results for O_2 and O_3. Hence the lines $O_1 J_1$, $O_2 J_2$ and $O_3 J_3$ are concurrent and the triangles are in perspective. ❑

There is one further useful result.

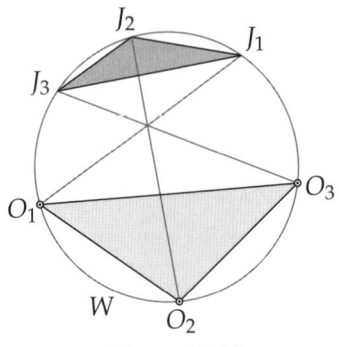

Figure 15.16

Theorem 15.11 *If X_1, X_2 and X_3 are three corresponding points of $\mathcal{F}_1$, $\mathcal{F}_2$ and $\mathcal{F}_3$, then triangle $\triangle X_1 X_2 X_3$ is in perspective with the invariable triangle and the perspector lies on the circle of similitude.*

PROOF By corollary 15.8, $J_1 X_1$, $J_2 X_2$ and $J_3 X_3$ are corresponding lines. Let $J_1 X_1$ and $J_2 X_2$ meet at W_3. The angle between these corresponding lines is θ_3, so W_3 lies on the circle of similitude. Similarly $J_1 X_1$ meets $J_3 X_3$ at W_2 and $J_2 X_2$ meets $J_3 X_3$ at W_1, and both of these points are also on the circle of similitude. Hence the three points W_1, W_2 and W_3 are identical. □

Examples

We illustrate these results using the orthic configuration.

(e) Consider all nine perpendicular bisectors, as defined in example (c) on page 207, which are concurrent in threes at A_1, B_1 and C_1.

By theorem 15.7, these nine lines pass through three invariant points on the circle of similitude. To identify these, consider the lines relating to $\triangle AFE$, which meet in its circumcentre. As $AFHE$ is cyclic, this is the midpoint of AH, the Euler point U (see figure 15.17).

Hence the invariant points of these three similar triangles are the Euler points U, V, W, and the invariant triangle is the Euler triangle $\triangle UVW$. By theorem 15.10, this is in perspective with the triangle of similitude $\triangle DEF$. This is clearly so and the perspector is H.

(f) The Euler lines of $\triangle AFE$, $\triangle DFB$ and $\triangle DCE$ are corresponding lines and therefore form a triangle of correspondence. They pass through

Chapter 15: Spiral similarities

Figure 15.17

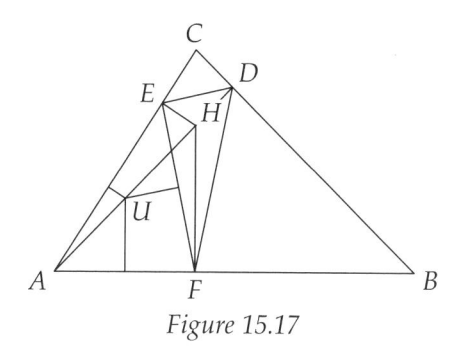

the circumcentres of the three triangles, which are the Euler points, and also the three orthocentres H_a, H_b and H_c (see figure 15.18). Hence, by theorem 15.11, they are concurrent on the nine-point circle.

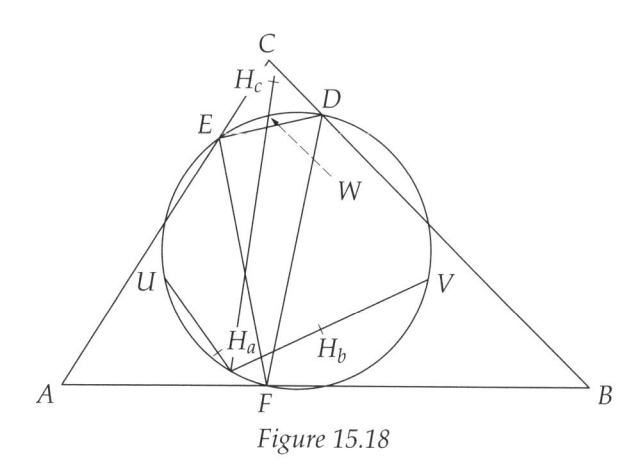

Figure 15.18

Exercise 15b

1. Let $\triangle DYX$ be the triangle of correspondence defined by corresponding cevians through A in $\triangle AFE$ and D in $\triangle DEC$. Prove that the perspector of $\triangle DYX$ and $\triangle DEF$ is the circumcentre of $\triangle DXY$.

2. Let $\triangle DYX$ be the triangle of correspondence defined by altitudes, as in example (b) on page 206. Prove that the perspector of $\triangle DYX$ and $\triangle DEF$ is the midpoint of BC.

Chapter 16

Brocard geometry

The ideas in this chapter are associated with the work of the French army officer, Henri Brocard, who in 1875 drew attention to the two points which bear his name. These were known some sixty years earlier, but their original discovery had been forgotten.

In fact, the configuration has already been encountered in exercise 13a on page 172, which explores conditions for a triangle to be congruent to its circumcevian triangle. Later on, we see that it is also possible to approach this material by using spiral similarities.

16.1 The Brocard points

The basic result of Brocard geometry can be viewed as a limiting case of theorem 4.8 on page 48, which concerns Miquel circles. Suppose we take P_1, P_2 and P_3 as B, C and A. Then the three circles which result are the 'circumcircles' of $\triangle AAC$, $\triangle BBA$ and $\triangle CCB$. Clearly this makes sense only if we interpret the circles as being tangential to the sides at the vertices. This is made precise in the following theorem.

Theorem 16.1 *Let S_A be the circle which passes through C and is tangent to AB at A, S_B the circle through A tangent to BC at B and S_C the circle through B tangent to CA at C. Then the three circles have a point Ω_1 in common, which has the property that $\angle \Omega_1 AB = \angle \Omega_1 CA = \angle \Omega_1 BC$.*

PROOF Suppose that S_A and S_B intersect at Ω_1 (see figure 16.1).

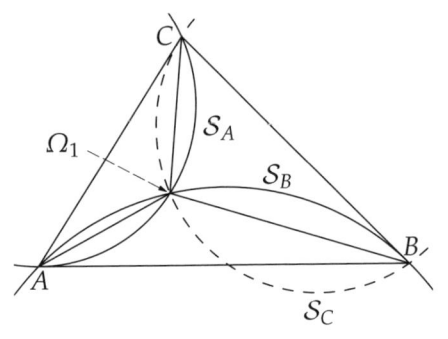

Figure 16.1

Then, by the alternate segment theorem, $\angle \Omega_1 AB = \angle \Omega_1 CA$ and $\angle \Omega_1 BC = \angle \Omega_1 AB$. It follows that $\angle \Omega_1 CA = \angle \Omega_1 BC$ and so Ω_1 lies on $\mathcal{S}_C$. □

Corollary 16.2 *An analogous result to theorem 16.1 holds if we define $\mathcal{S}_A^*$ to be the circle which passes through B and is tangent to CA at A, $\mathcal{S}_B^*$ the circle through C and tangent to AB at B, and $\mathcal{S}_C^*$ the circle through A tangent to BC at C. In this case the point of intersection is denoted by Ω_2, and we have $\angle CA\Omega_2 = \angle AB\Omega_2 = \angle BC\Omega_2$ (see figure 16.2).*

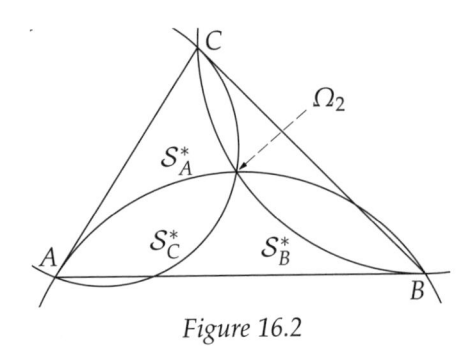

Figure 16.2

In terms of the treatment in exercise 13a, Ω_1 is the point in $\triangle ABC$ whose circumcevian triangle is congruent to $\triangle BCA$ and Ω_2 is the point whose circumcevian triangle is congruent to $\triangle CAB$.

The points Ω_1 and Ω_2 are known as the *first and second Brocard points* of the triangle, and the rays $A\Omega_1$, $B\Omega_1$, $C\Omega_1$ and $A\Omega_2$, $B\Omega_2$, $C\Omega_2$ are the

Chapter 16: Brocard geometry

first and second Brocard rays. By the manner in which they are constructed, these are clearly the only points which have the equal angle property. Note that the equal angles for the first Brocard point are adjacent to AB, BC and CA, whereas those for the second point are adjacent to AC, CB and BA, so we can remember the distinction as being between 'anticlockwise' and 'clockwise' angles.

For a particular triangle $\triangle ABC$, we shall denote by ω_1 and ω_2 the equal angles which are guaranteed by theorem 16.1 and corollary 16.2.

Theorem 16.3 *The two Brocard points are isogonal conjugates and* $\omega_1 = \omega_2$.

PROOF Consider the isogonal conjugate of Ω_1. This has the equal angle property of the corollary, and hence, by the uniqueness of the Brocard points, it is Ω_2. The equality of the angles ω_1 and ω_2 follows immediately. ❑

The common angle ω is known as the *Brocard angle* of $\triangle ABC$.

Theorem 16.4 $\cot \omega = \cot A + \cot B + \cot C$.

PROOF Let $B\Omega_1$ meet $\mathcal{S}_A$ again at X and define Y and Z to be the feet of the perpendiculars from A and X to BC (see figure 16.3).

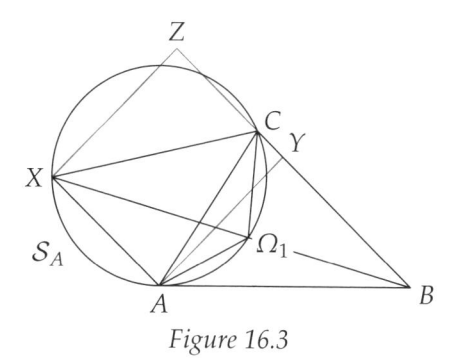

Figure 16.3

Then $\angle XBC = \angle \Omega_1 BC = \angle \Omega_1 CA = \angle \Omega_1 XA$. Hence AX is parallel to BC. Therefore $\angle A = \angle CAB = \angle CXA = \angle XCZ$.
Hence

$$\cot \omega = \cot \angle XBC = \frac{BZ}{XZ} = \frac{BY}{XZ} + \frac{YC}{XZ} + \frac{CZ}{XZ} = \cot B + \cot C + \cot A.$$

❑

Theorem 16.5 $\cot\omega = \dfrac{a^2+b^2+c^2}{4\Delta}$.

PROOF Set as question 4 of exercise 16a. ❏

Exercise 16a

1. Prove that $\triangle \Omega_1 O \Omega_2$ is isosceles with vertex angle 2ω.

2. Prove that Ω_1 is the Brocard point of its own pedal triangle.

3. If $\triangle ABC$ is right-angled at B, prove that $\omega \leq \tan^{-1}\left(\frac{1}{2}\right)$.

4. Prove theorem 16.5.

5. Prove that $\omega \leq 30°$.

6. Let $A\Omega_1$ meet BC at Ω_A. Prove that
$$\frac{B\Omega_A}{\Omega_A C} = \frac{b^2}{c^2}.$$

7. Prove that the first Brocard ray from A, the symmedian from B and the median from C are concurrent.

8. Prove that the second Brocard ray from A, the median from B and the symmedian from C are concurrent.

16.2 The Brocard triangles and circle

Define P as the point on $B\Omega_1$ which makes $\triangle CPB$ isosceles, and similarly define points Q on $C\Omega_1$ and R on $A\Omega_1$ which make $\triangle AQC$ and $\triangle BRA$ isosceles. These three triangles are similar since they all have base angles ω.

Alternatively, define P, Q, R as follows (see figure 16.4):

- P is the intersection of $B\Omega_1$ and A_1O;
- Q is the intersection of $C\Omega_1$ and B_1O;
- R is the intersection of $A\Omega_1$ and C_1O.

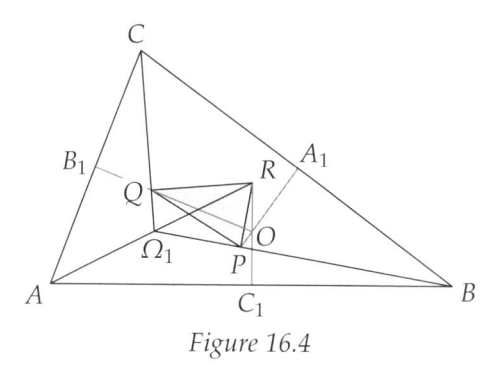

Figure 16.4

Then $\triangle PQR$ is the *first Brocard triangle* of $\triangle ABC$.

It turns out that there is a pleasing symmetry about this configuration.

Theorem 16.6 *The lines AQ, BR and CP concur at the second Brocard point.*

PROOF Let X be the intersection of AQ and CP (see figure 16.5).

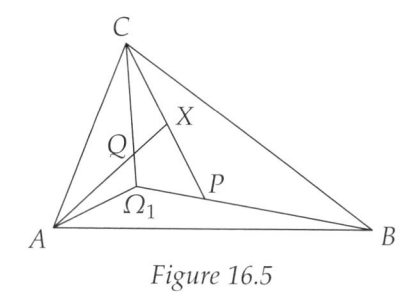

Figure 16.5

Then, since $\triangle AQC$ is isosceles, $\angle CAX = \angle ACQ = \angle AC\Omega_1 = \omega$. Also, since $\triangle BPC$ is isosceles, $\angle BCX = \angle CBP = \angle CB\Omega_1 = \omega$. Hence X is Ω_2, and B, R and Ω_2 are collinear. ☐

We now have a configuration involving both Brocard points and the first Brocard triangle (see figure 16.6):

♦ AR, BP and CQ meet at Ω_1;
♦ AQ, BR and CP meet at Ω_1.

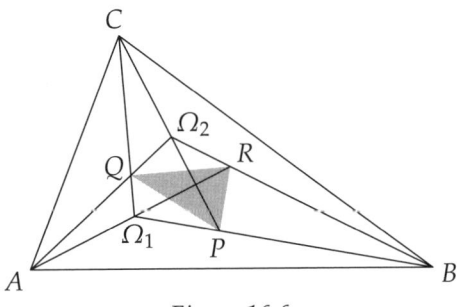

Figure 16.6

Surprisingly, it turns out that the symmedian point K plays a pivotal role in this configuration.

Theorem 16.7 *The line KP is parallel to BC.*

PROOF By corollary 8.3 on page 101, the perpendicular distance of K from BC is

$$\frac{2a\Delta}{a^2 + b^2 + c^2},$$

but, by theorem 16.5, this is $\tfrac{1}{2}a \tan \omega$. But this is the same as PA_1, the perpendicular distance of P from BC. ☐

Theorem 16.8 *The vertices of the first Brocard triangle lie on the circle with diameter OK.*

PROOF By theorem 16.7, KP is parallel to BC, so it is perpendicular to OA_1 (see figure 16.7).

Hence P, which lies on OA_1, lies on the circle with diameter OK, and, by a similar argument, so do Q and R. ☐

Chapter 16: Brocard geometry

Figure 16.7

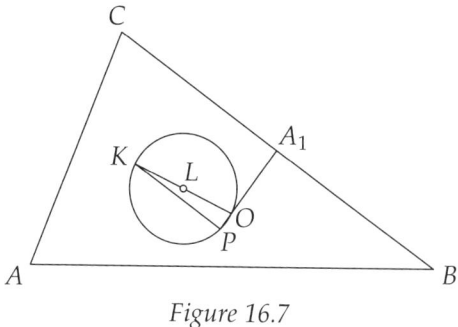

The circle with diameter OK is known as the *Brocard circle*, and the centre L is the *Brocard centre*. The line through O and K is called the *Brocard axis*.

Theorem 16.9 *Both the Brocard points lie on the Brocard circle.*

PROOF Since, by theorem 16.7, KP is parallel to BC, we have $\angle KP\Omega_1 = \angle CB\Omega_1 = \omega$ (see figure 16.8). But also KR is parallel to AB, so $\angle KR\Omega_1 = \angle BA\Omega_1 = \omega$. Hence, by angles in the same segment, quadrilateral $PRK\Omega_1$ is cyclic, and so Ω_1 is on the Brocard circle.

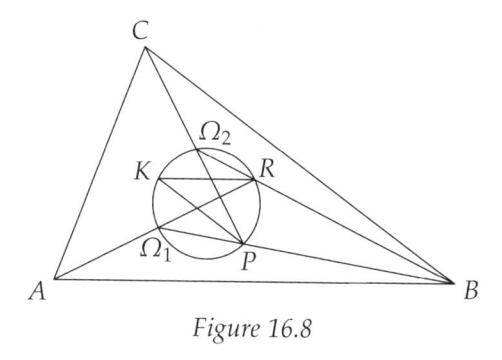

Figure 16.8

By the same argument, we have $\angle KP\Omega_2 = \angle BC\Omega_2$ and $\angle KR\Omega_2 = \angle AB\Omega_2$, and as both these angles are ω, Ω_2 is also on the Brocard circle. ☐

Corollary 16.10 *The first Brocard triangle is similar to* $\triangle ABC$.

PROOF Note that $\angle PRQ = 180° - \angle Q\Omega_1 P = \angle \Omega_1 BC + \angle BC\Omega_1 = \omega + \angle C - \omega = \angle BCA$. This, together with two similar results, is enough. ☐

With the circles which were used to define the two Brocard points, we can define another triangle.

Let P^* be the intersection of circles $\mathcal{S}_A$ and $\mathcal{S}_A^*$; the first of these is through C and tangential to AB at A, and the second is through B and tangential to CA at A. Similarly define Q^* and R^* (see figure 16.9). Then $\triangle P^*Q^*R^*$ is the *second Brocard triangle* of $\triangle ABC$.

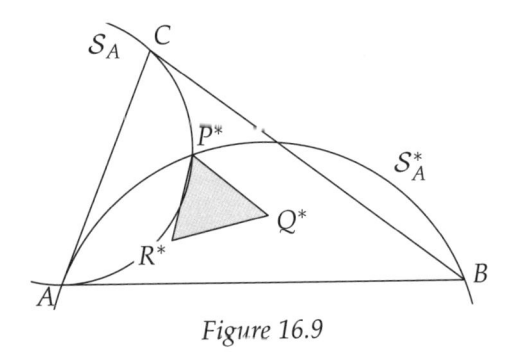

Figure 16.9

We have met P^* already in exercise 13a, as the point whose circumcevian triangle is similar to $\triangle ACB$. We noted there that P^* lies on the circumcircle of $\triangle BOC$, and this result forms part of the next theorem.

Theorem 16.11 *The vertices of the second Brocard triangle lie on the Brocard circle.*

PROOF By the alternate segment theorem, $\angle AP^*B$ and $\angle AP^*C$ are both $180° - \angle A$, so $\angle BP^*C = 2\angle A = \angle BOC$ (see figure 16.10). Hence BP^*OC is cyclic.

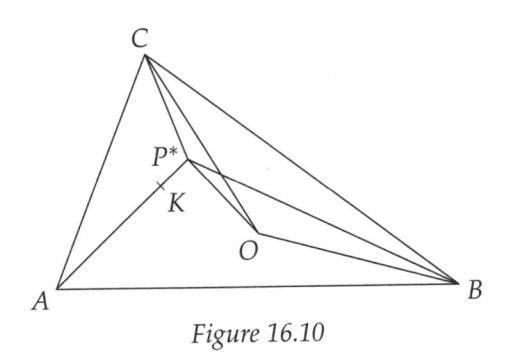

Figure 16.10

Now $\angle OP^*C = 180° - \angle OBC = 90° + \angle A$, and so $\angle AP^*O = 360° - \angle AP^*C - \angle OP^*C = 90°$. Also $\triangle AP^*B$ is similar to $\triangle CP^*A$, and so

$$\frac{\pi(P^*, AB)}{\pi(P^*, CA)} = \frac{c}{b}.$$

It follows by theorem 8.1 on page 100 that P^* is on the symmedian through A. Hence P^* lies on the circle with diameter OK, which is the Brocard circle. The same argument applies to Q^* and R^*. ❏

We now have ten significant points on the Brocard circle (see figure 16.11):

- the Brocard points Ω_1 and Ω_2;
- the symmedian point K;
- the circumcentre O;
- vertices P, Q and R;
- vertices P^*, Q^* and R^*.

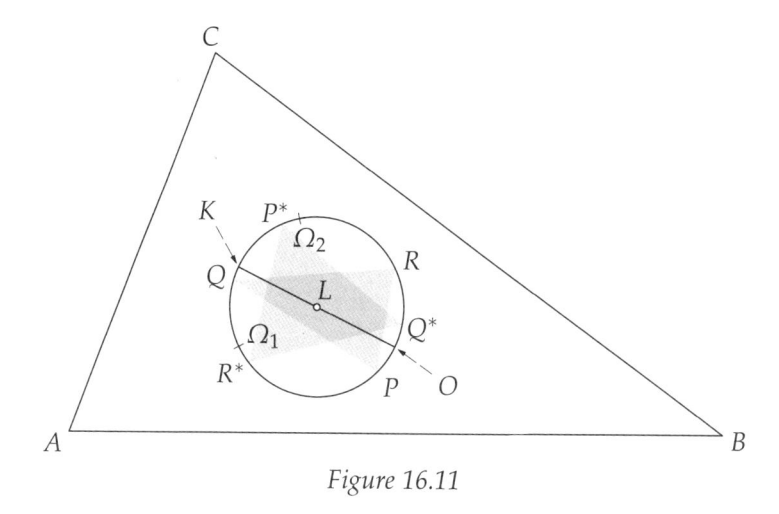

Figure 16.11

It is also worth summarising some definitions of the circles and points; see tables 16.1 and 16.2.

Circle	through point	tangential to	at point
S_A	C	AB	A
S_B	A	BC	B
S_C	B	CA	C
S_A^*	B	CA	A
S_B^*	C	AB	B
S_C^*	A	BC	C

Table 16.1

Point	Circle	Circle	Circle
Ω_1	S_A	S_B	S_C
Ω_2	S_A^*	S_B^*	S_C^*
P^*	S_A	S_A^*	$\triangle BOC$
Q^*	S_B	S_B^*	$\triangle COA$
R^*	S_C	S_C^*	$\triangle AOB$

Table 16.2

Exercise 16b

1. Prove that the sum of the areas of $\triangle CPB$, $\triangle AQC$ and $\triangle BRA$ is the area of $\triangle ABC$.

2. Prove that P^*, Q^* and R^* are the midpoints of the chords of the circumcircle of $\triangle ABC$ which consist of AK, BK and CK produced.

3. Prove that the medial point (the nine-point centre of the medial triangle) is the midpoint of the segment joining the Brocard centre to the symmedian point of the medial triangle. Also prove that the Brocard centre of the medial triangle is the midpoint of the segment joining the nine-point centre to the symmedian point of the medial triangle.

Chapter 16: Brocard geometry

16.3 Brocard triangles and perspective

Theorem 16.12 *The reference triangle $\triangle ABC$ is in perspective with the first Brocard triangle in three different ways, as $\triangle RPQ$, $\triangle QRP$ and $\triangle PQR$.*

PROOF The first fact is a consequence of the definition of the first Brocard triangle and the perspector is Ω_1. The second fact is theorem 16.6 and the perspector is Ω_2. The third perspectivity now follows from corollary 10.4 on page 137, but it is also a consequence of Kiepert's theorem (theorem 11.4 on page 147) with the triangles facing inwards. ❑

The three perspectors can be seen together in figure 16.12.

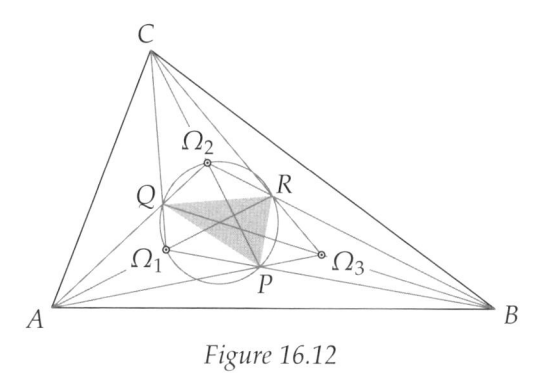

Figure 16.12

For reasons associated with the algebra of areal coordinates, the perspector of $\triangle ABC$ and $\triangle PQR$ is sometimes called the *third Brocard point* Ω_3.

We now prove a technical result on similar triangles, which will turn out to be appropriate for subsequent work.

Theorem 16.13 *If $\triangle ABC$ is a triangle and X, Y and Z are points such that the triangles $\triangle BCX$, $\triangle CAY$ and $\triangle ABZ$ are similar, then $G \triangle ABC = G \triangle XYZ$.*

PROOF Let X' be the reflection of X in A_1 (see figure 16.13). Then $BXCX'$ is a parallelogram and the centroid of $\triangle ABC$ divides AA_1 in the ratio $2:1$, so it is also the centroid of $\triangle AXX'$. Let W be the midpoint of AX'; then G divides XW in the ratio $2:1$.

Consider $\triangle YX'C$. We have, from the similarity of $\triangle AYC$ and $\triangle CXB$,

$$\frac{CY}{X'C} = \frac{CY}{BX} = \frac{CA}{BC}$$

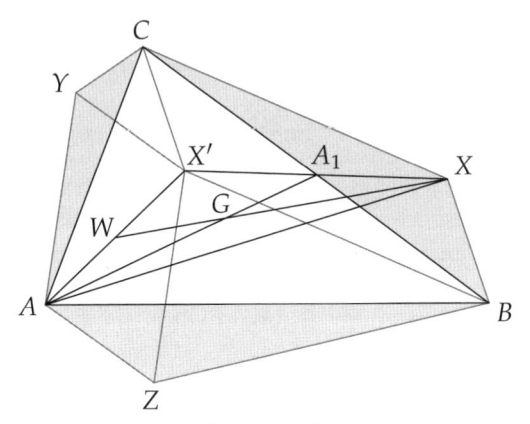

Figure 16.13

and, since $\angle ACY = \angle CBX = BCX'$, we also have $\angle YCX' = \angle ACB$. Hence the triangles $\triangle YX'C$ and $\triangle ABC$ are similar, and, by the same argument, so is $\triangle ZBX'$. Now, from $\triangle AYC$ and $\triangle BZA$,

$$\frac{AY}{ZB} = \frac{AC}{AB},$$

from $\triangle ABC$ and $\triangle YX'C$,

$$\frac{AC}{AB} = \frac{YC}{YX'}$$

and from $\triangle YX'C$ and $\triangle ZBX'$,

$$\frac{YC}{YX'} = \frac{ZX'}{ZB}.$$

We deduce that $AY = ZX'$. By a similar argument $AZ = YX'$, and so $AZX'Y$ is a parallelogram and W is the midpoint of ZY. Thus G is the centroid of $\triangle XYZ$. □

Corollary 16.14 *The centroid of the first Brocard triangle is G, the centroid of $\triangle ABC$.*

PROOF This follows by taking similar isosceles triangles facing inwards. □

Theorem 16.13 can now be used to prove some interesting results.

Theorem 16.15 *The first and second Brocard triangles are in perspective at G.*

PROOF Since $\triangle PQR$ and $\triangle ABC$ are similar and have the same centroid, $\angle RPG = \angle CAG$ (see figure 16.14).

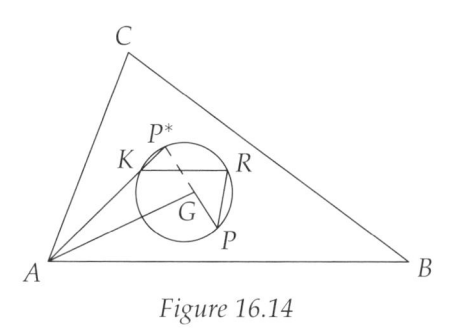

Figure 16.14

Since G and K are isogonal conjugates, $\angle CAG = \angle BAK$. But A, K and P^* are collinear, so $\angle BAK = \angle BAP^*$. Now, by theorem 16.8, RK and AB are parallel, so $\angle BAP^* = \angle RKP^*$. Then, by angles in the same segment, $\angle RKP^* = \angle RPP^*$.

Putting all this together, we see that $\angle RPG = \angle RPP^*$ and so G lies on PP^*. Similarly G lies on QQ^* and RR^* and the triangles are in perspective. ❏

Theorem 16.16 *Let H' be the orthocentre of the first Brocard triangle. Then the midpoint of KH' is the nine-point centre of $\triangle ABC$.*

PROOF By theorem 16.11, the circumcentre of the first Brocard triangle is L, the midpoint of OK (see figure 16.15). By corollary 16.14, the centroid of this triangle is G. Hence its Euler line is LGH', with $GH' = 2LG$. But $GH = 2OG$, so triangles $\triangle OLG$ and $\triangle HH'G$ are similar. Hence $H'H = 2LO = KO$ and HH' and KO are parallel. We conclude that $OKHH'$ is a parallelogram.

It follows that the diagonals of $OKHH'$ bisect one another, but the midpoint of OH is N, so the result follows. ❏

Figure 16.15

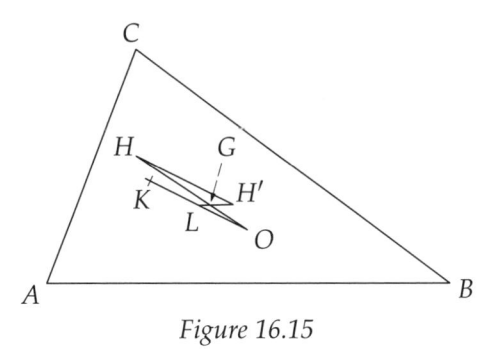

16.4 The Brocard configuration and spiral similarities

We now use the ideas of chapter 15 to obtain both some results we have already proved and some new ones on the Brocard configuration.

We begin with the configuration of theorem 16.13, in which similar triangles are erected externally on the sides of $\triangle ABC$ (see figure 16.16). Let the base angles be θ and ϕ, so that

$$\angle YAC = \angle ZBA = \angle XCB = \theta$$
$$\text{and} \quad \angle ACY = \angle BAZ = \angle CBX = \phi.$$

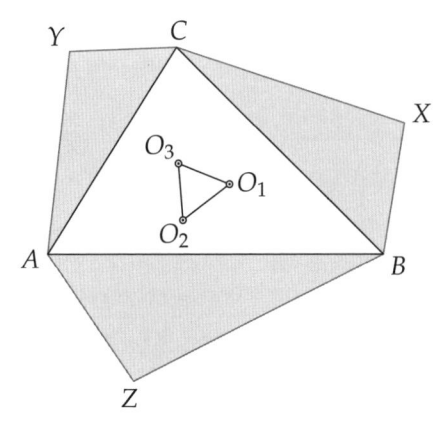

Figure 16.16

Chapter 16: Brocard geometry 231

In the terminology of section 15.3 on page 204, the triangles $\mathcal{F}_1$, $\mathcal{F}_2$ and $\mathcal{F}_3$ are $\triangle ACY$, $\triangle BAZ$ and $\triangle CBX$, and the three spiral similarities are as given in table 16.3.

Centre	Angle	Scale factor	From	To
O_3	$180° - \angle A$	$\dfrac{AB}{CA}$	$\triangle CAY$	$\triangle ABZ$
O_1	$180° - \angle B$	$\dfrac{BC}{AB}$	$\triangle ABZ$	$\triangle BCX$
O_2	$180° - \angle C$	$\dfrac{CA}{BC}$	$\triangle BCX$	$\triangle CAY$

Table 16.3

We begin by identifying the centres of similitude.

Theorem 16.17 *The triangle of similitude $\triangle O_1 O_2 O_3$ is the second Brocard triangle.*

PROOF Let P be the intersection of AY and ZB (see figure 16.17). Then, by theorem 15.1 on page 201, the intersection of the circumcircles of $\triangle PYZ$ and $\triangle PAB$ is O_3.

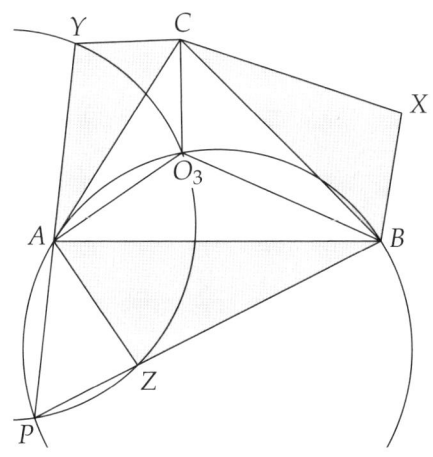

Figure 16.17

Now $\angle YAB = \theta + \angle A$ and $\angle APB = \theta$, so $\angle APB = \angle A$. Hence, by opposite angles of a cyclic quadrilateral, $\angle AO_3 B = 180° - \angle A$. Therefore the circle $\mathcal{S}_A^*$ passes through O_3. By exactly the same logic, but involving ϕ instead of θ, so does $\mathcal{S}_A$. Hence O_3 is the vertex P^* of the second Brocard triangle. ☐

Corollary 16.18 *The circle of similitude of $\mathcal{F}_1$, $\mathcal{F}_2$ and $\mathcal{F}_3$ is the Brocard circle.*

Theorem 16.19 *The invariable triangle $\triangle J_1 J_2 J_3$ is the first Brocard triangle.*

PROOF The perpendicular bisectors of the sides CA, AB and BC, which are corresponding lines, are concurrent at the circumcentre O (see figure 16.18).

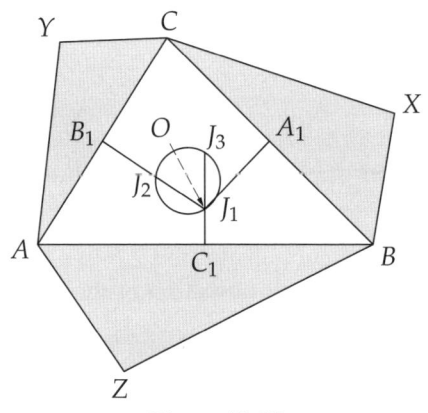

Figure 16.18

It follows from theorem 15.7 on page 212 that O lies on the Brocard circle and that the lines $B_1 O$, $C_1 O$ and $A_1 O$ cut the Brocard circle at the invariable points J_1, J_2 and J_3. But by theorem 16.8, these are the vertices of the first Brocard triangle. ☐

By theorem 15.1 on page 201, the first and second Brocard triangles are in perspective.

The bases CA, AB and BC of the similar triangles make a triangle of correspondence which is $\triangle BCA$ (see figure 16.19).

By theorem 15.4 on page 208, $\triangle ABC$ and the second Brocard triangle are in perspective, with centre on the circle of similitude. The point of concurrence is the symmedian point K.

Note that A, B and C are corresponding points of $\mathcal{F}_1$, $\mathcal{F}_2$ and $\mathcal{F}_3$. Hence, by theorem 15.10 on page 213, $\triangle ABC$ is in perspective with the

Chapter 16: Brocard geometry 233

Figure 16.19

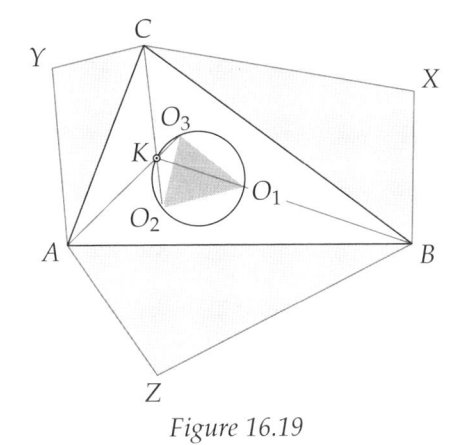

first Brocard triangle and the perspector is on the Brocard circle. We have already identified this as the second Brocard point Ω_2 (see figure 16.20).

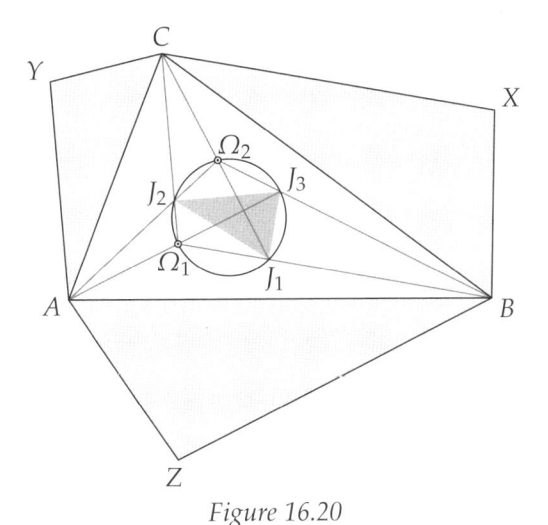

Figure 16.20

Moreover, we could also have started with corresponding points C, A and B, and the same argument shows that $\triangle CAB$ is in perspective with the first Brocard triangle, the centre being the first Brocard point Ω_1.

All of these results were familiar from earlier in the chapter, but in exercise 16c new results are obtained.

16.5 The Steiner and Tarry points

We now use the first Brocard triangle to create two new concurrencies.

Theorem 16.20 *The lines through A, B and C parallel to QR, RP and PQ are concurrent in a point on the circumcircle of $\triangle ABC$.*

PROOF By corollary 16.10 the first Brocard triangle is similar to $\triangle ABC$, in the order shown. Now let the lines through A and B parallel to QR and RP meet at a point Σ (see figure 16.21).

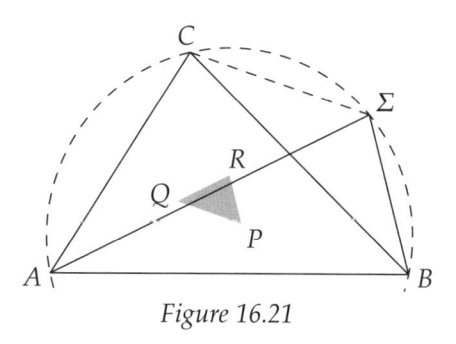

Figure 16.21

Then $\angle B\Sigma A = \angle QRP = \angle BCA$, so Σ lies on the circumcircle. Also $\angle C\Sigma A = \angle CBA = \angle RQP$ so $C\Sigma$ is parallel to PQ. ☐

The point Σ is known as the *Steiner point* of $\triangle ABC$.

Corollary 16.21 *The lines through A, B and C perpendicular to QR, RP and PQ are concurrent in a point on the circumcircle of $\triangle ABC$.*

PROOF This is immediate by considering the point on the circumcircle which is diametrically opposite to Σ. ☐

The point given by corollary 16.21 is called the *Tarry point* and will be denoted by T.

Theorem 16.22 *Let $\triangle A'B'C'$ be the first Brocard triangle of the first Brocard triangle $\triangle PQR$. Then $\triangle A'B'C'$ and $\triangle ABC$ are homothetic, with centre G.*

PROOF By corollary 16.14, applied twice, G is the centroid of $\triangle A'B'C'$ (see figure 16.22).

Chapter 16: Brocard geometry

Figure 16.22

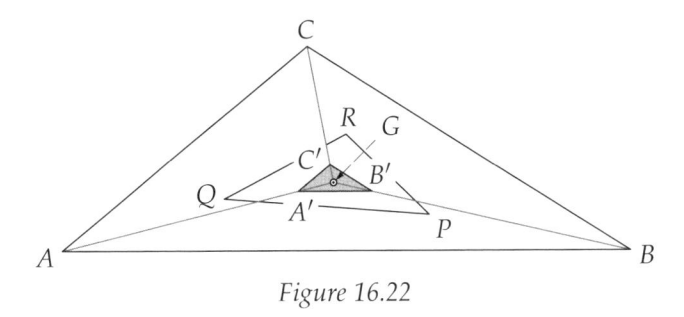

Since we have $\angle RPQ = \angle CAB$ and $\angle C'A'B' = \angle RPQ$, it follows that $\angle C'A'B' = \angle CAB$.

Now, since the process of forming $\triangle A'B'C'$ from $\triangle PQR$ is the same as that of forming $\triangle PQR$ from $\triangle ABC$, the angle between $A'B'$ and QR is the same as that between PQ and BC. This implies that $A'B'$ and AB are parallel and so the triangles are homothetic.

This homothecy takes $G \triangle A'B'C'$ to $G \triangle ABC$, but, since these points are identical, this is the homothetic centre. ❑

Corollary 16.23 *The Steiner point of $\triangle PQR$ is the symmedian point of $\triangle ABC$ and the Tarry point of $\triangle PQR$ is the circumcentre of $\triangle ABC$.*

PROOF The point $\Sigma \triangle PQR$ lies on the ray through P parallel to $A'C'$ and hence parallel to CA, which passes through K by theorem 16.7. Since the same is true for the other two rays, the result for the Steiner point follows.

Now $T \triangle PQR$ is diametrically opposite to $\Sigma \triangle PQR$ on the circumcircle of $\triangle PQR$, which is the first Brocard circle of $\triangle ABC$, and hence $T \triangle PQR$ is O. ❑

Exercise 16c

1. Let A', B' and C' be points on BC, CA and AB such that $BA' : A'C = CB' : B'A = AC' : C'B$. Prove that $\triangle A'B'C'$ is in perspective with the first Brocard triangle, with perspector on the Brocard circle.

2. Let the sides AB, BC and CA of $\triangle ABC$ be rotated about A, B and C through a fixed angle α to form a triangle $\triangle D_1D_2D_3$. Prove that

$\triangle D_1 D_2 D_3$ is in perspective with the second Brocard triangle, with perspector on the Brocard circle.

3. Prove that the triangle of orthocentres of $\triangle ACY$, $\triangle BAZ$ and $\triangle CBX$, the triangle of centroids of $\triangle ACY$, $\triangle BAZ$ and $\triangle CBX$ and the triangle of circumcentres of $\triangle ACY$, $\triangle BAZ$ and $\triangle CBX$ have a common perspector.

4. Let $\triangle P_1 Q_1 R_1$ be the medial triangle of the first Brocard triangle. Prove that $P_1 N$, $Q_1 N$ and $R_1 N$ are perpendicular to BC, CA and AB.

5. Prove that the Simson line of the Steiner point Σ is parallel to the Brocard diameter OK, and that of the Tarry point T is perpendicular to it.

Chapter 17

Lemoine, Tucker and Taylor circles

We now consider the Brocard configuration in the context of some more general results associated with the French geometer Emile Lemoine and an extension of that work due to the Englishmen Robert Tucker and Henry Taylor.

17.1 Lemoine circles

We begin by showing what happens when parallels and antiparallels to the sides are drawn through the symmedian point K of a triangle.

Theorem 17.1 *The parallels to the sides of $\triangle ABC$ through K cut the sides in six concyclic points.*

PROOF Let E_2D_1, F_2E_1 and D_2F_1 be lines through K parallel to AB, BC and CA (see figure 17.1).

Note first that, since AF_1KE_2 is a parallelogram, the diagonals AK and F_1E_2 bisect one another. But AK is a symmedian, so, by theorem 8.7 on page 106, F_1E_2 is antiparallel to BC and also F_2E_1. Hence the quadrilateral $E_1E_2F_1F_2$ is cyclic; by the same argument, so are $F_1F_2D_1D_2$ and $D_1D_2E_1E_2$.

Now we have $\angle D_1F_2B = \angle D_1CE_2 = \angle E_2F_1A = \angle F_1E_2D_1$, and so quadrilateral $F_2D_1E_2F_1$ is also cyclic. This, together with two similar results, is now enough to show that all three cyclic quadrilaterals have

Figure 17.1

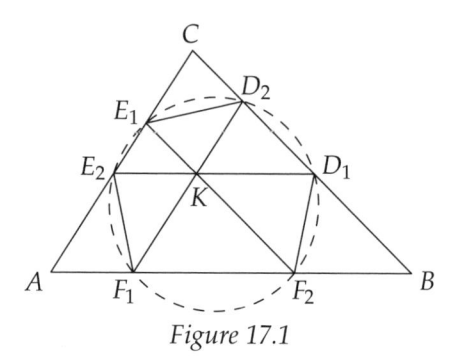

the same circumcircle, so the six points D_1, D_2, E_1, E_2, F_1 and F_2 are concyclic. ☐

It is tempting to try to curtail this proof by assuming that, since we have three cyclic quadrilaterals $E_1E_2F_1F_2$, $F_1F_2D_1D_2$ and $D_1D_2E_1E_2$, the six points are concyclic. But there is no reason why the three circles might be the same one; we need a 'bridging' quadrilateral such as $F_2D_1E_2F_1$ to enable us to make the final step in the proof. This situation will be addressed in general terms in chapter 18.

The circle containing the six points given by theorem 17.1 is known as the *first Lemoine circle* of $\triangle ABC$.

Theorem 17.2 *The centre of the first Lemoine circle is the Brocard centre.*

PROOF Let L be the midpoint of OK and J be the midpoint of F_1E_2 (see figure 17.2).

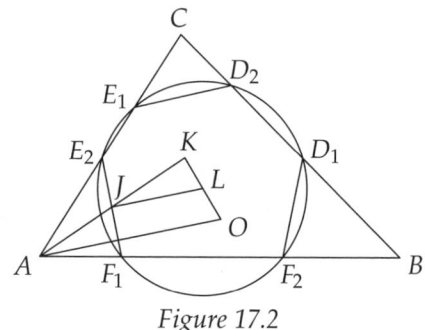

Figure 17.2

Chapter 17: Lemoine, Tucker and Taylor circles 239

Then JL is parallel to OA. But, by theorem 8.5 on page 105, this is perpendicular to F_1E_2 (which is antiparallel to BC). It follows that L lies on the perpendicular bisectors of three chords of the first Lemoine circle, so it is its centre. ❏

Theorem 17.2 shows that the Brocard circle and first Lemoine circle are concentric.

Corollary 17.3 *The third Brocard point is the isotomic conjugate of K.*

PROOF By theorem 16.7 on page 222, KP is parallel to BC. Hence this segment is part of the chord F_2E_1 of the first Lemoine circle (see figure 17.3).

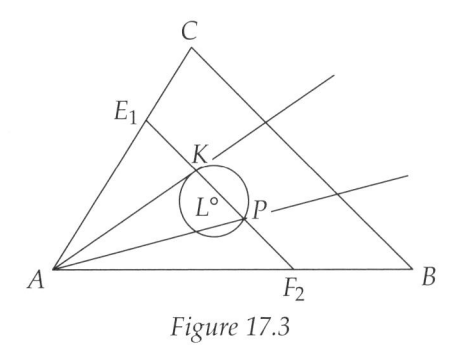

Figure 17.3

But, by theorem 17.2, the Brocard and first Lemoine circles are concentric, so $F_2K = PE_1$.

Hence AK and AP are isotomic conjugate rays, and the same is true for BK and BQ and for CK and CR. But, by theorem 16.12 on page 227, Ω_3 is the perspector of $\triangle ABC$ and $\triangle PQR$, so it is the isotomic conjugate of K. ❏

Theorem 17.4 *The antiparallels to the sides of $\triangle ABC$ through K cut the sides in six concyclic points.*

PROOF Denote the antiparallels by P_1Q_2, Q_1R_2 and R_1P_2 (see figure 17.4).

They they pass through K so by theorem 8.7 on page 106 they are bisected, and $P_1K = KQ_2$, $Q_1K = KR_2$ and $R_1K = KP_2$. Also, since BP_1Q_2A is cyclic, $\angle KP_1P_2 = \angle A$, and, for the same reason, $\angle KP_2P_1 = \angle A$, so $KP_1 = KP_2$. Similarly $KQ_1 = KQ_2$ and $KR_1 = KR_2$, so the six segments are equal in length, and the result follows. ❏

Figure 17.4

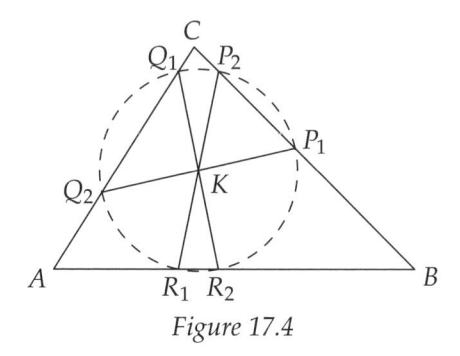

The circle given by theorem 17.4, which has centre K, is known as the *second Lemoine circle* of $\triangle ABC$. Note that $P_1P_2Q_2R_1$ is a rectangle with centre K. We can use this circle to provide an alternative proof of the result of question 1 of exercise 8c on page 110.

Theorem 17.5 *The symmedian point lies on the line joining the midpoint of a side to the midpoint of the corresponding altitude.*

PROOF Let X, M and Y be the midpoints of R_1P_1, AD and Q_2P_2. Then K is also the midpoint of the midline XY (see figure 17.5).

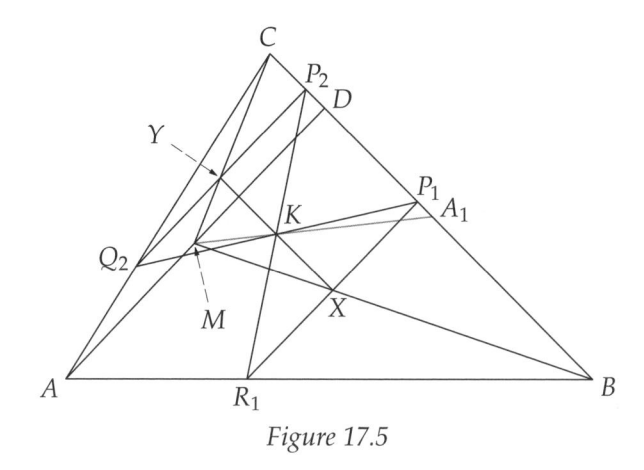

Figure 17.5

Hence M is the centre of an enlargement taking XY to BC, and therefore it maps the midpoint of one segment to the midpoint of the other. This is the required result. ❑

Chapter 17: Lemoine, Tucker and Taylor circles　　　　　　　　241

Exercise 17a

1. Prove that D_2E_1, E_2F_1 and F_2D_1 are equal chords of the first Lemoine circle.

2. Prove that, in the diagram for the first Lemoine circle (figure 17.1), $\triangle F_1D_1E_1$ and $\triangle E_2F_2D_2$ are directly similar to $\triangle ABC$.

3. Prove that, in the diagram for the second Lemoine circle (figure 17.4), R_1Q_2 is equal and parallel to P_1P_2.

4. Prove that the segments P_1P_2, Q_1Q_2 and R_1R_2, cut off on the sides of $\triangle ABC$ by the second Lemoine circle, are proportional to $\cos A$, $\cos B$ and $\cos C$. (For this reason, it is sometimes known as the *cosine circle*.)

5. Prove that, in the diagram for the second Lemoine circle (figure 17.4), $\triangle Q_1R_1P_1$ and $\triangle R_2P_2Q_2$ are directly similar to $\triangle ABC$.

6. In the configuration of theorem 9.15 on page 123, let $\triangle XYZ$ be the triangle formed by the lines Z_BY_C, Y_AX_B and X_CZ_A, with X, Y and Z opposite to A, B and C. Prove that the Gergonne point and Adams circle of $\triangle ABC$ are the symmedian point and first Lemoine circle of $\triangle XYZ$.

17.2 Miquel points

Theorem 17.6 *If $\triangle P_1P_2P_3$ is a Miquel triangle of the first Brocard point Ω_1 of $\triangle ABC$, then $\triangle P_3P_1P_2$ is similar to $\triangle ABC$ and Ω_1 is its first Brocard point.*

PROOF Recall that we can produce a Miquel triangle by choosing any point P_1 on BC and taking P_2 and P_3 to be the intersections of CA and AB with the circumcircles of $\triangle CP_1\Omega_1$ and $\triangle P_1B\Omega_1$ (see figure 17.6).
   We now have $\angle \Omega_1P_3P_1 = \angle \Omega_1BP_1 = \angle \Omega_1AP_3$ (since Ω_1 is the Brocard point) and also $\angle P_2P_3\Omega_1 = \angle P_2A\Omega_1$.

Figure 17.6

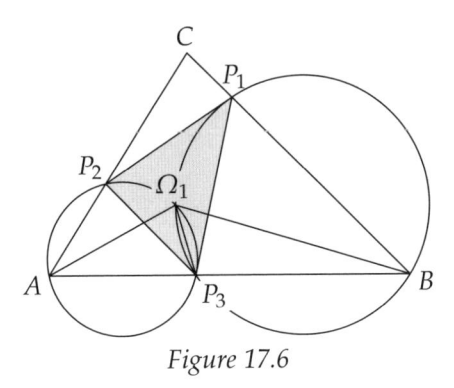

Hence $\angle P_2P_3P_1 = \angle A$, with analogous results for the other angles, giving the similarity. We have also shown relevant angles in $\triangle P_3P_1P_2$ are the equal Brocard angles. ❏

The corresponding result holds, with an identical proof, for the second Brocard point Ω_2, but this time it is $\triangle P_2P_3P_1$ which is similar to $\triangle ABC$ (see figure 17.7).

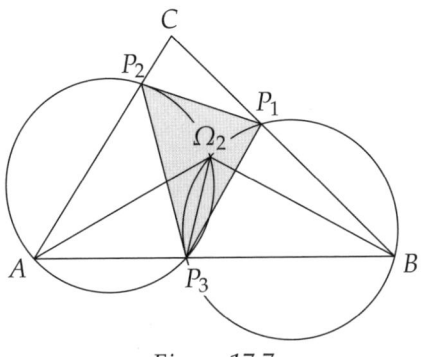

Figure 17.7

Theorem 17.7 *If a triangle $\triangle P_3P_1P_2$, with vertices on the sides AB, BC and CA of $\triangle ABC$, is similar to $\triangle ABC$, the Miquel point of $\triangle P_3P_1P_2$ is the first Brocard point of both triangles.*

PROOF Let X be the Miquel point (see figure 17.8).
We have $\angle P_2P_3P_1 = \angle P_2P_3X + \angle XP_3P_1 = \angle P_2AX + \angle XBP_1 = \angle A$, so $\angle XAP_3 = \angle XBP_1$. Since these are also equal to $\angle XCP_2$, X is the Brocard

Chapter 17: Lemoine, Tucker and Taylor circles   243

Figure 17.8

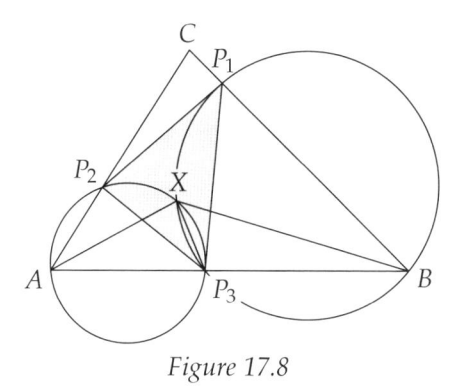

point Ω_1, and it is easy to check that it is also the first Brocard point of $\triangle P_1 P_2 P_3$. □

Naturally the analogous result is true for a triangle similar in the order $\triangle P_2 P_3 P_1$ and the second Brocard point.

We can now apply these results to triangles which arise in connection with the first and second Lemoine circles.

Corollary 17.8 *The first Brocard point of $\triangle F_1 D_1 E_1$ is the first Brocard point of $\triangle ABC$ and the second Brocard point of $\triangle E_2 F_2 D_2$ is the second Brocard point of $\triangle ABC$.*

Corollary 17.9 *The first Brocard point of $\triangle R_2 P_2 Q_2$ is the first Brocard point of $\triangle ABC$ and the second Brocard point of $\triangle Q_1 R_1 P_1$ is the second Brocard point of $\triangle ABC$.*

However, we can also identify the other Brocard points of the triangles associated with the first Lemoine triangle.

Theorem 17.10 *The symmedian point of $\triangle ABC$ is the first Brocard point of $\triangle E_2 F_2 D_2$ and the second Brocard point of $\triangle F_1 D_1 E_1$.*

PROOF (See figure 17.9.)
We have $\angle KE_2 F_2 = \angle E_2 F_2 F_1 = \angle KD_2 E_2 = \angle E_1 E_2 D_2 = \angle KF_2 D_2$ and a similar argument establishes the other result. □

Figure 17.9

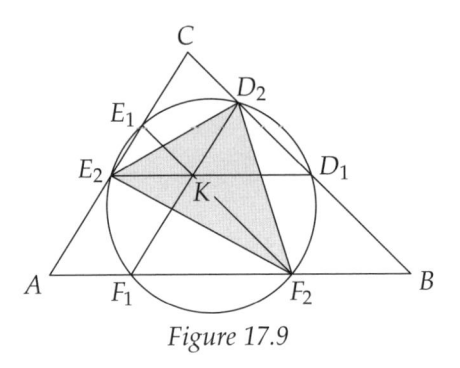

17.3 Tucker circles

In both Lemoine circles, the six concyclic points form a hexagon which consists of alternate parallels and antiparallels to the sides of $\triangle ABC$. This idea can be generalised. There are several different ways to begin, but we will make use of a homothecy centred on the symmedian point. With centre K, construct $\triangle A'B'C'$ to be homothetic to $\triangle ABC$ with scale factor k. Let $A'B'$ and $A'C'$ meet BC in D_1 and D_2, and similarly define points E_1, E_2, F_1 and F_2, as in figure 17.10.

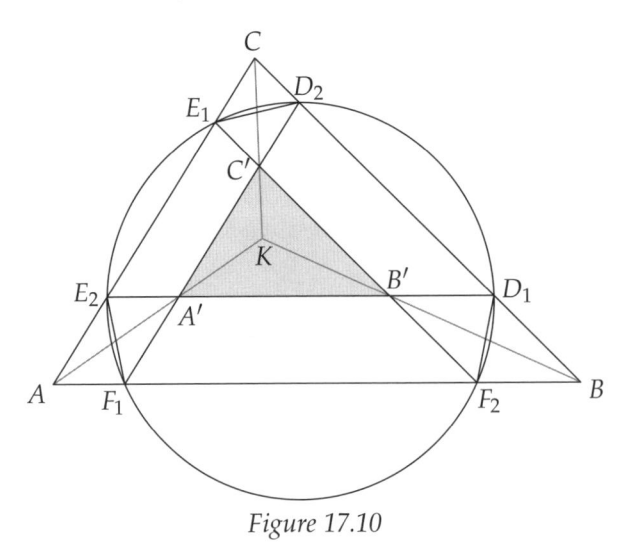

Figure 17.10

Theorem 17.11 *The hexagon $D_1 D_2 E_1 E_2 F_1 F_2$ is cyclic.*

Chapter 17: Lemoine, Tucker and Taylor circles   245

PROOF This proof is identical to that of theorem 17.1, but we will repeat it here. By construction, $AF_1A'E_2$ is a parallelogram, and so the diagonals AA' and F_1E_2 bisect one another. But AA' is a symmedian, so, by theorem 8.7 on page 106, F_1E_2 is antiparallel to BC and to F_2E_1. Hence the quadrilateral $E_1E_2F_1F_2$ is cyclic; by the same argument, so are $F_1F_2D_1D_2$ and $D_1D_2E_1E_2$. Now we have $\angle BF_2D_1 = \angle ACB = \angle AE_1F_2$ and so $F_1F_2E_1E_2$ is cyclic.

This, together with two similar results, is now enough to show that all three cyclic quadrilaterals have the same circumcircle, so the result follows. ❏

The circle defined by theorem 17.11 is known as a *Tucker circle*.

It is worth considering the polygon $D_1E_2F_1D_2E_1F_2$, noting carefully the order in which the vertices have been listed. The result is a hexagon, sometimes self-intersecting, whose sides are alternately antiparallel and parallel to the opposite sides of $\triangle ABC$. We call this a *Tucker hexagon*. It is not difficult to prove that such a hexagon is always closed, wherever we choose the starting point D. In fact, moving D has precisely the same effect as that of changing the value of the scale factor k. Hence we might have defined the Tucker circle by constructing a Tucker hexagon.

In figure 17.10, $k = 0.4$. There is, however, no need for k to be between 0 and 1. If $k > 1$ we obtain a Tucker circle which passes through the sides of the triangle produced (see figure 17.11), and if $k < 0$, the homothecy is indirect (see figure 17.12). The results in this chapter are valid for any k.

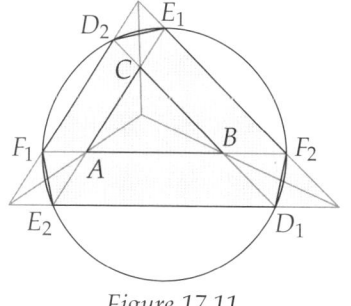

Figure 17.11 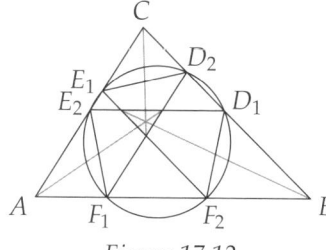   Figure 17.12

Corollary 17.12 $D_2E_1 = E_2F_1 = F_2D_1$.

PROOF This is a consequence of the angle-chasing we indulged in earlier. ❏

Note that around the edges of the configuration we have three isosceles trapezia, and that the exterior base angles are the angles of the original $\triangle ABC$. Yet another way of defining the Tucker circles is to begin by placing three isosceles trapezia inside (or outside) the triangle $\triangle ABC$.

Theorem 17.13 $\triangle D_1 E_1 F_1$ *is similar to* $\triangle BCA$ *and* $\triangle D_2 E_2 F_2$ *is similar to* $\triangle CAB$.

PROOF (See figure 17.13.)

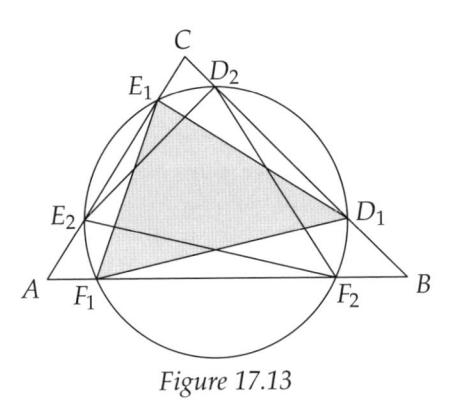

Figure 17.13

These results follow quickly from the existence of the Tucker circle and the parallel lines used to define it, using chains of reasoning such as $\angle D_1 E_1 F_1 = \angle D_1 D_2 F_1 = \angle BCA$. ☐

Corollary 17.14 *The first Brocard point of* $\triangle ABC$ *is the first Brocard point of* $\triangle D_1 E_1 F_1$ *and the centre of similitude of* $\triangle D_1 E_1 F_1$ *and* $\triangle BCA$. *Similarly, the second Brocard point of* $\triangle ABC$ *is the second Brocard point of* $\triangle D_2 E_2 F_2$ *and the centre of similitude of* $\triangle D_2 E_2 F_2$ *and* $\triangle CAB$.

PROOF The identity of the Brocard points follows from theorem 17.7. By theorem 17.13, the triangle $\triangle D_1 E_1 F_1$ is taken to $\triangle BCA$ by a spiral similarity, which maps the Brocard points of one triangle to the corresponding Brocard points of the other. However, these points are the same, so they are invariant under the spiral similarity, and hence they are the centres of similitude. ☐

Chapter 17: Lemoine, Tucker and Taylor circles 247

17.4 Tucker centres

We begin with a result which generalises that of theorem 2.22 on page 22.

Lemma 17.15 *The radii OA, OB and OC are perpendicular to E_2F_1, F_2D_1 and D_2E_1.*

PROOF (See figure 17.14.)

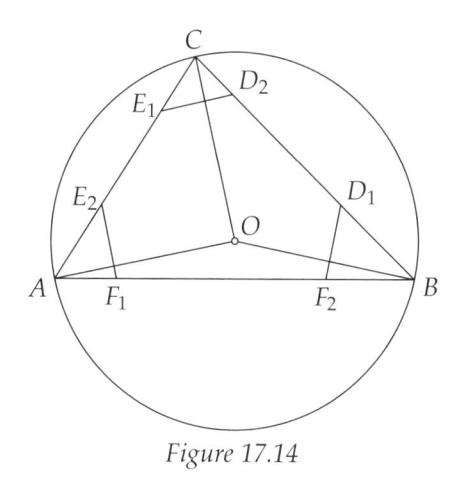

Figure 17.14

As F_1E_2 is antiparallel to BC, $\angle OAF_1 = 90° - \angle C = 90° - \angle AF_1E_2$ and the result follows. ❑

Theorem 17.16 *The centre of the Tucker circle is on the Brocard diameter of $\triangle ABC$.*

PROOF The symmedians AK, BK and CK bisect the segments E_2F_1, F_2D_1 and D_2E_1 at points U, V and W. Since these are also the midpoints of AA', BB' and CC', it follows that $KU : KA = KV : KB = KW : KC$. Hence K is the homothetic centre of triangles $\triangle UVW$ and $\triangle ABC$, and the enlargement maps the circumcentre O^* of $\triangle UVW$ to the circumcentre of $\triangle ABC$ (see figure 17.15).

Consequently O^* lies on KO, the Brocard diameter. Now, O^*U is parallel to AO, which, by lemma 17.15, is perpendicular to E_2F_1. Hence it is the perpendicular bisector of E_2F_1, and the same is true for O^*V and F_2D_1 and for O^*W and D_2E_1. Hence O^* is the centre of the Tucker circle.

Figure 17.15

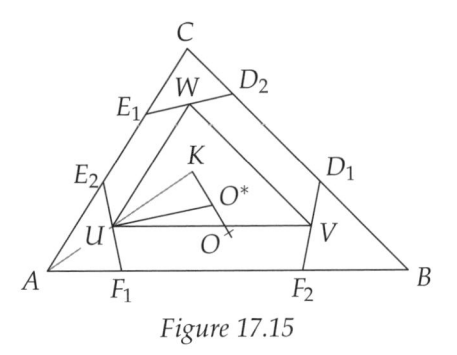

Note that it is quite possible for O^* to lie on KO produced; this depends on the value of k. ❏

Corollary 17.17 *The centre of the Tucker circle is the incentre of the triangle formed by producing the segments E_2F_1, F_2D_1 and D_2E_1.*

PROOF By corollary 17.12, the segments E_2F_1, F_2D_1 and D_2E_1 are equal, so $O^*U = O^*V = O^*W$. ❏

17.5 The Taylor circle

We now look at another circle which turns out to be a Tucker circle, although it is defined in a rather different way.

We begin with the orthic triangle $\triangle DEF$ and then draw perpendiculars from D, E and F to the other sides of the triangle $\triangle ABC$ (see figure 17.16).

The six points in the order shown define the *Taylor hexagon*.

Theorem 17.18 *The Taylor hexagon is a Tucker hexagon.*

PROOF Since AF_2DE_1 is cyclic, $\angle AF_2E_1 = \angle ADE_1 = 90° - \angle DAE_1 = \angle C$ and so F_2E_1 is antiparallel to BC (see figure 17.17).

Hence $\triangle AE_1F_2$ is similar to $\triangle ABC$, so

$$\frac{F_2E_1}{a} = \frac{AE_1}{c} = \frac{AD \sin C}{c} = 2R \times AD.$$

Hence $F_2E_1 = 4R\Delta$. It follows that the antiparallels F_2E_1, E_2D_1 and D_2F_1 are equal in length.

Chapter 17: Lemoine, Tucker and Taylor circles 249

Figure 17.16

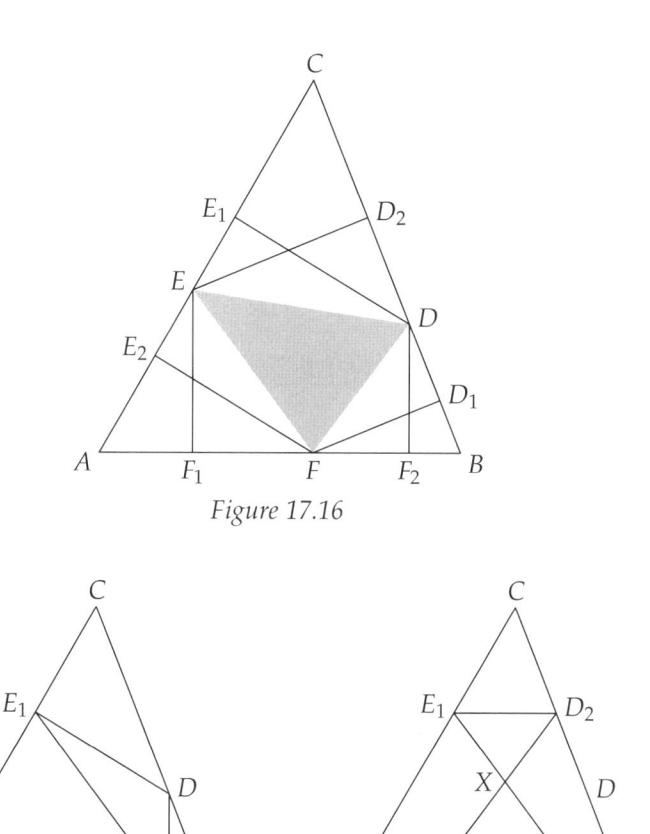

Figure 17.17

Figure 17.18

Let X be the point of intersection of E_1F_2 and F_1D_2 (see figure 17.18). Then $\angle XF_2F_1 = \angle C = \angle XF_1F_2$, so $XF_1 = XF_2$. Hence $XE_1 = XD_2$ and so $\triangle XE_1D_2$ and $\triangle XF_1F_2$ are similar isosceles triangles. It follows that the segment E_1D_2 is parallel to AB, and similarly for the other two such segments. Hence we do indeed have a Tucker hexagon. ❑

It follows that, by theorem 17.11, the six points are concyclic. This member of the Tucker family is called the *Taylor circle*.

Exercise 17b

1. Identify the Tucker circle corresponding to the following values of the scale factor k and determine the position of the centre on the Brocard diameter:
   (a) $k = 0$;
   (b) $k = 1$;
   (c) $k = -1$.

2. What is the condition on k for the centre of the Tucker circle to lie between K and O?

3. Prove that, in the diagram for the Tucker circle (figure 17.10), the circumcentre of $\triangle A'B'C'$ is the midpoint of KO.

4. Prove that the triangle $\triangle A''B''C''$ described in corollary 17.17 is homothetic to the tangential triangle $\triangle T_A T_B T_C$ and identify the homothetic centre.

5. Prove that, in figure 17.16, $E_1 F_2$ bisects the segments DE and DF.

6. Prove that the Spieker centre of the orthic triangle of $\triangle ABC$ is collinear with the symmedian point and circumcentre of $\triangle ABC$.

Chapter 18

Poles, polars and radical axes

In this chapter, we explore some key concepts in circle geometry. We begin with defining inverse points (although inversion is not introduced until chapter 20), and hence establish the relationship of pole and polar between a point and a line. This will turn out to be useful in discovering more collinearities and concurrences. We then introduce the important ideas of radical axis and radical centre, and conclude with a discussion of the properties of coaxal systems of circles.

Throughout this chapter, let S be a circle with centre O and radius r. Similarly S_i will be a circle with centre O_i and radius r_i, for $1 \leq i \leq 3$.

18.1 Pole and polar

Definition *The inverse of a point P with respect to S is the point P^* on the ray OP such that $OP \times OP^* = r^2$.*

Theorem 18.1 *Suppose that P and P^* lie on the diameter AB of a circle with centre O. Then P and P^* are inverse points if, and only if, they divide A and B harmonically (see figure 18.1).*

PROOF This is an immediate consequence of the definition and theorems 5.19 and 5.20 on page 61 and on page 62. ❑

Figure 18.1

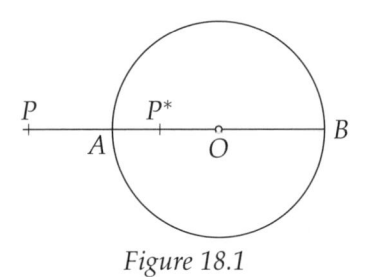

Theorem 18.2 *If P and P* are inverse points with respect to S, then any circle through P and P* is orthogonal to it.*

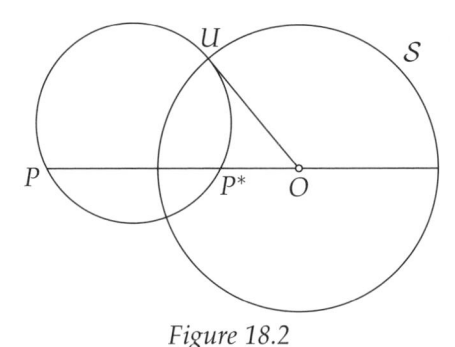

Figure 18.2

PROOF Let U be a point common to both circles (see figure 18.2). Since P and P^* are inverse points, $OP \times OP^* = OU^2$, and so OU is a tangent to the circle through U, P and P^*. But now the radius of one circle is tangent to the other, so the two circles are orthogonal. ❑

Definition *If P and Q are inverse points with respect to S, the line through Q perpendicular to OP is called the* **polar** *of P with respect to S, and P is called the* **pole** *of this line.*

Theorem 18.3 *If P lies outside S, then the polar of P is the chord of contact.*

PROOF Let PT be a tangent to S and TQ be perpendicular to OP (see figure 18.3). Since $\triangle PTO$ and $\triangle TQO$ are similar,

$$\frac{OQ}{OT} = \frac{OT}{OP}$$

Chapter 18: Poles, polars and radical axes 253

Figure 18.3

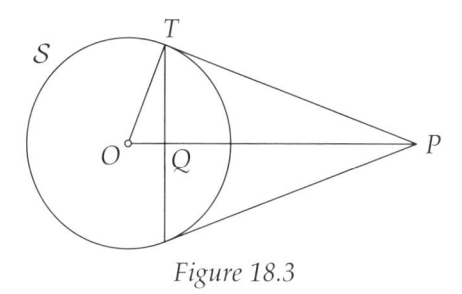

and so $OP \times OQ = r^2$ and Q is the inverse of P. Hence TQ is the polar of P. ❑

Theorem 18.4 *If Y lies on the polar of X with respect to S, then X lies on the polar of Y.*

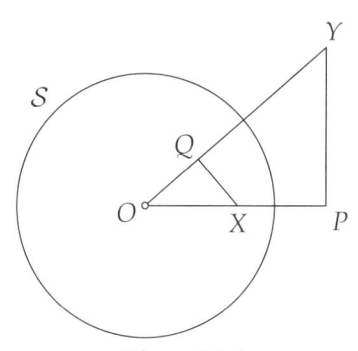

Figure 18.4

PROOF Let P be the foot of the perpendicular from Y to OX and let Q be the foot of the perpendicular from X to OY (see figure 18.4). If Y lies on the polar of X, then $OX \times OP = r^2$. Now quadrilateral $XPYQ$ is cyclic, so $\triangle OQX$ and $\triangle OPY$ are similar. Hence

$$\frac{OQ}{OP} = \frac{OX}{OY}$$

and so $OQ \times OY = r^2$ and X is on the polar of Y. ❑

Points such as X and Y are known as *conjugate points* with respect to S.

Corollary 18.5 *If the pole of the line p lies on line q, then the pole of line q lies on line p.*

PROOF This is simply a restatement of theorem 18.4. ❏

Lines such as p and q are known as *conjugate lines* with respect to S.

Exercise 18a

1. Prove that, if P and Q are inverse points with respect to S,
   (a) if P is inside S, Q is outside it, and *vice versa*;
   (b) if P is on S, it is its own inverse.

2. What is the polar of
   (a) a point on S?
   (b) the centre of S?

3. What is the pole of the diameter of S?

4. Let P be a point outside S and let the tangents from P touch it at A and B. A line through P intersects S in points X and Y. Prove that the tangents at X and Y meet on the line AB. What happens if P is actually on S?

5. Let P be a point outside S and let the tangents from P touch the circle at A and B. Suppose that OP and AB meet at Q, and let XY be any chord through Q. If the tangents at X and Y meet at T, prove that PT is perpendicular to OP.

6. Suppose that the line p is the polar of P and the line q is the polar of Q. Prove that PQ is the polar of the point where p and q meet. What happens if p and q are parallel?

7. Two circles S_1 and S_2 are orthogonal, and PQ is a diameter of S_1. The line O_2P cuts S_1 at R. Prove that QR is the polar of P with respect to S_2.

18.2 The radical axis

We return to the concept of the power of a point, which was introduced in section 3.6 on page 37.

Theorem 18.6 *Given two non-concentric circles S_1 and S_2, the locus of a point with equal power with respect to S_1 and S_2 is a line perpendicular to O_1O_2.*

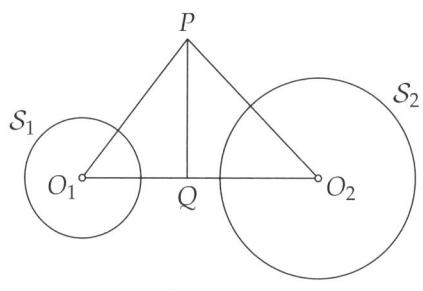

Figure 18.5

PROOF Suppose P is a point on this locus, and let Q be the foot of the perpendicular from P to O_1O_2 (see figure 18.5).

We assume, without loss of generality, that $r_2 \geq r_1$. Then

$$PO_1^2 - r_1^2 = PO_2^2 - r_2^2$$

and

$$O_1Q^2 - r_1^2 = O_2Q^2 - r_2^2$$

so that

$$\begin{aligned} r_2^2 - r_1^2 &= O_2Q^2 - O_1Q^2 \\ &= (O_2Q + O_1Q)(O_2Q - O_1Q) \\ &= O_1O_2(O_2Q - O_1Q). \end{aligned}$$

Hence $O_2Q - O_1Q$ is constant, and so is $O_2Q + O_1Q$, so it follows that O_2Q and O_1Q are fixed and so Q is a fixed point. Since this is true for any P on the locus, the locus is the line through Q perpendicular to O_1O_2. □

The line given by theorem 18.6 is known as the *radical axis* of S_1 and S_2. In order that any two circles have a radical axis, it is conventional to define it for two concentric circles as the line at infinity.

Theorem 18.7 *The radical axis of two intersecting circles is the line containing their common chord.*

PROOF Let the common chord be AB (see figure 18.6). It is clear that if P is on the common chord, then its power with respect to S_1 and S_2 is $PA \times PB$, and therefore it lies on the radical axis. ❑

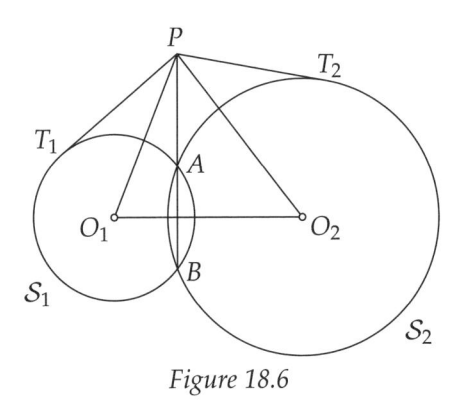

Figure 18.6

Theorem 18.8 *The part of the radical axis which is outside S_1 and S_2 is the locus of a point from which tangents to the two circles are equal.*

PROOF The power of P is the square of the length of the tangent, and so if P lies on the radical axis, we have $PT_1 = PT_2$. ❑

Theorem 18.9 *If a circle S, with centre O, is orthogonal to two other circles S_1 and S_2, then O lies on their radical axis. Conversely, circles with centres on the radical axis of S_1 and S_2 are orthogonal to both circles.*

PROOF The circle S is orthogonal to both circles if, and only if, the tangents from O to S_1 and S_2 are equal (see figure 18.7) and this happens if, and only if, O lies on their radical axis. ❑

Theorem 18.10 *The radical axes of three circles S_1, S_2 and S_3, with non-collinear centres, taken in pairs, are concurrent.*

Figure 18.7

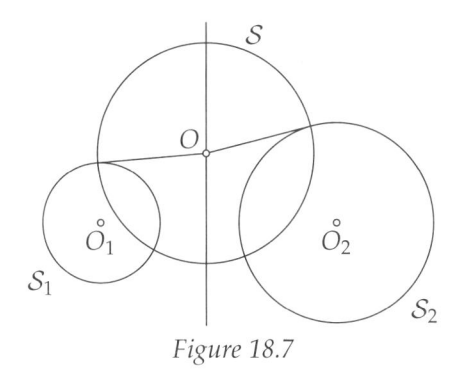

PROOF Since the radical axes are not parallel, two of them meet at a point P. Then P has equal powers with respect to S_1, S_2 and S_3, so it also lies on the third radical axis. ❏

The point given by theorem 18.10 is known as the *radical centre* of S_1, S_2 and S_3. If it lies outside all three circles, it is the only point from which the tangents to all three circles are equal. If it lies within all three, it is the intersection of the three common chords.

In the proof of theorem 17.1 on page 237, it was noted that you could not assume that the cyclic quadrilaterals $E_1E_2F_1F_2$, $F_1F_2D_1D_2$ and $D_1D_2E_1E_2$ were all identical, and, in order to complete the argument, it was necessarily to find a 'bridging' quadrilateral. We now know that the radical axes of three distinct quadrilaterals, taken in pairs, are concurrent. These are the lines D_1D_2, E_1E_2 and F_1F_2 and they are clearly not concurrent. Hence, without doing any extra work, we can now conclude that all three quadrilaterals have the same circumcircle.

Theorem 18.11 (Casey's power theorem) *Let S_1 and S_2 be non-concentric circles, with centres O_1 and O_2, and let P be any point. If Q is the foot of the perpendicular from P to the radical axis of S_1 and S_2 and the powers of P with respect to S_1 and S_2 are π_1 and π_2, then $|\pi_1 - \pi_2| = 2PQ \times O_1O_2$.*

PROOF Set as question 8 of exercise 18b. ❏

Exercise 18b

1. What is the radical axis of two tangential circles?

2. Prove that three circles, whose centres are collinear, have parallel or coincident radical axes. Conversely, if three circles, taken in pairs, have parallel or coincident radical axes, prove that their centres are collinear.

3. A point can be considered as a circle of zero radius (sometimes called a point-circle). What is
   (a) the radical axis of two distinct points?
   (b) the radical centre of three non-collinear points?
   (c) the radical axis of a circle and a point on it?

4. A point P lies outside a circle S. The radical axis of P and S cuts OP at Q, and the polar of P cuts OP at P^*. Prove that Q is the midpoint of PP^*.

5. Suppose that the power of the radical centre of S_1, S_2 and S_3 is positive. Prove that there is a unique circle which is orthogonal to all three circles.

6. Two circles S_1 and S_2 are given. If $r_1 > r_2$, prove that the radical axis of S_1 and S_2 is nearer to S_1 than to S_2 and nearer to O_2 than to O_1.

7. Prove that, if the radical axes of P and Q with respect to a circle intersect at a point R, then R lies on the perpendicular bisector of PQ.

8. Prove theorem 18.11.

9. Three circles touch each other externally in pairs. Prove that the tangents at the points of contact are concurrent and that the circle through the points of contact cuts each circle orthogonally.

10. Identify, with proof, the radical centre of three circles whose diameters are the sides of a triangle.

11. Let L, M and N be the intersections of a transversal with the sides BC, CA and AB of $\triangle ABC$. Prove that the orthocentres of $\triangle ABC$, $\triangle AMN$, $\triangle BNL$ and $\triangle CLM$ are collinear.

12. Prove that the radical axis of the circumcircle and nine-point circle of $\triangle ABC$ is the orthic axis.

13. For a triangle $\triangle ABC$, prove that the radical axis of the incircle and the excircle opposite to A passes through A_1.

14. Let a circle cut the sides AB and AC of triangle $\triangle ABC$ at internal points U and V. Identify, with proof, the radical axis of the circle through U tangential to BC at B and the circle through V tangential to BC at C.

15. Two non-intersecting circles have a line of centres which meets them in points A, B, C and D (in that order). Let P be any point on the radical axis. Let PA and PB meet the first circle at X and Y respectively, and let PC and PD meet the second circle at U and V respectively. Prove that
    (a) $YUVX$ is a cyclic quadrilateral;
    (b) AY, XB, VC and DU are concurrent;
    (c) XV and YU meet on the line of centres.

16. Prove that the symmedian point lies on the common chord of the two Lemoine circles, and that the first Lemoine circle bisects the circumference of the second.

17. A circle with centre P intersects $\triangle ABC$ at six points, which cut off three segments on the sides. Prove that the radical centre of the three circles with these segments as diameter is the isogonal conjugate of P.

18. In the notation of the Taylor configuration (see section 17.5 on page 248), prove that the circumcircles of $\triangle HD_1D_2$, $\triangle HE_1E_2$ and $\triangle HF_1F_2$ intersect in pairs at points on the altitudes of $\triangle ABC$.

18.3 Coaxal circles

A set of circles is said to be *coaxal* if they are all share the same radical axis. Note that the centres of the circles of a coaxal system all lie on a line perpendicular to the radical axis. There are two main types of coaxal system. (Later we will see that there are also some degenerate cases, but these are ignored at this stage.)

  I. Figure 18.8 shows four circles of a coaxal system in which two of the circles intersect.

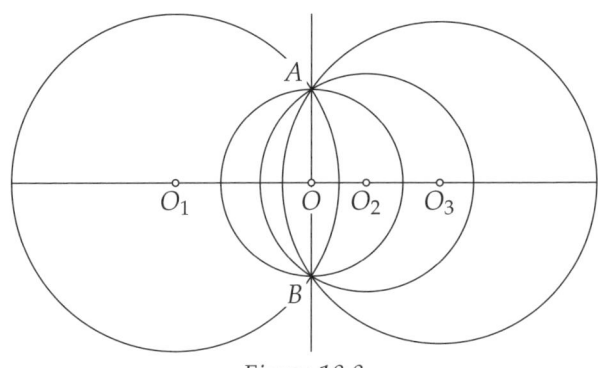

Figure 18.8

Since the radical axis is the common chord, *every* circle in the system passes through A and B, which are known as the *basic points*. There are infinitely many possible circles in this system and the one of smallest radius has its centre at O.

  II. In the second type of coaxal system, *none* of the circles intersect (see figure 18.9).

The condition for a circle to belong to this system is that the tangent from O to it has a fixed length.

It is easy to tell if a circle belongs to the first type of coaxal system, but a little harder to decide in the non-intersecting case.

Theorem 18.12 *In a non-intersecting coaxal system, let O be the point of intersection of the radical axis and the line of centres, and let t be the power of point O with respect to circles of the system. If a circle in the system has centre C, then its radius r satisfies $r^2 = OC^2 - t^2$.*

Chapter 18: Poles, polars and radical axes 261

Figure 18.9

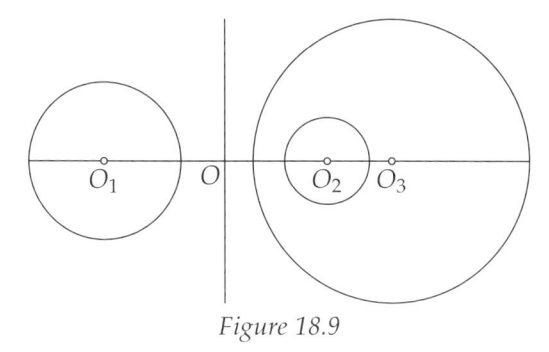

PROOF This is immediate from the definition since the power is given by $t^2 = OC^2 - r^2$. ❑

It is now clear that, to belong to the system, a (real) circle has to satisfy $OC > t$. There are therefore two points L_1 and L_2 on the line of centres at a distance of t either side of O which mark the nearest to O that the centres can be. These are known as the *limiting points* of the system, and it is conventional to consider two point circles of zero radius centred at these points as the limiting circles of the system.

Theorem 18.13 *Let C be a circle in a coaxal system with limiting points L_1 and L_2, and let X and Y be the intersections of C with the line L_1L_2. Then C is orthogonal to C_0, the circle on diameter L_1L_2, and X and Y are inverse points with respect to C_0.*

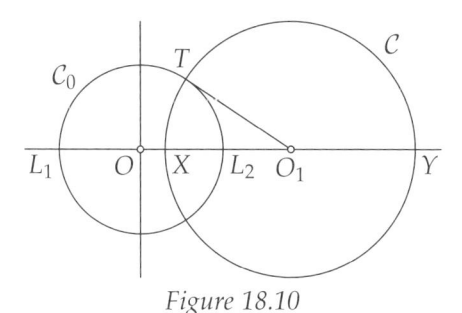

Figure 18.10

PROOF The orthogonality is immediate. Let T be a point of intersection of the circles (see figure 18.10). By the tangent-secant theorem, $OX \times OY =$

$OT^2 = OL_2^2$ and so, by theorem 5.20 on page 62, X and Y are harmonic conjugates with respect to L_1 and L_2. Hence, by theorem 18.1, they are inverse points with respect to C_0. ❑

Conversely, any circle orthogonal to C_0, with centre on the line of centres, belongs to the system.

The distinction between intersecting and non-intersecting systems of coaxal circles is slightly artificial, as is seen by the following result (see figure 18.11).

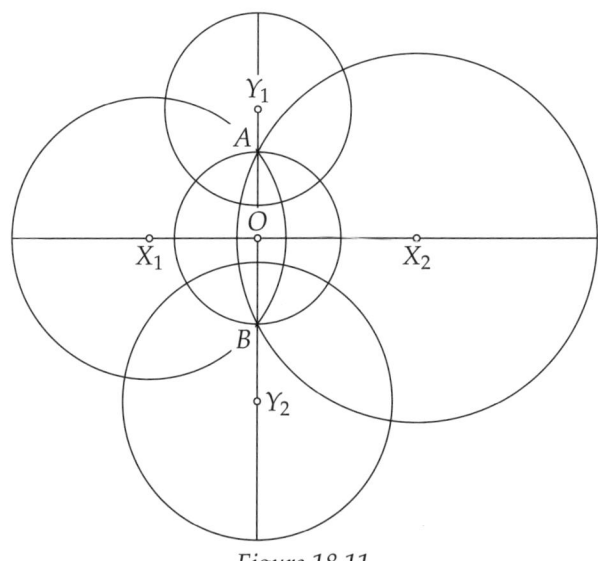

Figure 18.11

Starting with an intersecting system with base points A and B, we can take any point on the radical axis and draw a circle orthogonal to the circle on diameter AB. The set of all such circles forms a non-intersecting coaxal system with limiting points A and B.

The centres of the intersecting group are labelled X_1 and X_2 and those of the non-intersecting group Y_1 and Y_2. The line $X_1 X_2$ is the radical axis of the Y-group and the line $Y_1 Y_2$ is the radical axis of the X-group.

The two coaxal systems are said to be *conjugate* to one another.

Note that the circle on diameter AB is orthogonal to all the circles in this double system. In fact, we can say more than this.

Theorem 18.14 *Every circle of one system is orthogonal to every circle of the other system.*

PROOF Every circle of the intersecting system passes through the limiting points of the non-intersecting system, but these are inverse points with respect to every circle of the non-intersecting system, and so by theorem 18.2, the result follows. ❑

At this point, it is worth observing that we have already met this configuration in the work on centres of similitude and Apollonius circles in section 5.5 on page 64. If we start with two non-intersecting circles, then the centres of similitude are the limiting points of a coaxal system of which our circles are two members. The conjugate system consists of circles through the centres of similitude, and in question 8 of exercise 5e, it was shown independently that the two systems are orthogonal. For intersecting circles, we obtain another coaxal system, with the intersections as the limiting points of the conjugate system, and again this has been prefigured in question 7 of exercise 5e.

For completeness, it is worth stating that there are other types of coaxal system.

A special case of the intersecting and non-intersecting systems is where all the circles are tangential to the radical axis at O (see figure 18.12).

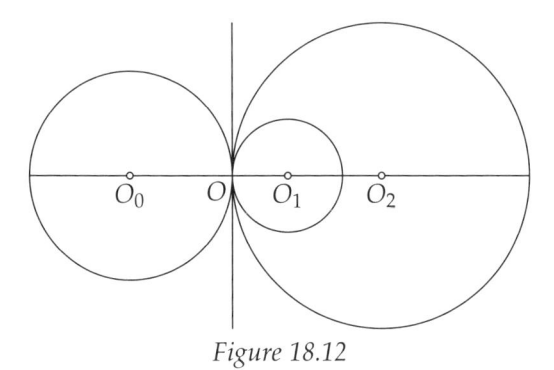

Figure 18.12

Another case is a set of concentric circles. The radical axis is the line at infinity (see figure 18.13).

It is conventional to allow these circles to have infinite radius, and therefore to treat a set of concurrent lines, and a set of parallel lines, as other limiting cases of a coaxal system.

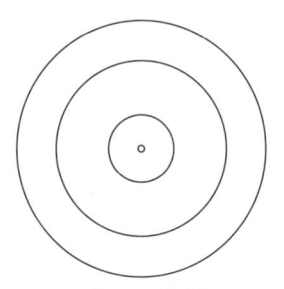

Figure 18.13

Theorem 18.15 *Let S_1 and S_2 be non-concentric circles. The locus of a point whose powers with respect to S_1 and S_2 are in a constant ratio is a circle coaxal with them.*

PROOF Set as question 2 of exercise 18c. ❑

Exercise 18c

1. In a non-intersecting coaxal system with limiting points L_1 and L_2, prove that the points of contact of tangents from L_1 to circles of the system lie on a fixed line, which should be identified.

2. Prove theorem 18.15.

3. Prove that the circle of similitude of two circles is coaxal with them and its diameter divides their line of centres harmonically.

4. Find the locus of a point whose powers with respect to two concentric circles are in a constant ratio (which is not equal to 1).

Chapter 19

The isodynamic points

We now explore a configuration of related circles which motivates the introduction of the isodynamic points of a triangle. This configuration also involves the circumcircle of $\triangle ABC$, the symmedian point, and the Brocard circle.

19.1 The Apollonius circles

In section 5.5, we encountered Apollonius circles in general. We now define three specific Apollonius circles associated with $\triangle ABC$.

Let X and X_1 be the intersections of the internal and external bisectors of $\angle BAC$ with BC, and let O_A be the midpoint of XX_1. The circumcircle of $\triangle AXX_1$, which has centre O_A, is called the *A-Apollonius circle* (see figure 19.1).

In a similar way, there are *B-* and *C-* Apollonius circles.

Theorem 19.1 *The Apollonius circles are orthogonal to the circumcircle.*

PROOF Note that $\angle O_A AX = \angle O_A XA = \angle B + \frac{1}{2}\angle A$. Hence $\angle O_A AC = \angle O_A AX - \frac{1}{2}\angle A = \angle B$ and so, by the alternate segment theorem, $O_A A$ is the tangent to the circumcircle at A. ❑

On page 131, we defined the axis of perspective of the tangential triangle and the reference triangle as the Lemoine line.

Figure 19.1

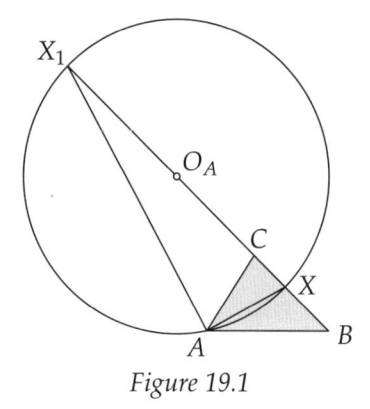

Theorem 19.2 *The centres of the three Apollonius circles are collinear on the Lemoine line.*

PROOF Let T_A and T_B be vertices of the tangential triangle $\triangle T_A T_B T_C$ (see figure 19.2).

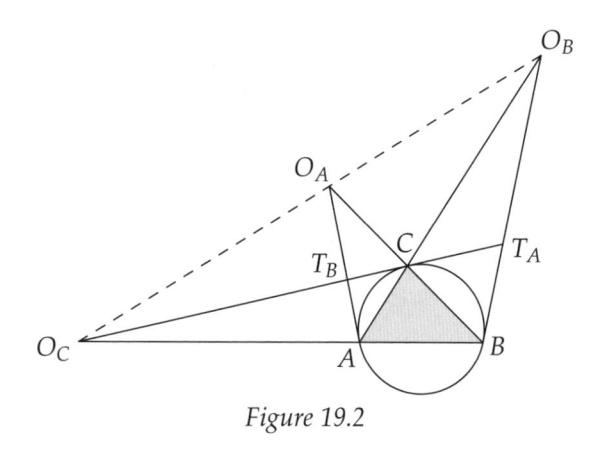

Figure 19.2

Since, from theorem 19.1, O_C lies on both the tangent $T_A T_B$ and the side AB, it lies on the axis of perspective of $\triangle T_A T_B T_C$ and $\triangle ABC$, and the same is true of O_A and O_B. ❑

Theorem 19.3 *The three Apollonius circles share the same common chord.*

Chapter 19: The isodynamic points

PROOF Consider the A- and B- Apollonius circles. Since A is inside the second and B is inside the first, these clearly intersect at two points, one of which, J_1, is inside and the other, J_2, outside (see figure 19.3).

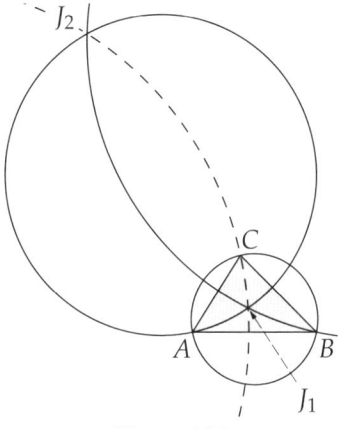

Figure 19.3

For either point, we have

$$\frac{JB}{JC} = \frac{AB}{AC} \quad \text{and} \quad \frac{JC}{JA} = \frac{BC}{BA}$$

and so

$$\frac{JA}{JB} = \frac{CA}{CB}.$$

Hence J also lies on the C-Apollonius circle. ∎

The points J_1 and J_2 are known as the *first and second isodynamic points* of $\triangle ABC$.

Corollary 19.4 *The distances of the isodynamic points from A, B and C are inversely proportional to a, b and c.*

PROOF Set as question 1 of exercise 19a. ∎

Exercise 19a

1. Prove corollary 19.4

2. Prove that the A-Apollonius circle is the locus of a point P whose pedal triangle $\triangle A''B''C''$ is isosceles with $A''B'' = A''C''$.

3. Prove that the points P and Q are inverse points with respect to the A-Apollonius circle if, and only if, their pedal triangles are inversely similar.

19.2 A coaxal system

Theorem 19.3 says the three Apollonius circles are part of an intersecting coaxal system, with basic points J_1 and J_2. The line $J_1 J_2$ is their common radical axis, and it is perpendicular to the Lemoine line, which by theorem 19.2 is the line of centres.

Theorem 19.5 *The symmedian through A is the polar of O_A with respect to the circumcircle of $\triangle ABC$.*

PROOF With respect to the circumcircle, the polar of A is AO_A, the tangent at A, and the polar of T_A is BC, the chord of contact (see figure 19.4).

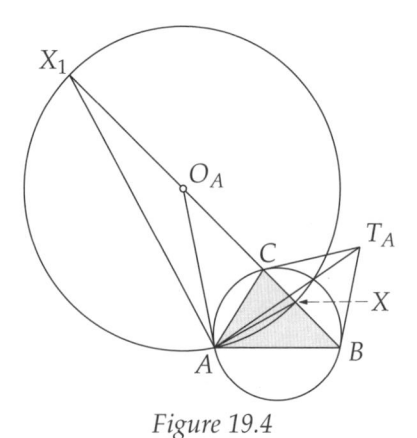

Figure 19.4

Hence, by theorem 18.4 on page 253, both A and T_A lie on the polar of O_A. But, by theorem 8.4 on page 101, the line AT_A is the symmedian through A. □

Chapter 19: The isodynamic points

Corollary 19.6 *The symmedian through A is the common chord of the circumcircle and the A-Apollonius circle.*

PROOF This is immediate from theorem 18.3 on page 252. ❏

Corollary 19.7 *The Lemoine line is the polar of the symmedian point K with respect to the circumcircle.*

PROOF By definition K is the intersection of the three symmedians. By theorem 19.5, it lies on the polar of O_A, and hence, by theorem 18.4 on page 253, its polar passes through O_A, and, by symmetry, through O_B and O_C as well. Therefore, by theorem 19.2, it is the Lemoine line. ❏

Corollary 19.8 *The Lemoine line is perpendicular to the Brocard axis.*

PROOF By definition, the polar of a point is perpendicular to the ray from the centre of the circle to the point.

In this case, the point is K, the polar, by corollary 19.7, is the Lemoine line, and the ray is the Brocard axis OK (see figure 19.5). ❏

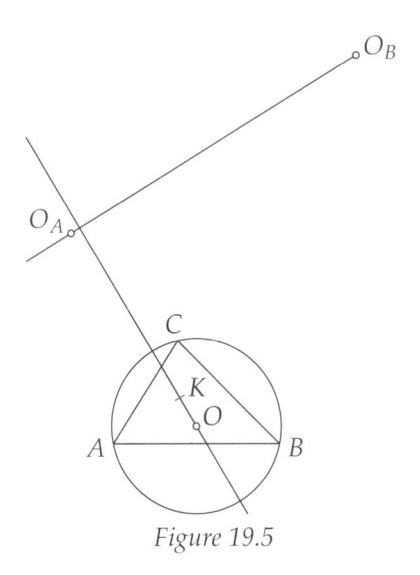

Figure 19.5

Corollary 19.9 *The symmedian through A is the polar of the circumcentre with respect to the A-Apollonius circle and it is perpendicular to OO_A.*

PROOF This is because the circles are orthogonal, by theorem 19.1, and the symmedian is the common chord, by corollary 19.6 (see figure 19.6). ❑

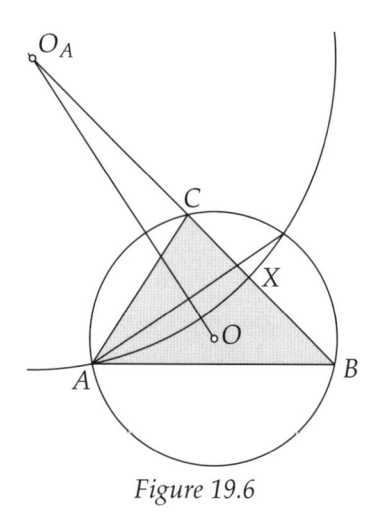

Figure 19.6

Theorem 19.10 *The Brocard circle is orthogonal to each of the Apollonius circles.*

PROOF Let AP be the common chord of the circumcircle and the A-Apollonius circle, which, by corollary 19.6, passes through K, and let M be its midpoint, which lies on the line of centres OO_A (see figure 19.7).

Hence $\angle OMA = 90° = \angle OMK$, and so, since the Brocard circle has diameter OK, M lies on this circle.

By corollary 19.9, O and M are inverse points with respect to the Apollonius circle, and hence, by theorem 18.2 on page 252, the Brocard circle is orthogonal to it. ❑

Theorem 19.11 *The Lemoine line is the radical axis of the Brocard circle and the circumcircle.*

PROOF By theorems 19.1 and 19.10, both the Brocard circle and the circumcircle are orthogonal to the Apollonius circle. Hence the tangents from O_A to these two circles are equal in length. Hence O_A lies on the radical axis, and by an identical argument so do OB and O_C. ❑

Chapter 19: The isodynamic points

Figure 19.7

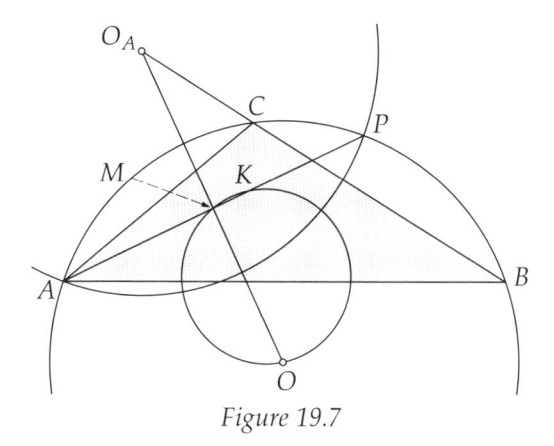

Theorem 19.12 *The isodynamic points lie on the Brocard axis.*

PROOF It is immediate that $J_1 J_2$ is perpendicular to the Lemoine line since a common chord is always perpendicular to the line of centres (see figure 19.8).

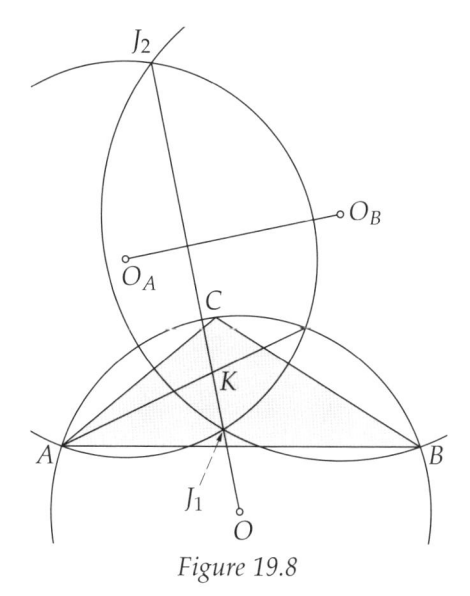

Figure 19.8

Now, by theorem 19.1, the circumcircle is orthogonal to each of the Apollonius circles, so, by theorem 18.9 on page 256, O lies on the radical axis, which is $J_1 J_2$. But a line through O perpendicular to the Lemoine line also passes through K and is the Brocard axis. ❑

It is worthwhile summarising what has been learnt so far and seeing the relationship between the various points and lines in a single diagram (see figure 19.9).

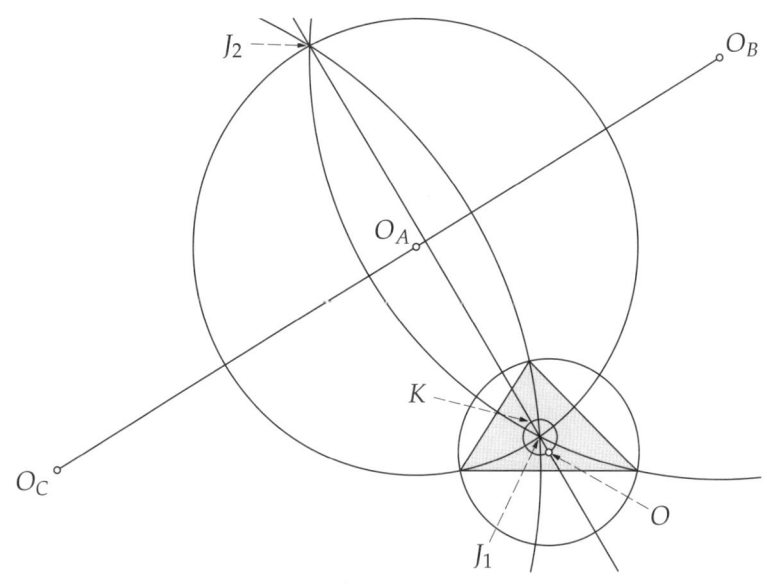

Figure 19.9

(i) The three Apollonius circles form an intersecting coaxal system.
(ii) The radical axis of this system is the Brocard axis OK.
(iii) The isodynamic points J_1 and J_2 are the basic points of this system.
(iv) The circumcircle and Brocard circle are part of the conjugate coaxal system, which is non-intersecting.
(v) The radical axis of the conjugate system is the Lemoine line $O_A O_B O_C$.
(vi) The isodynamic points J_1 and J_2 are the limiting points of the conjugate system, and are therefore equidistant from the Lemoine line.
(vii) The Brocard axis and Lemoine line are perpendicular.
(viii) J_1 and J_2 are inverse points with respect to the circumcircle and so O, J_1, K, J_2 is a harmonic range.

(ix) The common chords of each Apollonius circle with the circumcircle are concurrent at K.

19.3 The pedal triangles

The isodynamic points have a unique property which alone makes them worthy of inclusion in the list of important triangle centres.

Theorem 19.13 *The pedal triangles of the isodynamic points are equilateral (see figure 19.10).*

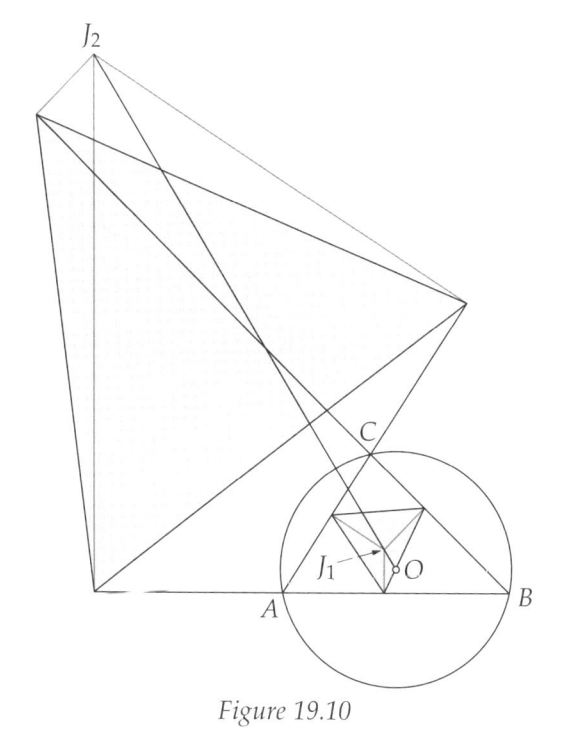

Figure 19.10

PROOF Consider the cyclic quadrilateral $CB''J_1A''$ (see figure 19.11).
The circumdiameter is CJ_1, so by the sine rule (twice) we have $A''B'' = CJ_1 \sin C = CJ_1 \times 2Rc$, and, by the result of corollary 19.4, this is the same for all three sides of the pedal triangle of J_1.

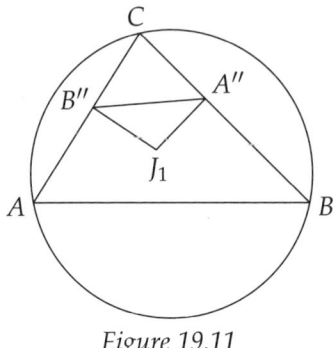

Figure 19.11

The argument for the pedal triangle of J_2 is identical. ❏

Corollary 19.14 *The circumcevian triangles of the isodynamic points are equilateral.*

PROOF This follows immediately from theorem 19.13 and theorem 13.1 on page 172. ❏

19.4 The isogonic centres and the isodynamic points

We are now aiming to relate the four points F_1, F_2, J_1 and J_2 to each other and to the Euler line of $\triangle ABC$.

Theorem 19.15 *The points F_1 and J_1 are isogonal conjugates, as are F_2 and J_2.*

PROOF Set as question 1 of exercise 19b. ❏

Theorem 19.16 *The outer Napoleon triangle and the pedal triangle of J_1 are homothetic.*

PROOF The proof of theorem 11.6 on page 149 showed that $N_A N_B$ is perpendicular to CF_1 (see figure 19.12).
 By theorem 7.8 on page 88, $X_1 Y_1$ is also perpendicular to CF_1. Since this is true for all three vertices of $\triangle ABC$, the two triangles are homothetic. ❏

Chapter 19: The isodynamic points 275

Figure 19.12

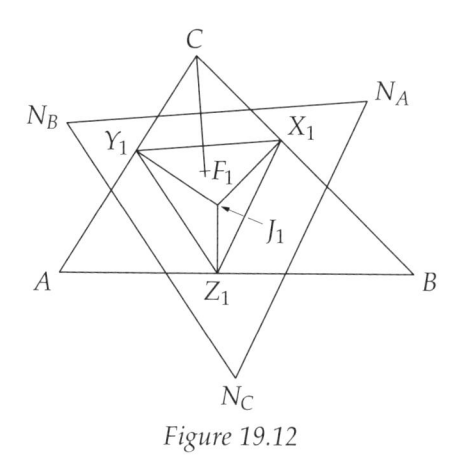

Theorem 19.17 *The inner Napoleon triangle and the pedal triangle of J_2 are homothetic.*

PROOF This is proved in exactly the same way as theorem 19.16. ☐

Theorem 19.18 *$F_1 J_1$ is parallel to the Euler line of $\triangle ABC$.*

PROOF Let D_1 be the centre of the homothecy of theorem 19.16, which maps centres of one triangle to centres of the other (see figure 19.13).

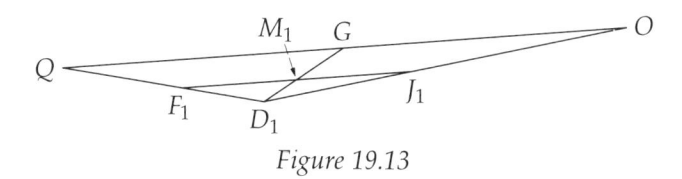

Figure 19.13

By theorem 11.7 on page 150, we have $O \triangle N_A N_B N_C = G$, and, by theorem 7.9 on page 89, $O \triangle X_1 Y_1 Z_1 = M_1$, the midpoint of $F_1 J_1$. Hence D_1, M_1 and G are collinear.

Now $N_A O$ and $X_1 J_1$ are both perpendicular to BC, so they are parallel. Since the same is true of $N_B O$ and $Y_1 J_1$, it follows that the homothecy maps O to J_1, and so D_1, J_1 and O are also collinear. Hence $M_1 J_1$ is parallel to GO, and it follows as well that Q, the centre of the orthocentroidal disc, is mapped to F_1, since G is the midpoint of OQ. ☐

We have a similar configuration involving the points F_2 and J_2 and the Euler line, with D_1 replaced by D_2, the centre of the homothecy of theorem 19.17. It follows that the three lines $F_1 J_1$, QO and $F_2 J_2$ are all parallel.

Theorem 19.19 *The Fermat axis and Brocard axis intersect at the symmedian point of $\triangle ABC$.*

PROOF By corollary 11.11 on page 154, F_1, Q and F_2 are collinear on the Fermat axis and, by theorem 19.12, O, J_1 and J_2 are collinear on the Brocard axis. Hence D_1 and D_2 coincide at the intersection of these two lines, which is marked D in figure 19.14.

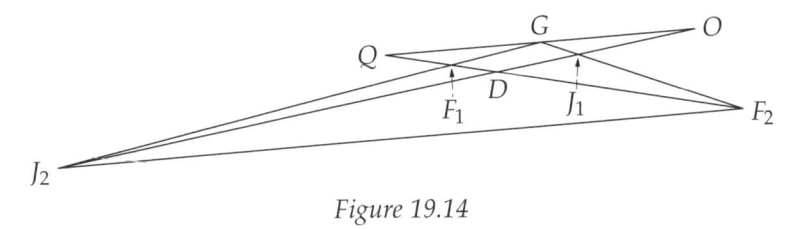

Figure 19.14

But now the points J_1, F_2, J_2 and F_1 form a quadrangle with diagonal triangle $\triangle QDO$.

It follows that J_2, D, J_1, O is a harmonic range. But, from item (viii) on page 272, this fixes D as the symmedian point K. ☐

Corollary 19.20 *The two isogonic centres separate the symmedian point and the centre of the orthocentroidal disc harmonically.*

PROOF This follows from the complete quadrangle identified in the proof of theorem 19.19. ☐

Exercise 19b

1. Prove theorem 19.15.

2. Prove that the tangents to the A-Apollonius circle at the isodynamic points, the Lemoine line and the symmedian through A are concurrent.

Chapter 20

Inversion

This chapter introduces a very powerful method of proof, based upon a transformation of the plane which takes a point P to an image point P_ι (where ι is the Greek letter iota). As the point P traces out some figure, which is usually either a straight line or a circle, P_ι traces out a new figure. In this way, the transformation maps a geometrical configuration to a different one.

Whilst the two configurations might appear to look nothing like one another, it turns out that certain geometrical properties are conserved under the mapping. If it is possible to prove results in the new configuration (by straightforward methods), then the corresponding results (which might be quite difficult to prove directly) are shown to be true in the original figure.

20.1 Transformation properties

We begin with a fixed circle S with centre O and radius r, which is called the *circle of inversion*. In practice, the centre turns out to be much more important, in most cases, than the radius.

We now recall the definition, from section 18.1, of inverse points P and P^*, namely $OP \times OP^* = r^2$. The result of mapping every point in a figure to its inverse point, in other words, taking P_ι to be P^*, is called the *inverse* of the original figure.

Note that inverse points come in pairs. In other words, if $P_\iota = Q$, then $Q_\iota = P$.

Our first task is to explore the rules which govern this transformation, known as *inversion*.

Lemma 20.1 *A line through O inverts to itself.*

PROOF This is obvious, but note that nearly every point on the line moves to a different point. Points inside the circle are sent to points outside it, and *vice versa*, with O itself being sent off to infinity. The only invariant points, which do not move under the inversion, are the intersections of the line with S. ❑

Lemma 20.2 *The inverse of a line not through O is a circle through O.*

PROOF Consider a line $\mathcal{L}$ not through O, and let A be the foot of the perpendicular to $\mathcal{L}$ from O. Let A_ι be the inverse of A and P_ι the inverse of P (see figure 20.1).

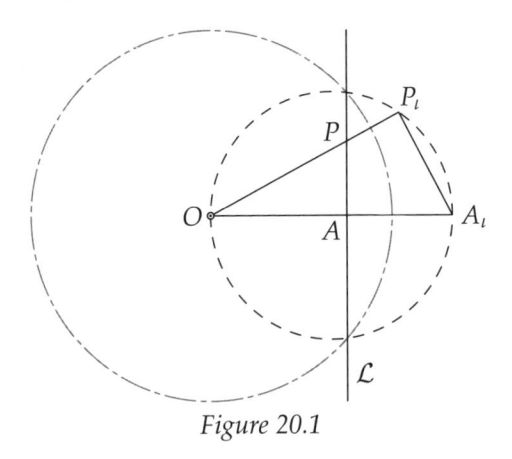

Figure 20.1

Then $OA \times OA_\iota = OP \times OP_\iota$, and so $PAA_\iota P_\iota$ is cyclic. Hence $\angle A_\iota P_\iota O = 90°$ and P_ι lies on the circle with diameter OA_ι. ❑

Lemma 20.3 *The inverse of a circle through O is a line not through O.*

PROOF This is just the converse of the preceding result. Start with the circle with diameter OA_ι and let A be the inverse of A_ι. Now let P_ι be an arbitrary point on the circle with diameter AA_ι. As before, P is the point on OP_ι such that $PAA_\iota P_\iota$ is cyclic, and this means that $\angle PAA_\iota = 90°$ and so P lies on the line $\mathcal{L}$. ❑

Chapter 20: Inversion 279

Lemma 20.4 *The inverse of a circle not through O is a circle not through O.*

PROOF There are two possible diagrams, according as O lies outside or inside the circle which is to be inverted (see figures 20.2 and 20.3).

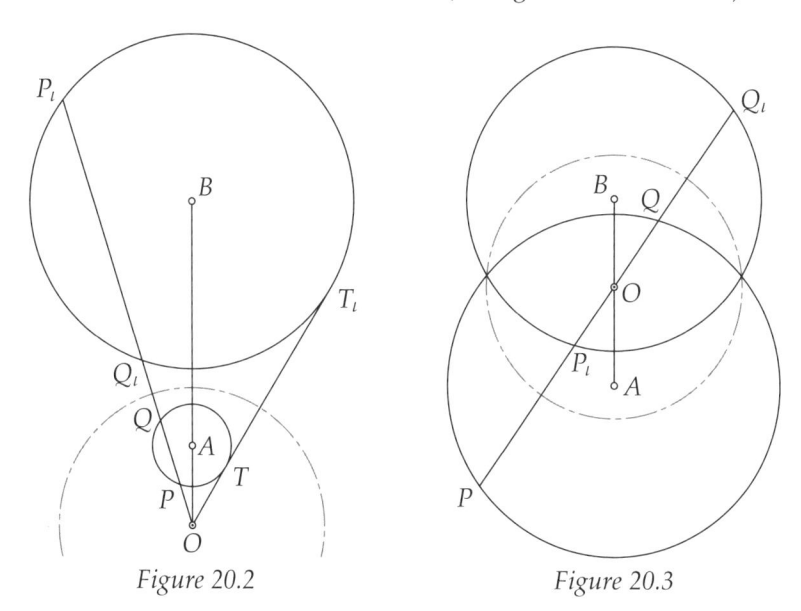

Figure 20.2 *Figure 20.3*

Let A be the centre of the circle to be inverted.

Consider a line through O cutting the circle at P and Q, and let P_I and Q_I be their respective inverses.

Let the power of O with respect to the circle with centre A be t; then $t > 0$ in figure 20.2 and $t < 0$ in figure 20.3.

Then $OP \times OQ = |t|$ and $OP \times OP_I = OQ \times OQ_I = r^2$. Hence

$$\frac{OP_I}{OQ} = \frac{r^2}{|t|} = \frac{OQ_I}{OP},$$

and so the locus of P_I (and of Q_I) is a circle homothetic to the circle with centre A, with centre B which lies on OA. ❏

In figure 20.2, O is the external centre of similitude of the two circles, and in figure 20.3 it is the internal centre of similitude. Also, in figure 20.2, let OT be the tangent from O to the circle with centre A; then OT is tangential to the image circle at a point T_I, which is the inverse of T.

Let the radius of the circle with centre A be R and that of the circle with centre B be R_ι, and let t_ι be the power of the image circle with respect to O.

Corollary 20.5 $R_\iota = R \times \dfrac{r^2}{|t|}$ and $tt_\iota = r^4$.

PROOF Note that
$$\frac{R_\iota}{R} = \frac{OP_\iota}{OQ}$$
and that $tt_\iota = OP \times OQ \times OP_\iota \times OQ_\iota$ and use the results in the proof of lemma 20.4. ❑

Corollary 20.6 *The inverse of A with respect to S is the inverse of O with respect to the circle with centre B.*

PROOF Set as question 4 of exercise 20a. ❑

Note that this means that centres of circles do not invert to centres.

Most work involving inversion focuses on properties of incidence and tangency. It is sometimes useful, however, to calculate distances, and there is a suitable formula. Suppose that points P and Q are mapped under the inversion to P_ι and Q_ι (see figure 20.4).

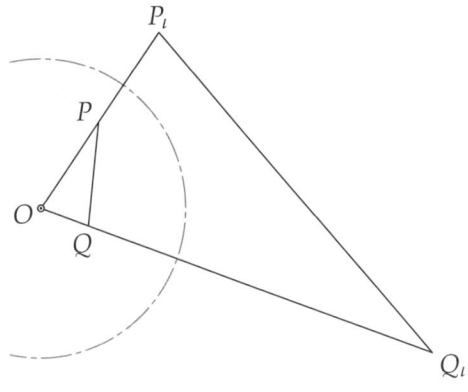

Figure 20.4

Since $OP \times OP_\iota = OQ \times OQ_\iota = r^2$, the quadrilateral $PQQ_\iota P_\iota$ is cyclic and so $\triangle OPQ$ and $\triangle OQ_\iota P_\iota$ are similar.

Theorem 20.7 (Inversion distance formula) $P_I Q_I = \dfrac{r^2}{OP \times OQ} QP.$

PROOF Set as question 5 of exercise 20a. ❑

To summarise, we now have these fundamental properties of inversion.

- The inverse of a line through O is itself.
- The inverse of a line not through O is a circle through O.
- The inverse of a circle through O is a line not through O.
- The inverse of a circle not through O is a circle not through O.

20.2 Angles and tangency

Theorem 20.8 *If O, Q and R are collinear and, under inversion with centre O, the points P, Q and R map to P_I, Q_I and R_I, then $\angle RPQ = \angle Q_I P_I R_I$.*

PROOF The quadrilaterals $PQQ_I P_I$ and $PRR_I P_I$ are cyclic (see figure 20.5).

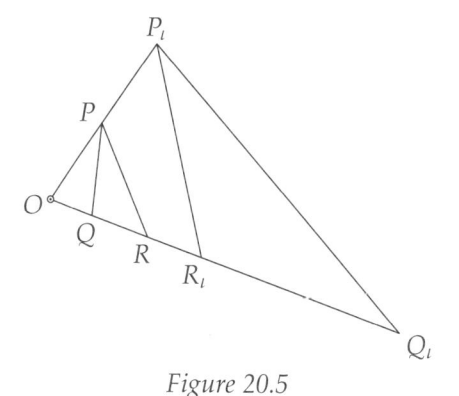

Figure 20.5

So

$$\angle RPQ = \angle RPO - \angle QPO$$
$$= \angle OR_I P_I - \angle OQ_I P_I$$
$$= \angle Q_I P_I R_I \qquad ❑$$

Corollary 20.9 *Two intersecting curves invert into curves intersecting at the same angle.*

PROOF Let QP and RP be chords of the two curves and allow Q and R to approach P; in the limit the chords become tangents. Then use the result of theorem 20.8. ☐

In particular, tangency and orthogonality are preserved under inversion.

Theorem 20.10 *If the points P, Q and R invert to P_I, Q_I and R_I, then $\angle POR = \angle P_I Q_I R_I + \angle PQR$ (see figure 20.6).*

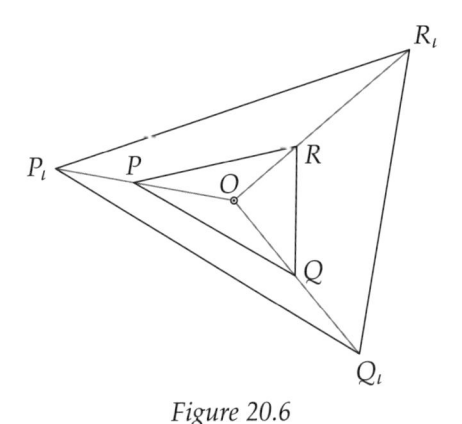

Figure 20.6

PROOF Using the external angles of cyclic quadrilaterals and of triangles, we obtain

$$\angle POR = \angle P_I Q_I O + \angle Q_I P_I O + \angle R_I Q_I O + \angle Q_I R_I O$$
$$= (\angle P_I Q_I O + \angle R_I Q_I O) + (\angle PQO + \angle RQO)$$
$$= \angle P_I Q_I R_I + \angle PQR.$$ ☐

This is a result which would benefit from the use of directed angles, since it is extremely diagram-dependent. As well as the stated form, the relationship could be either $\angle P_I Q_I R_I = \angle POR + \angle PQR$ or $\angle PQR = \angle P_I Q_I R_I + \angle POR$. Expressed in directed angles, this becomes $\angle P_I Q_I R_I =$

$\angle PQR + \angle POR$. The argument, however, is essentially exactly the same in all cases, with external angles being replaced by internal angles or angles in the same segment. The form given in theorem 20.10 is applicable when P is inside the two triangles, since that is what is needed below.

Theorem 20.11 *Let A_l, B_l and C_l be the images of the vertices of $\triangle ABC$ under an inversion with centre P. Then $\triangle A_l B_l C_l$ is similar to the pedal triangle $\triangle A''B''C''$ of P with respect to $\triangle ABC$ (see figure 20.7).*

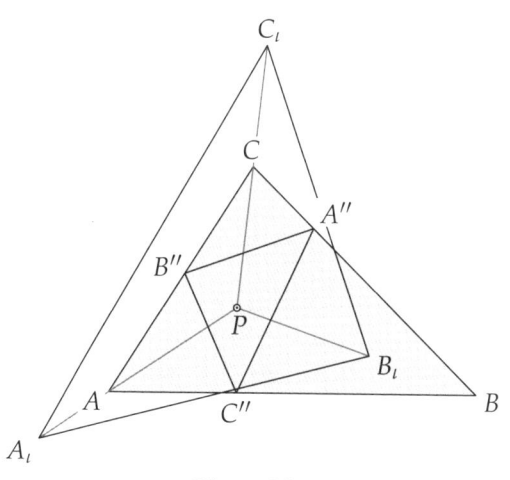

Figure 20.7

PROOF By theorem 20.10, we have $\angle BPC = \angle B_l A_l C_l + \angle BAC$ and by theorem 6.7 on page 77, $\angle BPC = \angle BAC + \angle B''A''C''$. Hence $\angle B_l A_l C_l = \angle B''A''C''$, and, with two more equalities of the same kind, the result follows. □

Exercise 20a

1. Prove that, if P_l and Q_l are the inverses of points P and Q, then the triangle $\triangle OPQ$ is similar to $\triangle OQ_l P_l$.

2. Given a line and a circle, prove that there are in general two centres of inversion which will map one to the other. In what circumstances is there only one centre?

3. Given any two circles, prove that they can be inverted to one another in two different ways.

4. Prove corollary 20.6.

5. Prove theorem 20.7.

6. Under what circumstances does a circle invert to itself?

7. Prove that, under an inversion with centre at one of the isodynamic points, triangle $\triangle ABC$ is mapped to an equilateral triangle.

20.3 Proof by inversion

Suppose we have a geometrical configuration and we wish to prove some result about it. By choosing an appropriate circle S, we can invert the whole of the configuration in S to create a new one, and the desired result becomes a new result. Then the task of proving the original result in the old configuration becomes that of proving the new result in the new configuration, which might be easier to do. The skill is in choosing the correct circle S. Usually the key choice is that of the *centre* of inversion; very often (but not always) the choice of the radius is less important.

We illustrate this process by proving the following.

Example *If AB and CD are direct common tangents to two circles which intersect at O, then the circumcircles of $\triangle ABO$ and $\triangle CDO$ are tangential (see figure 20.8).*

PROOF We invert in a circle with centre O, where the radius is immaterial. Let A_I, B_I, C_I and D_I be the images of A, B, C and D under the inversion (see figure 20.9). Note that the point O in both diagrams is the centre of inversion; its image O_I is, of course, at infinity.

The circles AOC and BOD become lines $A_I C_I$ and $B_I D_I$ and the lines AB and CD become circles $A_I O B_I$ and $C_I O D_I$. Since AB and CD are tangents to the circles AOC and BOD in the original diagram, $A_I C_I$ and $B_I D_I$ are tangents to the circles $A_I O B_I$ and $C_I O D_I$ in the image diagram.

Chapter 20: Inversion

Figure 20.8

Figure 20.9

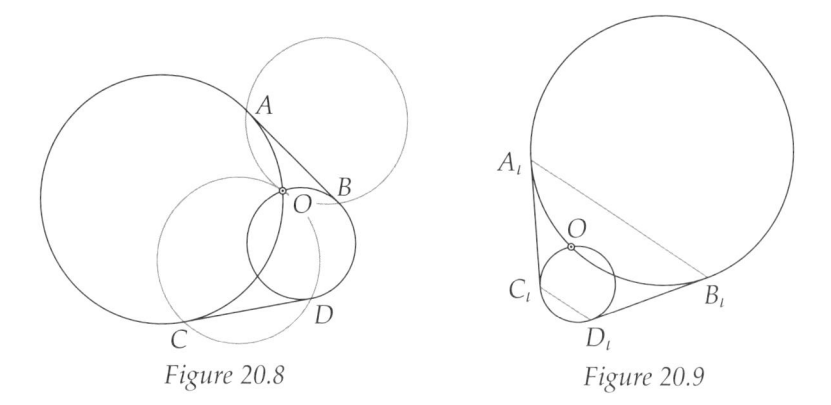

Finally, the circles AOB and COD become lines A_IB_I and C_ID_I. But these chords, being perpendicular to the line of centres, are parallel in the image diagram. It follows that the circles in the original diagram are tangential at O. Note that since the image of O is at infinity, this is equivalent to the parallel lines meeting at infinity. ❏

In the example, we have drawn two diagrams, one for the original configuration and one for the image under inversion. It would be quite in order to draw only one diagram since the points A_I, B_I, ... are just as 'real' as A, B, ..., but it often makes for greater clarity if two diagrams are used.

Exercise 20b

It is intended that the following questions are solved using inversion, although you might like also to attempt them using conventional methods of proof.

1. The circumcentres of $\triangle OBC$, $\triangle OCA$ and $\triangle OAB$ are X, Y and Z. If X lies on OA and Y lies on OB, prove that Z lies on OC.

2. The circumcircles of $\triangle ABC$ and $\triangle ABD$ are orthogonal. Prove that the circumcircles of $\triangle ACD$ and $\triangle BCD$ are also orthogonal.

3. The triangles $\triangle OBC$, $\triangle OCA$ and $\triangle OAB$ have circumradius R, and the circle with centre O and radius $2R$ touches their circumcircles at X, Y and Z. Prove that the circumcircles of $\triangle AOX$, $\triangle BOY$ and $\triangle COZ$ have a second point in common.

4. Points X, Y and Z are on the circumcircles of $\triangle OBC$, $\triangle OCA$ and $\triangle OAB$. Prove that the circumcircles of $\triangle AYZ$, $\triangle BZX$ and $\triangle CXY$ have a common point.

5. Points L, M and N are on the circumcircles of $\triangle OBC$, $\triangle OCA$ and $\triangle OAB$, such that the circumcircles of $\triangle OAL$, $\triangle OBM$ and $\triangle OCN$ have a second common point. Let L^*, M^* and N^* be the other intersections of circles OBC, OCA and OAB with the circumcircle of $\triangle LMN$. Prove that the circumcircles of $\triangle OAL^*$, $\triangle OBM^*$ and $\triangle OCN^*$ have a second common point.

20.4 The Kosnita and reflection triangles revisited

Recall from section 12.3 that the Kosnita triangle is formed from the circumcentres O_A, O_B and O_C of $\triangle OBC$, $\triangle OCA$ and $\triangle OAB$ and that the reflection triangle $\triangle A^*B^*C^*$ is obtained by reflecting the vertices of $\triangle ABC$ in the opposite sides.

We consider the effect of an inversion with centre O and radius R on the circumcircle of $\triangle BCO$. Since B and C invert to themselves, this will be the line BC.

Lemma 20.12 *Under this inversion, the point O_A inverts to O_a, the circumcentre of $\triangle A^*CB$.*

PROOF Let OO^* be the diameter of the circumcircle of $\triangle BCO$ which is perpendicular to BC (see figure 20.10).
As O^* inverts to A_1 it follows that $OA_1 \times OO^* = R^2$. Hence, since $OO_a = 2OA_1$, we have $OO_a \times OO_A = R^2$ and the result follows. □

Chapter 20: Inversion

Figure 20.10

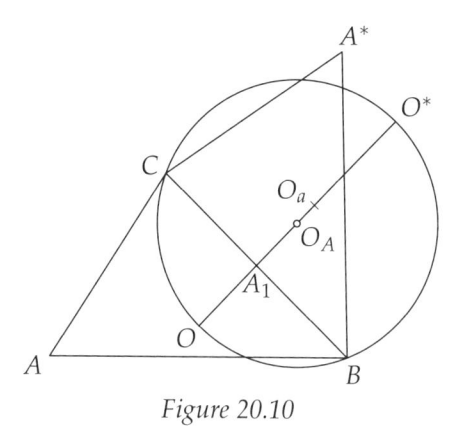

Theorem 20.13 *The circumcircles of $\triangle AOA^*$, $\triangle BOB^*$ and $\triangle COC^*$ are concurrent at a point K_* which is the inverse of the Kosnita point under the above inversion.*

PROOF Note first that the circumcircle of $\triangle AOA^*$ also passes through O_a. Under the inversion, A maps to itself and, by lemma 20.12, O_a maps to O_A, and hence the circumcircle inverts to the line AO_A. Hence the three circumcircles invert to AO_A, BO_B and CO_C. By theorem 12.9 on page 163, these lines are concurrent at K^*. It follows that the circumcircles are concurrent at the inverse of K^*. ❑

The point K_* is, for obvious reasons, known as the *inverse Kosnita point*. It follows, of course, that O, K^* and K_* are collinear, and that OA is a tangent to the circumcircle of $\triangle K^*AK_*$ (see figure 20.11).

The existence of the point K_*, as the second point of intersection of three circumcircles, can be shown without using inversion. Obviously O is on all three circles. The circumcentre of $\triangle AOA^*$ lies on the perpendicular bisectors of AO and AA^*, so it is the intersection of BC and O_BO_C, and the other two circumcentres are the intersections of CA and O_CO_A and of AB and O_AO_B. Hence the circumcentres lie on the axis of perspective of the Kosnita triangle $\triangle O_AO_BO_C$ and $\triangle ABC$. The axis of perspective is shown dashed in figure 20.11.

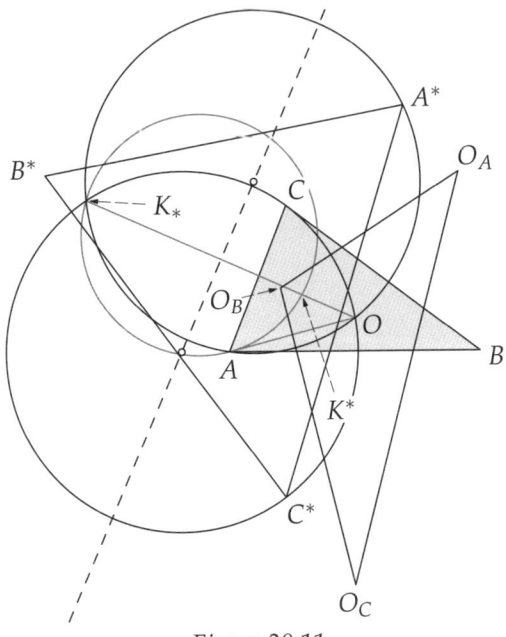

Figure 20.11

20.5 Inarc circles

When a triangle is circumscribed by a circle, we can think of the resulting configuration as three segments of the circle surrounding the triangle. An interesting problem is to locate the circles which are tangent to two of the sides of the triangle and to the circumcircle.

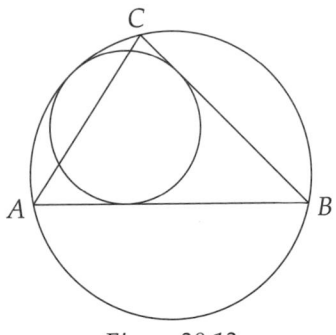

Figure 20.12

Chapter 20: Inversion

Figure 20.12 shows a circle which is tangential to BA and BC internally and also tangential internally to the circumcircle. We call this the *B-inarc circle*.

Note that there is also a circle, the *B-exarc circle*, which is tangential to BA and BC produced and also tangential externally to the circumcircle. We will focus on the inarc circles, since the treatment of the exarc circles is very similar.

Theorem 20.14 *If the B-inarc circle touches BA at R_b and BC at P_b, then the midpoint of $P_b R_b$ is the incentre of $\triangle ABC$.*

PROOF Let the incircle of $\triangle ABC$ touch BA and BC at P and R, and let the line through I perpendicular to BI meet BA and BC at J and K, so that I is the midpoint of JK (see figure 20.13).

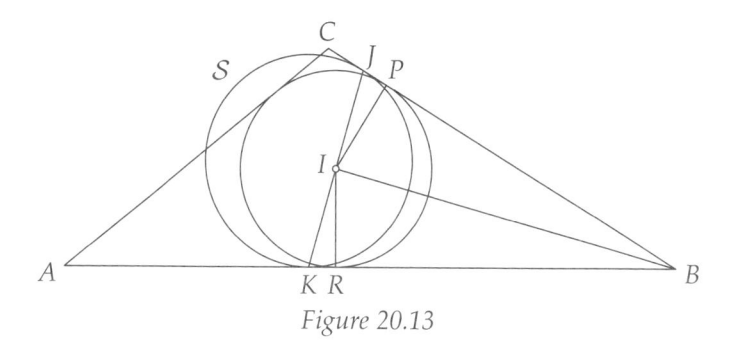

Figure 20.13

Invert in the circle with centre B and radius BI. Then, since $\triangle BPI$ and $\triangle BIJ$ are similar, we have $BP \times BJ = BI^2$, and so J and P are inverse points. Similarly so are K and R, and, of course, I is self-inverse. The incircle therefore inverts to the circle S which touches BA and BC at K and J.

Let A_l and C_l be the inverses of A and C, and let W be the incentre of $\triangle A_l B C_l$, which lies on BI (see figure 20.14).

Then $\angle A_l I W = \angle A_l I B = \angle BAI$, since $\triangle BIA_l$ is similar to $\triangle BAI$ by the inversion. Also note that $ACC_l A_l$ is cyclic, again by inversion. Therefore $\angle BAI = \frac{1}{2}\angle BAC = \frac{1}{2}\angle A_l C_l B = \angle A_l C_l W$. Hence $\angle A_l I W = \angle A_l C_l W$, and so $A_l I C_l W$ is cyclic. But WI is an axis of symmetry, so $\angle W A_l I = 90°$, and I is the excentre of $\triangle A_l B C_l$. Hence the incircle touches $A_l C_l$ at a point T (see figure 20.15).

Figure 20.14

Figure 20.15

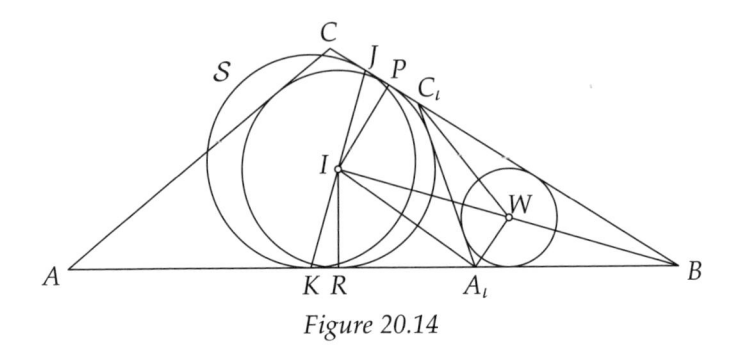

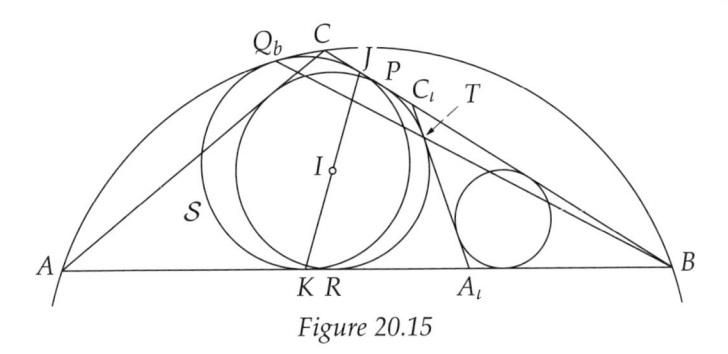

The inversion, however, takes $A_\iota C_\iota$ to the circumcircle of $\triangle BAC$, and so the circle S is tangential to the circumcircle at a point Q_b which is the inverse of T. Consequently the points J and K are the points P_b and R_b and S is the B-inarc circle. □

Theorem 20.14 gives a simple construction for the centres of the inarc circles, and it is interesting to see all three centres in the same diagram (see figure 20.16).

The centres of the exarc circles are constructed in exactly the same way, but beginning with the excentres. The analogous result to theorem 20.14 states that if the B-exarc circle touches BA at R_b^* and BC at P_b^*, then the midpoint of $P_b^* R_b^*$ is the B-excentre of $\triangle ABC$.

Figure 20.16

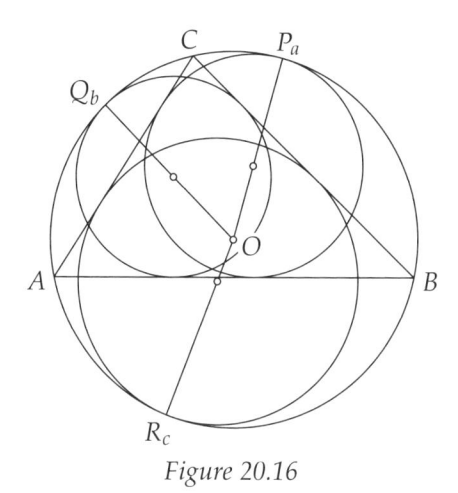

20.6 Poncelet's porism

Euler's formula, as given by theorem 3.8 on page 31, states that $IO^2 = R^2 - 2Rr$, and it concerns two circles, one with centre I and radius r and the other with centre O and radius R. Suppose now that we begin with two circles, satisfying the given relationship, and attempt to reconstruct the triangle which has the first as incircle and the second as circumcircle. In how many ways can this be done?

Surprisingly, it turns out that we can begin with *any* point on the outer circle, and, by drawing tangents to the inner circle, we always achieve a closed triangle. This is a special case of a much more general result which is known as *Poncelet's porism*.

Before embarking on a proof of this statement, it is worth seeing what happens when we begin with the configuration shown in figure 20.17, and perform an inversion with respect to the incircle $\mathcal{I}$.

The result, although not to the same scale, is shown in figure 20.18. The vertices of the intouch triangle $\triangle PQR$ are invariant under the inversion. The images A_ι, B_ι and C_ι of the vertices A, B and C are the midpoints of $\triangle PQR$, since, for example, AQ and AR are tangents to the incircle. Hence the line BC is inverted to the circumcircle of $\triangle IB_\iota C_\iota$, which has diameter IP and radius $\frac{1}{2}r$. The circumcircle of $\triangle ABC$ is mapped to the circumcircle of $\triangle A_\iota B_\iota C_\iota$, which is the nine-point circle of $\triangle PQR$ and hence also has radius $\frac{1}{2}r$. Note that all four of these circles are congruent.

Figure 20.17

Figure 20.18

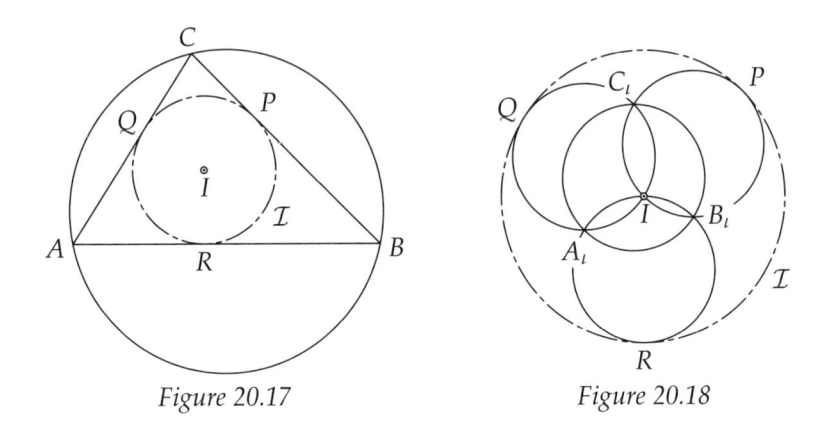

Now let us begin with just the incircle and the circumcircle S (see figure 20.19), and carry out the same inversion.

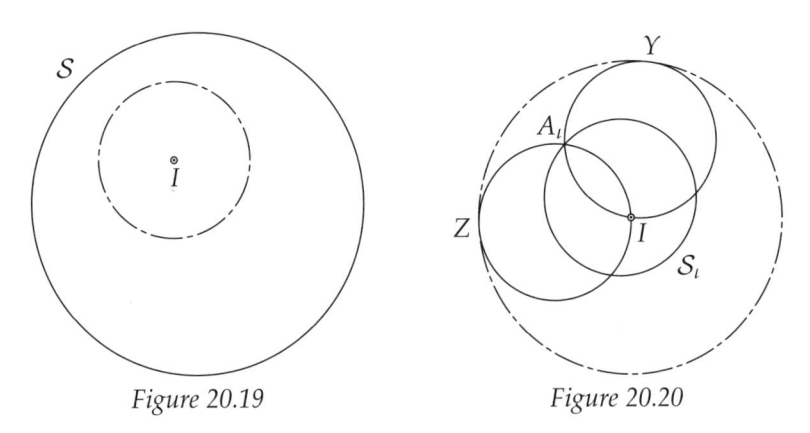

Figure 20.19

Figure 20.20

The circumcircle S inverts to a circle S_ι with radius R', where, by theorem 20.7,

$$R' = R \times \frac{r^2}{t} = R \times \frac{r^2}{|OI^2 - R^2|} = \tfrac{1}{2}r.$$

Now we select any point A_ι on the circle S_ι and construct two circles of radius $\tfrac{1}{2}r$ through A_ι and I (see figure 20.20).

Since these circles have diameters which are the radii of the incircle, they touch the incircle at points Z and Y. Also, note that since triangles $\triangle IA_\iota Z$ and $\triangle IA_\iota Y$ are congruent (RHS), A_ι is the midpoint of YZ.

Let B_l and C_l be the second intersections of these circles with S_l and let X be the intersection of ZB_l and YC_l. Then quadrilateral IC_lXB_l is cyclic, and its circumcircle has diameter IX (see figure 20.21).

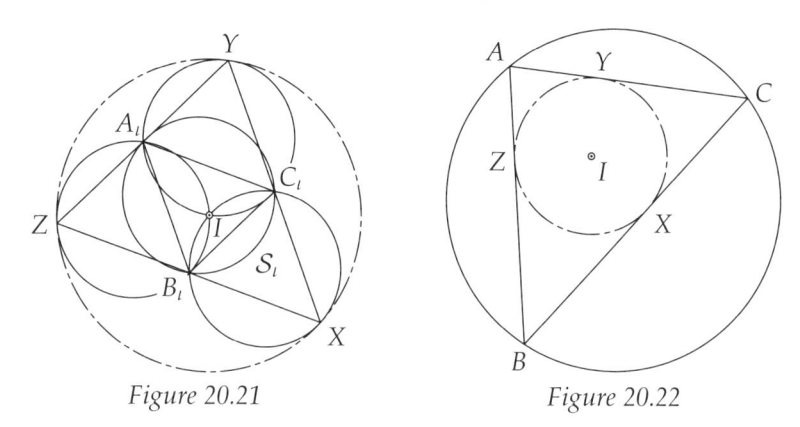

Figure 20.21 *Figure 20.22*

Now since A_lC_l is a common chord of circles of equal radius we have $\angle ZYX = \angle A_lYC_l = \angle C_lB_lA_l$, and, similarly, $\angle XZY = \angle B_lC_lA_l$. Hence $\angle C_lA_lB_l = \angle B_lXC_l$ and so the circumcircle of $\triangle B_lXC_l$ also has radius $\frac{1}{2}r$ and is tangential to the incircle at X.

Hence $\triangle A_lB_lC_l$ is the medial triangle of $\triangle XYZ$ and I is its orthocentre. We now invert in the incircle again. The three circles B_lXC_l, C_lYA_l and A_lZB_l become lines BXC, CYA and AZB tangential to the incircle, and the circle $A_lB_lC_l$ becomes the circumcircle of $\triangle ABC$ (see figure 20.22).

We have therefore shown that, starting from any point A on the outer circle, we can create a triangle $\triangle ABC$ which has the inner circle as its incircle.

Exercise 20c

1. Prove that the inverse Kosnita point K_* lies on the circumcircles of $\triangle C^*AB^*$, $\triangle A^*BC^*$ and $\triangle B^*CA^*$.

2. Prove that, if r_a is the radius of the A-inarc circle, then

$$r_a = r\sec^2 \tfrac{1}{2}A.$$

3. Prove that the lines AP_a, BQ_b, CR_c and IO are concurrent.

4. Prove that the lines AP_a^*, BQ_b^*, CR_c^* and IO are concurrent.

5. Prove that the length of the tangent from A to the A-inarc circle is $\dfrac{bc}{s}$.

6. Prove that the orthocentre and centroid of the intouch triangle $\triangle PQR$ are collinear with the incentre and circumcentre of $\triangle ABC$.

Chapter 21

The Feuerbach points

This chapter is centred around one of the gems of triangle geometry, a result which shows that the nine-point circle of a triangle is tangential to its incircles and excircles. The original proof used by Feuerbach calculated the distance between centres of the circles. The amount of algebra and trigonometry involved makes this method very ponderous.

We present several different approaches which are more elegant than this. The first is classical, in the sense that it uses standard Euclidean techniques and also constructs the position of the points of tangency. The second uses inversion and the third arises as a special case of a theorem on isogonal conjugates. In addition, we examine relationships between the Feuerbach triangle and the reference triangle.

21.1 Feuerbach's theorem

Theorem 21.1 (Feuerbach) *The nine-point circle is tangential to the incircle and the three excircles.*

PROOF The proof for the incircle is given as an extended exercise, using figure 21.1, in which the points A_1, D, I, I_A, N, O, P, P_A, U and X have their conventional meanings (see exercise 21a).

We must show that the nine-point circle is also tangential to the three excircles. We shall concentrate on the excircle opposite to A.

The line segment PXP_A is a transverse common tangent to the incircle and excircle, and X lies on their line of centres II_A. Hence the line TX is

Figure 21.1

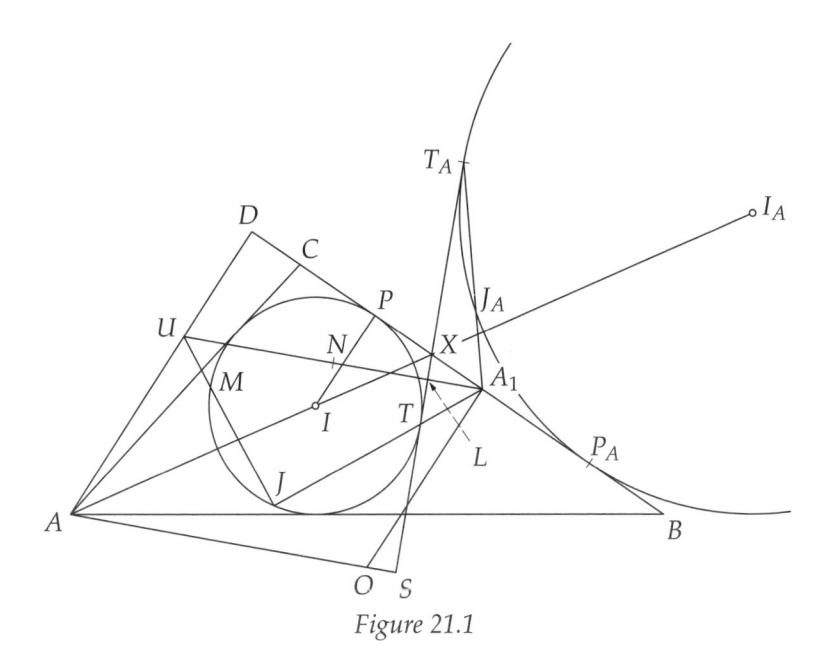

the other transverse common tangent, and we label the point of tangency with the A-excircle by T_A. Now let the intersection of $A_1 T_A$ with the excircle be J_A. We can now use an argument exactly similar to that of exercise 21a to show that the excircle and nine-point circle are tangential here. ❏

The strength of this 'classical proof' is that it identifies the points of tangency of the incircle and excircles with the nine-point circle. The point J is called the *Feuerbach point* of $\triangle ABC$ and J_A is called the *Feuerbach point of the A-excircle*, and there are, of course, analogous points J_B and J_C, giving four Feuerbach points in all. The triangle $\triangle J_A J_B J_C$ is known as the *Feuerbach triangle*, which obviously has circumcentre N.

Exercise 21a

1. (a) Show that D, P, X, P_A is a harmonic range.
   (b) Show that $A_1 X \times A_1 D = A_1 P^2$.
   (c) Show that AX bisects $\angle DAO$.

2. Let XT be the tangent from X to the incircle other than XP, meeting UA_1 at L and AO at S.
   (a) Show that AX bisects $\angle PXT$.
   (b) Show that XT is perpendicular to AO.
   (c) Show that $\angle XLU = 90°$.

3. Let $A_1 T$ meet the incircle again at J.
   (a) Prove that $A_1 L \times A_1 U = A_1 X \times A_1 D$.
   (b) Prove that $A_1 T \times A_1 J = A_1 P^2$.
   (c) Show that the quadrilateral $LUJT$ is cyclic.
   (d) Show that J lies on the nine-point circle.

4. Let UJ meet the incircle again at Y.
   (a) Prove that T, I and Y are collinear.
   (b) Prove that TY is parallel to UA_1.
   (c) Prove that N, I and J are collinear.
   (d) Hence prove that the nine-point circle is tangential to the incircle.

21.2 A proof using inversion

It is also possible to prove theorem 21.1 using inversion, and again this is presented as an exercise. This is a beautiful proof which has the merit of dealing with the incircle and excircles in a single argument, but it does not actually show where the points of tangency are.

Exercise 21b

1. Invert the figure consisting of the triangle $\triangle ABC$, the incircle, the A-excircle and the nine-point circle with respect to a circle S with centre A_1 and diameter PP_A.
   (a) What is the image of the incircle?
   (b) What is the image of the A-excircle?
   (c) What is the image of the line BC?
   (d) Prove that the nine-point circle inverts to a line $\mathcal{L}$ through the image of D.

2. We now identify this line $\mathcal{L}$; this is the nub of the proof.
   (a) What is the image of D under the inversion?
   (b) Prove that $\mathcal{L}$ is parallel to the tangent at A_1 to the nine-point circle.
   (c) Prove that $\mathcal{L}$ makes an angle of $|\angle C - \angle B|$ with BC.

3. Let $\mathcal{M}$ be the line through X perpendicular to AX.
   (a) Prove that $\mathcal{L}$ is the image of BC after reflection in $\mathcal{M}$.
   (b) Prove that $\mathcal{L}$ is the transverse common tangent to the incircle and A-excircle.

4. Prove Feuerbach's theorem.

21.3 Consequences

Now we can show an immediate but quite extraordinary consequence of theorem 21.1.

Corollary 21.2 *The sixteen incircles and excircles derived from the four triangles $\triangle ABC$, $\triangle BCH$, $\triangle CAH$ and $\triangle ABH$ are all tangent to the nine-point circle.*

PROOF From section 3.4 on page 34 we know that the four triangles of the orthocentric group have a common nine-point circle, and we simply apply the theorem to each of the triangles in turn. ❑

As a result of corollary 21.2, we obtain the splendid figure 21.2, in which the interior of the nine-point circle is shown cross-hatched.

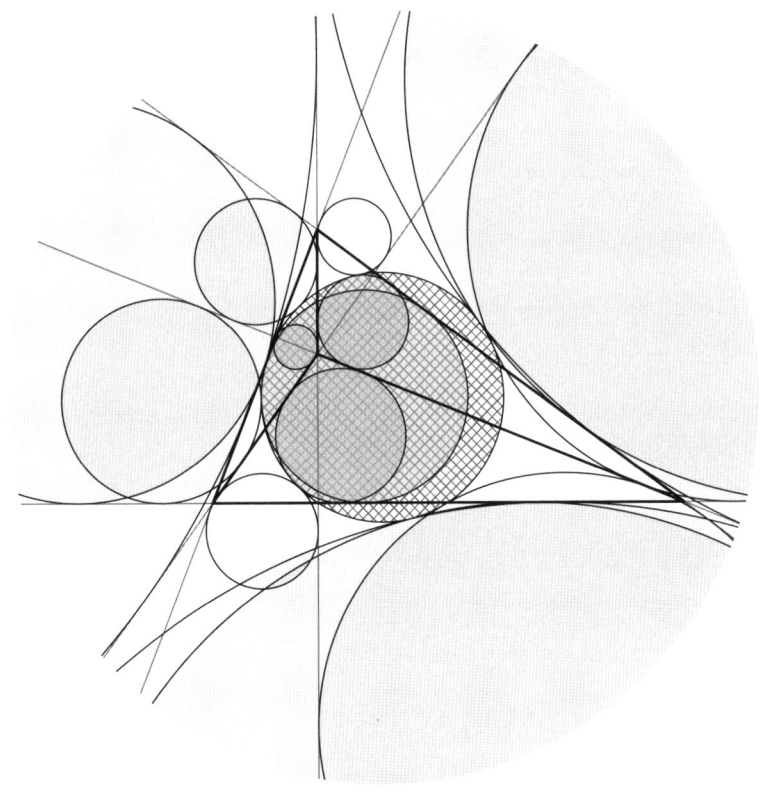

Figure 21.2

We can easily create situations in which the circumcircle of $\triangle ABC$ is the nine-point circle of some other triangle, and apply Feuerbach's theorem to this configuration. Some of these are explored in the following exercise.

Exercise 21c

1. Prove that the circumcircle of $\triangle ABC$ is tangential to the incircle and excircles of its anticomplementary triangle $\triangle A^*B^*C^*$.

2. Prove that, given a triangle formed by any three non-concurrent angle bisectors of $\triangle ABC$, the incircle and excircles are tangential to the circumcircle of $\triangle ABC$.

3. Prove that one of the lengths JA_1, JB_1 and JC_1 is the sum of the other two.

4. Prove that J lies on the Euler lines of $\triangle QAR$ (as in theorem 3.7 on page 30) and of the two triangles through B and C defined in an analogous way.

5. Prove that J lies on the nine-point circle of $\triangle HIM$, where M is the Nagel point.

6. Show that the orthocentre of any triangle which arises from Poncelet's porism lies on a fixed circle.

21.4 A proof using spiral similarities

A third approach to proving theorem 21.1 uses the theory of invariable points which was introduced in section 15.5 on page 212. As with the other examples in that chapter, we begin with the orthic configuration.

Theorem 21.3 *Let the points I_a, I_b and I_c be the incentres of $\triangle AEF$, $\triangle DBF$ and $\triangle DEC$, and let U, V and W be the Euler points of $\triangle ABC$. Then the lines $I_a U$, $I_b V$ and $I_c W$ are concurrent on the nine-point circle of $\triangle ABC$ (see figure 21.3).*

PROOF Let $\mathcal{F}_1$, $\mathcal{F}_2$ and $\mathcal{F}_3$ be the three similar triangles $\triangle AEF$, $\triangle DBF$ and $\triangle DEC$. Then I_a, I_b and I_c are corresponding points of $\mathcal{F}_1$, $\mathcal{F}_2$ and $\mathcal{F}_3$ and $\triangle UVW$ is the invariable triangle. The result now follows by theorem 15.11 on page 214. ☐

Figure 21.3

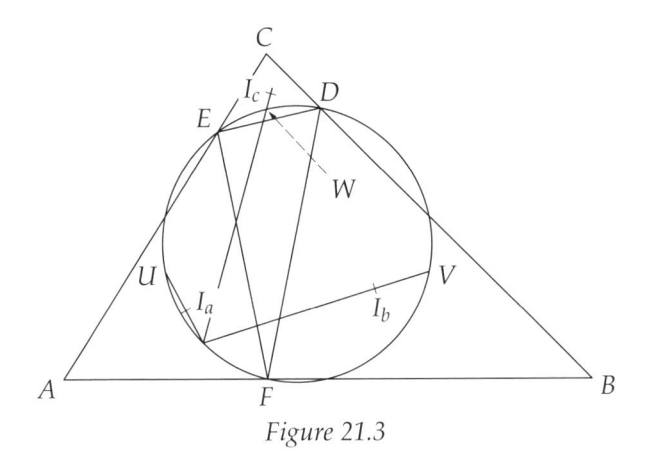

It will turn out that the point of concurrence is the Feuerbach point. To show this, we first prove a technical result.

Note that I_c lies on CI, the angle bisector at C. As in the proof of theorem 3.8 on page 31, let this meet the circumcircle again at Z', and let $Z'Z''$ be a diameter of the circumcircle.

Lemma 21.4 $\dfrac{II_c}{Z'I} = \dfrac{r}{R}$.

PROOF By the similarity of $\triangle DEC$ and $\triangle ABC$,

$$\frac{CI_c}{CI} = \frac{CE}{CB} = \cos C$$

so $CI_c = CI \cos C$. Hence $II_c = CI(1 - \cos C) = 2CI \sin^2 \tfrac{1}{2}C$. But $r = CI \sin \tfrac{1}{2}C$, so $CI \times II_c = 2r^2$.

Let the incircle touch CA at Q (see figure 21.4). Then $\triangle CQI$ is similar to $\triangle Z''AZ'$ so

$$\frac{CI}{IQ} = \frac{Z''Z'}{Z'A}$$

and, from the proof of theorem 3.8 on page 31, $Z'A = Z'I$. Hence $CI \times Z'I = IQ \times Z'Z'' = 2rR$. The result follows. ❑

Theorem 21.5 *The point of concurrence of I_aU, I_bV and I_cW is the Feuerbach point of $\triangle ABC$.*

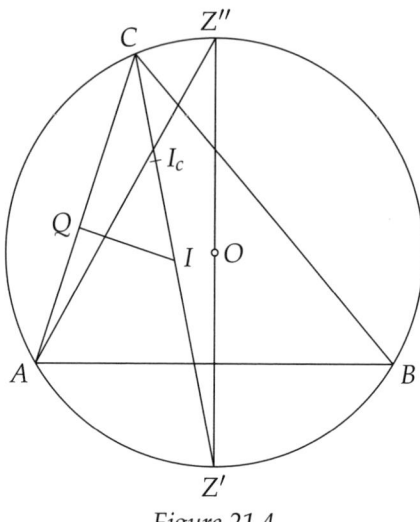

Figure 21.4

PROOF Let P be the point on WI_c such that IP is parallel to NW (see figure 21.5).

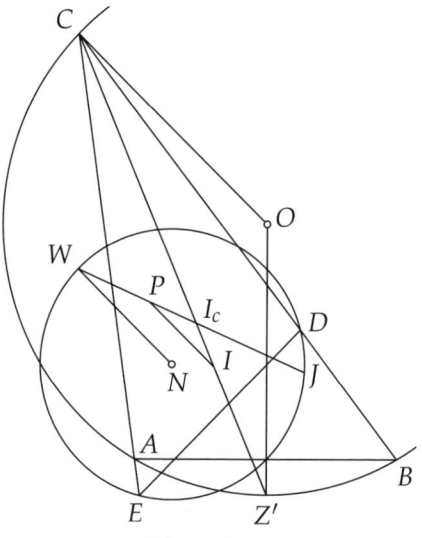

Figure 21.5

By the similarity of $\triangle DEC$ and $\triangle ABC$, $\angle CI_c W = \angle CIO$, and so $\angle II_c P = \angle Z'IO$. By theorem 2.22 on page 22, $CO \perp ED$ and so CO is parallel to IP. Hence $\angle I_c IP = \angle Z'CO = \angle IZ'O$ and $\triangle II_c P$ is similar to $\triangle Z'IO$. So
$$\frac{IP}{Z'O} = \frac{II_c}{Z'I} = \frac{r}{R}$$
by lemma 21.4. Hence $IP = r$ and P lies on the incircle.

Now $IP \parallel NW$, and they are radii of the incircle and nine-point circle. Therefore WP (and so $I_c W$) passes through their centre of similitude, which is the Feuerbach point. ❑

A similar argument shows that if I_{aA} is the A-excentre of $\triangle AEF$, I_{bD} the D-excentre of $\triangle DBF$ and I_{cD} the D-excentre of $\triangle DEC$, then $I_{aA}U$, $I_{bD}V$ and $I_{cD}W$ are also concurrent on the nine-point circle; this is, of course, the Feuerbach point J_A, the Feuerbach point of the A-excircle. The points J_B and J_C can be constructed in an analogous manner.

21.5 A proof using the Simson line

Recall from theorem 7.9 on page 89 that isogonal conjugates share the same pedal circle.

Theorem 21.6 *Let the points P and Q be isogonal conjugates which lie on a diameter of the circumcircle of $\triangle ABC$. Then their common pedal circle is tangent to the nine-point circle.*

PROOF Let XY be the diameter of the circumcircle through P and Q. By theorem 4.7 on page 46, the Simson lines of X and Y intersect at right-angles through a point on the nine-point circle which we label T. By theorem 7.9 on page 89, the centre O_P of the common pedal circle lies on this diameter at the midpoint of PQ.

Let X', P', Q' and Y' be the projections of X, P, Q and Y on BC, and note that A_1 is the projection of O (see figure 21.6).

The Simson lines of X and Y pass (by definition) through X' and Y', so A_1 is the centre of a circle with diameter $X'Y'$, which passes through T. Hence $A_1X' = A_1Y' = A_1T$. Now

$$\frac{A_1P'}{A_1X'} = \frac{OP}{R} \quad \text{and} \quad \frac{A_1Q'}{A_1Y'} = \frac{OQ}{R},$$

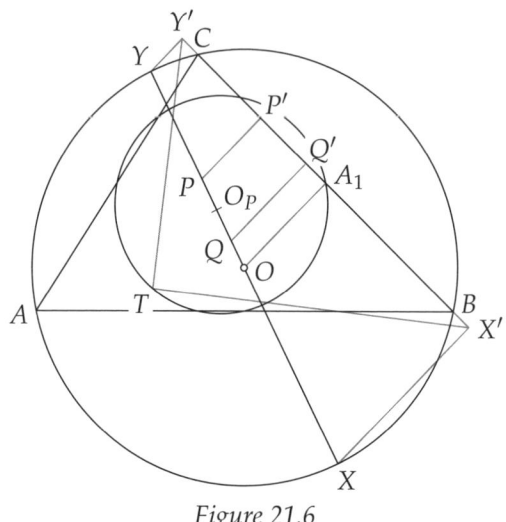

Figure 21.6

so

$$\frac{A_1P' \times A_1Q'}{A_1T^2} = \frac{OP \times OQ}{R^2}.$$

The numerator $A_1P' \times A_1Q'$ is the power of A_1 with respect to the common pedal circle; we shall denote this by $\pi(A_1)$. We can also think of A_1T^2 as the power of A_1 with respect to a point circle T, and will write this as $\pi_0(A_1)$. We can obtain similar equations for the projections on sides CA and AB, with the same right-hand side. It follows that

$$\frac{\pi(A_1)}{\pi_0(A_1)} = \frac{\pi(B_1)}{\pi_0(B_1)} = \frac{\pi(C_1)}{\pi_0(C_1)}.$$

Hence, by theorem 18.15 on page 264, the circle through A_1, B_1 and C_1 (the nine-point circle) is coaxal with the pedal circle and the point circle T.

Since T lies on the nine-point circle, this coaxal system consists of circles tangential to the radical axis, which is the tangent to the nine-point circle at T. It follows that the pedal circle is also tangential to the nine-point circle at T, and that O_P, N and T are collinear. ❑

Corollary 21.7 *The nine-point circle is tangential to the incircle and the three excircles.*

Chapter 21: The Feuerbach points

PROOF The incentre and excentres are their own isogonal conjugates, and their pedal circles are the incircle and excircles. ❏

This gives us another characterisation of the Feuerbach points, namely the points of intersection of the Simson lines at the ends of the circumdiameters through I, I_A, I_B and I_C.

21.6 The Feuerbach triangle

We now look at relationships between $\triangle J_A J_B J_C$ and $\triangle ABC$. Note that we can easily identify the Feuerbach points without drawing the incircle or excircles by showing where the nine-point circle intersects the four lines of centres NI, NI_A, NI_B and NI_C (see figure 21.7).

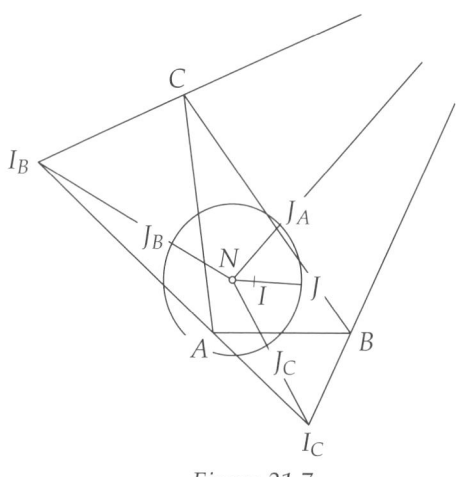

Figure 21.7

The external centre of similitude of the incircle and nine-point circle is their point of tangency, namely J, and the internal centre of similitude is the point J^* on NI such that N, J^*, I, J is a harmonic range.

Theorem 21.8 *The Feuerbach triangle $\triangle J_A J_B J_C$ is in perspective with the reference triangle $\triangle ABC$ and the perspector is J^*.*

PROOF Let AJ_A intersect the incircle at Q and IN at P (see figure 21.8).

Figure 21.8

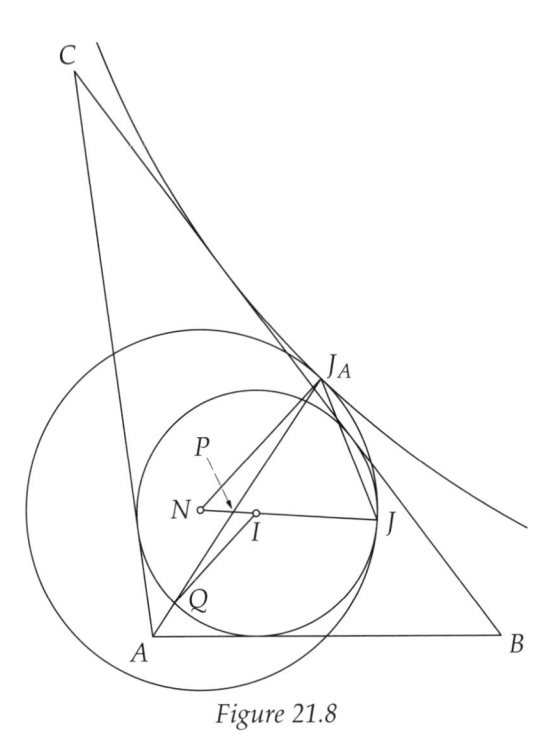

Since A is the centre of similitude of the incircle and the A-excircle, IQ is parallel to $I_A J_A$, and hence to NJ_A. So the triangles $\triangle IPQ$ and $\triangle NPJ_A$ are similar and
$$\frac{NP}{IP} = \frac{NJ_A}{IQ}.$$
Hence P is the internal centre of similitude J^* of the incircle and nine-point circle. But the same is true of BJ_B and CJ_C, so the results follow. □

The internal centre of similitude of the A-excircle and nine-point circle is J_A, their point of tangency, and so the external centre of similitude is the point J_A^* on $I_A N$ such that I_A, J_A, N, J_A^* is harmonic.

Theorem 21.9 *The triangles $\triangle JJ_CJ_B$ and $\triangle ABC$ are in perspective with perspector J_A^*.*

PROOF (See figure 21.9.)
Since N, J^*, I, J is harmonic (see the paragraph before theorem 21.8), the pencil $A(N, J^*, I, J)$ is harmonic. By theorem 5.8 on page 57, any

Chapter 21: The Feuerbach points 307

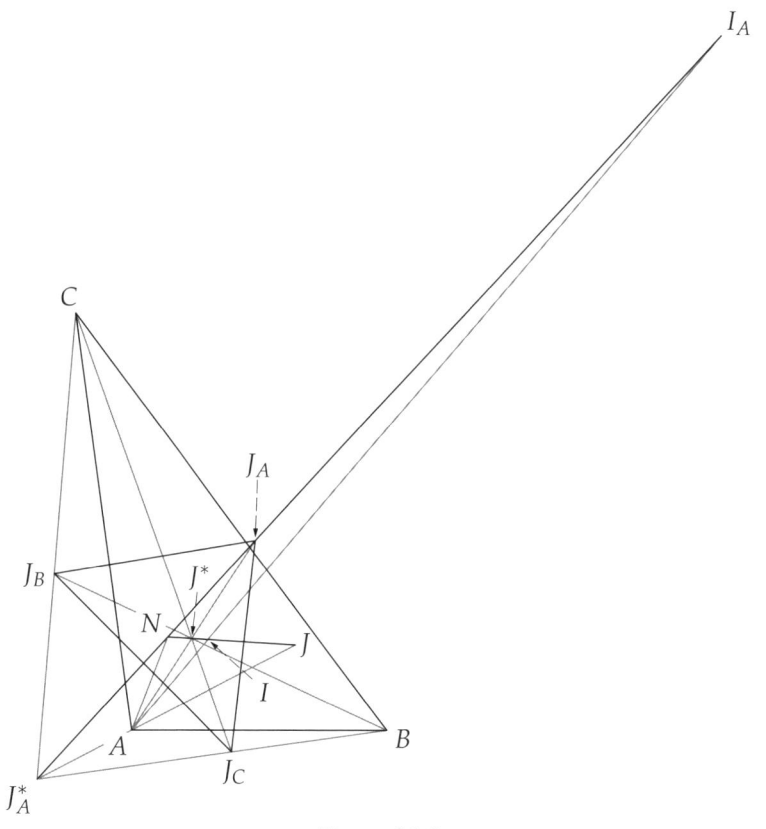

Figure 21.9

transversal of this pencil is harmonic. Note by theorem 21.8 that A, J^* and J_A are collinear. If we choose the transversal NI_A, this yields the range consisting of N, J_A, I_A and the point where JA intersects NI_A. Since this is a harmonic range, this point is J_A^*. Hence we have proved that J, A and J_A^* are collinear.

Now by definition J_A^* is the external centre of similitude of the A-excircle and the nine-point circle. By Feuerbach's theorem, J_B is the internal centre of similitude of the B-excircle and nine-point circle, and, by section 2.3 on page 15, C is the internal centre of similitude of the A- and B- excircles. Hence by theorem 6.6(ii) on page 75, J_A^*, J_B and C are collinear. A similar argument establishes that J_A^*, J_C and B are collinear, and this completes the proof. ❏

Exercise 21d

1. Prove that the triangles $\triangle BI_CJ_B$ and $\triangle CI_BJ_C$ are in perspective.

2. Prove that the triangles $\triangle BI_BJ_C$ and $\triangle CI_CJ_B$ are in perspective.

3. Prove that the triangles $\triangle BI_CJ_C$ and $\triangle CI_BJ_B$ are in perspective.

4. Prove that the Feuerbach triangle $\triangle J_AJ_BJ_C$ and the incentral triangle $\triangle XYZ$ are in perspective.

Chapter 22

Soddy circles

A famous problem due to the Greek geometer Apollonius is that of constructing all the circles which are tangential to three given circles. As the contact of the new circle with each of the originals can be either external or internal, there are, in general, eight solutions to this problem. Depending on how the original circles are related, there can in fact be any number of tangent circles between zero and eight.

In this chapter we look at a special case of the Apollonius problem where the three given circles touch each other externally.

22.1 Touching circles

For a given triangle $\triangle ABC$, there are three circles, externally tangential in pairs, centred at A, B and C. We shall call these the *base* circles and denote them by $\mathcal{S}_A$, $\mathcal{S}_B$ and $\mathcal{S}_C$. They are easy to construct.

Let P, Q and R be the points of tangency of the incircle with the three sides. Then the circles centred at A, B and C with radii $s - a$, $s - b$ and $s - c$ touch each other externally in pairs (see figure 22.1). This is a consequence of theorem 2.10 on page 16, with the circles touching at P, Q and R.

Our aim is to find a way of constructing two circles which are tangential to the base circles (see figure 22.2). These are known as the *inner* and *outer* Soddy circles of $\triangle ABC$. Their centres are known as the *inner* and *outer* Soddy points, and are denoted by S_i and S_o.

Figure 22.1

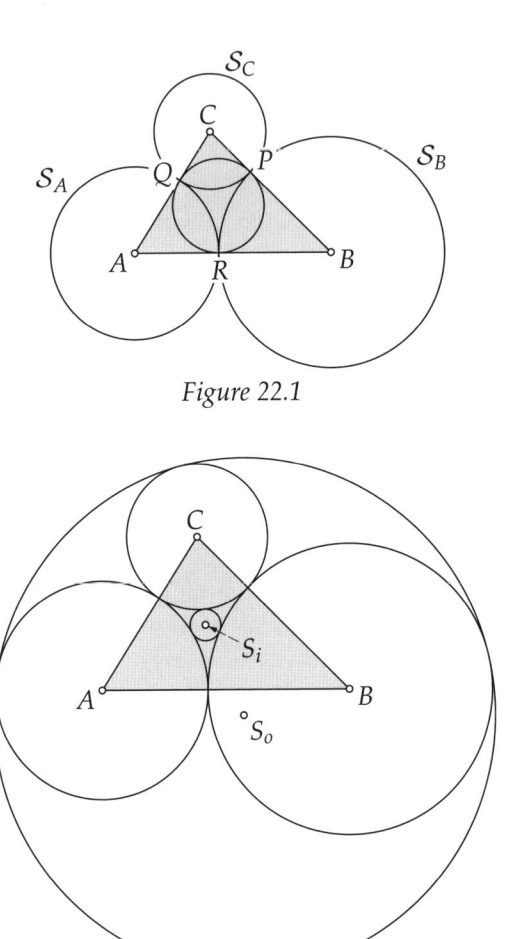

Figure 22.2

In figure 22.2, the inner Soddy circle is tangential to each of the base circles externally, and the outer Soddy circle is tangential to each of them internally. However, this does not always happen. Suppose that one of the angles of $\triangle ABC$, A for example, is allowed to grow in magnitude.

In figure 22.3, the outer Soddy circle touches the base circles externally. In between the two cases is a limiting one where the base circles have a common tangent (see figure 22.4). This is a 'degenerate' outer Soddy circle.

Chapter 22: Soddy circles 311

Figure 22.3

Figure 22.4

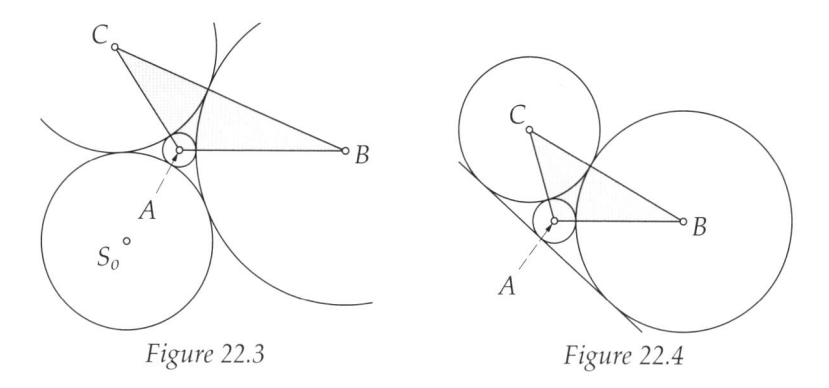

For convenience, we will refer to the two different configurations shown in figures 22.2 and 22.3 as the 'internal' and 'external' cases. Later we will analyse the conditions for each case to occur.

22.2 The Soddy circles

As the configuration contains several circles which are tangential to one another, a natural way of locating the Soddy circles is to use inversion. The ingenious step is to choose as the circle of inversion the circle which has centre P and is orthogonal to S_A, shown dashed in figure 22.5.

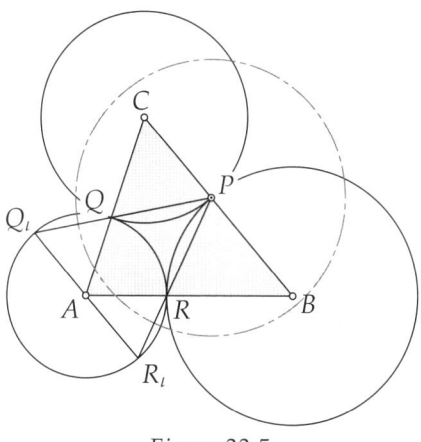

Figure 22.5

Let PQ meet $\mathcal{S}_A$ again at Q_ι. Then $\triangle AQQ_\iota$ is similar to $\triangle CQP$, as both are isosceles, and so AQ_ι is parallel to BC. Hence, if R_ι is defined in the same way, $R_\iota Q_\iota$ is a diameter of $\mathcal{S}_A$ parallel to BC.

Since it is orthogonal to the circle of inversion, $\mathcal{S}_A$ inverts to itself, with P and Q mapping to P_ι and Q_ι. Since the incircle passes through P it inverts to the line $R_\iota Q_\iota$.

The base circles $\mathcal{S}_B$ and $\mathcal{S}_C$ invert to lines which are perpendicular to BC and tangential to $\mathcal{S}_A$ (see figure 22.6).

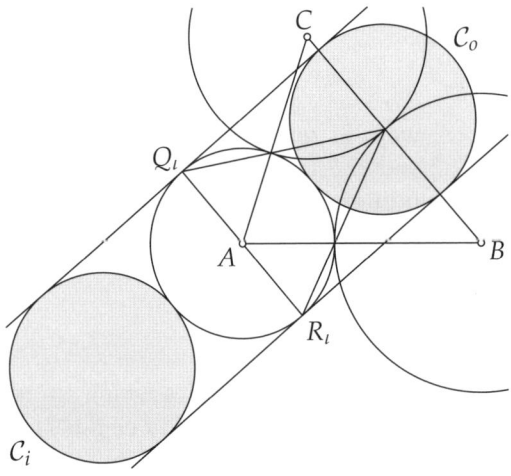

Figure 22.6

The inner and outer Soddy circles invert to circles which are tangential to $\mathcal{S}_A$ and to these lines. They are the two circles $\mathcal{C}_i$ and $\mathcal{C}_o$ shown shaded in figure 22.6, and they have the same radius as $\mathcal{S}_A$.

Now we can locate the original Soddy circles by inverting these two circles. The circle $\mathcal{C}_i$ inverts to the inner Soddy circle and $\mathcal{C}_o$ inverts to the outer Soddy circle.

We begin with $\mathcal{C}_i$, which touches $\mathcal{S}_A$ and the two lines at the points e_A, e_B and e_C. Then define E_A as the intersection of Pe_A with $\mathcal{S}_A$ and E_B and E_C similarly. The triangle $\triangle E_A E_B E_C$ is known as the *inner Soddy triangle* (see figure 22.7).

The inner Soddy circle is now the circumcircle of the inner Soddy triangle. It is tangential to the base circles at E_A, E_B and E_C, and so $\triangle E_A E_B E_C$ is in perspective with $\triangle ABC$ with perspector S_i, the centre of the inner Soddy circle.

Chapter 22: Soddy circles   313

Figure 22.7

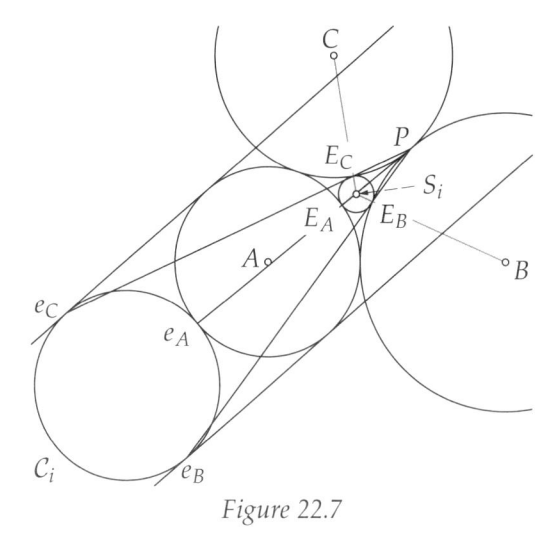

In exactly the same way we can construct the outer Soddy circle which has centre S_o. The point corresponding to e_A is e_A^* and the line Pe_A^* intersects $\mathcal{S}_A$ at E_A^*, and now the outer Soddy circle is the circumcircle of $\triangle E_A^* E_B^* E_C^*$, the *outer Soddy triangle* (see figure 22.8).

This construction works in both the internal and external case, since it depends only on tangency. Note that it can be undertaken without any knowledge of inversion, since e_A, e_B, e_C, e_A^*, e_B^* and e_C^* are simply the intersections of the altitudes of $\triangle ABC$ with the base circles.

Exercise 22a

1. Identify the radical centre of the base circles $\mathcal{S}_A$, $\mathcal{S}_B$ and $\mathcal{S}_C$.

2. What happens when the Soddy diagram is inverted in the incircle?

3. Let $\triangle ABC$ be isosceles with greatest angle $\angle A$ and $AB = AC$. Prove that the three base circles arising from $\triangle ABC$ share a common tangent if, and only if, $\angle BAC = 2\sin^{-1}\frac{4}{5}$.

Figure 22.8

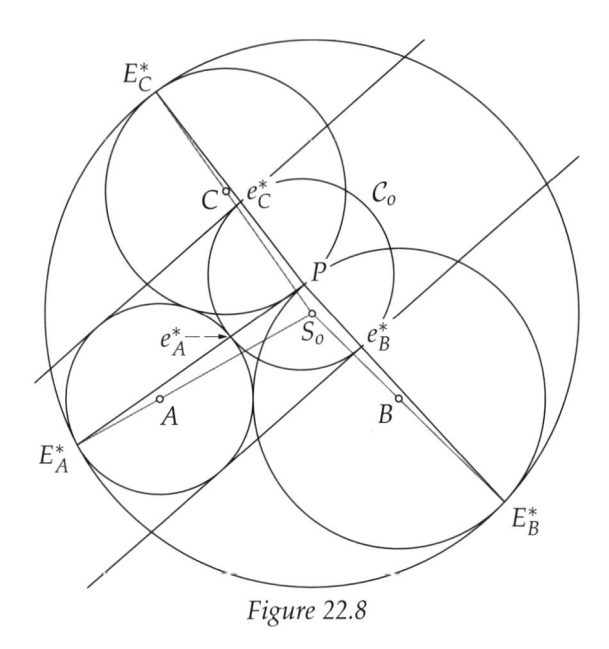

22.3 The Soddy radii

It is now straightforward to calculate the radii of the Soddy circles. Denote these by r_i and r_o.

Theorem 22.1 *The radii of the inner and outer Soddy circles are given by*

$$r_i = \frac{\Delta}{2s + 4R + r} \text{ and } r_o = \frac{\Delta}{|2s - 4R - r|}.$$

PROOF The two Soddy circles are the inverse images of the two circles C_i and C_i in figure 22.6. We will use the formula for the radius of the image of a circle under inversion given by corollary 20.5 on page 280. The circles to be inverted both have radius $s - a$. Let the radius of inversion be ρ. This is easily found by using the fact that the incircle, which has diameter $2r$, inverts to the line $R_\iota Q_\iota$, which is at a perpendicular distance of h_A from the centre of inversion P. Hence $\rho^2 = 2rh_A$. But $\Delta = \frac{1}{2}h_A a$ and, by theorem 2.12 on page 18, $rs = \Delta$, so

$$\rho^2 = \frac{4\Delta^2}{as} = \frac{4(s-a)(s-b)(s-c)}{a}$$

using Heron's formula. Finally we need to find the powers of the circles to be inverted with respect to P. We begin with the inner Soddy circle (see figure 22.9).

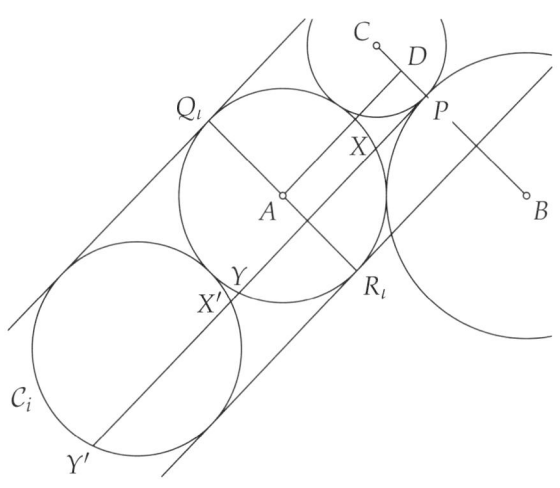

Figure 22.9

The power we need is $|t_i| = PX' \times PY'$. However, it is clear that $PX' = PX + 2(s-a)$ and $PY' = PY + 2(s-a)$. Also $PX \times PY = \rho^2$ and $PX + PY = AD = h_A$. Hence

$$|t_i| = \rho^2 + 4(s-a)h_A + 4(s-a)^2$$
$$= \rho^2 + 4(s-a)(h_A + s - a).$$

By corollary 20.5 on page 280 we now have

$$r_i = \frac{(s-a)\rho^2}{|t_i|}$$
$$= \frac{(s-a)\rho^2}{\rho^2 + 4(s-a)(h_A + s - a)}$$
$$= \frac{4(s-a)^2(s-b)(s-c)}{4(s-a)(s-b)(s-c) + 4a(s-a)(h_A + s - a)}$$
$$= \frac{(s-a)(s-b)(s-c)}{(s-b)(s-c) + a(h_A + s - a)}$$

and then using $a = (s-b) + (s-c)$ we have

$$r_i = \frac{(s-a)(s-b)(s-c)}{(s-b)(s-c) + (s-c)(s-a) + (s-a)(s-b) + 2\Delta}.$$

This can be simplified further, using theorem 2.12 on page 18 and then theorem 2.14 on page 19, to give

$$r_i = \frac{\Delta}{\frac{\Delta}{s-a} + \frac{\Delta}{s-b} + \frac{\Delta}{s-c} + \frac{2\Delta^2}{(s-a)(s-b)(s-c)}}$$

$$= \frac{\Delta}{r_A + r_B + r_C + 2s}$$

$$= \frac{\Delta}{2s + 4R + r}.$$

The argument for the outer Soddy circle is almost identical, except that we invert the circle $\mathcal{C}_o$, and so have $PX'' = PX - 2(s-a)$ and $PY'' = PY - 2(s-a)$. This has the effect of producing the formula for r_o. ❏

As a by-product, we have a simple condition for knowing whether we have the internal or external case for the outer Soddy circle.

Corollary 22.2 *The outer Soddy circle touches the base circles internally if $4R + r < 2s$ and externally if $4R + r > 2s$. If we have $4R + r = 2s$, the circle degenerates into a line.*

It is worth looking in some detail at the consequences of changing the angle at A.

When P is inside the circle $\mathcal{C}_o$, the circle inverts to the outer Soddy circle which circumscribes the base circles (see figure 22.10). This is the internal case and corresponds to the power t_o being negative, that is, to $4R + r < 2s$.

If $\angle A$ is increased, the circle $\mathcal{C}_o$ moves closer to A relative to P (and the other dimensions of the figure change at the same time). When X'' coincides with P, $t_o = 0$ and the circle $\mathcal{C}_o$ inverts to a line, which is the common tangent of the base circles. When P is outside the circle $\mathcal{C}_o$, the circle inverts to the external case of the outer Soddy circle. Now $t_o > 0$ and $4R + r > 2s$.

An alternative approach to the Soddy radii, depending on Descartes' circle theorem and involving the concept of *bends*, can be found in [8].

Figure 22.10

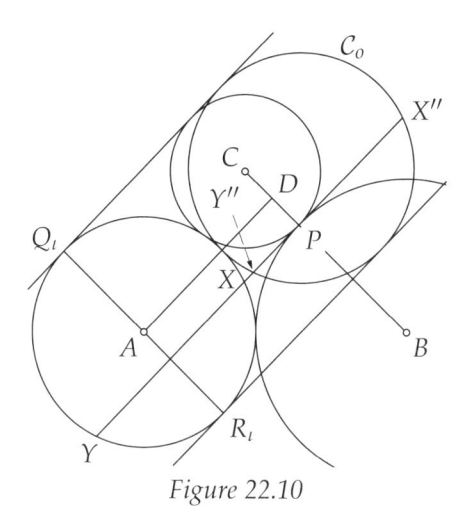

22.4 The isoperimetric and equal detour points

Theorem 22.3 *In the internal case, if $4R + r < 2s$, then the outer Soddy point has the property that the perimeters of the three triangles $\triangle S_o BC$, $\triangle S_o CA$ and $\triangle S_o AB$ are equal.*

For this reason, the outer Soddy point is also known as the *isoperimetric point*.

PROOF Set as question 1 of exercise 22b. ❏

Theorem 22.4 *The inner Soddy point has the property that the lengths of the three 'detours' $BS_i + S_iC - BC$, $CS_i + S_iA - CA$ and $AS_i + S_iB - AB$ are equal.*

For this reason, the inner Soddy point is also known as the *equal detour point*. In the external case, if $4R + r > 2s$, then the outer Soddy point also has this property.

PROOF Set as question 2 of exercise 22b. ❏

It is easy to check that exactly the same happens for the outer Soddy circle in the external case.

22.5 The Soddy line

Let C_A be the external centre of similitude of S_B and S_C, and define C_B and C_C similarly. By theorem 6.6 on page 75, these three points are collinear.

Theorem 22.5 *The lines BA, PQ, $E_B E_A$ and $E_B^* E_A^*$ are concurrent at C_C (see figure 22.11).*

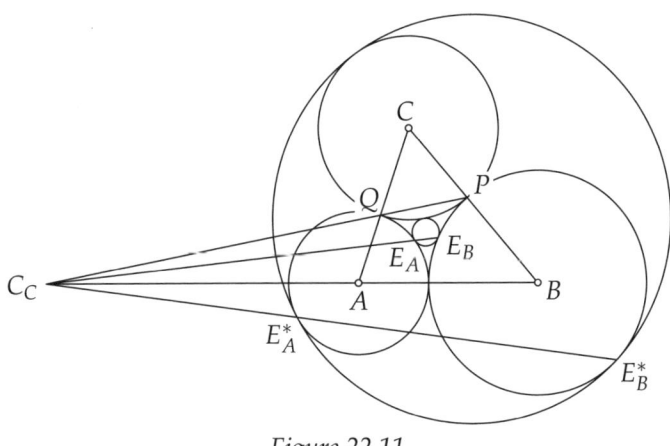

Figure 22.11

PROOF The external centre of similitude C_C lies on AB because it is the line of centres, and it lies on the other three lines by theorem 5.25 on page 64. ❑

Analogous results hold for the other centres of similitude C_A and C_B. It follows that $C_A C_B C_C$ is the axis of perspective of the reference triangle $\triangle ABC$ and the intouch triangle $\triangle PQR$. In section 10.1 on page 127 this was identified as the Gergonne line. Hence, by theorem 10.2 on page 130, the converse of Desargues' theorem, the four triangles $\triangle ABC$, $\triangle PQR$, $\triangle E_A E_B E_C$ and $\triangle E_A^* E_B^* E_C^*$ are in perspective in pairs.

- $\triangle ABC$ and $\triangle PQR$ have perspector Γ, the Gergonne point.
- $\triangle E_A E_B E_C$ and $\triangle E_A^* E_B^* E_C^*$ have perspector I, the incentre.
- $\triangle ABC$ and $\triangle E_A E_B E_C$ have perspector S_i, the inner Soddy point.
- $\triangle ABC$ and $\triangle E_A^* E_B^* E_C^*$ have perspector S_o, the outer Soddy point.

Chapter 22: Soddy circles

In addition, we have two new centres.

- The perspector of $\triangle PQR$ and $\triangle E_A^* E_B^* E_C^*$ is known as the *first Eppstein point* E_1.
- The perspector of $\triangle PQR$ and $\triangle E_A E_B E_C$ is known as the *second Eppstein point* E_2.

Corollary 22.6 *The points Γ, I, S_i, S_o, E_1 and E_2 are collinear.*

The line containing these points is known as the *Soddy line*.

PROOF This follows from theorem 10.9 on page 141. ❑

Theorem 22.7 *The radical axis of the Soddy circles is the Gergonne line.*

PROOF Let the ratio of the radii of $\mathcal{S}_A$ and $\mathcal{S}_B$ be k, let X be the second point of intersection of $C_C E_B$ with $\mathcal{S}_A$ and let Y be the second point of intersection of $C_C E_B^*$ with $\mathcal{S}_A$ (see figure 22.12).

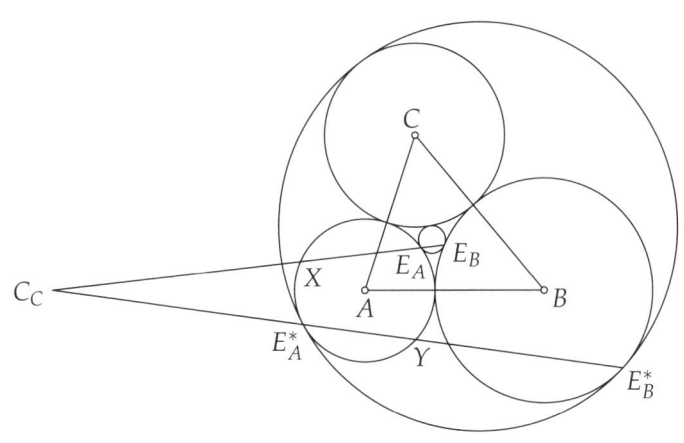

Figure 22.12

Then, since C_C is the centre of similitude of $\mathcal{S}_A$ and $\mathcal{S}_B$, $C_C E_B = k C_C X$ and $C_C E_B^* = k C_C Y$. Now we have

$$C_C E_A \times C_C E_B = k C_C E_A \times C_C X = k C_C Y \times C_C E_A^* = C_C E_A^* \times C_C E_B^*.$$

It follows that C_C is on the radical axis of the two Soddy circles, and, since the same argument applies to C_A and C_B, the Gergonne line is their radical axis. ❑

Corollary 22.8 *The Soddy line and the Gergonne line are perpendicular.*

PROOF Set as question 3 of exercise 22b. ☐

Exercise 22b

1. Prove theorem 22.3.

2. Prove theorem 22.4.

3. Prove corollary 22.8.

22.6 Gergonne's construction

The original approach to constructing the Soddy points and circles was due to Gergonne. It does not involve inversion, but instead employs the concepts of pole and polar.

Theorem 22.9 *The pole of the Gergonne line with respect to S_A lies on the line $E_A E_A^*$.*

PROOF The tangents to the two Soddy circles at E_A and E_A^* are also tangents to S_A. Therefore they are equal in length and meet on the radical axis of the Soddy circles, the Gergonne line, at a point Z. By theorem 18.3 on page 252, $E_A E_A^*$ is the polar of Z and Z is the pole of $E_A E_A^*$ with respect to S_A. Hence, by corollary 18.5 on page 254, the result follows. ☐

Clearly the same is true for the other two base circles.

Theorem 22.10 *The line $E_A E_A^*$ passes through the incentre of $\triangle ABC$.*

PROOF By theorem 5.25 on page 64, $E_A E_A^*$ passes through the internal centre of similitude of the two Soddy circles. Denoting this point by X, we have $XE_A^* \times XE_A = XR^2$, but that is also equal to $XE_B^* \times XE_B$. Continuing this process, we see that X is the radical centre of the three circles, as in question 1 of exercise 22a, which is the incentre of $\triangle ABC$. ☐

Now we have the *Gergonne construction*.
(i) Find the incentre I of $\triangle ABC$.
(ii) Find two of the external centres of similitude of $\mathcal{S}_A$, $\mathcal{S}_B$ and $\mathcal{S}_C$, thus determining the Gergonne line.
(iii) Find the poles of the Gergonne line with respect to $\mathcal{S}_A$, $\mathcal{S}_B$ and $\mathcal{S}_C$. This can be done by choosing two points on the line and finding the intersection of the two chords of contact.
(iv) The lines joining I to the three poles determine the points of tangency of the Soddy circles and thus the triangles $\triangle E_A E_B E_C$ and $\triangle E_A^* E_B^* E_C^*$.
(v) The Soddy points are the circumcentres of $\triangle E_A E_B E_C$ and $\triangle E_A^* E_B^* E_C^*$.

The proof of theorem 22.9 mentions a point Z on the Gergonne line where the tangents to the Soddy circles at E_A and E_A^* meet, but does not specify which point it is. In fact, it is C_A, the external centre of similitude of $\mathcal{S}_B$ and $\mathcal{S}_C$.

Theorem 22.11 *The line $C_A E_A$ is the common tangent to the inner Soddy circle and A-base circle, and the line $C_A E_A^*$ is the common tangent to the outer Soddy circle and the A-base circle.*

PROOF Let X be the intersection of the tangent at E_A^* with the line CB (see figure 22.13).

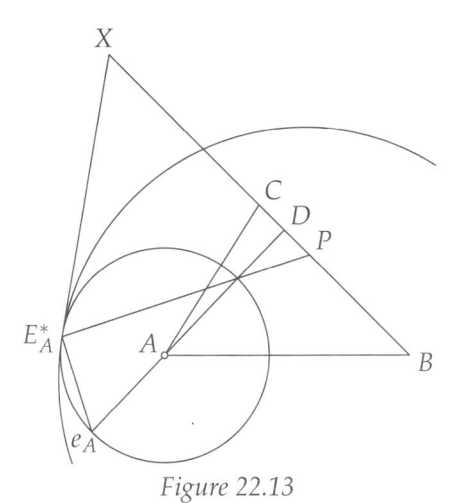

Figure 22.13

Note first that $\angle XPE_A^* = \angle De_A E_A^* = \angle PE_A^* X$ by the alternate segment theorem, so $XP = XE_A^*$.

Let $XP = x$. Then
$$x^2 = XA^2 - (s-a)^2$$
$$= (x - DP)^2 + AD^2 - (s-a)^2$$
and so
$$x = \frac{DP^2 + h_A^2 - (s-a)^2}{2DP}.$$
But $DP = (s-b) - c\cos B$ and $h_A = c\sin B$. So we have, using the cosine rule,
$$x = \frac{(s-b)^2 - 2c(s-b)\cos B + c^2\cos^2 B + c^2\sin^2 B - (s-a)^2}{2(s-b) - 2c\cos B}$$
$$= \frac{c(a-b) + c^2 - 2c(s-b)\cos B}{2(s-b) - 2c\cos B}$$
$$= \frac{2c(s-b) - 2c(s-b)\cos B}{2(s-b) - 2c\cos B}$$
$$= \frac{(s-b)(2ac - (a^2 + c^2 - b^2))}{a(c+a-b) - (a^2 + c^2 - b^2)}$$
$$= \frac{4(s-b)(s-a)(s-c)}{2(b-c)(s-a)}$$
$$= \frac{2(s-b)(s-c)}{b-c}.$$
Therefore
$$\frac{XC}{XB} = \frac{x + (s-c)}{x - (s-b)}$$
$$= \frac{2(s-b)(s-c) + (b-c)(s-c)}{2(s-b)(s-c) - (b-c)(s-b)}$$
$$= \frac{a(s-c)}{a(s-b)}$$
$$= \frac{s-c}{s-b},$$
which is the ratio of the radii of $\mathcal{S}_B$ and $\mathcal{S}_C$, so X is the external centre of similitude.

Chapter 22: Soddy circles

A similar argument applies to the common tangent to the inner Soddy circle and the A-base circle. ☐

We now have six lines concurrent at C_A (and also at C_B and C_C), including the tangent lines in theorem 22.11. These create two new triangles, the tangential triangles of $\triangle E_A E_B E_C$ and $\triangle E_A^* E_B^* E_C^*$, which we will call $\mathcal{T}$ and $\mathcal{T}^*$. It follows that $\mathcal{T}$ and $\mathcal{T}^*$ are in perspective with the inner and outer Soddy triangles and that the four perspectors lie on the Soddy line. It is in fact clear that $\mathcal{T}$ and $\triangle E_A E_B E_C$ are in perspective at the symmedian point of the inner Soddy triangle, and similarly for $\mathcal{T}^*$ and $\triangle E_A^* E_B^* E_C^*$. These two points are known as the *inner and outer Rigby points* R_1 and R_2. The perspector of $\mathcal{T}^*$ and $\triangle E_A E_B E_C$ is known as the *inner Griffiths point* G_1, and that of $\mathcal{T}$ and $\triangle E_A^* E_B^* E_C^*$ is the *outer Griffiths point* G_2.

Therefore we have fifteen pairs of triangles in perspective, with all the perspectors on the Soddy line. A list of the perspectors is given in table 22.1. Some of these results are stated without proof.

Perspector	Triangles
Γ	$\triangle ABC$, $\triangle PQR$
S_i	$\triangle ABC$, $\triangle E_A E_B E_C$
S_o	$\triangle ABC$, $\triangle E_A^* E_B^* E_C^*$
E_2	$\begin{cases} \triangle ABC,\ \mathcal{T} \\ \triangle PQR,\ \triangle E_A E_B E_C \end{cases}$
E_1	$\begin{cases} \triangle ABC,\ \mathcal{T}^* \\ \triangle PQR,\ \triangle E_A^* E_B^* E_C^* \end{cases}$
I	$\begin{cases} \triangle PQR,\ \mathcal{T},\ \mathcal{T}^* \\ \triangle E_A E_B E_C,\ \triangle E_A^* E_B^* E_C^* \end{cases}$
R_1	$\mathcal{T}$, $\triangle E_A E_B E_C$
G_2	$\mathcal{T}$, $\triangle E_A^* E_B^* E_C^*$
G_1	$\mathcal{T}^*$, $\triangle E_A E_B E_C$
R_2	$\mathcal{T}^*$, $\triangle E_A^* E_B^* E_C^*$

Table 22.1

22.7 Ratios on the Soddy line

Theorem 22.12 *The incentre I is the internal centre of similitude of the two Soddy circles if $2s > 4R + r$ and the external centre of similitude if $2s < 4R + r$.*

PROOF We will deal with the first case; the second is similar. Let the radii of the inner and outer Soddy circles be r_i and r_o and let X_i and X_o be the projections of S_i and S_o on BC (see figure 22.14).

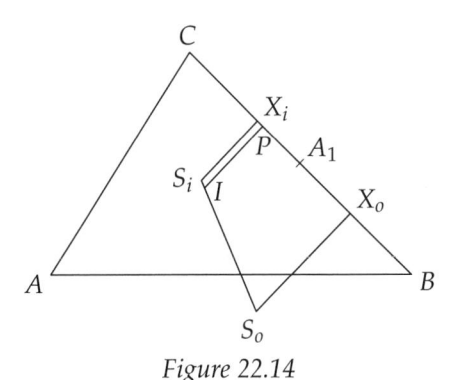

Figure 22.14

First consider the triangle $\triangle BCS_i$. By Pythagoras' theorem we have

$$S_iC^2 - S_iB^2 = X_iC^2 - X_iB^2,$$

but $S_iB = r_i + s - b$ and $S_iC = r_i + s - c$, and after a little algebraic manipulation we get

$$X_iA_1 = \frac{(b-c)(2r_i + a)}{2a}.$$

Similarly

$$A_1X_o = \frac{(b-c)(2r_o - a)}{2a}.$$

Therefore

$$X_iP = \frac{(b-c)(2r_i + a)}{2a} - \frac{b-c}{2}$$
$$= \frac{b-c}{a} r_i$$

and
$$PX_o = \frac{(b-c)(2r_o - a)}{2a} + \frac{b-c}{2}$$
$$= \frac{b-c}{a} r_o.$$

Hence
$$\frac{X_i P}{PX_o} = \frac{r_i}{r_o}$$

and the result follows. ❏

Theorem 22.13 *The de Longchamps point Λ lies on the Soddy line.*

PROOF Let Y be the projection of Λ on BC (see figure 22.15).

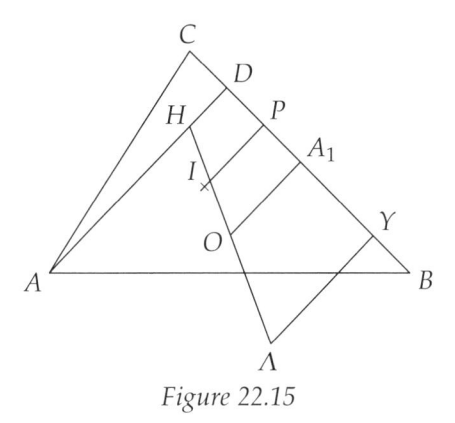

Figure 22.15

As O is the midpoint of $H\Lambda$, we have $DA_1 = A_1 Y$ and so $DY = a - c\cos B$ and
$$PY = a - c\cos B - (s-b)$$
$$= a - \frac{a^2 + c^2 - b^2}{2a} - \frac{a + c - b}{2}$$
$$= \frac{b^2 - c^2 + ab - ac}{2a}$$
$$= \frac{b-c}{a} s.$$

Now, from the proof of theorem 22.12,

$$X_iX_o = \frac{b-c}{2a}(2r_i + a + 2r_o - a)$$

$$= \frac{b-c}{a}(r_i + r_o)$$

and so $X_iX_o : PY = r_i + r_o : s$, which is independent of a. If we now carry out the same calculation, but with projections on CA (or AB), we obtain the same ratio. It follows that S_i, I, S_o, Λ are collinear. □

Theorem 22.14 *The Gergonne point Γ is the external centre of similitude of the two Soddy circles if $2s > 4R + r$ and the internal centre of similitude if $2s < 4R + r$.*

PROOF We will deal with the first case (see figure 22.16); the second is similar.

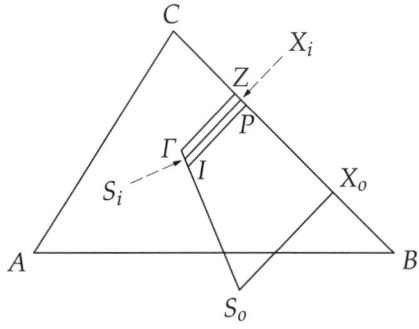

Figure 22.16

We need to show that
$$\frac{\Gamma S_i}{\Gamma S_o} = \frac{r_i}{r_o}.$$

By similar triangles,
$$\frac{\Gamma S_i}{\Gamma S_o} = \frac{ZX_i}{ZX_o}$$

$$= \frac{ZP - X_iP}{ZP + PX_o}$$

and
$$\frac{ZP}{\Gamma Z - r} = \frac{X_i P}{S_i X_i - r}.$$

We now summarise the formulae for various lengths. From the proof of theorem 22.13,
$$X_i P = \frac{b - c}{a} r_i$$
and
$$P X_o = \frac{b - c}{a} r_o$$
and from lemma 9.3 on page 114,
$$\Gamma Z = \frac{2 \Delta r_A}{a(4R + r)}.$$

We also need to calculate $S_i X_i$. Here we use the construction in section 22.2 which shows that P is the centre of similitude of the inner Soddy circle and the circle C_i. Hence
$$\frac{S_i X_i}{2(s - a) + h_A} = \frac{r_i}{s - a}$$
and so
$$S_i X_i = r_i \left(2 + \frac{h_A}{s - a} \right)$$
$$= 2 r_i \left(1 + \frac{r_A}{a} \right).$$

By theorem 22.1, we have
$$r_i = \frac{\Delta}{2s + 4R + r} \quad \text{and} \quad r_o = \frac{\Delta}{2s - 4R - r}$$
so
$$\frac{r_o r_i}{r_o - r_i} = \frac{\Delta}{2(4R + r)}$$
and
$$\frac{r_o + r_i}{r_o - r_i} = \frac{2s}{4R + r}$$
$$= \frac{2\Delta}{r(4R + r)},$$

using theorem 2.12 on page 18.

Now we are ready to start. Note that

$$\Gamma Z = \frac{2\Delta r_A}{a(4R+r)}$$

$$= \frac{2\Delta}{4R+r}\left(\frac{a+r_A}{a} - 1\right)$$

$$= \frac{4r_o r_i}{r_o - r_i}\left(\frac{a+r_A}{a}\right) - \frac{r(r_o + r_i)}{r_o - r_i}$$

Hence

$$(r_o - r_i)(\Gamma Z - r) = 4r_o r_i \frac{a+r_A}{a} - 2rr_o$$

$$= 2r_o S_i X_i - 2rr_o$$

and so

$$\frac{\Gamma Z - r}{S_i X_i - r} = \frac{2r_o}{r_o - r_i}.$$

Therefore

$$ZP = X_i P \left(\frac{\Gamma Z - r}{S_i X_i - r}\right)$$

$$= 2\left(\frac{b-c}{a}\right)\left(\frac{r_o r_i}{r_o - r_i}\right).$$

It follows that

$$r_o X_i P + r_i P X_o = 2r_o r_i \left(\frac{b-c}{a}\right)$$

$$= (r_o - r_i)ZP$$

so

$$r_i(ZP + PX_o) = r_o(ZP - X_i P)$$

and

$$\frac{\Gamma S_i}{\Gamma S_o} = \frac{ZP - X_i P}{ZP + PX_o}$$

$$= \frac{r_i}{r_o}$$

as required. □

Chapter 22: Soddy circles

Corollary 22.15 Γ, S_i, I, S_o is a harmonic range.

PROOF This is now immediate from theorems 5.21, 22.12 and 22.14. ❑

22.8 The limiting case

Finally we discuss an alternative approach to deciding whether the outer Soddy circle is internal or external to the base circles. The limiting case occurs when the base circles have a common tangent. In question 3 of exercise 22a, we considered the special case where $\triangle ABC$ was isosceles. In general, the analysis is a little harder.

Theorem 22.16 *Suppose that $\triangle ABC$ has greatest angle $\angle A$. The three base circles arising from $\triangle ABC$ share a common tangent if, and only if,*

$$\frac{1}{\sqrt{s-c}} + \frac{1}{\sqrt{s-b}} = \frac{1}{\sqrt{s-a}}.$$

PROOF (See figure 22.17.)

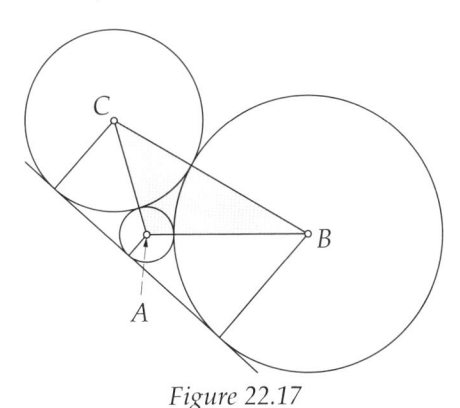

Figure 22.17

To begin with, call the three radii and r_a, r_b and r_c. The length of the common tangent between the circles with centres A, B is easily shown to be $\sqrt{r_a r_b}$. Hence there is a common tangent if, and only if,

$$\sqrt{r_a r_b} + \sqrt{r_c r_a} = \sqrt{r_b r_c}.$$

However, the three radii are actually $s-a$, $s-b$ and $s-c$. Therefore the relationship is

$$\sqrt{(s-a)(s-b)} + \sqrt{(s-c)(s-a)} = \sqrt{(s-b)(s-c)},$$

and so the result follows. ▫

Corollary 22.17 *A triangle will give rise to a degenerate outer Soddy circle if, and only if,*
$$\tan \tfrac{1}{2}A + \tan \tfrac{1}{2}B + \tan \tfrac{1}{2}C = 2.$$

PROOF We first use the identity
$$\alpha = \tan \tfrac{1}{2}A = \frac{r}{s-A}$$

(and two similar ones) to transform the condition in theorem 22.10 to $\sqrt{\alpha} = \sqrt{\beta} + \sqrt{\gamma}$. Now the outer Soddy circle will be degenerate if this condition holds for any of the three angles of the triangle, so
$$(\sqrt{\alpha} - \sqrt{\beta} - \sqrt{\gamma})(\sqrt{\beta} - \sqrt{\gamma} - \sqrt{\alpha})(\sqrt{\gamma} - \sqrt{\alpha} - \sqrt{\beta}) = 0.$$

Multiplying by the positive quantity $\sqrt{\alpha} + \sqrt{\beta} + \sqrt{\gamma}$, we obtain the equivalent form $\sum \alpha^2 = 2 \sum \alpha\beta$ and so $(\sum \alpha)^2 = 4 \sum \alpha\beta$. But, since $\angle A + \angle B + \angle C = 180°$,

$$\sum \tan \tfrac{1}{2}A \tan \tfrac{1}{2}B = \tan \tfrac{1}{2}A \tan \tfrac{1}{2}B + \tan \tfrac{1}{2}C \left(\tan \tfrac{1}{2}A + \tan \tfrac{1}{2}B \right)$$
$$= \tan \tfrac{1}{2}A \tan \tfrac{1}{2}B + \frac{\tan \tfrac{1}{2}A + \tan \tfrac{1}{2}B}{\tan \left(\tfrac{1}{2}A + \tfrac{1}{2}B \right)}$$
$$= \tan \tfrac{1}{2}A \tan \tfrac{1}{2}B + \left(1 - \tan \tfrac{1}{2}A \tan \tfrac{1}{2}B \right)$$
$$= 1,$$

and so the result follows. ▫

Note that the result of question 3 of exercise 22a is a special case of corollary 22.17. We have $\tan \tfrac{1}{2}A = \tfrac{3}{4}$ and $\tan \tfrac{1}{2}B = \tan \tfrac{1}{2}C = \tfrac{3}{4}$, so $\tan \tfrac{1}{2}B = \tan \tfrac{1}{2}C = \tfrac{1}{3}$. The condition is clearly met.

Corollary 22.18 *The outer Soddy circle touches the base circles internally if, and only if,*
$$\tan \tfrac{1}{2}A + \tan \tfrac{1}{2}B + \tan \tfrac{1}{2}C < 2.$$

PROOF The analysis is similar to that for the proof of corollary 22.17 but uses inequalities such as
$$\frac{1}{\sqrt{s-c}} + \frac{1}{\sqrt{s-b}} > \frac{1}{\sqrt{s-a}}$$

rather than equations. ▫

Chapter 23

The Mittenpunkt and the Clawson point

We now focus on configurations involving the excentral and extangents triangles of $\triangle ABC$. These turn out to have relationships with other triangles associated with the reference triangle, and lead to two new triangle centres and some interesting collinearities.

23.1 The excentral triangle

We have already encountered the excentral triangle $\triangle I_A I_B I_C$ several times. In section 9.6, the Bevan point Θ was defined as its circumcentre and theorem 9.14(i) showed that O was the midpoint of $I\Theta$.

Theorem 23.1 *The circumradius of the excentral triangle is* $2R$.

PROOF Set as question 1 of exercise 23a. ❏

Theorem 23.2 *The intouch and excentral triangle are homothetic.*

PROOF Since I is the centre of the incircle, and QR is the chord of contact from A, we have $IA \perp QR$ (see figure 23.1).
But $I_B I_C \perp IA$ and so $I_B I_C \parallel QR$. Since the same is true for the other sides, the triangles $\triangle I_A I_B I_C$ and $\triangle PQR$ are homothetic. ❏

Figure 23.1

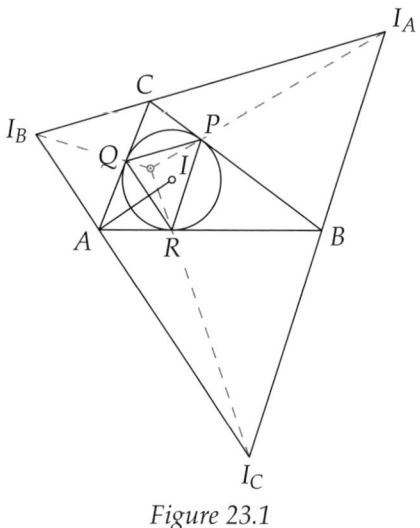

We use the notation μ for the homothecy between $\triangle PQR$ and $\triangle I_A I_B I_C$ and M_* for the homothetic centre.

Theorem 23.3 *The points I, O, Θ and M_* lie on the Euler line of the excentral triangle.*

PROOF Since $O = N \triangle I_A I_B I_C$, $I = H \triangle I_A I_B I_C$ and $\Theta = O \triangle I_A I_B I_C$ it follows that $OI\Theta$ is the Euler line of $\triangle I_A I_B I_C$, and the homothetic centre M_* lies on this line (see figure 23.2).

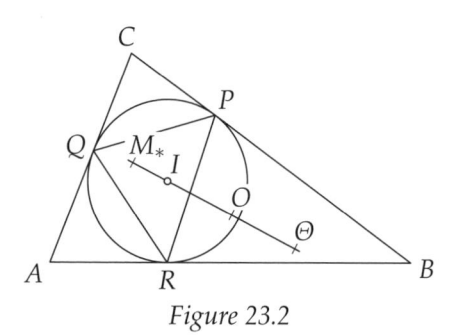

Figure 23.2

The centroid of the excentral triangle G_E is a new point, which also lies on this Euler line.

The Euler line of the intouch triangle goes through $I = O \triangle PQR$ and $O = O_T \triangle PQR$. Hence the intouch and excentral triangles share the same Euler line, although points on this line will represent different centres for the two triangles. The centroid of the intouch triangle is known as the *Weill point* G_I and its orthocentre will be denoted by H_I.

23.2 The Mittenpunkt

The *Mittenpunkt* is defined as the symmedian point of the excentral triangle and is denoted by M^*. It is useful to have a simpler characterisation of this point.

The tangential triangle of the excentral triangle is labelled $\triangle T_A^* T_B^* T_C^*$. Then, by theorem 8.4 on page 101, the Mittenpunkt is the perspector of $\triangle I_A I_B I_C$ and $\triangle T_A^* T_B^* T_C^*$ (see figure 23.3).

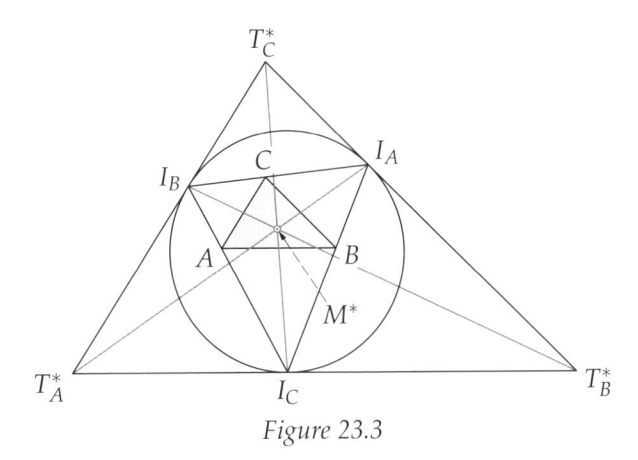

Figure 23.3

Theorem 23.4 *The Mittenpunkt is the perspector of the excentral triangle and the medial triangle.*

PROOF Set as question 2 of exercise 23a. ◻

Theorem 23.5 M_*, Γ and M^* *are collinear.*

PROOF Set as question 3 of exercise 23a. ◻

Theorem 23.6 *The Mittenpunkt is the Gergonne point of the medial triangle.*

PROOF Without loss of generality, suppose that $b > c$. Let $A_1 D_1$ be an altitude of the medial triangle and let $I_A A_1$ meet $B_1 C_1$ at P_1 (see figure 23.4).

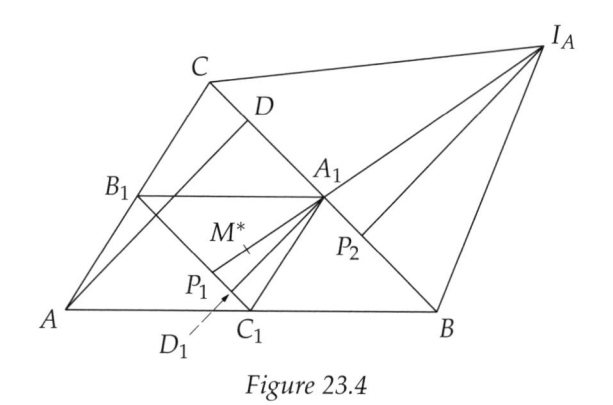

Figure 23.4

Then, by similar triangles

$$\frac{P_1 D_1}{A_1 D_1} = \frac{A_1 P_A}{I_A P_A} = \frac{b-c}{2r_A}$$

and since $A_1 D_1 = \frac{1}{2} h_A$,

$$P_1 D_1 = \frac{(b-c) h_A}{4 r_A} = \frac{(b-c)(s-a)}{2a}.$$

Also

$$D_1 B_1 = \tfrac{1}{2} BD = \tfrac{1}{2} c \cos B$$

and so

$$P_1 B_1 = \frac{(b-c)(b+c-a)}{4a} + \frac{a^2 + c^2 - b^2}{4a} = \frac{s-b}{2}.$$

This means that P_1 is the point where the incircle of $\triangle A_1 B_1 C_1$ touches $B_1 C_1$, and, since the same is true for the other sides of the medial triangle, the result follows. □

Theorem 23.7 M^*, Γ and G are collinear, with $\Gamma G : G M^* = 2 : 1$.

PROOF Set as question 4 of exercise 23a. □

Note that, by theorem 23.4, M_* also lies on the same line.

Theorem 23.8 *M^*, S and H are collinear.*

PROOF Set as question 5 of exercise 23a. ❑

Theorem 23.9 *M^* and M_* are isogonal conjugates.*

PROOF We prove this by calculating the perpendicular distances from M_* to the sides BC and CA (see figure 23.5).

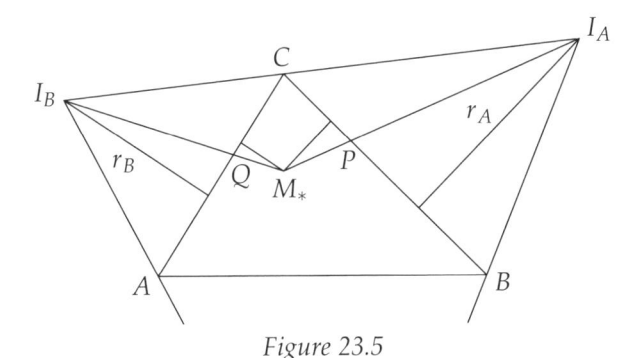

Figure 23.5

As M_* is the homothetic centre of $\triangle PQR$ and $\triangle I_A I_B I_C$, we have
$$\frac{M_* P}{PI_A} = \frac{M_* Q}{QI_B}.$$
But by similar triangles, the perpendicular distances p_A and p_B satisfy
$$\frac{p_A}{r_A} = \frac{M_* P}{PI_A} \quad \text{and} \quad \frac{p_B}{r_B} = \frac{M_* Q}{QI_B}$$
and so
$$\frac{p_A}{p_B} = \frac{r_A}{r_B} = \frac{s-b}{s-a}.$$
For the Mittenpunkt M^* this is more difficult. A short calculation using barycentric coordinates, to be found in appendix A, shows that, for the corresponding perpendicular distances p_A^* and p_B^*,
$$\frac{p_A^*}{p_B^*} = \frac{s-a}{s-b}.$$
Now, by theorem 7.6 on page 86, M^* and M_* are isogonal conjugates. ❑

As a consequence of theorem 23.9, M_* is called the *isogonal Mittenpunkt*.

Exercise 23a

1. Prove theorem 23.1.

2. Prove theorem 23.4.

3. Prove theorem 23.5.

4. Prove theorem 23.7.

5. Prove theorem 23.8.

23.3 The extangents triangle

The *extangents triangle* is the triangle externally tangent to the three excircles. The three vertices will be denoted by U_A, U_B and U_C (see figure 23.6). For simplicity, we shall assume that the triangle $\triangle ABC$ is acute, so that the extangents triangle surrounds the excentral triangle as in figure 23.6.

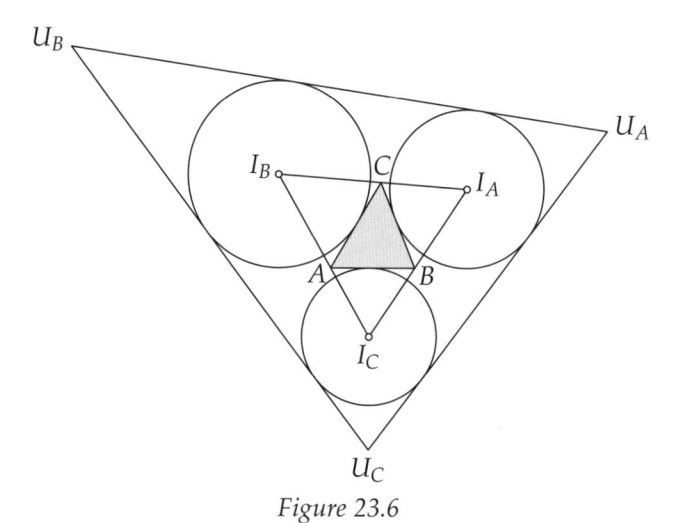

Figure 23.6

Theorem 23.10 *The extangents, excentral and reference triangles are in perspective in pairs and have a common axis of perspective.*

PROOF Note that the direct common tangents to the B- and A- excircles are BC and $U_B U_C$, and these meet, together with their line of centres $I_B I_C$ at their external centre of similitude. But by Monge's circle theorem (theorem 6.6 on page 75(i)), the external centres of similitude of the three excircles are collinear. The result now follows by the converse of Desargues' theorem (theorem 10.2 on page 130). ❑

The perspector of $\triangle ABC$ and $\triangle I_A I_B I_C$ is, of course, the incentre I.

Theorem 23.11 *The extangents and excentral triangles are in perspective at the Bevan point.*

PROOF Since $U_A I_A$, $U_B I_B$ and $U_C I_C$ are angle bisectors of the extangents triangle, they concur at its incentre, which is labelled X in figure 23.7.

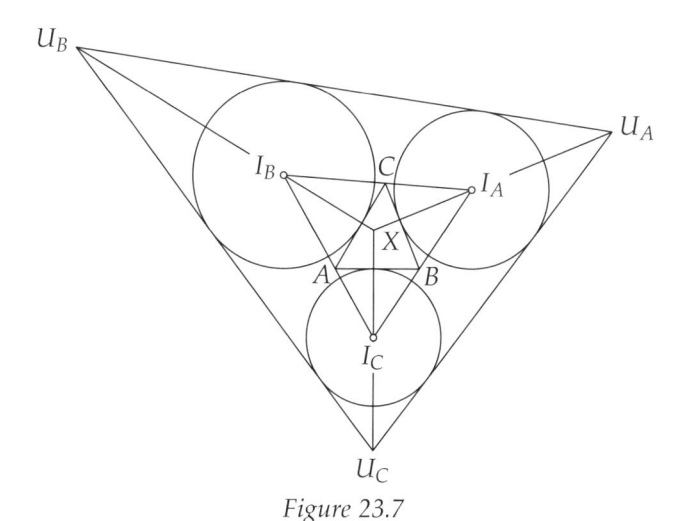

Figure 23.7

It remains to show that X is the circumcentre of $\triangle I_A I_B I_C$, the Bevan point.

Now $\angle I_B I_C I_A = \frac{1}{2}(\angle A + \angle B)$. The angle between $U_B U_C$ and $I_B I_C$, which is equal to that between $I_B I_C$ and BC, is $\frac{1}{2}\angle A + \angle B - 90°$. Now we have

$$\angle U_B U_C U_A = \left(\tfrac{1}{2}\angle A + \angle B - 90°\right) + \tfrac{1}{2}(\angle A + \angle B) + \left(\tfrac{1}{2}\angle B + \angle A - 90°\right)$$
$$= 2\angle A + 2\angle B - 180°$$
$$= 180° - 2\angle C.$$

Hence $\angle U_B U_C I_C = 90° - \angle C$ and, similarly, $\angle U_C U_B I_B = 90° - \angle B$. It follows that $\angle U_B X U_C = \angle B + \angle C$, and with two similar facts, the result follows. ☐

Corollary 23.12 *The Bevan point is the incentre of the extangents triangle.*

PROOF It follows from theorem 23.11 that $U_C \Theta$ is the internal angle bisector of $\angle U_B U_C U_A$. ☐

Corollary 23.12 was known in Japanese temple geometry [13] and was rediscovered by Neuberg [21].

We now calculate the inradius of $\triangle U_A U_B U_C$. The following technical result will turn out to be useful.

Lemma 23.13 *With the usual notation,* $r_A + 4R \cos A = r + r_B + r_C$.

PROOF Set as question 2 of exercise 23b. ☐

Theorem 23.14 *The inradius of the extangents circle is $r + 2R$.*

PROOF As shown in the proof of theorem 23.11, $\angle U_C U_A U_B = 180° - 2\angle A$, and so $\angle \Theta U_A U_B = 90° - \angle A$ (see figure 23.8).

Hence $I_A U_A = r_A \sec A$, and since $\Theta I_A = 2r$ by theorem 23.1 we have $\Theta U_A = 2R + r_A \sec A$. But the inradius of $\triangle U_A U_B U_C$ is $\Theta U_A \cos A$, which is $2R \cos A + r_A$. By lemma 23.13, this is $\tfrac{1}{2}(r_A + r_B + r_C + r)$, which is $r + 2R$ by theorem 2.14 on page 19. ☐

23.4 More on the intouch triangle

We now identify the perspector of the extangents and reference triangle. It is useful to begin with a result about the intouch triangle.

Let I_a, I_b and I_c be the images of I after reflection in QR, RP and PQ (see figure 23.9).

Figure 23.8

Figure 23.9

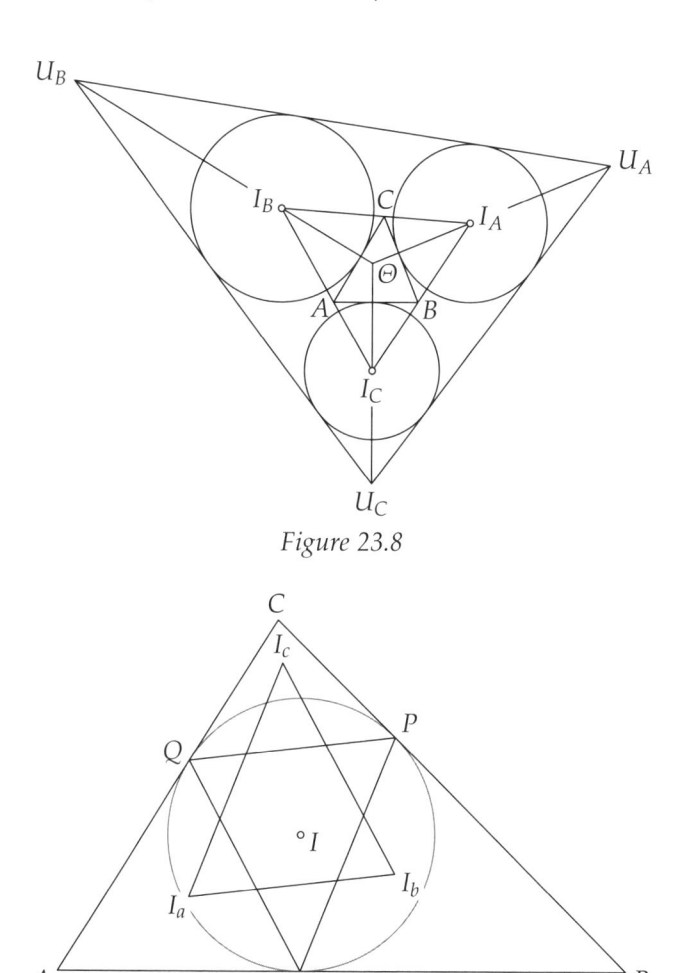

I discovered $\triangle I_a I_b I_c$ when browsing the website *Hyacinthos* [15], which discusses themes in triangle geometry. In view of the sources indicated there, perhaps a good name for it would be the *Emelyanov triangle*.

Theorem 23.15 *The triangles $\triangle PQR$ and $\triangle I_a I_b I_c$ are congruent and homothetic.*

PROOF As noted in section 23.1, $H_I I$ is the Euler line of the intouch triangle $\triangle PQR$ (see figure 23.10).

Figure 23.10

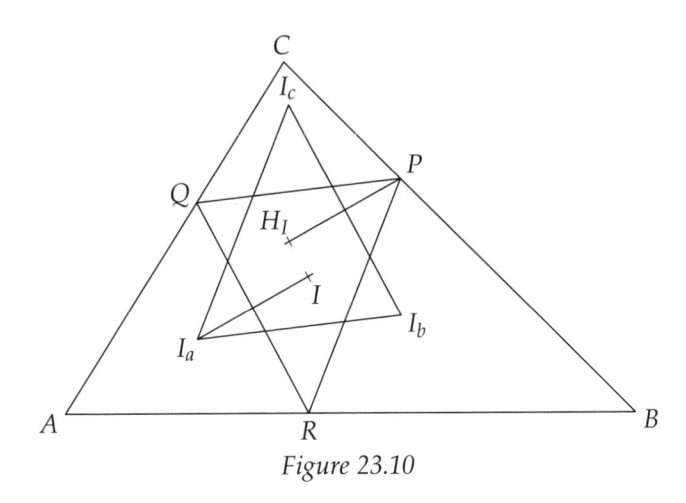

By theorem 3.2 on page 28, PH_I is parallel and equal to II_a. The result follows, and the homothetic centre is the midpoint of $H_I I$, which is the nine-point centre of the intouch triangle. ❑

Corollary 23.16 *The orthocentre of $\triangle I_a I_b I_c$ is I and its circumcentre is H_I.*

PROOF This follows from the homothecy of theorem 23.15. ❑

By theorem 23.3, $\triangle I_a I_b I_c$ is also homothetic to the excentral triangle $\triangle I_A I_B I_C$. In fact, this is easy to show directly (see figure 23.11).

Since QR is the chord of contact from A to the incircle, AI is its perpendicular bisector and so I_a lies on AI. But I_A also lies on AI, so I is the homothetic centre of $\triangle I_a I_b I_c$ and $\triangle I_A I_B I_C$.

The triangle $\triangle I_a I_b I_c$ shares the same Euler line with $\triangle PQR$ and $\triangle I_A I_B I_C$. It turns out, unexpectedly, to be very useful in identifying the perspector of the extangents triangle and the reference triangle. We introduce three more circles into the configuration (see figure 23.12).

The circle $\mathcal{C}_a$ has centre I_A and is tangential to AB and AC, and $\mathcal{C}_b$ and $\mathcal{C}_c$ are defined similarly. Note that the external centre of similitude of $\mathcal{C}_a$ and the A-excircle of $\triangle ABC$ is A.

The side BC is a direct common tangent of $\mathcal{C}_b$ and $\mathcal{C}_c$. Let the other direct common tangent be $\mathcal{T}_a$, and let $\mathcal{T}_b$ and $\mathcal{T}_c$ be defined similarly.

Theorem 23.17 *The lines $\mathcal{T}_a$, $\mathcal{T}_b$ and $\mathcal{T}_c$ are concurrent at H_I (see figure 23.13).*

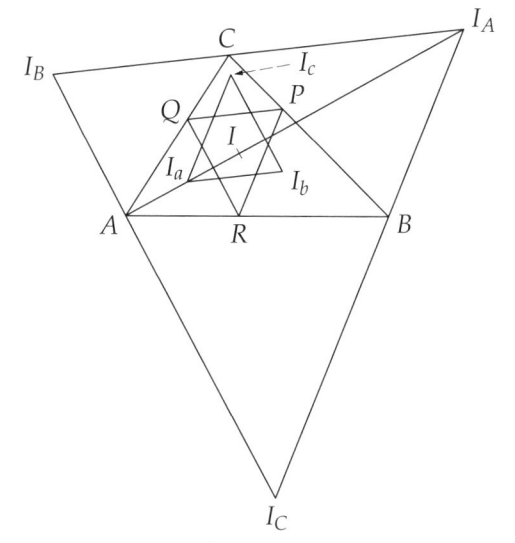

Chapter 23: The Mittenpunkt and the Clawson point 341

Figure 23.11

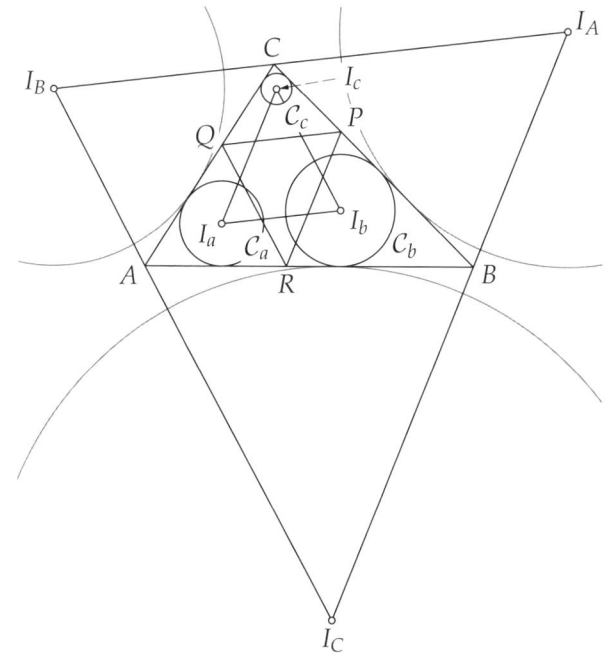

Figure 23.12

Figure 23.13

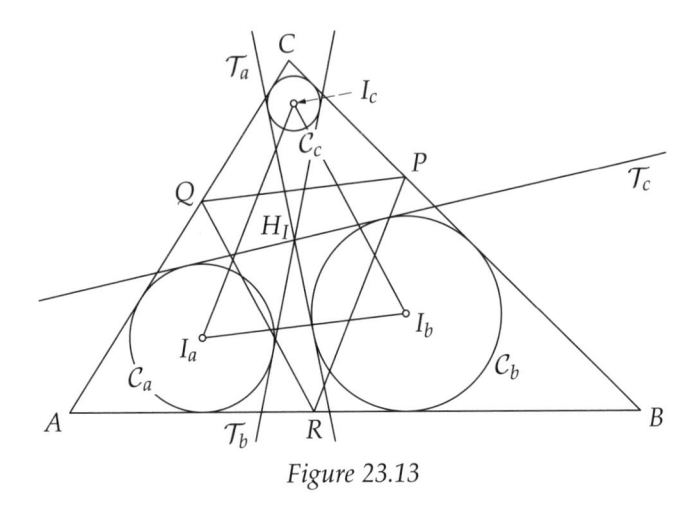

PROOF By theorem 23.15, H_I is the image of P when reflected in $I_b I_c$ and hence it lies on $\mathcal{T}_a$. Similarly it lies on $\mathcal{T}_b$ and $\mathcal{T}_c$. □

Lemma 23.18 *Under the enlargement from the centre of similitude B of $\mathcal{C}_b$ and the B-excircle, $\mathcal{T}_a$ and $\mathcal{T}_c$ map to the lines $U_B U_C$ and $U_A U_B$.*

PROOF Note first that $U_B U_C$ is obtained by reflecting BC in $I_B I_C$, and $\mathcal{T}_a$ is obtained by reflecting BC in $I_b I_c$. But $I_B I_C$ is parallel to $I_b I_c$ so $U_B U_C$ and $\mathcal{T}_a$ are also parallel. Now the enlargement from B takes $\mathcal{T}_a$ to a parallel tangent to the B-excircle, which must be the common tangent since it lies on the same side of BC as $\mathcal{T}_a$. □

Corollary 23.19 *The perspector of $\triangle ABC$ and $\triangle U_A U_B U_C$ is H_I.*

PROOF The intersection of $\mathcal{T}_a$ and $\mathcal{T}_c$ is H_I and that of $U_B U_C$ and $U_A U_B$ is B, so B, H_I and U_B are collinear. Similarly H_I lies on CU_C and AU_A. □

23.5 The Clawson point

Theorem 23.20 *The tangential and extangents triangles are homothetic.*

PROOF Note that $\angle T_B A I_B = \angle OAI = \frac{1}{2}\angle A + \angle B - 90°$ (see figure 23.14).
But by the proof of theorem 23.11, this is the same as the angle between $U_B U_C$ and $I_B I_C$. It follows that $T_B T_C$ is parallel to $U_B U_C$, as required. □

Figure 23.14

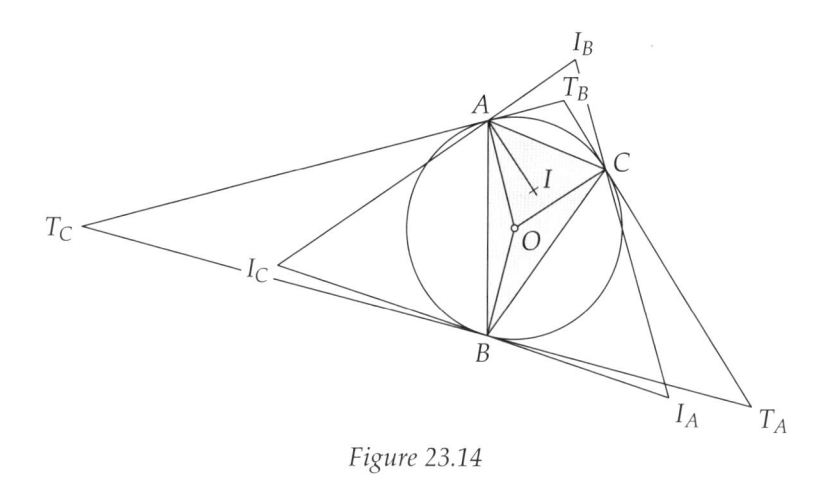

The homothetic centre given by theorem 23.20 turns out to be the point σ_i from page 181, the internal centre of similitude of the incircle and circumcircle of $\triangle ABC$. It is also the external centre of similitude of the circumcircle of $\triangle ABC$ and the incircle of $\triangle U_A U_B U_C$. To establish these facts requires the use of barycentric coordinates.

We now have seven significant points on the Euler line of the intouch and excentral triangles, which also have significance as perspectors or homothetic centres of pairs of triangles (see figure 23.15).

By theorem 12.15 on page 167, the tangential and orthic triangles are homothetic, with centre the Phi point Φ_1. Hence, by theorem 23.20, the extangents and orthic triangles are also homothetic. The homothetic centre is known as the *Clawson point* and will be denoted by C^*.

Corollary 23.21 *The points C^*, Φ_1 and σ_i are collinear.*

PROOF This follows from theorem 10.9 on page 141. ❏

Theorem 23.22 *The Clawson point is collinear with the orthocentre and the Bevan point.*

PROOF This follows from the homothecy with centre C^* from the orthic to the extangents triangle, since H is the incentre of $\triangle DEF$ and, by corollary 23.12, Θ is the incentre of $\triangle U_A U_B U_C$. ❏

Similar results are easy to achieve, although they do not on the whole involve points we have met before. For example, using circumcentres we

Figure 23.15

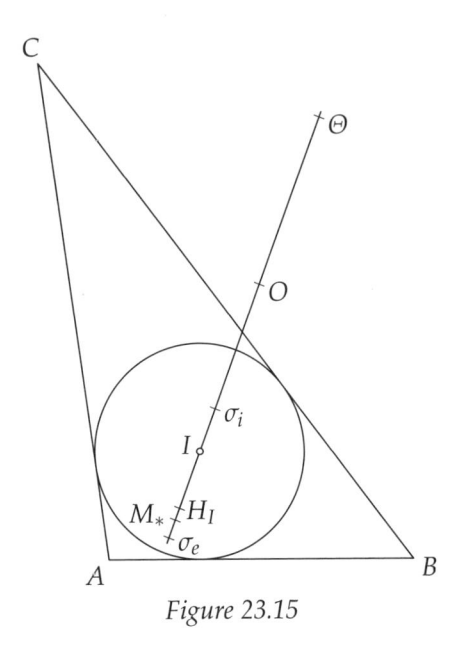

see that C^*, N and $O \triangle U_A U_B U_C$ are collinear, or using excentres, that C^*, A and $I_A \triangle U_A U_B U_C$ are collinear.

The following two results are proved in appendix A using barycentric coordinates.

Theorem 23.23 *M^* is collinear with I and K.*

Theorem 23.24 *M^* is collinear with H and C^*.*

Exercise 23b

1. Prove that the Bevan point is pedal-cevian.

2. Prove lemma 23.13.

3. With the notation of section 23.4, prove that I_a, I_b and I_c are the orthocentres of $\triangle ARQ$, $\triangle BPR$ and $\triangle CQP$.

4. With the notation of section 23.4, prove that I_a, I_b and I_c are the incentres of $\triangle AFE$, $\triangle BDF$ and $\triangle CEF$.

5. Prove that the quadrilaterals CI_cI_bB, AI_aI_cC and BI_bI_aA are cyclic.

6. Prove that the circumcircles of $\triangle PI_cI_b$, $\triangle QI_aI_c$ and $\triangle RI_bI_a$ share a common point on the incircle of $\triangle ABC$.

7. Prove that the circumcircles of $\triangle DI_cI_b$, $\triangle EI_aI_c$ and $\triangle FI_bI_a$ share a common point on the nine-point circle of $\triangle ABC$.

8. Prove that the quadrilaterals PDI_cI_b, QEI_aI_c and RFI_aI_b are cyclic, and hence identify the common points in questions 6 and 7.

Chapter 24

Partition triangles

We examine a method commonly used in creating configurations involving a triangle $\triangle ABC$.

Let X be a point, usually, but not necessarily, internal to $\triangle ABC$, and not on one of the sides. Consider the three triangles $\triangle XBC$, $\triangle XCA$ and $\triangle XAB$ formed by joining X to the vertices (see figure 24.1).

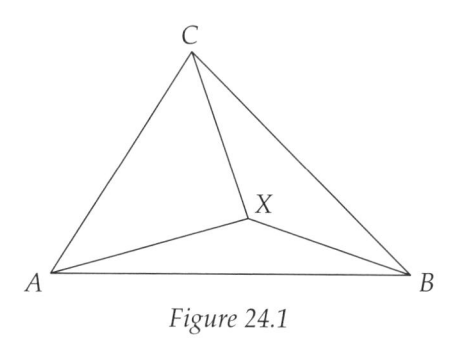

Figure 24.1

We shall say that X *partitions* the triangle $\triangle ABC$, and that $\triangle XBC$, $\triangle XCA$ and $\triangle XAB$ are the *partition triangles* of X.

It is worth introducing some notation. The set of three partition triangles of X will be denoted by $\triangle X$ and the triangle composed of the centres Y of these triangles will be denoted by $Y_\triangle X$. For example, the vertices of $O_\triangle G$ are the circumcentres of the triangles $\triangle GBC$, $\triangle GCA$ and $\triangle GAB$.

As a special case of this, the triangle $X_\triangle X$ will be denoted by $X_\triangle$.

24.1 Some easy facts about partitions

The triangle of centroids $G_\triangle X$, has a simple property whatever the choice of X.

Theorem 24.1 $G_\triangle X$ is homothetic to $\triangle ABC$, with centre which divides XG in the ratio $3 : 1$.

PROOF Let G_A, G_B and G_B be the centroids of $\triangle XBC$, $\triangle XCA$ and $\triangle XAB$ (see figure 24.2).

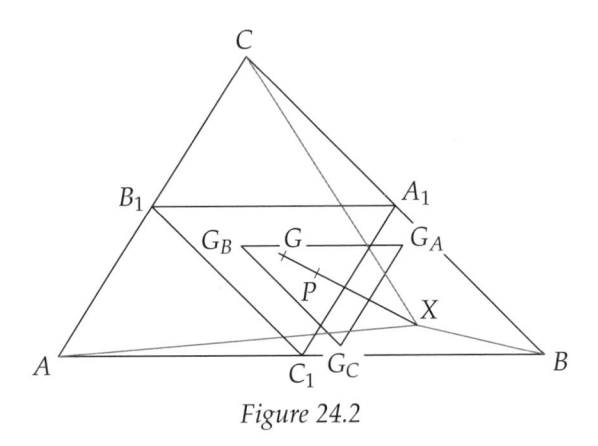

Figure 24.2

Since G_A divides XA_1 in the ratio $2 : 1$, it is clear that $\triangle G_A G_B G_C$ is mapped to $\triangle A_1 B_1 C_1$ by an enlargement with centre X and scale factor $\frac{3}{2}$. But $\triangle A_1 B_1 C_1$ is mapped to $\triangle ABC$ by an enlargement with centre G and scale factor -2.

Hence we need to combine these two homothecies with different centres to produce a single enlargement, with scale factor -3. The centre P will lie on the line segment XG, and is the fixed point of the two homothecies combined. If we let $XP = t$ and $PG = 1 - t$, then P is first mapped to P' with $XP' = \frac{3}{2}t$ and $GP' = \frac{3}{2}t - 1$. Then P' is mapped back to P by the other homothecy, so we have $PG = 2GP'$, thus $1 - t = 3t - 2$ and $t = \frac{3}{4}$, as claimed. □

As a result of theorem 24.1, the Euler lines of $G_\triangle X$ and $\triangle ABC$ are parallel and in opposite directions.

Chapter 24: Partition triangles 349

As a special case of this, we take X to be G. Now the two triangles have a common Euler line, with the same centroid. In figure 24.3 the other centres of $G_\triangle$ are denoted by O', N' and H'.

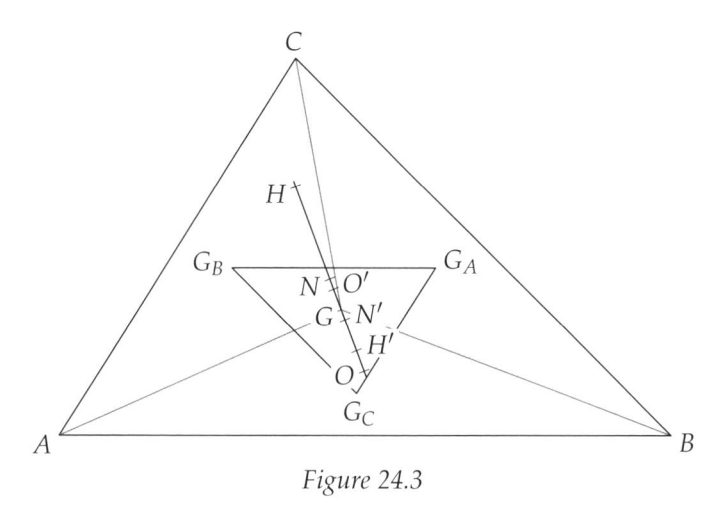

Figure 24.3

Let us summarise some facts about partitions which we know already, or which are consequences of theorem 24.1.

The partition triangles $\triangle H$ are familiar as the orthocentric group of triangles encountered in section 3.4.

- The Euler lines of the partition triangles $\triangle H$ are concurrent at N on the Euler line of $\triangle ABC$.

- The triangle $G_\triangle H$ is homothetic to $\triangle ABC$. The homothecy which takes $\triangle ABC$ to $G_\triangle H$ has centre N and scale factor $-\frac{1}{3}$.

- The triangle $O_\triangle H$ is homothetic to $\triangle ABC$ and the homothecy has centre N and scale factor -1.

- The triangle $N_\triangle H$ is degenerate as it consists of the single point N, so we might say that a homothecy with centre N and scale factor 0 takes $\triangle ABC$ to $N_\triangle H$.

- The triangle $H_\triangle$ is $\triangle ABC$.

The partition triangles $\triangle O$ are all isosceles.

- The Euler lines of $\triangle O$, being the angle bisectors at the circumcentre, are concurrent at O on the Euler line of $\triangle ABC$.

- By theorem 24.1, the triangle $G_\triangle O$ is homothetic to $\triangle ABC$. The homothecy which takes $\triangle ABC$ to $G_\triangle O$ has scale factor $-\frac{1}{3}$ and centre the midpoint of ON. This is is the nine-point centre of the medial triangle $\triangle A_1 B_1 C_1$.

- The triangle $O_\triangle$ is the Kosnita triangle of section 12.3, and is in perspective with $\triangle ABC$ at the Kosnita point K^*.

24.2 Some triangles in perspective

It is useful to generalise Kiepert's theorem, theorem 11.4 on page 147.

Theorem 24.2 *On the sides of $\triangle ABC$, triangles $\triangle CBX$, $\triangle ACY$ and $\triangle BAZ$ are constructed, facing all outwards or all inwards, so that $\angle ZBA = \angle CBX$, $\angle XCB = \angle ACY$ and $\angle YAC = \angle BAZ$. Then the lines AX, BY and CZ are concurrent.*

PROOF The proof is similar to that of Kiepert's theorem.

Let $\angle YAC = \alpha$, $\angle ZBA = \beta$ and $\angle ZCB = \gamma$ and let AX, BY and CZ meet BC, CA and AB at X', Y' and Z' (see figure 24.4).

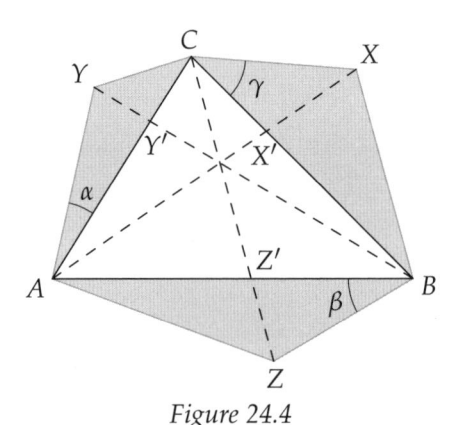

Figure 24.4

By the sine rule on various triangles we have

$$\frac{BX'}{X'C} = \frac{\sin \angle BXX'}{\sin \angle CXX'} = \frac{c \sin(B + \beta)}{b \sin(C + \gamma)}.$$

Now the result follows immediately from Ceva's theorem. □

Chapter 24: Partition triangles 351

Theorem 24.2 can be rephrased by saying that if (AY, AZ), (BZ, BX) and (CX, CY) are pairs of isogonal conjugates, then the triangles $\triangle ABC$ and $\triangle XYZ$ are in perspective.

Corollary 24.3 *The triangle $I_\triangle$ is in perspective with $\triangle ABC$.*

PROOF $I_\triangle$ is the triangle of incentres of the partition $\triangle I$ (see figure 24.5).

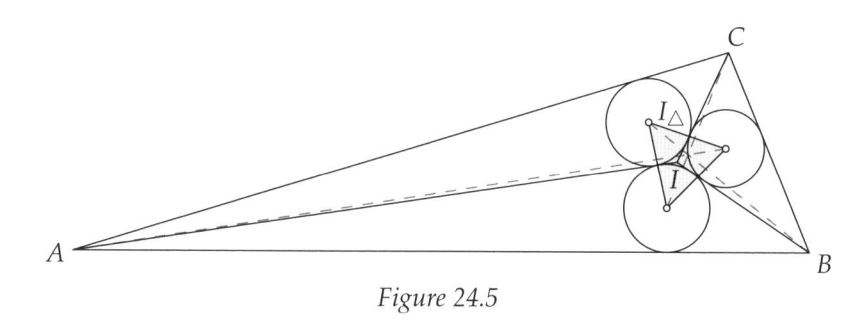

Figure 24.5

The result follows from theorem 24.2 by choosing $\alpha = -\frac{1}{4}A$, $\beta = -\frac{1}{4}B$ and $\gamma = -\frac{1}{4}C$. ❑

A degenerate case where $X_\triangle$ is in perspective with $\triangle ABC$ is when X is F_1, the first isogonic centre. If $\triangle ABC$ has no angle larger than 120°, then the isogonic centres of $(F_1)_\triangle$ are all at F_1, and if there is an angle larger than 120°, two are at F_1 and the third is at the obtuse vertex. The situation is similar for the second isogonic centre.

It also turns out that $K_\triangle$ is of some interest. It depends on a technical result about K_1, the symmedian point of the medial triangle $\triangle A_1 B_1 C_1$. This is the image of K under the homothecy θ with centre G and scale factor $-\frac{1}{2}$.

Lemma 24.4 *The lines BK_1 and BK_B are isogonal conjugates (see figure 24.6).*

PROOF The proof of this requires hard work involving barycentric coordinates and is not given here. ❑

Corollary 24.5 *The triangle $K_\triangle$ is in perspective with $\triangle ABC$.*

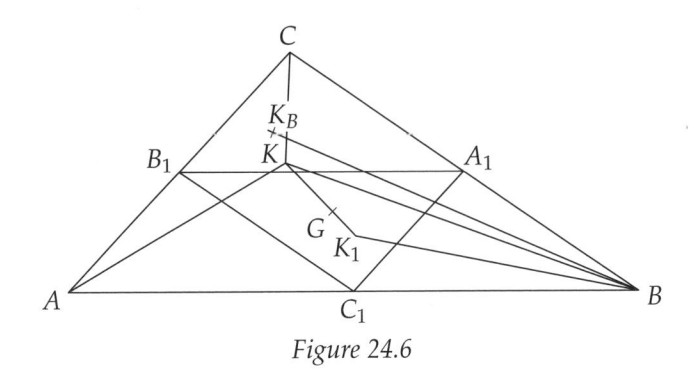

Figure 24.6

Exercise 24a

1. Prove that the triangle composed of the I-excentres of the partition $\triangle I$ is in perspective with $\triangle ABC$.

2. Prove that the triangle of incentres of the triangles $\triangle BCI_A$, $\triangle CAI_B$ and $\triangle ABI_C$ is in perspective with $\triangle ABC$.

24.3 Some concurrent Euler lines

We have already seen that the Euler lines for the triangles of $\triangle G$, $\triangle H$ and $\triangle O$ are concurrent. However, this is not true for $\triangle N$, but it is so for $\triangle I$. The common point is known as the *Schiffler point*, and is denoted by Y.

Theorem 24.6 *The three Euler lines of $\triangle I$ are concurrent on the Euler line of $\triangle ABC$.*

PROOF By theorem 2.13 on page 18, the circumcentres of the partition triangles are the vertices of the circummidarc triangle. However, the other centres on the Euler line are much harder to pin down, and, as a result, a Euclidean demonstration of this result seems difficult to achieve. A proof using barycentric coordinates can be found in appendix A. ❑

Another case, much easier to prove, concerns the partition triangles of the isogonic centres.

Chapter 24: Partition triangles　　　　　　　　　　　　　　　　　　353

Theorem 24.7 *The Euler lines of* △F_1 *and* △F_2 *are concurrent at G.*

PROOF We shall prove this for the first isogonic centre F_1; the argument for F_2 is similar. Let $\triangle ACY$ be the equilateral triangle on AC (see figure 24.7).

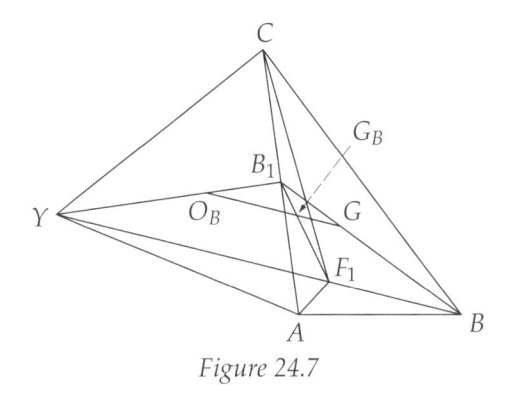

Figure 24.7

Let G_B and O_B be the centroid and circumcentre of $\triangle F_1 CA$. They trisect the segments $B_1 F_1$ and $B_1 Y$ so $O_B G_B$ is parallel to $Y F_1$ and meets $B_1 B$ at G, the centroid of $\triangle ABC$. Since the same is true for the other two partition triangles, the result follows. □

Theorem 24.7 shows that seven Euler lines pass through G, but Nikolai Beluhov has shown, in [3], that there are three more. The following proof is due to him.

Theorem 24.8 *The Euler lines of* $\triangle F_1 F_2 A$, $\triangle F_1 F_2 B$ *and* $\triangle F_1 F_2 C$ *are concurrent at G.*

PROOF Let $\triangle N_A N_B N_C$ and $\triangle N_a N_b N_c$ be the outer and inner Napoleon triangles, M the midpoint of $F_1 F_2$ and F_1' the reflection of F_1 in A_1 (see figure 24.8).
　　Note that $\angle BN_A C = 120°$, $\angle BF_1' C = \angle BF_1 C = 120°$ and $\angle BF_2 C = 60°$. Therefore F_2, B, N_A, F_1' and C are concyclic; in fact, the centre of this circle is N_a since it lies on the perpendicular bisector of BC and $\angle CN_a B = 120°$.
　　The circumcentre O_A of $\triangle F_1 F_2 A$ lies on the perpendicular bisectors of $F_1 A$ and $F_2 A$. These are $N_B N_C$ and $N_b N_c$, so O_A is the intersection of these two lines. Now let X be the intersection of $N_A N_C$ and $N_a N_c$. Since $\angle O_A N_b N_a = 60° = \angle O_A N_C X$, the quadrilateral $O_A N_C X N_b$ is cyclic. By theorem 11.7, G is the common centre of the two Napoleon triangles. It

Figure 24.8

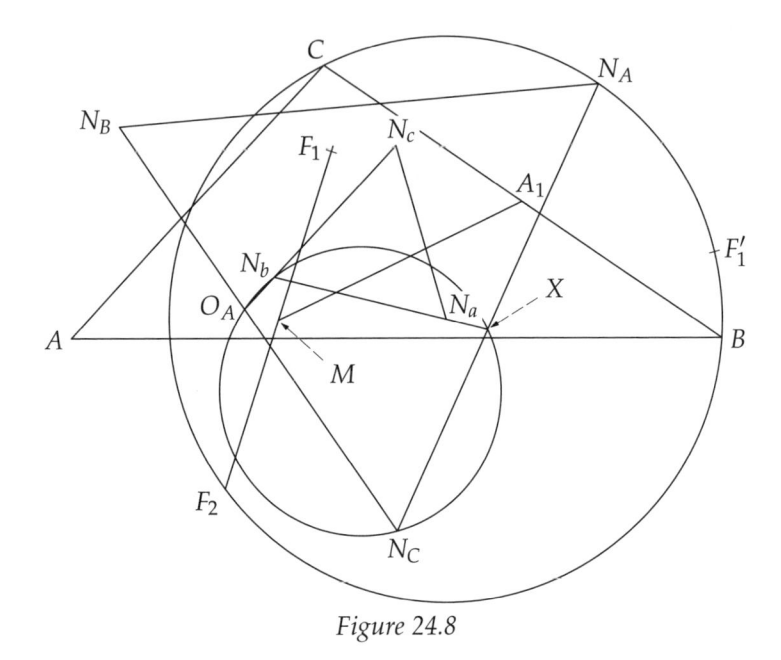

follows that $\angle XGO_A = 120°$ since a rotation by that angle takes $N_C N_B$ to $N_B N_A$ and $N_b N_c$ to $N_a N_b$. Hence G also lies on the circle $O_A N_C X N_b$.

Now we have

$$\begin{aligned}\angle N_C G O_A &= \angle N_C N_b O_A && \text{(angles in same segment)} \\ &= \angle N_A N_a X && \text{(rotation about } G\text{)} \\ &= \angle BCF_2 && \text{(rotation of } 90°\text{)} \\ &= \angle BF_1' F_2. && \text{(angles in same segment)}\end{aligned}$$

But BF_1' is parallel to $F_1 C$, which is perpendicular to $N_A N_B$, which is perpendicular to GN_C. Hence BF_1' is parallel to GN_C. It follows that GO_A is parallel to $F_1' F_2$.

If G_A is the centroid of $\triangle F_1 F_2 A$, then $G_A G$ is parallel to MA_1, which is in turn parallel to $F_1' F_2$. Hence O_A, G_A and G are collinear and the Euler line of $\triangle F_1 F_2 A$ passes through G. The analogous arguments for $\triangle F_1 F_2 B$ and $\triangle F_1 F_2 C$ completes the proof. ❑

An obvious problem is that of characterising the points P for which the triangles $\triangle P$ have concurrent Euler lines. Using an argument which employs areal coordinates, it can be shown that the locus of P is a curve of degree six. This argument also establishes that the point of concurrence is always on the Euler line of $\triangle ABC$.

24.4 Some connections between triangle centres

In this section, we collect together some results where particular centres of triangles $Y_\triangle X$ turn out to have significance in the context of $\triangle ABC$. Where I have not succeeded in proving these using the Euclidean methods favoured in this book, a vector approach has turned out to be appropriate.

Theorem 24.9 *The centroid of $O_\triangle G$ is the circumcentre of $\triangle ABC$.*

PROOF This is a special case of a more general result, which will be proved first. We shall assume, without loss of generality, that $\angle B > \angle C$.

Let P be the foot of the perpendicular from C_1 to AA_1, let CP meet OB_1 at X and let N be the intersection of $A_1 O$ and $C_1 X$ (see figure 24.9).

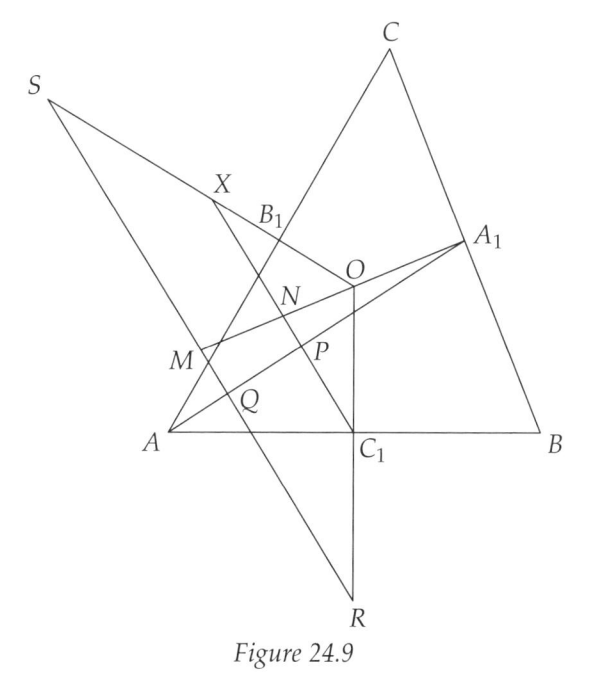

Figure 24.9

Then $\triangle C_1NO$ and $\triangle XNO$ are similar to $\triangle AA_1B$ and $\triangle AA_1C$ by considering rotations of 90°. Hence

$$\frac{C_1N}{NO} = \frac{AA_1}{A_1B} = \frac{AA_1}{A_1C} = \frac{XN}{NO}$$

so $C_1N = XN$ and N is the midpoint of C_1X.

But now let Q be any point of AA_1 and let the line through Q perpendicular to AA_1 meet OC_1 and OB_1 at R and S. Then the midpoint M of RS is on A_1O.

When Q is the midpoint of GA the points R and S are the circumcentres of $\triangle GAB$ and $\triangle GA$ (see figure 24.10).

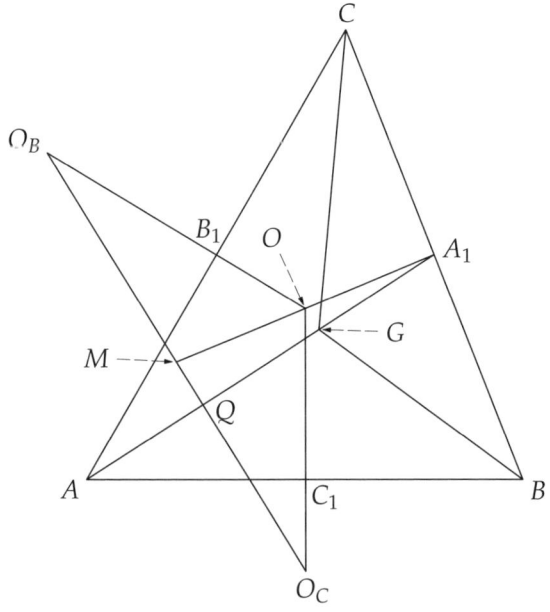

Figure 24.10

But A_1M is a median of $O_\triangle G$, which passes through O. As the same is true of the other two medians, the result follows. ☐

Theorem 24.10 *The centroid of $H_\triangle G$ is the orthocentre of $\triangle ABC$.*

PROOF We will use vectors with origin at the circumcentre of $\triangle ABC$. Let the position vectors of A, B and C be $3a$, $3b$ and $3c$. Then $OH = 3OG =$

$3a + 3b + 3c$. Similarly, if O_A, G_A and H_A are the circumcentre, centroid and orthocentre of $\triangle GBC$, $O_A H_A = 3 O_A G_A$. Let o_A, o_B and o_C be the position vectors of O_A, O_B and O_C; by theorem 24.9, $o_A + o_B + o_C = 0$.

Now $OG_A = \frac{1}{3}((a+b+c) + 3b + 3c)$, so $O_A H_A = 3(O_G O_A - OO_A) = a + 4b + 4c - 3o_A$ and $OH_A = a + 4b + 4c - 2o_A$. Hence the centroid of $\triangle H_A H_B H_C$ has position vector

$$3a + 3b + 3c - \tfrac{2}{3}(o_A + o_B + o_C) = OH,$$

so the result is proved. ☐

Theorem 24.11 *The centroid of $N_\triangle G$ is the nine-point centre of $\triangle ABC$.*

PROOF The proof is immediate from that of theorem 24.10, since $ON = \frac{1}{2}OH$ and $O_A N_A = \frac{1}{2} O_A H_A$, with minor modifications in the algebra. ☐

Theorem 24.12 *The orthocentre and circumcentre of $N_\triangle I$ are the incentre and nine-point centre of $\triangle ABC$.*

PROOF Again we use vectors with origin O and with the position vectors of A, B and C as $3a$, $3b$ and $3c$. By theorem 2.13 on page 18, the circumcentres of $\triangle I$ are the vertices of the circummidarc triangle $\triangle X'Y'Z'$, and the incentre of $\triangle ABC$ is the orthocentre of this triangle.

Let the position vectors of X', Y' and Z' be $3x$, $3y$ and $3z$, so $OI = 3x + 3y + 3z$. These vectors are, of course, related to the position vectors of A, B and C. First, OX' is perpendicular to BC, so $x \cdot (b - c) = 0$. Secondly, A, I and X' are collinear, so $3x - 3a = \lambda(3y + 3z)$. By taking dot products with $y - z$ and noting that $y \cdot y = z \cdot z$ since the points are on the circumcircle, we have $a \cdot (y - z) = x \cdot (y - z)$.

Now we can begin calculations. Let G_A and N_A be the centroid and nine-point centre of $\triangle IBC$. Then we have:

$$OG_A = b + c + x + y + z;$$
$$O_A G_A = b + c - 2x + y + z;$$
$$O_A N_A = \tfrac{3}{2}(b + c - 2x + y + z);$$
$$ON_A = \tfrac{3}{2}(b + c + y + z);$$
$$IN_A = \tfrac{3}{2}(b + c - y - z) - 3x;$$
$$\text{and} \quad N_C N_B = \tfrac{3}{2}(c - b + z - y).$$

In order to show that IN is perpendicular to $N_B N_C$, we calculate the dot product. This yields
$$IN_A \cdot N_C N_B = \tfrac{9}{4}(b+c-y-z-2x)\cdot(c-b+z-y)$$
so that
$$\begin{aligned}\tfrac{4}{9}IN_A \cdot N_C N_B &= (b+c)\cdot(c-b) + (b+c)\cdot(z-y) \\ &\quad - (y+z)\cdot(c-b) - (y+z)\cdot(z-y) \\ &\quad - 2x\cdot(c-b) - 2x\cdot(z-y) \\ &= (b+c)\cdot(z-y) - (y+z)\cdot(c-b) \\ &\quad - 2x\cdot(c-b) - 2x\cdot(z-y) \\ &= 2(b\cdot z - c\cdot y) - 2(c\cdot x - b\cdot x) - 2a\cdot(z-y) \\ &= 2(c-b)\cdot x + 2(a-c)\cdot y + 2(b-a)\cdot z \\ &= 0.\end{aligned}$$

As the same is true for the other two expressions, this shows that I is the orthocentre of $\triangle N_A N_B N_C$.

The centroid of $\triangle N_A N_B N_C$ has position vector $a+b+c+x+y+z$. Hence the circumcentre of $\triangle N_A N_B N_C$ has position vector
$$\frac{3(a+b+c+x+y+z) - 3(x+y+z)}{3-1} = \tfrac{3}{2}(a+b+c),$$
but this is the nine-point centre of $\triangle ABC$. □

There is more going on here than this unilluminating proof shows. In fact, $\triangle N_A N_B N_C$ is similar to $\triangle X'Y'Z'$ and in perspective with it, although they are not homothetic

24.5 Van Lamoen's circle

A triangle can also be partitioned into six smaller triangles using cevians. It is well-known that the medians divide a triangle into six parts of equal area. What is not so familiar is the following result which was only discovered in 2000.

Theorem 24.13 (van Lamoen) *The circumcentres of the triangles* $\triangle GBA_1$, $\triangle GA_1C$, $\triangle GCB_1$, $\triangle GB_1A$, $\triangle GAC_1$ *and* $\triangle GC_1B$ *are concyclic. (See figure 24.11.).*

Chapter 24: Partition triangles 359

Figure 24.11

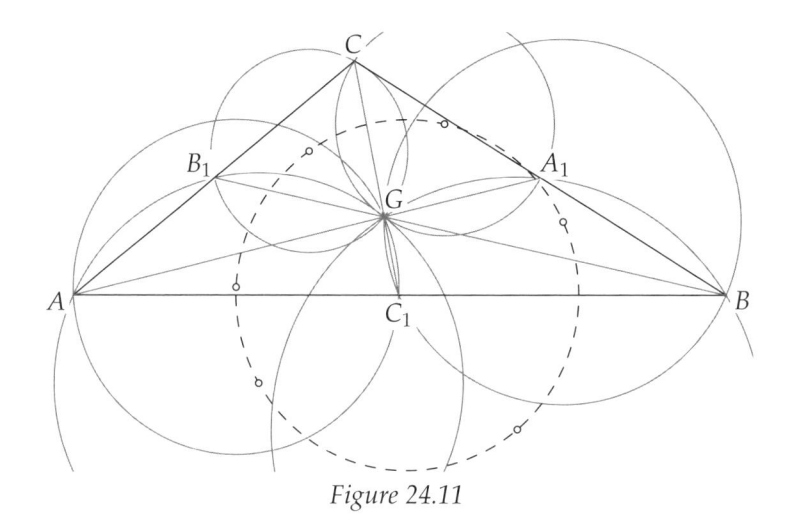

PROOF Let the circumcentres of the triangles in the order given be O_i for $1 \leq i \leq 6$ (see figure 24.12).

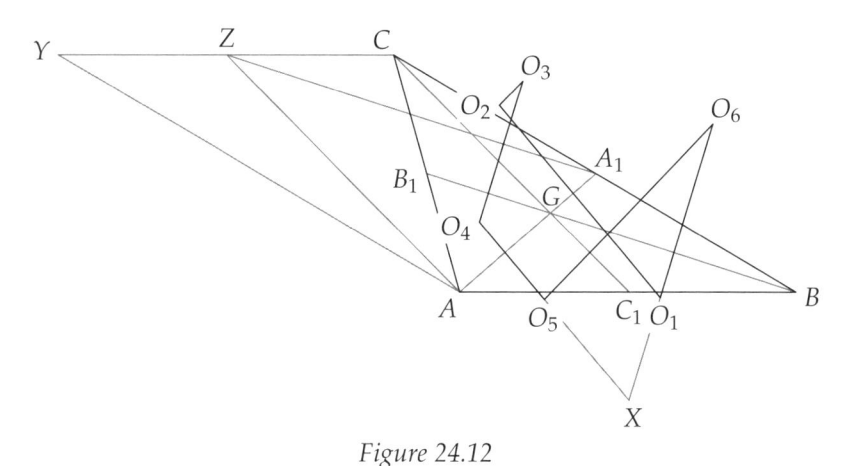

Figure 24.12

These form a hexagon, which in the diagram shown is self-intersecting, whose opposite sides are parallel. For example, O_1O_2 and O_4O_5 are parallel since they are both perpendicular to AA_1. Note also that the distance between these parallel lines is $\frac{1}{2}AA_1$.

Let O_4O_5 and O_1O_6 meet at X. The area of $\triangle XO_1O_4$ can be written in two ways, as $\frac{1}{4}(XO_1 \times BB_1)$ or as $\frac{1}{4}(XO_4 \times AA_1)$, so these expressions are

equal. Hence
$$\frac{BB_1}{AA_1} = \frac{XO_4}{XO_1}.$$

Construct the point Y such that $ABCY$ is a parallelogram, and let Z be the midpoint of CY. Then, as already noted in the solution to question 8 of exercise 2b, $\triangle AA_1Z$ has sides equal to the three medians of $\triangle ABC$. Now focus on the triangle $\triangle XO_6O_5$. By considering rotations through $90°$, $\angle XO_6O_5 = \angle BGC_1 = \angle A_1ZA$ and $\angle O_6O_5X = \angle C_1GA = \angle ZAA_1$. It follows that $\triangle XO_6O_5$ is similar to $\triangle A_1ZA$ and so

$$\frac{XO_6}{XO_5} = \frac{A_1Z}{A_1A} = \frac{BB_1}{AA_1}$$

So now we have $XO_1 \times XO_6 = XO_4 \times XO_5$, and it follows that O_1, O_4, O_5 and O_6 are concyclic. A similar argument shows that O_2 and O_3 also lie on this circle. ❑

We shall refer to the circle given by theorem 24.13 as the *van Lamoen circle*, labelling its centre O_{vL}.

Note that $O_1O_5O_4O_2$ is a cyclic trapezium, so $O_4O_1 = O_5O_2$. By the same argument, O_6O_3 has the same length. Therefore O_{vL} is equidistant from the lines O_4O_1, O_5O_2 and O_6O_3. In figure 24.13, this means that O_{vL} is the incentre of the triangle formed by the diagonals of the hexagon.

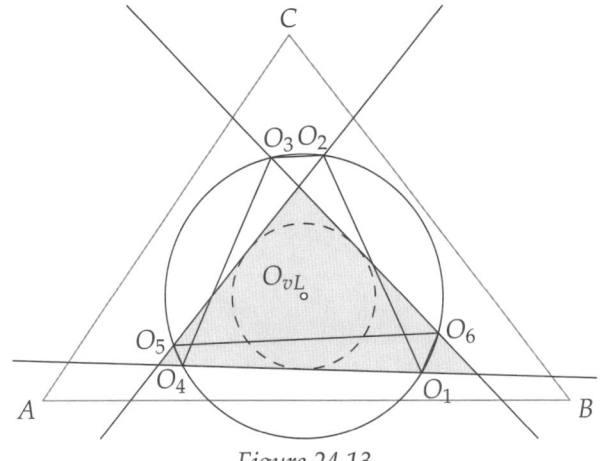

Figure 24.13

Chapter 24: Partition triangles 361

Figure 24.14

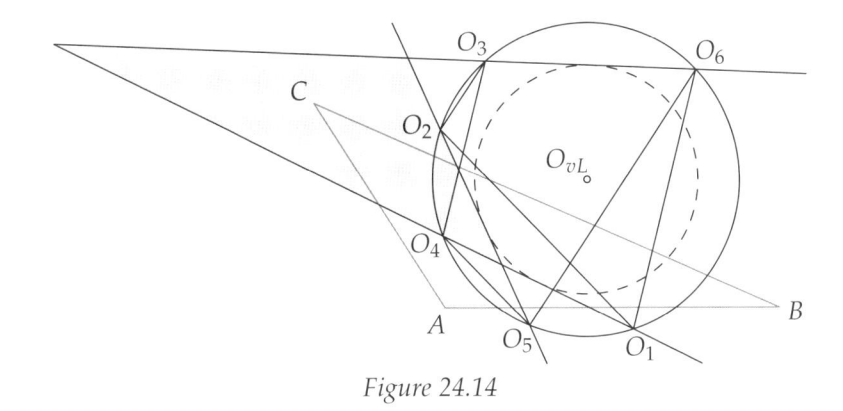

However, it is possible that O_{vL} is one of the excentres of the diagonal triangle; this is shown in figure 24.14.

It is, of course, possible that these three lines do not even form a triangle, since two of them might be parallel. This situation is the 'limiting case' between the two figures.

The van Lamoen circle is linked to the theory of Tucker circles from chapter 17.

Theorem 24.14 *The van Lamoen circle is the Tucker circle of $O_\triangle G$ with scale factor $-\frac{1}{2}$.*

PROOF Let P, Q and R be the midpoints of and GA, GB and GC and let O_A, O_B, O_C be the circumcentres of $\triangle GBC$, $\triangle GCA$ and $\triangle GAB$ (see figure 24.15).

Then $\triangle PQR$ is the pedal triangle of G with respect to $\triangle O_A O_B O_C$, and G is the centroid of $\triangle PQR$. Then, by theorem 8.9 on page 110, G is the symmedian point of $\triangle O_A O_B O_C$. The image of $O_B O_C$ under a homothecy with centre G and scale factor $-\frac{1}{2}$ is the line which intersects $O_A O_C$ and $O_A O_B$ at O_1 and O_2. Hence the result follows. ❑

This gives another characterisation of the centre of the van Lamoen circle. By theorem 17.16 on page 247, the centre of a Tucker circle of $\triangle O_A O_B O_C$ is on its Brocard diameter. The symmedian point of this triangle is G and the circumcentre is O^*, say. Then O_{vL} lies on GO^*.

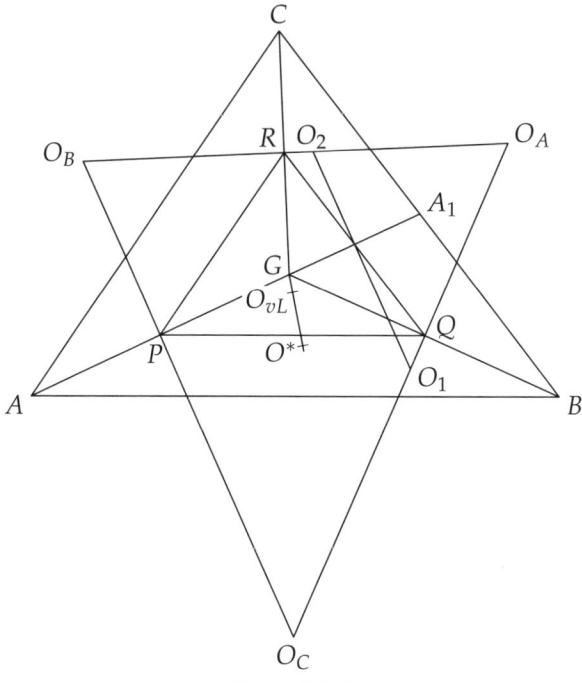

Figure 24.15

Exercise 24b

1. For what points P inside a triangle do the Euler lines of the partition triangles $\triangle P$ concur at P?

2. Prove that $\triangle ABC$ and $O_\triangle H$ have a common Euler line.

3. Prove that the tangents from A, B and C respectively to the circumcircles of $\triangle GBC$, $\triangle GCA$ and $\triangle GAB$ are equal in length.

4. Let the circumradii of $\triangle OBC$, $\triangle OCA$ and $\triangle OAB$ be R_a, R_b and R_c. Prove that
$$\frac{a}{R_a} + \frac{b}{R_b} + \frac{c}{R_c} = \frac{abc}{R^3}.$$

Chapter 25

What lies beyond

Anyone who browses Kimberling's remarkable book [18] or the website devoted to his work [17] will realise that the subject of triangle geometry is virtually inexhaustible. In this final chapter, I offer a tantalising glimpse into those areas which I not explored. This also offers a challenge to enterprising readers to provide proofs—preferably in the spirit of the methods championed by this book—for the results which are presented.

25.1 The equiparallelian point

Given a point P inside $\triangle ABC$, consider a line parallel to a side of the triangle through P, which cuts off intercepts on the other two sides (see figure 25.1). The segment so formed is known as a *parallelian*.

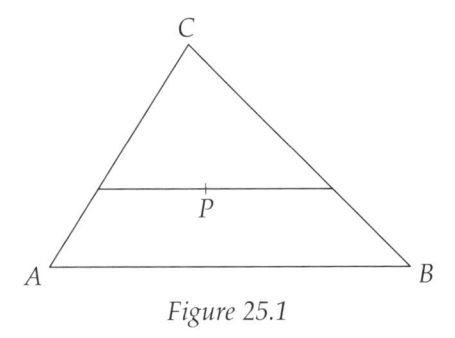

Figure 25.1

Is there a point for which the three parallelians are equal in length? It turns out that there is, and that this point is unique. Here are some properties of the *equiparallelian point*, which will be denoted by $P_=$ (see figure 25.2).

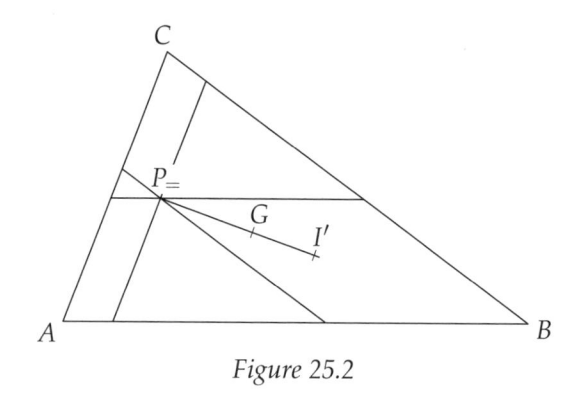

Figure 25.2

(i) Let I' be the isotomic conjugate of the incentre I. Then $P_=$ divides $I'G$ externally in the ratio $3 : -2$.
(ii) The common length of the equiparallelians is
$$\frac{2abc}{ab + bc + ca}.$$
(iii) The incentral triangle $\triangle XYZ$ and the anticomplementary triangle $\triangle A^*B^*C^*$ are in perspective and the perspector is $P_=$ (see figure 25.3).

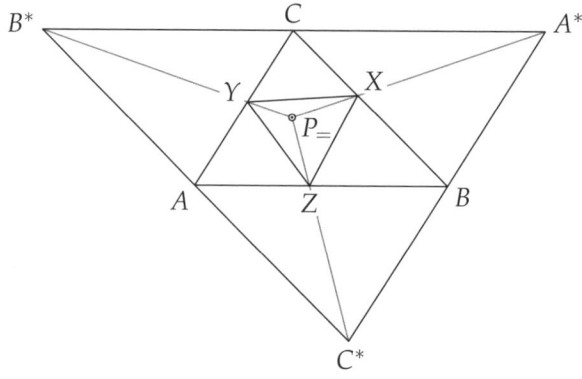

Figure 25.3

25.2 The Malfatti circles

Given a triangle $\triangle ABC$, it is possible to find three circles which are externally tangent to each other and internally tangent to the sides of the triangle (see figure 25.4). These are known as the *Malfatti circles*.

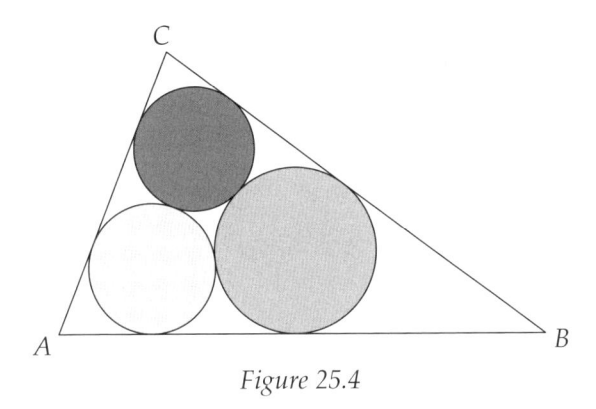

Figure 25.4

This configuration originally arose in the context of a problem set by Gian Francisco Malfatti in 1803, that of cutting three cylindrical columns out of a piece of marble in such a way as to maximise their total cross-sectional area. It was assumed for many years that the solution to the problem for a triangular piece of marble was the one shown in figure 25.4. Since then, however, it has been shown that this is *never* the optimal solution. However, the geometrical problem is interesting in its own right, and a simple construction for the circles was given by Jakob Steiner. In fact, the problem was known as early as the fourteenth century and this configuration occurred in Japanese temple geometry prior to Malfatti's challenge [13, page 293].

It turns out that there are two interesting concurrencies connected with this configuration. Consider the triangle $\mathcal{T}$ formed by the points of tangency between the three circles.

(i) The triangle $\mathcal{T}$ is in perspective with $\triangle ABC$ and the perspector is called the *first Ajima-Malfatti point* A_1^* (see figure 25.5).

(ii) The triangle $\mathcal{T}$ is also in perspective with the excentral triangle $\triangle I_A I_B I_C$, and the perspector is the *second Ajima-Malfatti point* A_2^* (see figure 25.6).

366   The Geometry of the Triangle

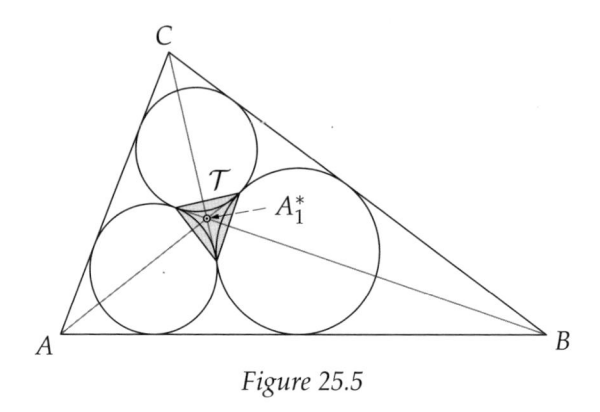

Figure 25.5

Figure 25.6

25.3 The Parry circle

The *Parry circle* is defined as the circumcircle of the triangle $\triangle GJ_1J_2$ consisting of the centroid and the isodynamic points of $\triangle ABC$ (see figure 25.7). The centre of the Parry circle is labelled P^*. The circle has a number of interesting properties.

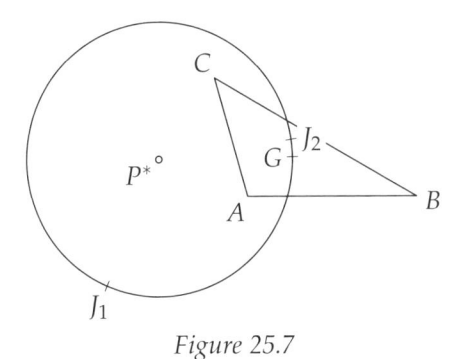

Figure 25.7

(i) The common chord of the Parry circle and the circumcircle passes through the symmedian point K (see figure 25.8).

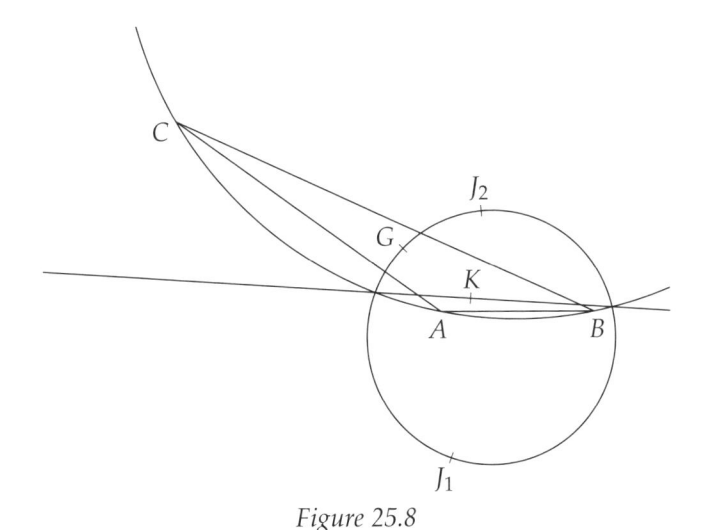

Figure 25.8

(ii) The circumcircle is orthogonal to the Parry circle. Consequently any ray through O meets the Parry circle in two points which are inverse with respect to the circumcircle.

(iii) The Brocard circle (which has diameter OK) is also orthogonal to the Parry circle (see figure 25.9).

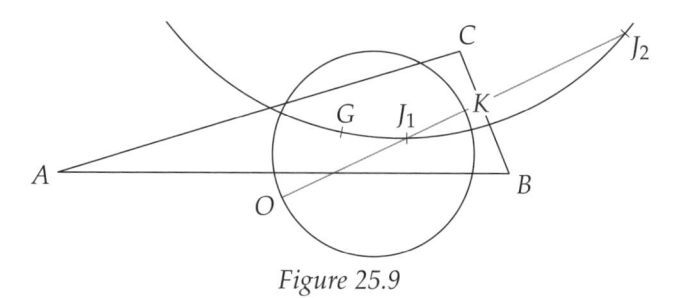

Figure 25.9

As a consequence of item (ii), the Euler line meets the Parry circle at G and a point G_l which is known as the *far-out point* (see figure 25.10).

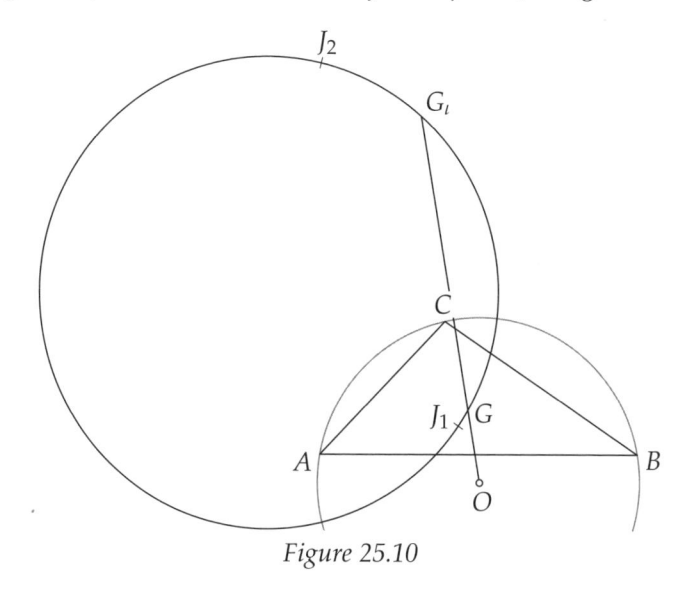

Figure 25.10

The reason for this name is clear when we realise that G_l is the inverse of G with respect to the circumcircle. Hence, as the triangle $\triangle ABC$ becomes equilateral, G_l moves further and further away from O on the Euler line.

25.4 The Apollonius point

In chapter 22, we encountered the Apollonius problem of drawing circles which are tangent to three fixed circles, and considered the special case using three base circles which were themselves mutually tangent. Another important example of this is to find the circle which is tangent to all three excircles of $\triangle ABC$ and encompasses them.

Note that, by Feuerbach's theorem (see page 295), we already have one circle which is externally tangent to the excircles, namely the nine-point circle of $\triangle ABC$. However, this is not the circle we are looking for, since it is encompassed by them. We now construct the circle $\mathcal{C}$ which is orthogonal to the three excircles; it helps to know that its centre is the Spieker centre of $\triangle ABC$. By inverting the nine-point circle in $\mathcal{C}$, we obtain another circle externally tangent to the excircles, which is the one we are looking for (see figure 25.11). It is known as the *Apollonius circle* of $\triangle ABC$.

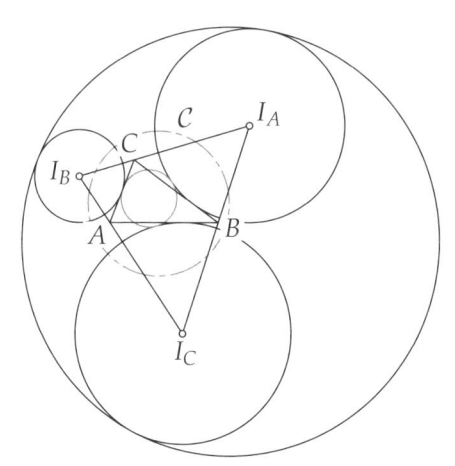

Figure 25.11

The Apollonius circle too has some interesting properties.

(i) Let $\mathcal{T}$ be the triangle formed by the three points of tangency with the excircles. Then $\mathcal{T}$ is in perspective with $\triangle ABC$, and the perspector is known as the *Apollonius point* A^* (see figure 25.12).

(ii) If r and s are, as usual, the inradius and semiperimeter of $\triangle ABC$, then the circle $\mathcal{C}$ has radius $\sqrt{r^2 + s^2}$ and the Apollonius circle has radius $\dfrac{r^2 + s^2}{4r}$.

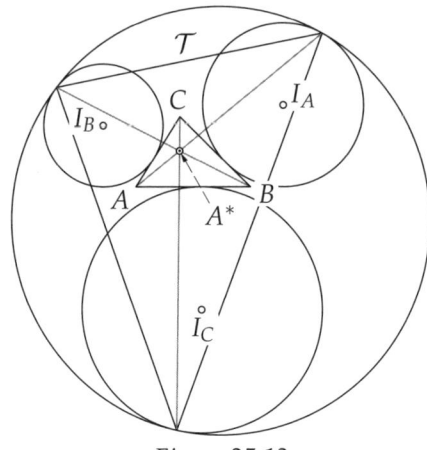

Figure 25.12

The Apollonius circle can also be constructed as a Tucker circle.

25.5 The Kenmotu point

This point has an interesting history. During the Edo period (1603–1867) in Japan, a tradition arose of painting geometrical configurations on wooden tablets, known as *sangaku*, and hanging these, as an act of devotion, in Buddhist temples and Shinto shrines. These problems were later collected and published [12], and they include the result of corollary 23.12 on page 338 and the Malfatti circles of section 25.2.

Another *sangaku* concerns the placement of three congruent squares within a triangle as indicated in figure 25.13. The three squares have a common point, which is known as the *(first) Kenmotu point* K_1^*.

This configuration has the following properties.

(i) The point K_1^* is the internal centre of similitude of the circumcircle and the second Lemoine circle. As a result of this, it lies on their line of centres, which is the Brocard axis .

(ii) The side length of the squares is

$$\frac{\sqrt{2}abc}{a^2 + b^2 + c^2 + 4\Delta}.$$

Chapter 25: What lies beyond

Figure 25.13

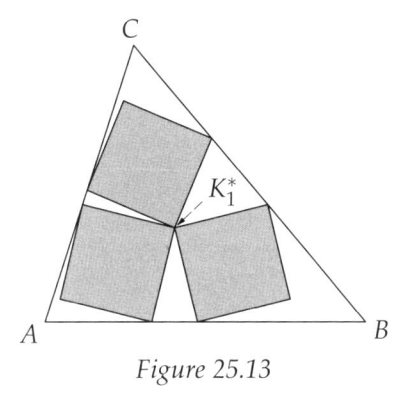

(iii) The three 'free' vertices of the squares form a triangle which is in perspective with $\triangle ABC$. The perspector is the external centre of similitude of the circumcircle and the second Lemoine circle, and is the *second Kenmotu point* K_2^* (see figure 25.14). As a consequence, O, K_1^*, K, K_2^* is a harmonic range.

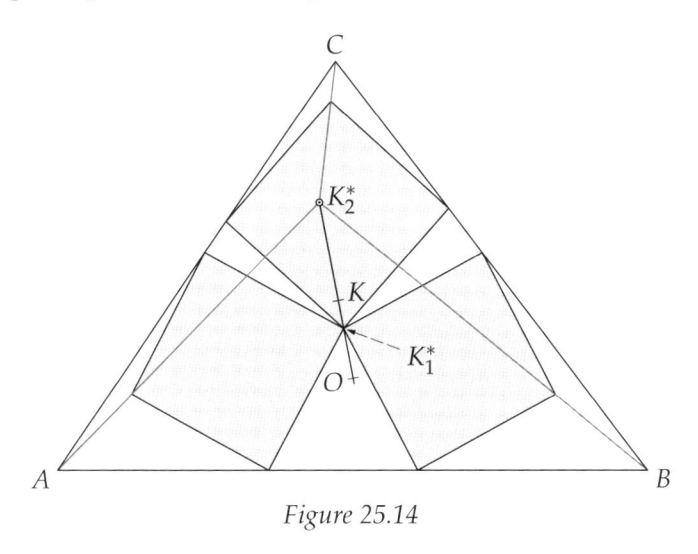

Figure 25.14

(iv) The first Kenmotu point K_1^* is the isogonal conjugate of the outer Vecten point.

This beautiful result seems like a good place to end our tour of triangle geometry.

Appendix A

Barycentric and areal coordinates

The intention in this book has been to avoid the use of coordinate methods wherever possible in deriving the results about triangle geometry, and the reasons for this are given in the preface. However, there are some results where it seems that this method cannot easily be avoided. For this reason, a brief account of the properties of such coordinates is now given. Fuller details can be found in [6], although the focus there is on areal coordinates.

Barycentric and areal coordinates are introduced in section 9.8, and some of the results below occur in exercise 9c on page 125. Unless otherwise indicated, coordinates are to be understood as barycentric.

Some important points

Table A.1 gives the barycentric coordinates of some significant points. Note that in some cases the side lengths alone are used, whereas in others it is convenient to use the angles of the reference triangle, or a mixture of both. Readers might like to check these by calculation; clearly it is sufficient to know the ratios in which the Cevians divide the sides.

Point	Label	Coordinates
Vertices	A, B, C	$(1,0,0), (0,1,0), (0,0,1)$
Midpoints	A_1, B_1, C_1	$(0,1,1), (1,0,1), (1,1,0)$
Centroid	G	$(1,1,1)$
Circumcentre	O	$(\sin 2A, \sin 2B, \sin 2C)$
Orthocentre	H	$(\tan A, \tan B, \tan C)$
Incentre	I	(a,b,c)
Excentres	I_A, I_B, I_C	$(-a,b,c), (a,-b,c), (a,b,-c)$
Nine-point centre	N	$(a\cos(B-C), b\cos(C-A), c\cos(A-B))$
Symmedian point	K	(a^2, b^2, c^2)
Gergonne point	Γ	$((s-b)(s-c), (s-c)(s-a), (s-a)(s-b))$
Nagel point	M	$(b+c-a, c+a-b, a+b-c)$
Spieker centre	S	$(b+c, c+a, a+b)$
Mittenpunkt	M^*	$(a(s-a), b(s-b), c(s-c))$
Feuerbach point	J	$(a[1-\cos(B-C)], b[1-\cos(C-A)], c[1-\cos(A-B)])$
Kosnita point	K^*	$(\sin A \sec(B-C), \sin B \sec(C-A), \sin C \sec(A-B))$
Clawson point	C^*	$(a\tan A, b\tan B, c\tan C)$

Table A.1

Appendix A: Barycentric and areal coordinates 375

The equation of a line

Suppose that $P_1(\lambda_1, \mu_1, \nu_1)$ and $P_2(\lambda_2, \mu_2, \nu_2)$ are the coordinates of two points in the plane of the triangle. They correspond to the centres of mass of masses λ_1, μ_1, ν_1 and λ_2, μ_2, ν_2 at the vertices of the triangle. A general point P on the line P_1P_2 is then the centre of mass of a linear combination of these masses (in other words $k\lambda_1 + (1-k)\lambda_2$ at A, $k\mu_1 + (1-k)\mu_2$ at B and $k\nu_1 + (1-k)\nu_2$ at C) and so it has coordinates $(k\lambda_1 + (1-k)\lambda_2, (k\mu_1 + (1-k)\mu_2, k\nu_1 + (1-k)\nu_2$. Eliminating k gives

$$(\mu_1\nu_2 - \nu_1\mu_2)x + (\nu_1\lambda_2 - \lambda_1\nu_2)y + (\lambda_1\mu_2 - \mu_1\lambda_2)z = 0,$$

which is the barycentric equation of the line containing $P_1(\lambda_1, \mu_1, \nu_1)$ and $P_2(\lambda_2, \mu_2, \nu_2)$. It is convenient to remember this in the form of a determinant

$$\begin{vmatrix} x & y & z \\ \lambda_1 & \mu_1 & \nu_1 \\ \lambda_2 & \mu_2 & \nu_2 \end{vmatrix} = 0.$$

It follows that the condition for the collinearity of three points P_1, P_2 and P_3 is

$$\begin{vmatrix} \lambda_1 & \mu_1 & \nu_1 \\ \lambda_2 & \mu_2 & \nu_2 \\ \lambda_3 & \mu_3 & \nu_3 \end{vmatrix} = 0.$$

In areal coordinates, that is, when the barycentric coordinates are normalised, this determinant represents the ratio

$$\frac{[P_1P_2P_3]}{[ABC]}$$

of triangle areas. It is now easy to interpret the collinearity condition in terms of a triangle of area zero.

The line at infinity has barycentric equation $x + y + z = 0$.

Isogonal conjugates

Let the point P have coordinates (λ, μ, ν) and let its isogonal conjugate be P'' with coordinates $(\lambda'', \mu'', \nu'')$. Then

$$\frac{\lambda}{\mu} = \frac{[BCP]}{[CAP]} = \frac{ap_A}{bp_B} \quad \text{and} \quad \frac{\lambda''}{\mu''} = \frac{[BCP'']}{[CAP'']} = \frac{aq_A}{bq_B},$$

where p_A, p_B, q_A and q_B are the perpendicular distances of P and P'' to the sides BC and CA. By theorem 7.6 on page 86, we have

$$\frac{p_A}{p_B} = \frac{q_B}{q_A}$$

and so

$$\frac{\lambda''}{\mu''} = \frac{a p_B}{b p_A} = \frac{a^2 \mu}{b^2 \lambda}.$$

It follows that we can take the coordinates of the isogonal conjugate to be

$$\left(\frac{a^2}{\lambda}, \frac{b^2}{\mu}, \frac{c^2}{\nu} \right).$$

Note that this accords with the fact that the incentre is its own isogonal conjugate and that the symmedian point is the isogonal conjugate of the centroid.

Conics

The general equation of a conic is a homogeneous equation of the second degree

$$ax^2 + by^2 + cz^2 + 2fyz + 2gzx + 2hxy = 0,$$

which may factorise into two linear factors (with real coefficients), in which case it is a line pair.

If the conic passes through A, B and C, then we have $a = b = c = 0$, and so the conic takes the simpler form

$$fyz + gzx + hxy = 0.$$

One way of telling whether this is an ellipse, a hyperbola or a parabola is to find its intersections with the line at infinity $x + y + z = 0$. This is equivalent to letting $z = 1$ and $y = -1 - x$, and will produce a quadratic in x which has either no, one or two real roots. These cases correspond to the conic being, respectively, an ellipse, a parabola or a hyperbola.

The Kiepert hyperbola

We begin with the configuration of Kiepert's theorem, which is theorem 11.4 on page 147, and calculate the locus of P, the perspector of

Appendix A: Barycentric and areal coordinates 377

$\triangle ABC$ and $\triangle XYZ$, as α varies. By the proof of theorem 11.4, we see that

$$\frac{[CPB]}{[BPA]} = \frac{a\sin(C+\alpha)}{c\sin(A+\alpha)},$$

and so on, and so the coordinates (x, y, z) of P are given by

$$\left(\frac{a}{\sin(A+\alpha)}, \frac{b}{\sin(B+\alpha)}, \frac{c}{\sin(C+\alpha)}\right).$$

Rearranging, we obtain

$$\sin A \cos\alpha + \cos A \sin\alpha = \frac{a}{x},$$

$$\sin B \cos\alpha + \cos B \sin\alpha = \frac{b}{y},$$

and $\sin C \cos\alpha + \cos C \sin\alpha = \frac{c}{z},$

which can be thought of as three equations in the two unknowns $\sin\alpha$ and $\cos\alpha$, which have a unique solution. Hence the determinant of coefficients is singular, so

$$\begin{vmatrix} \sin A & \cos A & \frac{a}{x} \\ \sin B & \cos B & \frac{b}{y} \\ \sin C & \cos C & \frac{c}{z} \end{vmatrix} = 0.$$

On multiplying out, we have

$$ayz\sin(B-C) + bzx\sin(C-A) + cxy\sin(A-B) = 0 \qquad (A.1)$$

Now, by the sine and cosine rules,

$$a\sin(B-C) = \frac{ab}{2R}\left(\frac{a^2+b^2-c^2}{2ab}\right) - \frac{ac}{2R}\left(\frac{c^2+a^2-b^2}{2ca}\right) = \frac{b^2-c^2}{2R},$$

so equation (A.1) becomes

$$(b^2-c^2)yz + (c^2-a^2)zx + (a^2-b^2)xy = 0,$$

which is the equation of the locus of P.

If the triangle $\triangle ABC$ is equilateral, the locus degenerates to a point, which is not surprising. If it is isosceles, say with $a = b \neq c$, it becomes $z(y - x) = 0$, which is a line pair consisting of the median through C and the line AB. In the scalene case, the locus is a conic through the three vertices of $\triangle ABC$.

We now substitute $z = 1$ and $y = -1 - x$ to check its nature. This produces the quadratic equation $(a^2 - b^2)x^2 + 2(a^2 - c^2)x + (b^2 - c^2) = 0$, and the discriminant of this is $2\sum (a^2 - b^2)$, which is positive. Hence the conic is a hyperbola. The condition for a circumscribing conic $\sum fyz = 0$ to be a rectangular hyperbola can be shown to be $\sum fbc \cos A = 0$. In this case, we have

$$\sum fbc \cos A = \sum (b^2 - c^2) bc \cos A = \tfrac{1}{2} \sum (b^2 - c^2)(b^2 + c^2 - a^2) = 0,$$

so this condition is satisfied. In fact, it is equivalent to $\sum f \tan B \tan C = 0$, which means that a circumscribing conic is a rectangular hyperbola if it passes through the orthocentre.

Conversely, any rectangular hyperbola which circumscribes a circle also passes through its orthocentre. This can be proved by elementary Cartesian methods. A result known as *Feuerbach's conic theorem* says that the locus of the centres of all such circumscribing rectangular hyperbolas is the nine-point circle. A special case of this result is that the centre of the Kiepert hyperbola, which can be shown to have coordinates

$$\left((b^2 - c^2)^2, (c^2 - a^2)^2, (a^2 - b^2)^2 \right),$$

lies on the nine-point circle of $\triangle ABC$. Of course, it also lies on the nine-point circle of any triangle whose vertices lie on the Kiepert hyperbola.

We know from Kiepert's theorem that the curve passes through the centroid G, orthocentre H, isogonic centres F_1 and F_2 and the Napoleon points Ψ_o and Ψ_i. Other points on the Kiepert hyperbola include the Spieker centre S and the Vecten points V_o and V_i.

The Lester circle

It is possible to tackle Lester's theorem by means of the Kiepert hyperbola and ordinary Cartesian methods, so the coordinates used in this section are Cartesians. Taking the centre of the hyperbola as the origin O and axes along the asymptotes, we parametrise a point on the hyperbola as

$$\left(t, \frac{1}{t}\right),$$

and choose the parameters of A, B, C, G and H to be a, b, c, g and h. It is easy to show that $abch = -1$. Since G is the centroid, we have

$$3g = a+b+c \quad \text{and} \quad \frac{3}{g} = \frac{1}{a} + \frac{1}{b} + \frac{1}{c}.$$

It follows that

$$ab + bc + ca = -\frac{3}{gh}.$$

If the first isogonic centre F_1 has parameter f, then using the usual gradient formula we have

$$\tan \angle BF_1 A = \frac{\frac{1}{fa} - \frac{1}{fb}}{1 + \left(\frac{1}{fa}\right)\left(\frac{1}{fb}\right)} = \frac{f(b-a)}{1 + f^2 ab}$$

and similarly

$$\tan \angle CF_1 B = \frac{f(c-b)}{1 + f^2 bc} \quad \text{and} \quad \tan \angle AF_1 C = \frac{f(a-c)}{1 + f^2 ca}.$$

These expressions are all equal, since $\angle BF_1 A = \angle CF_1 B = \angle AF_1 C$, so

$$\frac{f(b-a)}{1 + f^2 ab} = \frac{f(c-b)}{1 + f^2 bc} = \frac{f(a-c)}{1 + f^2 ca}.$$

As the numerators of these expressions sum to zero, the denominators do so as well. This yields

$$3 + f^2(ab + bc + ca) = 3 - \frac{3f^2}{gh} = 0,$$

so $f = \pm\sqrt{gh}$. This has given us the parameter for the second isogonic centre F_2 as well as that for F_1. As a consequence, we now know that the Fermat axis passes through the centre of the Kiepert hyperbola and the isogonic centres are equally situated on its two branches. It might be objected that this proof assumes that $\triangle ABC$ has all angles less than

120°, so that F_1 is the Fermat point. In fact, it is possible to rephrase the argument in terms of directed angles so that the angles between AF_1, BF_1 and CF_1 are either 120°, 120°, 120° or 60°, 60°, −120°. Then it is still true that the tangents of the directed angles are equal. This applies equally well to F_2.

Now the gradient of OF_1 is

$$\frac{1}{f^2} = \frac{1}{gh}.$$

The centre Q of the orthocentroidal disc is the midpoint of GH so it has coordinates

$$\left(\frac{g+h}{2}, \frac{g+h}{2gh}\right)$$

and the gradient of OQ is also $\dfrac{1}{gh}$.

It follows that O, Q, F_1 and F_2 are collinear, so we now know that the Fermat axis intersects the Euler line at Q.

Next we show that $QF_1 \times QF_2 = OG^2$. We have

$$4QG^2 = (g-h)^2 + \left(\frac{g-h}{gh}\right)^2$$

$$= (g-h)^2\left(1 + \frac{1}{f^4}\right),$$

$$QF_1^2 = \left(\frac{g+h}{2} - f\right)^2 + \left(\frac{g+h}{2f^2} - \frac{1}{f}\right)^2$$

$$= \left(\frac{g+h}{2} - f\right)^2\left(1 + \frac{1}{f^4}\right)$$

and $\quad QF_2^2 = \left(\dfrac{g+h}{2} + f\right)^2\left(1 + \dfrac{1}{f^4}\right)$

and so

$$QF_1^2 \times QF_2^2 = \left(\left(\frac{g+h}{2}\right)^2 - f^2\right)^2\left(1 + \frac{1}{f^4}\right)^2$$

$$= \tfrac{1}{4}((g+h)^2 - 4gh)^2\left(1 + \frac{1}{f^4}\right)^2$$

$$= \tfrac{1}{4}(g-h)^4\left(1+\frac{1}{f^4}\right)^2$$
$$= QG^2.$$

We can now proceed as in the proof on page 155 to prove Lester's theorem.

The Morley centres

We begin by calculating the coordinates of the vertices of the first Morley triangle. It will be convenient to denote $\tfrac{1}{3}\angle A$, $\tfrac{1}{3}\angle B$ and $\tfrac{1}{3}\angle C$ by α, β and γ.

Letting $BD = y$ and $CD = z$, we have $y\sin\beta = z\sin\gamma$. Then the areas of $\triangle BCD$, $\triangle CAD$ and $\triangle ABD$ are $\tfrac{1}{2}ay\sin 2\beta$, $\tfrac{1}{2}bz\sin 2\gamma$ and $\tfrac{1}{2}cx\sin 2\alpha$. If, then, we set $y\sin\beta = z\sin\gamma = 2$, the coordinates of D can be taken as $(a, 2b\cos\gamma, 2c\cos\beta)$. Similarly E is $(2a\cos\gamma, b, 2c\cos\alpha)$ and F is $(2a\cos\beta, 2b\cos\alpha, c)$.

Now the equations of the lines AD, BD and CD are $yc\cos\beta = zb\cos\gamma$, $za\cos\gamma = xc\cos\alpha$ and $xb\cos\alpha = ya\cos\beta$. Therefore the coordinates of M_2, which is the point common to these three lines, can be taken as $(a\sec\alpha, b\sec\beta, c\sec\gamma)$.

By theorem 14.5 on page 189, the Morley-Yff centre M_3 is the isogonal conjugate of M_2, so it has coordinates $(a\cos\alpha, b\cos\beta, c\cos\gamma)$.

The first Morley centre M_1 is the centroid of the equilateral triangle $\triangle DEF$. It might be thought that its coordinates can be calculated by simply adding (or averaging) the coordinates of D, E and F which have already been obtained, but this will not work since they are not normalised. It is easier to adopt a direct approach and calculate the perpendicular distances of M_1 from the sides. Without loss of generality, we set the side of the Morley triangle as 3. In the proof of theorem 14.1 on page 185, we note that $\angle BDF = 60° + \gamma$, $\angle DFB = \angle DEC = 60° + \alpha$ and $\angle CDE = 60° + \beta$ so by the sine rule

$$BD = \frac{3\sin(60°+\alpha)}{\sin\beta},\ BF = \frac{3\sin(60°+\gamma)}{\sin\beta}\ \text{and}\ CE = \frac{3\sin(60°+\beta)}{\sin\gamma}.$$

So the perpendicular distances of D, E and F from BC are $3\sin(60°+\alpha)$, $6\sin(60°+\beta)\cos\gamma$ and $6\sin(60°+\gamma)\cos\beta$ and hence the distance of M_1 is

$$\sin(60°+\alpha) + 2\sin(60°+\beta)\cos\gamma + 2\sin(60°+\gamma)\cos\beta.$$

Expanding by the addition formulae and using $\alpha + \beta + \gamma = 60°$, we obtain

$$\sin(60° + \alpha) + \cos\beta \sin\gamma + \cos\gamma \sin\beta + 2\sqrt{3}\cos\beta \cos\gamma$$
$$= \sin(60° + \alpha) + \sin(60° - \alpha) + 2\sqrt{3}\cos\beta \cos\gamma$$
$$= \sqrt{3}\cos\alpha + 2\sqrt{3}\cos\beta \cos\gamma$$

and it follows that the barycentric coordinates of M_1 can be taken to be

$$(a(\cos\alpha + 2\cos\beta \cos\gamma), b(\cos\beta + 2\cos\gamma \cos\alpha), c(\cos\gamma + 2\cos\alpha \cos\beta)).$$

Now it is possible to prove theorem 14.6 on page 189 using the coordinates of M_1, M_2 and M_3. It is convenient to denote $\cos\alpha$, $\cos\beta$ and $\cos\gamma$ by p, q and r respectively. We evaluate the determinant of coordinates to obtain

$$\begin{vmatrix} a(p+2qr) & b(q+2rp) & c(2+2pq) \\ \dfrac{a}{p} & \dfrac{b}{q} & \dfrac{c}{r} \\ ap & bq & cr \end{vmatrix}$$

$$= \begin{vmatrix} 2aqr & 2brp & 2cpq \\ \dfrac{a}{p} & \dfrac{b}{q} & \dfrac{c}{r} \\ ap & bq & cr \end{vmatrix} \quad (\text{row}_1' = \text{row}_1 - \text{row}_3)$$

$$= 0$$

since $\text{row}_1 = pqr \times \text{row}_2$, and the collinearity follows.

This illustrates how simple certain proofs become using barycentric methods (once the coordinates of specific points are calculated) but it cannot be said to give much insight as to why the collinearity occurs.

The Mittenpunkt

This is the intersection of the lines $I_a A_1$, $I_B B_1$ and $I_C C_1$. Since I_A is $(-a, b, c)$ and A_1 is $(0, 1, 1)$, the line has equation $(b-c)x + ay - az = 0$.

Appendix A: Barycentric and areal coordinates

We have

$$(b-c)a(s-a) + ab(s-b) - ac(s-c)$$
$$= ab(s-a+s-b) - ac(s-a+s-c)$$
$$= abc - abc$$
$$= 0$$

and so the point $(a(s-a), b(s-b), c(s-c))$ lies on $I_A A_1$. We can also check that it lies on $I_B B_1$ (and $I_C C_1$) so this is the Mittenpunkt M^*. In particular, we see that the perpendiculars from M^* to the sides are $s-a$, $s-b$ and $s-c$; this fact is used in the proof of theorem 23.9 on page 335.

We can also prove the two collinearities given by theorems 23.23 and 23.24 on page 344.

The barycentric coordinates of I, K and M^* are (a,b,c), (a^2, b^2, c^2) and $(a(s-a), b(s-b), c(s-c))$ respectively. Now we consider the determinant

$$\begin{vmatrix} a & b & c \\ a^2 & b^2 & c^2 \\ a(s-a) & b(s-b) & c(s-c) \end{vmatrix} = \begin{vmatrix} a & b & c \\ a^2 & b^2 & c^2 \\ as & bs & cs \end{vmatrix} \quad (\text{row}_3' = \text{row}_3 + \text{row}_2)$$
$$= 0$$

since $\text{row}_3 = s \times \text{row}_1$, and the collinearity follows.

The barycentric coordinates of H, C^* and M^* are $(\tan A, \tan B, \tan C)$, $(a \tan A, b \tan B, c \tan C)$ and $(a(s-a), b(s-b), c(s-c))$ respectively, so we must show that the expression

$$\begin{vmatrix} \tan A & \tan B & \tan C \\ a \tan A & b \tan B & c \tan C \\ a(s-a) & b(s-b) & c(s-c) \end{vmatrix} = \sum a(s-a)(c-b) \tan B \tan C$$

is zero. It is equal to

$$\frac{\tan A \tan B \tan C}{4R} \sum (s-a)(c-b) \cos A.$$

Now this sum is

$$\frac{2}{abc} \sum (b+c-a)(c-b)a(b^2+c^2-a^2),$$

so it is sufficient to multiply out the brackets and see that everything cancels. We have

$$\sum a(c^4 - b^4) - a^2(c-b)(b^2+c^2) - a^3(c^2-b^2) + a^4(c-b).$$

When this is summed, the first and last terms cancel as do the second and third terms.

The Schiffler point

We prove theorem 24.6 on page 352. The Schiffler point Y has barycentric coordinates

$$\left(a - \frac{a^2}{b+c}, b - \frac{b^2}{c+a}, c - \frac{c^2}{a+b}\right).$$

First, we show that this is on the Euler lines of the triangles $\triangle IBC$, $\triangle ICA$ and $\triangle IAB$.

The Euler line of $\triangle IBC$ passes through its centroid G_A and circumcentre O_A. O_A is the midpoint of II_A, so its coordinates are the mean of the normalised barycentric coordinates of I and I_A. As these are

$$\frac{(a,b,c)}{b+c+a} \text{ and } \frac{(-a,b,c)}{b+c-a},$$

the mean is

$$\frac{(-2a^2, 2b(b+c), 2c(b+c))}{(b+c+a)(b+c-a)}.$$

Therefore we can take unnormalised barycentric coordinates for O_A as $(-a^2, b(b+c), c(b+c))$. The coordinates of G_A are found by taking the mean of

$$\frac{(a,b,c)}{a+b+c}, (0,1,0) \text{ and } (0,0,1)$$

and these turn out to be $(a, a+2b+c, a+b+2c)$ in unnormalised form.

Appendix A: Barycentric and areal coordinates

We now show that Y is collinear with G_A and O_A. To do this, we consider the determinant

$$\begin{vmatrix} a & a+2b+c & a+b+2c \\ -a^2 & b(b+c) & c(b+c) \\ a-\dfrac{a^2}{b+c} & b-\dfrac{b^2}{c+a} & c-\dfrac{c^2}{a+b} \end{vmatrix}$$

$$= \begin{vmatrix} a & a+2b+c & a+b+2c \\ 0 & (a+b)(a+b+c) & (a+c)(a+b+c) \\ a-\dfrac{a^2}{b+c} & b-\dfrac{b^2}{c+a} & c-\dfrac{c^2}{a+b} \end{vmatrix}$$

$$(\text{row}_2' = \text{row}_2 + a\,\text{row}_1)$$

$$= a(a+b+c) \begin{vmatrix} 1 & a+2b+c & a+b+2c \\ 0 & a+b & a+c \\ 1-\dfrac{a}{b+c} & b-\dfrac{b^2}{c+a} & c-\dfrac{c^2}{a+b} \end{vmatrix}$$

$$(\text{factors of row}_2 \text{ and col}_1)$$

$$= a(a+b+c) \begin{vmatrix} 1 & b+c & b+c \\ 0 & a+b & a+c \\ 1-\dfrac{a}{b+c} & b-\dfrac{b^2}{c+a} & c-\dfrac{c^2}{a+b} \end{vmatrix}$$

$$(\text{row}_1' = \text{row}_1 - \text{row}_2)$$

$$= a(a+b+c) \begin{vmatrix} 1 & 0 & 0 \\ 0 & a+b & a+c \\ 1-\dfrac{a}{b+c} & a-c-\dfrac{b^2}{c+a} & a-b-\dfrac{c^2}{a+b} \end{vmatrix}$$

$$(\text{col}_2' = \text{col}_2 - (b+c) \times \text{col}_1,$$
$$\text{col}_3' = \text{col}_3 - (b+c) \times \text{col}_1)$$

$$= a(a+b+c)\Big(a^2-b^2-c^2-(a^2-c^2-b^2)\Big)$$

$$(\text{expand along row}_1)$$

$$= 0$$

and Y is on the Euler line of $\triangle IBC$, and similarly on the Euler lines of $\triangle ICA$ and $\triangle IAB$.

Finally, we need to show that Y is on the Euler line of $\triangle ABC$. The barycentric coordinates of G and O are $(1,1,1)$ and $(\sin 2A, \sin 2B, \sin 2C)$ respectively. From the sine and cosine rules the latter are equivalent to $\left(a^2(b^2+c^2-a^2), b^2(c^2+a^2-b^2), c^2(a^2+b^2-c^2)\right)$. The determinant of coordinates is thus

$$\begin{vmatrix} 1 & 1 & 1 \\ a^2(b^2+c^2-a^2) & b^2(c^2+a^2-b^2) & c^2(a^2+b^2-c^2) \\ a-\dfrac{a^2}{b+c} & b-\dfrac{b^2}{c+a} & c-\dfrac{c^2}{a+b} \end{vmatrix}$$

$$= \begin{vmatrix} 1 & 0 & 0 \\ a^2(b^2+c^2-a^2) & c^2(b^2-a^2)+a^4-b^4 & b^2(c^2-a^2)+a^4-c^4 \\ a-\dfrac{a^2}{b+c} & b-a+\dfrac{a^2}{b+c}-\dfrac{b^2}{c+a} & c-a+\dfrac{a^2}{b+c}-\dfrac{c^2}{a+b} \end{vmatrix}$$

$$(\text{col}_2' = \text{col}_2 - \text{col}_1$$
$$\text{col}_3' = \text{col}_3 - \text{col}_1)$$

$$= \begin{vmatrix} c^2(b^2-a^2)+a^4-b^4 & b^2(c^2-a^2)+a^4-c^4 \\ b-a+\dfrac{c(a^2-b^2)+a^3-b^3}{(b+c)(c+a)} & c-a+\dfrac{b(a^2-c^2)+a^3-c^3}{(b+c)(a+b)} \end{vmatrix}$$

(expand along row$_1$)

$$= (b-a)(c-a)$$
$$\times \begin{vmatrix} (b+a)(c^2-a^2-b^2) & (c+a)(b^2-c^2-a^2) \\ 1-\dfrac{c(a+b)+a^2+ab+b^2}{(b+c)(c+a)} & 1-\dfrac{b(c+a)+c^2+ca+a^2}{(b+c)(a+b)} \end{vmatrix}$$

(factors of col$_1$ and col$_2$)

$$= (b-a)(c-a) \begin{vmatrix} (b+a)(c^2-a^2-b^2) & (c+a)(b^2-c^2-a^2) \\ \dfrac{c^2-a^2-b^2}{(b+c)(c+a)} & \dfrac{b^2-c^2-a^2}{(b+c)(a+b)} \end{vmatrix}$$

$$= 0$$

since $\text{row}_1 = (b+c)(c+a)(a+b) \times \text{row}_2$. Therefore the three points are collinear and hence Y is on the Euler line of $\triangle ABC$.

Exercise A

1. Prove *Routh's theorem*:
   Let the sides of $\triangle ABC$, whose area is Δ, be divided by L, M and N in the ratios $\lambda : 1$, $\mu : 1$ and $\nu : 1$. Then AL, BM and CN form a triangle whose area Δ' satisfies
   $$\frac{\Delta'}{\Delta} = \frac{(\lambda\mu\nu - 1)^2}{(\lambda\mu + \lambda + 1)(\mu\nu + \mu + 1)(\nu\lambda + \nu + 1)}.$$

2. Explore the consequences of choosing $\lambda = \mu = \nu = k$ for integer $k \geq 1$.

3. Use Routh's theorem to prove Ceva's theorem and adapt the result to prove Menelaus' theorem.

4. Prove that the circumcentre and orthocentre are isogonal conjugates.

5. Prove that the centroid, circumcentre and orthocentre are collinear.

6. Prove that the barycentric equation of the Euler line is
   $$\sum \left(b^2 + c^2 - a^2\right)\left(b^2 - c^2\right)x = 0.$$

Appendix B

Solutions to the exercises

Exercise 2a

1. This is immediate from the fact that $\triangle ABC$ is the anticomplementary triangle of its medial triangle $\triangle A_1B_1C_1$.

2. By angles in the same segment, we have $\angle AX'Y' = \angle ABY' = \frac{1}{2}\angle B$, $\angle X'Y'B = \angle X'AB = \frac{1}{2}\angle A$ and $\angle BY'Z' = \angle BCZ' = \frac{1}{2}\angle C$. If P is the intersection of AX' and $Y'Z'$, we now have $\angle Y'PX' = 180° - \frac{1}{2}(\angle A + \angle B + \angle C) = 90°$ and so $X'A$ is an altitude of $\triangle X'Y'Z'$. Similarly so are $Y'B$ and $Z'C$.

3. (a) Let P be the point such that $\mathbf{OP} = \mathbf{OA} + \mathbf{OB} + \mathbf{OC}$. Then $\mathbf{AP} = \mathbf{OB} + \mathbf{OC}$ and $\mathbf{BC} = \mathbf{OC} - \mathbf{OB}$. Hence $\mathbf{AP} \cdot \mathbf{BC} = |\mathbf{OC}|^2 - |\mathbf{OB}|^2 = 0$ and so AP is perpendicular to BC. Similarly BP is perpendicular to CA, so P is the orthocentre H.
   (b) This follows from (a) together with theorem 2.7.

4. (See the figures.)
   The circumcircle of $\triangle BOC$ goes through H if, and only if, $\angle BOC = \angle BHC$. Now a short angle-chase shows that $\angle BHC = \angle C + \angle B$, and, by angle at the centre, $\angle BOC = 2 \times \angle A$. Hence $\angle BOC = \angle BHC$ if, and only if, $\angle A = 60°$.
   The circumcircle of $\triangle BOC$ goes through I if, and only if, $\angle BOC = \angle BIC$. Now $\angle BIC = 180° - \frac{1}{2}(\angle B + \angle C) = 90° + \frac{1}{2}\angle A$. So $\angle BIC = \angle BOC$ if, and only if, $90° + \frac{1}{2}\angle A = 2\angle A$, which is true if, and only

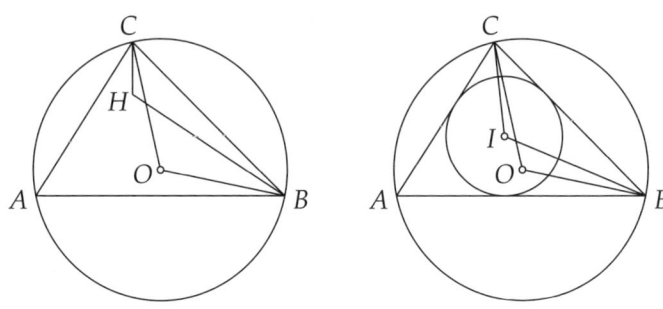

Exercise 2a question 4

if, $\angle A = 60°$ and the result follows.

5. Note that $\triangle ACT$ is similar to $\triangle BAT$, using the alternate segment theorem. Hence
$$\frac{b}{c} = \frac{CT}{AT} = \frac{AT}{BT}$$
and the result soon follows.

6. Defining T as in question 5, we have $\angle TAB = \angle C$ by the alternate segment theorem, so $\angle TAX = \angle C + \frac{1}{2}\angle A = \angle AXT$. Hence $\triangle ATX$ is isosceles with $AT = XT$. Since $\angle XAX_1 = 90°$, we have $\angle TAX_1 = \angle AX_1T$ and so $AT = X_1T$.

7. Extending AX to meet the circumcircle at X', we see that $\triangle ABX'$ is similar to $\triangle AXC$. Hence
$$\frac{AX}{b} = \frac{c}{AX'}$$
and so $AX \times AX' = bc$. But $AX' = AX + XX'$ and $AX \times XX' = BX \times XC$ by intersecting chords. Put these together to obtain the result.

8. The necessary and sufficient condition for concurrency follows from repeated use of Pythagoras' theorem. Now use this condition to establish that the common value of the fractions is 1. (I am grateful to Des MacHale for drawing my attention to this property of the circumcentre.)

9. Let O be the circumcentre of $\triangle ABC$. By the sine rule,
$$AO = \frac{BC}{2\sin \angle BAC},$$

Appendix B: Solutions to the exercises 391

which is constant. Hence the locus of O is a circle with centre C.

10. By the sine rule on $\triangle ABX$ and $\triangle ACX$,
$$AP = \frac{c}{2\sin \angle AXB} \quad \text{and} \quad AQ = \frac{b}{2\sin \angle AXC}.$$
Hence the two triangles have equal circumradii and the result follows.

11. Let L, M and N be the midpoints of AD, BD and CD (see the figure).

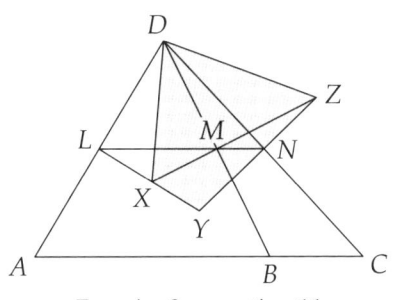

Exercise 2a question 11

These three points are collinear, as are L, X and Y, M, Z and X, and N, Y and Z. Also the quadrilaterals $LXMD$, $DMNZ$ and $LYND$ are cyclic. Hence $\angle LDX = \angle LMX = \angle NMZ = \angle NDZ$ and so $\angle XDZ = \angle LDN = 180° - \angle LYN = 180° - \angle XYZ$ so $XYZD$ is also cyclic.

12. It is enough to notice that PQ and SR are both perpendicular to BD and so are parallel. The same can be said about PS and QR.

13. Once you have drawn a decent diagram, everything falls into place (see the figure).

By external angles of cyclic quadrilaterals, $\angle PRB = \angle DCB$ and $\angle QRB = \angle DAB$, but these two angles are themselves supplementary, so it follows that P, R and Q are collinear.

14. $\angle O_1 Y O_2 = \angle O_1 X O_2 = 180° - \angle A - \angle B = \angle C$.

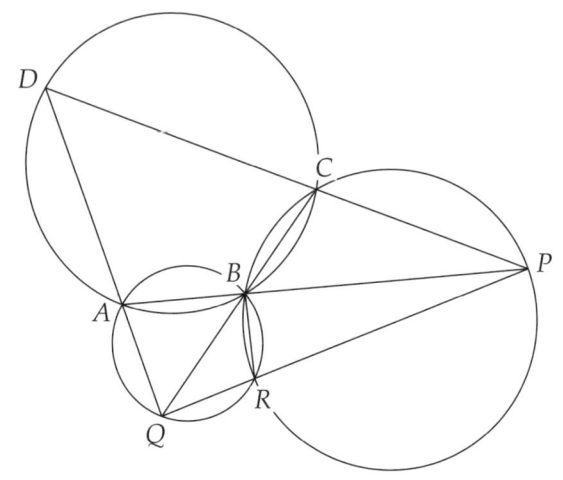

Exercise 2a question 13

Exercise 2b

1. Since the base BC is fixed, so is the midpoint A_1. The vertex A is now allowed to move on the fixed circle (see the figure).

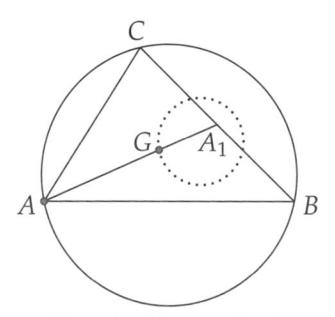

Exercise 2b question 1

The centroid G divides the line segment $A_1 A$ in the ratio $1 : 2$. Hence, as A traces out a circle, G will also trace out a circle of one third the radius. The centre will be a third of the way along $A_1 O$.

2. Let the line through G parallel to BC meet AB at X and AC at Y. Then the ratio of the area of $\triangle AXY$ to that of $\triangle ABC$ is $4 : 9$. The statement follows immediately from this.

Appendix B: Solutions to the exercises

3. (See the figure.) $\triangle BAA_1$ and $\triangle CAA_1$ have equal areas since they have the same base and the same height. So do $\triangle BXA_1$ and $\triangle CXA_1$, for the same reason.
   Hence, by subtraction, the areas of $\triangle BXA$ and $\triangle CXA$ are equal.
   By doubling their areas, we obtain $\beta c = \gamma b$.

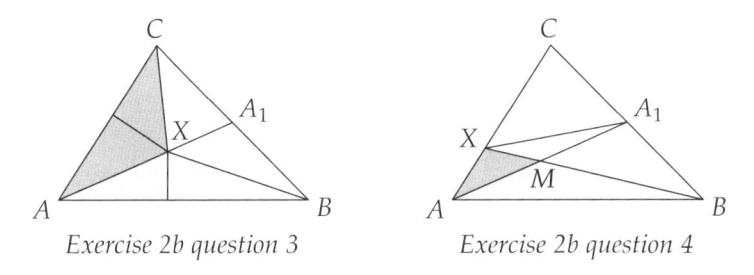

Exercise 2b question 3   *Exercise 2b question 4*

4. Let BM meet AC at X (see the figure).
   The areas of $\triangle BMA$ and $\triangle BMA_1$ are equal, as are those of $\triangle XMA$ and $\triangle XMA_1$, $\triangle ABA_1$ and $\triangle ACA_1$, and $\triangle BXA_1$ and $\triangle CXA_1$. So, setting $[BMA] = 1$ and $[XMA] = x$, we have $[ABC] = 4$ and $[XA_1C] = 2 - 2x$.
   Now $1 + x = 2 - 2x$, so $x = \frac{1}{3}$, and the ratio $AX : XC = \frac{4}{3} : \frac{8}{3} = 1 : 2$, as required.

5. Let the centroids of $\triangle PBC$, $\triangle PCA$ and $\triangle PAB$ be G_A, G_B and G_C (see the figure).

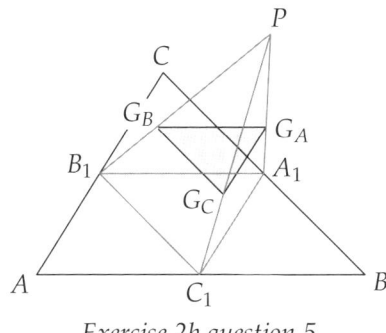

Exercise 2b question 5

Then G_A, G_B and G_C lie on the line segments PA_1, PB_1 and PC_1 and divide each in the ratio $2 : 1$. Hence $\triangle ABC$, $\triangle A_1B_1C_1$ and

$\triangle G_A G_B G_C$ are similar.

6. Let P' be the reflection of P in A_1 (see the figure).

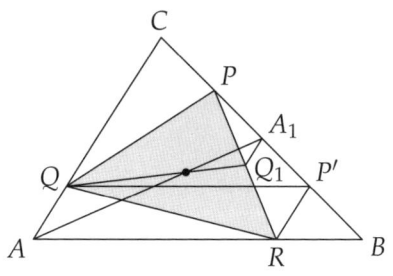

Exercise 2b question 6

Then
$$\frac{BP'}{P'C} = \frac{CP}{PB} = \frac{AQ}{QC} = \frac{BR}{RA}$$
and so $P'Q \parallel BA$ and $P'R \parallel CA$ and $P'QAR$ is a parallelogram. Let Q_1 be the midpoint of PR. Then $A_1 Q_1$ is parallel to $P'R$ and half its length, so it also parallel to QA and half its length.

Hence the segments AA_1 and QQ_1 meet at a point which divides both in the ratio 2 : 1, which must therefore be the centroid of $\triangle ABC$. Since it is on the median QQ_1, it is also the centroid of $\triangle PQR$.

7. Let $AG = 2$. Then $GA_1 = BA_1 = CA_1$, so A_1 is the circumcentre of $\triangle BCG$, and $\angle BGC = 90°$.

8. Let X be a point such that $ABCX$ is a parallelogram, and let Y be the midpoint of CX (see the figure).

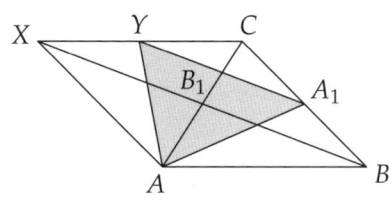

Exercise 2b question 8

Then $\triangle AA_1 Y$ has sides equal to the medians of $\triangle ABC$: AA_1 is a median; AY is a median of the congruent triangle $\triangle CXA$; and $A_1 Y = \frac{1}{2} BX = BB_1$.

Now $[ABA_1] = [AXY] = \frac{1}{4}[ABCX]$ and $[A_1CY] = \frac{1}{8}[ABCX]$. Hence $[AA_1Y] = \frac{3}{8}[ABCX] = \frac{3}{4}[ABC]$.

Exercise 2c

1. The similarity follows from the fact that $\angle I_A BR_A + \angle IBR = 90°$ and the deduction is immediate from theorems 2.10 and 2.11. Now Heron follows from this and theorem 2.12.

2. Theorem 2.12 shows that
$$\frac{1}{r} = \frac{s}{\Delta}, \quad \frac{1}{r_A} = \frac{s-a}{\Delta}, \quad \text{and so on;}$$
simply combine these and simplify for the first equality, and use $\Delta = \frac{1}{2}ah_A$, and so on, to get the second.

3. Let N be
$$s(s-b)(s-c) + s(s-c)(s-a) + s(s-a)(s-b)$$
$$- (s-a)(s-b)(s-c).$$
By factorising and expanding the brackets, we see that $N = abc$. Hence
$$r_A + r_B + r_C - r = \Delta\left(\frac{1}{s-a} + \frac{1}{s-b} + \frac{1}{s-c} + \frac{1}{s}\right)$$
$$= \Delta \frac{N}{s(s-a)(s-b)(s-c)}$$
$$= \frac{abc}{\Delta} = \frac{2Rab\sin C}{\Delta} = 4R.$$

4. This follows from the fact that $\angle I_C CI_B = \angle I_C BI_B = 90°$.

5. (See the figure.) By corollary 2.6, O, A_1 and X' are collinear, so $\angle X'OY' = 180° - \angle C$ and $\angle A_1X'Y' = \frac{1}{2}\angle C$.
Hence triangles $\triangle A_1 X'P$ and $\triangle QCP$ are equiangular, and so CI is perpendicular to $X'Y'$. The result now follows.

6. The external angle bisectors of B and C meet the circumcircle at Y'' and Z'' which are diametrically opposite to Y' and Z'. Hence $Y''Z''$ is parallel to $Z'Y'$ and the result follows.

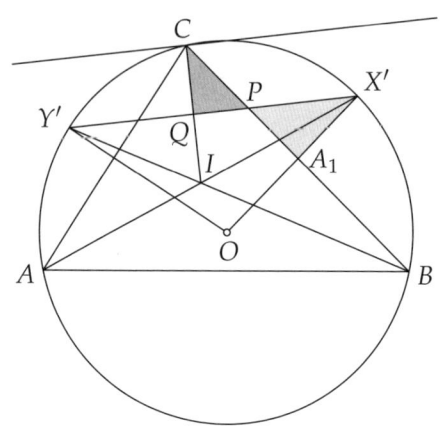

Exercise 2c question 5

7. This is just an angle chase.
8. Let one of the circles have diameter AQ.
9. First show that $AB + CD = AC + BD$, and then use theorem 2.10.
10. Writing $AP = d$, the distance of both points of tangency from A is easily calculated as $\frac{1}{2}(b + c + d - s)$.
11. Prove first that Y is an excentre of $\triangle ABX$ and hence calculate $\angle YXZ$.
12. The 'only if' part of this statement is trivial. The 'if' part is sometimes called the Steiner-Lehmus theorem. We actually prove a contrapositive statement, which is

> If, in $\triangle ABC$, $\angle C > \angle B$, then the angle bisector from $\angle B$ is longer than that from $\angle C$.

Let BY and CZ be the angle bisectors at $\angle B$ and $\angle C$, and take K on BY such that $\angle KCZ = \frac{1}{2}\angle B$ (see the figure).

Then by angles in the same segment $BCKZ$ is a cyclic quadrilateral. Now

$$\angle ZBC = \tfrac{1}{2}\angle B + \tfrac{1}{2}\angle B$$
$$< \tfrac{1}{2}\angle B + \tfrac{1}{2}\angle C$$
$$= \angle BCK$$

and so $CZ < BK < BY$ as required.

Appendix B: Solutions to the exercises

Exercise 2c question 12

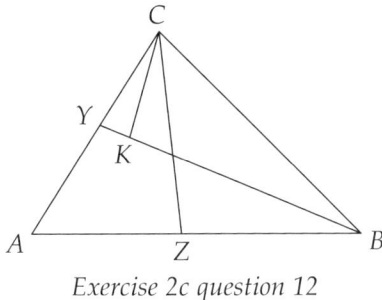

It follows that, if the angle bisectors are equal, then the triangle has two equal sides.

13. Let I_A, I_B, I_C and I_D be the incentres of $\triangle BCD$, $\triangle ACD$, $\triangle ABD$ and $\triangle ABC$ and let P, Q, R and S be the midpoints of the arcs AB, BC, CD and DA (see the figure).

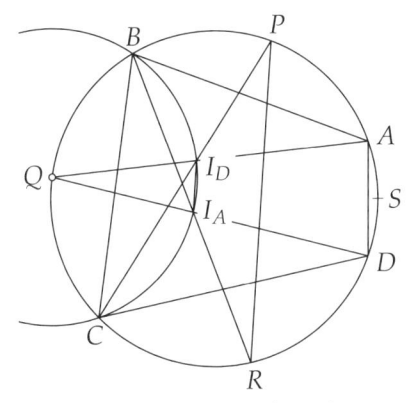

Exercise 2c question 13

Then I_A is the intersection of BR and DQ and I_D is the intersection of AQ and CP. By theorem 2.13, the circle with centre Q through B and C also passes through I_A and I_D. Hence $\angle I_A I_D C = \angle I_A BC = \angle RBC = \angle RPC$ and so $I_A I_D$ is parallel to RP, as is $I_B I_C$. Similarly $I_C I_D$ and $I_B I_A$ are parallel to SQ.

However, RP is perpendicular to SQ. (This can be proved by looking at angles subtended by arcs such as AP at the centre and circumference of the circle.) It follows that $I_A I_D$ is perpendicular to $I_B I_A$ and

$I_A I_B I_C I_D$ is a rectangle (see the next figure).

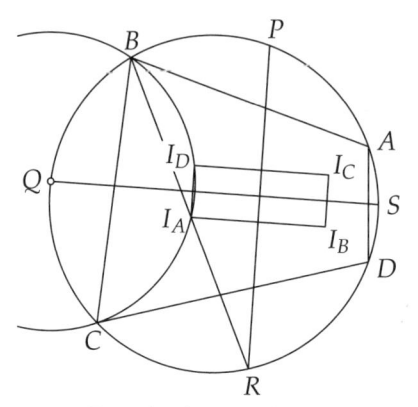

Exercise 2c question 13

Moreover, SQ bisects $I_A I_D$ and $I_B I_C$ because Q is the centre of a circle containing the chord $I_A I_D$. It follows that the intersection of PR and SQ is the centre of the rectangle $I_A I_B I_C I_D$.

This elegant result is due to Fuhrmann.

Exercise 2d

1. Note that $\angle E'BA = 90° - \angle A = \angle F'CA$, and that equal angles are subtended by equal arcs.

2. Note that $BCEF$ is cyclic, and the centre of the circumcircle is A_1. Now use the fact that radii which bisect chords are perpendicular to them.

3. (See the figure.) $\angle AOC = 2\angle B$ so $\angle OAE = 90° - \angle B$.
   But from corollary 2.20 $\angle AEF = \angle B$ so AO is perpendicular to EF.

4. By theorem 2.22, these are parallel to EF, FD and DE, so they are altitudes of the orthic triangle, and are hence concurrent at the orthocentre of $\triangle DEF$.

5. (See the figure.) By theorem 2.17, $\triangle DEF$ can be transformed onto $\triangle D'E'F'$ under an enlargement, centre H and scale factor 2. Hence the result of theorem 2.22 is mapped into a similar result

Appendix B: Solutions to the exercises

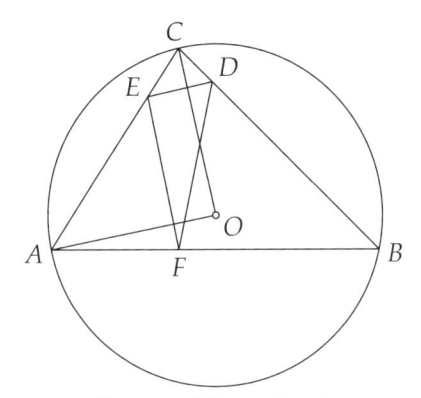

Exercise 2d question 3

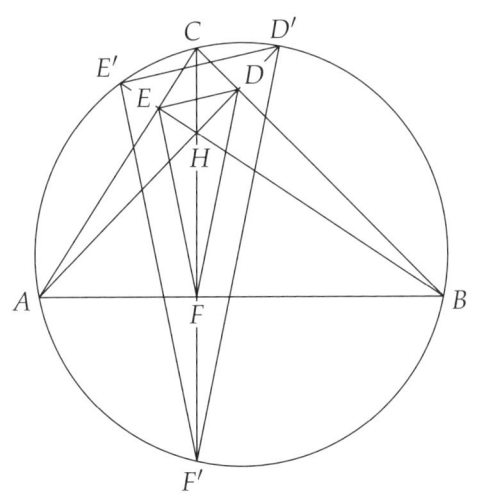

Exercise 2d question 5

in $\triangle D'E'F'$.

Note that the point of concurrence is the orthocentre of $\triangle D'E'F'$ and this is the image of the orthocentre of $\triangle DEF$ under the same enlargement and centre.

6. (See the figure.) Consider this as an incentre-excentre configuration, with base triangle $\triangle DEF$, B as the excentre opposite to E and C as the excentre opposite to F.

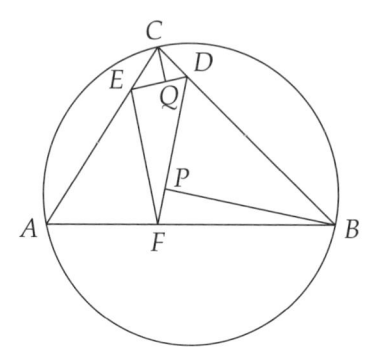

Exercise 2d question 6

Then P and Q become the points of tangency of the two excircles which are internal to the sides DF and DE. Now we use theorem 2.11, which evaluates both of EQ and FP as $s-a$, to achieve the desired result.

7. (See the figure.) Note that A_1 is the centre of circle $BCEF$ and so $\angle A_1 FB = \angle B$. But we also know that $\angle AEF = \angle B$ and hence, by the alternate segment theorem, $A_1 F$ is a tangent to circle $AEHF$.

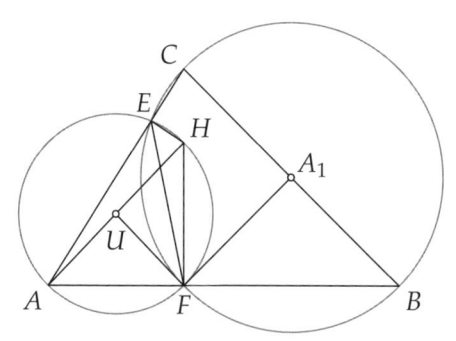

Exercise 2d question 7

So if U is the midpoint of AH, and hence the centre of circle $AEHF$, then UF and $A_1 F$ are perpendicular. But these are the radii of the two circumcircles in question, which are therefore orthogonal.

8. Let R be the foot of the altitude from Q to AB, and let S lie on PQ (possibly produced) so that IIS is parallel to AB (see the figure).

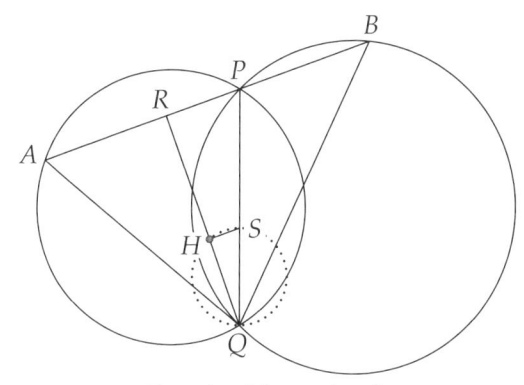

Exercise 2d question 8

First note that the angles of $\triangle ABQ$ are fixed. It follows from this that the ratio $QH : QR$ is fixed since it depends only on the angles, and so S is a fixed point on PQ. Hence the locus of H is a circle on diameter QS.

Exercise 2e

1. The perimeter is $D'D'' = 2AD \sin A$, but $AD = 2\Delta \div a$, and the result follows from the sine rule.

2. Consider the circumcircle of $CEFB$, which has diameter BC, and let F' be the image of F when reflected in BC, which lies on the circumference (see the figure).

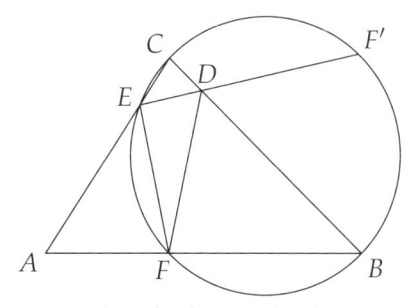

Exercise 2e question 2

Then, because $\angle BDF = \angle EDC = \angle FDB$, E, D and F' are collinear, and $FD = F'D$.

It follows that
$$DE + EF = F'D + DE = F'E \leq BC.$$
Equality is achieved if, and only if, the chord $F'E$ is a diameter of the circle, when $D = A_1$, and in that case $\triangle ABC$ is isosceles with $AB = AC$.

3. By theorem 2.23, the perimeter of the orthic triangle is less than or equal to that of the medial triangle. By the result of question 1, this gives
$$\frac{a+b+c}{2} \leq \frac{2\Delta}{R},$$
so, by theorem 2.12, $Rs \leq 2rs$ and the result follows. Alternatively, we can add three symmetrical versions of the result of question 2 to obtain $2(DE + EF + FD) \leq a + b + c$, and then proceed as before.

Equality occurs if, and only if, $\triangle ABC$ is equilateral. We will meet this important result again in section 3.3.

Exercise 3a

1. (a) It collapses to the point G. (b) It is the axis of symmetry. (c) It is the median from the right angle.

2. The Euler line is parallel to BC if, and only if, $OA_1 = HD$. But
$$OA_1 = \frac{a}{2\tan A} \text{ and } HD = \frac{c \cos B}{\tan C}.$$
Hence the equality is equivalent to $a \tan C = 2c \tan A \cos B$. Using the sine rule and some manipulation, we obtain
$$2 \cos B \cos C = \cos A = -\cos(B+C) = \sin B \sin C - \cos B \cos C,$$
which is equivalent to $\tan B \tan C = 3$.

3. The Euler triangle is similar to $\triangle ABC$ since it is the image of this triangle under an enlargement with centre H and scale factor $\frac{1}{2}$. The medial triangle is similar to $\triangle ABC$ since it is the image of this triangle under θ. Hence the two triangles are congruent to each other (but with opposite orientation).

4. Because OA_1 is equal and parallel to AU, AUA_1O is a parallelogram, and its diagonals bisect one another (so it is also true that AA_1 is bisected by OU).

5. (See the figure.) Since O is the midpoint of PP' and $GH = 2OG$, it follows that G is the centroid of $\triangle PP'H$. Hence X is the midpoint of HP'.

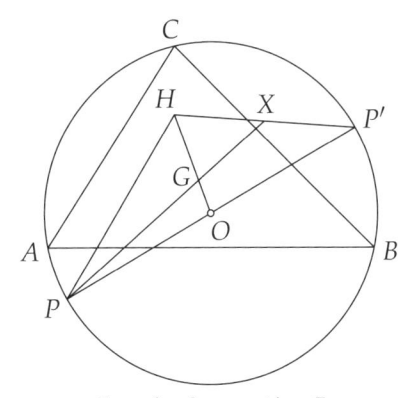

Exercise 3a question 5

6. Let X and Y be the midpoints of AB and CD, so that $OXPY$ is a rectangle (see the figure).

   Assume, without loss of generality, that $\angle ADB$ is acute and $\angle ACB$ is obtuse. The orthocentres H_D of $\triangle ABD$ and H_C of $\triangle ACB$ lie on DC with $DH_D = CH_C = 2OX$. Hence $H_D H_C = DC$.

   If Z is the midpoint of $H_D H_C$, then $YZ = DH_D = 2OX = 2YP$ and P is the midpoint of YZ. Let Q be the image of O in P, a fixed point.

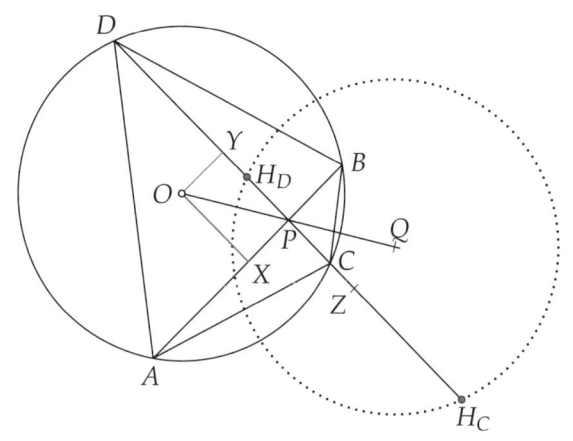

   Exercise 3a question 6

   Now $\triangle POX \cong \triangle PQZ$ and $\triangle QZH_C \cong \triangle OYD$. Hence $QH_C = QH_D = OD$, and so the locus of both orthocentres is a circle with centre Q and radius equal to that of the original circle.

7. Since $OG = \frac{1}{3}OH$, the locus of the centroids is also a circle of one-third the radius.

8. (a) It passes through the vertex with the right angle. (b) It touches the base of the isosceles triangle at its midpoint.

9. (See the figure.) The two triangles $\triangle AB_1C_1$ and $\triangle A_1B_1C_1$ are homothetic with scale factor -1 and centre the midpoint M of C_1B_1, which is also a point on both nine-point circles. The enlargement maps one nine-point centre to the other, and the line of centres passes through M, and hence the circles touch at that point.

10. By the alternate segment theorem the angle is $\angle B_1A_1C - \angle B_1C_1A_1 = \angle B - \angle C$ when, as in the diagram, $\angle B > \angle C$.

Appendix B: Solutions to the exercises 405

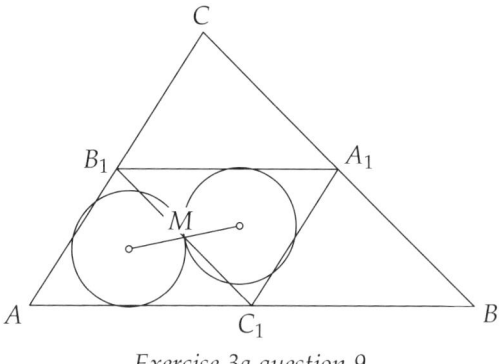

Exercise 3a question 9

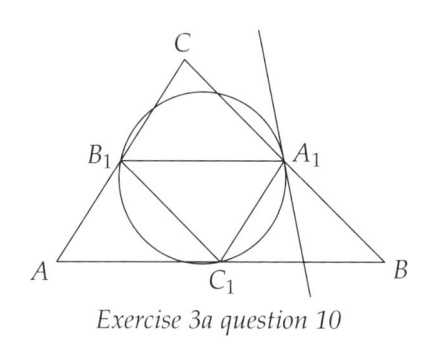

Exercise 3a question 10

11. Since $AH = 2OA_1 = OB = AO$, $\triangle AHO$ is isosceles and $\angle AHO = \angle AOH$ (see the figure).

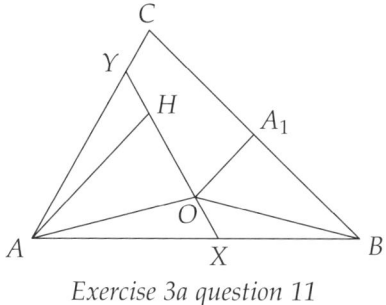

Exercise 3a question 11

But $\angle HAE = 90° - \angle C = \angle OAC_1$.

Hence $\angle HYA = \angle OXA$ and so $\triangle YAX$ is isosceles. But this also means that it is equilateral.

12. By considering the trapezium HDA_1O we have
$$2p_A = HD + OA_1 = c \cos B \cot C + R \cos A.$$
From the sine rule, and a little trigonometrical manipulation, this yields
$$\begin{aligned} 2p_A &= 2R \cos B \cos C + R \cos A \\ &= R(2 \cos B \cos C - \cos(B+C)) \\ &= R(\cos B \cos C + \sin A \sin B) \\ &= R \cos(B-C), \end{aligned}$$
as required.

13. Let Y and Z be the intersections of PQ and PR with the line through A parallel to BC (see the figure).

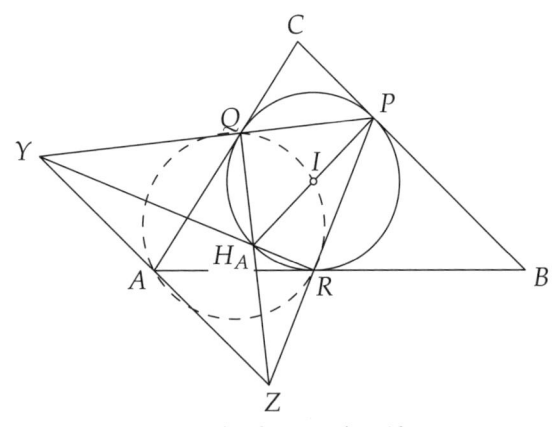

Exercise 3a question 13

Since $\angle AZR = \angle BPR = \angle PRB = \angle ZRA$, we have $AZ = AR$ and, similarly, $AY = AQ$. But $AR = AQ$, so A is the midpoint of YZ. Also A is the centre of the circumcircle of $\triangle QYZ$ and so $\angle ZQY = 90°$, and similarly $\angle ZRY = 90°$. Hence the circumcircle of $\triangle QAR$ is the nine-point circle of $\triangle PYZ$ and H_A is its orthocentre. Also I is the midpoint of the diameter H_AP of the incircle, so it is an Euler point of $\triangle PYZ$ and also lies on the nine-point circle.

Appendix B: Solutions to the exercises

Exercise 3b

1. By theorem 3.10, we have $R = 2r$ if, and only if, O and I are the same point. Then $\triangle ABC$ is equilateral, and now R and r are two sides of a (30°, 60°, 90°) triangle.

2. Since, by theorem 3.1, $ON = \frac{1}{2}OH$, we have $ON^2 = \frac{9}{4}R^2 - \frac{1}{4}(a^2 + b^2 + c^2)$.

   Alternatively, apply theorem 3.10 to the anticomplementary triangle; this has sides $2a$, $2b$, $2c$, circumradius $2R$, circumcentre H and nine-point centre O.

3. (a) First, we have
$$a^2 + b^2 + c^2 = 4R^2(\sin^2 A + \sin^2 B + \sin^2 C)$$
$$= 2R^2(3 - \cos 2A - \cos 2B - \cos 2C).$$

    But
$$\cos 2A + \cos 2B + \cos 2C$$
$$= 2\cos(A+B)\cos(A-B) + \cos 2(A+B)$$
$$= 2\cos(A+B)\cos(A-B) + 2\cos^2(A+B) - 1$$
$$= 4\cos(A+B)\cos A \cos B - 1$$
$$= -4\cos A \cos B \cos C - 1.$$

    Hence $a^2 + b^2 + c^2 = 2R^2(4 + 4\cos A \cos B \cos C)$. Combining this with the result of theorem 3.10, the result follows.

    (b) The inequality is an immediate consequence of (a).

    (c) The condition for equality is that O and H are the same point, so the triangle is equilateral.

4. Clearly the Euler line meets the median at the centroid. OG is perpendicular to OA if, and only if, $OA^2 = OG^2 + AG^2$. Now
$$AG^2 = \tfrac{4}{9}AA_1^2 = \frac{4}{9}\left(\frac{2b^2 + 2c^2 - a^2}{4}\right) = \frac{2b^2 + 2c^2 - a^2}{9}$$
by Apollonius' median theorem, and, by theorem 3.10,
$$OG^2 = \tfrac{1}{9}OH^2 = R^2 - \frac{a^2 + b^2 + c^2}{9}.$$
Putting these together, we have $b^2 + c^2 = 2a^2$, as required.

Exercise 3c

1. This is an immediate consequence of the enlargement with centre N and scale factor -1. The orthocentre of $\triangle ABC$ maps to O, which is therefore the orthocentre of the triangle of circumcentres.

2. Again, this follows from the enlargement with centre N and scale factor $-\frac{1}{3}$. The orthocentre of $\triangle ABC$ maps to G, which is therefore the orthocentre of the triangle of centroids.

3. The first fact is theorem 2.9 on page 16. The orthic triangle is $\triangle ABC$ and so the nine-point circle is the circumcircle of $\triangle ABC$. The common circumradius of the four triangles in the group is therefore double the radius of their nine-point circle, and this is $2R$.

4. (See the figure.) The nine-point centre of the excentral triangle is the circumcentre of its medial triangle, and this is O. By theorem 2.9 on page 16, the orthocentre of the excentral triangle is I. Let O_i be the circumcentre of the excentral triangle $\triangle I_A I_B I_C$. Then the Euler line of the excentral triangle is IOO_i and O is its midpoint.

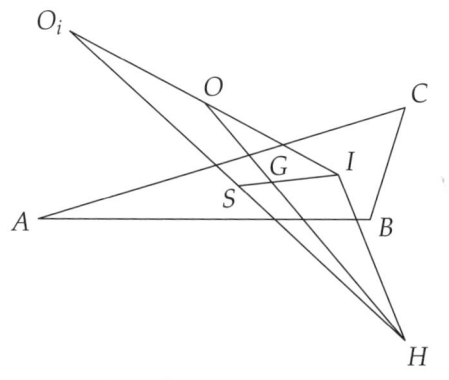

Exercise 3c question 4

Now consider $\triangle HIO_i$. Since G, which is on the Euler line of $\triangle ABC$, divides HO in the ratio of $2:1$, it is also the centroid of $\triangle HIO_i$.

Hence IG is a median of $\triangle HIO_i$ and it bisects HO_i at its midpoint S. But under an enlargement with centre G and scale factor $-\frac{1}{2}$, $\triangle ABC$ is mapped to its medial triangle, and hence S is the incentre of the medial triangle.

Appendix B: Solutions to the exercises

Exercise 3d

1. It is a concentric circle of radius $\sqrt{R^2 + p}$.
2. If two orthogonal circles with centres O_1 and O_2 intersect at A, then $O_1 A$ and $O_2 A$ are perpendicular, so the radius of the first circle is the tangent to the second.
3. This is immediate from the definition of power and Pythagoras' theorem.

Exercise 4a

1. Here the pedal triangle degenerates to the vertex and the foot of the altitude from it, so the Simson line is the altitude from the vertex.

2. Consider the point diametrically opposite to vertex A. Then the point M is B and N is C, whilst L lies on BC, and the Simson line is the side BC.

3. The Simson line intersects PH at its midpoint. But the enlargement with centre H and scale factor $\frac{1}{2}$ maps the circumcircle to the nine-point circle, and so the midpoint lies on the nine-point circle.

4. Let CO meet the circumcircle again at N'; then, by theorem 4.2, PN' is perpendicular to AB. Hence $\angle N'PC = 90°$ and so the result follows.

5. The direction is given by theorem 4.2 in a limiting case where A and L' coincide, so the chord AL' becomes a tangent. By theorem 2.17 on page 21, D is the midpoint of HD', and by theorem 4.3, this point lies on the Simson line.

6. QL' is a diameter since PL' is perpendicular to PQ. Hence AQ is perpendicular to AL', which, by theorem 4.2, is parallel to the Simson line of P.

7. The line AL' is parallel to the Simson line, so $\angle QAL' = 90°$ and hence $\angle QPL' = 90°$. But since $\angle BLP = 90°$, it follows that $QP \parallel BC$.

8. Consider the pedal triangle of D with respect to $\triangle ABC$, which is its Simson line. The quadrilateral $DMLC$ is cyclic with diameter DC, and ML subtends $\angle C$ at the circumference, so by the sine rule

$$LM = DC \sin C = \frac{DC \times c}{2R} \quad \text{and} \quad DC \times AB = 2R \times LM.$$

But $LM + MN = LN$, and Ptolemy's theorem follows immediately. With care, the converse of the Simson line property can be used to prove the converse of Ptolemy.

9. (See the figure.) The quadrilateral $BDAE$ is cyclic, and so we can consider D as a point on the circumcircle of $\triangle BEA$.
Then PQS is the Simson line of D with respect to this triangle. In a similar way, PRS is the Simson line of D with respect to $\triangle AFC$. Hence P, Q, R and S are collinear.

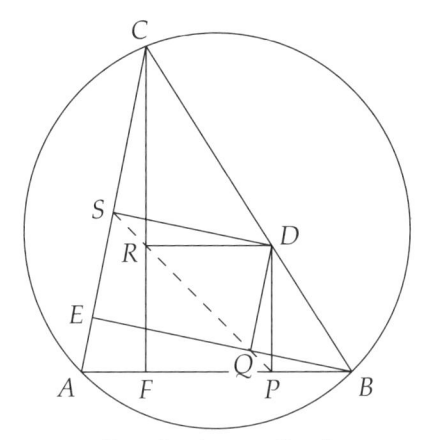

Exercise 4a question 9

10. This is simply a restatement of the Simson line theorem since L, for example, is the intersection of C_2 and C_3.

    It is possible to formulate a converse to this result.

11. Note that BC is the line of centres of two of these circles, so their common chord is at right angles to this side of $\triangle ABC$ (see the figure).

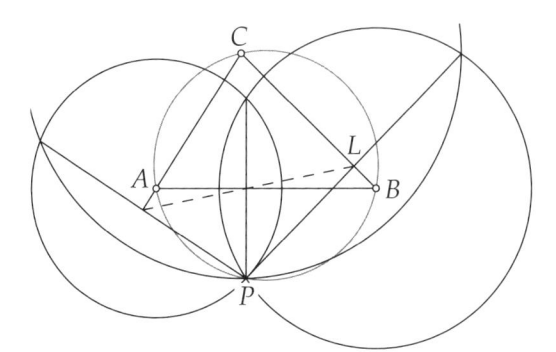

Exercise 4a question 11

The midpoint of the common chord is L, the foot of the perpendicular from P to BC. The same is true for the other two sides of $\triangle ABC$. Hence the three midpoints are on the Simson line of P with respect to $\triangle ABC$, and the other three intersections of the circles are on the parallel line through the orthocentre of $\triangle ABC$.

Exercise 4b

1. This is immediate from theorem 4.5.

2. (a) If the diameter perpendicular to BC is PP', then A_1 is the foot of the perpendiculars from P and P' to BC, so both Simson lines go through it.
   (b) The Simson line of A is AD. If AQ is the diameter through A, then $\angle QCA = \angle QBA = 90°$ and so the Simson line of Q is CB. Hence both Simson lines pass through D.
   (c) The line through P perpendicular to BC is a tangent to the circle, so the point L', as defined in theorem 4.2, is coincident with P. Hence the Simson line of P is parallel to AP (and that of Q is parallel to AQ). However, the Simson lines also pass through the midpoints of HP and HQ (see the figure).

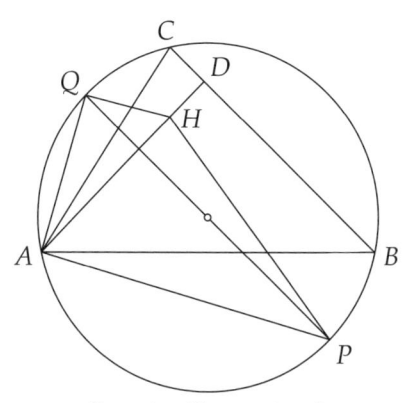

Exercise 4b question 2

Hence, by the midpoint theorem, they pass through the midpoint of AH, which is the Euler point U.

3. Denote the orthocentre of $\triangle ABC$ by H_D, and similarly with the other triangles (see the figure).
   But the segments AH_D and DH_A are both equal to $2R\cos A$, and, since they are parallel, $AH_D H_A D$ is a parallelogram. Hence the diagonals bisect one another, and so, by theorem 4.3, the Simson

Appendix B: Solutions to the exercises

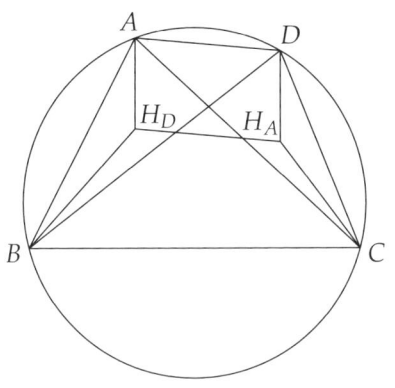

Exercise 4b question 3

lines of A with respect to $\triangle BCD$ and of D with respect to $\triangle ABC$ meet at this point.

Now we can go cyclically around the quadrilateral $ABCD$ to show that all four Simson lines are concurrent there. Moreover, this point is also on the four nine-point circles.

Exercise 4c

1. This is obvious from the three cyclic quadrilaterals since opposite angles are supplementary.

2. (See the figure.) For example,

$$\angle P_1 P_2 P_3 = \angle P_1 P_2 P + \angle P P_2 P_3$$
$$= \angle P_1 C P + \angle P A P_3$$
$$= \angle BCP + \angle PAB$$

and this depends only on the position of P within $\triangle ABC$.

3. Let O_1, O_2 and O_3 be the centres of the three Miquel circles. Note that $O_1 O_2$, the line of centres of two Miquel circles, is the perpendicular bisector of their common chord PP_3. Similarly, $O_2 O_3$ and $O_3 O_1$ are the perpendicular bisectors of PP_1 and PP_2 (see the figure).

Draw lines parallel to $O_3 O_1$ and $O_2 O_1$ through P_2 and P_3. These will intersect at a point A^* such that $\angle P_2 A^* P_3 = \angle O_3 O_1 O_2$. But $\angle PP_3 A^* = \angle PP_2 A^* = 90°$, so A^* is on the circumcircle of $\triangle P_3 PP_2$,

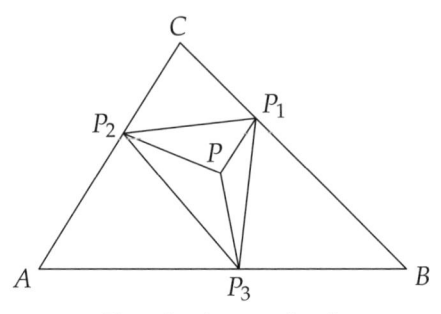

Exercise 4c question 2

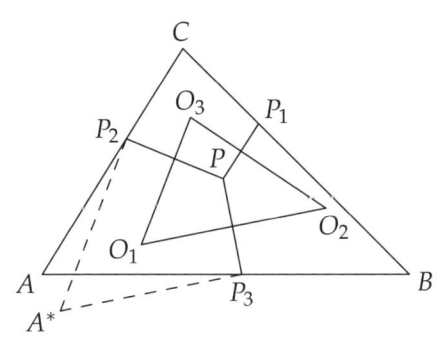

Exercise 4c question 3

which is the Miquel circle through A. Hence we have $\angle O_3 O_1 O_2 = \angle P_2 A^* P_3 = \angle A$. The result follows.

4. (See the figure.)
$$\begin{aligned}\angle BPC &= \angle BPP_1 + \angle P_1 PC \\ &= \angle BP_3 P_1 + \angle P_1 P_2 C \\ &= \angle P_3 AP_1 + \angle P_3 P_1 A + \angle P_2 AP_1 + \angle P_2 P_1 A \\ &= \angle A + \angle P_3 P_1 P_2.\end{aligned}$$

5. Let the orthocentres of $\triangle ABC$, $\triangle AMN$, $\triangle BNL$ and $\triangle CLM$ be H, H_A, H_B and H_C (see the figure). The common Simson line passes through the midpoints of PH, PH_A, PH_B and PH_C. Hence the orthocentres are also collinear.

Appendix B: Solutions to the exercises 415

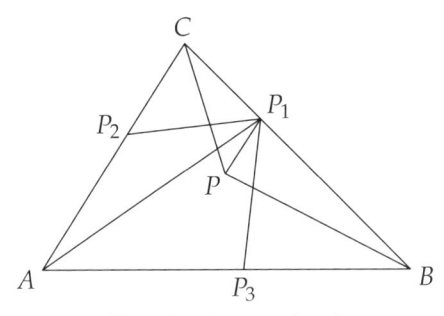

Exercise 4c question 4

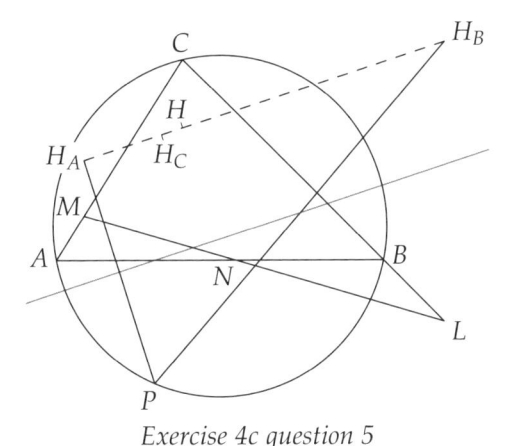

Exercise 4c question 5

6. Let O, O_B and O_C be the circumcentres of $\triangle ABC$, $\triangle BNL$ and $\triangle CLM$ (see the figure). Since the line of centres of two circles bisects the common chord at right angles, we see that $O_B O_C$, OO_B and OO_C (extended if necessary) are the perpendicular bisectors of PL, PB and PC. Since L, B and C are collinear the midpoints of PL, PB and PC are also collinear.

Now we appeal to the converse of the Simson line property to conclude that P lies on the circumcircle of $\triangle OO_B O_C$. But, as a similar property shows that P lies on the circumcircle of $\triangle OO_C O_A$, it follows that the five points P, O, O_A, O_B and O_C are all on the same circle.

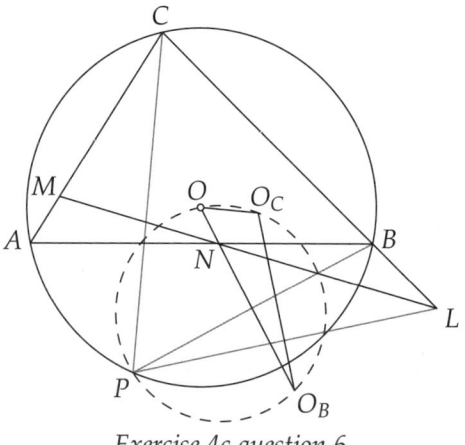

Exercise 4c question 6

Exercise 5a

1. It is worthwhile drawing a diagram showing the relative positions of A, B, C and D.

   (a) $(A,C;B,D) = \dfrac{1 \times -1}{1 \times 3} = -\dfrac{1}{3}.$

   ```
   |—— 1 ——|—— 1 ——|—— 1 ——|
   A       B       C       D
   ```

   (b) $(A,C;B,D) = \dfrac{2 \times -3}{1 \times 6} = -1.$

   ```
   |—— 2 ——|— 1 —|—— 3 ——|
   A       B     C       D
   ```

   (c) $(A,C;B,D) = \dfrac{-5 \times -6}{1 \times 2} = 15.$

   ```
   |— 1 —|———— 4 ————|—— 2 ——|
   B     C           A       D
   ```

2. $(A,C;B,D) = \dfrac{2 \times -x}{2(4+x)} = -\dfrac{1}{2}$ and so $CD = x = 4.$

   ```
   |—— 2 ——|—— 2 ——|———— x ————|
   A       B       C           D
   ```

3. $(A,C;B,D) = \dfrac{(3-x)(x-4)}{x(7-x)} = -1$ and so $x = 1$ or 6 and $AD = 1$ or 6.

   ```
   |—— 3−x ——|— x —|—— 4−x ——|
   A         B     C         D
   ```

4. (a) $\tfrac{2}{5}$.   (b) $\tfrac{5}{2}$.   (c) $\tfrac{5}{2}$.

5. This could only happen if $AD = BD$, so there is no such 'real' point D. However, it is convenient to imagine a 'point at infinity' on the line which satisfies this condition. Note that it is not necessary to have two points at infinity, one at either end of the line; one is sufficient.

6. Both these cross ratios are equal to -1.

Exercise 5b

1. Consider all the permutations with A in the first place, and let $(A, B; C, D) = x$.

   By theorem 5.8, $(A, B; D, C) = \dfrac{1}{x}$.

   By theorem 5.9, $(A, C; B, D) = 1 - x$.

   By the reciprocal theorem again, $(A, C; D, B) = \dfrac{1}{1-x}$.

   By the complement theorem again, $(A, D; B, C) + (A, B; D, C) = 1$ and so $(A, D; B, C) = 1 - \dfrac{1}{x} = \dfrac{x-1}{x}$.

   Again by the reciprocal theorem $(A, D; C, B) = \dfrac{x}{x-1}$.

   Now all the permutations with B, C or D first can be obtained from one of these by the reciprocal theorem, and therefore these six expressions represent all possible values of the cross-ratios. Note that we can start with any of these six values and call it x, obtaining the others by the same operations.

2. This is essentially the same result as the complement theorem, after multiplication throughout by $AD \times BC$. It can be thought of as a limiting case of Ptolemy's theorem for a cyclic quadrilateral $ABCD$ when the radius of the circumcircle has been allowed to grow to infinity.

3. Write the cross ratios out algebraically and cancel.

4. Write the left-hand side out algebraically and cancel to produce the right-hand side.

Exercise 5c

1. Suppose that $A'B'C'$ is parallel to VD (see the figure). Then D' is a point at infinity and

$$(A', C'; B', D') = \dfrac{A'B'}{B'C'}.$$

Now let A^*BC^* be parallel to VD, so

$$\dfrac{A'B'}{B'C'} = \dfrac{A^*B}{BC^*}.$$

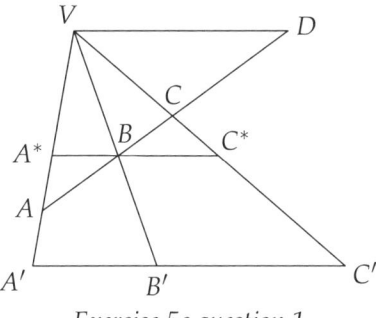

Exercise 5c question 1

By similar triangles,
$$\frac{DC}{CB} = \frac{VD}{BC^*} \quad \text{and} \quad \frac{DA}{AB} = \frac{VD}{A^*B}$$
Dividing, we obtain
$$\frac{DC}{CB} \times \frac{AB}{DA} = \frac{A^*B}{BC^*}$$
and so $(A', C'; B', D') = (A, C; B, D)$, as required.

2. (See the figure.) By theorem 5.8, we have
$$(A, C; B, D) = (A, C'; B', D') = (A, C''; B'', D'').$$
By theorem 5.11, $B'B''$, $C'C''$ and $D'D''$ are concurrent at some point X.

3. (See the figure.)
By theorem 5.8, $(A, C; B, D) = (A', C'; B', D') = (A'', C''; B'', D'')$. Now let C^*B^* meet UAV at A^*, and let $A^*B^*C^*$ meet UD'' at D_1^* and VD' at D_2^*.
Then, again by theorem 5.8,
$$(A^*, C^*; B^*, D_1^*) = (A', C'; B', D') = (A, C; B, D)$$
and
$$(A^*, C^*; B^*, D_2^*) = (A'', C''; B'', D'') = (A, C; B, D),$$
so that $(A^*, C^*; B^*, D_1^*) = (A^*, C^*; B^*, D_2^*)$. Hence the points D_1^* and D_2^* are identical, and, since they lie on both UD'' and VD', this point is D^*. Hence we have the required collinearity.

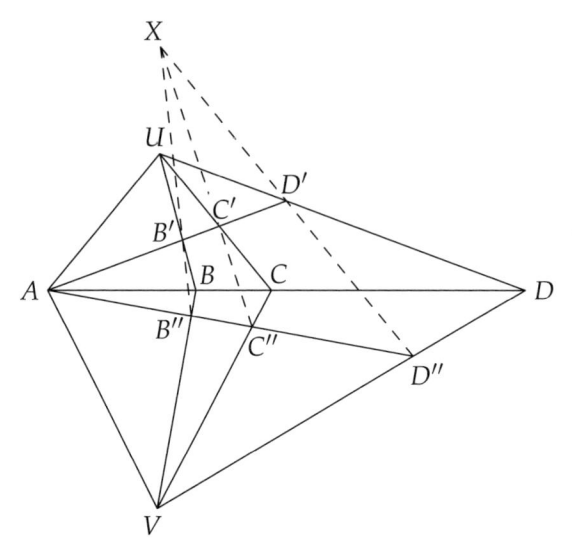

Exercise 5c question 2

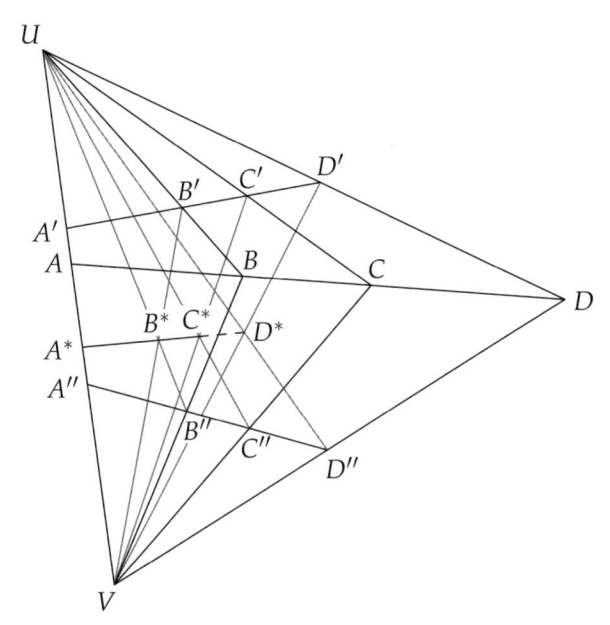

Exercise 5c question 3

Exercise 5d

1. With x, y, z defined as in the proof of theorem 5.19, we have $2xz = xy + yz$. Now divide by the non-zero xyz to get the required result. Algebraically, we say that y is the *harmonic mean* of x and z.

2. This is immediate from similar triangles.

3. This is the result of theorem 5.14, taking bisectors at $\angle ACX$.

4. Let O be the centre of the circle, and M the midpoint of BD (see the figure). Note that $APOQ$ is cyclic, and its circumcircle passes through M because M is the midpoint of a chord and so $\angle OMA = 90°$.

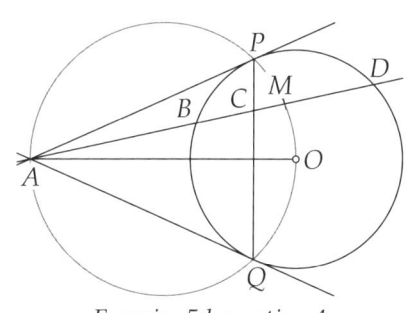

Exercise 5d question 4

Hence $AC \times CM = PC \times CQ = BC \times CD$. Now
$$BC \times CD = (BM - CM)(BM + CM) = BM^2 - CM^2$$
and
$$MC \times MA = MC^2 + MC \times CA = MC^2 + BC \times CD = BM^2$$
and theorem 5.20 ensures that A, B, C, D is harmonic.

5. Since $\mathcal{C}$ and the circle with centre C are orthogonal, we have $CP^2 = CA \times CB$; the result now follows from theorem 5.20.

Exercise 5e

1. C_i is the centroid and C_e is the orthocentre.

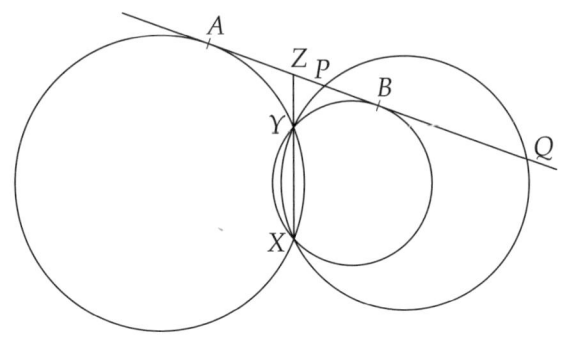

Exercise 5e question 2

2. Consider the point Z where the common chord XY meets the tangent (see the figure).

   By repeated use of the tangent-secant and intersecting chords properties, we have $ZP \times ZQ = ZY \times ZX = ZB^2 \times ZA^2$. It follows from theorem 5.20 that A, P, B, Q is a harmonic range.

3. It is enough to show that TA and TC are the internal and external bisectors of $\angle BTD$.

4. We treat the case of the external centre of similitude (see the figure); the argument is easily adapted to the internal centre.

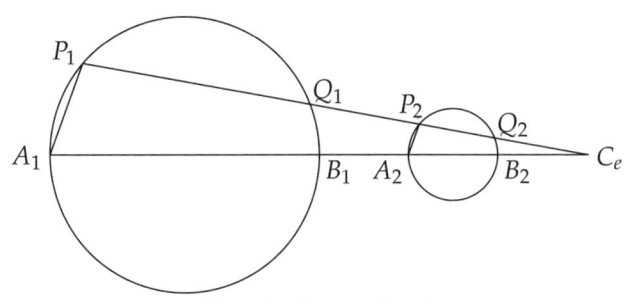

Exercise 5e question 4

By similar triangles,
$$\frac{C_e P_1}{C_e A_1} = \frac{C_e P_2}{C_e A_2} = \frac{C_e P_1 - C_e P_2}{C_e A_1 - C_e A_2} = \frac{P_1 P_2}{A_1 A_2},$$

and also
$$\frac{C_eQ_1}{C_eB_1} = \frac{Q_1Q_2}{B_1B_2}.$$
Hence, multiplying,
$$\frac{C_eP_1 \times C_eQ_1}{C_eA_1 \times C_eB_1} = \frac{P_1P_2 \times Q_1Q_2}{A_1A_2 \times B_1B_2}.$$
But, by intersecting chords, $C_eP_1 \times C_eQ_1 = C_eA_1 \times C_eB_1$ and so $P_1P_2 \times Q_1Q_2 = A_1A_2 \times B_1B_2$, which is constant.

Note that we can take the secant as a common tangent and obtain the result $T_1T_2^2 = A_1A_2 \times B_1B_2$.

5. We assume that the contact is external. Let X be the intersection of T_1T_2 and the line of centres (see the figure).

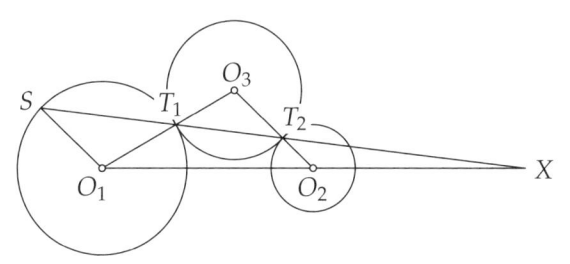

Exercise 5e question 5

A short angle chase shows that $\angle T_1SO_1 = \angle XT_2O_2$. Hence the two radii are equally inclined to the line of centres, and so X is the external centre of similitude.

The argument when the contact is internal is the same.

6. This is similar to the argument for question 5.

7. By theorem 5.22, the centres of similitude divide the line of centres O_1O_2 in the ratio $r_1 : r_2$. Hence, by theorem 5.23, the circle of similitude is an Apollonius circle, being the locus of all points for which $O_1P : O_2P = r_1 : r_2$. In particular, it passes through the intersections of the two circles.

8. (See the figures.) We begin with a special case where the circle has centre M, the midpoint of O_1O_2.

Because O_1, C_i, O_2, C_e is a harmonic range, by theorem 5.20 we have $MC_i \times MC_e = MO_2^2$. But $MO_2 = MA$, so, by the tangent-secant

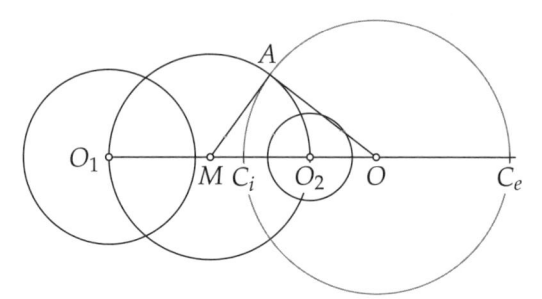

Exercise 5e question 8

theorem, MA is a tangent to the circle of similitude and $\angle MAO = 90°$. Note that, if $MA = a$ and $OA = c$, then $MO^2 = a^2 + c^2$.
Now let X be any point on the perpendicular bisector of O_1O_2.

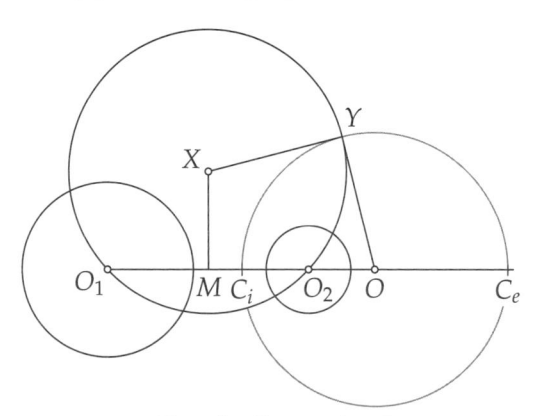

Exercise 5e question 8

Then
$$XO^2 = XM^2 + MO^2$$
$$= \left(XO_2^2 - a^2\right) + \left(a^2 + c^2\right)$$
$$= XO_2^2 + c^2$$
$$= XY^2 + OY^2$$

and hence XY is a tangent to the circle of similitude, as required.

Exercise 6a

1. For the angle bisectors, use the angle bisector theorem, and for the altitudes, use trigonometry.

2. This is immediate from Menelaus; if the triangle is isosceles, one of the points is at infinity.

3. Also immediate from Menelaus; if the triangle is equilateral, the line in question is the line at infinity.

4. By theorem 2.21 on page 22, the sides of the triangle are the external angle bisectors of the orthic triangle. The result now follows from that of question 3.

5. This is immediate from the definition of harmonic conjugate and Ceva's theorem.

6. The positions of L, M and N are fixed by the angle bisector theorem, and then the concurrency is easily proved by Ceva. The two points coincide if, and only if, the sides of the triangle subtend angles of $120°$ at P. (We will meet this point again later, in chapter 11.)

7. L', M' and N' are the harmonic conjugates of L, M and N with respect to the vertices; the result now follows from question 5.

8. Use the angle bisector theorem and similar triangles to show three results similar to
$$\frac{BL}{LC} = -\frac{c^2}{b^2}$$
then use Menelaus.

9. (a) The cevians are the medians, the cevian triangle is the medial triangle $\triangle A_1 B_1 C_1$ and the cevian circle is the nine-point circle.
   (b) The cevians are the altitudes, the cevian triangle is the orthic triangle $\triangle DEF$ and the cevian circle is the nine-point circle.
   (c) The cevians are the internal angle bisectors, the cevian triangle is $\triangle XYZ$, which is known as the *incentral triangle*, and the cevian circle is the *incentral circle*.

10. The simplest proof uses areas (see the figure).
$$\frac{BP}{PC} = \frac{[AOB]}{[AOC]} = \frac{\frac{1}{2}R^2 \sin 2C}{\frac{1}{2}R^2 \sin 2B} = \frac{\sin 2C}{\sin 2B}.$$

This fact is clearly sufficient to demonstrate the existence of the circumcentre, but the characterisation does not seem particularly useful.

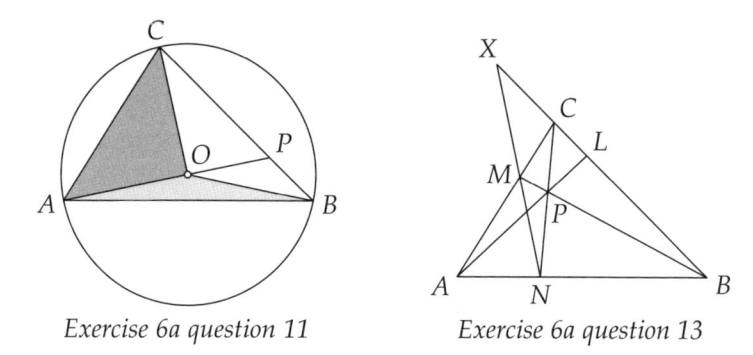

Exercise 6a question 11

Exercise 6a question 13

11. This is simply a matter of following the instructions.

12. The complete quadrangle $AMPN$ has B, C as two diagonal points (see the figure), so
$$\frac{BL}{LC} = -\frac{BX}{XC}$$
By Menelaus on NMX, we have
$$\frac{AN}{NB} \times \frac{BX}{XC} \times \frac{CM}{MA} = -1$$
and now Ceva follows immediately.

Exercise 6b

1. (a) The pedal triangle is the medial triangle $\triangle A_1 B_1 C_1$ and the pedal circle is the nine-point circle.
   (b) The pedal triangle is the orthic triangle $\triangle DEF$ and the pedal circle is the nine-point circle.
   (c) The pedal triangle is $\triangle PQR$, known as the *intouch triangle* (or sometimes the *contact triangle*) and the pedal circle is the incircle.

2. By theorem 6.9, this is a circle centred at the circumcentre.

3. By theorem 6.9, this is the circumcentre, and the area of the pedal triangle is $\frac{1}{4}\Delta$; as it is the medial triangle, this is not surprising.

4. By theorem 6.9, the point lies on the circumcircle; as the pedal triangle is degenerate and has zero area, this is also not a surprise.

Exercise 7a

1. By theorem 2.4 on page 11, it is the circumcentre.

2. It is the incentre since the cevians are angle bisectors.

3. Suppose, for the sake of argument, that the point P lies on the side BC. Then the cevian BP meets AC at C and the reflection of this in B_1 is A; similarly, the cevian CP meets AB at B and this also reflects (in C_1) to A. Finally the cevian AP reflects in A_1 to another line through A. It follows that, for any point P on the side BC, the isotomic conjugate is the opposite vertex A.

4. It is the centroid since the cevians cut the sides at their midpoints and hence are medians.

5. The cevians of the point A^* are the median AA_1 and the lines through B and C parallel to the opposite sides, which therefore intersect them on the line at infinity. None of these is affected by a reflection in A_1, so A^* is self-conjugate, though in a limiting sense.

6. The cevian triangle of the orthocentre is the orthic triangle, and its circumcircle is the nine-point circle. The other points of intersection are the midpoints of the sides, and so the cevians are the medians and the cyclocevian conjugate is the centroid.

7. The circumcircle of $\triangle LMN$ is tangential to the sides of $\triangle ABC$, so the point is the Gergonne point from theorem 6.5 on page 73.

Exercise 7b

1. The circumcircle of $\triangle P_a P_b P_c$ is the image under enlargement with centre P and scale factor 2 of the pedal circle of P (see the figure).
   But, by theorem 7.9, the latter has centre O_P, and this point maps to Q, the isogonal conjugate of P, under such an enlargement. Hence this result is simply a restatement of theorem 7.9. Note that we could start with Q and obtain exactly the same circle.

2. Let Q be the isogonal conjugate of P, which, by the the text preceding theorem 7.2, is on the line at infinity. The lines AQ, BQ and CQ are parallel and, by theorem 7.8, perpendicular to the sides of the pedal triangle of P. But this is degenerate and corresponds to the Simson

Appendix B: Solutions to the exercises 429

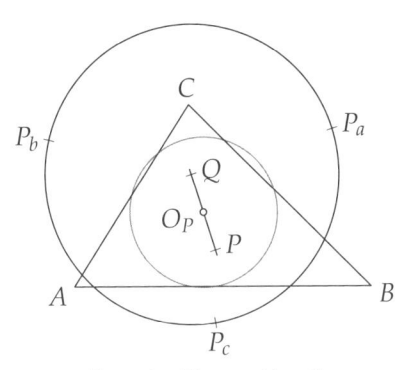

Exercise 7b question 1

line of P.

3. Use the sine rule on triangles $\triangle ABP^*$ and $\triangle ACQ_A$ to obtain the relationship involving AP^* and AQ_A. Then either repeat this method or call on the result of theorem 7.4 to obtain the other part of the relationship.

4. This comes from the sine rule on triangles such as $\triangle ABP_A$.

5. This follows from Menelaus' theorem and the result of question 4.

Exercise 7c

1. This is immediate from Menelaus and the definition of isotomic points.

2. (See the figure.)

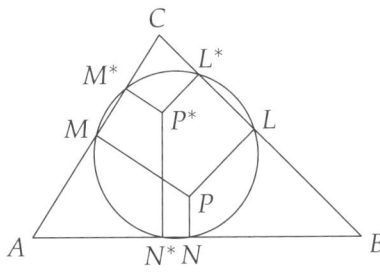

Exercise 7c question 2

By theorem 7.3, AL^*, BM^* and CN^* are concurrent. Let P and P^* be the Miquel points of $\triangle LMN$ and $\triangle L^*M^*N^*$. By corollary 4.9 on page 49,

$$\angle BPC = \angle A + \angle NLM$$
$$\text{and} \quad \angle BP^*C = \angle A + \angle N^*L^*M^*.$$

Hence $\angle BPC + \angle BP^*C = 2\angle A + \angle NLM + \angle N^*L^*M^*$.

But by theorem 7.12, this is $180° + \angle A$. Similarly $\angle CPA + \angle CP^*A = 180° + \angle B$ and $\angle APB + \angle AP^*B = 180° + \angle C$. So, by theorem 7.7, P^* and P are isogonal conjugates.

3. The pedal triangle of the incentre is formed by the points where the incircle touches the sides of $\triangle ABC$. By theorem 6.5 on page 73, this triangle is cevian and $\widehat{I} = \Gamma$.

4. Let P, with pedal triangle $\triangle DEF$, be the pedal-cevian point of $\widehat{P}$. Let the image of P under reflection in O be Q, with pedal triangle $D^*E^*F^*$ (see the figure).

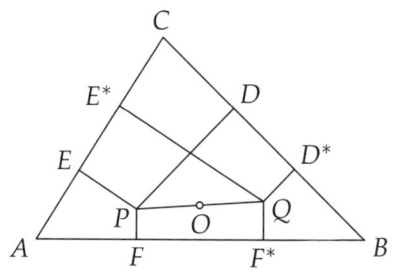

Exercise 7c question 4

Then D^*, E^* and F^* are the reflections of D, E and F in the midpoints of the sides. Hence the line segments AD^*, BE^* and CF^* are concurrent at $\widehat{Q}$, the isotomic conjugate of $\widehat{P}$.

5. Let P, with pedal triangle $\triangle DEF$, be the pedal-cevian point of $\widehat{P}$. Let the isogonal conjugate of P be Q, with pedal triangle $\triangle D^*E^*F^*$. Then by theorem 7.9, P and Q have the same pedal circle (see the figure).

The cevians AD, BE and CF are concurrent at $\widehat{P}$. Hence the line segments AD^*, BE^* and CF^* are also concurrent. Thus Q is pedal-cevian and $\widehat{Q}$ is the cyclocevian conjugate of $\widehat{P}$.

Appendix B: Solutions to the exercises　　　431

Exercise 7c question 5

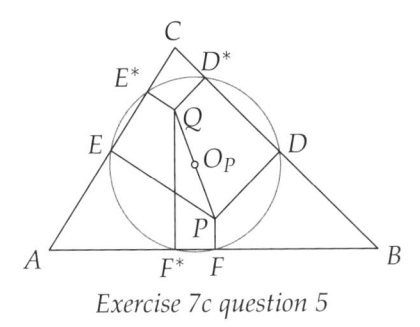

6. This follows from the fact that O is the midpoint of $H\Lambda$.

Exercise 7d

1. We will prove questions 1 and 2 together by producing a necessary and sufficient condition. Let P be any point on $C_1 B_1$ and let M be the midpoint of AD, which lies on $C_1 B_1$ (see the figure).

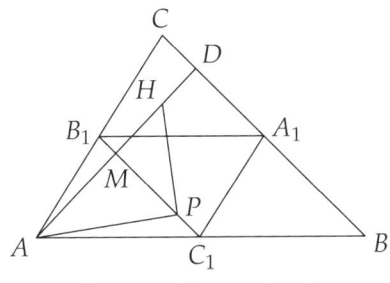

Exercise 7d question 1

Then
$$AP^2 = AM^2 + MP^2$$
$$= AM^2 + HP^2 - HM^2$$
$$= AH \times HD + HP^2,$$

but by theorem 2.16 on page 20, this expression is independent of the vertex chosen. Hence $AP = BQ = CR$ if, and only if, HP is constant, and so both results follow.

2. See the solution to question 1.

3. In the proof of question 1, $HP = \rho_0$ and $AP = \rho$, and the value $AH \times HD$ is given by theorem 3.14 on page 38.

4. The Droz-Farny circles arise when $\rho = AO = R$, so their radius is then ρ_0, which is given by

$$\rho_0^2 = 5R^2 - \tfrac{1}{2}(a^2 + b^2 + c^2).$$

Exercise 8a

1. From theorem 2.19 on page 22, $\triangle AEF$ is similar to $\triangle ABC$. Let X be the intersection of AK_A and EF (see the figure).

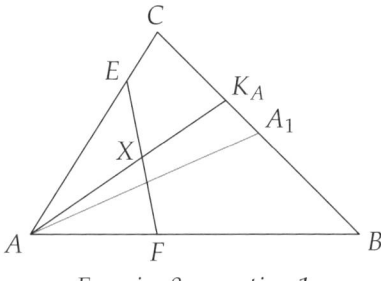

Exercise 8a question 1

Since AK_A is the symmedian of $\triangle ABC$ we have $\angle FAX = \angle BAK_A = \angle CAA_1$. Hence, under the similarity, the symmedian of $\triangle ABC$ is a median of $\triangle AEF$, and so X is the midpoint of FE.

2. It is sufficient to observe that the median of $\triangle ABC$ is the symmedian of $\triangle AEF$.

3. K lies on the altitude AD since $\angle BAD = \angle C = \angle CAA_1$ (see the figure).

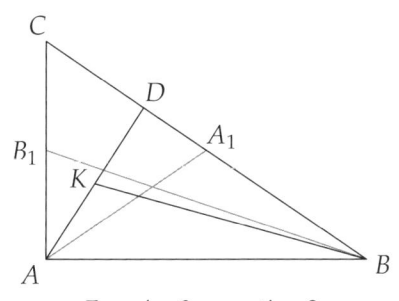

Exercise 8a question 3

Also $\triangle ADB$ is similar to $\triangle CAB$ and the symmedian of $\triangle CAB$ corresponds to the median of $\triangle ADB$; hence K is the midpoint of AD.

4. A neat argument uses the statics arguments for the centroid in section 1.4. Place masses of a^2, b^2 and c^2 at A, B and C. The two

masses at B and C can be replaced by a single mass of $b^2 + c^2$ at K_A, using corollary 8.2. Now the centre of mass of all three lies somewhere on the symmedian AK_A, but, since there is nothing special about A, it lies on all three symmedians and so is K. But now it follows that $AK : KK_A = b^2 + c^2 : a^2$.

5. Let k be the common value of the ratios in theorem 8.1, so the area of $\triangle BCK$ is $\frac{1}{2}ka^2$. By adding the three corresponding areas together, we have
$$\tfrac{1}{2}k(a^2 + b^2 + c^2) = \Delta.$$
The required result follows immediately.

6. This uses exactly the same idea as question 5, but now we must add two areas and subtract the third.

7. (See the figure.) By the result of question 4,
$$\frac{AK}{KK_A} = \frac{b^2 + c^2}{a^2},$$
so $b^2 + c^2 = 2a^2$ if, and only if, $AK = \frac{2}{3}AK_A$, which is equivalent to the fact that KG is parallel to BC and perpendicular to AH. Since O and H, and also G and K, are isogonal conjugates, it follows that $\angle OAG = \angle KAH$. Therefore $\angle OAG = \angle OKG$, and so $OAKG$ is cyclic. Hence $\angle OKA = 90°$.

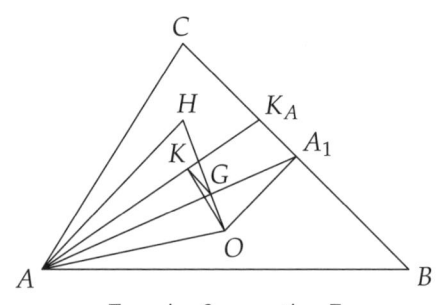

Exercise 8a question 7

Combining this with question 4 of exercise 3b, we see that the Euler line is perpendicular to the median through A if, and only if, the line OK is perpendicular to the symmedian through A. This result appeared in [9]. We will meet OK again in chapter 16 where it is known as the *Brocard axis*.

8. Let HA_1 meet $\mathcal{C}$ at A' and note, by theorem 2.17 on page 21, that $D'A'$ is parallel to BC (see the figure).

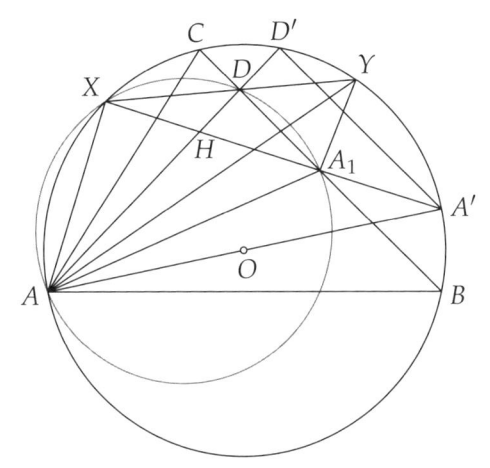

Exercise 8a question 8

Also, because $A_1O = \frac{1}{2}HA$, $A'A$ is a diameter of $\mathcal{C}$. It follows that $\angle A'XA = 90°$ and so the quadrilateral $AXDA_1$ is cyclic. Hence $\angle DXA_1 = \angle DAA_1$.

Therefore $\angle D'AY = \angle D'XY = \angle D'XA_1 - \angle DXA_1 = \angle D'AA' - \angle DAA_1 = \angle A_1AA'$ and so, since $\angle BAH = \angle OAC$ by theorem 2.4 on page 11, we have $\angle BAY = \angle A_1AC$, as required.

Exercise 8b

1. It is enough to observe that an isosceles trapezium is cyclic. Alternatively, the symmedian of an isosceles triangle is the same as the median.

2. Quadrilateral $BCEF$ is cyclic.

3. Any line antiparallel to BC is parallel to the tangent at A, which is perpendicular to the diameter through A.

4. Since $BCUV$ is cyclic, $\angle AUX_1 = \angle ABX$ (see the figure).
   If also $\angle AX_1U = \angle AXB$, we have $\angle UAX_1 = \angle VAX_1$ and so AX is an angle bisector.

Exercise 8b question 4

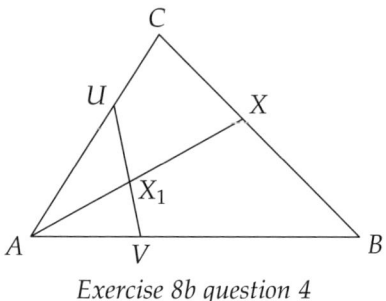

5. Let AX meet BC at Y and let YW and YR be parallel to VU and TS (see the figure).

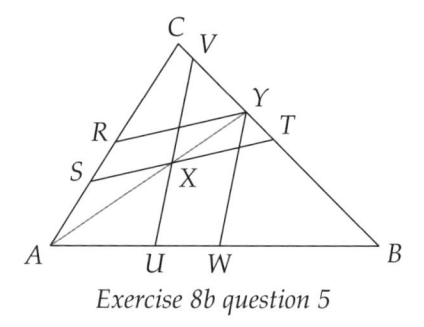

Exercise 8b question 5

Then $\angle XVT = \angle WYB = \angle A = \angle RYC = \angle XTV$ and so $XT = XV$. Hence $XU = XS$ and so $YW = YR$. The triangles $\triangle YBW$, $\triangle ABC$, $\triangle YRC$ are similar, so
$$BY = \frac{c}{b}YW \text{ and } YC = \frac{b}{c}YR$$
Hence
$$\frac{BY}{YC} = \frac{c^2}{b^2}$$
and so, by corollary 8.2, AY is the symmedian through A.

6. It is straightforward to check that quadrilateral $D'NBM$ is cyclic. Alternatively, the Simson line of D' is parallel to the tangent at A; this is a limiting case of theorem 4.2 on page 42.

Appendix B: Solutions to the exercises 437

Exercise 8c

1. Let T_A be the exsymmedian point opposite to A (see the figure).

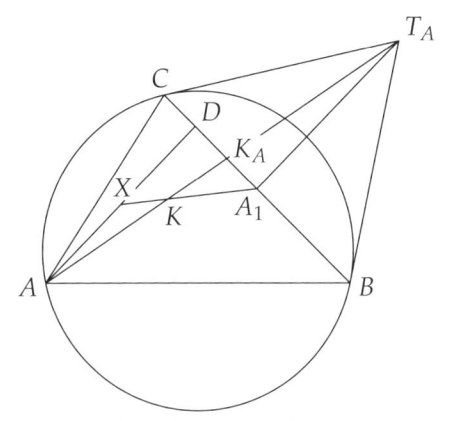

Exercise 8c question 1

Then, by the result of theorem 5.20 on page 62, the range A, K, K_A, T_A is harmonic. Hence $A_1(A, K, K_A, T_A)$ is a harmonic pencil. Now consider the transversal AD, which cuts this pencil in the points A, X, D and the point at infinity (since AD is parallel to A_1T_A). This is another harmonic range, and, since it contains a point at infinity, we have $AX = XD$.

2. Let A^*D^* be an altitude of the anti-complementary triangle, intersecting BC at X (see the figure).

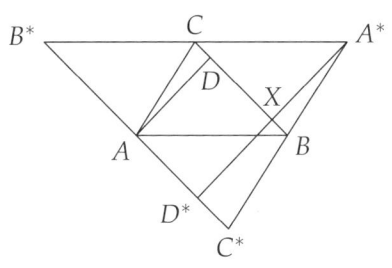

Exercise 8c question 2

Then, since $\triangle ABC$ can be mapped to $\triangle A^*B^*C^*$ under an enlargement with centre G and scale factor -2, we have $CX = BD$ and

X is the midpoint of A^*D^*. But A is the midpoint of B^*C^*, so by the result of question 1, AX is a symmedian of $\triangle A^*B^*C^*$. But the three altitudes of $\triangle ABC$ meet in its orthocentre, and the three symmedians of $\triangle A^*B^*C^*$ meet in its symmedian point, so the result follows.

3. A short angle chase shows that $\angle B^*A^*A = \angle B^*BA = \angle KBC'' = \angle KA''C''$ and similarly $\angle C^*A^*A = \angle KA''B''$ (see the figure).

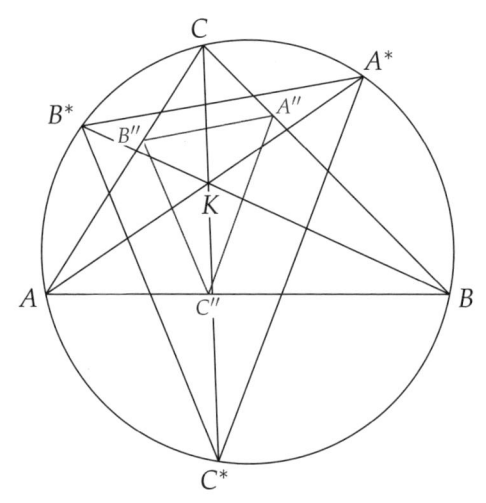

Exercise 8c question 3

Hence we have $\angle B^*A^*C^* = \angle B''A''C''$, and $\triangle B^*A^*C^*$ is similar to $\triangle B''A''C''$. By theorem 8.9, K is the centroid of $\triangle A''B''C''$. But, since $\angle C^*A^*A = \angle KA''B''$ and $\angle B^*A^*A = \angle KA''C''$, it follows that K is the isogonal conjugate of the centroid, namely the symmedian point, of $\triangle A^*B^*C^*$.

4. Let P be an internal point of $\triangle ABC$, let its pedal triangle be $\triangle XYZ$ and let XP and YZ meet at Q (see the figure). Also let the lengths of PX, PY and PZ be p_A, p_B and p_C.

Note that $\angle ZPQ = \angle B$ and $\angle QPY = \angle C$. By the sine rule on triangles $\triangle PQZ$ and $\triangle PYQ$, we have

$$\frac{p_C}{\sin \angle PQZ} = \frac{ZQ}{\sin B} \text{ and } \frac{p_B}{\sin \angle PQY} = \frac{QY}{\sin C}.$$

Appendix B: Solutions to the exercises 439

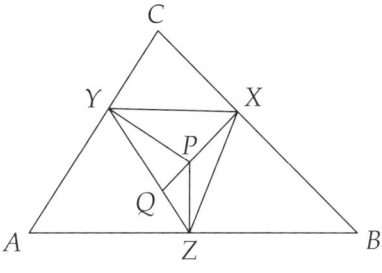

Exercise 8c question 4

It follows that
$$\frac{p_C}{p_B} = \frac{ZQ \sin C}{QY \sin B} = \frac{c \times ZQ}{b \times QY}.$$
Hence $ZQ = QY$ if, and only if,
$$\frac{p_C}{p_B} = \frac{c}{b},$$
and, by theorem 8.1, this is true if, and only if, AP is a symmedian of $\triangle ABC$. Since similar statements hold for the other two symmedians, the result follows.

The fact that the symmedian point has this property can be proved neatly without recourse to trigonometry.

Extend AA_1 to A_1' so that $AA_1' = 2AA_1$ and let the pedal triangle of K be triangle $\triangle A''B''C''$ (see the figure).

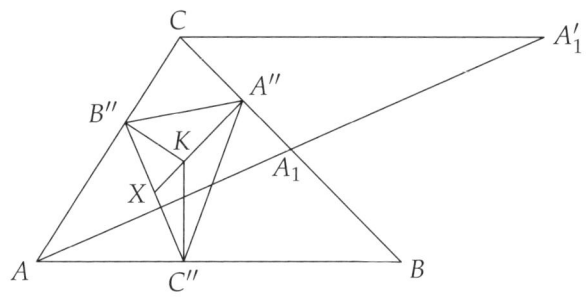

Exercise 8c question 4

Now the triangles $\triangle B''C''K$ and $\triangle AA_1'C$ are similar since, by theorem 7.8 on page 88, AA_1' is perpendicular to $B''C''$, $A_1'C$ is parallel to

BA which is perpendicular to $C''K$ and CA is perpendicular to KB''. Hence KX and CA_1 are corresponding line segments in these two figures, as they are perpendicular through corresponding vertices, and so X is the midpoint of $B''C''$ and $A''X$ is a median. As the same is true for the other two medians, the result is proved.

However, this argument does not seem to be easily reversible to show that the symmedian point is the only point with this property.

Appendix B: Solutions to the exercises

Exercise 9a

1. (See the figure.)

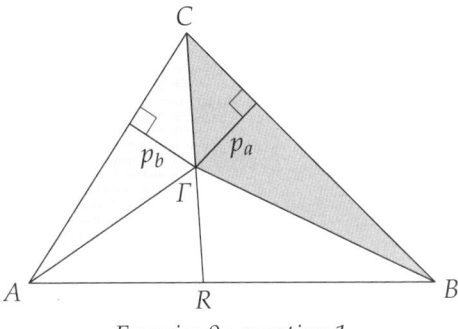

Exercise 9a question 1

It is clear from consideration of areas that
$$\frac{ap_A}{bp_B} = \frac{[\Gamma BC]}{[\Gamma CA]} = \frac{BR}{RA} = \frac{s-b}{s-c}.$$
The result follows.

2. We have $ap_A + bp_B + cp_C = 2\Delta$. Substituting by using lemma 9.2, we get
$$p_A = \frac{2(s-b)(s-c)\Delta}{a\big((s-b)(s-c) + (s-c)(s-a) + (s-a)(s-b)\big)}$$
$$= \frac{2\left(\frac{\Delta}{s-a}\right)\Delta}{a\left(\frac{\Delta}{s-a} + \frac{\Delta}{s-b} + \frac{\Delta}{s-c}\right)}$$
$$= \frac{2r_A\Delta}{a(r_A + r_B + r_C)}$$
using theorem 2.12 on page 18. The other form comes from using theorem 2.14 on page 19.

3. It is clear from consideration of areas that
$$\frac{ar_A}{br_B} = \frac{[MBC]}{[MCA]} = \frac{BR_C}{R_CA} = \frac{s-a}{s-b}.$$
The result follows.

4. Let A_1S meet AB at X (see the figure).

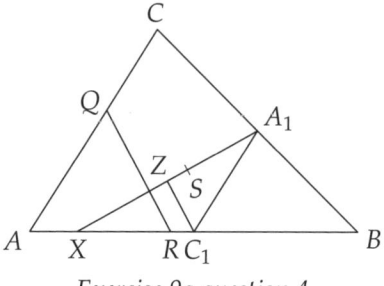

Exercise 9a question 4

By the proof of theorem 9.9, $C_1X = C_1A_1$, and so A_1X is perpendicular to C_1Z, the angle bisector of $\angle A_1C_1X$. But C_1Z makes an angle of $90° - \frac{1}{2}A$ with AB, so it is parallel to QR. Hence A_1X is perpendicular to QR, and the result follows.

5. Since, by theorem 9.12, they share the same incircle, the triangles $\triangle A_1B_1C_1$ and $\triangle UVW$ are homothetic, with centre S and scale factor -1 (see the figure).

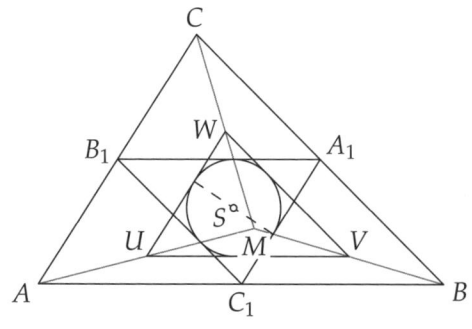

Exercise 9a question 5

It follows that the two radii from S which are perpendicular to A_1C_1 and UW are 'parallel' and therefore coincident in a single diameter. Hence the points of contact are diametrically opposite. This is clearly true for the other two diameters.

6. Let X be the midpoint of C_1B_1 and also the midpoint of the median AA_1 (see the figure).

By theorem 9.6, I is the Nagel point of $\triangle A_1B_1C_1$. Now $\triangle ABC$ is mapped to $\triangle AC_1B_1$ by an enlargement with centre A and scale

Appendix B: Solutions to the exercises

Exercise 9a question 6

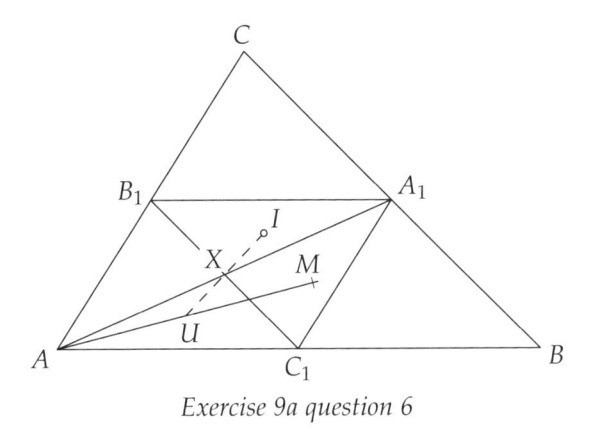

factor $\frac{1}{2}$, so U is the Nagel point of this triangle. But $\triangle AC_1B_1$ can be mapped to $\triangle A_1B_1C_1$ by an enlargement with centre X and scale factor -1, and this mapping takes U to I as they are both Nagel points.

7. Since $\triangle AGM$ and $\triangle A_1GI$ are similar, with scale factor 2 : 1, it follows that $AM = 2IA_1$ (see the figure).

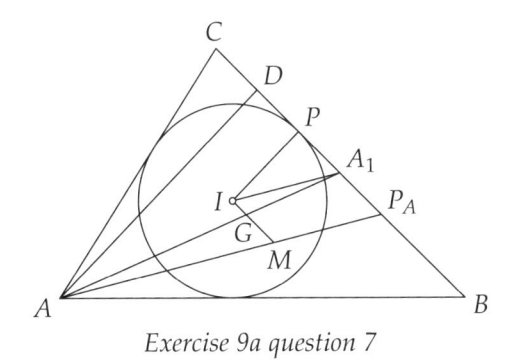

Exercise 9a question 7

Hence
$$\frac{AM}{AP_A} = \frac{2IA_1}{AP_A} = \frac{2IP}{AD} = \frac{2r}{AD}.$$
But $2\Delta = AD \times a$ and $rs = \Delta$, so
$$\frac{AM}{AP_A} = \frac{a}{s}.$$

Exercise 9b

1. By the argument in section 1.5 on page 6, $O \triangle A^*B^*C^* = H$.
2. Since the nine-point circle of $\triangle A^*B^*C^*$ is the circumcircle of $\triangle ABC$, $N \triangle A^*B^*C^* = O$.
3. By corollary 9.8, $I \triangle A^*B^*C^* = M$.
4. Since $\triangle ABC$ is the medial triangle of $\triangle A^*B^*C^*$, $S \triangle A^*B^*C^* = I$.
5. By theorem 9.1, $K \triangle PQR = \Gamma$.
6. By theorem 2.9 on page 16, $H \triangle I_A I_B I_C = I$.
7. By theorem 2.21 on page 22, $I \triangle DEF = H$.
8. By theorem 2.21 on page 22, $I_D \triangle DEF = A$.

Exercise 9c

1. Let U_1 be the point on AD such that $AU_1 = 2r$ (see the figure).

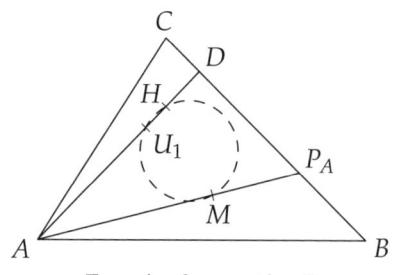

Exercise 9c question 1

Now
$$AD = c \sin B = \frac{2\Delta}{a},$$
so
$$\frac{AU_1}{AD} = \frac{ar}{\Delta}.$$
But, by theorem 2.16 on page 20, $rs = \Delta$, so
$$\frac{AU_1}{AD} = \frac{a}{s}.$$

Appendix B: Solutions to the exercises

However, by exercise 9a, question 7, this is also
$$\frac{AM}{AP_A}.$$
Hence $U_1 M \parallel DP_A$ and so $\angle HU_1 M = 90°$ and U_1 lies on the Fuhrmann circle.

2. This is immediate from the fact that $OIHF^*$ is a parallelogram, with N the midpoint of HO.

3. $A = (1, 0, 0)$, $B = (0, 1, 0)$, $C = (0, 0, 1)$, $A_1 = (0, 1, 1)$, $B_1 = (1, 0, 1)$, $C_1 = (1, 1, 0)$.

4. (a) (a, b, c); (b) $(-a, b, c)$. Both of these results follow from the angle bisector theorem.

5. (a) This is the symmedian point, by corollary 8.2 on page 100.
   (b) This is the Nagel point, by theorem 2.11 and theorem 9.4.
   (c) This is the Gergonne point, by theorem 2.10 and theorem 6.8 on page 16 and on page 78.
   (d) This is the Spieker centre. One approach is to note that this is equivalent to masses of $2a$, $2b$ and $2c$ at the midpoints A_1, B_1 and C_1, so the point is, by the result of question 4(a), the incentre of the medial triangle. Alternatively, we can superimpose the situations of masses a, b, c and $2(s-a)$, $2(s-b)$, $2(s-c)$ at the vertices, to produce masses of $2s$ at I and $2s$ at M, and then use the result of theorem 9.10.

6. This is the centroid since it is equivalent to equal masses at the midpoints, so it is the centroid of the medial triangle.

7. This is the Spieker centre since it is equivalent to masses a, b, c at the midpoints, and hence is the incentre of the medial triangle.

8. (a) By the result of question 10 of exercise 6a, the coordinates are $(\sin 2A, \sin 2B, \sin 2C)$.
   (b) We have
   $$BD : DC = c \cos B : b \cos C$$
   $$= \sin C \cos B : \sin B \cos C$$
   $$= \tan C : \tan B.$$

Hence $(\tan A, \tan B, \tan C)$ is a neat form for the barycentric coordinates.

Exercise 10a

1. By section 2.3 on page 15, this is the incentre.
2. By section 9.1 on page 113, this is the Gergonne point.
3. By theorem 9.4 on page 114, this is the Nagel point.
4. By theorem 8.4 on page 101, this is the symmedian point.
5. This is immediate from the diagram, and in each case the perspector is the omitted vertex of the quadrangle.

Exercise 10b

It is sensible to begin the process of 'translation' by reformulating the original statement in terms which make it very clear how the configuration is built up. Then apply the duality operation. In what follows, the original statements are given in parallel with the corresponding dual statements.

1. ORIGINAL

   We begin with a circle, on which there are six points.

   The points are joined by lines.

   Opposite sides meet at points which are collinear.

   DUAL

   We begin with a circle with six tangent lines.

   The tangents intersect in points.

   Opposite points are joined by lines, which are concurrent.

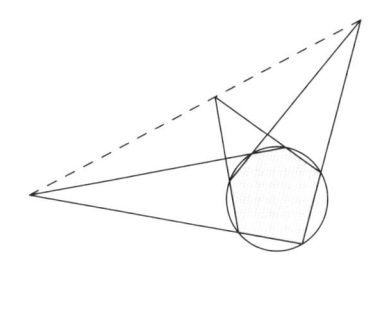

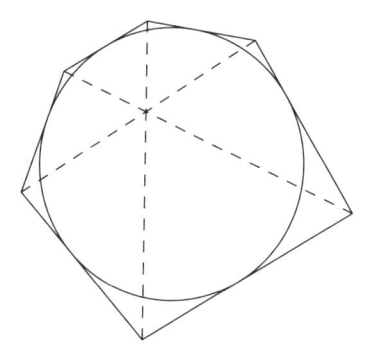

It is now possible to rephrase the dual result in more familiar and concise terms. If a hexagon is circumscribed about a circle, then the lines joining opposite vertices are concurrent.

The original result is *Pascal's theorem* (see section 10.3 on page 136) and the dual result is *Brianchon's theorem*.

2. ORIGINAL

We start with a circle with three tangent lines, meeting in pairs in three points.

We now identify the points of contact of the tangents.

Each contact point is joined to the opposite vertex by a line, and these three lines are concurrent.

DUAL

We start with a circle on which are three points, joined in pairs to form a triangle.

We now identify the tangents at the three points.

Each tangent meets the opposite side at a point, and these points are collinear.

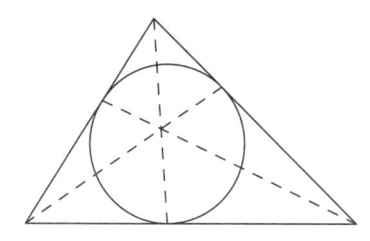

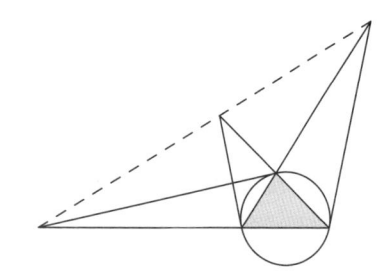

The dual result appeared as question 8 of exercise 6a. The tangents to the circumcircle of a triangle meet the opposite sides in three collinear points.

3. ORIGINAL

We begin with two fixed points A and B.

Through A there are two fixed lines $\mathcal{X}$ and $\mathcal{Y}$.

Through B there are two variable lines which create two points P and R on $\mathcal{X}$, and Q and S on $\mathcal{Y}$.

The intersection of the joins PS and QR is on a fixed line through A.

DUAL

We begin with two fixed lines $\mathcal{A}$ and $\mathcal{B}$.

On $\mathcal{A}$ there are two fixed points X and Y.

On $\mathcal{B}$ there are two variable points which create two lines $\mathcal{P}$ and $\mathcal{R}$ through X, and $\mathcal{Q}$ and $\mathcal{S}$ through Y.

The line joining the intersections $\mathcal{PS}$ and $\mathcal{QR}$ passes through a fixed point on $\mathcal{A}$.

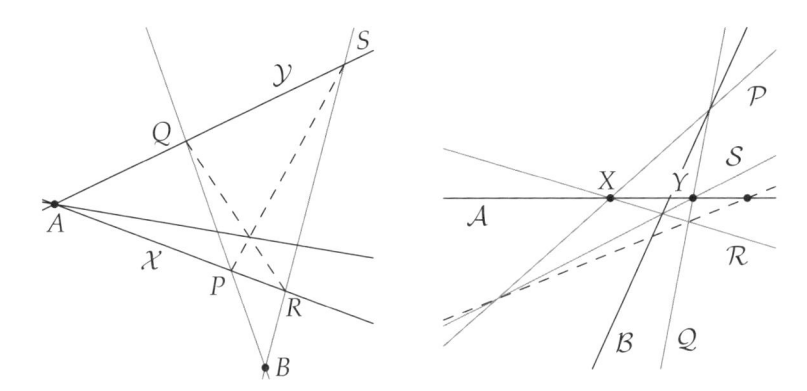

Appendix B: Solutions to the exercises 449

The dual result can be stated more succinctly as follows. Given two fixed lines, with fixed points B, C on one, and points P, Q on the other, let PB meet QC at U and let PC meet QB at V. Then, as P and Q vary, the line UV passes through a fixed point on BC.

Notice that in the original diagram, the point moves up and down a fixed line, whereas in the dual diagram, the line moves so that it always goes through a fixed point.

Exercise 10c

1. Since triangles $\triangle ABC$ and $\triangle LMN$ are in perspective, they have an axis of perspective PQR. Let P' be the midpoint of LP; then $P'N_1$ is parallel to PM and so P' is on the line M_1N_1. In the same way define Q' and R' (see the figure).

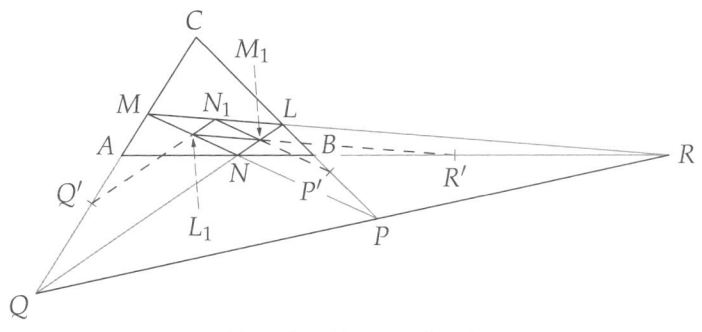

Exercise 10c question 1

By Menelaus for $\triangle LMN$ and the transversal PQR we have
$$\frac{LR}{RM} \times \frac{MP}{PN} \times \frac{NQ}{QL} = -1.$$
Hence
$$\frac{LR'}{R'M} \times \frac{MP'}{P'N} \times \frac{NQ'}{Q'L} = -1$$
and so P', Q' and R' are collinear. Therefore $\triangle ABC$ and $\triangle L'M'N'$ are in perspective.

This could also be tackled using theorem 10.3.

2. This is similar to question 1. Let P', Q' and R' be the midpoints of AP, BQ and CR.

3. Triangles $\triangle ABC'$ and $\triangle A'B'C$ are in perspective, so the points Q, P and N are collinear, where $N = AB \cap A'B'$ (see the figure).

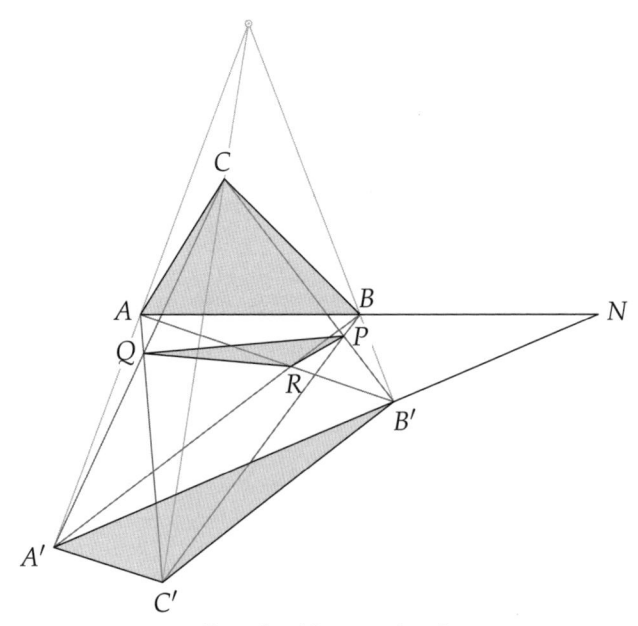

Exercise 10c question 3

A similar result holds, of course, for $M = AC \cap A'C'$ and $L = BC \cap B'C'$. Hence $\triangle PQR$ has the same axis of perspective LMN as $\triangle ABC$ and $\triangle A'B'C'$, and the three triangles are in perspective in

Appendix B: Solutions to the exercises 451

pairs. Hence, by theorem 10.8, the three perspectors are collinear.

4. By theorem 7.9 on page 89, P and P^* share the same pedal circle, with centre O_P, the midpoint of PP^*. Let E^*E_1 and F^*F_1 be diameters of this circle (see the figure). Then $\angle E_1EE^* = 90°$ so P lies on E_1E, and similarly on F_1F.

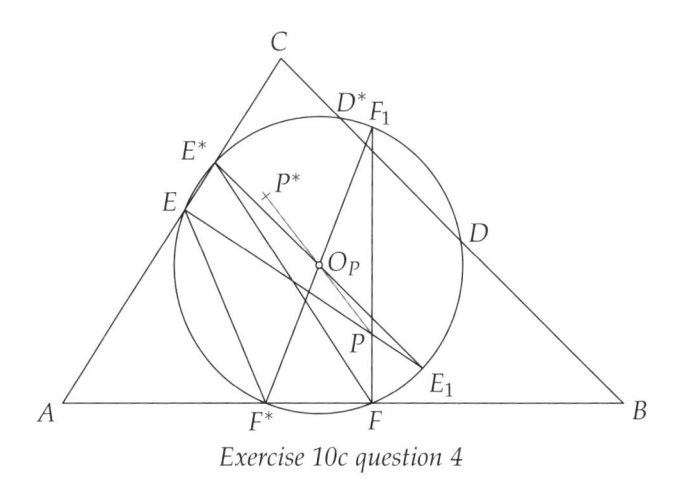

Exercise 10c question 4

Now apply theorem 10.5 to the hexagon $EE_1E^*FF_1F^*$.
But $E_1E^* \cap F_1F^* = O_P$ and $EE_1 \cap FF_1 = P$, and so $E^*F \cap F^*E$ is collinear with these two points, and hence lies on PP^*. Naturally the same is true of the other intersections.

Exercise 11a

1. One needs only to draw the diagram to see that this is obvious (see the figure).

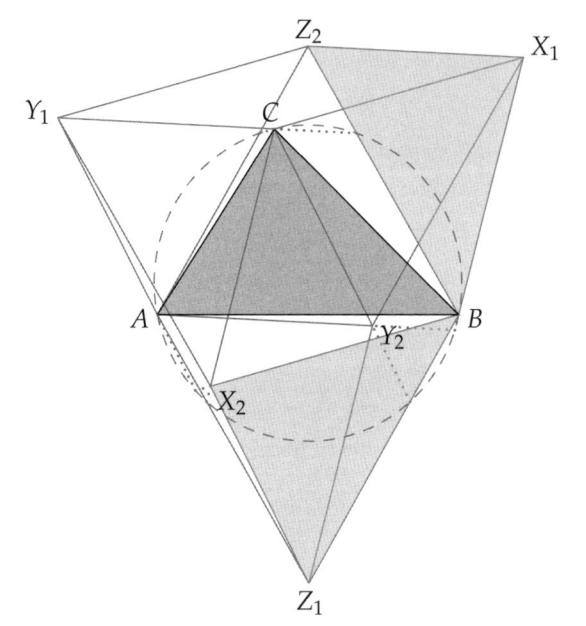

Exercise 11a question 1

Moreover, three of the triangles are the effect of rotating $\triangle ABC$ through 60° clockwise and another three are the effect of rotating through 60° anticlockwise.

Note also that the intersections (AY_2, BX_1), (AY_1, BX_2), (BZ_2, CY_1), (BZ_1, CY_2), (CX_2, AY_1), (CX_1, AY_2) all lie on the circumcircle of $\triangle ABC$. This can be proved by calculating appropriate angles.

2. Let K be the point on F_1X such that $F_1K = F_1C$ (see the figures). Then $\triangle F_1KC$ is equilateral, and so $\triangle CKX \cong \triangle CF_1B$ by SAS. It follows that $KX = F_1B$.

Hence $AX = AF_1 + F_1K + KX = F_1A + F_1B + F_1C$ as required.

In the case where $\angle A \geq 120°$, the proof works in exactly the same way until the final step. This becomes $AX = F_1K + KX - F_1A = F_1C + F_1B - F_1A$.

Appendix B: Solutions to the exercises 453

Exercise 11a question 2

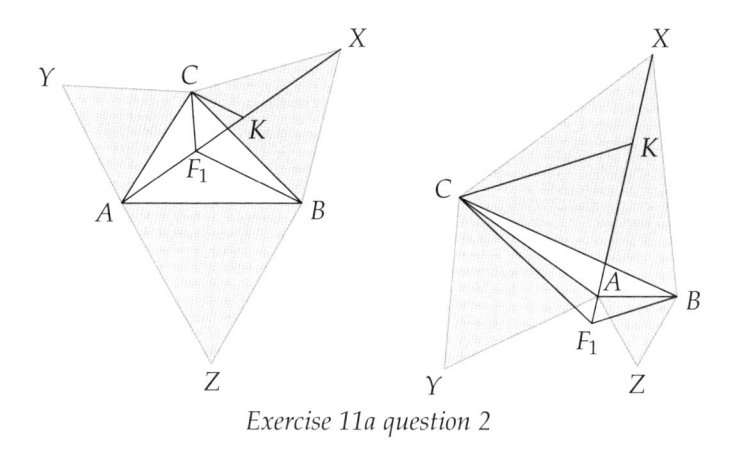

3. (See the figure.)

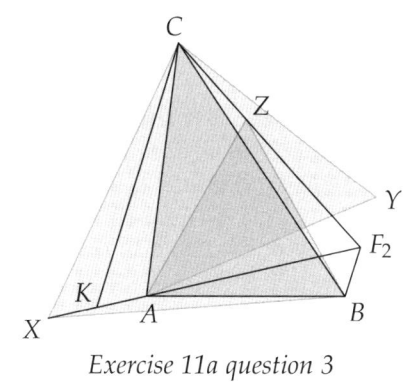

Exercise 11a question 3

Again, the argument is the same as question 2 until the final step, which now takes the form $AX = F_2K + KX - F_2A = F_2C + F_2B - F_2A$.

4. Since $\angle BAC = 60°$, the line YAZ is a straight line. Let D be on AB such that CD is parallel to YZ (see the figure). Then $\triangle CAD \cong \triangle CAY$.

Now triangles $\triangle AZD$ and $\triangle DXC$ are each congruent to $\triangle ABC$ by SAS. Then $\triangle BDZ \cong \triangle DBX$ (SSS).

The result follows.

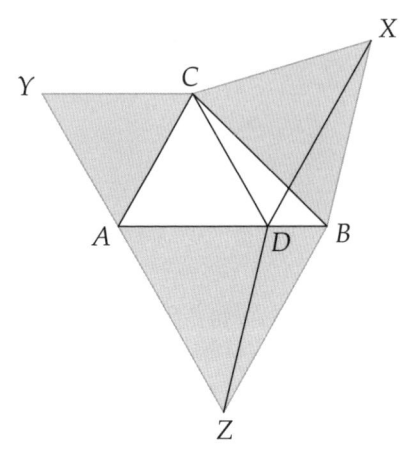

Exercise 11a question 4

5. Let two of the circumcircles—say those of $\triangle CBX$ and $\triangle ACY$—meet at a point P. Then a simple angle chase shows that $\angle BPA = 180° - \angle AZB$, so $BPAZ$ is cyclic.

   In the case where YAZ, ZBX and XCY are straight lines, this becomes an instance of Miquel's theorem. However, nothing is now being claimed about $\triangle ABC$ and $\triangle XYZ$ being in perspective.

6. This is a special case of the result in question 5.

Exercise 11b

1. The connectors of corresponding points are simply the perpendicular bisectors of BC, CA and AB, so the perspector is the circumcentre of $\triangle ABC$.

2. Note first that $AN_B = AN_b = R_B$, the circumradius of $\triangle CAY$, and, similarly, $AN_C = AN_c = R_C$, the circumradius of $\triangle ABZ$. Now we use the cosine rule on $\triangle AN_BN_C$ to calculate the side length N_BN_C of the outer Napoleon triangle, noting that $\angle N_B AN_C = A + 60°$. This gives

$$(N_BN_C)^2 = R_B^2 + R_C^2 - 2R_BR_C \cos(A + 60°)$$

Appendix B: Solutions to the exercises

and by a similar argument

$$(N_b N_c)^2 = R_B^2 + R_C^2 - 2R_B R_C \cos(A - 60°).$$

Now the area of an equilateral triangle of side k is $\frac{\sqrt{3}}{4}k^2$, so the difference of the areas of the two Napoleon triangles is

$$\tfrac{\sqrt{3}}{2} R_B R_C [\cos(A - 60°) - \cos(A + 60°)] = \tfrac{3}{2} R_B R_C \sin A,$$

using the factor formula. However, from the sine rule, $2b = R_B \sqrt{3}$ and $2c = R_C \sqrt{3}$, so this expression becomes $\frac{1}{2} bc \sin A$, which is the area of $\triangle ABC$.

3. Since the line of centres of two circles is the perpendicular bisector of their common chord, $N_B N_C$, $N_C N_A$ and $N_A N_B$ are perpendicular to $F_1 A$, $F_2 B$ and $F_3 C$ at U, V and W, their midpoints (see the figure).

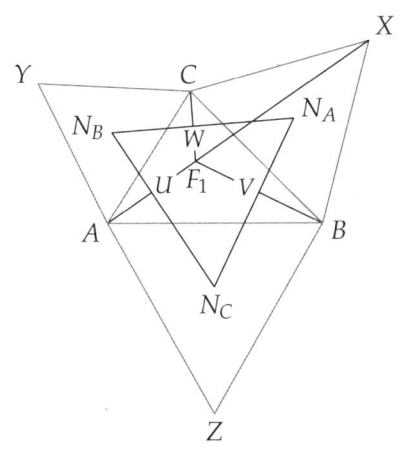

Exercise 11b question 3

But the angles at F_1 are each 120° so $\angle N_A N_B N_C$, $\angle N_B N_C N_A$ and $\angle N_C N_A N_B$ are all 60° and the triangle is equilateral.

4. By definition $\angle C N_a B = 120°$, and by theorem 11.1 $\angle C F_1 B = 120°$, so $BCN_a F_1$ is cyclic (see the figure).

Hence $\angle N_a F_1 C = 180° - \angle N_a BC = 150°$. Similarly $\angle C F_1 N_b = 150°$, and so $\angle N_a F_1 N_b = 60°$. But, by theorem 11.6, $\angle N_a N_c N_b = 60°$, so F_1 lies on circle $N_a N_c N_b$.

The other proof is similar.

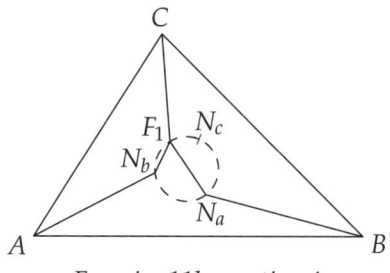

Exercise 11b question 4

Exercise 11c

1. Since $QG = QH$, we have $QH^2 = QF_1 \times QF_2$ from the proof of theorem 11.12, and the result follows.

2. This is a consequence of theorem 3.13 on page 37. The power of Q is $QF_1 \times QF_2$, which is QG^2, and the orthocentroidal disc has radius QG.

3. This is exactly the same proof as for question 2.

Appendix B: Solutions to the exercises

Exercise 12a

1. Let the homothetic centre be P (see the figure) and its perpendicular distances from AB, CA and BC be p_C, p_B and p_A.

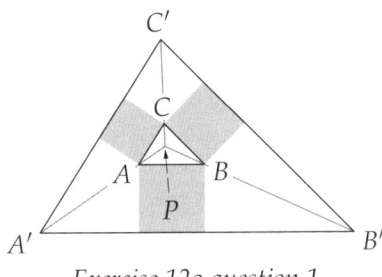

Exercise 12a question 1

Then, by similar triangles,
$$\frac{p_C}{p_B} = \frac{p_C + c}{p_B + b} = \frac{c}{b}$$
and so on. Hence
$$\frac{p_C}{c} = \frac{p_B}{b} = \frac{p_A}{a}.$$
The result follows by theorem 8.1 on page 100.

2. Note that
$$OV_A = OA_1 + A_1V_A = \tfrac{1}{2}a(1 + \cot A),$$
with similar results for OV_B and OV_C (see the figure).

The angle between OV_B and OV_C is $180° - \angle A$ and so the area of $\triangle OV_BV_C$ is $\tfrac{1}{8}bc(1 + \cot B)(1 + \cot C)\sin A$.

We have to add three such areas. Using the sine rule and some manipulation, the expression becomes
$$\tfrac{1}{2}R^2 \sin A \sin B \sin C \left(3 + 2\sum \cot A + \sum \cot A \cot B\right).$$

If $\angle A + \angle B + \angle C = 180°$, then it can be shown that $\sum \cot A \cot B = 1$. Also, the area of $\triangle ABC$ is $\tfrac{1}{2}ab \sin C = 2R^2 \sin A \sin B \sin C$. Finally
$$R^2 \sin A \sin B \sin C \sum \cot A = R^2 \sum \sin A \sin B \cos C.$$

458   The Geometry of the Triangle

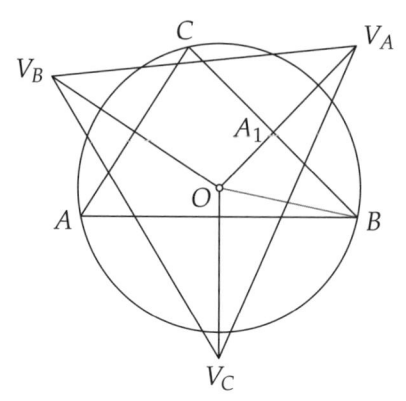

Exercise 12a question 2

But now the sine and cosine rules show that

$$R^2 \sin A \sin B \cos C = \tfrac{1}{4}ab\left(\frac{a^2+b^2-c^2}{2ab}\right)$$
$$= \tfrac{1}{8}(a^2+b^2-c^2)$$

and when all this is put together we obtain the desired formula.

For the inner Vecten triangle, simply replace the plus signs by minus signs in the formulae for OV_A and so on, to see that the area is $\Delta - \tfrac{1}{8}(a^2+b^2-c^2)$.

3. $\triangle AB_AB$ is congruent to $\triangle ACC_A$ (SAS) and is mapped onto it by a rotation of $90°$ with centre A, so BB_A is perpendicular to CC_A at a point X. But B_AC is a diameter of the circumcircle of ACB_CB_A, so X lies on this circle. Since AB_C is also a diameter we have $\angle AXB_C = 90°$. Since $\angle C_AXB = 90°$ the point X is also on the circumcircle of AC_AC_BB and so $\angle AXC_B = 90°$. Hence X also lies on B_CC_B.

4. By the proof of question 3, AX is the common chord of the circumcircles of the squares with centres V_B and V_C, and hence it is perpendicular to the line of centres V_BV_C. It follows by theorem 12.2 that AX passes through the outer Vecten point V_o, and so this is the perspector of $\triangle ABC$ and $\triangle XYZ$.

5. Rotate $\triangle B_AAB$ through $90°$ about V_B to $\triangle ACT$, noting that CT is perpendicular to AB and equal to it in length (see the figure).

Appendix B: Solutions to the exercises

Exercise 12a question 5

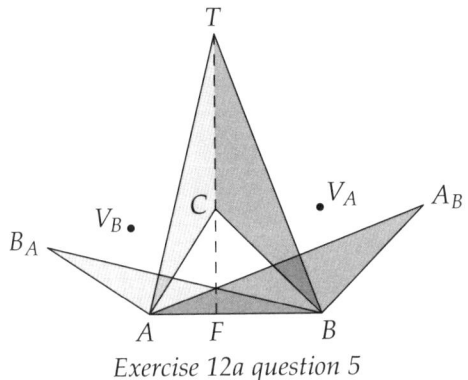

Now rotate $\triangle ABA_B$ clockwise through $90°$ about V_A. The image will be $\triangle TCB$.

Now note that TF, AA_B and BB_A are altitudes of $\triangle TAB$, and hence concurrent.

6. Let M be the midpoint of $A_B B_A$ and X and Y be the feet of the perpendiculars from B_A and A_B to AB (see the figure).

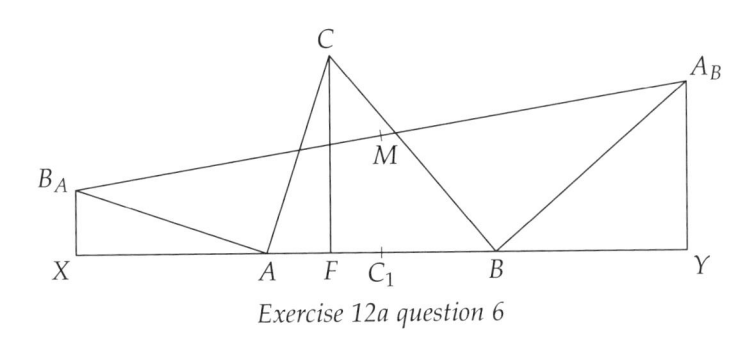

Exercise 12a question 6

Then $BY = CF = AX$, $A_B Y = BF$ and $B_A X = AF$, so C_1 is the midpoint of XY and MC_1 is perpendicular to AB.

Also $MC_1 = \frac{1}{2}(B_A X + A_B Y) = \frac{1}{2}(AF + FB) = \frac{1}{2}AB$, so the result follows.

Exercise 12b

1. This is immediate from theorem 12.7; the perspector is the orthocentre H.

2. This follows from the fact that a triangle is a flank of its own flank; the perspector is the centroid G.

3. Note that O_A is the midpoint of the segment AA' in question 1 of exercise 12a. It follows that the perspector is the symmedian point K. In fact, the two triangles are homothetic.

4. This follows from the fact that a triangle is a flank of its own flank; the perspector is the circumcentre O. However, the two triangles are not necessarily homothetic.

5. This is immediate from the fact that the internal angle bisectors of $\triangle ABC$ are also angle bisectors of the flanks. Hence the perspector is the incentre I.

Exercise 12c

1. (See the figure.)

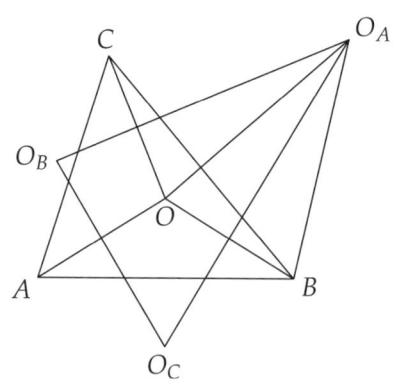

Exercise 12c question 1

It is enough to note that $\angle OBO_A = \angle O_A OB = \angle A$ and so $\angle CBO_A = \angle A - (90° - \angle A) = 2\angle A - 90°$.

Hence the result follows from lemma 12.8.

2. Let $\triangle A_1B_1C_1$ be the medial triangle, let the median AA_1 meet C_1B_1 at A_2, and let G' be the point on AA^* such that GG' is parallel to BC and C_1B_1 (see the figure).

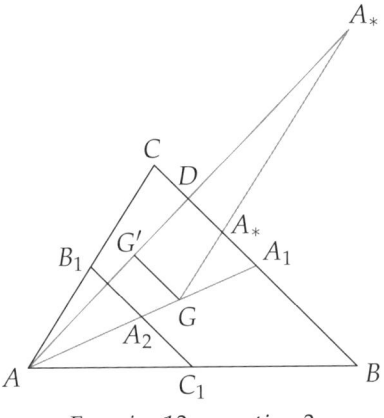

Exercise 12c question 2

Then
$$\frac{GA_*}{A_*A^*} = \frac{G'D}{DA^*} = \frac{G'D}{AD} = \frac{GA_1}{AA_1} = \frac{1}{3},$$
and so the result follows.

3. Consider the enlargement ϕ, with centre Φ_1, which takes $\triangle DEF$ to $\triangle T_A T_B T_C$. This maps $N = O \triangle DEF$ to $O_T = O \triangle T_A T_B T_C$ and $H = I \triangle DEF$ to $O = I \triangle T_A T_B T_C$, so

$$\frac{\Phi_1 O_T}{\Phi_1 N} = \frac{\Phi_1 O}{\Phi_1 H}$$
$$= \frac{\Phi_1 O_T - \Phi_1 O}{\Phi_1 N - \Phi_1 H}$$
$$= \frac{OO_T}{HN}$$
$$= -\frac{OO_T}{ON},$$

as required.

4. Denote the inradius of the orthic triangle by ρ and the inradius of the Kosnita triangle by r_H.

The homothecy α maps the incircle of $\triangle DEF$ to that of $\triangle T_A T_B T_C$, which is the circumcircle of $\triangle ABC$, so $r_H = \frac{1}{2}R$.

The homothecy λ maps the incircle of $\triangle DEF$ to that of $\triangle O_A O_B O_C$, so
$$\frac{\Lambda_1 H}{\Lambda_1 O} = \frac{\rho}{r_H}.$$

The homothecy ϕ maps the incircle of $\triangle DEF$ to the circumcircle of $\triangle ABC$, so
$$\frac{\Phi_1 H}{\Phi_1 O} = \frac{\rho}{R}.$$

Hence we have
$$\frac{\Lambda_1 H}{\Lambda_1 O} = 2\frac{\Phi_1 H}{\Phi_1 O}.$$

After a little algebraic manipulation, we obtain
$$\frac{\Lambda_1 \Phi_1}{\Lambda_1 H} = -\frac{\Lambda_1 O}{OH},$$

which is the required result.

Appendix B: Solutions to the exercises

Exercise 13a

In this exercise, it is sufficient to prove that $\triangle ABC$ is similar to the pedal triangle of P (in some orientation) since, by theorem 13.1, it is then similar to the circumcevian triangle as well. But similar triangles which have the same circumradius are in fact congruent.

We first prove a result for the general configuration.

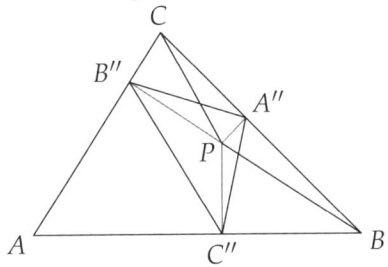

Using cyclic quadrilaterals, we see that

$$\angle C''A''B'' = \angle C''A''P + \angle PA''B''$$
$$= \angle C''BP + \angle PCB''$$
$$= \angle CBP + \angle PCB$$
$$= \angle CPB - \angle CAB.$$

1. If now $\angle C''A''B'' = \angle CAB$, we have $\angle CPB = 2\angle A$, and similarly $\angle APC = 2\angle B$ and $\angle BPA = 2\angle C$ (see the figure).

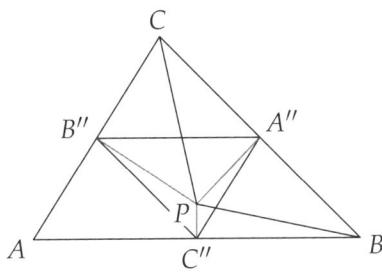

Exercise 13a question 1

As a result, P is the circumcentre of $\triangle ABC$. This argument is clearly reversible, so this is a necessary and sufficient condition.

2. Now we want $\angle C''A''B'' = \angle CAB$ as before, so $\angle CPB = 2\angle A$ and P lies on the circumcircle of $\triangle BOC$ (see the figure).

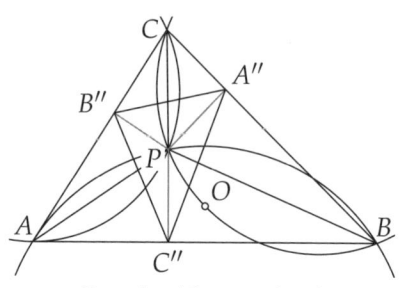

Exercise 13a question 2

Note that, since $PB''AC''$ is cyclic, $\angle PAB = \angle PAC'' = \angle PB''C''$ and, since $PA''CB''$ is cyclic, $\angle A''B''P = \angle A''CP = \angle BCP$. It follows that $A''B''C'' = \angle PAB + \angle BCP$. Hence the requirement that $\angle A''B''C'' = \angle ACB$ is equivalent to $\angle PAB + \angle BCP = \angle PCA + \angle BCP$ and so to $\angle PAB = \angle PCA$. This implies that P lies on the circle through C which is tangential to AB at A. By the same argument, P is also on the circle through B tangential to CA at A. This determines the point uniquely.

3. Now, by the same argument as in question 2, repeated, we want $\angle PAB = \angle PBC = \angle PCA$, and so P is the intersection of three circles (see the figure).

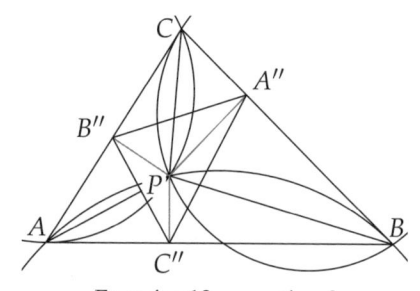

Exercise 13a question 3

One circle is through A and tangential to BC at B, the second is through B and tangential to CA at C and the third is through C and tangential to AB at A.

4. This is the same configuration as in question 2, with the vertices permuted. Hence P lies on the circumcircle of $\triangle AOB$, the circle

through B tangential to CA at C and the circle through A tangential to BC at C.

5. This is the configuration of question 3 reversed. P lies on circles through A tangential to BC at C, through B tangential to CA at A and through C tangential to BC at B.

6. This is like question 2, and this time P lies on the circumcircle of $\triangle COA$, the circle through C tangential to AB at B and the circle through A tangential to BC at B.

Exercise 13b

1. Let $\Lambda_1 A$ meet EF at X and $E'F'$ at Y, and let $E'F'$ meet CA at Z (see the figure).

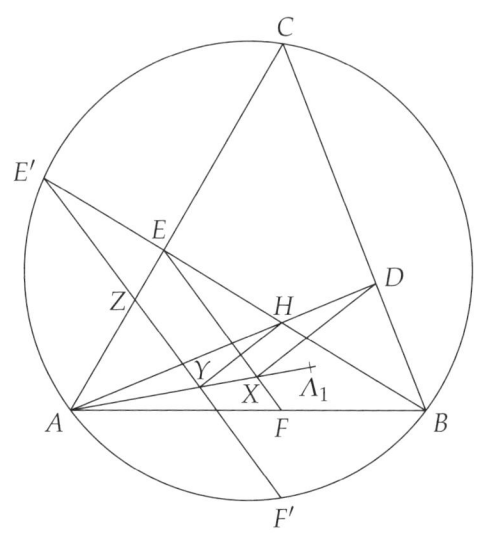

Exercise 13b question 1

By corollary 13.3, Y is on the orthic triangle of $\triangle D'E'F'$ and so $\angle HYF' = 90°$.

By similar triangles,
$$\frac{AX}{AY} = \frac{AE}{AZ} = \frac{HE \tan C}{HE \tan C - EE' \cot B},$$

but by theorem 2.17, $HE = EE'$, so
$$\frac{AX}{AY} = \frac{\sin B \sin C}{\sin B \sin C - \cos B \cos C} = \frac{\sin B \sin C}{\cos A}.$$
But we also have
$$\frac{AD}{AH} = \frac{c \sin B}{c \cos A \operatorname{cosec} C} = \frac{\sin B \sin C}{\cos A},$$
and so
$$\frac{AX}{AD} = \frac{AY}{AH}.$$

It follows that $\triangle AYH$ is similar to $\triangle AXD$, and hence DX is perpendicular to EF. By symmetry, the same is true beginning with E and F instead of D, so the result follows.

2. The OoI triangle is denoted by $\triangle D_I E_I F_I$ (see the figure).

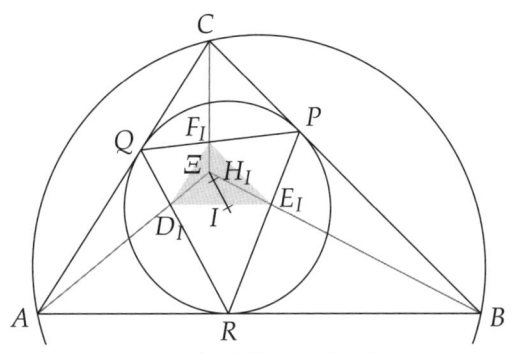

Exercise 13b question 2

If we think in terms of $\triangle PQR$, then $\triangle ABC$ is its tangential triangle and $\triangle D_I E_I F_I$ is its orthic triangle. Hence, by theorem 12.15 on page 167, these triangles are homothetic.

The homothetic centre Ξ lies on the Euler line of $\triangle PQR$, and this includes $O_{\triangle PQR} = I$ and $H_{\triangle PQR}$, which is denoted by H_I in the diagram.

3. This is immediate from the fact that both triangles are homothetic to $\triangle ABC$. Hence, by theorem 10.9 on page 141, the three homothetic centres are collinear.

4. The tangential triangle of the intouch triangle $\triangle PQR$ is the reference triangle $\triangle ABC$, and so, by theorem 12.20 on page 168, the

Appendix B: Solutions to the exercises 467

circumcentre of $\triangle ABC$ is on the Euler line of $\triangle PQR$.

But exactly the same is true for the three extouch triangles, so all four Euler lines pass through O. They are, of course, OI, OI_A, OI_B and OI_C.

Another way of looking at this is to think of the incentre I as the orthocentre of the excentral triangle $\triangle I_A I_B I_C$ and the circumcentre O as its nine-point centre (see the figure).

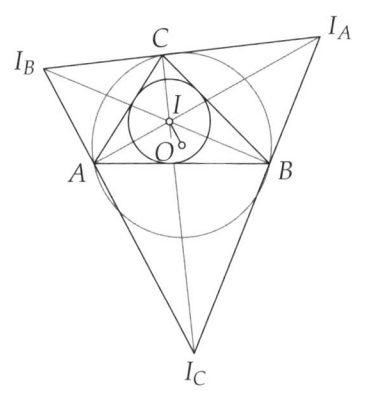

Exercise 13b question 4

5. By theorem 9.13 on page 120, the quadrilateral $HF_B F_A F_C$ is cyclic (see the figure).

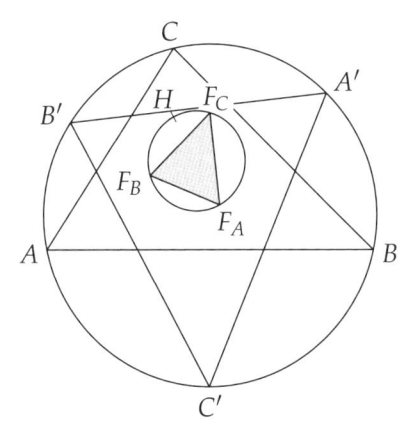

Exercise 13b question 5

Hence $\angle F_A H F_B = \angle F_A F_C F_B$. But, also from the proof of theorem 9.13, $F_A \parallel B'C'$ and $F_B H \parallel A'C'$, and so $\angle F_A H F_B = \angle A'C'B'$. By symmetry, the result follows.

Appendix B: Solutions to the exercises

Exercise 14a

1. Using the notation in the proof of theorem 14.1, we have, from the sine rule on $\triangle BFD$ and $\triangle BCD$, and also the fact that $\angle PFD = 120° - \frac{1}{3}\angle A$,
$$\frac{DF}{\sin \frac{1}{3}B} = \frac{BD}{\sin(120° - \frac{1}{3}A)}$$
and
$$\frac{BD}{\sin \frac{1}{3}C} = \frac{a}{\sin(\frac{1}{3}B + \frac{1}{3}C)} = \frac{2R}{\sin A}$$
so the result will follow if we can show that, writing $A = 3\alpha$,
$$\sin 3\alpha = 4 \sin \alpha \sin(60° - \alpha) \sin(120° - \alpha).$$
But by expanding the left-hand side in the form $\sin(\alpha + 2\alpha)$ and using a 'product formula' for the last two terms on the right-hand side, we may show these are both equal to $\sin \alpha (1 + 2 \cos 2\alpha)$.

2. From the proof of theorem 14.1, PD is the angle bisector of $\angle FDE$ (see the figure), so the segments PD, QE and RF concur at M_1, the incentre of $\triangle DEF$.

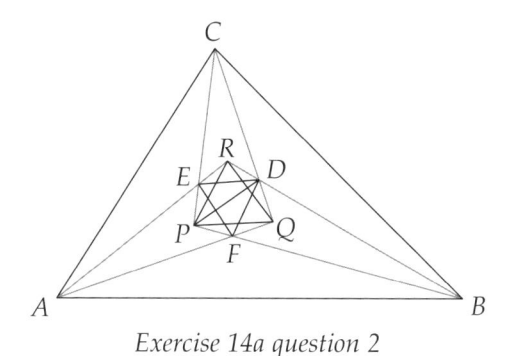

Exercise 14a question 2

3. Since M_1 is the circumcentre of the equilateral triangle $\triangle DEF$, all the angles around it are $60°$ (see the figure).
So
$$\angle PM_1R = \angle RM_1Q = \angle QM_1P.$$
This makes M_1 the first isogonic centre of $\triangle PQR$.

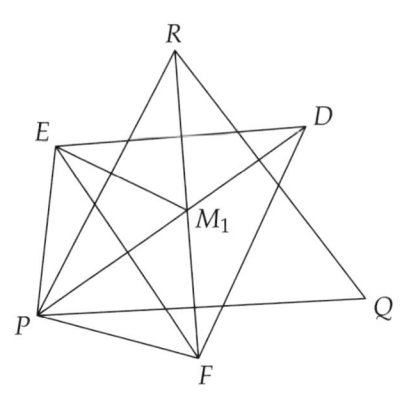

Exercise 14a question 3

4. Note that AF and AR are isogonally conjugate lines, as are BF and BR; it follows that F and R are isogonally conjugate as points. Hence CF and CR are isogonally conjugate lines, and similarly so are AD and AP and also BE and BQ. But by theorem 14.3, AD, BE and CF are concurrent, so it follows that AP, BQ and CR are also concurrent, and the perspectors of $\triangle PQR$ and $\triangle DEF$ are isogonally conjugate as points.

Exercise 14b

1. The proof is almost exactly that of theorems 14.1 and 14.7, with the following modifications (see the figure).
   The point D^{**} is the excentre of $\triangle P^{**}BC$. In the calculation, we have $\angle BCP^{**} = 60° - \frac{2}{3}\angle C$ and $\angle P^{**}BC = 60° - \frac{2}{3}\angle B$.
   Thus $\angle BP^{**}C = 60° + \frac{2}{3}(\angle B + \angle C)$ and $P^{**}F^{**}E^{**} = 60° - \frac{1}{3}(\angle B + \angle C) = \frac{1}{3}\angle A$. It follows that $\angle P^{**}F^{**}D^{**} = 60° - \frac{1}{3}\angle A = \angle P^{**}F^{**}Y$. Hence $\angle YF^{**}E^{**} = 60° - \frac{2}{3}\angle A = \angle F^{**}E^{**}X$.
   We now construct Z and show that it is the centre of a circle through A, Y, F^{**}, E^{**} and X and the proof is concluded in exactly the same way.

2. The angle between BC and $E^{**}F^{**}$ is $\frac{1}{3}\angle A - (60° - \frac{2}{3}\angle B) = \frac{1}{3}(\angle B - \angle C)$. So, by corollary 14.2, FE and $F^{**}E^{**}$ are parallel, with analogous results for the other two pairs of sides.

Appendix B: Solutions to the exercises 471

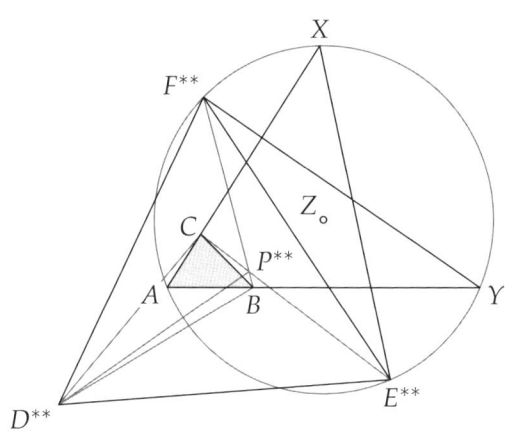

Exercise 14b question 1

Exercise 15a

1. This is simply theorem 4.10 on page 49 applied to $\triangle A'AX$ and the transversal $B'BY$. In other words, O is the Miquel point of the complete quadrilateral $AA'B'B$. Note that this is also saying that AA' and BB' are corresponding segments under the same spiral similarity, which is hardly surprising.

2. The fixed point A is the centre of a spiral similarity for which BC and $B'C'$ are corresponding segments, so, by the result of question 1, so are CC' and BB' (see the figure). But the direction of BB' is fixed. It follows that the direction of CC' is also fixed.

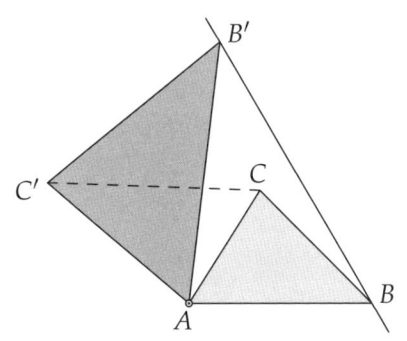

Exercise 15a question 2

3. First we prove this using elementary arguments.

    By the alternate segment theorem, $\angle CAD = \angle ABD$. Let BD meet the circumcircle again at F (see the figure). Now $\angle ABD = \angle ABF = \angle AEF$, so arc CE = arc AF. Hence arc FE = arc AC and so $EF = AC$.

    By the alternate segment theorem again, $\angle BAD = \angle ACD$, so $\angle ADC = \angle ADB = \angle FDE$, and hence $\triangle FDE \cong \triangle CDA$. It follows that $DE = DA$.

    However, the problem is actually about spiral similarities: D is the centre of similitude of a similarity which maps AB to AC, so $\triangle ABD$ is similar to $\triangle CAD$. Hence $\angle FED = \angle FBA = \angle CAD$ and $\angle DFE = \angle BAE = \angle ACD$, so $\triangle FED$ is similar to $\triangle CAD$. But also $CD = FD$ since the chords subtend equal angles, so the triangles are congruent and $DE = DA$.

Appendix B: Solutions to the exercises

Exercise 15a question 3

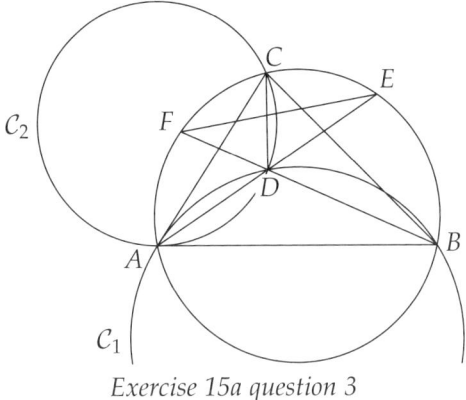

4. The perpendicular distances of D from AB and AC are in the ratio $c : b$ of their lengths, so by theorem 8.1 on page 100 it follows that AD is a symmedian.

Exercise 15b

1. Let K be the perspector of $\triangle DEF$ and $\triangle DYX$, and let L be the centre of similitude of $\triangle AFE$ and $\triangle DXY$. By theorems 15.4 and 15.6, both these points lie on the circle of similitude, which is the nine-point circle (see the figure).

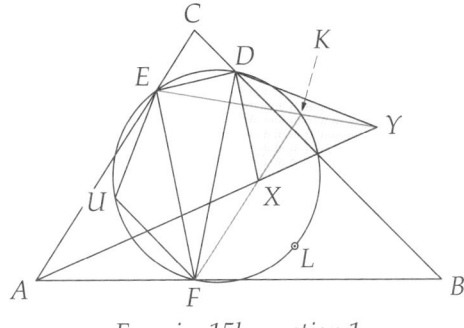

Exercise 15b question 1

Hence the points D, E, U, F, L and K are concyclic. Now $\angle LFU = 180° - \angle LDU = 180° - \angle LDA = 180° - \angle LXF$ since DX and AF

are corresponding segments, and now $180° - \angle LXF = \angle LXK$.

It follows that FU and XK are corresponding lines. Similarly, so are EU and YK. Hence U and K are corresponding points. But U is the circumcentre of $\triangle AFE$, so K is the circumcentre of $\triangle DXY$.

2. Note first that $\angle DXY = \angle DCA$, so X is on the cyclic quadrilateral $AFDC$ (see the figure). Hence $\angle DFX = \angle DAX = (90° - \angle B) - (90° - \angle C) = \angle C - \angle B$.

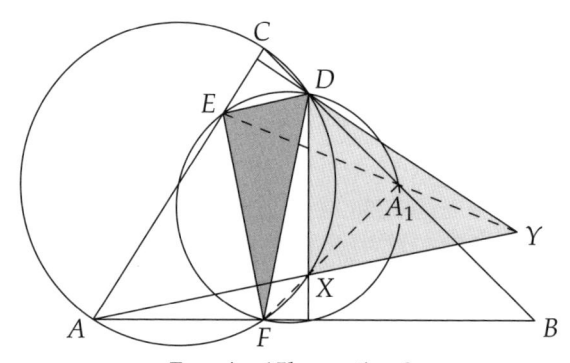

Exercise 15b question 2

Now A_1 is the centre of the circumcircle of $\triangle BCE$, so $A_1E = A_1C$ and so, from the nine-point circle, $\angle DFA_1 = \angle DEA_1 = \angle A_1EC - \angle DEC = \angle C - \angle B$.

It follows that A_1 lies on FX, and by a similar argument it lies on EY, as required.

Appendix B: Solutions to the exercises

Exercise 16a

1. Let $\triangle A'B'C'$ be $\oslash \Omega_1$ (see the figure).

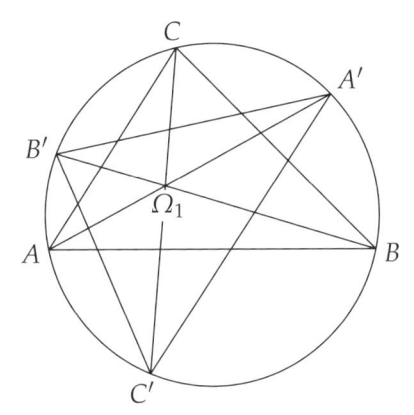

Exercise 16a question 1

Then $\angle A'C'C = \angle A'AC$ and $\angle CC'B' = \angle CBB' = \omega = \angle BAA'$, and so $\angle A'C'B' = \angle BAC$. With two similar results, this shows that $\triangle C'A'B'$ is congruent to $\triangle ABC$ and also that $\Omega_1 = \Omega_2 \triangle C'A'B'$. Also $\angle C'OA = 2\omega$, so $\triangle ABC$ is taken to $\triangle C'A'B'$ by a rotation of 2ω about O. Since this also takes Ω_2 to Ω_1, the result follows.

2. Let $\triangle XYZ$ be the pedal triangle of Ω_1 (see the figure).

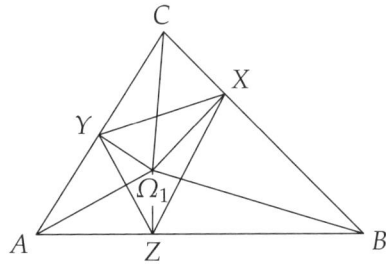

Exercise 16a question 2

Note that $\angle \Omega_1 YZ = \angle \Omega_1 AZ$, $\angle \Omega_1 ZX = \angle \Omega_1 BX$ and $\angle \Omega_1 XY = \angle \Omega_1 CY$, but each of these angles is equal to ω, so Ω_1 is the first Brocard point of $\triangle XYZ$.

3. Let $t = \tan A$. Then, by theorem 16.4 and the AM-GM inequality, $\cot \omega = t + \frac{1}{t} \geq 2$, with equality if, and only if, $t = 1$. Hence $\omega \leq \tan^{-1}\left(\frac{1}{2}\right)$, with equality when the triangle is isosceles.

4. First note that
$$\cot A + \cot B = \frac{c}{h_c}.$$
This is easy to prove, although it is necessary to consider separately the cases when $\angle C$ is acute and obtuse. But
$$h_c = \frac{2\Delta}{c},$$
so
$$\cot A + \cot B = \frac{c^2}{2\Delta},$$
and now the result follows from adding three such equations.

5. There are many ways of proving this, but a neat approach uses the inequality
$$\sin A \sin B \sin C \leq \frac{3\sqrt{3}}{8},$$
with equality if, and only if, $A = B = C = 60°$, which can be found in [4, result 9.8(ii)]. This can be rewritten, using the sine rule, as $abc \leq 3\sqrt{3}R^3$, and this can be rearranged to give
$$\sqrt[3]{a^2b^2c^2} \geq \frac{abc}{R\sqrt{3}}.$$
Now we use the AM-GM inequality to show that
$$a^2 + b^2 + c^2 \geq 3\sqrt[3]{a^2b^2c^2},$$
with equality if, and only if, $a = b = c$.

Putting these together, we have
$$a^2 + b^2 + c^2 \geq \frac{abc\sqrt{3}}{R},$$
and so, using theorem 16.5,
$$\cot \omega \geq \frac{abc\sqrt{3}}{4R\Delta}.$$
But $4R\Delta = abc$, so this gives $\cot \omega \geq \sqrt{3}$ and so $\omega \leq 30°$. This bound is achieved when the conditions above are met, which is

Appendix B: Solutions to the exercises

when $\triangle ABC$ is equilateral. The two Brocard points coincide at the circumcentre.

6. From the sine rule
$$\frac{C\Omega_A}{B\Omega_A} = \frac{b\sin(A-\omega)}{c\sin\omega}$$
(see the figure).

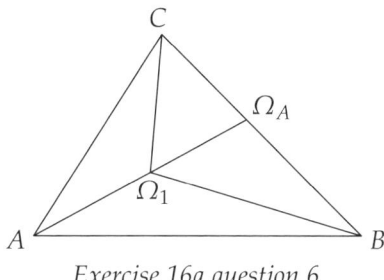

Exercise 16a question 6

But
$$\begin{aligned}
\frac{\sin(A-\omega)}{\sin\omega} &= \sin A \cot\omega - \cos A \\
&= \sin A(\cot A + \cot B + \cot C) - \cos A \\
&= \sin A(\cot B + \cot C) \\
&= \frac{a\sin A}{h_A} \\
&= \frac{a^2}{bc}
\end{aligned}$$
and the result now follows.

7. This is immediate from corollary 8.2 on page 100, the result of question 6 and Ceva's theorem.

8. The points of concurrency in this and question 7 are isogonal conjugates.

Exercise 16b

1. The area of $\triangle ABC$ is $\frac{1}{4}a^2 \tan\omega$, so the sum of the areas of all three triangles is $\frac{1}{4}(a^2+b^2+c^2)\tan\omega$. By theorem 16.5, this is Δ.

2. This is immediate from the fact that $\angle AP^*O = 90°$.

3. The figure shows the Euler line of $\triangle ABC$, with points O, G and N, and the Brocard diameter OLK.

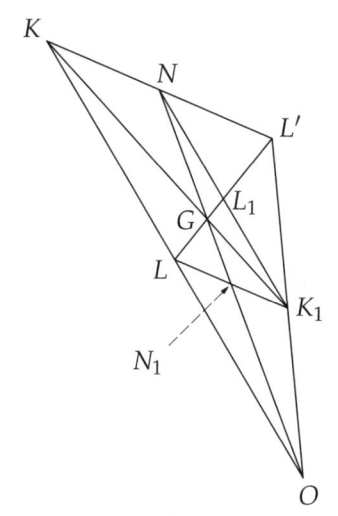

Exercise 16b question 3

The enlargement θ, with centre G and scale factor $-\frac{1}{2}$, takes O to N, N to N_1, the medial point, K to K_1, the symmedian point of the medial triangle, and L to L_1, the Brocard centre of the medial triangle.

Then NK_1 is parallel to KO and half its length, so OK_1 and KN meet at a point L', with N and K the midpoints of KL' and OL'. Now G is the centroid of $\triangle OKL'$, and so L, G, L_1 and L' are collinear. Also L, N_1 and K_1 are collinear, with midpoint N_1, and N, L_1 and K_1 are collinear, with midpoint L_1. In addition to proving everything required, we have also shown that L' is the symmedian point of the anticomplementary triangle of $\triangle ABC$.

Exercise 16c

1. This is immediate from theorem 15.11 on page 214, because A', B' and C' are corresponding points.

Appendix B: Solutions to the exercises

2. This follows from theorem 15.4 on page 208. When α is the Brocard angle, $\triangle D_1 D_2 D_3$ is degenerate and becomes the first Brocard point.

3. This follows from the fact that the three Euler lines are concurrent on the Brocard circle.

4. By corollary 16.14, G is the centroid of $\triangle PQR$. The enlargement θ takes P to P_1 and O to N (see the figure).

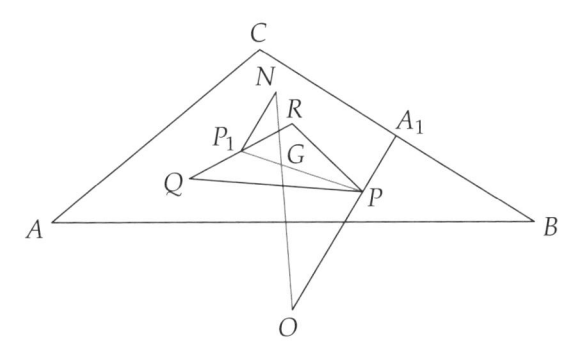

Exercise 16c question 4

Hence $P_1 N$ is parallel to OP, which, by construction, is perpendicular to BC. The same argument works for Q_1 and R_1.

5. As shown in section 7.1 (see page 82), the isogonal conjugate of any point on the circumcircle, such as Σ, is at infinity since the lines isogonal to ΣA, ΣB and ΣC are parallel. The direction of these lines is indicated by BX in the figure, and $\angle XBA = \angle CB\Sigma$.

But $B\Sigma \parallel PR$ and $BC \parallel PK$ by theorem 16.8, so $\angle CB\Sigma = \angle RPK = \angle ROK$.

The Simson line of Σ is its degenerate pedal triangle, which, by theorem 7.9 on page 89, is perpendicular to BX. However, $OR \perp AB$, by the definition of the Brocard triangle, so $OK \perp BX$, and the result follows. As the Tarry point is the diametric opposite of the Steiner point, their Simson lines are perpendicular.

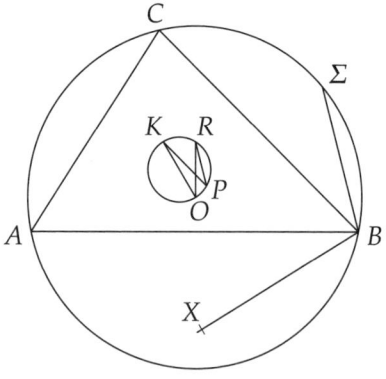

Exercise 16c question 5

Exercise 17a

1. In the proof of theorem 17.1, we showed that $D_1E_2F_1F_2$ is a cyclic trapezium (see the figure).

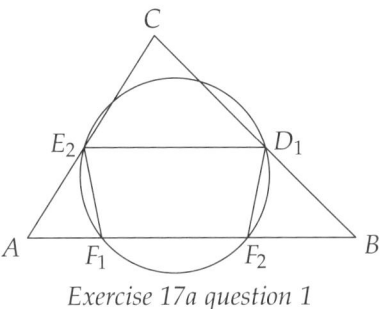

Exercise 17a question 1

Hence the base angles are equal and then the non-parallel sides are also equal.

2. Note that $\angle F_1E_1D_1 = \angle F_1D_2D_1 = \angle C$, and similar results for the other angles.

3. This follows from the fact that $R_1Q_2P_2P_1$ is a rectangle.

4. Since R_1P_2 is a diameter of the second Lemoine circle (see the figure), $\angle R_1P_1P_2 = 90°$, and, since AR_1P_2C is cyclic, $\angle R_1P_2P_1 = \angle A$.

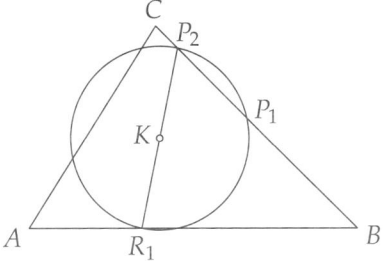

Exercise 17a question 4

Hence $P_1P_2 = 2R' \cos A$, where R' is the radius of the Lemoine circle.

5. This follows from the fact that Q_1R_1, R_1P_1 and P_1Q_1 are perpendicular to AB, BC and CA, with similar results for the other triangle.

6. By theorem 9.1 on page 113, Γ is the symmedian point of the intouch triangle $\triangle PQR$ (see the figure).

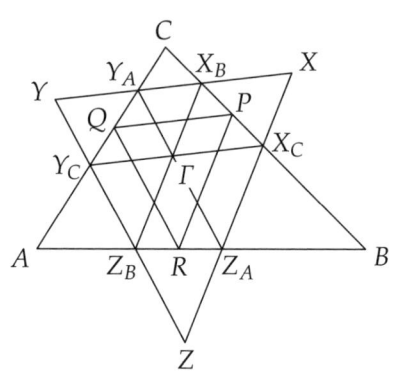

Exercise 17a question 6

The triangles $\triangle PQR$ and $\triangle XYZ$ are homothetic with centre of similitude Γ, so this is also the symmedian point of $\triangle XYZ$.

The Adams circle of $\triangle ABC$ is that through the six points X_C, X_B, Y_A, Y_B, Z_C and Z_A. But the first Lemoine circle of $\triangle XYZ$ is precisely this, since, for example, $Y_A Z_A$ is parallel to YZ.

Exercise 17b

1. (a) If $k = 0$, then the triangle $\triangle A'B'C'$ degenerates to K, the points U, V and W are the midpoints of KA, KB and KC and the Tucker circle is the first Lemoine circle. It follows that O^* is the midpoint of KO, as has already been shown in theorem 17.2.
   (b) If $k = 1$, then A', B' and C' coincide with A, B and C and also with U, V and W, and the Tucker circle is the circumcircle with centre O.
   (c) If $k = -1$, then the points U, V and W coincide with K, and the three antiparallels E_2F_1, F_2D_1 and D_2E_1 all pass through K. The Tucker circle is the second Lemoine circle, with centre K.

2. We have
$$\frac{KO^*}{KO} = \frac{KU}{KA} = \frac{k+1}{2}$$

Appendix B: Solutions to the exercises 483

by simple ratio calculations. Hence if $0 \leq \frac{KO^*}{KO} \leq 1$, it follows that $-1 \leq k \leq 1$. If $k > 1$, then O^* lies on KO produced, and if $k < -1$, it lies on OK produced.

3. Let the circumcentre of $\triangle A'B'C'$ be O'. Then by similar triangles
$$\frac{O'O^*}{O'O} = \frac{A'U}{A'A} = \tfrac{1}{2}.$$

4. Since both $T_B T_C$ and, by lemma 17.15, $B''C''$ are perpendicular to OA, the two triangles are homothetic (see the figure).

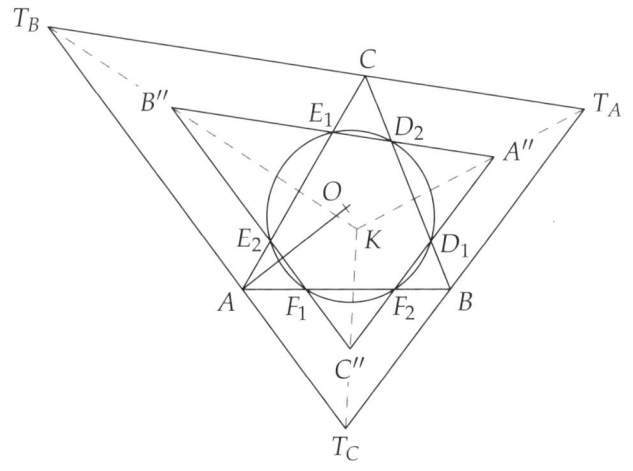

Exercise 17b question 4

By theorem 8.4 on page 101, T_A lies on the symmedian AK. By corollary 17.12, the antiparallels D_1F_2 and E_1D_2 are equal, so by the result of theorem 8.8 on page 107, their intersection A'' also lies on AK.

It follows that K is the homothetic centre.

5. Let E_1F_2 meet DF and DE at M and N (see the figure).
Since $AEHF$ and AE_1DF_1 are similar figures, F_2E_1 is parallel to FE. Hence $\angle MF_2F = \angle EFA = \angle C = \angle MFF_2$ and so $MF = MF_2$. But $\angle DF_2F = 90°$, so this implies that M is the midpoint of DF. Similarly N is the midpoint of DE.

6. By theorem 17.16, the centre of the Taylor circle (as a Tucker centre) lies on the Brocard diameter KO. But by corollary 17.17, it is also

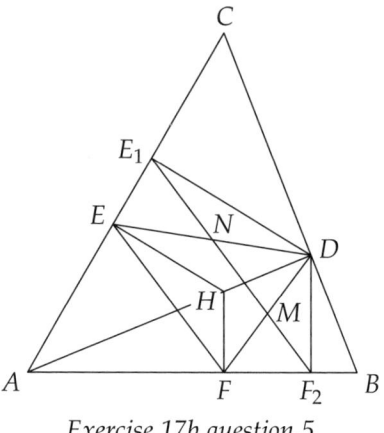

Exercise 17b question 5

the incentre of the triangle formed by D_1E_2, E_1F_2 and F_1D_2. Hence it is equidistant from them, and therefore it is also the incentre of the medial triangle of $\triangle DEF$. But this is its Spieker centre.

Appendix B: Solutions to the exercises

Exercise 18a

1. Both parts are immediate from the definition.
2. (a) It is the tangent at that point.
   (b) It is the line at infinity.
3. It is the point at infinity in the direction perpendicular to the diameter.
4. Let the tangents at X and Y meet at Q (see the figure).

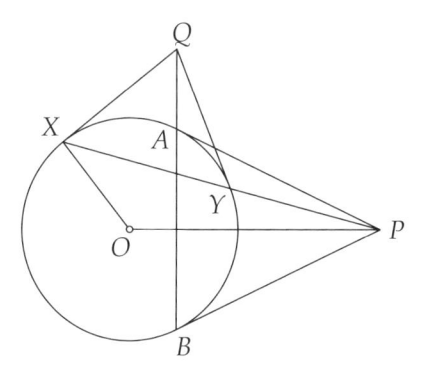

Exercise 18a question 4

Now P lies on the polar of Q, so by theorem 18.4, Q lies on the polar of P, which is AB.

If P lies on the circle, AB becomes the tangent at P, and Y coincides with P, so YQ is also the tangent at P, and the result becomes trivial.

5. (See the figure.).

Note that Q is on the polar of P, so, by theorem 18.4, P is on the polar of Q. Also Q is on the polar of T, so T is on the polar of Q. But P and Q are inverse points, so the polar of Q is the perpendicular to OP at P.

6. Let the two polars meet at R (see the figure).

Then, by theorem 18.4, both P and Q are on the polar of R. Hence PQ is the polar of R.

If p and q are parallel, O lies on PQ, which is a diameter of the circle. So, as in question 4, the pole of PQ lies on the 'line at infinity'.

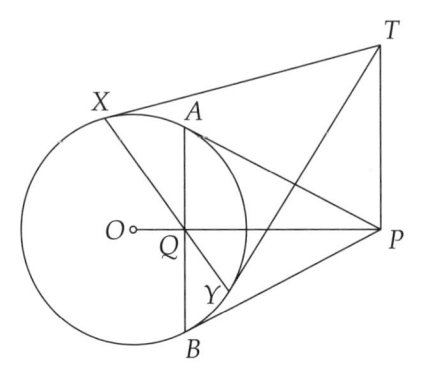

Exercise 18a question 5

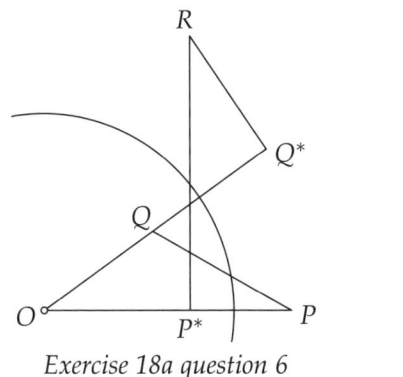

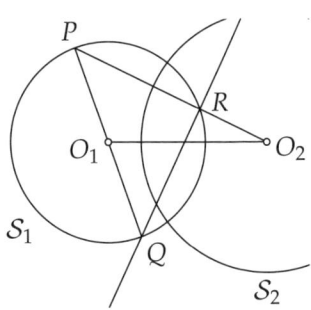

Exercise 18a question 6

Exercise 18a question 7

7. (See the figure.). Because the circles are orthogonal, the tangent to one circle is the radius of the other. Hence, by the tangent-secant theorem, $O_2 R \times O_2 P = r_2^2$, where r_2 is the radius of the circle with centre O_2.

So P and R are inverse with respect to this circle. But $\angle PRQ = 90°$ since PQ is a diameter, and hence the result follows from the definition of polar.

Exercise 18b

1. It is the common tangent.

2. Both these facts are immediate from the fact that the radical axis is perpendicular to the line of centres.

3. (a) It is the perpendicular bisector.
   (b) It is the circumcentre.
   (c) It is the tangent at the point.

4. Let the tangent from P to the circle be PT (see the figure).

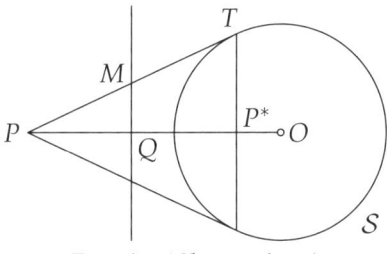

Exercise 18b question 4

Then the radical axis passes through the midpoint M (since the tangent from M to P is simply MP). But TP^* is the polar of P and it is immediate that Q is the midpoint of PP^*.

5. Since the power is positive, the radical centre lies outside all three circles, and it is the point for which the lengths of the tangents to all three circles are equal. Hence the circle with centre C through the six points of tangency is orthogonal to all three circles. It is unique since the centre of any such circle would be need to have equal power which respect to all three circles.

6. Taking O as the intersection of the radical axis and the line of centres, we have $OO_1^2 - r_1^2 = OO_2^2 - r_2^2$ and so $OO_1^2 - OO_2^2 = r_1^2 - r_2^2 > 0$, so $OO_1 > OO_2$. But also
$$\frac{OO_1 - r_1}{OO_2 - r_2} = \frac{OO_2 + r_2}{OO_1 + r_1} < 1$$
and so $OO_1 - r_1 < OO_2 - r_2$ and the larger circle is closer to the radical axis than the smaller.

7. The point R is the radical centre of the circle and the two point-circles, and hence it lies on the radical axis of the two points, which is their perpendicular bisector.

8. Let O be the intersection of the radical axis with O_1O_2 (see the figure).

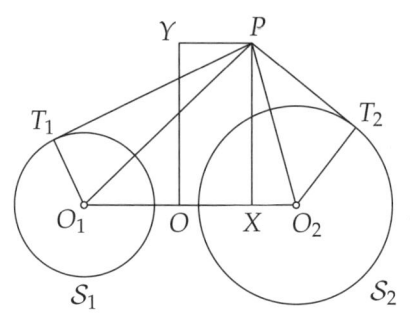

Exercise 18b question 8

Let the feet of the perpendiculars from P to the radical axis and line of centres be Y and X, and let the points of contact of tangents be T_1 and T_2. Then

$$PT_1^2 - PT_2^2 = PO_1^2 - PO_2^2 - r_1^2 + r_2^2$$
$$= XO_1^2 - XO_2^2 - r_1^2 + r_2^2$$
$$= O_1O_2(XO_1 - XO_2) - r_1^2 + r_2^2$$
$$= O_1O_2(2XO + OO_1 - OO_2) - r_1^2 + r_2^2.$$

But

$$OO_1^2 - r_1^2 = OO_2^2 - r_2^2,$$

so

$$r_2^2 - r_1^2 = OO_2^2 - OO_1^2$$
$$= O_1O_2(OO_2 - OO_1)$$

and hence

$$PT_1^2 - PT_2^2 = 2O_1O_2 \times PY,$$

as required.

9. The common tangents at the points of contact are the three radical axes, which are concurrent in the radical centre.

10. Using the fact that the angle in a semicircle is a right angle, the radical axes are the altitudes and the radical centre is the orthocentre. There is no need for the diameters to be sides of $\triangle ABC$; any cevians

AX, BY and CZ (not necessarily concurrent) would do as well (so long as they do not share the same radical axis). Note that the common power is given by theorem 2.16 on page 20 to be $AH \times HD$.

11. Let the circles on diameters AL, BM and CY be $\mathcal{S}_A$, $\mathcal{S}_B$ and $\mathcal{S}_C$. Then, by the previous result, H lies on the radical axes of $\mathcal{S}_B$ and $\mathcal{S}_C$, $\mathcal{S}_C$ and $\mathcal{S}_A$, and $\mathcal{S}_A$ and $\mathcal{S}_B$. But equally well we can consider the original triangle to be $\triangle AMN$ and the transversal to be BCL and conclude that the same three radical axes pass through H_A, the orthocentre of $\triangle AYZ$. By a similar argument, they also pass through H_B and H_C. But these four points are different, so the only conclusion is that the three circles have the same radical axis on which all four orthocentres lie.

12. Let BC and FE meet at X, which lies on the orthic axis of $\triangle ABC$ and $\triangle DEF$ (see the figure).

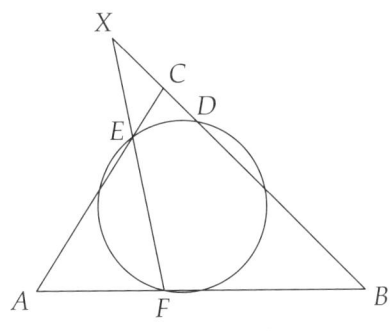

Exercise 18b question 12

Then, since $BCEF$ is cyclic, $XB \times XC = XF \times XE$, so X has the same power with respect to the circumcircle and nine-point circle, and it lies on their radical axis. Since this is true for three such points, the two lines are identical.

13. Note that BC is a common tangent to the incircle and excircle and, from a point on the radical axis, the tangents to both circles are equal in length. It follows that the radical axis passes through the midpoint of PP_A, which, by theorem 2.11 on page 17, is A_1.

14. Since $AU \times AB = AV \times AC$, A lies on the radical axis, and since BC is a common tangent, its midpoint A_1 also lies on it, so the radical axis is the median through A.

15. (a) (See the figure.).

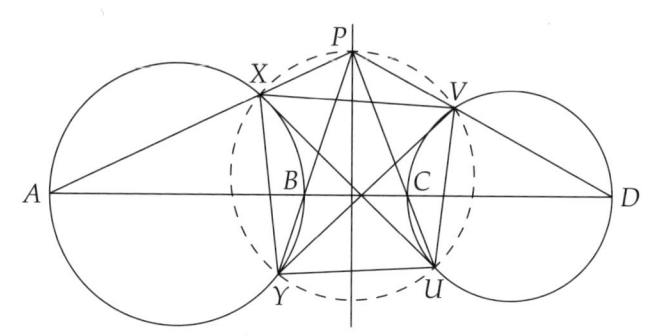

Exercise 18b question 15

Since P is on the radical axis, $PX \times PA = PV \times PD$ and so $ADVX$ is cyclic. Now $\angle PXV = \angle VDA = \angle VDC = \angle VUP$ and so $PXUV$ is cyclic, and by a similar argument so is $PXYV$. Hence $YUVX$ is cyclic.

(b) Since AB is a diameter $\angle BXP = 90°$. Now we have $\angle BXV = 90° - \angle VXP = 90° - \angle VDA = \angle VCD$ and so $BCVX$ is also cyclic. Hence, if XB and VC meet at Q we have $QB \times QX = QC \times QV$, and so Q lies on the radical axis (see the figure).

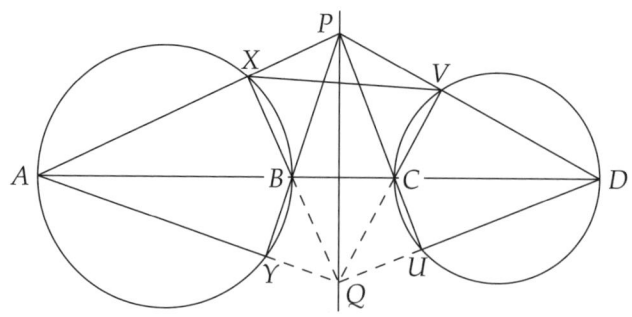

Exercise 18b question 15

But B is the orthocentre of $\triangle APQ$, so Q lies on AY, and similarly on DU.

We now see that $DAYU$ is cyclic. Now $\angle QYU = \angle UCD = \angle UVC = \angle QVU$ and so Q is also on the circumcircle of

Appendix B: Solutions to the exercises 491

PXYUV.

(c) Consider the circumcircles of the three quadrilaterals $ADVX$, $DAYU$ and $YUVX$ (see the figure).

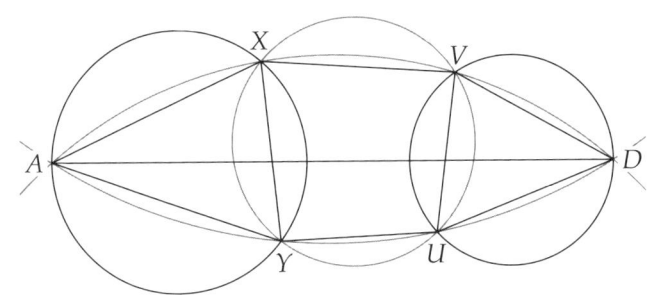

Exercise 18b question 15

The radical axis of $ADVX$ and $DAYU$ is AD, the radical axis of $ADVX$ and $YUVX$ is VX and the radical axis of $DAYU$ and $YUVX$ is YU. Hence these three lines are concurrent at the radical centre of these three circumcircles.

16. Consider the parallel F_2E_1 and the antiparallel R_2Q_1 to BC through K (see the figure).

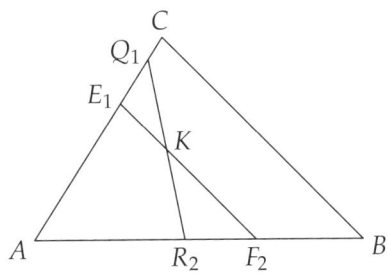

Exercise 18b question 16

The quadrilateral $E_1Q_1F_2R_2$ is cyclic, so by intersecting chords $F_2K \times KE_1 = R_2K \times DQ_1$. Hence K lies on the radical axis of the two circles, which is their common chord. But K is also the centre of the second Lemoine circle, so the common chord is a diameter and bisects its circumference.

17. Let the circle with centre P be $\mathcal{S}_P$, the midpoints of the three segments be X, Y and Z, and the circles with these segments as diam-

eters be S_X, S_Y and S_Z. Then the radical axis of S_P and S_X is BC and that of S_P and S_Y is CA. Hence C lies on the radical axis of S_X and S_Y. But this is perpendicular to the line of centres, so it is the perpendicular from C to XY. Similar results characterise the other two radical axes. Hence by theorem 7.8 on page 88, the radical centre is the isogonal conjugate of P.

18. Consider the circumcircles of $\triangle HD_1D_2$ and $\triangle HE_1E_2$, together with the Taylor circle T (see the figure).

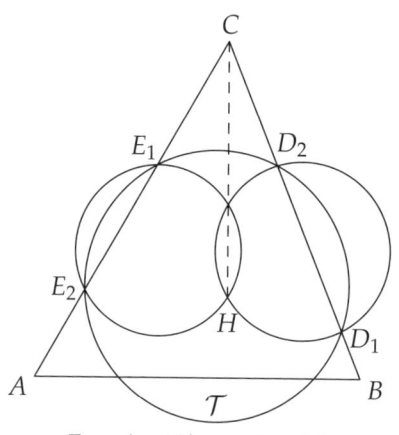

Exercise 18b question 18

The radical axis of the circle HD_1D_2 and T is their common chord BC, and similarly that of HE_1E_2 and T is AC, so C is the radical centre of all three circles. Hence the common chord of the circles HD_1D_2 and HE_1E_2 is HC.

Exercise 18c

1. The locus is the line through L_2 parallel to the radical axis. Let a circle of the system with centre O_1 meet this line at P (see the figure).

Since L_1, X, L_2, Y is a harmonic range, then by theorem 5.19 on page 61, $O_1L_1 \times O_1L_2 = OX^2 = OP^2$. It follows that OP is the tangent to the circumcircle of L_1L_2P, whose centre C is on the radical axis. Hence L_1P is perpendicular to O_1P as required.

Appendix B: Solutions to the exercises

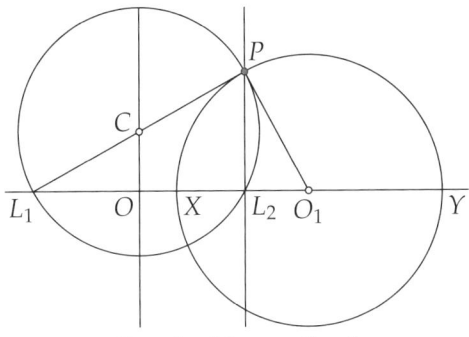

Exercise 18c question 1

2. Let the centres of S_1 and S_2 be O_1 and O_2. Let P be any point which satisfies the condition, and let O be the centre of the circle S through P which is coaxal with them. Let Q be the foot of the perpendicular from P to the radical axis of S_1 and S_2. The power of P with respect to S is zero. Let the powers of P with respect to S_1 and S_2 be π_1 and π_2. Then, by theorem 18.11, $|\pi_1| = 2PQ \times OO_1$ and $|\pi_2| = 2PQ \times OO_2$, and as a result $OO_1 : OO_2$ is constant. Hence O and the circle S are fixed.

In this argument, we should consider OO_1 and OO_2 as directed line segments. If one power is positive and the other negative, then O lies between O_1 and O_2. If the powers are both positive or both negative, then OO_1 and OO_2 are in opposite directions, and O lies outside the segment $O_1 O_2$.

3. Let the circles be S_1 and S_2 with centres O_1 and O_2 and radii r_1 and r_2, and let S be their circle of similitude. Let P be any point on S. Then, by theorem 5.24 on page 64, $O_1 P : O_2 P = r_1 : r_2$. If the powers of P with respect to S_1 and S_2 are π_1 and π_2, then $\pi_1 : \pi_2 = r_1^2 : r_2^2$ and hence by theorem 18.15, S is coaxal with S_1 and S_2. It divides $O_1 O_2$ harmonically because it has diameter $C_i C_e$ and, by theorem 5.22 on page 63, O_1, C_i, O_2, C_e is a harmonic range. In fact, it is possible to prove that this is the only circle with this property.

4. Let the centre of the two circles be O and their radii be r_1 and r_2. Then, if P is a point which satisfies the condition, with ratio $k \neq 1$, then $OP^2 - r_1^2 = k(OP^2 - r_2^2)$ and consequently OP is constant.

Hence the locus is a circle which is concentric with the two circles.
Note that this gives some justification for regarding concentric circles as forming a coaxal system.

Appendix B: Solutions to the exercises

Exercise 19a

1. This is immediate from the definition of an Apollonius circle as a locus.

2. By theorem 6.8 on page 78, $A''B'' = CP \sin C$ and $A''C'' = BP \sin B$ (see the figure).

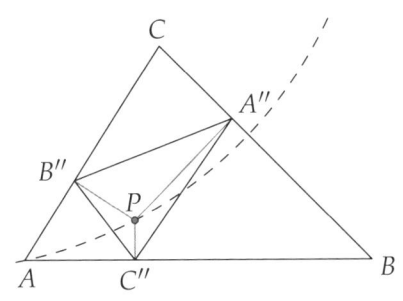

Exercise 19a question 2

Hence

$$A''B'' = A''C'' \Leftrightarrow CP \sin C = BP \sin B \Leftrightarrow \frac{BP}{CP} = \frac{\sin C}{\sin B} = \frac{c}{b},$$

which is the condition for P to lie on the A-Apollonius circle.

Note that it makes perfect sense for P to be an external point of the triangle (see the figure).

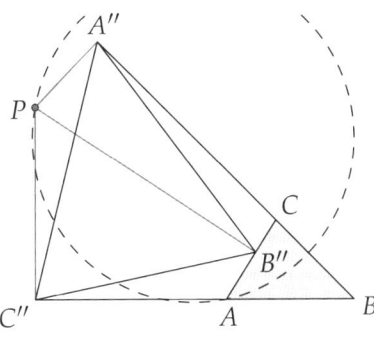

Exercise 19a question 2

3. Let P and Q be inverse points with respect to the A-Apollonius circle (see the figure).

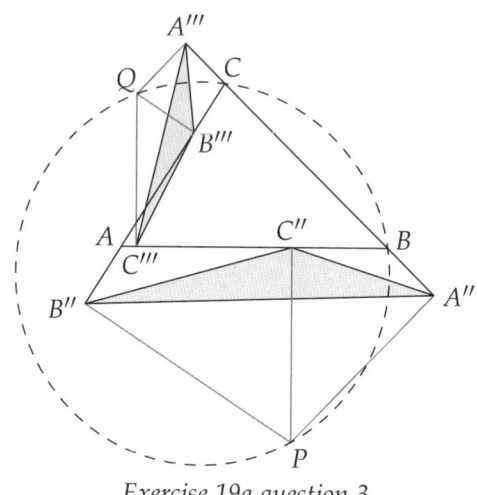

Exercise 19a question 3

If this circle has radius r, $O_A P \times O_A Q = r^2$. But by theorem 19.1, $O_A B \times O_A C = r^2$ and so P, Q, B and C are concyclic. Hence $\angle BPC = \angle BQC$. But $\triangle A''B''C''$ is a Miquel circle of P and so by corollary 4.9 on page 49, $\angle BPC = \angle A + \angle B''A''C''$. A similar argument applies to Q and so we have $\angle B''A''C'' = \angle B'''A'''C'''$. The result in one direction follows, and this argument is reversible.

Exercise 19b

1. Let J_1^* be the isogonal conjugate of J_1. Then, by theorem 7.8 on page 88, $\angle AJ_1^*B + \angle AJ_1B = 180° + \angle C$. But by theorem 6.7 on page 77, we have $\angle AJ_1B = \angle C + \angle C''A''B''$, and by theorem 19.13, $\angle C''A''B'' = 60°$. Putting these together, we have $\angle AJ_1^*B = 120°$, and clearly the same is true for the other angles around J_1^*, so it is the first isogonic point. A similar argument works for J_2.

2. By corollary 19.9, the polar of O with respect to the A-Apollonius circle is the symmedian AK, and, by corollary 19.7, the polar of K with respect to the circumcircle is the Lemoine line. Hence OK is the polar of the intersection of these two lines. But this is the point of intersection of the tangents at J_1 and J_2.

Appendix B: Solutions to the exercises 497

Exercise 20a

1. This is immediate from the fact that the quadrilateral PQQ_lP_l is cyclic.

2. Let XY be a diameter of the circle perpendicular to the line. Then either X or Y can be taken as the centre of inversion. If the line is tangent to the circle, there is only one centre, the point of contact.

3. The centre of inversion can be either of the centres of similitude, and then the radius of the inversion can be calculated from the formula $r^2 = OP \times OP_l$.

4. Let the inverse of O with respect to the circle centre B be O_l; then $BO_l \times BO = R_l^2$. Also let A_l be the inverse of A with respect to $\mathcal{S}$; then $OA_l \times OA = r^2$. Since O is the centre of similitude of the two circles, it follows from corollary 20.5 that

$$\frac{OB}{OA} = \frac{R_l}{R} = \frac{r^2}{|t|} = \frac{|t_l|}{r^2}.$$

Now we have

$$OO_l = |O_lB - OB_l| = \frac{|R_l^2 - OB^2|}{OB} = \frac{|t_l|}{OB} = \frac{r^2}{OA} = OA_l$$

and so $O_l = A_l$ as required.

5. Since $\triangle OQP$ and $\triangle OP_lQ_l$ are similar, we have

$$\frac{P_lQ_l}{QP} = \frac{OP_l}{OQ} = \frac{r^2}{OP \times OQ}.$$

6. Clearly the circle of inversion inverts to itself. Otherwise, the circle is orthogonal to the circle of inversion, since then $t = r^2$ and so, in terms of the notation of lemma 20.4, $P_l = Q$ and $Q_l = P$.

7. This follows immediately from theorems 19.13 and 20.11.

Exercise 20b

In these solutions, the inverse of a point P is denoted by P_l.

1. Invert in O, with any radius (see the figures).

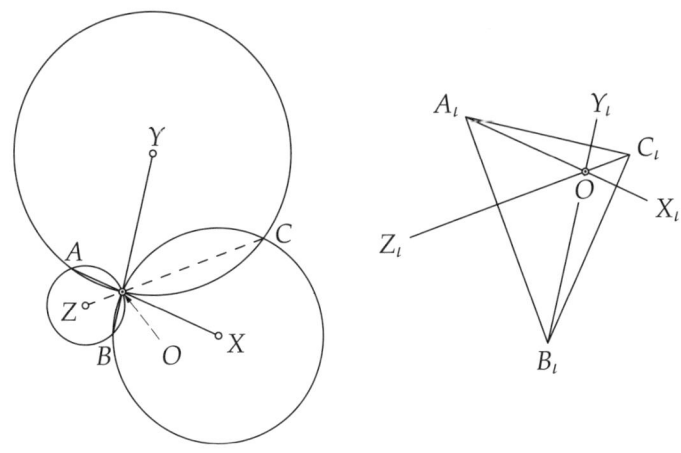

498   The Geometry of the Triangle

Exercise 20b question 1

The three circles map to the sides of the triangle $\triangle A_\iota B_\iota C_\iota$, where $A_\iota O X_\iota$ is perpendicular to $B_\iota C_\iota$ and $B_\iota O Y_\iota$ is perpendicular to $C_\iota A_\iota$. Hence O is the orthocentre of $\triangle A_\iota B_\iota C_\iota$ and $C_\iota O Z_\iota$ is perpendicular to $A_\iota B_\iota$. This implies the desired result in the original diagram.

2. Invert in A, with any radius (see the figures).

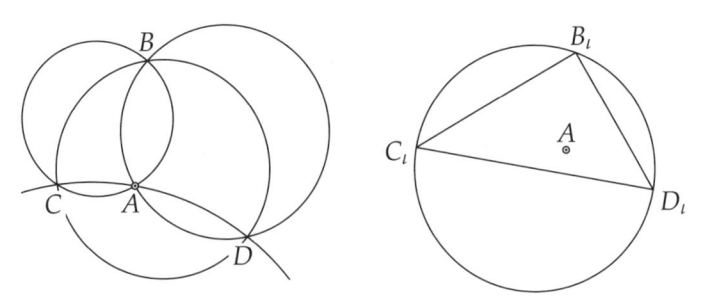

Exercise 20b question 2

Since the circles ABC and ABD are orthogonal, $B_\iota C_\iota$ and $B_\iota D_\iota$ are perpendicular. The circle ACD inverts to the line $C_\iota D_\iota$ and the circle BCD to the circle $B_\iota C_\iota D_\iota$, but these are orthogonal since $C_\iota D_\iota$ is a diameter. The result follows.

3. Invert in O with radius $2R$ (see the figures).

Appendix B: Solutions to the exercises 499

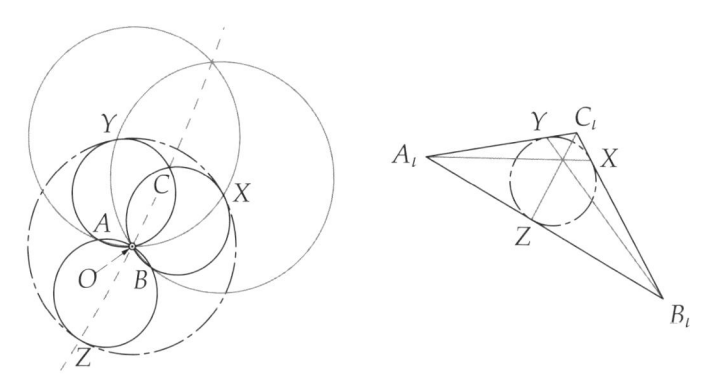

Exercise 20b question 3

The three circles invert to the sides of a triangle $\triangle A_l B_l C_l$ and the circle XYZ to the incircle. Then the circumcircles of $\triangle AOX$, $\triangle BOY$ and $\triangle COZ$ invert to lines $A_l X$, $B_l Y$ and $C_l Z$, which are concurrent at the Gergonne point of $\triangle A_l B_l C_l$, and the image of this under inversion is on all three circles.

4. Invert in O to produce a triangle $\triangle A_l B_l C_l$ (see the figures).

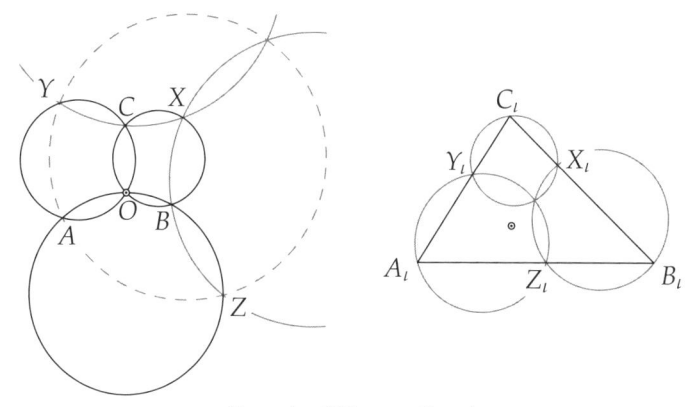

Exercise 20b question 4

Now X_l, Y_l and Z_l are arbitrary points on the sides $B_l C_l$, $C_l A_l$ and $A_l B_l$. The circles $A_l Y_l Z_l$, $B_l Z_l X_l$ and $C_l X_l Y_l$ intersect in the Miquel point.

5. Invert in O to produce a triangle $\triangle A_l B_l C_l$ (see the figures).

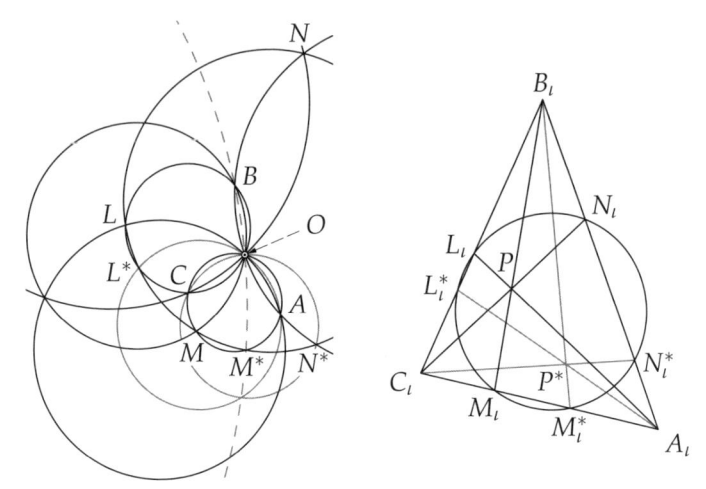

Exercise 20b question 5

Then we have cevians $A_l L_l$, $B_l M_l$ and $C_l N_l$ concurrent at a point P. Then the circumcircle of $\triangle L_l M_l N_l$ meets the sides at points L_l^*, M_l^* and N_l^* such that $A_l L_l^*$, $B_l M_l^*$ and $C_l N_l^*$ are concurrent at its cyclocevian conjugate P^*, and this is the image of the second common point on the three circumcircles.

Exercise 20c

1. First note that $\angle A^* K_* C^* = \angle A^* K_* O + \angle O K_* C^*$ (see the figure). Since $A^* K_* A O$ is cyclic,

$$\angle A^* K_* O = \angle A^* A O$$
$$= \angle A^* A B - \angle O A B$$
$$= (90° - \angle B) - (90° - \angle C)$$
$$= \angle C - \angle B.$$

Similarly, since $C K_* C^* O$ is cyclic, $\angle O K_* C^* = \angle A - \angle B$, and so $\angle A^* K_* B^* = \angle A - 2\angle B + \angle C$.
Now $\angle A^* B C^* = 3\angle B$, so

$$\angle A^* K_* B^* + \angle A^* B C^* = \angle A + \angle B + \angle C = 180°.$$

Appendix B: Solutions to the exercises

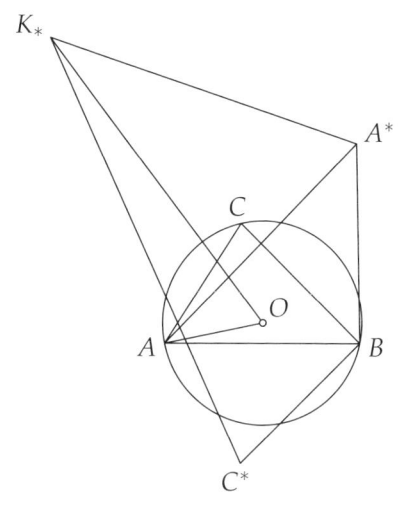

Exercise 20c question 1

But this shows that K_* lies on the circumcircle of $\triangle C^*AB^*$, and the same argument will work for the other two circumcircles.

2. This is a simple trigonometric calculation based on the construction of P_a.

3. From the proof of theorem 20.14, BQ_b is a cevian of $\triangle C_l BA_l$ which passes through its Nagel point. However, $\triangle C_l BA_l$ is similar to $\triangle ABC$ and so this corresponds to the isogonal cevian of $\triangle ABC$. Hence the three lines are concurrent in the isogonal conjugate of M, the Nagel point of $\triangle ABC$. From theorem 13.10 on page 183, this is σ_e, the external centre of similitude of the incircle and circumcircle, which lies on IO.

4. An argument which mirrors that of the solution to question 3 shows that the three lines are concurrent in the isogonal conjugate of Γ, the Gergonne point of $\triangle ABC$. From theorem 13.9 on page 182, this is σ_i, the internal centre of similitude of the incircle and circumcircle, which lies on IO.

5. From the construction in theorem 20.14, we see that the length of the tangent is

$$AI \sec \tfrac{1}{2}A = r \operatorname{cosec} \tfrac{1}{2}A \sec \tfrac{1}{2}A = \frac{2r}{\sin A} = \frac{2\Delta}{s} \times \frac{bc}{2\Delta} = \frac{bc}{s}.$$

6. The inversion in the incircle discussed in section 20.6 maps the circumcircle of $\triangle ABC$ to the nine-point circle of $\triangle PQR$. Hence the centres of these two triangles are collinear with the centre of the inversion, which is I. But now this line contains both the circumcentre and nine-point centre of the intouch triangle, so it is its Euler line. Hence it contains also the orthocentre and centroid of the intouch triangle.

Exercise 21a

1. (a) By corollary 5.15 on page 60, A, I, X, I_A is harmonic, so, by lemma 5.21 on page 62, the orthogonal projection onto BC is also a harmonic range. But the feet of the perpendiculars from A, I, and I_A on BC are D, P and P_A.
   (b) By theorem 2.11 on page 17, A_1 is the midpoint of PP_A, and now we use theorem 5.19 on page 61.
   (c) This is theorem 2.4 on page 11.

2. (a) This is because triangles $\triangle XIP$ and $\triangle XIT$ are congruent.
   (b) We now have $\angle DAX = \angle SAX$, $\angle AXD = \angle AXS$ and AX is common, so triangles $\triangle AXD$ and $\triangle AXS$ are congruent. But $\angle ADX = 90°$ and so $\angle ASX = 90°$. Hence AO and XT are perpendicular.
   (c) By theorem 3.2 on page 28 and the fact that U is the midpoint of AH, $A_1O = UA$, and the segments are parallel. It follows that AUA_1O is a parallelogram, and UA_1 is parallel to OA. But XS is perpendicular to OA, so it is also perpendicular to UA_1.

3. (a) The quadrilateral $UDXL$ is cyclic, with diameter UX, by virtue of the two right-angles. The result now follows from the intersecting chords theorem.
   (b) This is the tangent-secant theorem for the incircle.
   (c) Putting (a) and (b) together with question 1(b), we have $A_1L \times A_1U = A_1T \times A_1J$ and use the converse of the intersecting chords theorem.
   (d) Since, by question 2(b), $\angle ULT = 90°$, it follows that $\angle UJT = 90°$. But UA_1 is a diameter of the nine-point circle, so J lies on this circle.

4. (a) Since $\angle YJT = 90°$, it follows that YT is a diameter of the incircle and hence it passes through its centre I.
   (b) Since XT is a tangent to the incircle and YT a diameter, they are perpendicular, but UA_1 is also perpendicular to XS by question 2(c).
   (c) Since N is the midpoint of UA_1, JN is a median of $\triangle UA_1J$. By (b), TY is parallel to the base of this triangle, so its midpoint, I,

also lies on this median.

(d) NJ is a radius of the nine-point circle and IJ is a radius of the incircle, so the circles are tangential at J.

Exercise 21b

1. (a) The incircle is orthogonal to $\mathcal{S}$, so it inverts to itself.
   (b) The A-excircle is orthogonal to $\mathcal{S}$ so it also inverts to itself.
   (c) The line is orthogonal to $\mathcal{S}$, so it inverts to itself.
   (d) A circle through the centre of inversion A_1 inverts to a line not through A_1; since it passes through D, it inverts to a line through the image of D.

2. (a) Since D, P, X, P_A is harmonic, D inverts to X.
   (b) By lemma 20.2 on page 278, $\mathcal{L}$ is perpendicular to the diameter of the nine-point circle through A_1 and hence parallel to the tangent at A_1.
   (c) This is theorem 3.5 on page 29.

3. (a) Show that the angle between $\mathcal{M}$ and BC is $\frac{1}{2}|\angle C - \angle B|$ and use the result of question 2(c).
   (b) The line BC is one transverse common tangent, so its image under reflection is the other one.

4. Feuerbach's theorem follows immediately from the fact that inversion preserves angles, and hence tangency.

Exercise 21c

1. Since A, B and C are the midpoints of the sides of $\triangle A^*B^*C^*$, the circumcircle of $\triangle ABC$ is the nine-point circle of $\triangle A^*B^*C^*$. In fact, all we have here is an enlargement of the original diagram through the centroid of $\triangle ABC$.

2. By theorem 2.9 on page 16, $\triangle ABC$ is the orthic triangle of $\triangle I_A I_B I_C$, so the nine-point circle of $\triangle I_A I_B I_C$ is the circumcircle of $\triangle ABC$. Applying theorem 21.1 to $\triangle I_A I_B I_C$ shows that the circumcircle is tangential to the incircle and excircles of the excentral triangle. Finally, corollary 21.2 extends the result to the other triangles of the

orthocentric group.

3. (See the figure.)

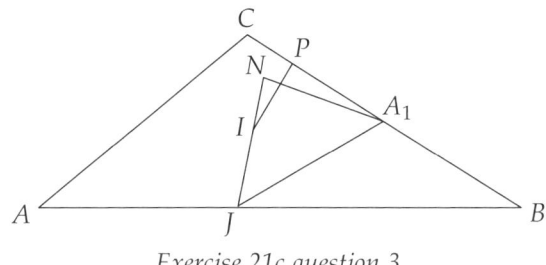

Exercise 21c question 3

If $\angle JNA_1 = \angle INA_1 = \alpha$, then $JA_1 = \frac{1}{2}R\sin\frac{1}{2}\alpha$ since it is a chord of the nine-point circle.
Now $NA_1 = \frac{1}{2}R$ and $IN = \frac{1}{2}R - r$. Also $IA_1^2 = r^2 + PA_1^2 = r^2 + \frac{1}{4}(b-c)^2$ so, by the cosine rule on $\triangle INA_1$, $r^2 + \frac{1}{4}(b-c)^2 = \frac{1}{4}R^2 + \left(\frac{1}{2}R - r\right)^2 - R\left(\frac{1}{2}R - r\right)\cos\alpha$ and, after a little algebra, we obtain

$$\cos\alpha = 1 - \frac{(b-c)^2}{2R(R-2r)}.$$

It follows that
$$\sin\tfrac{1}{2}\alpha = \frac{|b-c|}{2\sqrt{R(R-2r)}},$$
and the result now follows.

4. In the proof of theorem 3.7 on page 30, it was shown that I was on the nine-point circle of $\triangle RAQ$, which has diameter AI and orthocentre H_A. The nine-point centre of this triangle is N_A, the midpoint of AI, and its Euler line is $H_A N_A$ (see the figure).

Let H', N' and O' be points on this line such that $H'H$, $N'N$ and $O'O$ are perpendicular to BC. Note that A lies on $H'H$ and A_1 on $O'O$, and also that $AH = 2OA_1$ and $AH' = H_A I = r$. Hence $HH' = AH - AH' = 2OA_1 - r$ and $2NN' = HH' + OO'$.

Next we consider the excentre I_A, and note, by theorem 2.4 on page 11, that AI_A and OA_1 meet on the circumcircle at a point X' (see the figure). Then $OO' = X'O' - R$.

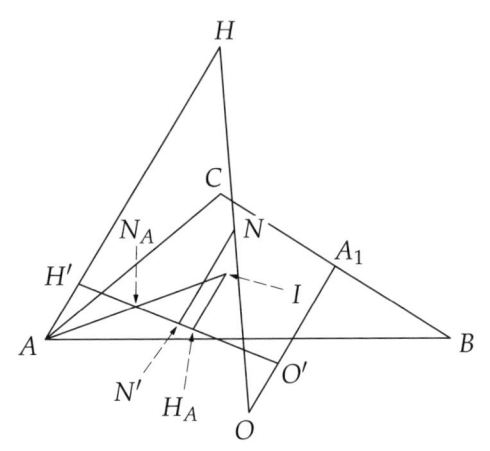

Exercise 21c question 4

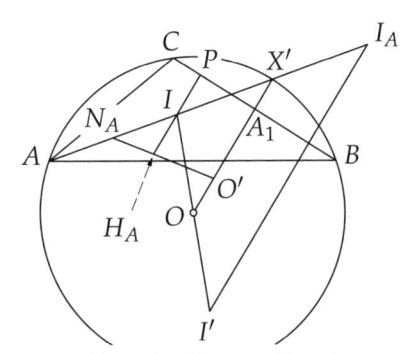

Exercise 21c question 4

By similar triangles,
$$\frac{X'O'}{IH_A} = \frac{X'N_A}{IN_A}.$$
But X' and N_A are the midpoints of $I_A I$ and IA, so this ratio is
$$\frac{I_A A}{IA} = \frac{r_A}{r},$$
and, since $IH_A = r$, we have $X'O' = r_A$.

Also, if I' is the reflection of I in O, then A_1 is the midpoint of PP_A, so $I'I_A = 2OX = 2R$ and $2OA_1 = IP + I'P_A = r + 2R - r_A$.

Putting all this together, we have $2NN' = (r + 2R - r_A) - r + (r_A - R) = R$. Hence NN' is a radius of the nine-point circle. It follows that the intersection of $N'H_A$ and NI is the external centre of similitude of the nine-point circle and incircle. But this is the Feuerbach point.

5. By theorem 9.13 on page 120, the Fuhrmann centre F^* is the midpoint of HM, the Spieker centre S is the midpoint of IM and F^*O, and IOF^*H is a parallelogram. Hence N, which is the midpoint of HO, is also the midpoint of IF^*. It follows that F^*, N, I and J are collinear. Let X be the midpoint of HI; then N is the midpoint of XS (see the figure).

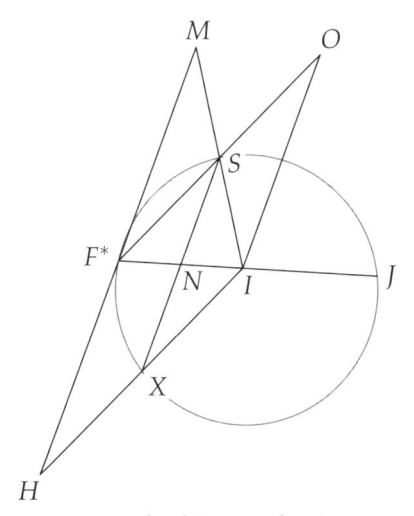

Exercise 21c question 5

Note that $IJ = r$ and $NJ = \frac{1}{2}R$, the radius of the nine-point circle. Then $F^*N \times NJ = NI \times \frac{1}{2}R = \frac{1}{2}R(\frac{1}{2}R - r) = \frac{1}{4}OI^2$ by Euler's formula. But $IO^2 = 4NS^2 = 4XN \times NS$. It follows that $F^*N \times NJ = XN \times NS$ and so, by intersecting chords, F^*XJS is cyclic. But the circumcircle of $\triangle XSF^*$ is the nine-point circle of $\triangle HIM$.

6. Let the incentre, circumcentre, nine-point centre and orthocentre of such a triangle be I, O, N and H. The first two points are, of course, fixed. Let X be the point on OI such that $OI = IX$; this point is also fixed. Now by Feuerbach's theorem, $IN = \frac{1}{2}r - R$, and by the midpoint theorem, $HX = 2IU = R - 2r$, which is constant. Hence

the locus of H is a circle with centre X and radius $R - 2r$.

Exercise 21d

1. We have three triangles which are in perspective in pairs, with perspectors as follows:

$$\begin{array}{ccc} \triangle ABC & \triangle J_A J_B J_C & J^* \\ \triangle ABC & \triangle I_A I_B I_C & I \\ \triangle J_A J_B J_C & \triangle I_A I_B I_C & N \end{array}$$

   Note also that the perspectors J^*, I and N are collinear. It now follows from theorem 10.8 on page 140 that the triangles have a common axis of perspective. This implies in turn that the lines BC, $J_B J_C$ and $I_B I_C$, which are corresponding sides of these triangles, are concurrent on this axis, and hence triangles $\triangle BI_C J_B$ and $\triangle CI_B J_C$ are in perspective. Note that the axis of perspective of these triangles passes through I_A.

2. This is precisely the same argument as question 1; this time the axis of perspective passes through I.

3. Again, this is the same argument as question 1, and now the axis of perspective is $I_A N J_A^*$.

4. Note that X is the internal centre of similitude of the incircle and A-excircle (see the figure).

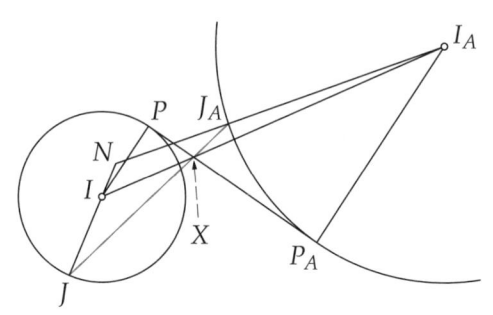

Exercise 21d question 4

So now, denoting the radius of the nine-point circle by ρ, we have
$$\frac{NJ}{JI} \times \frac{IX}{XI_A} \times \frac{I_A J_A}{J_A N} = \frac{\rho}{-r} \times \frac{r}{r_A} = \frac{r_A}{\rho} = -1$$
and so, by Menelaus' theorem on $\triangle NII_A$, we see that J_A, X and J are collinear.

As similar results are true for Y and Z as well, the required result follows, and the perspector of the two triangles is J.

Exercise 22a

1. This is the incentre I of $\triangle ABC$, because IP, IQ and IR are common tangents to the base circles taken in pairs.

2. The incentre is the radical centre of the circles and the incircle is orthogonal to all three of them. Consequently the inversion leaves the base circle alone. The Soddy circles must invert to themselves to preserve tangency, but they are clearly not invariant. Hence the inversion swaps the inner and outer Soddy circles.

3. Let the radii of the base circles centred at A and B be ρ and σ (see the figure).

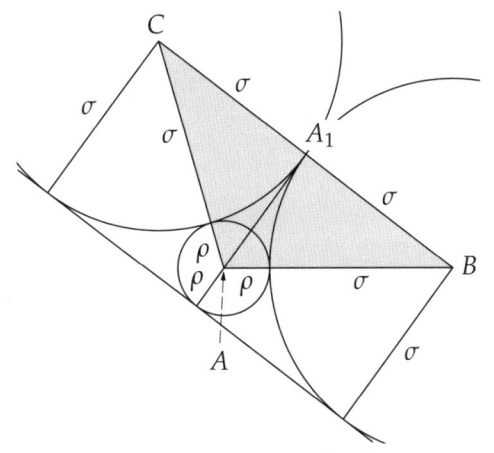

Exercise 22a question 3

Then there is a common tangent if, and only if, $\sigma = \rho + AA_1$. But $A_1B = \sigma$ and $AB = \rho + \sigma$, so, by Pythagoras' theorem, $(\sigma + \rho)^2 = (\sigma - \rho)^2 + \sigma^2$ and $\sigma = 4\rho$. Hence $\triangle BAA_1$ is a $(3, 4, 5)$-triangle and the result follows.

Exercise 22b

1. The perimeter of $\triangle S_o AB$ is $r_o - (s - a) + c + r_o - (s - b) = 2r_o$ (see the figure).

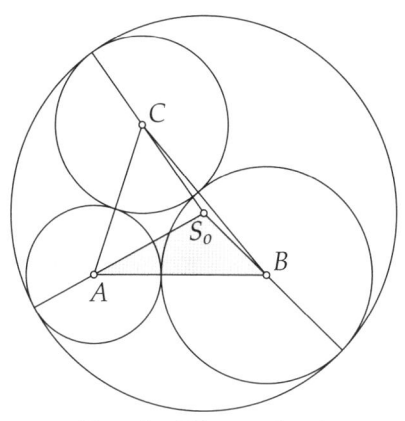

Exercise 22b question 1

Since we obtain the same expression for $\triangle S_o BC$ and $\triangle S_o CA$, the result follows.

2. The detour for $\triangle S_i AB$ is $r_i + (s-a) + r_i + (s-b) - c = 2r_i$ (see the figure).

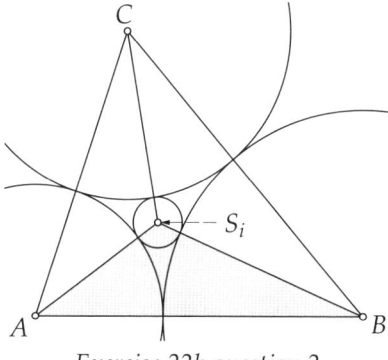

Exercise 22b question 2

Once again, this is the same for the other two triangles.

3. This is because the line of centres of two circles is perpendicular to their radical axis.

Exercise 23a

1. (See the figure.)

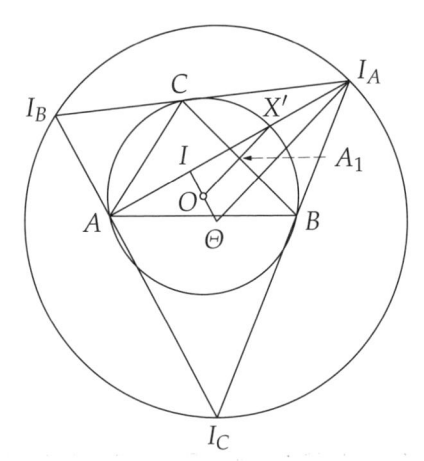

Exercise 23a question 1

By theorem 2.13 on page 18, X' is the midpoint of II_A. But O is the midpoint of $I\Theta$, so ΘI_A is parallel to OX' and twice its length.

2. Note that quadrilateral $BCI_B I_C$ is cyclic, so that BC is antiparallel to $I_C I_B$ with respect to I_A, and hence the symmedian through I_A bisects BC (see the figure).

   Hence the lines $I_A A_1$, $I_B B_1$ and $I_C C_1$ are concurrent at M^*.

3. The homothecy μ takes the symmedian point of the contact triangle, which by theorem 9.1 on page 113 is Γ, to that of the excentral triangle, which is M^*.

4. This follows from the homothecy θ with centre G and scale factor $-\frac{1}{2}$, which maps the Gergonne point of $\triangle ABC$ to that of $\triangle A_1 B_1 C_1$, and the result of theorem 23.6.

5. By corollary 22.6 on page 319 and theorem 22.13 on page 325, the points Γ, I and Λ are collinear on the Soddy line (see the figure).

   Now θ maps Λ to Γ (by section 3.5 on page 36), I to S (by section 9.3 on page 116) and Γ to M^* by theorem 23.7. Hence the result follows.

Appendix B: Solutions to the exercises

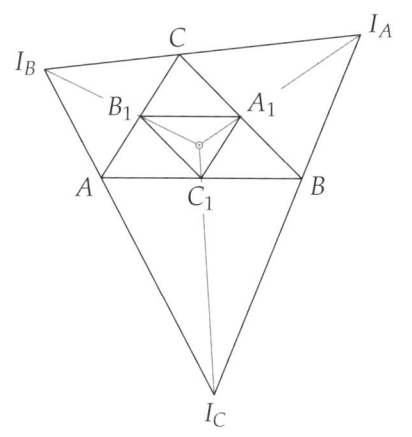

Exercise 23a question 2

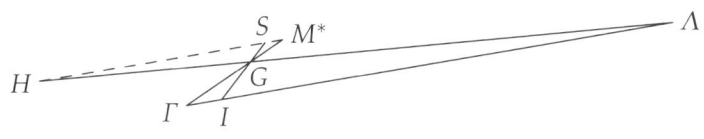

Exercise 23a question 5

Exercise 23b

1. By theorem 23.11, the pedal triangle of Θ is the extouch triangle $\triangle P_A Q_B R_C$ and, by theorem 9.4 on page 114, the cevians AP_A, BQ_B and CR_C are concurrent at the Nagel point, so $\widehat{\Theta} = M$.

2. Using theorem 2.12,

$$r_B + r_C - r_A + r = \frac{\Delta}{s-b} + \frac{\Delta}{s-c} - \frac{\Delta}{s-a} + \frac{\Delta}{s}$$

$$= \frac{a\Delta}{(s-b)(s-c)} - \frac{a\Delta}{s(s-a)}$$

$$= \frac{a\Delta}{s(s-a)(s-b)(s-c)}[s(s-a) - (s-b)(s-c)]$$

$$= \frac{a}{\Delta}[s(b+c-a) - bc]$$

$$= \frac{a}{2\Delta}[(b+c)^2 - a^2 - 2bc]$$

$$= \frac{a}{2\Delta}[b^2 + c^2 - a^2]$$

$$= \frac{abc}{\Delta}\cos A$$

$$= 4R\cos A.$$

3. Let AI meet QR at its midpoint U (see the figure).

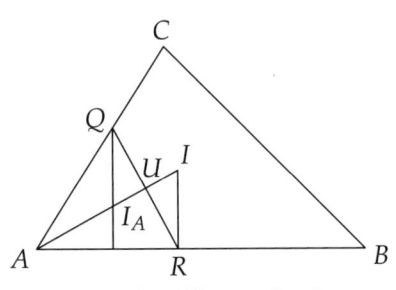

Exercise 23b question 3

Then $\triangle QI_AU$ is congruent to $\triangle RIU$, so QI_A is parallel to IR and hence is an altitude of $\triangle ARQ$. Similarly RI_A is an altitude and so I_A is the orthocentre of $\triangle ARQ$. The result follows by symmetry.

4. (See the figure.)

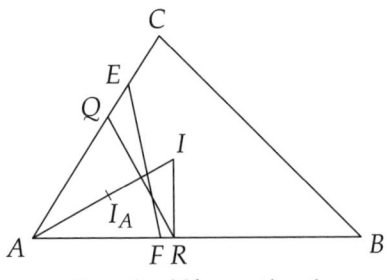

Exercise 23b question 4

Since $\angle QRI = \frac{1}{2}\angle A$, we have

$$II_A = 2r\sin\tfrac{1}{2}A = 2AI\sin^2\tfrac{1}{2}A$$

and so

$$AI_A = AI(1 - 2\sin^2\tfrac{1}{2}A) = AI\cos A.$$

But $\triangle AFE$ is similar to $\triangle ABC$, with scale factor $\cos A$, so I_A is its incentre.

5. (See the figure.)

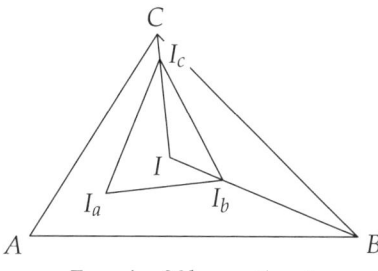

Exercise 23b question 5

By corollary 23.16, $I = H_{\triangle I_a I_b I_c}$, so
$$\angle I_b I_c I = 90° - \angle I_a I_b I_c.$$
But by theorem 23.2,
$$\angle I_a I_b I_c = \angle I_A I_B I_C = \tfrac{1}{2}(\angle A + \angle C)$$
so $\angle I_b I_c I = \tfrac{1}{2}\angle B$ and the result follows.

6. First note that, using the result of question 3,
$$\angle I_c Q I_a = 180° - \angle CQI_c - \angle I_a QA$$
$$= 180° - (90° - \angle C) - (90° - \angle A)$$
$$= \angle C + \angle A.$$
Let the circumcircles of $\triangle PI_c I_b$ and $\triangle RI_b I_a$ intersect at X (see the figure).

Now, again using question 3,
$$\angle I_c X I_a = \angle I_b X I_a - \angle I_c X I_b$$
$$= \angle I_b R I_a - (180° - \angle I_c P I_b)$$
$$= (180° - \angle C) - \angle A$$
$$= 180° - (\angle C + \angle A).$$
and so X also lies on the circumcircle of $\triangle QI_a I_c$.

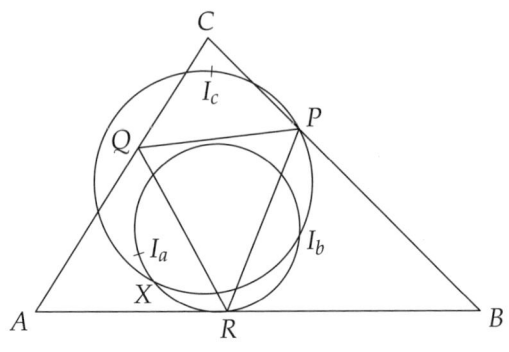

Exercise 23b question 6

Now we show that X lies on the incircle. We have, also using the result of question 5,

$$\angle PXR = \angle PXI_b + \angle I_b XR$$
$$= \angle PI_c I_b + \angle I_b I_a R$$
$$= \angle CI_c I_b - \angle CI_c P + \angle I_b I_a A - \angle RI_a A$$
$$= (180° - \angle I_b BP) - \angle CI_c P + (180° - \angle RBI_b) - \angle RI_a A$$
$$= (90° + \angle BPR) - (180° - \angle CQP)$$
$$\quad + (90° + \angle PRB) - (180° - \angle RQA)$$
$$= \angle B - \angle CQP - \angle RQA$$
$$= \angle PQR,$$

which is what we need.

This proof is diagram-dependent, but as usual the only changes which need to be made are to replace angles by their supplements. It can be presented using directed angles to avoid the need for this.

7. The proof is the same as that of question 6, although it uses different results. First we have, using the result of question 4,

$$\angle I_c EI_a = 180° - \angle CEI_c - \angle I_a EA$$
$$= 180° - \angle B$$
$$= \angle A + \angle C.$$

Let the circumcircles of $\triangle DI_c I_b$ and $\triangle FI_b I_a$ intersect at Y (see the figure).

Appendix B: Solutions to the exercises 517

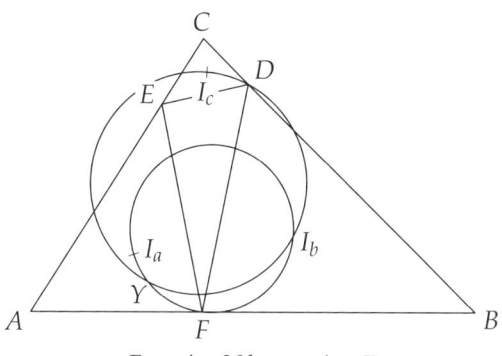

Exercise 23b question 7

Again using question 4,

$$\angle I_c Y I_a = \angle I_b Y I_a - \angle I_c Y I_b$$
$$= \angle I_b F I_a - (180° - \angle I_c D I_b)$$
$$= (180° - \angle C) - \angle A$$
$$= 180° - (\angle C + \angle A).$$

and so Y also lies on the circumcircle of $\triangle E I_a I_c$.

Now we show that Y lies on the nine-point circle. We have, also using the result of question 5,

$$\angle DYF = \angle DY I_b + \angle I_b YF$$
$$= \angle D I_c I_b + \angle I_b I_a F$$
$$= \angle C I_c I_b - \angle C I_c D + \angle I_b I_a A - \angle F I_a A$$
$$= (180° - \angle I_b BD) - \angle C I_c D + (180° - \angle FB I_b) - \angle F I_a A$$
$$= 360° - \angle B - (180° - \tfrac{1}{2}\angle C - \tfrac{1}{2}\angle A)$$
$$\qquad - (180° - \tfrac{1}{2}\angle C - \tfrac{1}{2}\angle A)$$
$$= \angle C + \angle A - \angle B$$
$$= 180° - 2\angle B$$
$$= \angle DEF,$$

which is what we need.

This proof is diagram-dependent, but as usual the only changes which need to be made are to replace angles by their supplements. It can be presented using directed angles to avoid the need for this.

8. By the proof of question 6, $\angle I_b P I_c = \angle B + \angle C$, and by that of question 7, $I_b D I_c = \angle B + \angle C$. It follows that P, D, I_c, I_b are concyclic. Hence the subject of questions 6 and 7 is the same triple of circles, and the points X and Y are identical. This point lies on both the incircle and the nine-point circle, so it is the Feuerbach point of $\triangle ABC$.

Exercise 24a

1. This follows from theorem 24.2 by choosing $\alpha = 90° - \frac{1}{4}\angle A$, $\beta = 90° - \frac{1}{4}\angle B$ and $\gamma = 90° - \frac{1}{4}\angle C$.

2. This follows from theorem 24.2 by choosing $\alpha = 45° - \frac{1}{4}\angle A$, $\beta = 45° - \frac{1}{4}\angle B$ and $\gamma = 45° - \frac{1}{4}\angle C$.

Exercise 24b

1. Suppose that the Euler line of $\triangle ABC$ passes through the vertex A. The circumcentre O is distinct from A, so the Euler line is OA. If O is A_1, $\triangle ABC$ is right-angled at A, and if it is not, the Euler line is perpendicular to BC, so the triangle is isosceles with apex A.

    Now consider a situation in which the three Euler lines of a partitioned triangle all pass through P. The triangles $\triangle PAB$, $\triangle PBC$ and $\triangle PCA$ would need to be either right-angled at P or isosceles with apex P. At most one can be right-angled, so other two are isosceles, and so all three are isosceles. Hence P is the circumcentre of $\triangle ABC$.

2. The two triangles share the same nine-point centre, and the circumcentre of one is the orthocentre of the other. Hence their Euler lines are reflections of each other in N.

3. Let the circumcentre of $\triangle GBC$ be O_A and the circumradius be R_A (see the figure).

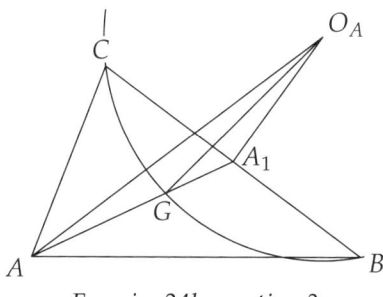

Exercise 24b question 3

We begin by using Stewart's theorem on $\triangle AA_1O_A$. This gives
$$O_AA^2 + 2O_AA_1^2 = 3O_AG^2 + AG^2 + 2A_1G^2$$
$$= 3R_A^2 + \tfrac{2}{3}AA_1^2.$$

By Apollonius' median theorem,
$$b^2 + c^2 = 2AA_1^2 + \tfrac{1}{2}a^2$$
and also
$$O_AA_1^2 = R_A^2 - \tfrac{1}{4}a^2.$$

Hence we have
$$AO_A^2 - R_A^2 = \tfrac{1}{3}(a^2 + b^2 + c^2).$$

Therefore the power of the circumcircle of $\triangle GBC$ with respect to A is a symmetric expression, and so the result follows.

4. Let the areas of $\triangle OBC$, $\triangle OCA$ and $\triangle OAB$ be Δ_a, Δ_b and Δ_c. Then, using the relationship
$$4\Delta = \frac{abc}{R}$$
and the fact that $\Delta = \Delta_a + \Delta_b + \Delta_c$, we obtain the desired result.

Appendix B: Solutions to the exercises 521

Exercise A

1. The line joining $A(1,0,0)$ to $L(0,1,\lambda)$ is clearly $\lambda y - z = 0$, and the other two cevians are $\mu z - x = 0$ and $\nu x - y = 0$. These intersect in the three points $(\mu, \mu\nu, 1)$, $(1, \nu, \nu\lambda)$ and $(\lambda\mu, 1, \lambda)$. In order to use the area formula, we must normalise these coordinates by dividing the sum of their components. It follows that the area ratio is given by the determinant

$$\begin{vmatrix} \mu & \mu\lambda & 1 \\ 1 & \nu & \nu\lambda \\ \lambda\mu & 1 & \lambda \end{vmatrix} = (\lambda\mu\nu - 1)^2$$

   divided by $(\lambda\mu + \lambda + 1)(\mu\nu + \mu + 1)(\nu\lambda + \nu + 1)$.

2. Setting $\lambda = \mu = \nu = k$ gives

$$\frac{(k^3 - 1)^2}{(k^2 + k + 1)^3} = \frac{(k-1)^2}{k^2 + k + 1}.$$

   When $k = 1$ this is zero, expressing the fact that the medians are concurrent. The sequence of values continues

$$\frac{1}{7}, \frac{4}{13}, \frac{3}{7}, \frac{16}{31}, \ldots$$

   The first of these is a well-known fact about the trisectors of the sides.

3. To obtain Ceva set $\lambda\mu\nu = 1$. For Menelaus, use a similar argument to show that
$$\frac{[LMN]}{\Delta} = \frac{\lambda\mu\nu + 1}{(\lambda + 1)(\mu + 1)(\nu + 1)}$$
   and then put $\lambda\mu\nu = -1$.

4. The barycentric coordinates of O are $(\sin 2A, \sin 2B, \sin 2C)$, so its isogonal conjugate has coordinates
$$\left(\frac{a^2}{\sin 2A}, \frac{b^2}{\sin 2B}, \frac{c^2}{\sin 2C}\right) = 2R^2(\tan A, \tan B, \tan C)$$
   and these are equivalent to the barycentric coordinates of H.

5. Expanding the determinant by the bottom row, we obtain

$$\begin{vmatrix} 1 & 1 & 1 \\ \sin 2A & \sin 2B & \sin 2C \\ \tan A & \tan B & \tan C \end{vmatrix} = \sum \tan A (\sin 2C - \sin 2B)$$

$$= 2 \sum \tan A \cos A \sin(B - C)$$
$$= 2 \sum \sin(B + C) \sin(B - C)$$
$$= 2 \sum (\cos 2C - \cos 2B)$$
$$= 0,$$

which is sufficient to show collinearity. Notice that the trigonometrical forms for the circumcentre and orthocentre make the calculation rather unpleasant.

6. We have

$$\tan A = \frac{abc}{R(b^2 + c^2 - a^2)}.$$

Now the barycentric equation is given by

$$0 = \frac{abc}{R} \begin{vmatrix} x & y & z \\ 1 & 1 & 1 \\ \frac{1}{b^2 + c^2 - a^2} & \frac{1}{c^2 + a^2 - b^2} & \frac{1}{a^2 + b^2 - c^2} \end{vmatrix}$$

$$= \frac{abc}{R} \sum x \left(\frac{1}{a^2 + b^2 - c^2} - \frac{1}{c^2 + a^2 - b^2} \right)$$

$$= \frac{2abc}{R(b^2 + c^2 - a^2)(c^2 + a^2 - b^2)(a^2 + b^2 - c^2)}$$
$$\times \sum x (b^2 + c^2 - a^2)(c^2 - b^2),$$

which is equivalent to the required equation.

Appendix C

An index of geometers

Adams circle Karl Adams (1811–1849) was a Swiss mathematician and teacher who specialised in synthetic geometry. His *Lehre von den Transversalen* contains the work on the circle which bears his name.

Apollonius circles Apollonius of Perga (c262–c190 BC) was known as 'the great geometer'. His treatise on conics introduced the terms parabola, ellipse and hyperbola and it included a definition of the circle using the ratio property. He is also credited with the result on medians which is a special case of Stewart's theorem.

Bevan point Benjamin Bevan (1773–1833) was a civil engineer and brewer in Leighton Buzzard. In 1804 he issued a challenge concerning the properties of the circumcentre of the excentral triangle, and the solution was found by one John Butterworth.

Brianchon's theorem Charles Julien Brianchon (1783–1864) was a French mathematician and chemist. He entered into the École Polytechnique in 1804 at the age of eighteen, and studied under Monge. After a spell as a lieutenant in Napoleon's artillery, he became a professor in the Artillery School of the Royal Guard at Vincennes.

Brocard points Pierre René Jean Baptiste Henri Brocard (1845–1922) was a French army officer, meteorologist and mathematician. Along with Neuberg and Lemoine, he is often cited as one of the founders of modern triangle geometry.

Casey's power theorem John Casey (1820–1891) was born in Kilkenny and lectured at the Catholic University of Ireland and University College, Dublin. His classic work was *A Sequel to the First Six Books of the Elements of Euclid* and he was elected as a Fellow of the Royal Society in 1875.

Ceva's theorem Giovanni Ceva (1647–1734) taught in Pisa and Mantua and published his result in his *De lineis rectis*. He also rediscovered Menelaus' theorem.

Clawson point John Wentworth Clawson (1881–1964) was born in Saint John, New Brunswick, Canada, and became the professor of mathematics and physics at Ursinus College in Collegeville, Pennsylvania.

Desargues' theorem Girard Desargues (1591–1661) was a native of Lyon and one of the founders of projective geometry. He first published his theorem on perspective triangles in 1648.

Droz-Farny circles Arnold Droz-Farny (1856–1912) taught physics and mathematics in the cantonal school of Porrentruy in his native Switzerland, after studying in Munich.

Eppstein points David Eppstein (b 1963) is professor of computer science at the University of California, Irvine.

Euler line Leonhard Euler (1707–1783), who was one of the most prolific of all mathematicians, needs no introduction. His demonstration of the collinearity of O, G and H was, however, entirely algebraic, and he certainly had no knowledge of the nine-point circle.

Fagnano's problem Giovanni Fagnano (1715–1797) was a cleric in the Adriatic city-state of Sinigaglia but he followed his father's interest in mathematics. His solution of the minimisation problem used calculus, but soon after its publication it was tackled by purely geometrical methods by others including Hermann Schwarz and Lipót Féjer.

Fermat point Pierre de Fermat (1601–1665) was a lawyer and government official in Toulouse but soon gained a reputation as one of the leading mathematicians in the world; his work includes important contributions to number theory, analysis, algebra, geometry and optics.

Fuhrmann circle Wilhelm Fuhrmann (1833–1904) studied and worked as a teacher in Königsberg. He wrote about the circle in *Synthetische Beweise Planimetrischer Sätze* in 1890.

Gergonne point Joseph Diaz Gergonne (1771–1859) served as a soldier in various Napoleonic campaigns before settling down as professor of mathematics at Nîmes and Montpellier, where he worked on algebra, analysis and geometry.

Grebe point Ernst Wilhelm Grebe (1804–1874) taught mathematics at the Gymnasium at Kassel. In 1847 he published a paper which introduced the symmedian point. He was thus 26 years ahead of Lemoine, but in fact the point had already been noted in 1809 by the Swiss geometry Simon L'Huilier.

Griffiths points Griffiths was the author of a paper published in 1857 which proved that if a point lies on a fixed line through the circumcentre of a triangle, its pedal circle passes through a fixed point on the nine-point circle. This is the inner Griffiths point.

Heron's formula Hero(n) of Alexandria (c10–c70) was a Greek engineer and mathematician resident in Egypt. The formula for the area of a triangle appeared in his *Metrica* but perhaps can be traced back to Archimedes. There is no indication of any method of proof.

Kiepert hyperbola Ludwig Kiepert (1846–1934) was professor of mathematics at Hannover from 1879 to 1921.

Kosnita triangle Nothing appears to be known about this name. There are various rumours on the internet that it refers to a Rumanian mathematician, but there are also suggestions that it might even be a place-name in Bulgaria or Moldova.

Lemoine circles Emil Michel Hyacinthe Lemoine (1840–1912) was famous for his work on the symmedian point, but he was by profession a civil engineer. He was also a competent amateur musician.

Lester circle June Lester is currently researching the online teaching of mathematics at Simon Fraser University in British Columbia, Canada.

de Longchamps point Gaston de Longchamps (1842–1906) was born in Alençon and became a teacher of mathematics in the Lycée Saint-Louis in Paris.

Malfatti circles Gian Francesco Malfatti (1731–1807) taught mathematics in a school in Ferrara before becoming professor at the university there. He worked on quintic equations, probability and mechanics as well as posing the geometrical problem for which he is most famous.

Menelaus' theorem Menelaus of Alexandria (c70–c130) also worked in Rome. Not much is known of his life, apart from his work in spherical geometry and astronomy.

Miquel circles Auguste Miquel (*fl* 1830–1850) lived in Nantua and published the result about intersecting circles in 1838, but he was not the first to discover them. The result was first stated by William Wallace in 1799.

Monge's circle theorem Gaspard Monge (1746–1818) was born in Beaune and showed early expertise in technical drawing. He was a strong supporter of the French Revolution, becoming Minister of the Marine in 1792. Later he became director of the École Polytechnique and travelled with Napoleon to Egypt. He is considered to be one of the founders of differential geometry.

Nagel point Christian Heinrich von Nagel (1803–1882) was born in the city of Stuttgart in Germany, but spent all of his life teaching mathematics in Tubingen, as well as working as a clergyman.

Napoleon points Napoleon Bonaparte (1729–1821) was Emperor of the French from 1804 to 1815. Although he enjoyed mathematics at school and kept in touch with the leading mathematicians of his day, such as Fourier, Monge, Laplace and Berthollet, there is no evidence at all that he was responsible for the result which bears his name.

Parry circle Cyril Parry, who died in 2005, was an English geometer who collaborated with Martyn Cundy and Clark Kimberling on a number of significant papers.

Appendix C: An index of geometers

Pascal's theorem Blaise Pascal (1623–1662) was eminent as a philosopher, natural scientist, inventor and writer. He discovered the theorem on the 'mystic hexagon' at the age of 16 and his later work did much to establish the foundations of probability theory, but he decided, after a mystical experience in 1654, to abandon mathematics and to devote himself to Catholic theology.

Ptolemy's theorem Claudius Ptolemaeus (c85–c165), known as Ptolemy, was a Helleno-Egyptian mathematician, astronomer and geographer. The theorem on cyclic quadrilaterals appears in his *Almagest*.

Pythagoras' theorem Pythagoras of Samos (c569–c475 BC) was one of the most celebrated of the Greek geometers, but also a figure shrouded in mystery. He also made important contributions to the theory of music.

Rigby points John Rigby was Reader in Pure Mathematics at the University of Wales, Cardiff until his retirement. His particular interests include Japanese temple geometry and the role of geometrical patterns in art.

Routh's theorem Edward John Routh (1831–1907) was born of English parents in Quebec. He was the senior wrangler in the Cambridge Tripos, was elected a fellow of Peterhouse College, and became one of the most successful mathematical coaches in the university's history.

Schiffler point Kurt Schiffler (1896–1986) was an accomplished amateur geometer. He introduced the point which is named after him in a problem in *Crux Mathematicorum* in 1985.

Simson line Robert Simson (1687–1768) was a Scottish mathematician who observed the convergence of successive ratios from the Fibonacci sequence, but there is no evidence that the line which bears his name was known to him. The ascription was made by Poncelet, but the line was in fact discovered by fellow Scot William Wallace (1768–1843). Wallace's mother was in fact called Janet Simson, but again there seems to be no connection to Robert, who was unmarried.

Soddy circles Frederick Soddy (1877–1956) was an English radiochemist who received the Nobel Prize for Chemistry in 1921. He rediscovered the theorem about tangent circles, due originally to Descartes, in 1936, publishing it along with a poem, *The Kiss Precise*.

Spieker centre Theodor Spieker (1823–1913), was a high school teacher in Potsdam. His geometry text, *Lehrbuch der ebenen Geometrie*, greatly influenced the 12-year old Albert Einstein.

Steiner point Jakob Steiner (1796–1863) was a Swiss mathematician who became professor at the University of Berlin, where he worked primarily in geometry, but also made contributions to combinatorics.

Taylor circle Henry Martin Taylor (1842–1927) was born in Bristol and became a Fellow of Trinity College, Cambridge. He discussed his circle in 1882, but it was certainly known earlier in France and Belgium. In later life, he became blind and developed Braille as well as serving as Mayor of Cambridge.

Tarry point Gaston Tarry (1843–1913) was born near Aveyron and studied mathematics at high school before joining the civil service in Algeria. He was a gifted amateur mathematician who confirmed Euler's conjecture on the non-existence of the 6×6 Graeco-Latin square.

Torricelli's solution Evangelista Torricelli (1608–1647) did important work in hydrodynamics, optics and mechanics as well as the mathematics of curves and solids. His solution to the Fermat problem was geometrical in nature rather than analytic.

Tucker circles Robert Tucker (1832–1905) was born in Walworth in Surrey and studied mathematics at Cambridge before teaching at University College School, Hampstead. He became the secretary of the London Mathematical Society, serving under nineteen different presidents, and was particularly involved in publishing and editing the geometrical papers of W K Clifford.

van Lamoen circle Floor van Lamoen (b 1966) is a mathematics teacher in Goes, Holland, and is the editor of the internet-based journal *Forum Geometricorum*. As a former athlete, he gained several national medals in the discipline of fast walking.

Appendix C: An index of geometers

Vecten points (Jean-François?) Vecten (*fl* 1810-1824) was a teacher at the Lycée at Nîmes, and published work in the *Annales* edited by Gergonne.

Weill point Emile Weill (*fl* 1880s) was a French geometer who published papers in the journal *Nouvelles Annales de Mathématiques*.

Bibliography

[1] Nathan Altshiller-Court. *College Geometry. An Introduction to the Modern Geometry of the Triangle and the Circle.* Dover, 2009. ISBN: 978-0-486-45805-2.

[2] Nikolai Ivanov Beluhov. "An elementary proof of Lester's theorem". In: *Journal of Classical Geometry* 1 (2012), pp. 53–56. URL: http://jcgeometry.org/Articles/Volume1/JCG2012V1pp53-56.pdf.

[3] Nikolai Ivanov Beluhov. "Ten concurrent Euler lines". In: *Forum Geometricorum* 9 (2009), pp. 271–274. URL: http://forumgeom.fau.edu/FG2009volume9/FG200924index.html.

[4] C. J. Bradley. *Introduction to Inequalities.* UKMT, 2010. ISBN: 978-1-906001-11-7.

[5] C. J. Bradley. *The Algebra of Geometry.* UKMT, 2007. ISBN: 978-1-906338-00-8.

[6] Christopher J. Bradley. *Challenges in Geometry. For Mathematical Olympians Past and Present.* Oxford University Press, 2005. ISBN: 978-0-19-856692-2.

[7] John H. Conway. "The Power of Mathematics". In: *Power.* Ed. by Alan Blackwell and David J. C. MacKay. 2004. URL: http://www.cs.toronto.edu/~mackay/abstracts/conway.html.

[8] H. S. M. Coxeter. *Introduction to Geometry.* Wiley Classics Library. John Wiley & Sons, 1989.

[9] Michael Goldenberg and Mark Kaplan. "Problem 1855". In: *Mathematics Magazine* 84.4 (Oct. 2011), p. 301.

[10] Darij Grinberg. "On the Kosnita point and the reflection triangle".
In: *Forum Geometricorum* 3 (2003), pp. 105–111. URL: http://forumgeom.fau.edu/FG2003volume3/FG200311index.html.

[11] Richard K. Guy. "The lighthouse theorem, Morley & Malfatti—a budget of paradoxes".
In: *American Mathematical Monthly* 114.2 (2007), pp. 97–141.

[12] Fukagawa Hidetoshi and John Rigby. *Traditional Japanese Mathematics Problems of the 18th and 19th Centuries.*
Singapore: SCT Publishing, 2002. ISBN: 978-981-04-2759-7.

[13] Fukagawa Hidetoshi and Tony Rothman.
Sacred Mathematics. Japanese Temple Geometry.
Princeton University Press, 2008.

[14] Ross Honsberger.
Episodes in Nineteenth and Twentieth Century Euclidean Geometry.
Anneli Lax New Mathematical Library.
The Mathematical Association of America, 1996.
ISBN: 978-088385-639-0.

[15] *Hyacinthos.*
URL: http://tech.groups.yahoo.com/group/hyacinthos/.

[16] Roger Johnson. *Advanced Euclidean Geometry.* Dover, 1960.

[17] Clark Kimberling. *Encyclopedia of Triangle Centers.* URL: http://faculty.evansville.edu/ck6/encyclopedia/ETC.html.

[18] Clark Kimberling. *Triangle Centers and Central Triangles.*
Congressus numerantum 129.
Utilitas Mathematica Publishing, 1998.

[19] Gerry Leversha. *Crossing the Bridge.* UKMT, 2008.
ISBN: 978-1-906001-06-3.

[20] E. A. Maxwell. *Geometry for Advanced Pupils.*
Oxford Clarendon Press, 1949.

[21] Joseph Neuberg. "Problem 1078". In: *Mathesis* (1896), p. 193.

[22] Geoff Smith and Gerry Leversha. "Euler and triangle geometry".
In: *The Mathematical Gazette* 91 (Nov. 2007), pp. 436–452.

[23] Floor van Lamoen. "Friendship among triangle centres".
In: *Forum Geometricorum* 1 (2001), pp. 1–6. URL: http://forumgeom.fau.edu/FG2001volume1/FG200101index.html.

[24] Ian Warburton. "Bride's Chair revisited again!"
In: *Mathematical Gazette* 80 (Nov. 1996), pp. 557–558.

[25] I. M. Yaglom. *Geometric Transformations II*. Trans. by A. Shields.
New Mathematical Library 21.
Mathematical Association of America, 1968. ISBN: 978-0-88385-621-5.

[26] Paul Yiu.
"The Circles of Lester, Evans, Parry, and their Generalizations".
In: *Forum Geometricorum* 10 (2010), pp. 175–209. URL: http://forumgeom.fau.edu/FG2010volume10/FG201020index.html.

Index

A-Apollonius circle, 265
Adams circle, 123
adjunct Morley triangle, 189
Ajima-Malfatti
    first $\sim$ point, 365
    second $\sim$ point, 365
angle
    $\sim$ bisector, 3
    Brocard $\sim$, 219
    directed $\sim$, xvii
anti-complementary triangle, 6
antiorthic axis, 131
antiparallel, 104
Apollonius
    $\sim$ circle, 369
    $\sim$ point, 369
areal coordinates, 125
axis
    $\sim$ of perspective, 128
    antiorthic $\sim$, 131
    Brocard $\sim$, 223, 434
    Fermat $\sim$, 146
    orthic $\sim$, 73
    radical $\sim$, 255

barycentric coordinates, 125
basic points, 260
bends, 316
Bevan point, 122
bisector
    angle $\sim$, 3

perpendicular $\sim$, 2
Brianchon's theorem, 448
Brocard
    $\sim$ angle, 219
    $\sim$ axis, 223, 434
    $\sim$ centre, 223
    $\sim$ circle, 223
    $\sim$ point, 218
    $\sim$ ray, 219
    first $\sim$ triangle, 221
    second $\sim$ triangle, 224
    third $\sim$ point, 227

Casey's power theorem, 257
centre
    $\sim$ of perspective, 128
    $\sim$ of similitude, 3
    Brocard $\sim$, 223
    external $\sim$ of similitude, 63
    first isogonic $\sim$, 145
    first Morley $\sim$, 189
    Fuhrmann $\sim$, 120
    homothetic $\sim$, 3
    internal $\sim$ of similitude, 63
    medial $\sim$, 36
    Morley $\sim$, 185
    Morley-Yff $\sim$, 189
    nine-point $\sim$, 28
    radical $\sim$, 257
    second isogonic $\sim$, 146
    second Morley $\sim$, 188

Spieker ∼, 35, 116
cevian
  ∼ circle, 72
  ∼ triangle, 72
cevians, 72
circle
  ∼ of inversion, 277
  ∼ of similitude, 63, 205
  A-Apollonius ∼, 265
  Adams ∼, 123
  Apollonius ∼, 369
  Brocard ∼, 223
  cevian ∼, 72
  cosine ∼, 241
  Droz-Farny ∼s, 94
  exarc ∼, 289
  first Lemoine ∼, 238
  Fuhrmann ∼, 120
  inarc ∼, 289
  incentral ∼, 425
  inner Napoleon ∼, 150
  inner Soddy ∼, 309
  Lester ∼, 154
  Malfatti ∼s, 365
  Miquel ∼s, 49
  Monge's ∼ theorem, 76
  Morley ∼, 185
  nine-point ∼, 28
  outer Napoleon ∼, 150
  outer Soddy ∼, 309
  Parry ∼, 367
  pedal ∼, 77
  second Lemoine ∼, 240
  Spieker ∼, 116
  Taylor ∼, 249
  Tucker ∼, 245
  van Lamoen ∼, 360
circumcevian triangle, 172
circumcircle, 3
circummedial triangle, 172
circummidarc triangle, 172
circumorthic triangle, 172

circumradius, 3
Clawson point, 343
coaxal, 260
conic, Feuerbach's ∼ theorem, 378
conjugate, 262
  ∼ lines, 254
  ∼ points, 253
  cyclocevian ∼, 83
  isogonal ∼, 81
  isotomic ∼, 82
construction, Gergonne ∼, 321
contact triangle, 426
coordinates
  areal ∼, 125
  barycentric ∼, 125
correspondence, triangle of ∼, 205
cosine circle, 241
cross-ratio, 53
  ∼ of a pencil, 57
  harmonic ∼, 59
cyclocevian conjugate, 83

de Longchamps point, 36
diagonal triangle, 66, 134
dilative reflection, 203
directed angle, xvii
directly similar, 4
disc, orthocentroidal ∼, 36
Droz-Farny circles, 94
dual statements, 132
duality, principle of ∼, 132

Emelyanov triangle, 339
Eppstein
  first ∼ point, 319
  second ∼ point, 319
equal detour point, 317
equiparallelian point, 364
Euler
  ∼ line, 27
  ∼ triangle, 30
exarc circle, 289
excentral triangle, 16

Index

Exeter point, 177, 179
exmedians, 109
exsymmedian points, 109
exsymmedians, 109
extangents triangle, 336
external centre of similitude, 63
externally, 28
extouch triangle, 131

far-out point, 368
Fermat
 ∼ axis, 146
 ∼ point, 145
Feuerbach
 ∼ point, 296
 ∼ triangle, 296
Feuerbach's conic theorem, 378
first
 ∼ Ajima-Malfatti point, 365
 ∼ Brocard triangle, 221
 ∼ Eppstein point, 319
 ∼ Kenmotu point, 370
 ∼ Lemoine circle, 238
 ∼ Morley centre, 189
 ∼ Morley line, 189
 ∼ Morley triangle, 190
 ∼ isodynamic point, 267
 ∼ isogonic centre, 145
Fuhrmann
 ∼ centre, 120
 ∼ circle, 120
 ∼ triangle, 120

Gergonne
 ∼ construction, 321
 ∼ line, 131
 ∼ point, 73, 136
glide reflection, 203
Grebe point, 99
Griffiths
 inner ∼ point, 323
 outer ∼ point, 323
group, orthocentric ∼, 34

harmonic
 ∼ cross-ratio, 59
 ∼ mean, 421
 ∼ pencil, 59
 ∼ range, 59
hexagon
 Taylor ∼, 248
 Tucker ∼, 245
homology, 199
homothecy, 4
homothetic, 3
 ∼ centre, 3

inarc circle, 289
incentral
 ∼ circle, 425
 ∼ triangle, 425
incircle, 3
infinity, line at ∼, 57
inner
 ∼ Griffiths point, 323
 ∼ Napoleon circle, 150
 ∼ Napoleon point, 149
 ∼ Napoleon triangle, 150
 ∼ Rigby point, 323
 ∼ Soddy circle, 309
 ∼ Soddy point, 309
 ∼ Soddy triangle, 312
 ∼ Vecten point, 159
 ∼ Vecten triangle, 159
inradius, 3
inscribable, 19
internal, 3
 ∼ centre of similitude, 63
internally, 28
intouch triangle, 426
intouch-of-circumorthic triangle, 175
intouch-of-orthic triangle, 184
invariable
 ∼ points, 212
 ∼ triangle, 212

inverse, 251, 277
    ∼ Kosnita point, 287
inversely similar, 4
inversion, 278
    circle of ∼, 277
isodynamic
    first ∼ point, 267
    second ∼ point, 267
isogonal
    ∼ Mittenpunkt, 335
    ∼ conjugate, 81
isogonic
    first ∼ centre, 145
    second ∼ centre, 146
isoperimetric point, 317
isotomic conjugate, 82

Kenmotu
    first ∼ point, 370
    second ∼ point, 371
Kosnita
    ∼ point, 163
    ∼ triangle, 163
    inverse ∼ point, 287

Lambda point, 167
Lemoine
    ∼ line, 131
    ∼ point, 99
    first ∼ circle, 238
    second ∼ circle, 240
Lester circle, 154
limiting points, 261
line
    ∼ at infinity, 57
    ∼ segment, 1
    conjugate ∼s, 254
    Euler ∼, 27
    first Morley ∼, 189
    Gergonne ∼, 131
    Lemoine ∼, 131
    second Morley ∼, 192
    Simson ∼, 42

Soddy ∼, 319
third Morley ∼, 193

Malfatti circles, 365
mean, harmonic ∼, 421
medial
    ∼ centre, 36
    ∼ triangle, 5
Miquel
    ∼ circles, 49
    ∼ point, 49
    ∼ triangle, 49
Mittenpunkt, 333
    isogonal ∼, 335
Monge's circle theorem, 76
Morley
    ∼ centre, 185
    ∼ circle, 185
    ∼ triangle, 185
    adjunct ∼ triangle, 189
    first ∼ centre, 189
    first ∼ line, 189
    first ∼ triangle, 190
    second ∼ centre, 188
    second ∼ line, 192
    second ∼ triangle, 190
    third ∼ line, 193
Morley-Yff centre, 189

Nagel point, 114
Napoleon
    inner ∼ circle, 150
    inner ∼ point, 149
    inner ∼ triangle, 150
    outer ∼ circle, 150
    outer ∼ point, 149
    outer ∼ triangle, 149
nine-point
    ∼ centre, 28
    ∼ circle, 28
normalised, 125

orthic
    ∼ axis, 73
    ∼ triangle, 20
orthic-of-intouch triangle, 184
orthic-of-orthic triangle, 184
orthocentric
    ∼ group, 34
    ∼ quadrilateral, 34
orthocentroidal disc, 36
orthogonal, 23
outer
    ∼ Griffiths point, 323
    ∼ Napoleon circle, 150
    ∼ Napoleon point, 149
    ∼ Napoleon triangle, 149
    ∼ Rigby point, 323
    ∼ Soddy circle, 309
    ∼ Soddy point, 309
    ∼ Soddy triangle, 313
    ∼ Vecten point, 158
    ∼ Vecten triangle, 158

parallelian, 363
Parry circle, 367
Pascal's theorem, 448
pedal
    ∼ circle, 77
    ∼ sum, 110
    ∼ triangle, 25, 77
pedal-cevian point, 92
pencil, 133
    ∼ of rays, 56
    cross-ratio of a ∼, 57
    harmonic ∼, 59
perpendicular bisector, 2
perspective, 128
    axis of ∼, 128
    centre of ∼, 128
perspector, 128
Phi point, 167
Pi point, 175

point
    Apollonius ∼, 369
    basic ∼s, 260
    Bevan ∼, 122
    Brocard ∼, 218
    Clawson ∼, 343
    conjugate ∼s, 253
    de Longchamps ∼, 36
    equal detour ∼, 317
    equiparallelian ∼, 364
    Exeter ∼, 177, 179
    exsymmedian ∼s, 109
    far-out ∼, 368
    Fermat ∼, 145
    Feuerbach ∼, 296
    first Ajima-Malfatti ∼, 365
    first Eppstein ∼, 319
    first isodynamic ∼, 267
    first Kenmotu ∼, 370
    Gergonne ∼, 73, 136
    Grebe ∼, 99
    inner Griffiths ∼, 323
    inner Napoleon ∼, 149
    inner Rigby ∼, 323
    inner Soddy ∼, 309
    inner Vecten ∼, 159
    invariable ∼s, 212
    inverse Kosnita ∼, 287
    isoperimetric ∼, 317
    Kosnita ∼, 163
    Lambda ∼, 167
    Lemoine ∼, 99
    limiting ∼s, 261
    Miquel ∼, 49
    Nagel ∼, 114
    outer Griffiths ∼, 323
    outer Napoleon ∼, 149
    outer Rigby ∼, 323
    outer Soddy ∼, 309
    outer Vecten ∼, 158
    pedal-cevian ∼, 92
    Phi ∼, 167

Pi ∼, 175
power of a ∼, 37
Schiffler ∼, 352
second Ajima-Malfatti ∼, 365
second Eppstein ∼, 319
second isodynamic ∼, 267
second Kenmotu ∼, 371
Steiner ∼, 234
symmedian ∼, 99
Tarry ∼, 234
third Brocard ∼, 227
Weill ∼, 333
polar, 252
pole, 252
　Simson ∼, 43
Poncelet's porism, 291
porism, Poncelet's ∼, 291
power
　∼ of a point, 37
　Casey's ∼ theorem, 257
principle of duality, 132
projections, 62

quadrangle, 66, 133
quadrilateral, 133, 134
　orthocentric ∼, 34

radical
　∼ axis, 255
　∼ centre, 257
range, 53, 133
　harmonic ∼, 59
ray, 1
　Brocard ∼, 219
　pencil of ∼s, 56
reference triangle, 1
reflection
　∼ triangle, 164
　dilative ∼, 203
　glide ∼, 203
Rigby
　inner ∼ point, 323
　outer ∼ point, 323

Routh's theorem, 387

Schiffler point, 352
second
　∼ Ajima-Malfatti point, 365
　∼ Brocard triangle, 224
　∼ Eppstein point, 319
　∼ Kenmotu point, 371
　∼ Lemoine circle, 240
　∼ Morley centre, 188
　∼ Morley line, 192
　∼ Morley triangle, 190
　∼ isodynamic point, 267
　∼ isogonic centre, 146
segment, line ∼, 1
similar
　directly ∼, 4
　inversely ∼, 4
similarity, spiral ∼, 199
similitude
　centre of ∼, 3
　circle of ∼, 63, 205
　external centre of ∼, 63
　internal centre of ∼, 63
　triangle of ∼, 205
Simson
　∼ line, 42
　∼ pole, 43
Soddy
　∼ line, 319
　inner ∼ circle, 309
　inner ∼ point, 309
　outer ∼ circle, 309
　outer ∼ point, 309
Spieker
　∼ centre, 35, 116
　∼ circle, 116
spiral similarity, 199
squares, Vecten ∼, 157
Steiner point, 234
symmedian, 99
　∼ point, 99

tangential triangle, 102
Tarry point, 234
Taylor
    ∼ circle, 249
    ∼ hexagon, 248
theorem
    Brianchon's ∼, 448
    Casey's power ∼, 257
    Feuerbach's conic ∼, 378
    Monge's circle ∼, 76
    Pascal's ∼, 448
    Routh's ∼, 387
third
    ∼ Brocard point, 227
    ∼ Morley line, 193
    ∼ Morley triangle, 192
transversal, 56
triangle, 132
    ∼ of correspondence, 205
    ∼ of similitude, 205
    adjunct Morley ∼, 189
    anti-complementary ∼, 6
    cevian ∼, 72
    circumcevian ∼, 172
    circummedial ∼, 172
    circummidarc ∼, 172
    circumorthic ∼, 172
    contact ∼, 426
    diagonal ∼, 66, 134
    Emelyanov ∼, 339
    Euler ∼, 30
    excentral ∼, 16
    extangents ∼, 336
    extouch ∼, 131
    Feuerbach ∼, 296
    first Brocard ∼, 221
    first Morley ∼, 190
    Fuhrmann ∼, 120
    incentral ∼, 425

inner Napoleon ∼, 150
inner Soddy ∼, 312
inner Vecten ∼, 159
intouch ∼, 426
intouch-of-circumorthic ∼, 175
intouch-of-orthic ∼, 184
invariable ∼, 212
Kosnita ∼, 163
medial ∼, 5
Miquel ∼, 49
Morley ∼, 185
orthic ∼, 20
orthic-of-intouch ∼, 184
orthic-of-orthic ∼, 184
outer Napoleon ∼, 149
outer Soddy ∼, 313
outer Vecten ∼, 158
pedal ∼, 25, 77
reference ∼, 1
reflection ∼, 164
second Brocard ∼, 224
second Morley ∼, 190
tangential ∼, 102
third Morley ∼, 192
trilateral, 133, 134
tritangent, 15
Tucker
    ∼ circle, 245
    ∼ hexagon, 245

van Lamoen circle, 360
Vecten
    ∼ squares, 157
    inner ∼ point, 159
    inner ∼ triangle, 159
    outer ∼ point, 158
    outer ∼ triangle, 158
vertex, 56

Weill point, 333